FREEDO[

The Lower Mississippi Valley is more than just a distinct geographical region of the United States; it was central to the outcome of the Civil War and the destruction of slavery in the American South. Beginning with Lincoln's 1860 presidential election and concluding with the final ratification of the Thirteenth Amendment in 1865, *Freedom's Crescent* explores the four states of this region that seceded and joined the Confederacy: Tennessee, Mississippi, Arkansas, and Louisiana. By weaving into a coherent narrative the major military campaigns that enveloped the region, the daily disintegration of slavery in the countryside, and political developments across the four states and in Washington DC, John C. Rodrigue identifies the Lower Mississippi Valley as the epicenter of emancipation in the South. A sweeping examination of one of the war's most important theaters, this book highlights the integral role this region played in transforming United States history.

John C. Rodrigue is the Lawrence and Theresa Salameno Professor in the Department of History at Stonehill College. His book *Reconstruction in the Cane Fields* received the Kemper and Leila Williams Prize from the Louisiana Historical Association. He is also a co-editor of one of the volumes of *Freedom: A Documentary History of Emancipation, 1861–1867*. In 2016–2017, he served as the President of the Louisiana Historical Association.

CAMBRIDGE STUDIES ON THE AMERICAN SOUTH

Series Editors:
Mark M. Smith, *University of South Carolina, Columbia*
Peter Coclanis, *University of North Carolina at Chapel Hill*

Editor Emeritus:
David Moltke-Hansen

Interdisciplinary in its scope and intent, this series builds upon and extends Cambridge University Press's longstanding commitment to studies on the American South. The series offers the best new work on the South's distinctive institutional, social, economic, and cultural history and also features works in a national, comparative, and transnational perspective.

Titles in the Series

John C. Rodrigue, *Freedom's Crescent: The Civil War and the Destruction of Slavery in the Lower Mississippi Valley*

Elijah Gaddis, *Gruesome Looking Objects: A New History of Lynching and Everyday Things*

Damian Alan Pargas, *Freedom Seekers: Fugitive Slaves in North America, 1800–1860*

Sebastian N. Page, *Black Resettlement and the American Civil War*

Hayden R. Smith, *Carolina's Golden Fields: Inland Rice Cultivation in the South Carolina Lowcountry, 1670–1860*

Wilson Jeremiah Moses, *Thomas Jefferson: A Modern Prometheus*

Joan E. Cashin, *War Stuff: The Struggle for Human and Environmental Resources in the American Civil War*

David Stefan Doddington, *Contesting Slave Masculinity in the American South*

Lawrence T. McDonnell, *Performing Disunion: The Coming of the Civil War in Charleston, South Carolina*

Enrico Dal Lago, *Civil War and Agrarian Unrest: The Confederate South and Southern Italy*

Daniel J. Vivian, *A New Plantation World: Sporting Estates in the South Carolina Low Country, 1900–1940*

Eugene D. Genovese, ed. Douglas Ambrose, *The Sweetness of Life: Southern Planters at Home*

Donald G. Mathews, *At the Altar of Lynching: Burning Sam Hose in the American South*

Keri Leigh Merritt, *Masterless Men: Poor Whites and Slavery in the Antebellum South*

Katherine Rye Jewell, *Dollars for Dixie: Business and the Transformation of Conservatism in the Twentieth Century*

Sarah Gardner, *Reviewing the South: The Literary Marketplace and the Southern Renaissance, 1920–1941*

William Thomas Okie, *The Georgia Peach: Culture, Agriculture, and Environment in the American South*

Karlos K. Hill, *Beyond the Rope: The Impact of Lynching on Black Culture and Memory*

William A. Link and James J. Broomall, eds., *Rethinking American Emancipation: Legacies of Slavery and the Quest for Black Freedom*

James Van Horn Melton, *Religion, Community, and Slavery on the Colonial Southern Frontier*

Damian Alan Pargas, *Slavery and Forced Migration in the Antebellum South*

Craig Friend and Lorri Glover, eds., *Death and the American South*

Barton A. Myers, *Rebels against the Confederacy: North Carolina's Unionists*

Louis A. Ferleger and John D. Metz, *Cultivating Success in the South: Farm Households in Postbellum Georgia*

Luke E. Harlow, *Religion, Race, and the Making of Confederate Kentucky, 1830–1880*

Susanna Michele Lee, *Claiming the Union: Citizenship in the Post–Civil War South*

Kathleen M. Hilliard, *Masters, Slaves, and Exchange: Power's Purchase in the Old South*

Ari Helo, *Thomas Jefferson's Ethics and the Politics of Human Progress: The Morality of a Slaveholder*

Scott P. Marler, *The Merchants' Capital: New Orleans and the Political Economy of the Nineteenth-Century South*

Ras Michael Brown, *African-Atlantic Cultures and the South Carolina Lowcountry*

Johanna Nicol Shields, *Freedom in a Slave Society: Stories from the Antebellum South*

Brian Steele, *Thomas Jefferson and American Nationhood*

Christopher Michael Curtis, *Jefferson's Freeholders and the Politics of Ownership in the Old Dominion*

Jonathan Daniel Wells, *Women Writers and Journalists in the Nineteenth-Century South*

Peter McCandless, *Slavery, Disease, and Suffering in the Southern Lowcountry*

Robert E. Bonner, *Mastering America: Southern Slaveholders and the Crisis of American Nationhood*

FREEDOM'S CRESCENT

The Civil War and the Destruction of Slavery in the Lower Mississippi Valley

JOHN C. RODRIGUE
Stonehill College

To Melissa, Henry, & Nathalie:

With fond memories of our visit to Davis while working on this book, & with much love & very best wishes,

John

CAMBRIDGE
UNIVERSITY PRESS

University Printing House, Cambridge CB2 8BS, United Kingdom

One Liberty Plaza, 20th Floor, New York, NY 10006, USA

477 Williamstown Road, Port Melbourne, VIC 3207, Australia

314–321, 3rd Floor, Plot 3, Splendor Forum, Jasola District Centre,
New Delhi – 110025, India

103 Penang Road, #05–06/07, Visioncrest Commercial, Singapore 238467

Cambridge University Press is part of the University of Cambridge.

It furthers the University's mission by disseminating knowledge in the pursuit of education, learning, and research at the highest international levels of excellence.

www.cambridge.org
Information on this title: www.cambridge.org/9781108424097
DOI: 10.1017/9781108539715

© John C. Rodrigue 2023

This publication is in copyright. Subject to statutory exception and to the provisions of relevant collective licensing agreements, no reproduction of any part may take place without the written permission of Cambridge University Press.

First published 2023

A catalogue record for this publication is available from the British Library.

Library of Congress Cataloging-in-Publication Data
Names: Rodrigue, John C., author.
Title: Freedom's crescent : the Civil War and the destruction of slavery in the lower Mississippi Valley / John C. Rodrigue, Stonehill College, Massachusetts.
Other titles: Civil War and the destruction of slavery in the lower Mississippi Valley
Description: Cambridge, United Kingdom ; New York, NY : Cambridge University Press, 2023. | Series: Cambridge studies on the American South | Includes bibliographical references and index.
Identifiers: LCCN 2022034272 (print) | LCCN 2022034273 (ebook) | ISBN 9781108424097 (hardback) | ISBN 9781108539715 (ebook)
Subjects: LCSH: African Americans – History – 1863–1877. | Freed persons – United States – History – 19th century. | Slaves – Emancipation – United States – History – 19th century. | Reconstruction (U.S. history, 1865–1877) – Mississippi River Valley. | African Americans – Mississippi River Valley – Social conditions – 19th century. | Slavery – Mississippi River Valley – History – 19th century. | Mississippi River Valley – History – Civil War, 1861–1865.
Classification: LCC E185.2 R63 2023 (print) | LCC E185.2 (ebook) | DDC 973.7/14–dc23/eng/20220823
LC record available at https://lccn.loc.gov/2022034272
LC ebook record available at https://lccn.loc.gov/2022034273

ISBN 978-1-108-42409-7 Hardback
ISBN 978-1-108-43934-3 Paperback

Cambridge University Press has no responsibility for the persistence or accuracy of URLs for external or third-party internet websites referred to in this publication and does not guarantee that any content on such websites is, or will remain, accurate or appropriate.

to Sylvia

It may look like boasting – but what I tell you is truth – I began to reflect how magnificent a thing it was to die in such a manner, and how foolish it was in me to think of so paltry a consideration as my own individual life, in view of so wonderful a manifestation of God's power. I do believe that I blushed with shame when this idea crossed my mind. After a little while I became possessed with the keenest curiosity about the whirl itself. I positively felt a *wish* to explore its depths, even at the sacrifice I was going to make; and my principal grief was that I should never be able to tell my old companions on shore about the mysteries I should see. These, no doubt, were singular fancies to occupy a man's mind in such extremity – and I have often thought since, that the revolutions of the boat around the pool might have rendered me a little light-headed.

        Edgar Allan Poe, "A Descent into the Maelström" (1841)

CONTENTS

List of Figures   *page* xi
Acknowledgments   xii
List of Abbreviations   xvi

Introduction   1

Prologue: Life – and Labor – on the Mississippi   22

PART I   From War for Union to Military Emancipation, 1860–1862

1 "An Independent Power"   43
2 Of Stampedes and Free Papers   65
3 "Broken Eggs Cannot Be Mended"   82
4 "The Unsatisfactory Prospect Before Them"   100

PART II: From Military Emancipation to State Abolition, 1863

5 "The Return of the Seceded States to This Union as Slave States"   115
6 "Repugnant to the Spirit of the Age"   132
7 "The Greatest Question Ever Presented to Practical Statesmanship"   145
8 "The Name of 'Slavery'"   165
9 "Repudiating the Emancipation Proclamation and Reestablishing Slavery"   185

PART III: Abolition: State and Federal, 1864

10 "Slavery Is Incompatible with a Republican Form of Government"   223

11	Of Foul Combinations and the Common Object	237
12	"The Jewel of Liberty"	252
13	"The Virus of Slavery Is As Virulent As It Ever Was"	268
14	"No Longer Slaves but Freedmen"	282
15	"So Long As a Spark of Vitality Remains in the Institution of Slavery"	297
16	"Freedom, Full, Broad and Unconditional"	318
17	"To Resolve Never Again to Be Reduced to Slavery"	337

PART IV: **The Destruction of Slavery, 1865**

18	"The Tyrants Rod Has Been Broken"	359
19	"This Cup of Liberty"	377
20	"Establish Things as They Were Before the War"	396
21	"The Institution of Slavery Having Been Destroyed"	414
22	"Americans in America, One and Indivisible"	437

Epilogue: Memphis and New Orleans: May 1–3 and July 30, 1866   457

Bibliography   473
Index   501

FIGURES

1. The lower Mississippi valley   *page* xviii
2. The percentage of slaves in the total population, by county (or parish), 1860   xx
3. Emancipation and abolition in the lower Mississippi valley   xxi
4. Fugitive slaves enter Union lines   204
5. Baton Rouge contraband camp   204
6. Ulysses S. Grant   205
7. John Eaton   205
8. Samuel R. Curtis   206
9. Frederick Steele   206
10. Benjamin F. Butler   207
11. Nathaniel P. Banks   207
12. Lorenzo Thomas addresses freed people   208
13. Nathaniel P. Banks addresses Louisiana planters   208
14. Abraham Lincoln   209
15. James M. Ashley   210
16. Henry Winter Davis   210
17. Andrew Johnson   211
18. William G. "Parson" Brownlow   211
19. Isaac Murphy   212
20. William M. Fishback   212
21. Edward W. Gantt   213
22. Michael Hahn   214
23. J. Madison Wells   214
24. The inauguration of Michael Hahn   215
25. William B. Campbell   216
26. Emerson Etheridge   216
27. Christian Roselius   217
28. William H. Grey   218
29. Black troops mustered out, Arkansas, 1866   218
30. Memphis massacre   219
31. New Orleans massacre   219

ACKNOWLEDGMENTS

Given that this book has turned out to be a much more ambitious undertaking – and has consequently taken far longer to complete – than I had originally intended, it is a pleasure finally to be able to thank all of the persons who have helped to bring it to fruition. I first began to develop the idea for this book while working on my previous one, *Lincoln and Reconstruction*. It occurred to me then that there was a larger story than I was able to tell at the time. Little did I know how much larger, and it took me a while to figure things out, but I thank everyone who was associated with that book for this one as well.

A chance encounter with David Moltke-Hansen at the 2016 annual meeting of the Organization of American Historians (OAH) in Providence, Rhode Island, first steered me in the direction of Cambridge University Press's Studies on the American South series. David had previously edited the series with Mark M. Smith, but it now was being edited, David informed me, by Mark and Peter A. Coclanis. I thank David for the suggestion (which never would have occurred to me). I cannot express my appreciation enough to Mark and Peter for all of their support, encouragement, and patience during these last few years, especially when the length of the manuscript was beginning to cause, as Mark so eloquently put it, "some heartburn."

I would like to express special gratitude to everyone I have had the privilege of working with at Cambridge University Press. Deborah Gershonowitz first assumed responsibility for this project, and she offered important advice and support during my early association with the press (in addition to enabling me to get to self-importantly say that "I have a meeting with my editor in New York"). Cecelia Cancellaro subsequently inherited stewardship of this project, and I especially appreciate her guidance, support, and saintly patience in bringing a long and unwieldy manuscript to completion. I also thank the anonymous outside reviewers of the original book proposal and, later, the manuscript for their challenging but helpful insights, questions, and – yes – criticisms, all of which made the book much better. As things got down to the wire, Victoria Phillips handled my innumerable questions with aplomb. Thanks to the members of the Press's outstanding production department – Melissa Ward and Vidya Ashwin and her team, especially copy editor Vinod Kumar – who made this book a truly global endeavor.

ACKNOWLEDGMENTS

I had the opportunity to present parts of this work before various audiences over the years, much to my benefit. I had the special privilege of presenting an early version of the project in April 2015 before a symposium in honor of Ira Berlin at the University of Maryland, College Park. The reaction from the audience suggested to me that I might in fact be on to something, but I am especially grateful for the comments and responses from Steven F. Miller (my former colleague on the Freedmen and Southern Society Project [FSSP]), Lawrence N. Powell, Thavolia Glymph, Steven Hahn, and Ira himself. That gathering, for various reasons, truly was a highlight of my career. I had the opportunity to present the Tennessee dimension of this story at a conference at the University of Memphis in May 2016 marking the sesquicentennial of the 1866 Memphis massacre. I would like to thank Susan E. O'Donovan (another former FSSP colleague who was present at the Ira event) for refusing to take no for an answer when she invited me to participate in the conference. I also thank Susan and Beverly Greene Bond for putting together a brilliantly conceptualized program, and the other participants and audience members for their questions, suggestions, and positive vibes.

I gave a much-abbreviated version of the Louisiana story in my presidential address before the 2017 annual meeting of the Louisiana Historical Association (LHA) in Shreveport. I greatly appreciate the response to my address from LHA friends and associates far too numerous to name here, but I would especially like to thank my dear friends Chuck Shindo and Michael Fontenot for traipsing all the way up from Baton Rouge to hear my address, and Faye Phillips for all of her support throughout my academic career, dating back to when we first met in the spring of 1988 at the Louisiana State University special collections, as I was just commencing my dissertation research.

Louis Ferleger, another dear friend of more than thirty years and one of my most earnest advocates, made me the proverbial offer I couldn't refuse by insisting that I present before the American Political History Institute of Boston University's History Department. I thank Lou and Bruce J. Shulman, who administers the Institute, for the invitation to speak in September 2018. I also greatly appreciate the challenging questions and words of encouragement that I received from Nina Silber, Sarah T. Phillips, and the other contributors to our collegial discussion.

I had the great honor, along with Edward Ayers, of participating in the Distinguished Scholars Series at Nicholls State University in Thibodaux, Louisiana, in March 2019. I greatly appreciate the invitation from David D. Plater, author of a fine book on the Butler family of south Louisiana, to give the talk. I asked David what he needed me for if he already had Ed Ayers lined up, but he insisted, and for that I thank him. I would also like to thank Paul Wilson, Chair of the Department of History and Geography; Jay Clune, President of Nicholls State; Tom Becnel, retired faculty member in the Nicholls history department; and the entire Nicholls State/Thibodaux community for their gracious hospitality. It is always nice to go back to Louisiana.

I presented an early version of this project at a Dean's Forum at Stonehill College. I would like to thank the friends, colleagues, and students who attended the presentation and who asked probing and challenging questions and offered helpful advice and suggestions. I also thank those of my Stonehill colleagues who offered encouragement and support during some trying times. Moreover, two separate sabbatical leaves (yet another indication of how long this project took) also provided me with the time, in both instances at critical junctures, to undertake significant but essential revisions of the manuscript.

I thank the staffs of the various archives I have visited over the years for their assistance and of the repositories from which I secured illustrations for reproducing them and for permission to use them. The Stonehill College library's interlibrary loan staff likewise provided invaluable aid in tracking down materials. Tom Willcockson created the excellent maps.

I unabashedly abused the friendship of Paul A. Cimbala (fellow Emory grad and New Jersey guitarist), Michael W. Fitzgerald, the aforementioned Lou Ferleger, and Joseph P. Reidy in taking them up on their gracious offers to read a ramshackle manuscript. I'd like to think our friendships have survived, but I owe each of them a tremendous debt of gratitude for offering advice and suggestions that greatly improved what I was trying to say. They really did make the book better, and there was simply no getting around the fact that I had to have sympathetic but discerning readers look at it. I hope to be able to repay the debt. Steven Hahn also read parts of the manuscript and provided sagacious advice, in addition to his general support and encouragement. Richard Frank (my uncle-in-law) graciously read the entire manuscript – the long version – and made a number of good catches.

I thank Michael Vorenberg for his assistance on a couple of specific matters that made a big difference. He may not remember it, but James Oakes offered a reassuring endorsement when this book was barely a two-paragraph proposal.

Friends with whom I have discussed this project over the years also offered advice, suggestions, and encouragement, or just helped to keep me sane. They include Mike Ross (whose insistence that I include Alabama, since "people write songs about Alabama," I ultimately had to take a pass on); Scott Marler (whose excellent book on New Orleans helped me greatly); Andrew Slap; Mark Schantz; Paul Cimbala (again) and Elizabeth Vozzola; Rex Palmer and Claudia Rizzini; and Gloria and Ken Nykiel. Jim Roark, my dissertation adviser from back in the day and longtime friend, also read parts of the manuscript and was willing to talk endlessly – on those all-too-rare occasions we are able to get together anymore, and on the phone – about the project. In an entirely different realm of my existence, Jim Thorpe, Dave Betten, Don Distaso, Wayne Jarger, Tom Tozzi, and Tony Chibaro, as always, kept it real.

My friend John Merriman has served as an unindicted co-conspirator on this project. In the nearly forty years since we first met at Emory University in preparing for the fall 1986 semester, John has been a dear and true friend, a comrade, and an intellectual partner. Even though he now lives half a world away, our regular phone conversations have helped to shape my thinking on this book and on many other things. And once again, John generously gave of his time and worked his magic on the footnotes and bibliography. When it comes to historiographical or bibliographic matters, he can virtually read my mind. Any errors in "the notes and bib" are on me, but such virtues as they may have are owing to John's selfless efforts.

I would again like to express my deepest appreciation to the late Lawrence Salameno and to Theresa Salameno for creating the professorship that I have been privileged to hold and for their support of Stonehill College. Despite Larry's passing, I always had him in mind as my ideal reader and intended audience: someone who held an abiding passion for history and understood its importance, and who, though not an academic, could appreciate the finer points of serious, scholarly debate. I do miss Larry and our conversations about history, the Yankees, the cats, and other matters.

Several other friends and family members have sadly passed away in the years I was working on this book, two of whom I must mention. My father, John Rodrigue, was diagnosed with cancer in early 2017, just as I was preparing to give my LHA presidential address, and he passed a year later. A dear friend from my Louisiana days, Rex Stem, was taken much too soon. An April 2013 trip to northern California with my wife Sylvia – for the OAH meeting in San Francisco, to do a couple of days of research at Stanford, and to visit with Rex, Melissa, and their children Henry and Nathalie in Davis – remains a treasured memory. I miss these and all of the loved ones who have passed in recent years.

I would like to express my deepest appreciation to my family members, including my mother Maureen, my sisters Ann-Marie and Terry, my various in-laws, and my nieces and nephews Kelly, Glen, Jackie, Eddie, Abigail, and Emily, for all of their love and support. Thanks too to Granite, Zydeco, Mr. Friendly, Minnie, Maxx, and Shadow for greatly enriching Sylvia's and my lives (and to Mr. Friendly and Maxx in particular for their thoughtful emendations while strolling across the computer keyboard).

The dedication of this book acknowledges a bond that I deeply treasure.

ABBREVIATIONS

Full citations for published material are provided in the Bibliography

ALP	The Papers of Abraham Lincoln, Library of Congress
CG	*Congressional Globe*
CWL	*The Collected Works of Abraham Lincoln* (Basler)
Freedom: BME	*Freedom: A Documentary History of Emancipation. Series 2: The Black Military Experience*
Freedom: DS	*Freedom: A Documentary History of Emancipation. Series 1. Volume 1: The Destruction of Slavery*
Freedom: L&L-1865	*Freedom: A Documentary History of Emancipation. Series 3. Volume 1: Land and Labor, 1865*
Freedom: WGFL-LS	*Freedom: A Documentary History of Emancipation. Series 1. Volume 3: The Wartime Genesis of Free Labor: The Lower South*
LSU	The Louisiana and Lower Mississippi Valley Collections, Hill Memorial Library, Louisiana State University
OR	*Official Records of the War of the Rebellion*
PAJ	*The Papers of Andrew Johnson*
UNC	The Southern Historical Collection, Wilson Library, University of North Carolina at Chapel Hill

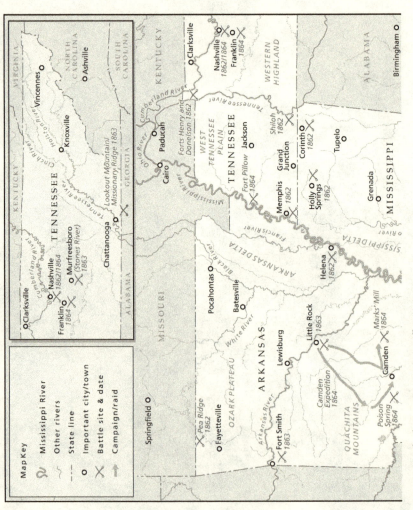

Figure 1 The lower Mississippi valley

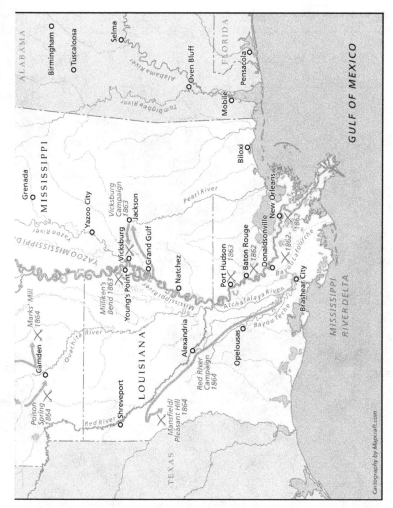

Figure 1 (Cont.)

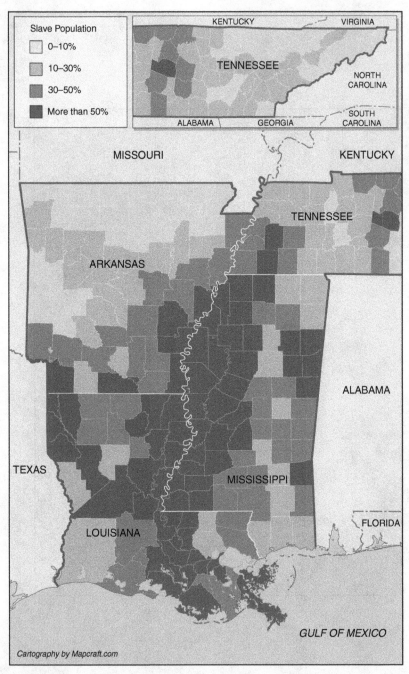

Figure 2 The percentage of slaves in the total population, by county (or parish), 1860

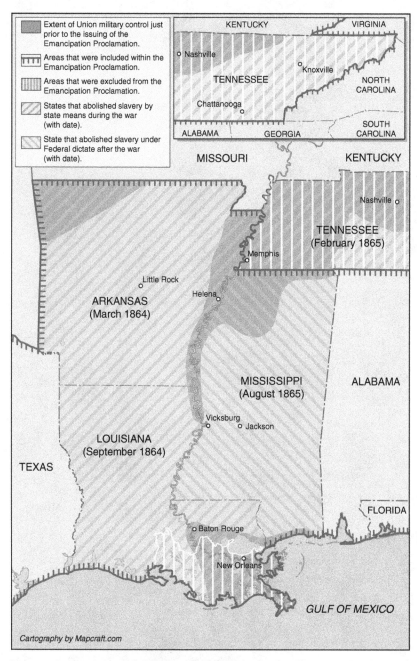

Figure 3 Emancipation and abolition in the lower Mississippi valley. **Note:** The Thirteenth Amendment, which became operative in December 1865, prohibited slavery in all of the states and in all territory under Federal jurisdiction.

Introduction

The legacy of slavery continues to haunt the national conscience, and questions surrounding race remain among the nation's most intractable challenges. Despite – or indeed because of – the dramatic transformations that American society has undergone in recent decades, along with concomitant changes in the historical profession and historical scholarship, any attempt to understand the nation's past, or present, revolves more than ever around the study of slavery and its destruction, and scholarly interest in these topics shows no signs of abating. Slavery, it is well understood, was not tangential to – or somehow an aberration of – the American experience. It was central, and its overthrow precipitated a fundamental reordering of every aspect of US society. Nothing was immune to slavery's – or emancipation's – consequences. Paradoxically, while notions of race, as the historical record has amply demonstrated, are "constructs" that evolve over time, racism and racialist thinking also appear to be immutable elements of modern society. To this day, Americans continue to grapple with slavery's bitter legacy. They probably always will.

As part of the effort to understand that legacy, this book examines the destruction of slavery in the lower Mississippi valley – the vast geological basin drained by the Mississippi River and its main tributaries and distributaries south of the confluence with the Ohio River – during and immediately following the US Civil War. Beginning with Abraham Lincoln's election as president in November 1860 and ending with final ratification of the Thirteenth Amendment in December 1865, it focuses on the four states of the region that seceded from the Union and joined the Confederate States of America – Arkansas, Louisiana, Mississippi, and Tennessee. In particular, this study places special emphasis on the parts of those states where slavery and plantation agriculture predominated, including west and central Tennessee, the southeasterly half of Arkansas, and the western half of Mississippi, as well as almost all of Louisiana. Of these states, only Mississippi did not abolish slavery during the war or experience wartime Reconstruction. The lower Mississippi valley encapsulated the destruction of slavery in the rebellious states as a whole, something that can be said of no other part of the Confederacy.

Even taking into account D. W. Meinig's observation that "[m]ost geographic regions are abstractions and approximations," this book considers the lower Mississippi valley as a distinct geopolitical entity.[1] From this vantage point, it integrates into a coherent narrative the military experience, political developments in the four states and Washington, DC, and the undermining of slavery "from the bottom up" in examining what was undoubtedly the greatest social revolution in US history. The lower Mississippi valley boasts of a universe of scholarship on various aspects of the Civil War and the destruction of slavery, and scholars have long understood the centrality of the region to the war's outcome and to slavery's downfall. Considering how much has been written on the lower Mississippi valley during the war, it seems remarkable that no single book examines the ending of slavery in this distinct and vitally important region. This book attempts to fill that gap.[2]

While framed as a chronological narrative, this book puts forward two overarching themes. First, it argues that the multidimensional nature of emancipation and abolition in the lower Mississippi valley elucidates the various means by which slavery was brought to an end in the United States. Second, it contends that the destruction of slavery in the United States was even more contingent than previous scholarship has allowed for, and that the exigencies of war, emancipation, and wartime Reconstruction in the states of the lower Mississippi valley proved integral to this process. The first theme pulls together the myriad strands of a story with which scholars of emancipation are familiar, while the second offers a revision of what might be considered the standard account of the destruction of slavery in the United States.

---

[1] Meinig, *The Shaping of America*, xvii. Although Americans during the nineteenth century employed the term Mississippi valley imprecisely, they had a general awareness of the area as a distinct geographical region.

[2] One crucial exception is Armstead L. Robinson's 1977 dissertation, "Day of Jubilo." The story of this work is legendary in the scholarship on emancipation. The book that was eventually published posthumously (in 2005) was very different from Robinson's dissertation, though the lower Mississippi valley figures prominently in both works. Robinson's *Bitter Fruits of Bondage* takes a much more expansive view of the Mississippi valley than does mine, incorporating almost the entire area from the Appalachian Mountains to Texas. It also focuses most of its attention on the first two years of the war, until the Confederacy's 1863 military losses at Vicksburg and Chattanooga. While the ending of slavery is obviously critical to Robinson's analysis, he examines the (lower) Mississippi valley as a means of demonstrating that class conflict among white Southerners over slavery was the primary cause of Confederate defeat. As will be seen, my examination of the lower Mississippi valley seeks to explain how the formal abolition of slavery came about. Ironically, Robinson's dissertation probably had a more profound impact on the scholarship on slavery, emancipation, and the Civil War than did the book when it finally appeared. Nonetheless, all of this scholarship since the late 1970s owes a tremendous debt of gratitude to Robinson's truly pathbreaking dissertation.

The first theme maintains that the lower Mississippi valley experienced all of the five major dimensions of wartime emancipation and abolition. First, parts of all four states witnessed the liberating of slaves by Union military forces – or *limited military emancipation* – under various Federal edicts prior to Lincoln's issuing of the Emancipation Proclamation on January 1, 1863. Although circumscribed in theory, such emancipation was widespread in practice. Second, the freeing of all slaves in designated geographical areas – or *universal military emancipation* – under the Emancipation Proclamation took place throughout all of Arkansas and Mississippi and most of Louisiana, including parts of all three states that Union military forces controlled when the proclamation was issued. Third, the region experienced *exclusions* from the proclamation, including southern Louisiana and all of Tennessee, as a concession to southern Unionists in those states who were attempting to organize loyal governments. Fourth, *state-level abolition*, as part of wartime Reconstruction, occurred in Arkansas and Louisiana in 1864 and in Tennessee in early 1865. These actions provided constitutional sanction to the freedom former slaves had gained via military emancipation, and they abolished slavery as an institution, something the Emancipation Proclamation could not do. Finally, *Federal civil authority* definitively ended slavery. Mississippi essentially abolished slavery under Federal dictate after the war, while the Thirteenth Amendment prohibited any state to reintroduce slavery. Other Confederate areas experienced one or more of these dimensions of emancipation, but none experienced all of them. It would not be an overstatement to say that the destruction of slavery in the South as a whole can be understood by looking at the lower Mississippi valley.[3]

The second theme, which requires greater elaboration than the first, seeks to revise the conventional narrative that explains how the Civil War was transformed, for most Northerners, from a war to preserve the Union into one both to preserve the Union and to end slavery. It also calls for a deeper appreciation of the difficulties that were involved in translating military emancipation – or the freeing of slaves as a *consequence* of suppressing the rebellion – into the political

---

[3] Possible exceptions to this generalization include the Virginia–West Virginia situation and Kentucky. Although Virginia established a Unionist government that abolished slavery and was instrumental in creating the state of West Virginia, wartime Reconstruction in that state was of far less significance than in the lower Mississippi valley. Because Kentucky (which was excluded from the Emancipation Proclamation) did not abolish slavery during the war, and was not required to abolish slavery as a condition for restoration to the Union (since it did not secede), slavery only ended in the state with final ratification of the Thirteenth Amendment in December 1865. During the war, Kentucky experienced other modes of Federal emancipation particular to its circumstances: in April 1864, the War Department approved an order allowing for the recruitment of male slaves in Kentucky (thereby emancipating them) with their owners' permission; in March 1865, Congress approved a resolution freeing the wives and children of black soldiers and future recruits, a policy that was enforced widely in Kentucky. These measures still did not abolish slavery in the state. *Freedom: BME*, 193, 196–97.

objective of abolishing slavery as an institution (which also includes state means, not just the Thirteenth Amendment). These difficulties, this book further suggests, were rooted in the shortcomings of abolitionist thought and the antislavery movement in general. Historians of the Civil War and emancipation have traditionally immersed themselves in the "war-for-Union to war-for-freedom" narrative. Yet they have generally demonstrated less awareness of the problem – which became a central one for antislavery advocates during the war – of transforming military emancipation into constitutional abolition. Whereas developments throughout the slave states contributed to the advent of universal military emancipation, the lower Mississippi valley was at the epicenter of the transformation of military emancipation into constitutional abolition.

The "standard" account of how the Civil War became a war to end slavery focuses overwhelmingly on the process by which Lincoln came to issue the Emancipation Proclamation. Historians have traditionally viewed the proclamation, quite correctly, as one of the truly transformative moments in US history. It is almost impossible to overstate the proclamation's significance to the outcome of the war and to Americans' historical consciousness. Yet many historians equate *emancipation* with *abolition*, or they presuppose that the former inevitably led to the latter.[4] Despite excellent work on the Thirteenth

---

[4] The scholarship on the destruction of slavery is so vast that it would be impossible to cite the many works that demonstrate this emphasis on the Emancipation Proclamation over constitutional abolition. While there are some exceptions, the equating of military emancipation with abolition, or the assumption that abolition inevitably followed the proclamation, pervades the literature. The same is true of the scholarship on Lincoln, which almost by definition highlights the proclamation. Standard accounts of the ending of slavery in the western hemisphere, which are essential to any understanding of the destruction of slavery in the United States, include Blackburn, *American Crucible*; Davis, *Problem of Slavery in the Age of Emancipation*; and Drescher, *Abolition*. Older works on the proclamation or on Federal wartime antislavery policy that emphasize emancipation include Franklin, *Emancipation Proclamation*, and Gerteis, *From Contraband to Freedman*. The more recent, generally excellent, scholarship on emancipation or abolition in the United States also displays this tendency to accentuate the proclamation, and military emancipation generally, over constitutional abolition. Works that situate the long-term project of ending slavery in the United States in hemispheric perspective include Berlin, *Long Emancipation*; Hahn, *Political Worlds of Slavery and Freedom*; Rael, *Eighty-Eight Years*, esp. chap. 7; and Sinha, *The Slave's Cause*. Recent works on wartime emancipation and the destruction of slavery, or on Lincoln and emancipation, that devote most of their attention to the proclamation include Blair and Younger, *Lincoln's Proclamation*; Blair and Broomall, *Rethinking American Emancipation*; Finkelman and Kennon, *Lincoln, Congress, and Emancipation*; Foner, *Fiery Trial*; Guelzo, *Lincoln's Emancipation Proclamation*; Holzer and Gabbard, *Lincoln and Freedom*; Holzer, Medford, and Williams, *Emancipation Proclamation*; Masur, *Lincoln's Hundred Days*; Medford, *Lincoln and Emancipation*; Medford, "Day of Jubilee"; Oakes, *Freedom National*; and Williams, "Under Cover of Liberty." In one of the essays in Holzer and Gabbard, *Lincoln and Freedom*, Herman Belz perhaps comes closest to pinpointing the difficulty of transforming military emancipation into constitutional abolition. However, even in this essay, Belz tends to equate emancipation with abolition, and he takes the idea of abolishing slavery by

Amendment by Michael Vorenberg, Leonard L. Richards, and Rebecca E. Zietlow, historians of emancipation tend to relegate the formal abolition of slavery almost to an afterthought.[5] They may disagree on *how* the shift to

> amending the Federal Constitution almost as a given. (Belz, "Constitution, the Amendment Process, and the Abolition of Slavery.") The legal historian Gerald T. Dunne goes so far as to suggest that the Thirteenth Amendment was "largely unnecessary," owing to the Emancipation Proclamation and "state action at the grass roots" (Dunne, "Reconstruction Amendments," 179). As arguably the most authoritative recent account of the wartime destruction of slavery, Oakes's *Freedom National* deserves special commentary. Oakes devotes approximately 80 percent of his nearly 500 pages of text to the year and a half leading up to the proclamation and to its implementation, and 20 percent to the almost three years that were subsequently needed to abolish slavery. Oakes includes two incisive chapters that trace the challenges of abolishing slavery after the proclamation had been issued, but by far his focus is on the proclamation as the culmination of Union military emancipation policy that began, he posits, at the very start of the war. Although I disagree with Oakes's contention that Republicans, including Lincoln, were generally committed to a war against slavery right from the start, my intellectual debt to his extraordinary work will be obvious. In *The Second Founding*, Eric Foner makes the distinction between military emancipation and constitutional abolition, though mostly to show why an abolition amendment to the Federal Constitution was necessary. Foner also notes, however, that the Emancipation Proclamation "did not mean the end of Lincoln's quest for state-by-state abolition," both as a means of winning the war and abolishing slavery in the seceded states (23–28; quotation, 27). A central theme of Chandra Manning's *Troubled Refuge* is the contingent nature of wartime emancipation and the possibility of slavery surviving the war. There have been many instances throughout history, Manning notes, in which slavery was critically weakened during war only to survive and become even stronger. Ironically, Manning may take this argument a bit *too* far in maintaining that it was not the Thirteenth but the *Fourteenth* Amendment that finally guaranteed the demise of US slavery, since, as she observes, "it is far more difficult to enslave a citizen than a noncitizen." She continues: "the Fourteenth Amendment helped to ensure the permanence of emancipation in the United States, in contrast to most instances of wartime emancipation throughout world history, which more often resulted in reenslavement or the perpetuation of slavery" (282). For recent overviews on the scholarship on emancipation and abolition, see Brooks, "Reconsidering Politics in the Study of American Abolitionists"; Emberton, "Unwriting the Freedom Narrative"; and Kolchin, "Reexamining Southern Emancipation." Kolchin correctly notes the difficulty of pinning down the precise "moment of emancipation," but he then jumps ahead from the proclamation to the Thirteenth Amendment. Although Kolchin allows for "self-emancipation" and slave flight throughout the war, abolition seems to follow emancipation almost inevitably. "If the Emancipation Proclamation indicated an intent to move toward emancipation," he writes, "the Thirteenth Amendment appeared almost an afterthought by the time it was ratified, endorsing what had already occurred in fact" (9–10). While there are certainly exceptions, the scholarship on the destruction of slavery focuses overwhelmingly on the Emancipation Proclamation, assumes slavery was doomed following Union military victory, and treats the abolition of slavery as a virtual formality. If slavery were indeed dead by the time the Thirteenth Amendment was finally ratified, it was only because of the fierce struggle over its fate – driven, as this book will show, by the fear that it might very well survive Union military victory – in the nearly three years between January 1, 1863, and December 1865.

[5] Vorenberg, *Final Freedom*; Richards, *Who Freed the Slaves?*; and Zietlow, *Forgotten Emancipator*. In contrast to Oakes, Vorenberg focuses overwhelmingly on the amendment

a war for freedom came about (witness the endless debate over "who freed the slaves?"), but they generally concur that such a shift took place. To be sure, some of them challenge this narrative. Gary Gallagher, for instance, claims that the war always remained a war primarily for Union for most Northerners, while James Oakes's monumental *Freedom National* contends that Republicans began acting against slavery almost immediately.[6] Nonetheless, historians largely adhere to this "war-for-Union to war-for-freedom" trajectory, even if they differ on the impulses behind it. Placing far more emphasis on the proclamation than on later developments, they almost assume that once Lincoln issued it, pending Union military victory, slavery was doomed.[7]

following its December 1863 introduction into Congress, devoting approximately 20 percent of its 250 pages of text to the amendment's antebellum and wartime background. This observation is offered as a basis for comparison, not as criticism. Vorenberg provides a number of key insights that I have used and expanded upon in my analysis. My debt to his work will also be obvious. Although Richards takes greater account of the amendment's background than does Vorenberg, Richards seems to assume the preexisting idea of a Federal abolition amendment, something, as Vorenberg shows, very few Americans subscribed to before the Civil War. Zietlow's study of Ohio US Representative and Radical Republican James M. Ashley, who shepherded the Thirteenth Amendment through the House, provides an example of one of the rare Republicans or antislavery advocates who called for such an amendment before the war. See also Samito, *Lincoln and the Thirteenth Amendment*.

[6] Gallagher, *Union War*.
[7] Mention must also be made of the groundbreaking work of the Freedmen and Southern Society Project, which has produced the multi-volume, documentary editing series, *Freedom: A Documentary History of Emancipation, 1861–1867*, along with the similar scholarship, both before and after it, that cast emancipation as a social revolution. While these works hardly ignored official policy, laws, and the like, they were more concerned with emancipation as a social and historical *process*, one in which the slaves themselves played a central role, than with policy. The starting point for this view is Du Bois, *Black Reconstruction*, but see also Aptheker, *Negro in the Civil War*. Important titles of the post–World War II period include Litwack, *Been in the Storm So Long*; McPherson, *Negro's Civil War*; Quarles, *Negro in the Civil War*; and Rose, *Rehearsal for Reconstruction*. No attempt is made here to cite the vast body of local or community studies on the ending of slavery that this previous scholarship has inspired, but important works along these lines for the South (and the nation) as a whole include Foner, *Reconstruction*; Hahn, *Nation Under Our Feet*; and Reidy, *Illusions of Emancipation*. Reidy has further questioned approaches to emancipation that are framed around the "linear" evolution of policy. This viewpoint fits within his larger argument that individuals experienced both time and place in essentially malleable and radically different ways amidst the upheaval and strife of war. "As I argue throughout this book," Reidy writes (371, n. 38), "understanding emancipation as a linear succession of official actions obscures more than it illuminates." While I do not disagree with Reidy's key insight that individuals experienced time differently under different circumstances, the account presented here, admittedly, is firmly rooted in the "linear" evolution of policy. The classic account of the slaveholders' response to emancipation for the South as a whole is Roark, *Masters without Slaves*. Finally, in the vast literature on the Confederacy, important recent works that attribute its failure to the crisis over slavery include Levine, *Fall of the House of Dixie*; McCurry, *Confederate Reckoning*; and Robinson, *Bitter Fruits of Bondage*.

Yet this fixation on the Emancipation Proclamation has led to historical misunderstanding. Although scholars have long recognized the many limitations of the proclamation, they have not fully appreciated its most important shortcoming or the implications thereof. Even allowing for its unquestioned legality and full implementation, the proclamation did not – *could* not – abolish slavery as an institution. It was a military directive that freed certain slaves. Among the many questions it left unanswered, it said nothing about how slavery would factor into the rebellious states' return to the Union. It was also entirely silent on the future of slavery. The proclamation could have freed every single slave in the seceded states and yet still have left slavery legally in place. Because of the proclamation's inability to end slavery as an institution, there remained the possibility of the seceded states being restored to the Union without having to abolish it, and of slavery therefore surviving the war. If such a possibility seems remote in hindsight, it was not so to many contemporaries, both for and against abolition. (As often noted, the vast majority of the Confederacy's 3.5 million slaves were still enslaved when the war ended.) Assuming slavery's destruction to be inevitable after the proclamation, and upon Union victory, historians have overlooked the significance of the shift to constitutional abolition – and thus have missed an important part of the story.

As historians have well understood, Republicans were committed to the eradication of slavery after January 1, 1863, and many before then. Yet it was not at all clear how – or whether – Lincoln's emancipation policy would be turned into abolition. This situation, in many respects, was a logical outgrowth of the prewar antislavery movement. For all of the abolitionists' success before the war in shaping northern public opinion on the enormity of slavery, they had never really developed any concrete, coherent plan for how to end it. Neither had the advocates of an antislavery Constitution – or what historians call "antislavery constitutionalism" – made much headway in devising a strategy to eliminate slavery in the states under peacetime conditions. The principle of "freedom national" – the idea that slavery, as a strictly local or state institution, enjoyed no legal existence wherever Federal authority prevailed – had gained widespread support before the war. Yet even this idea offered no way to end slavery. Indeed, the so-called Federal consensus – which may well have been the most sacrosanct constitutional principle before the Civil War, and to which even most abolitionists subscribed – held that because slavery was a state matter, the Federal government possessed no authority to act against it in the states. Only a *state* could abolish slavery. Lincoln himself swore by this principle and only deviated from it near the end of the war. It is perhaps ironic that wartime military emancipation, however inadvertently, exposed this essential flaw in the entire abolitionist project.

Abolitionists and many Republicans saw the start of the war as a golden opportunity to challenge slavery, but they still faced seemingly insurmountable obstacles in turning this goal into reality. Abolitionists had talked for decades about freeing slaves in any potential civil war. Yet in response to the age-old question "What is to be done?," antislavery advocates had no plan. While considering Reconstruction legislation early in the war, Republicans began to debate the fate of slavery, but they made little progress. So long as the war was about preserving the Union, in any event, the question of slavery's fate was moot. Once Lincoln issued the proclamation, the general presumption remained that the *states* would abolish slavery. They would perhaps accomplish this task as part of the process of state restoration, under the auspices of Federal legislation, though even then Republicans continued to disagree on the basis for such legislation. Many contemporaries simply assumed that the fate of slavery would be postponed until the rebellion had been defeated. Owing to traditional notions of federalism, including the Federal consensus (from which even rebellious states evidently benefitted), most opponents of slavery held that abolition by *state* means, carried out in conjunction with the other practical considerations relating to state restoration, was a more viable method of ending slavery than by a Federal mandate imposed on the states against their will.

Moreover, as Michael Vorenberg has demonstrated, few Americans before the Civil War, and for the first two years during it, would have supported the idea of abolishing slavery – or carrying out any social reform – by amending the Federal Constitution. This document, as the work of the "Founders," was generally thought to be beyond substantive revision. Overturning this mindset would take time and was itself a product of the war. Plus, with fifteen slave states, there was no hope of such a measure ever being ratified. In a few instances in the decades before the war, abolitionists had suggested a Federal abolition amendment. But this idea was a pipedream – so outlandish, even by abolitionist standards, that it stood no chance of implementation. Once the war began, many antislavery proposals were put forward, both before and after the Emancipation Proclamation, to end slavery – so many as almost to preclude any consensus from developing. Debate over the fate of slavery in any prospective postwar settlement further intensified after the Union victories at Vicksburg and Gettysburg. Even after the various proposals to make emancipation universal coalesced into a Federal abolition amendment in early 1864 (the "Thirteenth Amendment"), many of the amendment's supporters harbored grave doubts about its prospects for success. Neither did they necessarily view it as a substitute for state action. The idea of the amendment as a stand-alone measure giving constitutional sanction to the proclamation, overriding state concerns, has become essential to our understanding of the destruction of slavery, but it does not accurately convey how most contemporaries saw the problem of securing universal emancipation.[8]

---

[8] Americans' aversion to the idea of amending the Constitution before the Civil War is an important theme in Vorenberg's *Final Freedom*, but see esp. 5–7. For one suggestion

The transformation of military emancipation into constitutional abolition, I argue, was as fraught with difficulty – and as historically contingent – as had been the transformation of a war to preserve the Union into a war of universal military emancipation. The shift from "war-for-Union to war-for-freedom" was not a one-step process but rather a two-step process: war for Union to Emancipation Proclamation, and Emancipation Proclamation to constitutional abolition. The second step of this process was as essential to ending slavery as had been the first. However, the first – for various reasons, including the story of how the Emancipation Proclamation was adopted and the slaves' role therein, and the lionization of Lincoln as "the Great Emancipator" – has traditionally received much more scholarly attention. By contrast, the excellent recent work on the Thirteenth Amendment tends to accentuate the circumstances surrounding the amendment itself, once it had been introduced into Congress, rather than its antecedents or background. There is clearly something missing in the standard account of the destruction of slavery. The Emancipation Proclamation freed slaves but did not abolish slavery as an institution. That was an entirely different problem, as was that of state restoration. In much the same way that the abolitionists had devised no viable plan to end slavery before the war, the path from military emancipation to constitutional abolition was not nearly as clear, direct, or inevitable for contemporaries as later generations have assumed.

If this shift from military emancipation to constitutional abolition was more the product of wartime contingencies than of theories antislavery advocates had developed before the war, I further contend, it also pivoted on the lower Mississippi valley. The abolition of slavery as a wartime political objective arose as a direct consequence of Federal military success in the region during the first half of 1862. Since the start of hostilities, northern policymakers and other interested parties had debated the problem of "state restoration," which involved the myriad practical difficulties – in addition to ending slavery – that would have to be addressed in restoring the rebellious states to the Union. Congress had considered legislation regarding these matters in early 1862, and halting initiatives had been undertaken in Virginia and North Carolina. By June, however, Federal military forces had conquered and occupied New Orleans and southern Louisiana; Memphis, Nashville, and much of west and central Tennessee; and parts of northern and eastern Arkansas. Federal military success in the western theater made concrete the abstract problem of state restoration even as the fate of slavery further complicated it.

before the war, Oakes, *The Crooked Path to Abolition*, 176–80. Again, James M. Ashley is something of an outlier here. Indeed, Ashley was also one of the few northern antislavery political leaders who rejected the idea of the Federal consensus before the war and argued that the Constitution already empowered the Federal government to abolish slavery in the states, a position he would have to reconcile with the Thirteenth Amendment itself. Zietlow, *Forgotten Emancipator*, 89.

Following these military gains, amorphous Unionist movements in Louisiana and Tennessee began to take shape. They included slaveholders and antislavery advocates as well as Unionists of various stripes and even former secessionists. The failure of what many Northerners had believed was latent southern Unionism to seize the initiative has long been recognized as a key factor in Lincoln's decision to issue the Emancipation Proclamation, although Lincoln eventually excluded southern Louisiana and Tennessee from the proclamation. Initially, Unionists in each of these two states worked together toward state restoration, and their primary goal throughout 1862 was to initiate reorganization efforts before the Federal government became fully committed to destroying slavery. However, the proclamation drove a wedge into southern Unionism, dividing Unionists in both states into proslavery and free-state factions.

Throughout 1863 and most of 1864, rival Unionist factions in Tennessee and Louisiana vied for control of the state restoration process. Free-state forces attempted to organize state governments and write free-state constitutions, while "conservative Unionists" undertook to restore their states to the Union under their antebellum constitutions in hopes of preserving slavery. Seeking to gain legitimacy, both sides repeatedly appealed to Lincoln and to Congress. Although Republicans and other antislavery advocates had already begun to link abolition to state restoration by early 1863, the contest over state reorganization in the lower Mississippi underscored the essential limitations of military emancipation, and thereby helped to catalyze the freeing of slaves into constitutional abolition. With conservative Unionism as a viable political alternative and the survival of slavery a distinct possibility, Republicans eventually developed a consensus around incorporating immediate abolition into the process of state restoration. If the Federal government could not abolish slavery in the states, it could require rebellious states – as a result of the specific circumstances of civil war – to enact free-state constitutions. The situation in the lower Mississippi valley was not the sole factor in this transition. However, owing to the strategic significance of the lower Mississippi valley and to Federal military success there, and because state restoration efforts had advanced further there than anywhere else in the rebellious states, the region assumed special salience in the debate over wartime Reconstruction and in establishing the abolition of slavery as an essential requirement for restoring the seceded states to the Union. Wartime Reconstruction in the lower Mississippi valley, in short, forced northern antislavery advocates to resolve the fundamental problem that had plagued the antebellum abolitionist movement almost from its very inception.[9]

---

[9] James Oakes observes in *The Crooked Path to Abolition* (194): "Lincoln's sustained efforts to get states to abolish slavery, *after* the Emancipation Proclamation had been issued, remains one of the least-understood features of his presidency." I would argue that the

Again, the idea of slavery somehow enduring after Confederate military defeat seems absurd in hindsight. The trope that "slavery would never survive the war" had become widespread by mid-1863, and historians have readily accepted it. Yet no person at the time, upon sober reflection, would have considered slavery's demise a certainty before it was formally abolished. Proslavery Unionists, in trying to keep slavery alive, were hardly delusional; antislavery advocates, in warning that slavery might survive the war, were not paranoid. (The widespread belief among white Southerners, even *after* military defeat, that slavery could still be salvaged only lends further weight to the conservative-Unionist program.) Lincoln and congressional Republicans categorically opposed such an outcome, but preventing the rebellious states from returning with slavery was not the same thing as abolishing slavery in them. So long as slavery continued to exist legally, so long as large numbers of slaves who had been declared free by the Emancipation Proclamation remained enslaved, so long as conservative Unionism remained a genuine threat in the Union-occupied South, and so long as northern War Democrats opposed an abolitionist war, the possibility of some form of slavery surviving the rebellion – even following northern military victory – could not be dismissed.

Insofar as the North was fighting a war solely to preserve the Union, the question commonly thought of as "Reconstruction" was more accurately one of state restoration. Once the Union adopted military emancipation, however, the fate of slavery converged with – and eventually became inseparable from – the issue of state restoration. Thus, it was the conjoining of abolition to state restoration following the Emancipation Proclamation – precipitated by the contest between free-state and conservative Unionists in the lower Mississippi valley – that gave rise to *Reconstruction*. Moreover, because Republicans came to see the end of slavery as inseparable from state restoration, they likewise viewed the Federal abolition amendment as an essential *complement* to Reconstruction legislation, not as a stand-alone measure. Such legislation would address, in addition to the consequences of abolition, the numerous other issues resulting from Confederate military defeat. Congressional Republicans eventually agreed that the seceded states, although technically never having left the Union, would nonetheless be required to meet certain conditions before being restored to it, and that those conditions would include

---

scholarship on emancipation has almost completely *ignored* how the internal dynamics within the Union-occupied rebellious states – the lower Mississippi valley especially – influenced the shift toward constitutional abolition. Oddly, Rebecca E. Zietlow's otherwise thorough study of James M. Ashley, which devotes considerable attention to his theories of Reconstruction, almost entirely skips over the crucial period between the issuing of the Emancipation Proclamation and the convening of the Thirty-Eighth Congress in December 1863, when the idea of a Federal abolition amendment was taken up. This time gap includes the second session of the Thirty-Seventh Congress, from December 1862 to March 1863. Zietlow, *Forgotten Emancipator*, esp. the shift from chap. 5 to chap. 6.

the state-level abolition of slavery. After first entertaining notions of "territorialization" – the idea that the seceded states had reverted to territories and thus could be ruled directly by Congress – in justifying this requirement, most Republicans gravitated around the concept that slavery was incompatible with the constitutional provision enjoining the Federal government to guarantee to the states a "republican form of government." The amendment, then, was originally part of what Michael Vorenberg has called a "two-pronged method," which would also include a Reconstruction bill, for restoring the Union without slavery.[10]

There is a certain irony here. The conventional account of the destruction of slavery holds that formal abolition was meant to be carried out by Federal means, and that the states that abolished slavery during the war (Arkansas, Louisiana, Tennessee, Maryland, Missouri, Virginia, and West Virginia) constituted the exception, not the rule. After all, the Thirteenth Amendment abolished slavery in most of the former Confederate states, as well as in Kentucky and Delaware (although Andrew Johnson also required the rebellious states to abolish slavery in their state constitutions, in addition to ratifying the amendment). However, that was not the case. Once the war became an assault against slavery, most Americans, including antislavery advocates, assumed that slavery would be abolished via *state* means, carried out by local Unionists working under Federal oversight as part of the process of state restoration – precisely how slavery was abolished in three of the states of the lower Mississippi valley.[11] In other words, the process of ending slavery in most of the lower Mississippi valley more closely approximated how contemporaries envisioned slavery's abolition than did the manner in which it was ended in the other Confederate states, save Virginia.[12] Only after Lincoln's reelection in November 1864 did the main focus shift to Federal abolition.

This post hoc logic would later be applied to the story of slavery's end. As Peter L. Kolchin has observed, the destruction of slavery in the United States

---

[10] Vorenberg, *Final Freedom*, 51.
[11] Oakes argues in *The Crooked Path to Abolition*, chap. 6, that Lincoln and Republicans eventually came to adopt a three-pronged strategy for ending slavery that included military emancipation, state-level abolition, and the Federal abolition amendment. This argument has much validity. However, in framing this policy in many respects as the fulfillment of a vision that antislavery advocates had developed decades earlier, Oakes's argument, I believe, misses the deeply contingent nature by which this strategy unfolded. Insofar as Lincoln and Republicans adopted a coherent plan, the plan was itself the product of the circumstances of war, even if some of the concepts that informed it had been developed earlier.
[12] An important qualifier here, as will be seen, is that most slavery opponents insisted that this process was to be implemented under congressional authority, via legislation, and not by executive authority under a presidential proclamation (and worse, through military power).

was "post-planned."[13] The central challenges regarding slavery during most of the war had been the emergence of military emancipation, the translating of military emancipation into formal abolition, and the convergence of state restoration and abolition. Only in early 1865 did the Thirteenth Amendment emerge as the crowning achievement of abolition, or what Lincoln called "a King's cure for all the evils." Whereas the main northern objective had been state restoration at the start of the war, and whereas abolition and state restoration converged during it, the amendment came to supersede state restoration as the war neared its end. The amendment was being sent to the states before the decision had been made as to what role the rebellious states would play in the ratification process. For several reasons in early 1865, including the story of House passage of the amendment, the failure of Lincoln and congressional Republicans to agree on Reconstruction legislation before the war ended, and Lincoln's assassination, the idea of the amendment as an independent measure designed to give constitutional sanction to the Emancipation Proclamation – having nothing to do with state restoration – came to be applied retroactively to the amendment's origins. This retrofitted idea has been central to the story of slavery's destruction ever since. Working from the assumption that it had been part of the plan all along, some scholars have even anachronistically attributed it to antebellum abolitionists.

* * *

At the risk of violating the dictum "never explain," I offer certain caveats that may enable the reader to better understand my intentions and modus operandi. First, while this book is firmly grounded in primary sources, many of which are now readily accessible online, it also relies heavily on the extensive secondary literature on the wartime lower Mississippi valley and on the various other topics it examines. I readily acknowledge my debt to my predecessors' efforts and insights. Also, I originally intended the notes to include comprehensive surveys of this secondary literature. However, it quickly became evident that such a strategy would add considerable bulk to what promised to be a lengthy manuscript. Because I wanted to devote such space as I had to the presentation of my argument, and not to long, exhaustive (and exhausting) footnotes, I have employed a "minimalist" approach to the citations (aside from the aforementioned literature on emancipation). The bibliography is likewise selective, being mostly limited to works cited. I trust the reader will recognize those instances in which I signal my awareness of the large scholarly literature – sometimes by the use of a particular word or phrase – on a given topic. It would not be an overstatement to say that I have been working on this book – unbeknownst even to myself – during more than thirty years of research, reading, and teaching.

---

[13] Kolchin, "Reexamining Southern Emancipation," 15. (Quotation marks in the original.)

There is also the issue of terminology. Scholars customarily use the term *emancipation* to signify the cluster of issues arising from the destruction of New World slavery. Thus, they speak of the nineteenth century as "the Age of Emancipation." (This term, of course, has even wider applicability.) This study employs emancipation in this sense when the meaning is clear. However, because my argument hinges so keenly on distinguishing between the freeing of slaves and the formal abolition of slavery, I generally maintain this distinction. I am not suggesting that historians have been incorrect to use emancipation in its more generic sense, and I often do so myself. Nonetheless, I generally distinguish between *emancipation* (or *military emancipation*) when referring to the freeing of slaves without ending slavery as an institution and *abolition* (and abolish, etc.) when referring to the legal and constitutional eradication of slavery.

Although focused mostly on formal politics, this book includes a series of four chapters (8, 13, 17, and 20), beginning with the 1863 agricultural year, that trace the disintegration of slavery as a labor system and the emergence of a new one to replace it. These *plantation-labor* chapters complement the political narrative but also constitute an essential element of the analysis. They demonstrate that the advent of wartime free labor propelled the transformation from military emancipation to constitutional abolition in two ways. First, responsibility fell primarily to Federal authorities to make freedom meaningful to the freed people in their daily working lives and in the care of the nonproductive members of their communities, matters over which the slaveholders had previously wielded total authority. Second, wartime free labor revealed the limits of military emancipation, or the freeing of slaves, and demonstrated the need for formal abolition. This "on-the-ground" experience, whatever shortcomings it exposed, was essential to ending slavery. These chapters, moreover, rest heavily on the volumes of *Freedom: A Documentary History of Emancipation, 1861–1867*, the documentary editing project with which all scholars of emancipation are familiar (and on which I have been an editor). In addition to offering both temporal and geographical specificity, the wealth of readily accessible source material in *Freedom* provides an unparalleled range of perspectives and affords scholars a veritable historical kaleidoscope through which to view the process of emancipation.

Although an essential thread running through the plantation-labor chapters is the importance of "ordinary" men and women in shaping their own destinies, this book also argues that their "on the ground" experience had to be translated into society's institutional structure in order to be secured. This book thereby attests to the significance of institutions and formal politics to the historical process. Individual choices and actions are shaped by this institutional structure – by laws, policies, proclamations, orders, amendments, and the like, and by everything required for their enforcement. But individuals also push constantly against it. Even in instances where men and women demonstrated an incorrect understanding of policy, the fact that they invoked it or protested against it is of historical value. A society's institutional structure, then, works in conjunction with human agency to make history. This emphasis on institutions is not to deny the central role of the slaves in destroying slavery, which stands as one of the great historiographical revolutions and conceptual breakthroughs in all of the writing of US history. Instead, both the slaves' historical agency *and* formal institutions were essential to the destruction of slavery.

By the same token, because this book places much emphasis on formal politics, there are stretches where the African American experience is not at the center of the narrative. Nonetheless, my analysis rests on the basic supposition that emancipation amounted to a social revolution in which the slaves played an essential role. Despite their apparent powerlessness, the slaves, as historians have well established, shaped slavery in integral ways. Likewise, once hostilities commenced and the nation descended into civil war, the slaves' response to the opportunities that war presented – in their efforts to free themselves and their loved ones and to bring down the slave regime – serves as the foundation on which the entire endeavor is predicated. Enslaved and formerly enslaved historical actors do not appear in every scene in the drama presented here, but there is little that they, to one degree or another, did not cause.

Along those same lines, critics of my argument might contend that once the Union adopted the Emancipation Proclamation and large numbers of slaves gained their freedom, slavery was doomed. The genie, as it were, could never have been returned to the bottle. I would counter that the process by which the political consensus materialized that slavery would not be allowed to survive the war was contingent, not inevitable. It was an act of political will that was contested at every step of the way and could have been derailed at any juncture. Even allowing that slavery's demise, as the abolitionists argued, was historically fated, the manner in which it ended was hardly a foregone conclusion. It is possible – even necessary – to envision alternate scenarios. Some modified version of slavery might have survived the war, for example, only to end through a patchwork of various state-sponsored measures extending over decades. Anyone who doubts how far the slaveholders and their fellow travelers were willing to go to preserve slavery, to salvage some shred of their former authority, and to reassert racial dominance once they had half a chance need only peruse the historical record. This is not a moral judgment. Their actions followed from the logic of their own worldview. If the story of emancipation and its consequences could have had a better outcome, it could also have had a worse one.

This book also contends that no matter how limited freedom ultimately ended up being for the former slaves, and no matter how overwhelming the economic and racial power they faced, legal freedom marked an essential break with chattel slavery. The violence, odium, and hatred that the freed people suffered at the hands of their former oppressors, and the animosity, cynicism, and betrayal they endured at the hands of their liberators are well known. The assumption, central to nineteenth-century liberalism, that everything would fall into place once slavery had been eliminated seems deeply delusional in hindsight. Nonetheless, I respectfully disagree with some recent works – excellent pieces of scholarship – that offer more pessimistic assessments of emancipation's consequences.[14] Likewise, while I recognize the contributions of the scholarship on "the second slavery," I suspect that this approach can also be taken too far. The argument that the so-called Age of Emancipation of the late eighteenth and early nineteenth centuries actually witnessed a revitalization of slavery has some merit, as does the view that this second slavery, when finally defeated later in the nineteenth century, was replaced by the quasi-freedom of the Age of Capital.[15] Yet this argument also misses the essential adaptability that had always infused New World slavery. From its very beginnings in the western hemisphere, racial slavery had constantly evolved. The ostensible "second slavery" was more a continuation of this process of evolution than a new historical formation. Moreover, as this book contends, a system of political economy based on chattel slavery differed qualitatively from one predicated on the principle of "no property in man." Formal freedom was not nearly enough, but it was an essential first step, without which nothing else was possible.

This book does not systematically address the border states of Missouri and Kentucky, but it incorporates developments in them as necessary. Historians have long recognized the internal divisions within antebellum northern and southern society, and the recent scholarship on slavery and the Civil War era has embraced the "borderlands" as an analytical concept.[16] Before the war, conventional antislavery thought had held that the border states would lead the way in abolishing slavery, to be followed first by the upper-South and then by the lower-South states. The start of hostilities exacerbated tensions within the

---

[14] See, for example, Downs, *Sick from Freedom*. Downs offers an essential corrective to the story of emancipation as a sort of liberal triumphalist narrative. Historians have hardly been unfamiliar with the shortcomings of Federal wartime policy toward the former slaves. Yet Downs shows that these shortcomings did not simply cause hardship but rather cost tens of thousands of innocent persons their lives. Other recent works that depict the hardships of emancipation while drawing less pessimistic conclusions include Taylor, *Embattled Freedom*, and Manning, *Troubled Refuge*. The essential question all of these works raise is whether the suffering caused by Federal emancipation policy was systematic (if unintentional) or incidental.

[15] It is not necessary to cite the literature on "the second slavery." For a thoughtful essay suggesting that insights from this literature – along with those from recent works on slavery and capitalist development in nineteenth-century US society – can be applied to emancipation, see Mathisen, "Second Slavery," esp. the works cited at 694–96, n. 12–21.

[16] There is an extensive literature on the border states that does not need to be cited here, but see especially, Phillips, *Rivers Ran Backward*, and his essay, "Southern Cross, North Star."

borderlands as much as it accentuated differences between the slave and free states, and the stance of the border states was immediately seen as integral to the outcome of the war. "To lose Kentucky is nearly the same as to lose the whole game," Lincoln famously declared in 1861. Likewise, ending slavery in the border states was soon incorporated into Lincoln's strategic vision, since slave states that began to embrace abolition, he believed, would be unlikely to join the rebellion.

That being said, this book maintains that the lower Mississippi valley provides a sharper image for understanding this era than do the border states, and that the conflict between the free and slave states better encapsulates the meaning of the war than does the internal chaos of the borderlands.[17] Whereas Lincoln had been keenly solicitous of the border states during the war's early phase, he effectively wrote them off in deciding to issue the Emancipation Proclamation. Because they did not secede, the border states did not experience the process of state restoration and its various exigencies. The border states no doubt witnessed fierce internal conflict, but it was in the lower Mississippi valley where the challenge of restoring the seceded states while abolishing slavery had to be worked out. As essential as the border states had been to the long-term vision of ending slavery, the states of the lower Mississippi valley eventually leap-frogged over them in achieving this objective. The one thing this book does share with the recent borderlands scholarship, however, is the importance of the western theater to the war's outcome. Given the significance of the Mississippi River to American development before the Civil War, many contemporaries intuited at the start of hostilities that control of the river would prove decisive, and they were right. Just as some military historians argue that the Civil War was decided in the western theater, much about the destruction of slavery and its consequences can be told by looking at the lower Mississippi valley.[18]

Finally, it is necessary to return to the question of the Constitution and slavery. Generations of Americans before the Civil War debated whether this document was "proslavery" or "antislavery," and scholars have continued this debate ever since. The Constitution reflected any number of compromises on

---

[17] Some work on the borderlands has had the unintended consequence of deemphasizing the differences between northern and southern society and thus minimizing slavery as a cause of the war. By contrast, Edward L. Ayers's work on Franklin County, Pennsylvania, and Augusta County, Virginia, shows these two communities to be virtually mirror images of each other, with the crucial exception of *accentuating* slavery as the key difference between them. See Ayers, *In the Presence of Mine Enemies* and *Thin Light of Freedom*.

[18] Hess, *Civil War in the West*, esp. 317–19. On the role of Union officers in bringing on military emancipation in the western theater: Teters, *Practical Liberators*. This is not to deny the importance of the eastern theater to the outcome of the war or to emancipation. Brasher, *Peninsular Campaign and the Necessity of Emancipation*.

slavery, including the three-fifths clause, the fugitive slave provision, and the eventual prohibition of the international slave trade. However, the most important principle the Constitution incorporated with regard to slavery, I would argue, was the Federal consensus – the idea that slavery in the states was secure from Federal interference. Whatever regulatory powers Congress may have enjoyed over slavery in the territories, or elsewhere, Americans almost universally believed that the Federal government possessed no authority to regulate or "interfere with" slavery in the states. Ironically, this principle, which arguably did more to shape the debate over slavery than any other single idea, as James Oakes has observed, "was not even in the Constitution." Americans had essentially made up – though not without reason – the concept that would have perhaps the most profound repercussions for what was inarguably the most divisive issue they faced before the Civil War. Because only the states could end slavery, the citizens of the slave states would have to be convinced to carry out this objective voluntarily. This was the central challenge the abolitionists confronted.[19]

Despite the excellent recent scholarship on antislavery constitutionalism and on abolitionism, historians have been less successful in reconciling the antislavery movement with the Federal consensus. For all of the ingenious arguments that the advocates of an antislavery Constitution were able to concoct, and for all of the moral condemnation that the abolitionists heaped on slavery, antislavery advocates never resolved the central problem that only the states could abolish slavery. In showing – often very cleverly – how specific provisions of the Constitution could be interpreted from an antislavery perspective, such as the fugitive slave clause, the abolitionists and their allies were still only hitting around the periphery. They were essentially talking about freeing individual slaves, but they were not getting at the main problem – abolishing slavery as an institution. Confronted with the Federal consensus, the antislavery movement never developed a concrete, feasible plan for ending slavery in the states under peacetime conditions. To be sure, as Sean Wilentz convincingly argues, the opponents of slavery achieved the crucial victory at the constitutional convention of preventing the principle of property in man from gaining constitutional sanction. This victory, moreover, later undergirded the abolitionist movement. Yet even antislavery advocates who denied the constitutional sanction of property in man nonetheless accepted the Federal consensus. For all of the pressure the abolitionists could level against the slave states and the slaveholders, there was *nothing* either the free states or the Federal government could do to compel the slave states to end slavery

---

[19] It is not necessary to cite the voluminous literature on the Constitution and slavery. I have found the recent works on antislavery constitutionalism, in particular Wilentz, *No Property in Man*, and Oakes, *The Crooked Path to Abolition* (quotation, 19), to be persuasive, though, as I note, not without their own difficulties.

against their will. The proslavery advocates, whenever the battle was going against them, could always retreat to the bunker of the Federal consensus.[20]

Admittedly, the abolitionists had developed something of a long-term vision for eradicating slavery, or what James Oakes calls "the Antislavery Project." It involved, he notes, "a series of specific policies that were designed to stop and then reverse the expansion of slavery," putting slavery on the course (quoting Lincoln) to "ultimate extinction." Among these measures were stopping the spread of slavery into the territories and prohibiting the admission of any more slave states; ending all support for slavery wherever Federal authority prevailed, and restricting slavery to local authority (or "freedom national"); limiting the scope of Federal fugitive slave laws by providing fugitive slaves with due process protections; pressuring the border states and upper-South states to end slavery while also making available to them Federal assistance and encouragement; and, finally, convincing the lower-South states – surrounded by a *cordon sanitaire* and with no other choice – to abolish slavery. In a larger sense, the project entailed giving an antislavery reading to every provision of the Constitution, and to the document as a whole, and following this reading through to its logical conclusion. By the 1850s, Oakes contends, the abolitionists had succeeded "in restoring the problem of slavery to the heart of American politics," and Lincoln's victory in 1860 was a major step in fulfilling this vision.[21]

The only problem with this plan, and it was a crippling one, was that anybody who took the time to listen to the white South on the topic – especially its political, cultural, and intellectual leadership – would have realized that the chances of the slave states voluntarily ending slavery at any point in the foreseeable future were virtually nil. And amending the Constitution, as noted, was not an option. Some critics of the abolitionists charged that their tactics were counterproductive and actually hardened the South's commitment to slavery. This may have been true. But by the time "second wave," or "immediate," abolitionism emerged in the early 1830s, the white South had already begun shifting from the "necessary evil" to the "positive good" defense of slavery. To be sure, there was an "other" South, as Carl N. Degler and other historians have maintained, that included dissidents against slavery. Also, the fear that social and economic class divisions among white Southerners might

---

[20] Wilentz, *No Property in Man*, and Oakes, *The Crooked Path to Abolition*. Manisha Sinha's monumental and otherwise exhaustive analysis of the abolitionist movement, *The Slave's Cause*, for instance, contains no substantive discussion of any abolitionist plan to end slavery. Her study examines just about every other issue relevant to abolitionism, but not this crucial one. This observation is not intended as a criticism of Sinha's excellent work, but the omission reflects the political dead end in which the abolitionists found themselves.

[21] Oakes, *The Crooked Path to Abolition*, xiv. For other recent work on antislavery constitutionalism, Zietlow, *Forgotten Emancipator*, chap. 2, and "Ideological Origins."

cause nonslaveholders to turn against slavery, as various historians have argued, was a main driving force behind secession. Nonetheless, given everything white Southerners said about slavery after 1830, and arguably well before, as a wealth of historical scholarship has demonstrated, it is almost impossible to envision a scenario in which the slave states ever would have abolished slavery of their own volition. Neither political power nor moral suasion seemed to offer a way out.[22]

The tragic but indisputable fact remains that the very fabric of the antebellum constitutional system – in particular, the Federal consensus and the difficult amending process – allowed for no viable means to end slavery. Precisely because the war came, James Oakes has again observed, "there's no way to know whether the [Antislavery Project] would have worked in peacetime." However, we can be fairly certain that it would *not* have worked, because the constitutional system – combined with the white South's unstinting commitment to slavery – would not have permitted it. In perhaps a cruel irony, the Constitution contained no sanction of the principle of "property in man," but neither did it include any realistic method for putting slavery on the path to "ultimate extinction." Due process protections or the writ of habeas corpus might have benefitted the handful of slaves in the upper South who managed to escape to free territory, but what good would these precepts do the hundreds of thousands of enslaved persons in the Deep-South plantation belt that extended from South Carolina to Louisiana? Indeed, had the war not intervened, the more likely outcome would have been a Supreme Court decision, as Lincoln had warned, effectively nationalizing slavery by mandating that slaveholders could not be prohibited to bring their slave property into the "free" states. The frightening reality is that had white Southerners not panicked in response to Lincoln's election, a strategy many supporters of slavery advocated during the secession crisis, slavery conceivably could have gone on indefinitely. To say that the abolitionists provoked the South into a war that resulted in the destruction of slavery – a war that could easily have produced a very different outcome – is not a very persuasive argument for the efficacy of abolitionism as a political movement, or of antislavery constitutionalism as a political doctrine. The claim that the abolitionists ultimately carried the day is predicated, however implicitly, on a kind of historical determinism.[23]

Once hostilities started, the issue of whether states that were in rebellion against the national authority would continue to enjoy constitutional protections, including the ban on Federal interference with slavery in the states, emerged as one of the war's central conundrums, and as one of the key difficulties antislavery advocates would have to overcome. Much as the

---

[22] Degler, *Other South*. It is not necessary to cite here the voluminous literature on proslavery thought, a topic discussed in the Prologue.

[23] Oakes, *The Crooked Path to Abolition*, xxviii.

abolitionists had lacked a plan to end slavery before the war, Republicans and other antislavery advocates now had to figure out a way to move beyond the freeing of individual slaves, even in large numbers, to abolishing slavery as an institution. This book attempts to explain – by examining war, emancipation, and wartime Reconstruction in the lower Mississippi valley – how they accomplished that goal.

PROLOGUE

Life – and Labor – on the Mississippi

One of the world's longest and most powerful rivers, the Mississippi River has always been central to the American experience. For millions of years before human beings set eyes on it, the river and the many tributaries and distributaries that make up the Mississippi River basin carved and recarved the landscape. This massive geological drainage system encompasses nearly half of the continental United States, from the Appalachians to the Rockies, and covers more than a million square miles. Within it, the *lower* Mississippi valley – the area south of the confluence with the Ohio River – constitutes a distinct geological entity.

Before there was a United States, the river and its adjoining lands shaped the lives of the indigenous populations and framed European imperial rivalries. The earliest inhabitants of the lower Mississippi valley arrived between 10,000 and 12,000 years ago, and their descendants dwelled for centuries in hemispheric isolation before European contact. The process by which they and the other indigenous peoples of the western hemisphere were dispossessed of these lands – and their populations decimated and their cultures nearly erased – marked one of the major turning points of human history. By the early nineteenth century, the landscape had already undergone massive political, cultural, and physical reconfiguration, as the European settlers and their descendants partitioned the land into political entities and personal fiefdoms while commanding the productive capacities and lives of persons of African descent. The first half of the nineteenth century witnessed the extension of plantation agriculture and racial slavery – grounded in notions of racial supremacy and "Manifest Destiny" – and the further destruction or removal of the various American Indian tribal groups. By the 1850s, as Walter Johnson has demonstrated, the lower Mississippi valley lay at the epicenter of what slavery's most zealous advocates envisioned as a slave-based, global empire, one that would colonize Central America and the Caribbean basin while extending its suzerainty across the Atlantic and Pacific oceans. These "dark dreams," however delusional in hindsight, exerted powerful influence at the time, and they pivoted on the lower Mississippi valley.[1]

---

[1] Johnson, *River of Dark Dreams*, esp. chaps. 11–14; Hahn, *Nation Without Borders*, 2.

As a distinct region, the lower Mississippi valley epitomized the antebellum South. It could almost be thought of as a living organism, with the Mississippi River and its auxiliaries serving as the nervous system. Although the region exhibited much internal diversity, the one feature of life on the Mississippi that trumped almost any other consideration before the Civil War was the commitment of the region's white inhabitants to racial slavery.

I

The states within the lower Mississippi valley, as with almost all geopolitical bodies, are defined by boundaries that conform to geographical contours or markers but are also somewhat arbitrary. At its most basic level, the region can be divided into the lower-lying alluvial areas and the uplands. This distinction, in turn, largely corresponds to geographical areas that were more conducive to plantation agriculture and large slaveholdings and areas that were less so – in short, areas that lay within or outside the South's plantation belt.[2]

From its confluence with the Ohio River, the Mississippi flows between southwestern Kentucky and southeastern Missouri before forming Tennessee's western border. Tennessee has traditionally consisted of three distinct regions – west, middle, and east – that are legally recognized as the Grand Divisions of Tennessee. From their sources in the Appalachian Mountains, the Tennessee and Cumberland Rivers, as major tributaries of the Ohio that join it near the confluence with the Mississippi, follow a westerly course and also belong to the lower Mississippi valley system. The Cumberland Plateau is a massive geological formation that forms the boundary between east and middle Tennessee, while the western reach of the Tennessee River divides middle and west Tennessee. The plantation economy and slavery assumed increasing importance as one moved from the mountainous east to the rolling hills and fertile valleys of middle Tennessee to the low-lying west.[3]

If Tennessee comprises three distinct regions, Arkansas is made up of two. An imaginary diagonal line running from southwest to northeast bisects the state. The uplands, including the Ozark and Ouachita Mountains, lie to the north and west, and the alluvial regions, including the Arkansas Delta, to the south and east. Southwest and south-central Arkansas also features elevated areas and less fertile soil than the Delta. Plantation agriculture predominated in the southeast and farming in the northwest. Arkansas's four main rivers – the Arkansas, Red, Ouachita, and White – generally flow from the northwest uplands in a southeasterly direction toward the Gulf. The state's

---

[2] Rothstein, "Antebellum South as a Dual Economy." Robinson, *Bitter Fruits of Bondage* (48–49), notes the correlation between soil fertility, large slaveholdings, and plantation agriculture.

[3] Ash, *Middle Tennessee Society Transformed*, chap. 1.

most important river is the Arkansas, which enters west-central Arkansas and cuts the state in half, slithering between the Ozark and Ouachita Mountains and continuing through the Arkansas Delta, past Little Rock and Pine Bluff, before emptying into the Mississippi. The White River flows from north-central Arkansas and joins the Mississippi a few miles upriver from the mouth of the Arkansas. The Red River briefly slices through Arkansas's southwest corner before entering northwest Louisiana.[4]

Mississippi and Louisiana lie almost entirely within the Mississippi River's alluvial plain. The Yazoo and Big Black Rivers are the Mississippi's main tributaries within the state of Mississippi. The Yazoo–Mississippi Delta, also known as the Mississippi Delta, is a distinct region of northwest Mississippi, lying between the Mississippi River and the Yazoo River, which empties into the Mississippi just above Vicksburg. Much of this region remained undeveloped until after the Civil War.[5] The state's southwest corner consists of what was once commonly known as the Natchez District. Centered around the city of Natchez, it extended southward to the Louisiana–Mississippi latitudinal boundary and northward to Vicksburg. The area along the Tombigbee River, in east-central Mississippi, constituted the terminus of the Black Belt that extended from central Georgia to Mississippi. Only the piney woods of southeastern Mississippi, east of the Pearl River, and the hill country of the northeast were largely beyond the sphere of plantation agriculture.[6]

One of only two states, along with Minnesota, that the Mississippi River courses internally, Louisiana consists almost entirely of the alluvium of the Mississippi and Red Rivers. The Red River and the Ouachita River, one of the Red's main tributaries, are not technically tributaries of the Mississippi, but the Red and Mississippi Rivers were effectively connected during the nineteenth century, and the Atchafalaya River functions as a distributary of both. (Today, the convergence of the Mississippi, Red, and Atchafalaya Rivers is controlled by the Old River Control Structure, which prevents the Mississippi from changing course to the Atchafalaya and bypassing New Orleans.) The Red River runs southeasterly through northwest and central Louisiana before joining the Mississippi River above Baton Rouge. The region below the confluence of the Mississippi and Red Rivers, especially east of the Atchafalaya, is home to the state's sugar country. This area includes bayous Lafourche and Teche, which serve as important distributaries of the Mississippi, but it also consists of much swampland and marsh that are not conducive to agricultural development. Plantation agriculture was also less prominent in

---

[4] McNeilly, *Old South Frontier*, 1–10.
[5] There is an extensive literature on the society and culture of the Yazoo–Mississippi Delta, most of which focuses on the postbellum period. For the prewar period, see Saikku, *This Delta, This Land*, chaps. 1–2; Cobb, *Most Southern Place on Earth*, 3–29.
[6] Bond, *Political Culture in the Nineteenth-Century South*, chap. 1.

the north-central hill country, between the Red and Ouachita Rivers, and in the Florida Parishes, the area between the Mississippi and Pearl Rivers that consists of the same piney woods of southeastern Mississippi. ("Parishes" are Louisiana's equivalent of counties.) Yet even in these latter areas, small slaveholdings were common and plantations not unknown. Only in southwestern Louisiana, largely coastal prairie, were slavery and plantation agriculture negligible.[7]

In his famous work *Life on the Mississippi*, published in 1883 but in part a memoir of his days on the river before the war, Mark Twain observed:

> One who knows the Mississippi will promptly aver – not aloud, but to himself – that ten thousand River Commissions, with the mines of the world at their back, cannot tame that lawless stream, cannot curb it or confine it, cannot say to it, Go here, or Go there, and make it obey; cannot save a shore which it has sentenced; cannot bar its path with an obstruction which it will not tear down, dance over, and laugh at.[8]

Twain was right. For all of humanity's hubris, the river will do what it wants. But over millennia, the immense destructive power of the Mississippi River also created a natural environment that proved to be ideal for the production of cotton, sugarcane, and other commodities. This undertaking would require a form of social relations in which one group of people systematically expropriated the productive and reproductive capacities of another group of people. To facilitate this task, the members of the former group would construct a political and legal order devoted to the preservation of those social relations, and they would formulate a body of ideas to rationalize practices that appeared to violate the most basic human instincts. The latter group, by contrast, would face the challenges of resisting their oppression in what few ways were available to them, and of finding meaning in what seemed an absurd existence.

In other words, these rivers had helped to lay the foundations of the plantation economy and racial slavery that dominated the lower Mississippi valley of the mid-nineteenth century. But once this society joined the attempt to create an independent nation, dedicated to the perpetuation of slavery as a way of life, these rivers would be a key factor in the aspiring nation's undoing.

II

Population figures for 1860 demonstrate the importance both of slavery to the lower Mississippi valley and of the lower Mississippi valley to what would become the Confederate States of America (CSA). The four states of

---

[7] Howard, *Political Tendencies in Louisiana*. On the Florida parishes, Hyde, *Pistols and Politics* and *Fierce and Fractious Frontier*.

[8] The Mississippi River Commission, which still exists, was created by Congress in 1879 and charged with the oversight of virtually all topics relating to the Mississippi River, including, perhaps most importantly, flood control.

the lower Mississippi valley had a total population, excluding free persons of color, of 3,017,694 persons, of whom 1,155,191, or 38.3 percent, were enslaved and 1,862,503, or 61.7 percent, were white. The percentage of slaves in each state's population adhered to the traditional divide between the lower South and upper South, with slaves making up 55.2 percent of the population in Mississippi and 48.1 percent in Louisiana, as opposed to 25 percent each in Arkansas and Tennessee. The total population of the eleven CSA states was nearly 9 million persons, of whom just over 3.5 million, or 38.9 percent, were enslaved, and just under 5.5 million, or 61.1 percent were white. Thus, the breakdown between slaves and whites in the lower Mississippi valley effectively matched that of the CSA overall, while the region accounted for approximately one-third of both the CSA's slave and white populations.[9]

Within the lower Mississippi valley, aggregate county-level or parish-level population data confirm the link between alluvial areas, slaveholding, and plantation agriculture.[10] In Tennessee, where one-fourth of white households owned slaves overall, slaves made up less than 30 percent of the population in every county in the eastern part of the state, and in many of these counties less than 10 percent, although some larger holdings occurred along the eastern reaches of the Tennessee River valley. In middle Tennessee, more moderate slaveholdings generally prevailed. Most of the counties in the Nashville Basin,

---

[9] Unless otherwise indicated, the free black populations have been excluded from the discussion of population in this section, since the main purpose here is to draw comparisons between the white and slave populations. Louisiana was notable for its free black population before the Civil War, but even this population (fewer than 20,000 in 1860) was demographically negligible compared to the other groups. The figures in this section have been calculated from the following sources: Kennedy, *Population of the United States* and *Agriculture of the United States*; Paullin, *Atlas of the Historical Geography of the United States: Population, 1790–1930: Slaves: 1860* (https://dsl.richmond.edu/historicalatlas/68/b; accessed July 2019); The Civil War Home Page: Dedicated to the Participants, both North and South, in the Great American Civil War, 1861–1865 (www.civil-war.net/census.asp?census=Total; accessed July 2019). The *Atlas of the Historical Geography of the United States* is an interactive website that allows the user to click on a particular county for the number of slaves and their percentage of the total populations. The categories used for that map for percentages of slaves in the total population (0–10, 10–30, 30–50, and 50+) have largely been retained here. Slight discrepancies exist between some figures in the Civil War Home Page tables and those produced by the US Census. The map created by the Department of the Interior in 1861, showing the percentages of slaves in the total population for every county in the slave states, has also been consulted, although there are also slight discrepancies between it and the *Atlas of the Historical Geography of the United States*.

[10] Although aggregate data do not allow for identifying concentrations of slaveholdings *within* counties, it provides a rough approximation of the primary zones of slavery and plantation agriculture at the state level. Such data also tend to underestimate the extent of plantation agriculture. Low percentages of slaves at the county level generally indicate an absence of plantations, but such counties might still include small clusters of plantations.

in the heart of the state, included populations of between 30 and 50 percent slave, while the peripheral areas had slave populations less than 30 percent. Although only one county in middle Tennessee, Williamson, hosted a population more than 50 percent slave, several counties in this region had slave populations in excess of 40 percent. West Tennessee, where slavery and the plantation system were more prevalent, also revealed internal distinctions. Slaves constituted between 30 and 50 percent of the population, and in two cases more than 50 percent, in the six-county cluster in the state's southwestern corner, but only between 10 and 30 percent of the rest of the region.

Similarly, in Arkansas, where only 20 percent of white households owned slaves, the lowest of any CSA state, the distribution of slaves conformed to the state's topography. In no county in the state's northwestern section did slaves account for as much as 30 percent of the population, and in many counties they accounted for less than 10 percent. Such large holdings as existed in this region were along the Arkansas River. By contrast, in only two counties in southeastern Arkansas did slaves not make up at least 30 percent of the population, and in most of these counties the percentages were solidly in the mid-to-high thirties. In the heart of the Arkansas Delta, along the Mississippi and the lower reaches of the Arkansas and White Rivers, slaves made up more than 50 percent of the population, as they did in two counties along the Red and Ouachita Rivers, in southwestern and south-central Arkansas. Although slaves were a majority in only six of Arkansas's fifty-five counties, slavery was widespread in the southeastern half of the state.

Whereas Tennessee and Arkansas demonstrated limited large-scale slaveholding in the upper South, Louisiana and Mississippi likewise demonstrated the prevalence of larger holdings – and of slavery in general – in the lower South. In all but five of Louisiana's forty-eight parishes, slaves made up at least 30 percent of the population. In thirty-five of Louisiana's forty-eight parishes, slaves made up more than half the population. In a few instances the total populations were fairly small and the slave majorities slight, but in the large majority of cases the slave populations were substantial. Slaveholding was heaviest along the main waterways. Nearly every parish along the Mississippi, Red, Ouachita, and Atchafalaya Rivers and bayous Teche and Lafourche held populations of more than 50 percent slave. In the Natchez District, Tensas and Concordia parishes were more than 90 percent slave each, and in the sugar region, several parishes exceeded 70 percent slave. Along the Red River, slaveholdings were slightly more modest, generally in the 50–60 percent range. There were few areas in Louisiana where slavery was not widespread.

The population of Mississippi greatly resembled that of Louisiana, with the important exception of New Orleans. Despite vast stretches of the Yazoo-Mississippi Delta having remained unsettled before the Civil War, the entire line of counties along the western third of Mississippi held large – in many cases overwhelming – slave majorities. The four counties on the Mississippi side of the Natchez District had slave percentages lower than those on the Louisiana side (Wilkinson, 82 percent; Claiborne, 78 percent; Adams, 70 percent; and Warren, 66 percent), yet they were complemented by the counties of the Yazoo–Mississippi Delta, where many of the slave percentages were comparable or higher. Bolivar County was 87 percent slave, Washington County 92 percent, and Issaquena County 93 percent. In addition to the aforementioned section of east-central Mississippi near the Tombigbee River, which hosted a slave majority, slaves made up between 30 and 50 percent of the population of the rest of the state, save for four counties in central Mississippi and the southeastern and northeastern corners of the state.

Paradoxically, nearly half (twenty-nine of sixty) of Mississippi's counties had a white majority, a much higher percentage than Louisiana's 27 percent, even though the proportion of slaves in Mississippi's total population, at 55 percent, outpaced Louisiana's 48 percent. Only South Carolina's 57 percent was higher among the CSA states. At first glance, slaveholding also appeared to be more widely distributed in Mississippi, where 49 percent of white households owned slaves (the highest percentage of any CSA state), than in Louisiana, where only 29 percent did so. However, these percentages are significantly skewed by the 40 percent of Louisiana's white population that lived in New Orleans, where slaveholding was much less common than in the countryside. No equivalent city existed in Mississippi. Excluding New Orleans, slaves made up nearly 60 percent of the population of the rest of Louisiana, and the proportion of white households that owned slaves jumps to almost 43 percent. Despite the apparent differences between them, Mississippi and Louisiana were very similar once the unique situation of New Orleans is taken into account.

This demographic profile of the lower Mississippi valley allows for two larger conclusions. First, a virtually unbroken configuration of counties and parishes, inhabited by slave majorities and centered along the Mississippi River, stretched from southwest Tennessee to the mouth of the Mississippi River, and along the Red River valley all the way into southwest Arkansas. In addition, a penumbral region in which slaves made up between a third and half of the population further outlined this slave-majority expanse. These two areas combined, covering just over 100,000 square miles, constituted the heart of the lower Mississippi valley, and they were home to the overwhelmingly large majority of the region's more than one million slaves. Second, the process of secession in the four states of the lower Mississippi valley would largely follow the region's demographic profile. The two upper-South states would be deeply divided over disunion, with these divisions conforming to slaveholding patterns, while the lower-South states would demonstrate much greater unity.

III

By 1860, the lower Mississippi valley was the product of forces at work for more than a century and a half. From the late seventeenth century through the early nineteenth century, the land west of the Mississippi River, along with New Orleans and the surrounding Isle of Orleans, formed the colony of Louisiana. Although Louisiana always remained peripheral within the French and Spanish empires, New Orleans developed during the eighteenth century into an important commercial and political center.[11] Meanwhile, Louisiana's Florida Parishes and much of today's Mississippi, Alabama, and west Tennessee made up West Florida, which Spain and Great Britain alternately possessed between the 1760s and 1780s. By the early nineteenth century, as a result of the Louisiana Purchase and other circumstances, the United States had secured control of the entire lower Mississippi valley, setting off migrations of Anglo-Americans to the region. In addition, the invention of the cotton gin and the advent of commercial sugar production in southern Louisiana during the 1790s precipitated the plantation revolution of the ensuing decades. As a result of individual migration and the interstate slave trade, more than one million enslaved persons would be transported from the eastern seaboard states to the southwest before the Civil War. These developments transformed the region from a society with slaves into a *slave society*.[12]

Like the rest of the South, the lower Mississippi valley consisted of innumerable localities, each of which possessed its own identity and character. Arkansas and Tennessee, as upper-South states, were not as wedded to the plantation economy as were the lower-South states, but their political commitment to slavery was beyond question. East Tennessee would remain stubbornly Unionist during the war but still strongly supported slavery. Middle Tennessee spawned a genuinely mixed economy, with plantation agriculture coexisting with middling farms, smaller slaveholdings, diversified agriculture, and even a nascent industrial sector. Political allegiances would be deeply divided here during the war, and the region reflected much of the internal

---

[11] The literature on early Louisiana and New Orleans society is extensive. Important works include Din, *Spaniards, Planters, and Slaves*; Faber, *Building the Land of Dreams*; Hall, *Africans in Colonial Louisiana*; Ingersoll, *Mammon and Manon in Early New Orleans*; Johnson, *Slavery's Metropolis*; Milne, *Natchez Country*; Narrett, *Adventurism and Empire*; Powell, *Accidental City*; Smith, *Louisiana and the Gulf South Frontier*; Usner, *Indians, Settlers, and Slaves*; and Vidal, *Louisiana*.

[12] Ira Berlin's name is most closely associated with the distinction between societies with slaves and slave societies. See his *Many Thousands Gone* and *Generations of Captivity*. On the domestic slave trade, especially to the southwest, see Berlin, *Making of African America*, chap. 3; Deyle, *Carry Me Back*; Gudmestad, *Troublesome Commerce*; Johnson, *Soul by Soul*; Tadman, *Speculators and Slaves*. On the opening and development of the lower Mississippi valley and the southwest, see Johnson, *River of Dark Dreams*; Moore, *Emergence of the Cotton Kingdom*; Rothman, *Slave Country*.

chaos of the border states. West Tennessee was much more strongly defined by the plantation economy, but farming and smaller slaveholdings were also common in the region.[13]

Although eastern Arkansas experienced much development after the Louisiana Purchase, major stretches of it remained unsettled before the Civil War. Even in the developing areas, conditions often more closely resembled the frontier than a mature plantation society. Notwithstanding significant slave populations in much of the Arkansas Delta by 1860, the region displayed few ostentatious mansions or other markers of an established and self-assured elite. Statehood in 1836 had brought stability to Arkansas society, and the 1850s witnessed dramatic increases in the number of slaves, improved acreage, and the production of cotton. Still, eastern Arkansas probably remained the least developed section of the lower Mississippi valley's plantation belt before the war.[14]

Slave society in many respects had advanced much further across the river, in the Yazoo–Mississippi Delta. Although conditions there were often similar to those in Arkansas, the planters of the Mississippi Delta by mid-century had achieved considerable affluence. This was truer still for planters in the Natchez District, who were some of the largest slaveholders in the entire South and some of the wealthiest individuals in the nation. As was true of large slaveholders elsewhere in the South, especially along the rivers and in areas where internal improvements were of special concern, these planters eschewed fire-eating disunion, which was more closely associated with southern Democrats, in favor of Whig moderation. The mid-1850s demise of the Whig Party left them with nowhere to go, and most of them drifted reluctantly toward the Democrats. During the secession crisis, many hedged their bets until their state seceded. When the war finally came to their doorsteps, many fled to the Confederate interior, but others stayed put, either claiming to have been loyal all along or quickly resuming their former allegiance.[15]

Toward the northern end of the Natchez District, about thirty miles below Vicksburg, at a sharp bend in the river that has long since been cut off, was located one of the most extraordinary communities in the entire South. The

---

[13] Ash, *Middle Tennessee Society Transformed*, chap. 1.

[14] McNeilly, *Old South Frontier*; Whayne and Gatewood, *Arkansas Delta*; Whayne, *Delta Empire* and *Shadows Over Sunnyside*; Jones, "Seeding Chicot," 147–64; Moore, "'Keeping All Hands Moving'"; Walz, "Arkansas Slaveholdings and Slaveholders in 1850." For an overview of Arkansas as a slave society, see Bolton, "Slavery and the Defining of Arkansas."

[15] On the Mississippi Delta, see Cobb, *Most Southern Place on Earth*, chap. 1; Harris, *Deep Souths*, 38–49. On the Natchez District, see Brazy, *American Planter*; Davis, *Good and Faithful Labor*, chap. 2; James, *Antebellum Natchez*; Kaye, *Joining Places*; Wayne, *Reshaping of Plantation Society*, chap. 1. On the Natchez planters' political allegiances, see Cole, *Whig Party in the South*, chap. 3, esp. 66–72; Bettersworth, *Confederate Mississippi*, 4–5.

neighborhood of plantations known as "Davis Bend" had been pioneered by Joseph Davis, the eldest brother of Jefferson Davis – who was Joseph's junior by twenty-four years and to whom Joseph was more a father figure. Joseph acquired some 11,000 acres of land in 1818 and had inherited several slaves but focused mostly on his Natchez legal practice. Only after becoming familiar with the ideas of British utopian reformer Robert Owen in the early 1820s did Davis turn his attention to agriculture. Retaining 5,000 acres, which he named "Hurricane" plantation, Davis sold the rest to friends whom he wanted as good neighbors and later gave the adjoining Brierfield estate outright to his brother Jefferson.

Joseph's administration of Hurricane was as successful as it was unorthodox, and for the next thirty-five years he boasted of one of the most prosperous plantations in the lower Mississippi valley. By 1860 he owned more than 350 slaves and worked 1,700 improved acres. Utilizing Robert Owen's reformist principles, Davis allowed his slaves considerable autonomy, encouraging them to develop skills and to engage in their own economic activities, and permitting them discretion in naming practices. The Hurricane slaves exercised a form of self-government which included a slave jury that heard testimony and adjudicated complaints. Meeting weekly in a "Hall of Justice," the jury arbitrated all manner of cases. Even overseers were forbidden to inflict punishment without jury approval. Yet the cooperative ethos on which this community was based could never be reconciled with slavery. Davis's slaves enjoyed better material conditions and treatment than most other slaves, and they almost never ran away. But they were deprived of any meaningful self-determination, and Davis seems never to have manumitted a single enslaved person. If Joseph Davis, a man born in the eighteenth century whose hero was Thomas Jefferson, viewed slavery as a "necessary evil," he lived in a world characterized by the views of his brother Jefferson, a full generation younger, for whom slavery was a "positive good."[16]

Perhaps the only group that could rival the cotton lords of the Natchez District for their economic, political, and cultural dominance consisted of the sugar barons of southern Louisiana. Sugar production was by definition big business, requiring high concentrations of land and labor, and several planters owned both Natchez District cotton plantations and sugar plantations. Sugar making was also among the heaviest capitalized industries in the slave South, and the sugar mills represented some of the most technologically advanced agricultural operations in the entire country before the war, even if the large majority of mills employed antiquated techniques. The tariff on imported sugar gained the Whig Party the support of the sugar planters, who, as Richard Follett contends, subscribed to a capitalist ethos that they managed to instill, at least in part, in their enslaved workers. The geographical limits of

---

[16] Hermann, *Pursuit of a Dream*, chap. 1.

the sugar region also infused the planters with a unity of purpose and collective identity that cotton planters could never achieve. Once the war came and New Orleans fell to Federal forces, a number of sugar planters would lead the effort to restore Louisiana to the Union in hopes of preserving slavery.[17]

As an overwhelmingly rural and agricultural society, the antebellum South never developed an urban network akin to that of the North. In addition to Memphis, the cities and major towns of Helena, Vicksburg, Natchez, and Baton Rouge on the Mississippi, along with Little Rock, Nashville, Jackson, Alexandria, and Shreveport on the region's other major rivers, played a commanding role in the commercial, political, and cultural life of their surrounding regions, but their primary function was to complement the plantation economy. The one exception was New Orleans. The nation's sixth most populous city in 1860 (counting Brooklyn and New York City – today's Manhattan – separately) and by far the South's largest, New Orleans was home to nearly 145,000 whites, 14,000 slaves, and nearly 11,000 free people of color, and it served as a vital commercial center to the lower Mississippi valley, the trans-Appalachian west, and the nation at large. Despite the opening of the Erie Canal and other internal improvements, much of the trade of the upper Midwest still made its way down the Ohio and Mississippi Rivers for transshipment through New Orleans. The proportion of the South's total cotton trade that was handled in New Orleans steadily increased from roughly a third in the mid-1820s to more than half by the 1850s. The rise of midwestern cities by 1860, and the advent of the railroad trunk lines, already signaled the reorientation of the nation's trade along an east–west axis. As Scott P. Marler has also demonstrated, the prosperity of the 1850s masked deeper, underlying inefficiencies in the plantation economy. Yet there was no reason to suspect – the Panic of 1857 notwithstanding – that the flush times were about to end. Given the city's strategic location, political and commercial importance, and symbolic significance, its capture by Federal forces would fundamentally alter the course of the war.[18]

IV

The nearly 350,000 slaveholders of the antebellum South – including the slightly more than 100,000 in the lower Mississippi valley – were by 1860 the most economically and politically powerful group of slaveholders in the western hemisphere and the world. The nearly four million enslaved

---

[17] Follett, *The Sugar Masters*; Heitmann, *Modernization of the Louisiana Sugar Industry*, chap. 2; Plater, *Butlers of Iberville Parish*, chaps. 3–8; Rehder, *Delta Sugar*; Rodrigue, *Reconstruction in the Cane Fields*, chap. 1; Sitterson, *Sugar Country*, chaps. 3–5.

[18] Marler, *Merchants' Capital*, chap. 2; Reed, *New Orleans and the Railroads*; Reinders, *End of an Era*.

men, women, and children whom they considered their property, inhabiting the fifteen slave states from Delaware to Texas, along with the District of Columbia, represented a capital investment of almost $4 billion at the time. The disproportionate political influence that the slave states and the slaveholders wielded at the national level has been well established. As Steven Hahn has maintained, "the principal struggle of the period" was less between the North and the South over the western territories than between the Northeast and the Mississippi valley "for control of the continent and, perhaps, the hemisphere." Which section, in effect, was going to direct the expansionist impulses of this "nation without borders"? In hindsight, the outcome of this contest seems inevitable, and the answer to this question self-evident. Yet in 1860 few rational observers would have bet against the slaveholding class or the lower Mississippi valley in shaping the destiny of the nation.[19]

Historians have intensely debated the essential nature of this slaveholding elite and its role in southern society. Although this debate has evolved over time, it centers on whether the slaveholders exhibited the characteristics of a modern, acquisitive ruling class operating within the capitalist world market, and on whether their outlook was at variance with the world capitalist order of the mid-nineteenth century. The slaveholders no doubt subscribed to certain practices and beliefs characteristic of modern capitalist society, including profit maximization, economic efficiency, and absolute property rights. Yet they also espoused what scholars have described as *paternalism* in their relationship with their slaves. This philosophy imbued the slaveholders with a fundamental concern for the slaves' moral and material welfare, which also aligned with their economic self-interest, and it shaped their behavior toward the slaves in substantive ways. Paternalism could be – and was – cruel and oppressive, and it had devastating psychological consequences for its supposed beneficiaries. It always functioned primarily to justify the slaveholders' authority as well as their power, dominance, and control over the slaves. As is true of the belief systems of all ruling classes, it was a self-serving ideology, designed to rationalize both the slaveholders' status as owners of human property and their position in southern society. Nonetheless, this outlook impelled the slaveholders to conceptualize the relationship with their slaves in ways fundamentally different from that of northern employers under "free labor." Moreover, this outlook permeated southern society, even influencing the slaves themselves; and it anchored a worldview that rejected notions of the relationship between "capital" and "labor" that prevailed, however imperfectly, in northern society.[20]

[19] Hahn, *Nation Without Borders*, 2–6 (quotation, 3). Hahn addresses the southern slaveholders' loss of national power after the war in "Class and State in Postemancipation Societies." On the importance of Louisiana to US history, see Powell, "Why Louisiana Mattered."

[20] The argument that the slaveholders adhered to something akin to "paternalism," that such thinking shaped their behavior, and that their worldview differed fundamentally from that of the northern propertied classes is most closely associated with Eugene

While scholars have always contested this view, a new body of literature emphasizes the brutally exploitative character of slavery. Denying, usually implicitly, that notions of benevolence or paternalism influenced the slaveholders' behavior, this new work highlights the slaveholders' sheer avariciousness; and it contends, perhaps more importantly, that slavery was integral to the rise of modern capitalism in the United States. In terms of their day-to-day operations, their specific business practices, and their overall conceptualization of the plantation system, the slaveholders were decidedly modern, and they greatly resembled in their thought and behavior the capitalist classes of the North. Much the same can also be said of the domestic slave trade and slave traders. These scholars disagree on many particular points, but they maintain that the brutality of slavery went hand in hand with what they see as the unbridled rapaciousness of modern capitalism. Previous interpretations hardly romanticized slavery, even those contending that the planters practiced some form of paternalism. Yet this newer scholarship – sometimes dubbed "slavery's capitalism" – paints a much grimmer picture of life under slavery. It calls into question the slaves' historical agency, for instance, and their ability to resist their enslavement in any meaningful way.[21]

D. Genovese, along with, later, Elizabeth Fox-Genovese. Much of the scholarship on slavery, the slaveholders, and antebellum southern society since the 1970s has been in response to this thesis, such that it would be impossible to cite the many works for and against it. While the debate over paternalism lacks its previous intensity, and while the more recent scholarship on slavery has moved in different directions, the question of how slavery and the plantation economy of the US South fit within the world capitalist system of the mid-nineteenth century is still vital. Genovese and Fox-Genovese articulated this thesis in a number of works, both individually and together. See especially, for Genovese: *Political Economy of Slavery*; *World the Slaveholders Made*; *Roll, Jordan, Roll*; *In Red and Black*; *Southern Front*; *A Consuming Fire*. For Fox-Genovese, see *Within the Plantation Household*. For Fox-Genovese and Genovese, see *Fruits of Merchant Capital*; *Mind of the Master Class*; *Slavery in White and Black*; *Fatal Self-Deception*. Important works that disputed this argument include Degler, *Place Over Time*; Fogel and Engerman, *Time on the Cross*; Oakes, *Ruling Race*; Scarborough, *Masters of the Big House*; Shore, *Southern Capitalists*; and Walker, *Deromanticizing Black History*. For an excellent critical appraisal of Genovese's work, see Harris, "Eugene Genovese's Old South," which argues persuasively that Genovese underappreciated the role of race and racism to the slaveholders' outlook.

[21] These works do not necessarily discount the slaves' efforts to exercise historical agency or to shape their own destinies. However, they generally share this skepticism toward – if not a complete rejection of – the idea that paternalism or anything like it influenced the slaveholders' thinking or behavior toward their slaves. Indeed, the conditions the slaves had to endure were so brutal as to preclude any kind of meaningful response to their enslavement, though this scholarship does not always fully explore the implications of this finding. The more important works within this scholarly trend include Baptist, *Half Has Never Been Told*; Beckert, *Empire of Cotton*; Beckert and Rockman, *Slavery's Capitalism*; Berry, *Price for Their Pound of Flesh*; Dattel, *Cotton and Race*; Johnson, *River of Dark Dreams*; Rosenthal, *Accounting for Slavery*; Rothman, *Flush Times*;

This newer work has served as a corrective to any tendency to understate the horrific nature of slavery or slavery's destructive consequences for generations of men, women, and children – although neither slavery's cruelty nor the link between slavery and modern capitalism is an original insight.[22] Nonetheless, there remained one essential feature of modern capitalism to which the slaveholders could not subscribe: under no circumstances could they envision operating their plantations under a system in which the laborers enjoyed the absolute legal freedom to sell their labor-power as a commodity within the capitalist market. This commodification of their workers' productive capacity contradicted everything the slaveholders understood about the plantation economy and their entire social and political order. For planters to have to purchase the labor-power of workers who enjoyed legal authority over their own bodies and productive capacity was unthinkable, as were the possibilities that planters and laborers would bargain as equals in a relationship that state power would sanction and maintain. If there were anything the slaveholders could do about it, and there was indeed a lot, this was never going to happen.

Race was an essential element of this reasoning. Planters – and all white Southerners – believed that black people lacked the internal motivation necessary for self-support and self-improvement. Black people would work productively only under the threat of corporal punishment, white Southerners insisted, and were incapable of meeting the responsibilities of freedom. Yet in a larger sense, the slaveholders found inconceivable a social order in which capital and labor were bound to each other by nothing more than economic interests. Because every organized society, as a constellation of hierarchical relationships, required a laboring class to perform the necessary drudgery of life, the idea of ostensibly equal parties relating to each other solely as the buyers and sellers of labor-power was both immoral and logically absurd. The

---

Schermerhorn, *Money over Mastery* and *Business of Slavery*. Despite my disagreement with the underlying premises of much of this scholarship, I have found some of it – especially the work of Sven Beckert and Walter Johnson – helpful in my thinking on these issues.

[22] "Cruel, unjust, exploitative, oppressive" is how Genovese describes slavery in the very opening of *Roll, Jordan, Roll*, 3. Both Marxian and non-Marxian scholars have long appreciated the relationship between slavery (and other coercive labor systems) and capitalism, and between slavery and US economic development before the Civil War. See, for instance, Williams's classic, *Capitalism and Slavery*; North, *Economic Growth of the United States*. This older scholarship, it is worth noting, is part of a larger debate, again involving scholars of various perspectives, over the transition from feudalism and other "pre-capitalist" modes of production to modern capitalism. See, for instance, Aston and Philpin, *Brenner Debate*; Dobb, *Studies in the Development of Capitalism*; Hilton, *Transition from Feudalism to Capitalism*. Not only does the newer literature on "slavery's capitalism," by minimizing the differences between the North and the South, offer no explanation for the Civil War, but it also seems to limit its critique of modern capitalism to capitalism's association with slavery, as though capitalism has historically had nothing else to answer for.

slaveholders defended slavery as a viable solution to one of the central challenges of the modern world: the role of "labor" in society. One did not have to be a Marxist to appreciate the threat that class conflict presented to capitalist society. Slavery – racial slavery – provided an alternative to free labor within the modern capitalist system, and it enabled southern society to circumvent all of free labor's attendant ills. The proslavery theorists never quite worked out how to solve this problem in a society that did not enjoy what they considered the benefit of racial slavery. It was in this sense that notions of paternalism influenced the slaveholders' thinking and behavior. To be sure, the slaveholders paid for labor in the human beings they purchased and in the slaves' upkeep and depreciation, as property. But they did not engage labor directly as equals. If key features of capitalist society include the legal freedom of labor, the principle of voluntary contracts between equal parties, and the commodification of labor-power, then the slaveholders utterly rejected these notions as the basis for society.

For all of this theorizing, however, the slaves remained property – bought and paid for. In the antebellum South, "labor" was the private property of individual men and women, as the ancient practice of slavery, which has historically assumed innumerable forms over time and place, became inextricably linked to the idea of absolute property rights that was a product of the European Age of Enlightenment. This "chattel principle" applied to the slaves' bodies, productive and reproductive capacities, and the fruits of their labor, all of which could be bought, sold, and disposed of at the virtually unrestricted discretion of their owner. New World slavery, moreover, was infused with distinctly modern notions of race and racial subordination, which, as scholars have demonstrated, were also consequences of the Enlightenment.[23] Slaveholders and white Southerners told themselves that enslaved persons, while clearly human beings, were inferior and worthy of enslavement. They defended their system to anyone who would listen, in every way they could – through politics, religion and theology, economics, the law, sociology (which the proslavery theorists helped create), science and medicine, and philosophy. In the slave states, these ideas manifested themselves in the higher arts and in common, everyday parlance, and they enjoyed full legal and constitutional sanction. All of the power white Southerners could array – local, state, and national – was dedicated to maintaining the distinct social order that these ideas rationalized. By 1860, this social order very much appeared to be on the march, not weakening.

Nonetheless, however invincible the "slave power" seemed at the time, it could not withstand the simple proposition of "no property in man." The vindication of this idea, and the destruction of the social and political order it had been framed to challenge, would be the most thoroughgoing social

[23] Eze, *Race and the Enlightenment*; Guyatt, *Bind Us Apart*; Thomas, *In Pursuit of Civility*.

revolution the nation has ever experienced. Legal freedom would prove insufficient in so many ways. Yet the commodification of the former slaves' labor-power, along with the decommodification of their bodies and reproductive capacity, would mark a *fundamental* break with the past, not a minor disruption along a larger continuum of oppressive social relations linking the antebellum to the postbellum South. Accomplishing these objectives – despite the efforts of slavery's defenders to prevent such an outcome – would compel the members of the world's most powerful slaveholding class to abandon some of their most cherished ideals and to reconcile themselves to a worldview they found reprehensible.

Historians of slavery in the US South have identified a paradox within the slaveholding experience. Whereas the large majority of slaveholders, who were a minority of the white population, qualified as small-scale slaveholders, owning fewer than twenty slaves each, the large majority of slaves lived on plantations or in areas characterized by high concentrations of slaveholdings. Thus, the "typical" slaveholder owned only a few slaves, and would have been considered more of a farmer than a planter, while the typical slave lived and worked among large numbers of his or her enslaved brethren. Even within the plantation belt, the planter elite generally constituted a minority of the slaveholders. In the four states of the lower Mississippi valley as a whole, 14,115 out of 101,301 slaveholders (13.9 percent) owned at least twenty slaves each. Even within the Natchez District, which was characterized by larger holdings, only a third of slaveholders (1,403 out of 3,766, or 37.3 percent) owned twenty or more slaves each. In the Louisiana sugar region, the *large* planters – owners of fifty or more slaves – constituted just over one-tenth of the slaveholders (525 out of 4,177, or 12.6 percent), but they owned over two-thirds of the region's nearly 90,000 slaves (excluding New Orleans). Despite their small numbers, the planter elite owned a vastly disproportionate share of the land, slaves, and other forms of wealth in their communities, and they translated that economic dominance into political, social, and cultural power and influence at the local, state, and regional levels.[24]

---

[24] On the planter elite of the lower Mississippi valley, see Ash, *Middle Tennessee Society Transformed*, chaps. 1–3; Bond, *Political Culture in the Nineteenth-Century South*, chaps. 1–3; Cimprich, *Slavery's End in Tennessee*, chap. 1; Moneyhon, *Impact of the Civil War and Reconstruction on Arkansas*, chaps. 1–4; Rodrigue, *Reconstruction in the Cane Fields*, 20–29; Wayne, *Reshaping of Plantation Society*, 5–15. The numbers (and percentages) of slaveholders who owned at least twenty slaves each in the states of the lower Mississippi valley are as follows: Arkansas: 1,363 of 11,481 (11.9 percent); Louisiana: 3,925 of 22,033 (17.8 percent); Mississippi: 5,895 of 30,943 (19.0 percent); Tennessee: 2,932 of 36,844 (8.0 percent). Kennedy, *Agriculture of the United States*, 224, 230, 232, 238–39, 247. For the Natchez District and the Louisiana sugar region: Wayne, *Reshaping of Plantation Society*, 8 (table 1); Rodrigue, *Reconstruction in the Cane Fields*, 21–22 (tables 1–2).

If the planter elite wielded economic and political power, the slaves in the plantation belt converted their demographic preponderance into a rich cultural life. Central to this culture was the slaves' devotion to their families and extended kin networks, both real and fictive, that offered the deepest sense of identity and belonging. It included the folklore and stories they told one another, often conveying a moral or transmitting their history and heritage, and the songs they sang, both secular and sacred. It encompassed their fervent religiosity, especially the variants of Afro-Christianity or other syncretic traditions (such as voodoo) they practiced; the economic activities they conducted on their own time – or the "slaves' economy" – and the modest accumulations of "property" and the meanings they attached to it; their healing practices and other forms of medical care, especially by enslaved women; their clandestine efforts to become "self-taught" and to pursue literacy and knowledge; the "joining places" that slaves on adjacent plantations fashioned and that instilled in them a sense of place and comradery; and the sheer act of running away, or risking punishment by assisting runaways. Even when subject to the domestic slave trade, which constituted perhaps the most psychologically alienating and traumatizing of all aspects of American slavery, the slaves relied on one another for essential support, and they cultivated a sense of community despite conditions and circumstances that defy imagination.[25]

Throughout the antebellum South, but especially in areas of large slaveholdings, this community and culture provided the slaves with a measure of autonomy and with the moral and material resources to resist their enslavement. Manifesting itself in virtually every aspect of life and labor, the slaves' culture gave their lives meaning even as it laid the foundations for black institutional life after emancipation. It also arguably imparted to the slaves a quasi-political consciousness that enabled them, however intuitively, to challenge their oppressors. Scholars may disagree as to whether this cultural life empowered the slaves to mount an existential threat to the slave regime, or whether it ultimately helped to solidify the regime by providing an outlet for the psychological torment the slaves had to endure. But if nothing else, the organic community that the slaves had managed to cobble together would serve as a springboard – once the nation descended into Civil War and the opportunity presented itself – for what W. E. B. Du Bois would call "the general strike" for freedom.[26]

[25] It would be impossible to cite the vast scholarship on the slave community and the slaves' cultural life. A selection of such works that are centered on the lower Mississippi valley include Bolton, *Fugitivism*; Kaye, *Joining Places*; Malone, *Sweet Chariot*; McDonald, *Economy and Material Culture of Slaves*; and Wilkie, *Creating Freedom*. Johnson, *Soul by Soul*, offers rich testimony of the slaves' efforts to navigate, in what limited ways they could, the domestic slave trade.

[26] Du Bois, *Black Reconstruction*, chap. 4. Genovese, in *Roll, Jordan, Roll* (280–84), argues that the slaves' culture, Afro-Christianity in particular, provided the groundwork for

It is also paradoxical, though hardly coincidental, that the lower Mississippi valley provides compelling evidence for all of these foregoing developments. The region's large slaveholdings gave rise to particularly complex slave communities and to an especially vibrant culture that helped the slaves to survive. Yet what Walter Johnson calls the region's "carceral landscape" offered ideal conditions for some of the most intensive – and dehumanizing – forms of labor exploitation and economies of scale to be found anywhere in the antebellum South. Further still, the cotton lords and sugar barons of the region testified, however self-servingly, to paternalism's moderating influence over the slaveholders' thinking and behavior, and to the absurdity of grafting notions of "free labor" onto the plantation system. Save perhaps for the South Carolina lowcountry and the Virginia tidewater, nowhere else did life and labor in the Old South achieve a higher stage of historical development than in the lower Mississippi valley. Plantation slavery may well have been "less a business than a life," in the still-relevant words of U. B. Phillips, making "fewer fortunes than it made men." But it was a business, and in the making of many fortunes, it devoured the lives of untold thousands of enslaved men, women, and children.[27]

* * *

The final word, before the descent into the maelstrom, belongs to Solomon Northup, a northern free black man who was infamously kidnapped and sold into slavery. Northup endured a dozen long, brutal years on Louisiana cotton and sugar plantations, from 1841 to 1853, before finally regaining his freedom. His harrowing chronicle of those experiences, *Twelve Years a Slave*, published soon after his deliverance, has long been considered a classic in the genre of first-person accounts of slavery. One passage would prove to be especially prophetic. "During the Mexican war I well remember the extravagant hopes that were excited. The news of victory filled the great house with rejoicing, but produced only sorrow and disappointment in the cabin," Northup recalled. "In my opinion – and I have had the opportunity to know something of the feeling of which I speak – there are not fifty slaves on the shores of Bayou Boeuf, but would hail with unmeasured delight the approach of an invading army."[28]

---

a "protonational consciousness" but also undermined any revolutionary impulse to challenge the regime. Hahn, in *Nation Under Our Feet* (chap. 1), contends that the slaves developed a politicized – and potentially revolutionary – consciousness. See also Hahn, *Political Worlds of Slavery and Freedom*, chap. 2.

[27] Johnson, *River of Dark Dreams*, chap. 8; Phillips, *American Negro Slavery*, 401.

[28] Northup, *Twelve Years a Slave*, 190. For a recent study of the attorney who helped Northup regain his freedom, see Riddle, *The Life and Diary of John P. Waddill*.

PART I

From War for Union to Military Emancipation, 1860–1862

1

"An Independent Power"

The secession crisis revealed to the white inhabitants of the lower Mississippi valley their fundamental unity of interests, and to the black inhabitants the faintest possibilities for change. The area encapsulated the crisis in the southern states at large, with Mississippi and Louisiana representing the lower South in their commitment to slavery and southern independence, and Tennessee and Arkansas reflecting the upper South. The start of hostilities solidified the bond between the two Souths, while tearing away the border states, and enabled them to overcome their internal divisions over disunion. By mid-1861, all four states had joined the Confederate States of America, a slaveholding republic with Mississippi slaveholder Jefferson Davis as its president. This new nation – which rested on the "cornerstone" of racial slavery, as Confederate Vice President Alexander Stephens famously pronounced, and was the first in world history founded on the "great physical, philosophical, and moral truth" that slavery was the "natural and normal condition" of persons of African descent–now embarked upon its own War of Independence.[1]

As this slaveholding republic attempted to gain its footing during the remainder of 1861, the people of the lower Mississippi valley experienced the Civil War largely by proxy. Decisions and actions elsewhere established the broad contours of Federal policy toward the seceded states and slavery in the war's initial phase. Yet even as the valley's inhabitants processed these far-off changes, events closer to home – in Missouri and Kentucky, and at Second Creek, Mississippi – augured the dangers for a slave society at war. By year's end, many Northerners were already beginning to rethink the war and the fate of slavery.

I

Abraham Lincoln's election in November 1860 ignited the paroxysm of secession. All of the states that eventually seceded – save South Carolina – witnessed brief but intense campaigns between "immediate secessionists," who argued

---

[1] Cleveland, *Alexander H. Stephens in Public and Private*, 717–29.

that each state should act as a sovereign entity in immediately leaving the Union, and "cooperationists," who called for the southern states to coordinate with one another before acting. Cooperationists defended the right to secede but argued that such action should only be undertaken as a last resort. The main difference between the two groups thus involved means and not ends. The cooperationists also included the South's few "unconditional" Unionists, who enjoyed little public support and had nowhere else to go. The large majority of white Southerners had long since decided that disunion was the only honorable response to a Republican presidential victory. Secession was carried out relatively quickly in the lower South. Yet public opinion in Mississippi and Louisiana was at first divided, and cooperationists and Unionists offered some resistance. In Arkansas and Tennessee, secession was much more contentious – especially outside the plantation belt. Immediatists and cooperationists were more evenly split, and unconditional Unionists were more numerous, in the upper South, and Arkansas and Tennessee seceded only after hostilities commenced.[2]

Despite a vigorously contested presidential election in Mississippi, Southern Democrat John C. Breckenridge won a large majority of the popular vote over Constitutional Unionist John Bell and Northern Democrat Stephen A. Douglas. Lincoln's name, as was the case in the lower South, did not appear on the ballot. Secessionists wasted little time in mobilizing. In response to Governor John J. Pettus's mid-November call for a special legislative session, to convene on November 26, the legislature immediately authorized an election for delegates to a state convention on December 20, with the convention to meet on January 7, 1861. Although many white Mississippians privately expressed misgivings and some communities witnessed spirited debate, immediate secession was a foregone conclusion. The election on December 20, the very day South Carolina seceded, resulted in the immediatists winning nearly seventy of the one-hundred seats.[3]

In complete control of the proceedings, the immediatists elected the convention president and formed a committee to draft an ordinance of secession. Hoping to stave off the inevitable, cooperationists offered various amendments – calling for the state to remain in the Union while a compromise was being pursued; proposing that secession not become effective until other lower-South states seceded; or requiring secession to receive voter approval – that were resoundingly defeated. In the final vote on January 9, the ordinance

---

[2] Barney, *Secessionist Impulse*, chap. 6; Potter, *Impending Crisis*; Freehling, *Road to Disunion, vol. 2: Secessionists Triumphant*.

[3] Burnham, *Presidential Ballots*, 552; Wooster, *Secession Conventions*, 27–29, 32, 35–37; Rainwater, *Mississippi*, 135–75; Powell and Wayne, "Self-Interest and the Decline of Confederate Nationalism," 30–32; Bettersworth, *Confederate Mississippi*, 14–17; Smith, *Mississippi Secession Convention*, 20; Davis, *Rise and Fall*, 57–58; O. R. Singleton to W. T. Walthall, July 14, 1877, in Davis, *Jefferson Davis*, 7: 560–62.

of secession was approved, 84 to 15, with about half of the thirty or so cooperationists voting in favor. Mississippi became the second state to secede. Many Natchez cotton planters, fearing they had the most to lose, had initially opposed secession. Yet aware of the need for unity and recognizing where their interests lay, even they now overwhelmingly supported it.[4]

Louisiana's secession proceeded a bit more slowly and initially provoked greater opposition, but the outcome was the same. Unionist sentiment there was owing to the tariff on sugar, essential to the state's planters; to the transplanted Northerners in New Orleans, though many had resided there for decades; and to the importance of New Orleans and the Mississippi River to the nation's economy.[5] Breckenridge won the state with a slim plurality of the popular vote, yet the election pushed the public mood decisively toward secession. Governor Thomas O. Moore, previously a moderate but now an avowed secessionist, immediately called for a special session of the legislature, to meet on December 10. "At this period it is entirely safe to declare that there exists no Union party in Louisiana," insisted a New Orleans newspaper that had previously advised caution. In a widely publicized Thanksgiving sermon, delivered in New Orleans and titled "Slavery a Divine Trust," the Presbyterian Minister Benjamin M. Palmer urged the formation of "a new and homogeneous confederacy." Upon convening in December, the legislature set an election for delegates on January 7 and a convention to meet on January 23, although the Louisiana constitution required popular approval of a convention.[6]

An intense campaign took hold of the state but soon petered out, the result inevitable. On election day, immediatists won 80 – or nearly two-thirds – of the 130 convention seats. Even New Orleans, once considered a center of political moderation, voted overwhelmingly immediatist and was now deemed "the hot-bed of Secession." The popular vote was much closer than the delegate count, with immediatists receiving nearly 21,000 votes and all others just over 17,000. Some Northerners misinterpreted this result as evidence of latent Unionism. The wealthy slaveholding and cotton parishes, especially along

---

[4] *Journal of the State Convention and Ordinances and Resolutions Adopted in January, 1861*, 6–7, 9, 14–16; Bettersworth, *Confederate Mississippi*, 4–5, 8–9; James, *Antebellum Natchez*, 291–92; Barney, *Secessionist Impulse*, 289–96, 308–9; Rainwater, *Mississippi*, 202–17; Degler, *Other South*, 177–78; Fulkerson, *Civilian's Recollections*, chap. 1; Woods, "Sketch of the Mississippi Secession Convention of 1861."

[5] Sitterson, *Sugar Country*, 178; Chenault and Reinders, "The Northern-born Community of New Orleans in the 1850s"; Marler, *Merchants' Capital*, 3–4, 16–17.

[6] "Proclamation," *New Orleans Daily Crescent*, November 24, 1860; "Governor's Message to the State of Louisiana," *New Orleans Daily Crescent*, December 12, 1860; Dumond, *Southern Editorials*, 338; Palmer, *Slavery a Divine Trust*, 17; Palmer, "A Vindication of Secession and the South"; Nguyen, "Preaching Disunion"; Wooster, *Secession Conventions*, chap. 7; Shugg, *Origins of Class Struggle in Louisiana*, 157–70; Winters, *Civil War in Louisiana*, 3–14; Caskey, *Secession and Restoration of Louisiana*; Taylor, *Louisiana: A History*, 87–89.

the Mississippi and Red Rivers, went solidly immediatist, whereas the opposition centered on the sugar parishes – which were evenly split – and the north-central hill country.[7]

By the time the delegates gathered in Baton Rouge later in January, Mississippi, Florida, Alabama, and Georgia had joined South Carolina in seceding. As in Mississippi, the outcome was academic, but the opponents of immediate secession put up a fight. The immediatists elected the convention president and formed a committee to draw up a secession ordinance, sweeping aside any efforts at delay. On January 26, the convention approved the ordinance, 113 to 17, with thirty-three of the fifty opponents of immediate secession voting in favor. The convention president proclaimed Louisiana "a free, sovereign, and independent power." Even before the vote, Governor Moore had ordered state officials to begin seizing Federal property, an action the convention overwhelmingly endorsed. Louisiana was the sixth and next-to-last state to secede, followed by Texas on February 2, before the start of hostilities.[8]

Even as they were separately seceding, the seven lower-South states took steps toward uniting as an independent republic. Responding to a call from Alabama, the various state conventions elected delegates to a convention of the seceded states, to be held in Montgomery in early February, to organize a new government. This convention unanimously elected Jefferson Davis as provisional president and drafted a national constitution, which each of the seceded states eventually ratified in formally joining the Confederate States of America. Meanwhile, the eight other slave states were deeply divided on disunion, and the secessionist impulse had stalled. By Lincoln's March 4 inauguration, stalemate prevailed, and the nation awaited the new administration's response to the crisis. Yet the white residents of Mississippi and Louisiana by and large considered themselves gone. Lemuel P. Conner, member of a prominent Natchez-District family and delegate to the Louisiana convention, expressed hope that the seceded states would gain recognition "as an Independent power" by what he called "the old United States."[9]

---

[7] Wooster, *Secession Conventions*, 104; Dumond, *Southern Editorials*, 338; "Public Sentiment," *New Orleans Bee*, December 17, 1860; Dew, "The Long-Lost Returns"; Dew, "Who Won the Secession Election in Louisiana?"

[8] *Official Journal of the Proceedings of the Convention of the State of Louisiana*, 4–5, 13, 15–18; Shugg, "A Suppressed Co-operationist Protest against Secession"; Winters, *Civil War in Louisiana*, 12–13; Taliaferro, *Protest Against the Ordinance of Secession*; Bearss, "Seizure of the Forts."

[9] Lemuel P. Conner to [Frances Elizabeth Conner], March 18, 1861, Conner Family Papers, LSU. A large literature exists on the formation of the Confederate national government. See esp. Davis, "*A Government of Our Own*"; Thomas, *Confederate Nation*, chap. 3; McCurry, *Confederate Reckoning*, chap. 2; Robinson, *Bitter Fruits of Bondage*, chap. 1.

II

Abraham Lincoln and many Northerners misjudged the meaning of these events, interpreting cooperation in the lower South and stalled secessionism in the upper as genuine Unionism. Lincoln had said almost nothing during the presidential campaign and as president-elect, and when he finally spoke, in dozens of speeches during his well-publicized February trip from Springfield to Washington, DC, he clearly underestimated the crisis, referring to it repeatedly as "artificial." White Southerners were at pains to point out this error. "[T]he North is wholly insensible to the truth that there is no Union party in some ten or more slaveholding States," insisted a New Orleans newspaper just before Louisiana's secession convention. The belief in southern Unionism "confounds Co-operationists with Unionists," it continued, assuring its readers that the vast majority of cooperationists were "heartily in favor of secession." The slow, torturous process by which Lincoln and the northern public disabused themselves of this fallacy would help to redefine the American Civil War.[10]

For now, Lincoln attempted to strike a balance between firmness and conciliation in his Inaugural Address. The Federal government was powerless under the Constitution to interfere with slavery in the states, he assured white Southerners. He foreswore unprovoked coercion and pledged to exercise discretion in maintaining the national authority. The southern states would continue to enjoy their traditional rights, including enforcement of the Fugitive Slave Act. At the same time, Lincoln affirmed the perpetuity of the Union, vowed to enforce the Constitution and laws of the United States and uphold Federal authority, and insisted that slavery would not be permitted to spread to the territories. "One section of our country believes slavery is *right*, and ought to be extended, while the other believes it is *wrong*, and ought not to be extended," Lincoln observed. "This is the only substantial dispute." Lincoln had said almost nothing new. Slavery was safe where it existed but would be barred from expanding; the national authority would be maintained but undue coercion would not be employed; and the slaveholders' rights would be defended but only within the framework of an indivisible Union.[11]

Nonetheless, secessionists read Lincoln's determination to maintain Federal authority in the South as a virtual declaration of war. His refusal to surrender any more Federal property in the seceded states, including Fort Sumter in Charleston Harbor, all but compelled Confederates to resort to force. The firing on Fort Sumter on April 12, 1861, destroyed what little hope remained for a peaceful settlement to the crisis, and it was cathartic to both North and

---

[10] Holzer, *Lincoln President-Elect*, chaps. 10–12, esp. 328 (quotation), 329, 341, 376; Dumond, *Southern Editorials*, 410; Potter, *Lincoln and His Party*, 315–23; Craven, *Coming of the Civil War*, 480, n. 23; Stampp, *And the War Came*, chap. 2.

[11] CWL, 4: 262–71 (quotation, 268–69).

South. The outbreak of hostilities also galvanized secessionism in the upper South after weeks of stalemate, as did Lincoln's proclamation of April 15, which the upper South deemed coercive.[12]

With the dubious benefit of historical hindsight, Lincoln's April 15 proclamation seems remarkably limited. Because the laws of the United States had been obstructed in certain states "by combinations too powerful to be suppressed" by ordinary civil authority, Lincoln called forth 75,000 state militia troops "to suppress said combinations" and to execute the laws. These troops' primary duty would "probably" be to repossess seized Federal property, but they were enjoined "to avoid any devastation, any destruction of, or interference with, property, or any disturbance of peaceful citizens." Lincoln beseeched loyal persons in these states to support the Federal government and ordered anyone opposing its authority to "retire peaceably" within twenty days. Lincoln thus called for 75,000 troops, whose terms were limited to thirty days by law, to restore the national authority over an area from South Carolina to Texas and bound to extend further. The problem that would become known as "Reconstruction" involved nothing more than suppressing "combinations" of individuals in the seceded states and restoring the national authority. Lincoln and most Northerners envisioned neither a war of desolation nor an overturning of the southern social order. Yet by calling Congress into special session on July 4, Lincoln also signaled more to come. "The time for argument and mere declamation has passed," announced a Nashville newspaper. "War has been solemnly proclaimed by the President's proclamation and is being waged with all the energy and resources of the Government."[13]

III

In truth, much time would pass before the Federal government marshaled its resources in suppressing the rebellion, but the editorial identified a central truth: Fort Sumter and Lincoln's response meant war, and the remaining slave states, including Tennessee and Arkansas, would have to choose sides. For neither the first nor the last time, outside events shaped destinies in the lower Mississippi valley while its people, both black and white, formulated their response.

Although an upper-South state, Arkansas gave a clear majority of its popular vote to Breckenridge in the presidential election. In the struggle to follow, the opponents of immediatism were dubbed "Unionists" but equated to cooperationists elsewhere. The legislature was scheduled to meet soon after the election, so no need existed for a special session. Governor Henry Rector – recently

---

[12] Lemuel P. Conner to [Frances Elizabeth Conner], March 4–5, 1861, Conner Family Papers, LSU; Cooper, *Jefferson Davis*, 340; Crofts, *Reluctant Confederates*, esp. chap. 13.
[13] *CWL*, 4: 331–33; Dumond, *Southern Editorials*, 506, 508.

inaugurated and a moderate on disunion – recommended holding a state convention, but with cooperation prevailing, the legislature at first took no action, and debate roiled the state for the next month. Not until mid-January did the legislature authorize an election for February 18 that would simultaneously decide on holding a convention and elect delegates to it. The election was not a foregone conclusion, and Arkansas witnessed a vibrant campaign between immediatists and various "Unionists." Since many of the latter demanded a means to express their views, the convention was overwhelmingly approved, and Unionists won a small majority of the seventy-seven delegates. The popular vote and delegate count were fairly evenly split, and the election – and public opinion generally – reflected Arkansas's geographical divide, with the southeasterly half voting immediatist and the northwesterly half voting Unionist. Of the ten counties where slaves made up at least 40 percent of the population, only Crittenden voted Unionist.[14]

The convention, which began its work in early March, included delegates who were destined to play critical roles in wartime Arkansas. Isaac Murphy, of Madison County in the northwest, would serve as Unionist governor in 1864 and 1865. William M. Fishback, a Little Rock attorney, would be elected in 1864 to the US Senate but not seated. In his message to the convention, in which he delivered a more strident defense of secession than he had in November to the legislature, Governor Rector also offered an unqualified endorsement of slavery. "Does there exist inside the borders of Arkansas any diversity of sentiment, as to the religious or moral right of holding negro slaves?" he asked rhetorically. "God in his omnipotent wisdom, I believe, created the cotton plant – the African slave – and the lower Mississippi valley, to clothe and feed the world, and a gallant race of men and women produced upon its soil to defend it, and execute that decree." Nonetheless, the convention elected a Unionist president and debated secession for the next two weeks. It reached a compromise on March 20, putting secession to a popular vote in early August – more than four months hence. The convention adjourned with the proviso that the president could reconvene it if necessary. Unionists had stemmed the secessionist tide, but a number of them expressed little hope for reconciliation. With Arkansas deeply divided, the convention postponed its decision and awaited developments elsewhere.[15]

---

[14] DeBlack, *With Fire and Sword*, 18–21; Scroggs, "Arkansas in the Secession Crisis"; Moneyhon, *Impact of the Civil War and Reconstruction on Arkansas*, 94–96; Dougan, *Confederate Arkansas*, chaps. 3–5; Woods, *Rebellion and Realignment*, chaps. 7–9; Wooster, *Secession Conventions*, chap. 10; Wooster, "The Arkansas Secession Convention." Wooster's article contains a helpful map (189), not included in the monograph, that clearly shows the geopolitical divide.

[15] "Governor's Message," March 2, 1860, in *Journal of Both Sessions of the Convention of the State of Arkansas*, March session, 41–49 (quotations, 44–45), 90–91, 101–2; DeBlack, *With Fire and Sword*, 24–25.

Fort Sumter and Lincoln's proclamation revolutionized public opinion. The convention reassembled on May 6, and secessionists overwhelmed what little remained of Unionism. The convention immediately drew up a secession ordinance and approved it almost unanimously. Only Isaac Murphy was opposed. He was soon driven into exile and fled to Missouri, where – along with the brothers Dr. James M. Johnson and Frank Johnson, and many other north Arkansans – he eventually signed on with the Union military. Arkansas became the ninth state to secede, following Virginia's secession in April. The convention elected members to the Confederate Congress and later ratified the Confederate Constitution before adjourning in early June. Arkansas now belonged to the Confederate States of America.[16]

It was also in early June that Tennessee became the last state of the lower Mississippi valley – and the last of the eleven Confederate states – to secede. Tennessee was also the only state to secede legislatively rather than by state convention, and it experienced the most contentious secession of any Confederate state, befitting its strategic importance. The state was deeply divided along its three sections, with west Tennessee strongly supporting secession, east Tennessee vehemently resisting it, and middle Tennessee initially opposing it until hostilities dramatically altered public sentiment.[17]

At the time of the presidential election, Democrats and their leader, US Senator Andrew Johnson, dominated Tennessee politics. But remnants of the old Whig party remained viable, and favorite son John Bell, the Constitutional Union candidate, won a slim plurality of the popular vote. (Only Tennessee, Kentucky, and Virginia supported Bell.) Following Lincoln's election, Governor Isham G. Harris, essentially a cooperationist but moving toward immediatism, waited until December 7 to call for a special session of the legislature, to meet on January 7, the same date of Mississippi's convention and Louisiana's election for convention delegates. The state intensely debated secession during the next month. When the legislature convened, Harris delivered a stridently states-rights address but also recommended voter approval of a state convention and expressed hope for compromise. For two weeks, the legislature deliberated, as one lower-South state after another seceded. On January 19, the legislature authorized an election, to be held on February 9, in which the voters would decide simultaneously whether to

---

[16] *Journal of Both Sessions*, May session, 113–14, 121–24, 132–35, 180–87, 452–53; Smith, *Courage of a Southern Unionist*, chap. 3; DeBlack, *With Fire and Sword*, 25–28.

[17] This account of Tennessee's secession is based, in addition to the sources indicated, on Wooster, *Secession Conventions*, chap. 11; Ash, *Middle Tennessee Society Transformed*, chap. 4; Cimprich, *Slavery's End in Tennessee*, 6–12; Fertig, *Secession and Reconstruction of Tennessee*, chap. 1; Atkins, *Parties, Politics, and the Sectional Conflict in Tennessee*, chap. 8; Frisby, "The Vortex of Secession."

hold a convention and select delegates to it. On February 4, the legislature adjourned.[18]

A vibrant contest over secession ensued, though it focused on whether slavery could better be preserved within or outside the Union. Staunch Unionists proclaimed themselves slavery's strongest defenders. "Any man with half a man's reasoning power can see that the friends of the existing Government are the only true friends of slavery," announced a Nashville newspaper, adding that "that institution has depended mainly for its existence upon the protection afforded it by the Constitution." Unionist editor William G. "Parson" Brownlow sounded a similar theme. "You correctly interpret the Union men of the border Slave States when you pronounce them 'pro-Slavery men,'" he wrote to a northern correspondent. "I am a pro-Slavery man, and so are the Union men generally of the border Slave States." Over the next four years, separating Unionism from slavery in Tennessee proved difficult.[19]

The election on February 9 resulted in a resounding defeat for the convention, 69,387 to 56,932. The vote confirmed the state's geographical divide. In middle Tennessee, a slim majority – out of more than 55,000 votes cast – opposed the convention, while east Tennessee overwhelmingly opposed it and west Tennessee overwhelmingly approved it. Although support for the convention was generally equated with immediate secession, a significant number of antisecessionists evidently voted *for* the convention, since the overall vote for convention delegates produced an even more lopsided repudiation of secessionist candidates – 91,803 to 24,749 – than did the vote on the convention itself. Disunion in Tennessee seemed dead.[20]

That is, until Fort Sumter triggered a political earthquake. "The great revolution in public sentiment in Tennessee, which has been inaugurated by the hostile attitude of the Lincoln Government and its dangerous usurpations of authority," a Nashville newspaper announced following Lincoln's April 15 proclamation, "has culminated in an almost universal sentiment of resistance, and a conviction that Tennessee must separate herself from a Union, thus perverted to the purposes of tyranny, and must unite herself at once with the Confederate States." A Memphis newspaper likewise applauded the "*perfect* unanimity among our population" that resulted from "the northern tyrant's manifesto." Pro-southern rallies were being held throughout the city, and former Unionists now universally urged resistance. "Party lines were

---

[18] Burnham, *Presidential Ballots*, 742; "Proclamation," *Daily Nashville Patriot*, December 11, 1860; *House Journal of the Extra Session of the Thirty-Third General Assembly of the State of Tennessee*, 4–17, 116; *Senate Journal of the Extra Session of the Thirty-Third General Assembly of the State of Tennessee*, 6–19, 65.

[19] Dumond, *Southern Editorials*, 425–26; Ash, *Secessionists and Other Scoundrels*, 57.

[20] *Nashville Union and American*, March 3, 1861; Wooster, *Secession Conventions*, 181, Table 43.

obliterated," the paper proclaimed, "and Memphis now stands a UNIT for the South!"[21]

After weeks of stalemate, matters now moved quickly. On April 18, Governor Harris summoned the legislature into special session. When it convened on April 25, he recommended that the legislature handle secession – presumably rather than again risk a popular vote on a state convention. But Harris also advised that any secession ordinance go to the voters. Having rejected Lincoln's call for state militia troops, Harris declared that Civil War had begun and Tennessee must now sever its ties to the Union. Yet even then, the legislature needed another two weeks to hammer out a secession ordinance, which it passed on May 6, the same day Arkansas seceded, pending voter approval in a June 8 referendum. Meanwhile, the legislature authorized the appointment of Confederate commissioners, whom Harris named and dispatched to Montgomery, still the Confederate capital, to sign a military alliance with the Confederacy. The legislature confirmed their appointment on May 7, and the state prepared for war.[22]

Secession in Tennessee may not have amounted to a coup d'état, as one historian has suggested, but the voters were being asked to endorse a fait accompli. Brownlow contended that the state was "in the midst of a reign of terror" following the legislature's action. Whether that were true, the voters approved secession by a vote of 104,913 to 47,238 – better than two-to-one. East and west Tennessee again, respectively, opposed and endorsed secession overwhelmingly. The major shift occurred in middle Tennessee, which now supported secession in a landslide. North Carolina's secession on May 20 took place after the Tennessee legislature had approved the secession ordinance, as did Virginia's popular approval of secession on May 23. But voter ratification of secession in early June made Tennessee the eleventh Confederate state.[23]

The process of secession would have important implications for "Reconstruction" once the lower Mississippi valley came under Federal military control. Mississippi, which had witnessed some cooperationism but little unconditional Unionism, would experience no meaningful attempt at wartime Reconstruction. In Louisiana, the primary center of opposition to immediatism – New Orleans and its environs – would undergo substantive Federal

---

[21] Dumond, *Southern Editorials*, 507; *Memphis Daily Appeal*, April 16, 1861, 2.

[22] "Proclamation by the Governor," *Daily Nashville Patriot*, April 21, 1861; *House Journal of the Second Extra Session of the Thirty-Third General Assembly of the State of Tennessee*, 4–11, 42, 54–55, 77–79; *Senate Journal of the Second Extra Session of the Thirty-Third General Assembly of the State of Tennessee*, 5–13, 42, 60–61, 68; "Convention between the State of Tennessee and the Confederate States of America," *House Journal of the Second Extra Session*, 78, and *Senate Journal of the Second Extra Session*, 67–68.

[23] Nevins, *War for the Union, vol. 1: The Improvised War*, 105; Ash, *Secessionists and Other Scoundrels*, 60; Wooster, *Secession Conventions*, 188–89; "Proclamation," *Nashville Union and American*, June 25, 1861.

military occupation, and Louisiana experienced the most extensive wartime Reconstruction of any seceded state. The Federal military would occupy those parts of Arkansas and Tennessee within the plantation belt and where support for secession was strongest. In short, Federal military occupation corresponded with potential Unionism in Louisiana but with secessionism in Arkansas, Tennessee, and Mississippi – save for the Natchez District. Despite these differences, wartime Reconstruction in these states, except Mississippi, would include genuine Unionists, conditional Unionists, cooperationists, and even immediate secessionists. But for many individuals, the allegiance to slavery outweighed everything else.

IV

These events were still unfolding when developments in the Virginia tidewater foreshadowed the revolutionary transformation that was to come. Only weeks after hostilities commenced, slaves began taking flight and seeking refuge behind Federal lines at Fortress Monroe, near the mouth of the James River. In doing so, they gave their own meaning to the conflict. Few white Americans, North or South, would have allowed the slaves any substantive role in the war. Even Northerners who opposed remanding runaways to disloyal slaveholders did not necessarily envision widespread emancipation. Union military personnel soon discovered, however, that secession enjoyed broad support, even in the upper South, and that distinguishing between the slaves of loyal and disloyal slaveholders was almost impossible. In mobilizing the South's resources, moreover, Confederate authorities impressed slaves as military laborers, using them in direct furtherance of treason. The slaveholders' demands for the return of their fugitive slaves, including slaves who had directly contributed to the Confederate war effort, demonstrated the absurdity of suppressing a slaveholders' rebellion without interfering with slavery.[24]

The commander at Fortress Monroe was General Benjamin F. Butler, a leading Massachusetts Democrat and "political general" destined to play a brief but crucial role in the lower Mississippi valley. Butler was no abolitionist but had zero tolerance for disloyalty, and he improvised an approach to the fugitive slave problem that helped redefine the war. Realizing the incongruity of returning runaways who might be used to support the rebellion, he argued that slaveholders in the seceded states had forfeited the protection of Federal fugitive slave laws. Instead, he seized the fugitives as "contraband" – enemy property taken for military purposes – and began employing able-bodied men as military laborers. Butler forswore the legal authority to emancipate fugitives and left open the possibility of loyal slaveholders later reclaiming them, but he had established the groundwork for a policy of military emancipation, though

[24] Nelson, "Confederate Slave Impressment."

limited at this point. As a means of suppressing rebellion, the Federal government might seize, employ, and perhaps even emancipate slaves in the seceded states. Fugitives who were assumed to serve no military function – women (incorrectly), children, the elderly – posed a different problem, but Butler maintained that they deserved shelter on humanitarian grounds. The Lincoln administration sanctioned Butler's policy, and by July nearly a thousand fugitives had secured refuge at Fortress Monroe. The term "contraband" quickly caught on with antislavery advocates, and it has ever since been integral to the lexicon of the Civil War and emancipation.[25]

Nearly a year would pass before Federal contraband policy came to be applied to the lower Mississippi valley, but two contradictory actions taken by the special session of Congress further underscored the impossibility of avoiding slavery. In late July, a resolution sponsored by John J. Crittenden of Kentucky in the House and Andrew Johnson in the Senate affirmed the Federal government's goals of preserving the Union and defending the Constitution while disavowing any intention "of overthrowing or interfering with the rights or established institutions" of the states. The "Crittenden Resolution" customarily serves as Exhibit A for the case that the North first went to war to preserve the Union and not to free the slaves. The measure reflected the need for northern solidarity over the war and the delusion that the slavery issue could be circumvented, but Butler's contraband policy rendered it moot.[26]

So did Congress's other important action: the 1861 Confiscation Act, passed on August 6 and signed immediately by Lincoln. Judged by everything that would later happen, its significance is easily overlooked. Yet as James Oakes argues, it underscored the emerging Republican consensus that interfering with slavery, though not the war's purpose, would be embraced as a *consequence* of suppressing rebellion. It declared as "forfeit[ed]" the claim of any slaveholder to the labor or service of any slave used in furtherance of the rebellion. The act did not technically emancipate such slaves, but in reality it did. It also applied only to slaves who had been used directly for military purposes and had subsequently escaped to Union lines, not to slaves still under Confederate authority. Although all slaves in the seceded states, and many in the border states, were arguably being used to support the rebellion, Congress did not intend the act to have such universal applicability. This policy of

---

[25] *OR*, ser. 2, vol. 1, 750; Marshall, *Private and Official Correspondence*, 1: 26. Every history of emancipation includes the origins of Butler's contraband policy, but see Masur, "A Rare Phenomenon of Philological Vegetation." For a nuanced examination of the many assumptions embedded in the term "military emancipation": Manning, *Troubled Refuge*, chap. 3.

[26] *CG*, 37th Cong., 1st Sess., 209 (July 23, 1861, Crittenden, quotation), and 243 (July 24, 1861, Johnson); McPherson, *Battle Cry of Freedom*, 311–12; Oakes, *Freedom National*, 128–31; Belz, *Reconstructing the Union*, 24–28. For contrasting views, see Hyman, *More Perfect Union*, 41–47; Hyman and Wiecek, *Equal Justice*, 22–23.

limited military emancipation nonetheless effectively freed any escaped slave who had been used in the Confederate war effort, even slaves whom Confederate authorities had impressed against their owners' wishes. The act did not distinguish between loyal and disloyal slaveholders, and neither did it distinguish between seceded and loyal slave states. Whatever its ambiguities and limitations, the act vitiated the Crittenden resolution.[27]

Moreover, the War Department's instructions for implementing the act prohibited Federal military personnel to distinguish between fugitive slaves who had been employed in support of the rebellion and those who had not, thereby ignoring a central provision of the act. This policy, along with the act's equating of loyal and disloyal slaveholders, essentially precluded the return of *any* fugitive slave who had reached Union lines. The 1861 Confiscation Act and the War Department's instructions dictated Federal antislavery policy for the next several months, but the Federal military's descent into the lower Mississippi valley in early 1862 revealed both the act's strengths and its weaknesses.[28]

In the meantime, developments closer to home also presaged the potential conflict over slavery for the inhabitants of the lower Mississippi valley. By summer 1861, General John C. Frémont commanded Union forces in Missouri. "The Pathfinder" to the west and the first Republican presidential candidate in 1856, Frémont boasted of antislavery credentials that put him in favor with the Radical Republicans and abolitionists, but he also displayed imperiousness and administrative incompetence. Facing a volatile situation in a bitterly divided state, Frémont issued an order in late August instituting martial law, threatening to shoot disloyal civilians, and declaring free the slaves of disloyal Missouri slaveholders. The order contravened the Confiscation Act, which confiscated only slaves employed in furtherance of the rebellion. When Frémont refused Lincoln's private request in early September to modify his order so as to comply with the Confiscation Act, Lincoln ordered him to do so.[29]

Lincoln's action sparked outrage throughout the North. While his counter-response is perhaps best known for asserting that Frémont's order would have driven the border states, especially Kentucky, out of the Union, Lincoln also maintained that Frémont, in emancipating slaves, had addressed a "*purely political*" question. This was something only Congress could do (legislate in principle; not free slaves). Frémont's proclamation, Lincoln insisted, "assumes that the general may do *anything* he pleases – confiscate the lands and free the slaves of *loyal* people, as well as disloyal ones." Although Lincoln reaffirmed

---

[27] *Statutes at Large*, 12: 319; Oakes, *Freedom National*, chap. 4; Siddali, *From Property to Person*, chaps. 3, 4.
[28] *OR*, ser. 2, vol. 1, 761–62; Oakes, "Reluctant to Emancipate?"
[29] *OR*, ser. 1, vol. 3, 466–67; *CWL*, 4: 506–7, 517–18.

the distinction between loyal and disloyal slaveholders, though in a border state, he also seemed to question even the *president's* legal authority to "make permanent rules of property by proclamation." He would later reverse himself on this point.[30]

Lincoln insisted that principle, not expediency over Kentucky, prompted him to countermand Frémont. Yet Kentucky was very much on his mind, given the state's strategic significance. Indeed, Lincoln's apprehension at provoking disunion had compelled him earlier to respect Kentucky's "armed neutrality." Even as the Frémont imbroglio was playing out in early September, Confederates under General Leonidas Polk violated that neutrality by seizing Columbus, a key railroad terminus on the Mississippi River, fearing that Union forces led by General Ulysses S. Grant at nearby Cairo, Illinois, would seize it first. Grant reacted by occupying Paducah, Kentucky, gaining control of the strategically crucial Tennessee and Cumberland Rivers. Both sides had entered Kentucky, but Polk was first. The Confederate "invasion" of Kentucky was a political disaster, causing Jefferson Davis far more grief than Frémont had caused Lincoln. The state had seemed to be leaning toward secession before Polk's precipitous maneuver, but it now experienced a Unionist upsurge. By late 1861, Confederates held southwestern Kentucky but Federals controlled the rest of the state. Not only had Confederates failed to honor a state's sovereignty, but they had also enabled Union forces to gain strategic positions in Kentucky without being deemed the aggressor. These gains would open the way in early 1862 to the conquest of the lower Mississippi valley.[31]

V

By fall 1861, Confederate authorities throughout the lower Mississippi valley had spent months severing their states' ties to the Union, integrating their states into the new Confederate nation, and mobilizing the region's resources for war. The Mississippi River was essential to the Confederacy's strategic defense, and extensive measures were undertaken to secure the river from invasion at either end. In particular, Confederate authorities impressed slaves to serve as military laborers, often without their owners' consent. No Federal military forces had yet arrived to which these slaves could escape, but this mobilization exposed numerous slaves to the wider world beyond their home plantations. It also raised conflict between the property rights of individual slaveholders and the Confederacy's national interests even as it threatened to

---

[30] *CWL*, 4: 531–33; Foner, *Fiery Trial*, 176–81.
[31] McPherson, *Battle Cry of Freedom*, 293–97; Oakes, *Freedom National*, 159–63; Hess, *Civil War in the West*, 11–17; Horn, *Leonidas Polk*, chap. 14; Phillips, *Rivers Ran Backward*, 139.

undermine the master–slave relationship and the slave system as a whole. A Pandora's box was being opened.[32]

This mobilization included militarily organizing several dozen New Orleans free men of color into the Louisiana "Native Guard." In offering their services to the Confederacy, these men undoubtedly sought cover in dangerous times. Governor Moore accepted the offer and enrolled them into the state militia, but thus ended their Confederate military careers. They would play a much larger role in the Union army after the fall of New Orleans.[33] However improbable, the very idea of black men fighting for the Confederacy underscored the reality that this new nation was predicated on the preservation of slavery. Americans, North and South, were aware of how a society's mobilizing for war might produce unanticipated consequences. In the South, therefore, heightened vigilance remained essential against any threat to the slave regime. The southern white mindset oscillated between the happy, contented slaves and the savage beasts ready to slit their masters' throats, and moments of crisis turned paranoia into hysteria. The slaveholders' apparent complaisance could never mask their unease over not really knowing what their slaves thought. "We live on a mine that the Negroes are suspected of an intention to spring on the fourth of next month," observed Kate Stone of Louisiana, whose concerns were prompted in part by the impending special session of the US Congress on July 4. From Carroll County, in west-central Mississippi, another plantation mistress told of local slaves having planned an insurrection, with at least one of them having been whipped to death as a result. But other people's slaves could never be trusted as one's own. "Our negroes are as humble and well behaved as they have always been," she assured herself.[34]

These reports were but part of a larger phenomenon of slave restiveness during 1861 throughout the lower Mississippi valley and the other slave states. Set off by the secession crisis, it would never really die down. If the valley's slaves could not abscond to Union lines, they could embark upon a mobilization of their own, and among the most wrenching episodes of this initial phase of slave unrest was the Second Creek conspiracy, near Natchez,

---

[32] On mobilization throughout the lower Mississippi valley, see Winters, *Civil War in Louisiana*, chaps. 2, 3; Smith, *Mississippi in the Civil War*, 29–35; DeBlack, *With Fire and Sword*, 29–43; Moneyhon, *Impact of the Civil War and Reconstruction on Arkansas*, 101–6, 115–16; Cimprich, *Slavery's End in Tennessee*, 14–16. Slaveholders' resistance to slave impressment is a key element of Armstead Robinson's argument that class conflict among white Southerners over slavery ultimately doomed the Confederacy: *Bitter Fruits of Bondage*, esp. 106–9.

[33] There is an extensive literature on the Louisiana Native Guard, but for an effective overview, see Hollandsworth, *Louisiana Native Guards*.

[34] Anderson, *Brokenburn*, June 19, 1861, p. 28; Dimond and Hattaway, *Letters from Forest Place*, 233; Cimprich, *Slavery's End in Tennessee*, 12–14. Historians have noted slave insurrection scares from Maryland to Texas during 1861, but see McCurry, *Confederate Reckoning*, 27–34, and Faust, *Creation of Confederate Nationalism*, chap. 4, esp. 71–72.

Mississippi. Although the episode probably originated in Fort Sumter's tumultuous aftermath, authorities did not discover it for months. As was so often true of rumored slave insurrections, it remains impossible to know what the Second Creek conspiracy entailed. The record, though fragmentary, is rich for a slave conspiracy, owing to an account kept by Natchez-District planter Lemuel P. Conner of some of the interrogations. The conspiracy no doubt consisted of something other than phantoms in the white mind, but it did not go beyond talk. No overt act took place; no white person was killed or attacked; nothing appears to have happened beyond the crafting of vague outlines. What *is* known is that between mid-September and late October 1861, at least twenty-seven slaves, and no doubt many others, were hanged – after brutal interrogation – as the plot was ruthlessly ferreted out. The executions of enslaved persons would continue in the area for nearly two more years.[35]

The plot centered on several plantations along Second Creek, a small stream just southeast of Natchez. There may have been no single plot but rather a series of overlapping schemes or proto-conspiracies. Conspiracies are by definition secret, and people who were illiterate concocted this one. White society wanted to get to the bottom of things but then suppressed all knowledge of the plot once it had been crushed. The accused slaves – suffering unspeakable torture – would have told their accusers anything they wanted to hear. Many of them were guilty under the law – as it stood at the time – of plotting servile insurrection, but others simply refused to betray their friends, though also a crime. Some were mere braggarts, but just talking insurrection was a matter of life and death.

The plot may have been hatched as early as April, the start of hostilities. Although their masters had talked about virtually nothing else for months, the slaves had somehow gotten the impression that Abraham Lincoln intended to free them. The conspiracy may have been linked to an insurrection scare in early May near Fayette, a town twenty-five miles northeast of Natchez, where a number of planters formed themselves into an investigative committee. They hanged at least four slave carriage drivers – men who occupied positions of responsibility and privilege, enjoyed the opportunity to move about and communicate with slaves on other estates, and possessed knowledge of the wider world – and probably executed several other slaves before "order" was restored. Once the Second Creek conspiracy came to light in early-to-mid-September, white society mobilized to destroy an internal threat. The official institutions of state and local government were bypassed, and the episode

---

[35] Jordan, *Tumult and Silence at Second Creek*; Behrend, "Rebellious Talk." Jordan's work provides transcriptions of a number of primary source documents on the conspiracy, including Lemuel Conner's account of the interrogations. On white Southerners' deeper fears of slave insurrection as a crucial factor in bringing on the Civil War, see Paulus, *Slaveholding Crisis*; Rugemer, *Problem of Emancipation*.

never entered the public record. Instead, several community leaders constituted themselves as the "Examination Committee," which carried out its gruesome business, including ordering an unknown number of hangings, during the second half of September.

In early October, upon discovery that slaves in Natchez may have been involved, the committee moved its operations to a racetrack on the eastern edge of the town, where it conducted its investigation and executed slaves throughout the month. By early November, the episode appeared to be over. "I am glad to hear that the finishing touch has been put to the investigations of the committee appointed to try the negroes who took part, or were suspected of having taken part, in the proposed insurrection," wrote one area resident, then serving in the Confederate army in Virginia, for whom the distinction between slaves involved in the plot and those only suspected of having been involved made no difference. "I am sincerely rejoiced to know that the last of the wretches have been hung."[36]

Although many particulars of the conspiracy remain shrouded in mystery, Lemuel Conner's account sheds light on others. The conspiracy's leadership, however amorphous, possessed both a hierarchical structure, including ranks and titles, and a military quality. The conspirators thought of themselves as equivalent to the Federal forces that, they assumed, were coming to free them, and with which they would be entering into an alliance. They were aware that a General Scott headed the Union military – in fact General Winfield Scott was general-in-chief – and that on September 10, the supposed date of the uprising, he would lead Union forces in capturing New Orleans. The conspirators also demonstrated an awareness of the Union naval blockade, and a belief – not entirely implausible, as it happened – that Federal gunboats were just up the Mississippi River. But much time would pass, and much suffering endured, before the army of liberation arrived.

Testifying before a very different investigative body, the Southern Claims Commission, in the mid-1870s, Rebecca A. Minor, widow of Natchez cotton planter and Louisiana sugar planter William J. Minor, who died in 1869, recalled that her husband had been "perfectly horrified" by the cruelty he witnessed during the interrogations at the racetrack. "It was one of the most unpleasant and disagreeable scenes, I have heard my husband say, that he ever witnessed, and he determined that he would never own a negro afterwards if such barbarity, and conduct, was attempted." She insisted that other white people threatened her husband because he objected to the methods being used, and that the conspirators "would have been more severely dealt with if Mr. Minor had not taken a stand against it."[37]

---

[36] Jordan, *Tumult and Silence at Second Creek*, 322.
[37] Jordan, *Tumult and Silence at Second Creek*, 331–32.

William Minor's plantation journal during this period offers no corroborating evidence that he objected to the interrogations. Yet what remains beyond doubt is that a self-appointed group of leading citizens, including some of the South's largest slaveholders, inflicted unspeakable suffering on human beings whom they suspected of having planned a revolt, and that more than two dozen of the conspirators, real and alleged, and probably many more, were hanged. From the perspective of white society, the Examination Committee had no choice, for what the slaves had in mind represented the violation of everything white Southerners held dear. Many of the Minor slaves had belonged to the family for generations, and William Minor, a life-long slaveholder, had always been, according to his widow, "an exceedingly lenient master." But no master could afford leniency in the face of insurrection. The Confederate states had declared their independence in part to forestall the very thing Second Creek embodied. Slavery had required constant vigilance and relentless violence even when the slave states enjoyed the full power of the Federal government to sustain it. Now, with an external enemy at the gates, the mere specter of insurrection required all of the force the slave regime could muster. The Second Creek conspiracy was ruthlessly suppressed, as were all other hints of servile insurrection, but the slaveholders could do nothing once the Union army finally arrived, as the slaves knew it would.

Yet even here the story did not end. Whether the slaves at Second Creek had conspired during the spring and summer of 1861 to organize a revolt, the slaveholders were responding to what Justin Behrend calls "a different kind of rebellion." Although the initial hysteria had died down by the fall, the slaves faced interrogation and execution until Union forces finally captured Vicksburg in July 1863. The slaveholders – and later, Confederate military authorities – were attempting to root out not conspiracy plots but rather any expression of slave support for the Union cause. Slaves conveyed these sentiments along deep and complex communication networks – the "grapevine" – that extended throughout the Natchez area. By 1863, more than 200 persons may have lost their lives in what Behrend labels "perhaps the largest series of slave executions in U.S. history." The large majority of these victims had not conspired to revolt but had simply expressed the hope that the Union would win the war and they would be freed. But, under the circumstances, saying this was tantamount to violent rebellion. The slaveholders, as Behrend further observes, "came to realize that talk of freedom represented as grave a threat to their lives and livelihoods as did a conspiratorial plot." But they also ultimately found, as have oppressors throughout history, that they could not execute an idea.[38]

---

[38] Behrend, "Rebellious Talk," 19 (first quotation), 20 (third quotation), and 21 (second quotation). For Behrend's estimates of the number of executions, 21, n. 9, and 50–51.

VI

By the fall, the implications of freeing slaves – if only as a consequence of suppressing rebellion – for the conduct of the war and for restoring the seceded states to the Union remained entirely unclear. Despite the upheaval that Federal antislavery policy portended, Lincoln and most Unionists adhered to a narrow vision of the war. Lincoln was determined to maintain a coalition that included Democrats who supported a war solely for the Union and antislavery radicals who advocated an abolitionist war. He also could not risk alienating the deeply divided border states of Delaware, Maryland, Kentucky, and Missouri, especially their influential slaveholders.[39]

Lincoln was also acting on his own understandings of federalism, the Constitution, and secession. He articulated these views, among other pronouncements, in his Inaugural Address, his April 15 proclamation, and his address to the special session of Congress. Maintaining the legal fiction that the seceded states had never left the Union, and the belief in Unionist majorities in them, Lincoln envisioned a war to restore the national authority over the seceded states. The process of restoring those states to the Union would be equally limited, Lincoln and the moderate Republicans whom he typified argued, and it might be more accurately described as *restoration* than as Reconstruction. Because *individuals* had carried out secession, acting through the framework of state governments, state restoration consisted of returning loyalists to power and reestablishing the seceded states' prior relations with the Union. This approach emphasized the distinction between the loyal and disloyal elements in the seceded states, and it upheld those states' essential integrity. The war was being fought to restore the old Union and not to recast the southern social order or redefine the relations between the states and the Federal government. Although slaves were being freed, Lincoln and most Northerners largely advocated this restorationist vision during the war's opening phase.[40]

While pushing for a war against slavery, by contrast, Radical Republicans and abolitionists also began to visualize an approach to state restoration more akin to *Reconstruction*. The Confederate national government was obviously illegitimate, but so were the state governments. Rejecting the idea that individuals alone had committed treason, Radicals contended that secession enjoyed broad support and that the governments of the seceded states, as the embodiments of the will of their citizens, ceased to exist as political entities. The seceded states had not left the Union, since doing so was illegal, but they had abrogated their relations with it, and those relations would have to be restored.

---

[39] There is a voluminous literature on the border states, and even on Lincoln's policies toward them, but for an excellent overview, see Harris, *Lincoln and the Border States*.

[40] CWL, 4: 421–41, esp. 426–28, 432–37; Belz, *Reconstructing the Union*, 8–10; Rodrigue, *Lincoln and Reconstruction*, 15–21.

Employing a concept that would become known as "territorialization," Radicals argued that the seceded states had reverted to territories, and that the Federal government would administer them directly and determine the conditions they must meet before gaining "readmission" to the Union. Territorialization was less concerned with the distinction between rebels and Unionists, seeing the former in the vast majority, and it drew a direct line between disunion and slavery. While its advocates often disagreed among themselves on particular points, territorialization allowed for Federal intervention in the states' internal affairs. This position was by far the minority one among Republicans, and while abolitionists immediately commenced petitioning Congress, once it convened in regular session in December, to take further measures against slavery, few Republicans had given serious consideration to how military emancipation would affect the problem of state restoration.[41]

Still, military emancipation, and what he later called the "friction and abrasion" of war, prodded Lincoln to address slavery's future. By the fall, Lincoln had begun to outline plans for two interrelated initiatives: gradual, compensated abolition for the border states – with compensation for *slaveholders*, not slaves – and colonization, or the resettlement of free black people, voluntarily or not, under public and/or private sponsorship, beyond US borders. Both initiatives had long been axiomatic to northern antislavery thought. Border-state abolition, along with prohibiting slavery's extension into the territories, had been considered essential steps toward eradicating slavery throughout the United States, whereas colonization dealt with the consequences. If neither idea was new, the war gave them greater salience. Lincoln formulated a gradual, compensated abolition proposal for Delaware, where slavery was essentially defunct, during the fall. Although the plan went nowhere, he developed a more ambitious proposal for all of the border states that he would recommend to Congress in early 1862 and advocate throughout the spring. Similarly, Lincoln recommended in his December 1861 message to Congress that "steps be taken" toward colonization. Congress demurred, but Lincoln and other Republicans continued to endorse the idea. Gradual abolition was predicated on the assumption that slavery remained a state matter, and Lincoln expressly denied that his border-state plan established any Federal claim to interfere with slavery in the states. The plan was designed in part to prevent the border states from joining the Confederacy, but Lincoln had dared to formulate a concrete proposal to end slavery as an institution, if only in the loyal slave states.[42]

---

[41] Belz, *Reconstructing the Union*, 10–13; McKitrick, *Andrew Johnson and Reconstruction*, chap. 5.

[42] *CWL*, 5: 29–31, 48 ("steps"), 144–46, 318 ("friction"); Williams, *Slavery and Freedom*; Reed, "Lincoln's Compensated Emancipation Plan." There is a considerable literature on

But none of this mattered without military success. As the reality sank in by late 1861 that the war would extend into a second fighting season, Lincoln and most Northerners were already envisioning a different kind of war. General-in-Chief Winfield Scott had devised the North's original strategy, the "Anaconda Plan," which called for placing the South under naval blockade while a Union strike-force captured the Mississippi River and split the Confederacy in two. The rebellion would then slowly be squeezed to death while avoiding major casualties or large-scale destruction. The plan was never really attempted, and by late October General George B. McClellan had replaced the aging Scott. Yet the plan anticipated – when combined with more aggressive methods that included engaging Confederate armies in traditional battles and destroying the South's infrastructure and resources – what eventually became the North's strategic vision. It underscored the significance of the Mississippi River and the western theater in general, and it envisaged using the South's rivers to gain entry into the Confederate heartland. By year's end, the Anaconda Plan had been scrapped, and Lincoln and his generals had yet to unite on a single vision. But Lincoln was already beginning to conceptualize a strategy that would capitalize on the North's superior resources by attacking the Confederacy simultaneously on multiple fronts. The lower Mississippi valley would prove pivotal to that strategy.[43]

The Union took no action along the Mississippi River before the year ended. Most of the war's first year in the west had focused on thwarting the secessionist impulse in Missouri, without which any river campaign further south was meaningless. Neither could Union forces move against the valley from the north without violating Kentucky's neutrality, and Polk's seizing of Columbus ensured southern control of the river. Despite these difficulties, Lincoln and Navy Secretary Gideon Welles had been persuaded during the fall to approve an expedition against New Orleans from the Gulf of Mexico. The War and Navy Departments cobbled together forces under Flag Officer David G. Farragut and General Benjamin F. Butler, originator of the Union's contraband policy, who would command a proposed Department of the Gulf. Butler had been recruiting regiments in New England in hopes of securing another command, having been relieved from duty at Fortress Monroe. Late 1861 and early 1862 saw Federal forces assemble on Ship Island, off the Mississippi coast, preparing to invade the valley. By April, they were ready.[44]

Lincoln and colonization, but for a good overview, see Foner, "Lincoln and Colonization," in Foner, *Our Lincoln*.

[43] Scott's plan appears in *OR*, ser. 1, vol. 51, pt. 1, 369–70. Also see Eisenhower, *Agent of Destiny*, chap. 35; Stoker, *Grand Design*, 60.

[44] Hearn, *When the Devil Came Down to Dixie*, chap. 3, 52–59; Hess, *Civil War in the West*, 75–77; McPherson, *Battle Cry of Freedom*, 290–93.

Meanwhile, with Congress and the northern public clamoring for action, Lincoln in late January 1862 ordered "a general movement of the Land and Naval forces" against the insurgents, to commence on February 22. No such general movement took place, much to Lincoln's dismay, but by that date, the commanders of one of the joint forces, General Grant and Flag Officer Andrew H. Foote, had delivered two major victories in Tennessee. The Union campaign against the lower Mississippi valley had begun.[45]

* * *

By early 1862, Federal military emancipation – in the guise of Butler's contraband policy, along with the Confiscation Act and the War Department's orders for its enforcement – had led to the freeing of slaves in Virginia, the border states, and the South Carolina Sea Islands, which Federals had captured during the fall. Though technically limited, it was being broadly applied. As Union forces prepared to invade the lower Mississippi valley during the spring of 1862, enslaved men and women in various parts of the region would seize upon Federal antislavery measures to secure the freedom that – as the slaves of Second Creek had demonstrated – they knew must come. In doing so, they would show themselves to be not the mere victims of their owners' paranoia and vengeance but the shapers of larger events – nothing less than the course of the war and the fate of slavery. Indeed, they would precipitate the *one* thing the Confederacy – this "Independent Power" – had been designed to prevent.

---

[45] *CWL*, 5: 111–12.

2

Of Stampedes and Free Papers

Although most of the people of the lower Mississippi valley experienced the first year of the Civil War vicariously, the region by early 1862 began to assume central significance in determining the course of the war and the fate of slavery. Utilizing the South's rivers to their advantage, Union military forces made inroads into western and central Tennessee during the winter and into Arkansas and southern Louisiana during the spring. They captured New Orleans in late April, Memphis in early June, and Helena, Arkansas, in mid-July. For the first time in the war, Federal forces descended into the maelstrom of the Confederate interior and – save for the South Carolina Sea Islands – the Deep-South plantation belt. Despite attempts by Federal commanders to evade the issue of slavery, the Federal presence spawned what observers would customarily call a "stampede" of enslaved persons toward Union lines. Those who remained behind contributed to slavery's undoing from within.

Throughout the first half of 1862, circumstances in the lower Mississippi valley created new challenges for Federal military commanders and civilian policymakers. Some of these challenges were the result of scale, whether geographical or demographic, such as the size of the slave population, whereas others derived from new pressures on earlier policies. While the occupation of large parts of the valley by midyear revealed the contradictions of Federal policy toward slavery in the Confederacy, Abraham Lincoln and congressional Republicans were implementing a more direct attack on slavery.

I

Although Lincoln's hope for a broad military mobilization in early 1862 came to naught, one of his generals showed resolve. Having previously seized the junctures of the Tennessee and Cumberland Rivers with the Ohio River, General Ulysses S. Grant further secured control of those two rivers by respectively capturing, on February 6 and February 16, forts Henry and Donelson. By February 25, Nashville capitulated without a fight, threatened by Grant and a second Union force to the north. The capital of the last state to secede thus became the first to surrender to Federal forces. Confederates soon thereafter abandoned Columbus, Kentucky, previously taken at such high political and military cost but now useless. These victories were of immeasurable strategic importance, securing Federal control of central and western Tennessee, and western Kentucky, and opening the way into the lower Mississippi valley. The hostility Federal forces encountered from the white population also demonstrated the rebellion's popular support and the need to suppress it through more than conciliation.[1]

The Federals' arrival prompted the full spectrum of reactions from the region's slaveholders and slaves. In a phenomenon that had already become familiar but was about to explode, the slaves took flight from the plantations and sought refuge with the Union troops whom they saw as liberators, thereby underscoring the link between disunion and slavery. Many slaves bided their time, weighing the risks, which were formidable, against the benefits, while others fled at the first opportunity. These seekers of freedom tested the limits of Federal contraband policy and the Confiscation Act. Many slaveholders also fled, but in the other direction, dragging their slaves with them. Because Confederate authorities had employed some of these enslaved men and women in aiding the rebellion, their owners knew they were subject to confiscation. Other slaveholders stayed put, professing loyalty and trusting in Federal commanders' promises not to interfere with slavery, and trying as best they could to keep their human property from bolting. In attempting to recover fugitives, some slaveholders demonstrated a keen awareness of the Confiscation Act, denying that their slaves had been used to support the rebellion. In adjudicating these competing claims, Federal commanders in Tennessee confronted the same questions that bedeviled their counterparts elsewhere, only on a scale that dwarfed previous experience. Were the masters of fugitives loyal? Had the slaves been used in furtherance of rebellion? Were the fugitives from a seceded or loyal slave state? Did any of this matter?[2]

Although many Northerners had already begun to visualize a different war, prevailing military policy in the west had been designed to avoid the slavery issue. Having replaced John C. Frémont in November 1861, General Henry W. Halleck commanded an area that included Missouri, Arkansas, and western Kentucky. Halleck was no abolitionist, but neither was he sympathetic to slaveholders, and he genuinely wanted to prevent the army from becoming mired in the slavery controversy. Quickly growing frustrated with slaveholders' appeals for their fugitives' return, and fearing that vital military information was being leaked, Halleck in late November ordered that all fugitive slaves and "unauthorized persons of every description" be barred from entering Union camps. Halleck's order was poorly worded, and members

---

[1] Smith, *Grant Invades Tennessee*; Hess, *Civil War in the West*, chap. 3; McPherson, *War on the Waters*, 2, 37–42; Sternhell, *Routes of War*, chap. 3.

[2] *Freedom: DS*, 251–56, 271–75 (docs. 83–85), 523–25 (doc. 200); *OR*, ser. 1, vol. 10, pt. 2, 15; Siddali, *From Property to Person*, chap. 3.

of Congress criticized it upon reconvening in December. Indeed, it was couched so broadly that some of Halleck's subordinates used it to prohibit *all* fugitives from Federal lines – including those who had been used in support of the rebellion – once Union troops entered Tennessee. Halleck had not intended his order to be so broadly construed, and although he issued several revisions of it, he had failed to avoid the tumult over slavery.[3]

In western Tennessee, Grant struggled to reconcile Halleck's order with the conditions he faced. He issued an order in late February specifying that Halleck's directive was "still in force and must be observed," and that the slaveholders' requests to enter Union lines in search of runaways necessitated the exclusion of all fugitives. Grant had also returned certain fugitive slaves in Kentucky. However, Grant directed that slaves who had already gained refuge within Union lines when Fort Donelson was captured, or who had been used "in any way hostile to the Government," would not be returned but instead would be employed by the Federal military. Although Grant's order was less restrictive than those of other officers, its exclusionary provisions still violated the Confiscation Act. As much as Federal commanders in the lower Mississippi valley hoped to avoid dealing with fugitive slaves, that objective only proved more unworkable the deeper Union troops descended into slave country.[4]

In the weeks ahead, Federal forces expanded and solidified their hold over the northern reaches of the lower Mississippi valley. In late February and early March, forces under General Samuel R. Curtis entered northwestern Arkansas, where they routed Confederates in the Battle of Pea Ridge, of March 6–8. Although Curtis pulled his own battered army back into Missouri to recuperate, Confederate authority in northern Arkansas had been significantly weakened. A month later, the Confederate attack at Pittsburg Landing caught Grant off guard, but the bloodbath at Shiloh, on April 6–7, failed to dislodge the Federals from the valley. The following day, Union forces captured the Confederate stronghold at Island No. 10 on the Mississippi River, leaving only Fort Pillow to defend Memphis. By mid-April, the Federal expedition against New Orleans was about to commence, further exposing the limits of Federal antislavery policy.[5]

---

[3] Oakes, *Freedom National*, 181–89; *Freedom: DS*, 251–52, 256–59, 275–76 (doc. 86), 279–81 (doc. 89), 417 (doc. 157); Marszalek, *Commander of All Lincoln's Armies*, 111–12; Engle, *Don Carlos Buell*, 201–3.

[4] *Freedom: DS*, 270 (doc. 82); Simon and Marszalek, *Papers of Ulysses S. Grant*, 4: 290–91; *OR*, ser. 1, vol. 7, 668, and vol. 52, pt. 2, 309; Hess, *Civil War in the West*, 38–39, 44–45; Manning, *Troubled Refuge*, 109–22.

[5] McPherson, *Battle Cry of Freedom*, 404–17; Hess, *Civil War in the West*, 45–49, 57–58; Moneyhon, *Impact of the Civil War and Reconstruction on Arkansas*, 124–25; DeBlack, *With Fire and Sword*, 43–50; *OR*, ser. 1, vol. 13, 28–48.

II

While Northerners were rethinking the Union war effort and the role of slavery in it during early 1862, congressional Republicans further accelerated the war's transformation. When the Thirty-Seventh Congress convened in regular session in December 1861, it seemed as though the world had been turned upside down since the special session of the previous summer. Attitudes on slavery in particular had shifted dramatically in the interim. Republicans were in a foul humor over Frémont's emancipation imbroglio and Halleck's fugitive slave order. The House, based on Republican votes, refused to reaffirm the Crittenden–Johnson resolution, and events in Tennessee and elsewhere demonstrated its absurdity. If anything, more extensive measures against slavery than the existing Confiscation Act, now seen as inadequate, were needed. Republicans went to work almost immediately on a new one, although it would only be enacted at the end of the session in July 1862.[6]

Congress also addressed for the first time the political status of the seceded states and their restoration to the Union. Whereas Republicans and War Democrats worked together on legislation to prosecute the war, bipartisanship disintegrated – and Republican factionalism became apparent – over "Reconstruction." Despite their revised thinking on the nature of the war, Lincoln and most moderate Republicans tended to maintain their "restorationist" approach to the seceded states. They still hoped that southern Unionists might seize the opportunity that Federal military protection afforded them to organize loyal governments. By contrast, several of the more radically inclined Republicans, such as Representative James M. Ashley of Ohio, who was destined to play a central role in the abolition of slavery, introduced a number of measures in late 1861 and early 1862 predicated on territorialization. While these proposals contained important differences, they all initiated the legislative attack on slavery by establishing provisional governments in the seceded states that would have been prohibited from legally recognizing or sanctioning slavery or involuntary servitude. Or, as Herman Belz observes, these bills "were alike in imposing on the rebel states territorial governments capable of abolishing slavery." None of the measures came close to passing, however, a harbinger of conflict over Reconstruction that would outlast the war itself. Northern Democrats – who contended that the seceded states should immediately resume their place in the Union once resistance to Federal authority ended – would have much success in playing Republicans off against one another. Nonetheless, although Congress would adjourn in July

---

[6] *CG*, 37th Cong., 2nd Sess., 1179 (March 12, 1862); Richards, *Who Freed the Slaves?*, 42; Siddali, *From Property to Person*, 227–50; Oakes, *Freedom National*, 226–39; McPherson, *Battle Cry of Freedom*, 442–53.

without enacting Reconstruction legislation, a Republican consensus was emerging that linked the fate of slavery and state restoration.[7]

It was perhaps to preempt territorialization legislation – while also safeguarding executive initiative and reaffirming his own approach to state restoration – that Lincoln initiated the policy of appointing military governors for the seceded states where Union forces made territorial gains. The appointing of military governors for areas where civilian government already existed was unprecedented in American history, and it sparked some backlash. Military governors would provide protection and guidance to southern loyalists in organizing state governments and restoring their states to the Union. They would also allow for the reassertion of Unionist sentiment that Lincoln believed secessionists had suppressed a year earlier, even if he was losing faith in a loyalist majority, and serve as a temporary expedient toward state restoration. Lincoln would encourage the military governors and other Federal officials to collaborate with local Unionists in establishing civilian governments and in organizing congressional elections. His goal was still to restore the seceded states as quickly as possible.[8]

In March 1862, Lincoln appointed Andrew Johnson as military governor of Tennessee with the rank of brigadier general. (He later appointed George Shepley for Louisiana, who played a subordinate role to the military department commanders; appointees for Arkansas, North Carolina, and Texas had little impact.) Johnson entered a volatile situation, as Tennessee was experiencing its own inner civil war. Federals held parts of secessionist west and central Tennessee, whereas Confederates controlled east Tennessee, having suppressed a Unionist uprising the previous fall. A rock-ribbed Unionist of the Jacksonian persuasion, and the only US Senator from a rebellious state not to resign or be expelled, Johnson was appointed for his presumed ability to galvanize Unionists in that bitterly divided state. For the next three years, he demonstrated tremendous personal bravery and fortitude in striving toward that goal. As a leading Unionist – along with William G. "Parson" Brownlow, Horace Maynard, Emerson Etheridge, William B. Campbell, Thomas A. R. Nelson, and others – Johnson enjoyed much support in Washington and at home. But as an east Tennessee Democrat who had advocated a Federal invasion of that region over west and central Tennessee, he also elicited criticism from former Whigs. Johnson deemed disunion the work of a cabal, contending that white Tennesseans had been denied the chance to express their views during the secession crisis. An advocate of

---

[7] Wilson, *History of the Antislavery Measures*, 337–39; Belz, *Reconstructing the Union*, 40–83 (quotation, 60); Zeitlow, *Forgotten Emancipator*, 89, 100–101, and "Ideological Origins," 404–7; *CG*, 37th Cong., 2nd Sess., 815 (February 14, 1862; bill by Ira Harris of New York), 1193 (March 12, 1862; bill by Ashley).

[8] Belz, *Reconstructing the Union*, 66–73; Harris, *With Charity for All*, 40–57, 105–12.

the white yeomanry who always maintained that slavery did more harm to them than to the slaves, Johnson held the planter elite responsible for the war. He would come to endorse the abolition of slavery as punishment for rebels as strongly as he opposed racial equality.[9]

Lincoln's instructions authorized Johnson to exercise "the powers, duties and functions" of military governor until Unionists had formed a loyal civilian government. It was not at all clear, however, what those powers were, how the military governor stood in relation to military commanders, or how the transition from military to civilian government would take place. One of Johnson's first acts was to issue "An Appeal to the People of Tennessee," in which he spelled out the conciliatory policy he planned to follow. Yet Johnson soon displayed the invective toward "traitors" for which he would become known. He demanded that all officeholders swear an oath of allegiance and imprisoned those who refused to do so, along with anyone who dared express Confederate sympathies.[10]

Johnson proved to be a polarizing figure, even among Unionists, and the shortcomings of his administration soon became apparent. He remained almost entirely focused on nurturing loyalism in central Tennessee and liberating east Tennessee, taking little interest in west Tennessee, where slavery was most deeply entrenched. Johnson never visited Memphis during the war. He devoted nearly all of his attention to state restoration efforts and virtually ignored slavery until well into 1863, allowing civil officials, especially in west Tennessee, to enforce parts of the slave code. His squabbles with military commanders often resulted in appeals to Lincoln or Secretary of War Edwin M. Stanton. Treading cautiously in such disputes, Lincoln expressed full confidence in Johnson and allowed him considerable latitude, but Johnson's stance that state restoration must await east Tennessee's liberation caused Lincoln and others much consternation. Johnson's main problem was that central and west Tennessee, where Federal control was strongest, remained stridently disunionist. The phrase that would become his defining mantra – "Treason must be made odious and traitors punished" – demonstrated the extent of both "treason" and "traitors" in the state. Confederate guerrilla raids also caused much dislocation and suffering. If Unionism in Tennessee

---

[9] An extensive literature exists on Johnson, owing to his later career as president and importance to postwar Reconstruction. But a significant scholarship covers his career as military governor, including the introductions to volumes 6 and 7 of the *PAJ*, Bergeron, *Andrew Johnson's Civil War and Reconstruction*, chaps. 1–4, and Cimprich, "Military Governor Johnson and Tennessee Blacks." All biographies cover these years, especially Trefousse, *Andrew Johnson*, chaps. 8, 9. The best insight into Johnson remains McKitrick's *Andrew Johnson and Reconstruction*, esp. chap. 4.

[10] *PAJ*, 5: 177–78, 209–12; Harris, *With Charity for All*, 50; Hess, *Civil War in the West*, 62–70.

depended on Federal military success, Confederate activity consistently undermined it.[11]

In the meantime, as Congress wrestled with both Reconstruction legislation and a new Confiscation Act, Republicans secured two critical measures in March that greatly expanded the boundaries of "limited" military emancipation. An article of war prohibited Union soldiers to decide upon the claim of any fugitive seeking refuge behind Union lines, even on the essential question, per the Confiscation Act, of whether said slave had been used to support the rebellion. In effect, Union soldiers were forbidden from returning any fugitives to their owners. Congress only now caught up to the War Department's instructions implementing the Confiscation Act. Republicans also spearheaded legislation prohibiting the military from enforcing the Fugitive Slave Act and authorizing criminal prosecution for military personnel who assisted in enforcing state fugitive slave laws. Federal officers and soldiers now possessed no legal authority to facilitate the return of any fugitive slave, just as large swathes of the lower Mississippi valley, including its two key cities, were about to come under Union control.[12]

III

By late March, the Union expedition against New Orleans from the Gulf of Mexico, under General Benjamin F. Butler and Flag Officer David G. Farragut, was ready. After surmounting the sandbars at the mouth of the Mississippi, the Union flotilla in mid-April approached Forts Jackson and St. Philip, about seventy miles below New Orleans. Federal gunboats tried for nearly a week to pound the forts into submission before Farragut decided to run past them on the night of April 23-24. With both sides exchanging furious fire, Farragut maneuvered all but three of his seventeen ships past the forts, and within days the Federal fleet anchored at New Orleans. Farragut then steamed further upriver, while Butler assumed control of the city.[13]

Throughout his career the irascible Butler stirred up trouble everywhere he went. This was never truer than during his eight-month tenure, which was to become the stuff of legend, as commander of the Department of the Gulf. Both Lincoln and General-in-Chief George B. McClellan seemed primarily motivated to get rid of Butler in sending him to New Orleans. If Lincoln hoped still to placate white Southerners, Butler, as the author of the Union's contraband policy, was hardly the man for the job. Butler genuinely wanted to conciliate

---

[11] *CWL*, 5: 302-3, 313; Johnson to Lincoln, July 10, 1862, ALP; *PAJ*, 5: 534; Harris, *With Charity for All*, chap. 2; Atkins, "Failure of Restoration," 302-3.

[12] *Statutes at Large*, 12: 354; *CG*, 37th Cong., 2nd Sess., 958 (February 25, 1862), 1143 (March 9, 1862); *Freedom: DS*, 22; Oakes, *Freedom National*, 186-89.

[13] Winters, *Civil War in Louisiana*, chap. 7, provides an effective account of the capture of New Orleans, which has received much scholarly attention.

Confederates who resumed their former loyalty but dealt harshly with those who did not. He pledged to protect the property rights of citizens who took the oath of allegiance and threatened to treat all others as "enemies" of the United States. He forcefully suppressed any expression of rebel sentiment, hanging a Confederate sympathizer who tore down the US flag and issuing an order threatening to arrest and charge with prostitution any woman who disrespected Union military personnel. His championing of the poor and working class, or what Scott P. Marler calls Butler's "campaign of class warfare," alienated the city's elite and doomed any chance of winning over the New Orleans mercantile community. Butler seemed to believe that his measures, which earned him the epithet "Beast" and white New Orleanians' undying hatred, would encourage loyalists to come forward and restore Louisiana to the Union.[14]

Butler demonstrated little nuance toward the politics of occupation, but the number of fugitive slaves in southern Louisiana trumped anything he had seen in Virginia. The parishes along the Mississippi River were home to the region's sugar planters and to more than 50,000 slaves. From this moment on, life for these people would never be the same. In their letters, memoirs, and other accounts, Union soldiers and sailors told of slaves discretely waving to them as gunboats and transports ascended the Mississippi. Witnessing this display of the military might of their enemy's enemy, and of their enemy's impotence in the face of it, the slaves saw their day of deliverance at hand. Decades later, many of them would recollect Lincoln personally telling them they were free.[15]

This constructed memory spoke to an essential truth. Yet the slaves did not need Lincoln to tell them what to do. No sooner had Federal ships appeared on the Mississippi than slaveholders told of slaves running off to the "Lincolnites." As in Virginia and elsewhere, this flight from the plantations started tentatively, by individuals or small groups, but soon became bolder, as plantation discipline broke down and the slaves realized there was little their owners could do about it. Before long, the "stampede" was underway; slavery and everything required to sustain it were coming apart. The sheer number of fugitives threatened to overwhelm the Federal army's resources, since they could not all be employed as military laborers or adequately fed and sheltered. Slaveholders in southern Louisiana responded to the situation in a variety of ways. Resorting to scorched earth, some indignant slaveholders deliberately compounded the problem by preemptively driving their slaves away before the

---

[14] *OR*, ser. 1, vol. 6, 717–20; Marler, *Merchants' Capital*, chap. 5, esp. 161–67 (quotation, 161); Hearn, *When the Devil Came Down to Dixie*; Butler, *Butler's Book*, 257–58.

[15] Louisiana Works Progress Administration, State Library of Louisiana, Louisiana Digital Library (https://louisianadigitallibrary.org/islandora/object/state-lwp%3A8595; accessed August 2019). This collection offers various initial reactions to the Federal arrival. Botkin, *Lay My Burden Down*, 16–19, includes instances in other places in the South of Lincoln personally informing slaves of their freedom.

slaves could leave. They were by far the exception. Unlike their counterparts in other areas, especially the South Carolina Sea Islands, Louisiana slaveholders largely remained on their estates, taking their chances with the conquerors rather than fleeing to the Confederate interior. Some had genuinely opposed secession, while others had been lukewarm supporters. Many who *had* supported secession now eagerly swore the oath of allegiance if it meant keeping their slaves.[16]

But perhaps what was most distinctive – and revealing – about the situation in southern Louisiana was the very dynamics of emancipation. The slaves were fleeing to Union lines, to be sure, but the Union army had also come to *them*. Under the circumstances, the current Federal antislavery policy was useless. Congress had decided that no fugitives would be returned to their owners. But to what extent would the Union army, as an occupation force, assume responsibility for maintaining discipline on the plantations? Would it, in other words, prop up the slave regime?

Butler spelled out these difficulties and requested instructions in late May from Secretary of War Stanton. In other Union-held areas, the question of "the state of negro property" could be easily settled, but not in southern Louisiana. Here, the citizens had largely resumed their allegiance and had returned to peaceful pursuits, or so Butler wanted to believe, and, as such, had been promised "protection and inviolability of the rights of property." Butler then got to the crux of the matter. "Now, many negroes, slaves, have come within my lines," he noted. "Loyal and disloyal masters have lost them alike." To permit "a virtual confiscation" of these fugitives by providing them refuge, Butler insisted, amounted to "an actual confiscation of all property," since any planter deprived of labor was doomed to economic ruin. The fugitive slave problem in southern Louisiana, as Butler saw it, entailed not just remanding individual slaves but also the viability of slavery and the economic survival of loyal slaveholders. Butler was not so much sympathizing with loyal planters as identifying the contradictory logic of Federal policy. In restoring Federal authority, was the army maintaining the slave regime or undermining it? And how could the Federal government cultivate southern Unionism while destroying slavery? "What would be the state of things if I allowed all the slaves from the plantations to quit their employment and come within the lines," Butler asked. If these were strange words from the man who had coined the term "contraband," they also suggest that the lessons of the Virginia situation of a year earlier did not apply to Louisiana.[17]

Butler wrote to Stanton in part because some of his own subordinates not only imagined an end to slavery but also worked to bring it about. General

---

[16] *Freedom: DS*, 191–95; Rodrigue, *Reconstruction in the Cane Fields*, 33–35.
[17] *Freedom: DS*, 203–8 (doc. 61). On the problem of the Union army as an occupational force in general, Lang, *In the Wake of War*, esp. chaps. 2, 3.

John W. Phelps was a Vermont abolitionist who commanded Camp Parapet, several miles upriver from New Orleans. A West Point man and life-long reformer, Phelps contended that military necessity justified the emancipation of *all* slaves in the seceded states and even empowered the president to abolish slavery entirely. Phelps wanted to admit all fugitives to Union lines, not just those used to support the rebellion, despite Butler's express orders to the contrary. He also refused to allow any slaves to be returned – even those who had not been used in rebellion and whose owners had taken the loyalty oath. Phelps's policy induced slaves to flee from plantations in localities where Federal authority had already been secured, and where Butler had given planters to understand – or so they thought – that traditional order would be upheld. Under such circumstances, enforcing discipline on the plantations was an exercise in futility. Owing to Phelps's policy, one officer complained, "it is utterly impossible to call upon the negroes for any labor, as they say they have only to go to the Fort to be free and are therefore very insolent to their masters."[18]

What Phelps was doing essentially accorded with Federal antislavery measures, including Butler's contraband policy at Fortress Monroe. There, however, Butler dealt with hundreds of slaves; here, thousands. And, as Butler explained to Stanton, the entire context of the Louisiana situation was unprecedented. As fugitives flocked to Union lines, despite attempts to discourage them, even Phelps seemed to entertain second thoughts. By the time Butler wrote to Stanton, congressional debate over a new Confiscation Act was intensifying.[19]

IV

While Butler's troops were securing control of southern Louisiana, Federal forces to the north also tightened their hold. Following the near disaster at Shiloh, General Henry Halleck assumed field command and devoted nearly a month to assembling a massive force in northern Mississippi. In early May, the Federal behemoth began finally to lurch toward Corinth, which Confederates abandoned later that month for Tupelo, fifty miles to the south. The loss of Corinth handed the Federals a direct rail link to Memphis and exposed Fort Pillow to land attack. The Confederate evacuation of the latter site in early June left Memphis virtually defenseless. A small Confederate river fleet provided the city some protection, but a brief naval engagement on June 6 resulted in its almost complete destruction. Memphis was in Federal

---

[18] *Freedom: DS*, 203 (doc. 60), 208–9 (doc. 62; quotation, 208).

[19] *Freedom: DS*, 192–95, 199–202 (doc. 58), 209–17 (doc. 63); *OR*, ser. 1, vol. 15, 485–91; Oakes, *Freedom National*, 218–23, 245–47. On the contraband experience in and around New Orleans, Manning, *Troubled Refuge*, 102–6.

hands, and the Union navy could navigate the Mississippi all the way to Vicksburg.[20]

Although Union forces had been operating in western Tennessee and northern Mississippi for months, the fall of Memphis threw the countryside as far south as Vicksburg into chaos. In the weeks ahead, Memphis was transformed by thousands of slaves who either sought refuge on their own or were hauled off by Union troops. "[The Yankees] are taking all the negro men and horses they can find in the country," noted a resident of northern Mississippi. In northeastern Louisiana, the mother of Kate Stone had the enslaved men on the plantation called up and instructed that "if the Yankees came on the place each Negro must take care of himself and run away and hide. We think they will." Stone was right, but not in the way she thought. In the ensuing days, she noted slaves absconding on their own or with Federal raiding parties and planters deserting their estates. One slaveholder who decided it was time to go was Confederate president Jefferson Davis's older brother Joseph. When he attempted to remove the slaves from their Davis Bend plantations into the Mississippi interior, the result was near insurrection. Davis eventually convinced more than a hundred people to leave, but many stayed behind, looting the places after he departed. A Federal raid in late June by Farragut's sailors destroyed most of what remained, including the mansion at Joseph's Hurricane plantation. Joseph Davis never returned, and his model community lay in shambles.[21]

Joseph Davis was a unique slaveholder but his experiences were not. The capture of Memphis amplified conflicts that had already pitted against one another the various players in this developing saga: loyal and disloyal slaveholders; fugitive slaves who had been used in support of the rebellion and those who had not, or those who could provide labor for the Union army and those who could not; and Union commanders who sympathized with the slaves and those who did not. Yet even conservative-minded commanders were coming to the same conclusion that Republicans and many Northerners had long since reached: the slaves were allies, and the masters, or most of them, were enemies. Increasingly, the key issue for field commanders was no longer whether a fugitive *slave* had been used to support the rebellion but whether the *master* was loyal. The 1861 Confiscation Act punished masters whose slaves had been employed in furtherance of rebellion by emancipating, implicitly, only those slaves so used. Now, disloyal masters whose slaves had not been used to support the rebellion deserved no quarter. "The slaves of our enemies," Union General William S. Rosecrans, who was no abolitionist, observed in

---

[20] Hess, *Civil War in the West*, 49–51, 59–60.
[21] Agnew Diary, UNC, June 4 and 5, 1862; Anderson, *Brokenburn*, 125–28 (June 29–July 5, 1862); Hermann, *Pursuit of a Dream*, 38–40.

late July, "deserve more at our hands than their masters." In time, even the master's loyalty would not matter.[22]

Across the river in Arkansas, Federal military progress during the spring was slower but the attack against slavery steadier. Having pulled back into southwestern Missouri after his March victory at Pea Ridge, General Samuel Curtis only in late April ventured again into Arkansas. As Curtis's army trampled through northern Arkansas, via the White River, Confederate authority disintegrated. Lacking the resources to move against his intended target of Little Rock, however, Curtis encamped in early May at Batesville, in northeastern Arkansas. Not until late June did he again move south along the White, hoping to secure supplies from a naval fleet at De Vall's Bluff before marching on Little Rock. As Curtis proceeded in late June and early July, he found his progress impeded by burned bridges, blocked roads, and other obstructions – almost all of it the work of slaves impressed from surrounding plantations. Failing to secure the anticipated resources, Curtis abandoned the Little Rock campaign and marched east to the Mississippi River, capturing Helena in mid-July.[23]

Curtis was frustrated over the Confederates' use of impressed slaves, whom he called "the most efficient foes" he encountered. Even before reaching Helena, Curtis began issuing "free papers" to fugitives who had been employed militarily, declaring them to be "forever emancipated" under the Confiscation Act. As word of Curtis's policy spread, slaves throughout the Arkansas Delta threw down their axes and flocked to Union lines, resulting in yet another "general stampede," as Curtis put it, and the almost complete breakdown of slavery in the area. Among the fugitives who received their papers were many whom Confederate military authorities had not actually impressed. Certain of Curtis's practices – emancipating slaves who had been used in support of the rebellion, and harboring all fugitives who voluntarily sought shelter behind Union lines – were clearly consistent with Federal policy. Others – enticing slaves to leave their plantations or carrying them off wholesale, and emancipating "forever" fugitive slaves who obviously had not been used for military purposes – just as clearly were not. Operating in a context very different from southern Louisiana, Curtis precipitated the very situation Benjamin Butler had feared. Just as Congress was about to pass a new Confiscation Act, Curtis, along with Phelps and others, anticipated some of its key provisions.[24]

---

[22] *Freedom: DS*, 254 (Rosecrans), 276–78 (doc. 87), 278–79 (doc. 88), 281–82 (doc. 90); *OR*, ser. 1, vol. 17, pt. 2, 97; Starr, *Jennison's Jayhawkers*, chap. 9; Sherman, *Memoirs*, 1: 176–77; Marszalek, *Sherman*, 126; Manning, *Troubled Refuge*, 132–34.

[23] *OR*, ser. 1, vol. 13, 30, 141; Moneyhon, *Impact of the Civil War and Reconstruction on Arkansas*, 124–25; *Freedom: DS*, 259–60; DeBlack, *With Fire and Sword*, 53–62; Schultz, *March to the River*; Bearss, "White River Expedition."

[24] *Freedom: DS*, 259–60, 285–87 (doc. 92), 292 (doc. 95); *OR*, ser. 1, vol. 13, 525; DeBlack, *With Fire and Sword*, 60–62; Hess, "Confiscation and the Northern War Effort." On the

V

By mid-1862, Abraham Lincoln and most Republicans had dramatically revised their thinking on the nature of the rebellion and the war. Because disunion enjoyed popular support throughout the seceded states, they were coming to realize that a war of conquest – a "hard" war – would have to replace one of conciliation. Lincoln had also reached the conclusion – as the historical record amply demonstrates – that some kind of general emancipation policy for the seceded states was necessary, both as a pragmatic military measure and as part of the ideological transformation of the war. Despite these changes, Lincoln and moderate Republicans had yet to modify their "restorationist" approach to Reconstruction. They hoped still to induce Confederates to resume their former allegiance and to restore the rebellious states without significant Federal involvement in their internal affairs. Although territorialization legislation had attracted some centrist-Republican support during the second half of the congressional session, between March and July, Democrats and conservative Republicans had combined to defeat it. The failure of McClellan's Peninsula campaign made Reconstruction moot, but western military success would make the question unavoidable.[25]

If Republicans had yet to reconcile military emancipation with state restoration, they continued to press the attack on slavery. Toward that end, the 1862 – or "second" – Confiscation Act illustrated the war's transformation for most Northerners during the previous year. Introduced at the opening of the congressional session in December, the act only passed as the session ended in July. Its fourteen sections were far more complicated than its predecessor's four, and its complexity matched the legislative wrangling needed to secure its passage. Debate reflected the sharp disagreement between northern and border-state Democrats and Republicans, and among Republicans themselves, over the conduct of the war, confiscating property, congressional power to legislate emancipation, and the president's authority to free slaves. Approval required intense negotiations among Republicans, especially during the session's final weeks, and the measure had to overcome several last-minute objections from Lincoln. The matter of confiscating real or personal property – and even property in slaves – proved especially problematic in light of the constitutional prohibition against bills of attainder. Although Republicans crafted the act with all forms of property in mind, slavery stood unambiguously at its core, and some of them believed emancipation to be its only enforceable feature.[26]

---

contraband experience at Helena: Manning, *Troubled Refuge*, 106–9. Helena also figures prominently in Taylor, *Embattled Freedom*, but see esp. chap. 4.

[25] Belz, *Reconstructing the Union*, chap. 4; Richards, *Who Freed the Slaves?*, 55–57.

[26] *Statutes at Large*, 12: 589–92, for the text of the act, which has received significant scholarly treatment, including Siddali, *From Property to Person*, chap. 6; Hamilton, *Limits of Sovereignty*, chaps. 2–4; Oakes, *Freedom National*, chap. 7; and Richards, *Who*

However convoluted the new act's language, many Republicans intended it to emancipate as many slaves as possible. Unlike the previous act, it expressly freed slaves, and it shifted the rationale for emancipation from the slave's status to the master's. Now, the slaves of disloyal masters would be freed, regardless of whether said slaves had been used to support the rebellion. Even as the new act explicitly distinguished between loyal and disloyal slaveholders, its framers assumed all slaveholders to be disloyal, so it amounted to general emancipation in Union-held areas of the seceded states. In redefining the war, Lincoln and Republicans were on the cusp of abandoning the distinction between loyal and disloyal slaveholders.

For now, though, the distinction would be maintained, at least theoretically, and rebellious slaveholders would be severely punished. Much of the act relied on the courts and required convictions for treason in order to set in motion its punitive provisions, but the emancipation sections were far less encumbered. The sixth section provided that all persons who failed to resume their allegiance and who aided the rebellion in any way – sixty days after a presidential cease-and-desist proclamation that the act called for – would have all of their property seized and sold by the Federal government. (This proclamation is not to be confused with the preliminary Emancipation Proclamation.) The slaves of slaveholders who continued to support the rebellion would thus be effectively emancipated. The act did not explicitly *require* this proclamation, but Lincoln would hardly have signed the bill and then not issued it.

Section six could be considered prospective emancipation, but section nine conceivably applied to areas, such as the lower Mississippi valley, that had *already* come under Union control. This complicated section attempted to cover the many contingencies regarding emancipation that had taken place in the seceded states, and it gave legal sanction to the various emancipatory tactics that Union military personnel were already employing in the field. It deemed as "captives of war" and declared "forever free of their servitude" all slaves who escaped from, were "captured from," or were "deserted by" disloyal slaveholders, and who subsequently gained refuge behind Union lines or came under Federal control. Disloyal persons were defined in this section as those "who shall hereafter be engaged in rebellion" or "who shall in any way give aid or comfort thereto." By allowing for the freeing of enslaved persons "captured from" disloyal slaveholders, the act countenanced the Union army's enticing of slaves from plantations, a practice that prompted slaveholders' cries of anguish. This section also freed all slaves of disloyal slaveholders in areas

Freed the Slaves?, 66–70. In general, bills of attainder are legislative acts that impose penalties upon persons, especially for high offenses such as treason, without those persons having been convicted in court. Article III, Section III of the Constitution prohibits Congress from imposing penalties, such as confiscation of property, on the family members or descendants of persons who had been guilty of treason, without themselves having been so convicted.

that had previously been "occupied by rebel forces" and later came under Federal military control. This provision applied to many parts of the seceded states, but none so extensive as the lower Mississippi valley.

Despite its carefully crafted language, section nine was not without ambiguity. Whether the terms "hereafter" and "shall," in defining disloyal slaveholders, were intended to refer only to future actions and allegiances remained unclear. Presumably, they were, otherwise the act could have been considered an ex post facto law. Slaveholders who took the loyalty oath *after* the Union army's arrival – as did many in western Tennessee or southern Louisiana – but *before* the act had been passed, or at least within the prescribed sixty-day window, could claim exclusion from the act. Neither did this provision clearly specify whether it applied to areas the Union army had occupied before the act's passage. In essence, would this section retroactively emancipate slaves, such as those in southern Louisiana, who had remained on the plantations when the Union army took control, and whose owners, having sworn the oath before the act's passage, were "loyal"? Slaveholders who had taken Butler up on his offer to swear allegiance in return for the protection of their property, including slaves, or who had resumed their loyalty within the sixty-day window, could rightly claim exemption from the act. And then, as Lincoln noted in his message to Congress identifying the act's shortcomings, the act provided no means for determining whether slaves belonged to loyal or disloyal owners, as defined by the ninth section. (Lincoln also denied Congress's legal authority to emancipate slaves.) Nonetheless, congressional Republicans overwhelmingly agreed that the act freed the slaves of disloyal slaveholders in all slave states, that it applied to former rebel areas *already* occupied by Federal forces when enacted, and that all slaveholders in the seceded states were essentially disloyal.[27]

The act included other important provisions. Reinforcing the article of war passed in March, it forbade all Federal military personnel, "under any pretense whatever," to decide on the validity of any slaveholder's claim to a fugitive or to remand any fugitive to any claimant. Thus, no fugitive slave could be returned to any slaveholder under any circumstances. Although this provision was framed within a larger one effectively nullifying the Fugitive Slave Act, it also mooted the ostensible distinction between loyal and disloyal slaveholders. The measure also authorized the president "to employ as many persons of African descent as he may deem necessary and proper for the suppression of this rebellion," and to "organize and use them in such manner as he may judge best for the public welfare." All adult slaves could now be employed in suppressing the rebellion, not only fugitives who had been used in support of it. This provision – along with the Militia Act, passed the same day, which provided for the employment of black men in "any military or naval service for which they may be found competent," and freed them and any family members owned by

---

[27] *CWL*, 5: 328–31; Oakes, *Freedom National*, 226–39.

disloyal slaveholders – would allow for enlisting black men in the armed services. Finally, the act authorized the president to pursue the voluntary colonization of all persons freed by it – provided the receiving country consented to their settlement and protection, "with all the rights and privileges of freemen."

Despite reservations over certain aspects of the bill, Lincoln signed it and took swift action. Several days after approving it, on July 22, he famously presented his Cabinet with a draft of the Emancipation Proclamation, which he was persuaded to delay issuing until the Union had achieved a military victory. The original draft of the Emancipation Proclamation began by citing section six of the 1862 Confiscation Act – which authorized confiscation following a presidential cease-and-desist proclamation and sixty-day grace period – and ended by promising to impose universal emancipation on all areas in rebellion on January 1, 1863. On July 25, Lincoln issued the proclamation that the Confiscation Act called for. Again citing section six of the act as authorization, it ordered all persons to whom that section might apply "to cease participating in, aiding, countenancing, or abetting the existing rebellion, or any rebellion," against the United States, and "to return to their proper allegiance ... on pain of forfeitures and seizures." Sixty days would give insurgents until September 23 to comply or risk losing their property. (This date would be one day after Lincoln issued the preliminary Emancipation Proclamation, though he had no idea at this point that he would issue it on that date.)[28]

In debating the 1862 Confiscation Act, as James Oakes argues, Republicans had crossed a crucial threshold, moving from emancipating slaves as a consequence of preserving the Union to attacking slavery itself. With the 1861 Act, emancipating certain slaves was accepted, grudgingly by some, in suppressing rebellion. The very point of the 1862 Act was to undermine slavery.[29] Such a shift was undoubtedly taking place. Yet this new approach could only go so far. Even though Republicans were coming to see emancipation and reunion as inseparable, there still remained a chasm – ideological as well as practical – between the kind of emancipation envisioned in the 1862 Confiscation Act and the eradication of slavery as an institution. Freeing individual slaves was not the same thing as abolishing slavery. Moreover, the new Confiscation Act had nothing at all to do with state restoration. Republicans would have to come up with a way of incorporating abolition into the process of restoring the seceded states to the Union – of translating military emancipation into constitutional abolition. Few people at this point would have seriously considered an amendment to the Federal Constitution

---

[28] *CWL*, 5: 336–38, 341–42.
[29] Oakes, *Freedom National*, 240–45.

abolishing slavery. If slavery were to end, it would have to be done by *state* means, and within the parameters of traditional federalism.

* * *

It remains impossible to know how many enslaved persons in the lower Mississippi valley gained their freedom during the first half of 1862. As Union military forces established varying degrees of control over the region, gains offset by the failure of McClellan's Peninsula campaign, military success gave rise to new circumstances. Federal commanders witnessed white Southerners' fervent support for secession, while the slaves displayed their own fervor for freedom. Thousands of enslaved men, women, and children were liberated – however tentatively – under Federal antislavery measures as a matter of military necessity and as a consequence of preserving the Union.

Because the lower Mississippi valley witnessed the first substantive Federal occupation of the lower-South plantation belt, aside from the Sea Islands, conflicts over slavery there infused the larger debate over its fate elsewhere. The 1862 Confiscation Act tried to address the various contingencies that Federal commanders confronted in the field, but the act was not without ambiguities, and it could not resolve underlying questions about slavery as an institution. Indeed, despite the new act, Federal policy toward the slaves of loyal slaveholders – once Confederate territory came under Union control – remained unclear. This situation was especially problematic when these slaves, in Benjamin Butler's words, "quit their employment" and sought refuge behind Union lines. In essence, what was to become of slavery once the rebellion had been suppressed? However difficult, this question was still seen as distinct from that of state restoration, which Federal military advances in the lower Mississippi valley had also brought to the fore. Even as Lincoln and Republicans moved toward a policy of universal military emancipation during the second half of 1862, they had barely begun to fathom its implications for state restoration.

3

"Broken Eggs Cannot Be Mended"

In the weeks following passage of the 1862 Confiscation Act, conflict over fugitive slaves in the lower Mississippi valley vivified the larger battle over slavery itself. This conflict reached a culmination of sorts in September when Abraham Lincoln redefined the war by issuing the preliminary Emancipation Proclamation. The collapse of slavery in places trodden upon by Federal troops contributed vitally to Lincoln's decision on emancipation. So did the failure of southern Unionism, especially in the lower Mississippi valley. By July 1862, just as Lincoln was informing his Cabinet that he intended to issue a proclamation of emancipation for the rebellious states, he gave evidence of his reasoning in uncharacteristically scathing comments about southern – especially Louisiana – Unionists' lack of resolve in their moment of truth. "Broken eggs cannot be mended," he warned these ostensible Unionists, prodding them to act. Lincoln would still need to work with southern Unionists on state restoration, but his September proclamation marked an all-out assault on slavery. The remainder of 1862 witnessed the initial efforts to establish formal systems of "free labor" in the lower Mississippi valley, either on abandoned plantations under Federal supervision or with resident planters who agreed to government-mandated labor arrangements. But neither wartime free labor nor Lincoln's proclamation would determine the fate of slavery as a legal institution.

I

As military emancipation in the lower Mississippi valley intensified during the summer and fall of 1862, the dismantling of slavery left a void that would have to be filled. The process by which an alternative to slavery as a labor system took root varied from one locality to the next, but it also revealed certain patterns. As the problem of fugitive slaves threatened to become a humanitarian crisis, Federal officials resorted to improvised tactics that would later yield to institutionalized policies. The Union army eventually employed thousands of able-bodied men and women as military laborers, while also establishing "contraband camps" and other places of refuge for their families and others. Many of these formerly enslaved persons would be put to work – some voluntarily, some not – on abandoned plantations under Federal military authority, whereas others remained on their home plantations and worked under labor arrangements overseen by Federal officers. Although neither the fate of slavery nor the legal status of many former slaves had been decided, the faintest outlines of new labor relations began to emerge.[1]

In Union-held western Tennessee and northern Mississippi – areas that were to be encompassed within the military Department of the Tennessee – many slaveholders "refugeed" to the Confederate interior, trying to take their slaves with them. Many others swore the oath of allegiance in a desperate bid to preserve their institution. Still others tightened discipline, or tried to, hoping to maintain power over their slaves or deluding themselves into thinking that the slaves had remained "faithful." Some relented to the new reality and began redefining their relationship with persons whom they had once considered their property, offering various inducements to get them to stay. With Federal troops nearby in many cases, (former) slaves did not have to leave their home plantations to benefit from new arrangements. Having been previously forced into the Mississippi interior, for instance, a number of former slaves of Jefferson and Joseph E. Davis managed to return home and began working the devastated Davis Bend lands on their own.[2]

The ratcheting up of the attack on slavery also further compelled commanders unsympathetic to emancipation to modify their views. Upon assuming command of Memphis in late July, General William Tecumseh Sherman, who would be called many things but never an abolitionist, issued a series of orders vigorously enforcing recent antislavery measures and providing for the employment of able-bodied men as military laborers.[3] This outlook reflected how dramatically Federal policy on slavery had been transformed. Far from prohibiting soldiers to interfere with slavery, it now virtually directed them to do so in the name of military necessity. But this was not the case everywhere. Some officers continued to discourage fugitives from seeking Federal refuge, especially those incapable of productive labor. In early August, General Ulysses Grant, who had recently assumed overall command in the west when Henry Halleck was promoted to general-in-chief, issued an order that, among other things, enjoined Federal soldiers from "enticing Slaves to leave their Masters." Still, the new Confiscation Act, along with the actions of the slaves themselves, effectively turned Union soldiers into slave stealers.[4]

---

[1] Downs, *Sick from Freedom*; Taylor, *Embattled Freedom*; Manning, *Troubled Refuge*.

[2] *Freedom: WGFL-LS*, 622–23; Agnew Diary, UNC, August 18 and 21, 1862; Hermann, *Pursuit of a Dream*, 38–40.

[3] *Freedom: DS*, 289–91 (doc. 94), 438–41 (doc. 171). For orders and other documents showing Sherman's shift, see *Freedom: DS*, 289–97 (docs. 94–98). See also *Freedom: WGFL-LS*, 623–24, 658–59 (doc. 148); Marszalek, *Sherman*, 191–93.

[4] *Freedom: DS*, 256; *Freedom: WGFL-LS*, 671n (quotation).

The consequences soon became apparent. The able-bodied – men and women – could be employed as military laborers, but the many others who arrived at Union lines destitute and starving portended a crisis. As the latter were shunted off to the outskirts of military camps, those not already ill soon succumbed to diseases and sickness. Chaplains and surgeons tried to alleviate suffering and improve living conditions, while northern benevolent societies also provided relief. But the situation required broad measures, not piecemeal initiatives. The Union army could hardly allow – even encourage – slaves to leave their masters only to let them waste away. At the same time, many Federal officials were obsessed with preventing former slaves from becoming dependent upon the government for their sustenance, whereas others, working in conjunction with northern reformers, were intent on demonstrating their capacity for self-support. Several attempts to relocate former slaves to destinations further upriver or to points in the upper Midwest sparked the predictable backlashes. Federal military officials had already established contraband camps and similar centers of refuge in central and western Tennessee, with a portion of military laborers' earnings going to the support of their families and nonproducers. Officials would establish others in the weeks ahead, but these places of refuge were as much the product of improvisation as of a coordinated policy.[5]

However difficult the situation east of the Mississippi, conditions in Arkansas were more chaotic. Confederate authority had never entirely solidified in northern Arkansas, and Union General Samuel R. Curtis's army further destabilized that authority as it advanced along the Arkansas and White Rivers en route to Helena. As fugitive slaves overwhelmed the Federal lines at that city, the quartermaster there complained in late July of "a perfect 'Cloud' of negroes being thrown upon me for Sustenance & Support." Curtis put hundreds of men to work on fortifications, but that still left many people needing assistance. "There are also here otherwise unprovided for, 500 women & children who are refugees from their masters," reported the post commander in early September. "They are in a most deplorable condition suffering for both food and covering." Many of them had traveled great distances and could not return home even if they so desired. Curtis established an accounting system in which he sold the cotton that many fugitive slaves had hauled with them into Federal lines to pay for their support. Viewing the fugitives' plight less sympathetically, Arkansas Military Governor John S. Phelps alleged in late September that Curtis had issued free papers solely on the fugitives' word and had ordered defensive works constructed mainly "to give employment to the slaves."[6]

---

[5] *Freedom: DS*, 255–56; *Freedom: WGFL-LS*, 625–26, 666 (doc. 153), 667–70 (doc. 154); Manning, *Troubled Refuge*, 109–13, 123–32.

[6] *Freedom: WGFL-LS*, 659–60 (doc. 149; quotation), 665 (doc. 152; quotation). On Curtis's accounting system, and on the cotton that fugitive slaves in Arkansas claimed to own, see

Whether Curtis had created a Federal make-work program, he displayed greater concern for the former slaves' welfare than did most generals. By the time of Phelps's complaint, however, Curtis had already been replaced by General Frederick Steele, who would play an essential role in Arkansas affairs for the next two-plus years. Steele proved to be more solicitous of would-be Unionists – including slaveholders – than Curtis. He even refused to abide by Curtis's promise to pay military laborers who had helped build the Helena fortifications the nearly $50,000 they were collectively owed, claiming not to know whether they or their owners should receive payment. Though not overtly hostile to the former slaves, Steele had little sympathy for them. Complaints of various abuses committed against black people by Federal soldiers and officers under his command – and of wretched conditions at Helena – would eventually prompt northern protests.[7]

The situation in southern Louisiana also remained unsettled through the summer. General Benjamin F. Butler struggled to rein in radical or abolitionist subordinates such as General John W. Phelps, whose run-ins with Butler would bring about his resignation from the service in early September. Butler also faced the challenge of mediating conflict between laborers who insisted on being treated as free and planters who, having taken the oath of allegiance, were determined to preserve their old authority. Even after Union forces had established a presence in certain neighborhoods, slaves fled, often incited by officers such as Phelps. The results, as elsewhere, were fears of a humanitarian crisis, the challenges of employing able-bodied fugitives as military laborers, and concerns over the support of nonproducers. At Carrollton, near New Orleans, former slaves were organized under strict rules ostensibly intended for their benefit. "For the welfare of the contrabands, and to save them from idle and vicious habits, it is necessary that they should work," the post commander imperiously ordered, "and as they are yet too ignorant, thoughtless and improvident to think and act judiciously for themselves, they must be subjected to wholesome rules and restraints."[8]

While former slaves naturally bristled at regulations predicated on such assumptions, policy toward them was part of a larger problem in southern Louisiana. In short, what was to be done with the thousands of slaves who continued to reside on plantations under the authority of their owners, who, claiming loyalty, expected the Union army to preserve order on their estates? The 1862 Confiscation Act had not settled that question. One planter informed

---

Freedom: WGFL-LS, 622–24, 660–64 (doc. 151). A military court of inquiry later concluded that Curtis had acted improperly. See also, Hess, "Confiscation and the Northern War Effort."

[7] *Freedom: WGFL-LS*, 628–29, 674–77 (doc. 157); [Unsigned] to [General Frederick Steele], November 1, 1862, Steele Papers, Stanford; DeBlack, *With Fire and Sword*, 86–87; Manning, *Troubled Refuge*, 106–9; Taylor, *Embattled Freedom*, chap. 4.

[8] *Freedom: WGFL*, 350–51, 377–80 (doc. 64), 380–82 (doc 65; quotation, 380).

Federal military officials in late September of the "state of insurrection" that prevailed in his neighborhood and asked that an officer be assigned to "restore peace & good order." But at what point did the restoration of "order" become the maintenance of slavery? In another episode, an entire planter family, claiming always to have been loyal, requested protection against several slaves, who, they alleged, having previously run away, had recently returned home with an order from General Phelps to the other slaves on the estate "to rise and murder the whole family – and plunder and burn the Plantation."[9]

Such requests reflected the paranoia or hysteria that had always colored the slaveholders' outlook, but neither were they pure fabrication. Slaveholders' entreaties to Federal officials revealed an essential truth: their slaves were rejecting their authority and the social order on which it rested. Some slaves equated all forms of labor with enslavement and refused to work, whereupon military authorities often dealt with them harshly. What now *former* slaves objected to most, however, was any attempt to restore the way things were before the Federals arrived. One formerly enslaved woman announced that she would "go anywhere else to work, but you may shoot me before I will return to the old plantation." The laborers on another estate, according to a report, "have driven the overseer off the plantation and swear they will not allow any white man to put his foot on it." Were Federal military personnel supposed to encourage or discourage such attitudes and behavior?[10]

II

The disintegration of slavery in the wake of Federal occupation was but one of several factors that ultimately convinced Abraham Lincoln to issue the Emancipation Proclamation. Others included Lincoln's own long-held hatred of slavery, the abolitionists' push to attack slavery from the start, and the border states' rejection of gradual abolition. Then there was the failure of McClellan and other generals to prosecute the war vigorously, apprehension over the possibility of foreign recognition of the Confederacy or European intervention, the revolution in the northern mindset over slavery and the war, and the actions of the slaves themselves. Each contributed to Lincoln's decision. But perhaps nothing influenced Lincoln more than the failure of southern Unionism. Although Lincoln had finally awakened from the fantasy of loyalist majorities in the seceded states, southern Unionists' loss of nerve caused him no end of grief. The true allegiance of professedly loyal slaveholders, who expressed greater concern with preserving slavery than the Union, also confounded hopes for the Unionist resurgence to which Federal military success in

---

[9] *Freedom: DS*, 219–21 (doc. 66B), 224–25 (doc. 68).
[10] *Freedom: WGFL-LS*, 351 (quotation); *Freedom: DS*, 221–22 (doc. 67A; quotation). For one episode of slaves murdering an overseer, see *Freedom: WGFL-LS*, 389–93 (doc. 69).

the lower Mississippi valley had given rise. To judge by his unusually acerbic language, Lincoln may well have considered the southern Unionists' inability to act, especially in Louisiana, the last straw.

Conditions in Louisiana had seemed ripe for cultivating southern Unionism. Cooperationism had been strong during the secession crisis. Many sugar planters had opposed secession outright until Louisiana seceded, even though their Unionism, however genuine, paled against their commitment to slavery. The situation in New Orleans had also seemed promising. Although boasting of a secessionist majority, the city was home to transplanted northerners, immigrants, free persons of color, intellectuals, and other real or potential Unionists. The mercantile community had only moderately supported disunion. Butler recently described the white population of occupied Louisiana as quiescent to Secretary of War Stanton. If Unionism could flower anywhere in the Deep South, Lincoln might have thought, it would be here.

Lincoln encouraged Military Governor George Shepley and Butler – directly, and through Stanton and Treasury secretary Salmon P. Chase, who had officials working out of the New Orleans Custom House – to assist local Unionists in organizing. Soon, a number of men who would play integral roles in Louisiana political life for the next several years came to the fore, including unconditional Unionists Michael Hahn and Benjamin F. Flanders and conditional Unionist Thomas J. Durant, later a leading radical. Butler organized these men into a loosely affiliated Union association, while local Union clubs, some of which were made up of free men of color, sprouted up throughout the city. It was too early at this point for the factionalism that later plagued Louisiana Unionism to manifest itself, but these Unionists had very different ideas on slavery and state restoration. Also, taking advantage of Butler's pledge to protect their property rights, some 10,000 residents of the area swore the oath of allegiance by July, including many planters who would form the core of conservative Unionism. However encouraging, these activities did not signify an outpouring of loyalty. The motives of many Unionists, especially the planters, were at best questionable.[11]

Lincoln needed no reminding of the quandary he faced over slavery. Military officials such as General Phelps were doing everything in their power to undermine the slave regime; the slaves were pushing against the limitations of Federal antislavery policy; and "loyal" slaveholders were demanding that the Federal government deliver on its promise to protect their property rights. The situation was already complicated enough. But when slaveholders began appealing to Lincoln, usually indirectly, for relief from various war-related disruptions, his exasperation began to show. By late July, three months after the fall of New Orleans, Lincoln was expressing annoyance over Louisiana affairs and signaling growing doubts about loyal

---

[11] Butler's loyalty-oath order: *OR*, ser. 1, vol. 6, 717–20.

slaveholders and southern Unionists in general. He gave vent to these sentiments in a series of letters that – although written *after* he had already committed to a policy of general military emancipation – demonstrate how the inability of southern Unionists to take the initiative influenced his thinking. Nowhere else was Lincoln's vexation over this failure more evident – and nowhere else with more profound consequences for the fate of slavery – than in Louisiana.

Lincoln forcefully responded, for instance, to criticism of the Louisiana situation by Reverdy Johnson, a conservative Democrat but firm Maryland Unionist and one of the nation's foremost jurists. When Johnson alleged in mid-July that Unionism in Louisiana had been undermined by the actions of abolitionist officers such as General Phelps, a clearly annoyed Lincoln riposted by defending Phelps. Denying that he had ever "had a wish to touch the foundations" of southern society or to threaten slaveholders' property rights, Lincoln nonetheless issued a stern warning. If the people of Louisiana "can conceive of anything worse than General Phelps, within my power, would they not better be looking out for it?" All they had to do was to return to the Union "upon the old terms," Lincoln insisted, but if they refused, "should they not receive harder blows rather than lighter ones?" If this threat were not enough, Lincoln concluded with a stronger one. "I must save this government if possible," he warned. "What I *cannot* do, of course I *will* not do; but it may as well be understood, once for all, that I shall not surrender this game leaving any available card unplayed."[12]

Lincoln leveled an even more forceful rebuke at southern Unionists – and employed almost identical logic – in response to criticism from Thomas J. Durant, who alleged, among other charges, that the Federal military's attack on slavery had violated various constitutional guarantees. Lincoln replied by castigating Unionists for failing to seize the initiative, especially since they now enjoyed Federal protection. But what angered him most was their apparent willingness to sacrifice the Union over slavery, rather than vice versa. It was as though they were waiting out the conflict to see who won, "without loss to themselves." If these purported Unionists wanted their property protected, Lincoln reasoned, all they had to do was to establish a loyal state government "upon the old Constitutional terms." But if they refused to undertake this "very simple and easy" task, he warned, then "you scarcely need to ask what I will do." Indeed, what would you have me do, Lincoln asked in a series of rhetorical questions. "Would you drop the war where it is? Or, would you prosecute it in future, with elder-stalk squirts, charged with rose water? Would you deal lighter blows rather than heavier ones? Would you give up the contest, leaving any available means unapplied[?]" Lincoln's exasperation with allies such as

---

[12] CWL, 5: 342–44. Johnson had been appointed by the State Department to investigate complaints by foreign consuls against Butler but went beyond his writ.

these was unmistakable. "I shall not do *more* than I can, and I shall do *all* I can to save the government, which is my sworn duty as well as my personal inclination," he concluded.[13]

If there remained any ambiguity over Lincoln's disappointment with southern Unionists, his late-July response to criticism from "a very wealthy and influential planter" who desired "a reconstruction of the Union" would have dispelled it. Advising Lincoln to take a "decisive course," the writer insinuated that his "vacillating policy" had alienated potential Unionists. "Now is the time, if ever, for honest men who love their country to rally to its support," the planter insisted. "Why will not the North say officially that it wishes for the restoration of the Union as it was?"

Few things angered Lincoln more than the accusation that he failed to articulate a clear policy. But he let it be known that he was fed up with these so-called honest men of the South. "Broken eggs cannot be mended; but Louisiana has nothing to do now but to take her place in the Union as it was, barring the already broken eggs," Lincoln advised. "The sooner she does so, the smaller will be the amount of that which will be past mending." In other words, slavery had already suffered much damage, and the seceded states could minimize further harm by ending the war. But should they fail to act, and soon, the question would no longer be one of damage control. "This government cannot much longer play a game in which it stakes all, and its enemies stake nothing," Lincoln cautioned. "Those enemies must understand that they cannot experiment for ten years trying to destroy the government, and if they fail still come back into the Union unhurt." The point of no return would soon be upon them, and time was short. "If they expect in any contingency to ever have the Union as it was," Lincoln concluded, "I join with the writer in saying, 'Now is the time.'"[14]

Lincoln's reading of Louisiana affairs by mid-1862 demonstrates the extent to which the failure of the state's Unionists had influenced his decision to issue a proclamation of general emancipation. Yet Lincoln was also guilty of sending mixed signals, since his use of conciliatory language – suggesting that "the Union as it was" or "the old Constitutional terms" might still be

---

[13] *CWL*, 5: 344–46. The letter was to Cuthbert Bullitt, a Kentucky acquaintance of Lincoln who at the time was a loyalist in New Orleans, where he would later hold various Federal posts. Durant's original letter to Bullitt of July 15, 1862, to which Lincoln was replying, was enclosed in a letter of the same date from Bullitt to William H. Seward, both of which are in the William Henry Seward Papers at the University of Rochester. Seward no doubt brought Durant's letter to Lincoln's attention, and Lincoln, in replying to Bullitt, evidently paraphrased some of Durant's complaints. Tregle, "Thomas J. Durant," 498, esp. n. 51.

[14] *CWL*, 5: 350–51. The original letter from the planter was addressed to New York financier August Belmont, who forwarded an extract from it to Thurlow Weed, a close confident of William H. Seward. Belmont characterized the writer as "a very wealthy and influential planter" in a reply to Lincoln of August 10.

restored – counterpoised his ominous warnings. Lincoln had to know that no such restoration could take place. How exactly does one mend broken eggs? Union territorial gains in the seceded states, especially in the lower Mississippi valley, along with the confiscation acts and other Federal antislavery measures, had virtually precluded any reestablishing of the old Union, however "simple and easy" a task. Even so, Lincoln had no choice but to hope that these warnings might goad both real and potential Unionists to act. Lincoln and many Northerners may have overcome their misconception of loyal majorities in the seceded states, but they still believed that a combination of incentives and threats could induce potential Unionists and avowed Confederates to resume their old allegiance. Little could Lincoln have anticipated that his frustration with Louisiana Unionists – those who wanted either to end slavery or to preserve it – was just beginning.

III

By late summer 1862, Lincoln had concluded that he could no longer defer a proclamation of universal military emancipation for areas in rebellion. He had indicated several times throughout the spring and summer that he possessed the constitutional authority to emancipate slaves in suppressing the rebellion and that he intended to wield it. When Seward had persuaded him in July to postpone announcing the proclamation, Lincoln hardly expected the delay to extend to two long months. Following the Confiscation Act and presidential cease-and-desist proclamation it called for, Northerners had anxiously awaited for weeks some further action against slavery. McClellan's repulsing of the Confederate invasion of Maryland at Antietam finally allowed Lincoln on September 22 to issue the preliminary Emancipation Proclamation, thereby redefining the war.[15]

The proclamation began by declaring that the war was being prosecuted "for the object of practically restoring the constitutional relation between the United States, and each of the states, and the people thereof." This had always been the point of the war for Lincoln and always would be. After reaffirming his commitment to compensated abolition for loyal slaveholding states and voluntary colonization, Lincoln announced that on January 1, 1863, "all persons held as slaves" within the rebellious states or parts thereof "shall be then, thenceforward, and forever free." Lincoln would formally designate – by a subsequent proclamation on that date – those states or parts thereof whose peoples were in rebellion against the United States. Any state that "in good faith" enjoyed congressional representation – by members chosen at elections in which a majority of the state's electorate had participated – would be

---

[15] Oakes, *Freedom National*, 316–17; *CWL*, 5: 433–36, for the preliminary proclamation.

deemed not in rebellion. In effect, any state represented in Congress on January 1, 1863, would be spared the proclamation.

This mechanism for determining loyalty raised several practical difficulties. Although Lincoln had carefully distinguished between entire states and parts thereof in announcing his intention to emancipate slaves in states designated as rebellious, his language in requiring congressional elections did not maintain this distinction. It instead called for "elections wherein a majority of the qualified voters of such state shall have participated." Consequently, in Union-occupied parts of the seceded states where no congressional elections had taken place as of January, or in which, technically, a majority of the state's *entire* electorate had not participated, or whose members-elect had not been seated, all slaves would be declared free. It was hardly realistic, under the circumstances, to expect congressional elections to be organized that would attract a majority of a rebellious state's qualified voters, or even a majority in parts thereof, allowing for a distinction Lincoln himself did not make, or to expect Congress to seat any members-elect. Would allowances be made if a significant number of a state's electorate participated but not a majority, or if a majority participated in Union-held areas or within particular congressional districts? And then, putting aside the congressional prerogative over seating members-elect, Lincoln included the qualifier "in the absence of strong countervailing testimony" in judging a state not to be rebellious. This provision placed the burden of proof on persons who claimed a state was *not* disloyal, the assumption being that it was unless proven otherwise.

After calling attention to the March congressional article of war, which prohibited Federal military personnel to return fugitive slaves, Lincoln ordered all such personnel "to observe, obey, and enforce" sections nine and ten of the 1862 Confiscation Act, and he incorporated the entire text of both sections into the proclamation. Section nine legalized the many emancipation measures that Federal forces had already undertaken, including freeing the slaves of disloyal slaveholders in insurgent areas that came under Federal control. Section ten restricted enforcement of the Fugitive Slave Act and reiterated the ban on Federal military personnel from returning fugitives under any circumstances.

The provision ordering enforcement of section nine of the 1862 Confiscation Act posed other difficulties. As noted, it remained unclear whether this section was limited to Confederate areas that came under Union control, or to persons who supported the rebellion, *after* the act had been passed, or after the presidential cease-and-desist proclamation and sixty-day grace period, or whether it also applied to areas that had already been occupied, or to persons already engaged in rebellion, when the act was passed. In short, did it provide only for *prospective* emancipation based on future disloyalty or also for *retroactive* emancipation based on past disloyalty? Yet even restricting the Confiscation Act to future disloyalty, so as to avoid ex post facto issues, it still conflicted with the preliminary Emancipation

Proclamation. By ordering enforcement of section nine, this provision of the proclamation implicitly recognized the distinction between loyal and disloyal slaveholders, whereas the proclamation's earlier provision, emancipating all slaves in entire geographically designated areas, did not. Many slaveholders in west Tennessee and southern Louisiana had already taken the oath of allegiance when Lincoln announced the preliminary proclamation; how might the proclamation affect them? Lincoln doubted their professions of loyalty. Still, many Louisiana slaveholders had been working with Butler on state restoration prior to the preliminary proclamation. They would redouble their efforts, holding congressional elections in hopes of gaining exclusion from the January 1 proclamation. Tennessee would be another matter.

Federal military forces had been assisting slaves in gaining their freedom since the start of the war, but the preliminary proclamation marked a cataclysmic shift in northern thinking on it. Whereas Lincoln had originally defined secession as the work of "combinations" of individuals, he would now declare entire geographical areas to be in rebellion. For the purpose of suppressing the rebellion, *all* slaves in those areas – regardless of the loyalties of their owners – would be declared free. As far as Lincoln and most Northerners were concerned, the Confederacy had assumed a collective identity, and the distinction between loyal and disloyal slaveholders in the seceded states no longer mattered. Lincoln pledged to support compensation for loyal slaveholders once the rebellion had ended, but even they would lose their slaves. The war was still being conducted "for the object of practically restoring the constitutional relation" between the Federal government and the rebellious states, but the underlying rationale for the war had been fundamentally altered. Because Unionists were so few and ineffectual in the seceded states, because slaveholders in those states were overwhelmingly disloyal, and because slavery and disunion were indivisible, the preservation of the Union was now inseparable from the destruction of slavery.

Nonetheless, the preliminary proclamation was meant to induce Confederates to end the rebellion by offering them the chance to avoid universal military emancipation. "In no just sense of the term is this an Abolition war. By no fair construction of its language can the President's proclamation be deemed an Abolition paper," remarked the *New York Times*. "It warns the rebels that if they persist in rejecting the Constitution, they shall be deprived of the protection it gives them. But it also gives them notice that if they will return to its jurisdiction, they shall have the full benefit of the guarantees which it embodies." The insurgents held the fate of slavery entirely in their own hands: "*They* can save Slavery, if they choose to do so; if they refuse, they will have only themselves to blame." Other mainstream northern periodicals expressed similar views. Ultimately, implementation of the final proclamation in the lower Mississippi valley would fail to comport with Lincoln's own specifications in the preliminary version, and neither would the proclamation be quite the last chance Lincoln had intended.[16]

IV

Enforcement of the Emancipation Proclamation hinged on the war's outcome, and the rest of 1862 witnessed two major military initiatives in the western theater: the initial phase of the Union's Vicksburg campaign, and the Confederate's fall offensive in Kentucky. Neither would achieve its objective. In late May, Federal gunboats under David G. Farragut, coming upriver from New Orleans, had demanded Vicksburg's surrender. Lacking infantry support, however, they were rebuffed. Failing to bombard the city into submission, Farragut withdrew in late July. Meanwhile, Federal forces had taken Baton Rouge – the second Confederate state capital to fall – soon after capturing New Orleans. Following a failed attempt to regain Baton Rouge in early August, Confederates entrenched at Port Hudson, some thirty miles north, to anchor their southerly defense of the river. (The Federals subsequently abandoned Baton Rouge before reoccupying it again for good in December 1862.) The stretch of river between Vicksburg and Port Hudson would tether the two halves of the Confederacy for the next year.

Even as these events unfolded, Confederates prepared to seize the strategic initiative in the west. In September, a Confederate incursion from east Tennessee into Kentucky enjoyed considerable success before being halted at Perryville on October 8, whereupon the Confederates pulled back into east Tennessee. Also in early October, Federal forces repulsed a major Confederate attack at Corinth, in northern Mississippi. Taken together, Perryville and Corinth effectively ended the Confederacy's western offensive.

By early November, Ulysses Grant prepared to resume the Union campaign against Vicksburg. He intended to march overland toward Jackson while William Tecumseh Sherman led a river-borne column against Vicksburg. By early December, Grant had advanced to Oxford. Descending into the lower South, he encountered ardent secessionism and large numbers of fugitive slaves, who were unequivocally emancipated under the 1862 Confiscation Act but never safe from remand. A Confederate raid at Holly Springs resulted in the recapture of some 300 liberated slaves. With his supply lines stretched dangerously thin and incurring Confederate raids against his rear, Grant decided to fall back to Tennessee. Unaware of Grant's action, Sherman continued downriver before ascending the Yazoo River, hoping to reach the high

---

[16] "Slavery and the War," *New York Times*, November 21, 1862, 4. See also Hazewell, "The Hour and the Man," *Atlantic Monthly* 10, no. 61 (November 1862), 631–33; "Not an Abolition War," *Harper's Weekly*, September 27, 1862, 611. Conversely, *Harper's* ran an editorial the next week (October 4, 1862) entitled "Slavery Practically Abolished" (626).

ground north of Vicksburg from which to launch an attack. He was repulsed in late December at Chickasaw Bayou and retreated to Milliken's Bend, abandoning the offensive.

Although Grant's initial effort against Vicksburg had failed, this defeat was partly offset by the Union victory at Stones River, or Murfreesboro, fifty miles southeast of Nashville. Taking place from December 31 to January 2, the bitterly fought battle solidified Federal control of central Tennessee and allowed the Federals to hold the strategic advantage in the west. Neither the Union nor Confederate side had achieved its military objective by year's end, but the Confederate position in the lower Mississippi valley was increasingly precarious.[17]

V

"[N]egro running is fashionable now-a-days," remarked an exasperated northern Mississippi slaveholder, who likewise complained of "these stampeding times" as Grant's troops slogged through the area. Grant's first foray against Vicksburg ended in disappointment, but it further swelled the maelstrom of emancipation. It now almost became noteworthy when slaves did *not* run away. Seeking instructions from Halleck regarding the "wagon loads" of fugitives who came into his lines, Grant was directed to employ those who were capable as military laborers and – with the cotton harvest already well underway – to put the rest to work on abandoned plantations. In mid-November, Grant appointed Colonel John Eaton, chaplain of an Ohio infantry regiment, to take charge of all fugitives in the vicinity of La Grange, Tennessee, and to establish a contraband camp at nearby Grand Junction. There, the fugitives "will be suitably cared for and organized into companies and set to work picking, ginning and baling all cotton now out standing in the Fields." Grant later named Eaton General Superintendent of Contrabands for the entire Department of the Tennessee, directing him to organize fugitives for similar purposes and to employ them "in any way where their service can be made available." Grant also authorized Eaton to hire fugitives to private employers, but under no circumstances, beyond military necessity, were they to be forced into government service or "enticed away from their homes." While insisting that the former slaves provide for themselves as far as possible out of their own earnings, Grant also directed Eaton to oversee the distribution of items donated by northern charitable organizations for their benefit.[18]

[17] Hess, *Civil War in the West*, 79–83, 92–109, 112–23, 126–33. On the recapture of fugitive slaves at Holly Springs, see *Freedom: DS*, 260, n. 19, and Agnew Diary, UNC, December 24, 1862.

[18] Agnew Diary, UNC, October 31, 1862, November 1, 1862 (quotation), November 25, 1862; *Freedom: WGFL-LS*, 626, 670–71 (doc. 155; quotations); Oakes, *Freedom National*, 321–22; Szcodronski, "From Contraband to Freedmen."

Eaton's appointment marked a significant shift in Federal antislavery policy and in the emergence of new labor arrangements in the lower Mississippi valley. Although he often displayed the condescension common to white reformers of the era, Eaton would prove to be among the former slaves' most stalwart advocates within the Federal military establishment. He soon engaged a number of subordinate superintendents, most of whom were also army chaplains, to administer contraband affairs. By the end of 1862, they had assumed responsibility for almost 25,000 former slaves in west Tennessee, northern Mississippi, and northeastern Louisiana. These formerly enslaved men and women were employed as military laborers or on abandoned plantations, or they were hired out to local planters or employers in a fledgling contract-labor system supervised by the superintendents. Eaton and his men believed it their responsibility to transform what they saw as degraded, dependent ex-slaves – adrift in what he called a "veritable moral chaos" – into independent citizens, capable of engaging in voluntary labor and competing in free society. "To make the Negro a consciously self-supporting unit in the society in which he found himself," as Eaton later put it, "and start him on the way to self-respecting citizenship, – that was the beginning and the end of all our efforts."[19]

Over time, these centers of refuge – "contraband camps," "home colonies," and abandoned plantations – evolved into nascent communities from which would emerge the central institutions of black life after emancipation. Of the roughly 300 such centers established under Federal auspices in the South by the end of the war, the vast majority of them were located in the lower Mississippi valley, especially along the Mississippi River. To be sure, as Chandra Manning has observed, these sites of freedom exhibited a more temporary quality in the western theater, owing to the armies' frequent movement, than in the eastern theater. Nonetheless, by the fall of 1862, something approaching a coordinated plan for the maintenance of former slaves in the lower Mississippi valley was beginning to take shape.[20]

In addition to Confederate raids, potential reenslavement, and uprooting by Federal authorities in the name of military necessity, other challenges jeopardized these burgeoning communities and the attempt to construct a new labor system. Nonpayment of wages was common, as Federal officials withheld disbursements to persons whose legal status remained unclear, while fraud, corruption, or bureaucratic incompetence prevented others from receiving their due. Predictably, former slaves often resisted their assignments, compelling some military officials, notwithstanding Grant's original orders to Eaton,

---

[19] Eaton, *Grant, Lincoln, and the Freedmen*, chaps. 1–3 (quotations, 2, 34); *Freedom: WGFL-LS*, 626–29.

[20] Manning, *Troubled Refuge*, chap. 2. On the number of contraband camps and other centers of refuge, see Taylor, *Embattled Freedom*, 6.

to resort to impressment. Yet perhaps the greatest difficulty involved instituting "equitable relations," as Eaton put it, between former slaveholders and former slaves. As the latter looked to Federal military authorities for protection, planters resented having to operate their estates under the new labor arrangements. "A good deal of friction resulted," Eaton concluded, with considerable understatement, "some of which assumed a somewhat personal character." This was only the beginning.[21]

Perhaps nowhere else in the lower Mississippi valley – or in the entire South, save for the South Carolina Sea Islands – were both the progress and challenges of new labor arrangements more evident by late 1862 than in southern Louisiana. With the problem of slavery's future in Union-held territory still unresolved, the efforts of Federal officials to reconcile the conflicting claims of planters and former slaves were compounded by the approaching harvest. In response, General Benjamin F. Butler instituted the first system of compensated labor for the area's sugar plantations. Fugitive slaves "are now coming in by hundreds, say thousands, almost daily," Butler informed Halleck in early September, while plantations along the Mississippi River were deserted, and "crops of sugar-cane are left standing to waste which would make a million of dollars' worth of sugar." Halleck advised Butler that putting idle persons to work on the plantations would salvage a lucrative crop, teach the former slaves to become self-sufficient, and finance any government aid they received.[22]

Since the start of his administration, Butler had dealt harshly with rebel slaveholders while exercising leniency toward persons who resumed their former allegiance. He had not originally intended to emancipate the slaves or disrupt the operations of loyal planters in Louisiana. Neither did he envision himself the apostle of slavery's demise. Nonetheless, facing the very real challenges of limiting assistance, reviving agricultural production, and sheltering the fugitives of disloyal owners, Butler began to improvise a response that would significantly weaken slavery. In October, he appointed Charles A. Weed to supervise the harvesting of the sugar crop on abandoned plantations near New Orleans, with most of the proceeds going to the Federal government. Weed was among a number of Northerners drawn to the region in search of financial gain. Butler authorized Weed to requisition workers from contraband camps and to draw supplies and rations from the army. Weed, in turn, appointed other Northerners to manage abandoned plantations, and he provided workers to yet others who entered into private partnerships with local planters.[23]

---

[21] *Freedom: WGFL-LS*, 628–29, 677–79 (doc. 158); Eaton, *Grant, Lincoln, and the Freedmen*, 24; Manning, *Troubled Refuge*, 109–22.
[22] *OR*, ser. 1, vol. 15, 558, 572. See also *Freedom: WGFL-LS*, 350.
[23] *Freedom: WGFL-LS*, 352.

In late October, with the sugar harvest imminent, Butler drew up an agreement with the loyal planters of the parishes downriver from New Orleans, providing the framework under which they would operate their estates. Acknowledging the conflicting claims of slaveholders and of "persons held to service and labor," and recognizing the need "to preserve the crops and property of loyal citizens" while providing employment to former slaves, the agreement specified that the United States would "employ all the persons heretofore held to labor on the several plantations," under the supervision of loyal planters and overseers, "as they have heretofore been employed." In effect, cooperating planters would work their estates under Federal supervision. Able-bodied male laborers would receive wages of $10 per month, which was the same rate for military laborers, while women and children received lesser amounts. Workers and their immediate family members would receive food and medical care. The hours and days of labor were explicitly defined, and each laborer's hours would be recorded. Corporal punishment was prohibited, but planters could call upon the military in cases of "insubordination or refusal to perform suitable labor." Disloyal planters or those who refused to comply with the agreement would have their plantations seized, and the laborers of such planters could hire themselves to other employers. Nothing was said about how the plantations would actually operate; the assumption was that they would do so more or less as they always had.

Demurring to rule on "the legal rights of either master or slave," Butler left "the question of freedom or slavery" to be determined "by considerations wholly outside of the provisions of this contract." The agreement – to which the former slaves themselves notably were not party – also conspicuously avoided the question of slavery's fate as an institution. But it obliterated the master–slave relationship and laid the groundwork for new labor arrangements in one of the South's wealthiest plantation districts. Its reverberations would be felt for decades.[24]

Even as Butler hammered out this agreement, his subordinate, General Godfrey Weitzel, prepared to lead an invasion of the Bayou Lafourche region, west of New Orleans. The operation brought an additional swath of rich plantation country under Federal control, and it prompted another "stampede" of slaves to Union lines, more cries of "insurrection" from slaveholders, and a field commander again asking "What shall I do with the Negroes?" This time there was no question as to the fugitives' legal status, since the recent Confiscation Act unequivocally emancipated them. "[H]aving come from rebel masters into our lines in occupation of rebel territory since the passage of that act they are free," Butler correctly observed. Acknowledging that Federal officials could not remand the fugitives against their will, Butler advised Weitzel to induce them to return home voluntarily. "Put them as far

---

[24] *Freedom: WGFL-LS*, 352, 383–85 (doc. 67).

as possible upon plantations; use every energy to have the sugar crop made and preserved for the owners that are loyal, and for the United States where the owners are disloyal." Butler also alerted Weitzel to his recent labor agreement, and he soon thereafter created a three-member Sequestration Commission to administer plantation affairs in the Lafourche district.[25]

The 1862 rolling season, conducted amidst wartime conditions, was disorganized and left almost everyone dissatisfied. The output of 87,000 hogsheads of sugar amounted to less than a third of late antebellum standards.[26] Butler, however, read the results optimistically. Responding to an inquiry from Lincoln about the new labor arrangements, he maintained in late November that the experiment in making sugar with voluntary labor was "succeeding admirably." He forwarded to Lincoln "a barrel of the first sugar ever made by *free black labor* in Louisiana," adding that "the fact that it will have no flavor of the degrading whip will not I know render it less sweet to your taste." While acknowledging difficulties, and admitting that gradual emancipation would have been preferable to immediate, Butler nonetheless emphasized how quickly "this great change in a social and political system" had been carried out. "Black labor can be as well governed, used, and made as profitable in a state of freedom as in slavery," he insisted. "Slavery is doomed."

But Butler also had to admit that all was not well. The planters had been struck with what he called "a sort of Judicial blindness," and some of them had abandoned their estates rather than work them with free labor. Butler had offered the planters the opportunity to harvest their crops on the basis of his labor agreement, but many rejected it "because they would not relinquish the right to use the whip." Yet the problem went deeper than plantation discipline or corporal punishment: it extended to the slaveholders' larger worldview. "Many of the planters here while professing loyalty and I doubt not feeling it, if the 'institution' can be spared to them," Butler observed, "have agreed together not to make any provision this Autumn for another crop of sugar next season." They had instead driven their slaves off the plantations once the harvest had been completed, to the care of Federal authorities. This was not a good omen. Butler may have exaggerated the progress of free labor in the Louisiana sugar country, but he also identified a harbinger of future difficulties. The slaveholders' loyalty, such as it was, rested on the preservation of slavery.[27]

* * *

---

[25] *OR*, ser. 1, vol. 15, 162–63, 170; *Freedom: DS*, 230n; Frazier, *Fire in the Cane Fields*, chaps. 12–14; *Freedom: WGFL-LS*, 352, 383–88 (doc. 67).

[26] *Freedom: WGFL-LS*, 382–401 (docs. 66–73) speaks to the difficulties of the 1862 sugar harvest.

[27] *CWL*, 5: 487–88; *Freedom: WGFL-LS*, 394–97 (doc. 70).

Wartime emancipation was less a specific event that happened at a singular moment in the life of a slave than a process that extended over days, weeks, even months. It was a journey that included many reverses, hardships, and dead ends. In addition to the ambiguities of Federal antislavery policy, there remained the problem of arbitrary enforcement and the danger of reenslavement. For thousands of enslaved persons, the journey ended in sickness and death – sometimes before, sometimes after having reached Union lines. So long as the war lasted, freedom was a possibility for the enslaved. Yet once achieved, it was still never certain.

Far from settling the uncertainty of emancipation, the preliminary Emancipation Proclamation contributed to it. In declaring impending universal military emancipation in rebellious areas, Lincoln seemed to spell out carefully the criteria that the seceded states would have to meet in order to be deemed loyal. But the terms that Lincoln decreed were ambiguous, and even then he ended up not adhering to them. Because Federal military success in the lower Mississippi valley had spawned the first state restoration efforts in southern Louisiana and Tennessee, Lincoln would exclude those areas from the final proclamation. These exemptions would be partly negated by the "on-the-ground" undermining of slavery, but they would also enable slaveholders and other proslavery Unionists to begin a fierce campaign to preserve it. Although Lincoln would encourage southern Unionists to hold congressional elections, as the preliminary proclamation had specified, this process only highlighted the overriding concern of ostensibly loyal slaveholders, as Butler had put it, with sparing their "institution."

4

"The Unsatisfactory Prospect Before Them"

In announcing his intention to declare free all slaves in rebellious areas on January 1, 1863, Abraham Lincoln gave the seceded states one last chance to preserve slavery. All they had to do was submit to Federal authority and end the war. Whatever Lincoln's motives in employing this tactic, his actions toward the lower Mississippi valley for the rest of 1862 demonstrate unequivocally that he had made the offer in good faith. Slavery was no doubt disintegrating. Yet Unionists in Federally held Louisiana, Tennessee, and, to a lesser extent, Arkansas attempted – with Lincoln's blessing – to secure exemptions from the proclamation in hopes that those states might stave off what Lincoln understatedly called "the unsatisfactory prospect before them."

At the same time, Lincoln put forward a proposal in his Annual Message to Congress that attempted to entice the rebellious states to return to the Union and undertake the long-term eradication of slavery. It won little support, North or South, but it helped to transform the national discussion from emancipating slaves in the seceded states, or from abolishing slavery in the border states, to abolishing slavery in the seceded states. When Lincoln issued the final proclamation, his decisions to exclude certain parts of the lower Mississippi valley did not comport with the criteria he had spelled out in the preliminary version. The proclamation did not abolish slavery, and, as events would show, the transition from emancipation to abolition would require a different kind of crusade. But the proclamation put to rest, for Republicans and their antislavery allies, the war solely to preserve the Union.

I

While updating Abraham Lincoln in late November on labor arrangements in Louisiana, General Benjamin F. Butler included observations on political conditions there, which Lincoln had also solicited. Despite southern Unionists' lack of initiative on state restoration, Lincoln still hoped to cajole them into action. The whole point of the preliminary Emancipation Proclamation had been to induce the people of the seceded states to hold congressional elections before the January deadline. Lincoln may well have believed that the threat of universal emancipation, along with the chance to preserve slavery, might goad

Confederates to return to the Union. He might also have made the offer as political cover, knowing white Southerners would never accept it. Either way, Lincoln had to allow them the opportunity. Restoring the seceded states to the Union with slavery was a gambit he was willing to risk.

Working with Military Governor George Shepley and other Federal officials, Butler could report some progress on state restoration. Unionists in New Orleans had formed a "Union Association," and thousands of citizens had taken the oath of allegiance. The organization's members generally agreed – following Lincoln's own logic – that secession had been illegal and that Louisiana, having never left the Union, should resume its rightful place within it. They wanted to elect members to Congress and organize a loyal state government as soon as possible. This organization included, as Butler had noted, slaveholders wanting to preserve slavery. But it also consisted of others who, while not explicitly advocating abolition, assumed that slavery would eventually be eliminated once Louisiana had rejoined the Union. Just as "Unionism" had meant different things before secession, Unionists now were hardly of one mind on slavery.[1]

But with restoration efforts in Louisiana lagging, Lincoln, not for the last time, tried to hurry things along. He met in mid-October with John E. Bouligny and dispatched him to Louisiana with instructions for Butler, Shepley, and other officials. A Louisiana native, Bouligny had refused to resign his US House seat when the state seceded. Lincoln directed these officials to provide Bouligny – and anyone else who wished to "avoid the unsatisfactory prospect before them," obviously referring to emancipation, and who desired "peace again upon the old terms" under the US Constitution – with assistance in holding congressional elections and organizing a state government. Lincoln wanted the elections to reflect the popular will and to be lawful, "but at all events get the expression of the largest number of people possible," he noted. Time was running short, and persons who wanted the state restored needed to move quickly.[2]

If Lincoln had offered secessionists the opportunity to avoid emancipation in the expectation that they would never avail themselves of it, his actions during this period did not reflect such a mindset. On November 21, having heard of little progress from Louisiana in more than a month, an impatient Lincoln penned two letters to Shepley in which he expressed much frustration over the delay. He wrote the first after meeting with Dr. Hugh Kennedy, a New Orleans pharmacist and archconservative who would assume a leading role among proslavery Unionists. Kennedy complained that congressional elections were indeed being organized but that Federal military officers rather than citizens were being put forward as candidates. Lincoln was not pleased. He

---

[1] Taylor, *Louisiana Reconstructed*, 15–16.
[2] *CWL*, 5: 462–63.

wanted this movement to consist of the "respectable citizens of Louisiana," he told Shepley in no uncertain terms. "To send a parcel of Northern men here, as representatives, elected as would be understood, (and perhaps really so,) at the point of the bayonet, would be disgusting and outrageous," he insisted.

Lincoln reiterated these sentiments in his second letter to Shepley of the same date. Prompted by an early-November report from Shepley to Secretary of War Edwin M. Stanton that made no mention of congressional elections, Lincoln admitted to annoyance over the matter. He wanted congressional elections to take place in Louisiana, but they must be a genuine "movement of the people" and not "a movement of our military and quasi-military, authorities there." Such elections would not be in strict accordance with the law, Lincoln acknowledged, since no regular elections were scheduled before the January deadline. "These knots must be cut," he insisted. If the loyal people of Louisiana "stand idle not seeming to know what to do," then Shepley was to organize elections himself. Do not waste any more time, Lincoln ordered, "but, fix the election day early enough that we can hear the result here by the first of January." These do not sound like the words of someone who hoped his deadline would not be met.[3]

By the time Lincoln wrote these letters, Shepley had already announced the elections. In a mid-November letter that Lincoln had not yet received, Shepley acknowledged receipt of Lincoln's mid-October letter, transmitted by Bouligny, and informed Lincoln that he had scheduled elections for early December for New Orleans and the surrounding area. Both Shepley and Butler assured Lincoln that unconditional Unionists would be elected, although Bouligny would not be one of them, Butler noted, since he had made the mistake of running for local office under Confederate authority. Instead, Butler predicted that Benjamin F. Flanders would win election, "and a more reliable or better Union man cannot be found." A New Hampshire native who had settled in New Orleans some twenty years earlier, Flanders had been forced to leave Louisiana after secession because of his outspoken Unionism but had since returned. He would become a leading radical in Louisiana during and after the war. Another top candidate was Michael Hahn. Born in Bavaria in 1830, Hahn had migrated to New Orleans with his family at age ten. After graduating from college and studying law, he joined the Democratic Party but remained a firm Unionist during the secession crisis. Destined in 1864 to become Louisiana's first free-state governor, he would lead the state's moderate Unionists. Several other candidates pursued the two seats, and the brief campaign focused almost entirely on the various candidates' loyalties during and after secession.[4]

---

[3] *CWL*, 5: 504–5 (both letters).
[4] *CWL*, 5: 505n; *Freedom: WGFL-LS*, 394–97 (doc. 70; quotations, 395–96); Simpson and Baker, "Michael Hahn."

In early December, Flanders and Hahn were, respectively, elected to Louisiana's first and second congressional districts. The nearly 7,800 votes cast amounted to far more than a majority of the districts' voters, even though many registered voters were currently serving in the Confederate army. The preliminary Emancipation Proclamation had specified that exclusion from the final proclamation would require a majority of a *state's* voters to participate in congressional elections. Neither would Flanders and Hahn actually be seated by January 1. Still, Lincoln would exclude southern Louisiana from the proclamation on the basis of these results, and Congress in early 1863 would seat both claimants.[5]

Despite this and other successes, Butler's time in New Orleans was ending. His confrontational style, along with allegations of corruption, enraged white New Orleanians, but his dealings with foreign consuls and resident aliens proved his undoing. Wartime relations with the European powers were fraught, especially before the Emancipation Proclamation, and many British and French nationals in New Orleans were even more sympathetic to the Confederacy than were their own governments. The art of diplomacy had never been Butler's strong suit, but his style as applied to international relations was disastrous. With foreign governments protesting the treatment of their subjects, Butler was replaced in mid-December by another Massachusetts political general, the far more accommodating Nathaniel P. Banks.[6]

II

Although Confederates controlled east Tennessee and the state failed to meet the criteria for exclusion (eight of the state's ten US House seats and both Senate seats remained vacant), Lincoln exempted all of Tennessee from the Emancipation Proclamation, believing that Unionism was gaining ground and that including the state would undermine it. He may also have concluded that Federal antislavery measures, along with the war itself, were weakening slavery. Dating back to the secession crisis, Tennessee Unionists had argued that the Federal government would respect the property rights, including slave property, of loyal citizens, yet military emancipation had rendered those assertions increasingly moot. Even as Tennessee's two US congressmen tried to fend off Federal antislavery measures, some Unionists began to move cautiously toward emancipation. Nonetheless, Unionism and slavery continued to coexist amicably in Tennessee. Thousands of former Confederates in west and central Tennessee, including many slaveholders, had taken the oath of allegiance, and

---

[5] Taylor, *Louisiana Reconstructed*, 15–17; Harris, *With Charity for All*, 77–79; Hearn, *When the Devil Came Down to Dixie*, 217.

[6] Taylor, *Louisiana Reconstructed*, 17–18; Hearn, *When the Devil Came Down to Dixie*, 213–19. For an overview of the European powers in the Civil War, see Foreman, *World on Fire*.

the state's white population stood firmly behind slavery. However politically necessary, the exclusion would bolster slavery's defenders in Tennessee.[7]

Tennessee's exclusion was not a given. Indeed, with white Tennesseans fearing that the final proclamation would include the state, the preliminary proclamation sparked a disunionist backlash. Horace Maynard, one of Tennessee's two congressional representatives, castigated Lincoln for the dual travesties of emancipation and the failure to liberate east Tennessee. Former Confederates violated their oaths and resumed the rebellion, and some erstwhile Unionists converted to the other side. The preliminary proclamation also generated a groundswell of support for congressional elections, which Unionists repeatedly petitioned Johnson to authorize. On October 21, Lincoln urged Johnson, Grant, and others, as he had Butler and Shepley in Louisiana, to hold elections and avoid the "unsatisfactory prospect" of emancipation. In late November, some Unionists discussed holding elections without Johnson's blessing if necessary.[8]

The calls for elections put Johnson in a bind. Sending representatives to Congress by the January deadline seemed to be the only way to secure exclusion from the proclamation. But Johnson feared that elections so hastily organized could result in Confederate sympathizers claiming seats in Congress. They would not necessarily be seated, but such embarrassing results could undo months of hard work in cultivating Tennessee Unionism. Paradoxically, elections would also allow predominantly secessionist west Tennessee to avoid the proclamation, while Unionist east Tennessee would be included. Johnson remained transfixed on liberating east Tennessee and opposed any restoration efforts until that objective had been secured. His concern over Confederates hijacking a restoration initiative that excluded east Tennessee was no doubt genuine, but he also legitimately worried that Lincoln's emancipation policy would weaken Unionism throughout the state.

Notwithstanding his reservations, Johnson relented and authorized elections for late December, though only for two congressional districts in west Tennessee. Such elections would seemingly fail to secure the exclusion of Union-held Tennessee – let alone the entire state – from the proclamation, and neither could the claimants possibly be seated by January 1. The election announcement also spawned a campaign not far from the kind Johnson had apprehended. At least two candidates denounced emancipation, and a Unionist meeting instructed the district's prospective representative to oppose antislavery measures and strengthen fugitive slave laws. This outcome

---

[7] Harris, *With Charity for All*, 46–53.
[8] Cimprich, *Slavery's End in Tennessee*, 98–101; Harris, *With Charity for All*, 54–55; *CWL*, 5: 470–71; Bergeron, *Andrew Johnson's Civil War and Reconstruction*, 24–25.

was clearly not what Lincoln had had in mind. The Confederate raids that greatly disrupted the vote probably came as a blessing in disguise.⁹

By the time of this "election," Lincoln had already decided to exclude Tennessee. At roughly the same time that Johnson authorized the election, former governor William B. Campbell of central Tennessee proposed that Unionist leaders petition Lincoln to exempt the state on the grounds that Confederate raids would prevent free and fair elections. Unionists had already been urging Lincoln to exclude the state. Johnson agreed to the proposal, and he and Campbell were among the forty signers of the petition. Congressman Maynard and William G. "Parson" Brownlow also endorsed it. On December 23, Emerson Etheridge, the state's other congressman and a west Tennessee Unionist, and the Clerk of the House of Representatives, presented the petition to Lincoln, who realized he had no choice but to comply with the request. Whatever misgivings Lincoln may have had, he could take solace in having shored up Unionism. "The Exception in favor of Tennessee will be worth much to us," Johnson reassured him in early January. Although thousands of slaves had already been emancipated in the state, slavery had won a reprieve.¹⁰

Since state restoration had made little headway in Arkansas and none in Mississippi, the inclusion of those states in the proclamation required less attention. Mississippi was the one state of the lower Mississippi valley for which exclusion, despite Federal control of some areas, was never contemplated. Arkansas was another story. After the Federal capture of Helena, Lincoln appointed John S. Phelps the state's military governor. A long-serving Democratic member of the US House from Missouri, Phelps had been among the border-state representatives who had rejected Lincoln's compensated abolition proposal. Arriving in Helena later that summer, Phelps set up a rudimentary government, but Federal military success did not carry over to the second half of 1862, and the anticipated conquest of Little Rock never materialized. Discouraged and in ill health, Phelps withdrew to St. Louis. Even then, Lincoln did not give up. In mid-November, he urged Phelps and General Frederick Steele to organize elections, and he ordered William M. McPherson, a prewar resident, to the state for that purpose. After consulting with Phelps and other Arkansas Unionists in St. Louis, McPherson initially believed the state might be salvaged, and he proposed extending the January deadline. When he visited Arkansas in person, however, he found the situation too unsettled, and his report convinced Lincoln to include the entire state in the proclamation. Lincoln

---

⁹ Cimprich, *Slavery's End in Tennessee*, 101.
¹⁰ *PAJ*, 6: 46–47, 85–86, 114 (quotation); Harris, *With Charity for All*, 54–56; Cimprich, "Military Governor Johnson and Tennessee Blacks," 462.

eventually revoked Phelps's appointment as military governor, and Reconstruction in Arkansas would remain on hold for almost another year.[11]

III

Even as these events were unfolding, Lincoln was putting together one last attempt to induce the rebellious states to return to the Union. In his annual message to Congress in early December, among the oddest documents of his presidency, Lincoln called for compensating any state that abolished slavery by 1900 and for Federally funded, voluntary colonization. Since gradual, compensated abolition and colonization had long infused antislavery thought, the proposal broke no new ground. It stood little chance of success, especially so late in the day, and attracted no substantive interest. But by proposing the outright abolition of slavery, for both the loyal and disloyal slave states, Lincoln crossed an important threshold between military emancipation and constitutional abolition.

The proposal centered on three constitutional amendments: offering Federal bonds in an amount to be determined to any state that abolished slavery by 1900; guaranteeing the freedom of all slaves liberated during the war and compensating loyal owners; and authorizing congressional funding for voluntary colonization. The proposal conformed to conventional wisdom. The states themselves – not the Federal government – would abolish slavery, doing so by any means and at any time within the specified period. Any state receiving Federal bonds and later reintroducing slavery would have to refund them, plus interest, but otherwise the plan included no enforcement mechanism. (The fact that Lincoln could even consider the possibility of a later reintroduction of slavery speaks volumes of the contingent nature of abolition and of Federal impotence against slavery in the states.) The plan said nothing about seceded states returning to the Union but not abolishing slavery by 1900. Neither did it require the seceded states to return to the Union by January 1 in order to avail themselves of it; Lincoln assumed that they would do so. Although the plan was a recommendation and not a requirement for state restoration, Lincoln seemed to believe that its adoption would obviate both the war and the Emancipation Proclamation. "Nor will the war, nor proceedings under the proclamation of September 22, 1862, be stayed because of the *recommendation* of this plan," he observed. "Its timely *adoption*, I doubt not, would bring restoration and thereby stay both."[12]

---

[11] Harris, *With Charity for All*, 83–85; Cowen, "Reorganization of Federal Arkansas," 35–36; Moneyhon, *Impact of the Civil War and Reconstruction on Arkansas*, 156–58; *CWL*, 5: 500.

[12] *CWL*, 5: 518–37 for the Message to Congress, with the discussion of the gradual abolition plan at 529–37. Every biography of Lincoln and study of emancipation examines the proposal.

If the proposal would not "stay" the impending proclamation, how were the two supposed to work together? Three constitutional amendments could never be ratified in less than a month, and Lincoln assured leading House radical James M. Ashley that the proposal would not delay emancipation. Lincoln offered no clarification in the annual message as to how adoption of the plan could possibly halt implementation of the proclamation once the latter had been issued. Presumably, the seceded states might still return to the Union and take advantage of the plan after January 1, but the proclamation would hardly serve as an inducement for them to pursue this option. Indeed, how could gradual abolition – or abolition that could be postponed until 1900 – be implemented once the proclamation had declared *all* slaves free in certain areas, effective immediately? Lincoln may have reasoned that he offered the seceded states genuine incentives to return to the Union before he imposed universal military emancipation on them. But his proposal only previewed the difficulties of moving from military emancipation to abolition.

Even so, Lincoln dangled gradual, compensated, and state-directed abolition before the rebellious states as an alternative to immediate and uncompensated universal military emancipation. He likewise helped to shift the terms of debate, however subtly, from freeing slaves to abolishing slavery. Lincoln's proposal called for the end of slavery not through military means but through a long-term process that the states would control. This was an important transition. While deeming his plan "a poor one," for instance, one northern journal credited Lincoln with being the first American president who "has risen to the conception of universal emancipation," and the "first among American statesmen ... to strive that reconstruction shall not mean a new lease for the human bondage." Yet if the proposal represented an important turning point in northern thinking, it was not a very attractive alternative to people who were actually fighting to *keep* slavery. So long as the rebellious states could maintain armies in the field – a point reinforced by the Federal disaster at Fredericksburg in mid-December – they had no reason to accept Lincoln's offer.[13]

Lincoln and congressional Republicans initiated or endorsed other antislavery measures in the weeks before the Emancipation Proclamation. In

---

[13] "The President's Message," *The Living Age*, vol. 76 (January–March 1863), no. 973 (January 24): 178–80 (quotations, 179, 180). On Lincoln's reassurance to Ashley regarding the Emancipation Proclamation, see Richards, *Who Freed the Slaves?*, 81. Burlingame, *Abraham Lincoln*, 439–43, discusses the range of contemporary reaction to the proposal, including how it was supposed to work in conjunction with the proclamation. Oakes, *The Radical and the Republican*, discusses the proposal mostly with reference to the border states, but he notes: "The amendments he now proposed were designed to secure the freedom of every slave in the United States" (199). Foner, *Fiery Trial*, 237–38, contends that the plan signaled an important shift from emancipation to abolition and thus marked a "crucial moment of transition" for Lincoln.

November, Lincoln allowed to stand a ruling by Attorney General Edward Bates that free black people were American citizens, effectually nullifying the *Dred Scott* decision and substantiating the legal freedom of thousands of former slaves. Antislavery Unionists in Maryland and Missouri – though often bitterly divided – continued efforts to abolish slavery in their states, and Congress considered proposals, which came to naught, to provide Federal assistance toward that objective. Lincoln and Republicans also moved forward with creating the state of West Virginia, which would be admitted to the Union in June 1863 with the stipulation that the state constitution provide for the abolition of slavery. West Virginia served as an inadequate model for restoring the seceded states, but by late 1862 that question was moot. With the seceded states showing no interest in returning to the Union, Lincoln on January 1, 1863, signed the Emancipation Proclamation.

The Emancipation Proclamation was a military measure, issued by Lincoln in his capacity as commander-in-chief, "in time of actual armed rebellion against authority and government of the United States, and as a fit and necessary war measure for suppressing said rebellion." It declared immediately free all slaves in entire geographical areas determined to be in rebellion. The proclamation was revolutionary and conservative, earth-shattering and limited. It marked a major break in Federal antislavery policy and a continuation of practices dating to the start of the war. Just as events in the lower Mississippi valley had contributed integrally to the proclamation, its implementation there would prove to be more complicated than perhaps anywhere else in the seceded states.[14]

Lincoln began the proclamation by calling attention to his proclamation of September 22, quoting in full its two essential paragraphs: the one in which he stated his intention to declare free all slaves in states, or parts thereof, in which the people were in rebellion on January 1; and the second, in which he announced that on that date he would officially designate, by proclamation, those states that were in rebellion while also spelling out the criteria by which he would determine states, or parts, to be loyal. In accordance with the stated purpose of the earlier proclamation, Lincoln formally designated ten of the eleven seceded states, excluding only Tennessee, "as the States and parts of States wherein the people ... are this day in rebellion against the United States." Arkansas and Mississippi were included in their entirety. The thirteen parishes of southern Louisiana, including New Orleans, were excluded, while Union-held areas of northeast Louisiana were included. (Lincoln also excluded the counties that were about to become West Virginia, along with several other counties in eastern Virginia.)

---

[14] Richardson, *Messages and Papers*, 8: 3358–60. For a discussion of the voluminous scholarship on the proclamation, see the Introduction.

Having officially designated the rebellious areas, Lincoln formally proclaimed "that all persons held as slaves within said designated States, and parts of States, are, and henceforward shall be free." The "forever" of the preliminary proclamation was dropped. He also ordered "the Executive government of the United States," including the armed forces, to "recognize and maintain the freedom of said persons." In the final two sections of the proclamation, Lincoln enjoined emancipated persons to refrain from violence, "unless in necessary self-defense," and recommended that "they labor faithfully for reasonable wages." He further announced that "such persons of suitable condition" – meaning black men – would be accepted into the armed forces of the United States. The proclamation mentioned neither colonization nor compensation for loyal slaveholders.

Despite its limitations, the Emancipation Proclamation imposed universal military emancipation, with few exceptions, throughout ten of the eleven insurgent states. In the lower Mississippi valley, it declared free the slaves in all of Arkansas and Mississippi, and in all but the excluded parts of Louisiana. In reality, the large majority of these slaves, living under Confederate authority, remained enslaved; the proclamation, in declaring them free, would enable them to gain their actual freedom once Federal troops arrived. Lincoln also hoped that the proclamation would further encourage slaves in Confederate areas to flee to Union lines. Many would attempt to do so, some successfully, but taking flight for most slaves in Confederate areas was not a realistic possibility. To all intents and purposes, freedom for slaves in the seceded states depended on Federal military success. As often noted, the proclamation transformed the Union army into an army of liberation, since Union forces would henceforward secure the freedom of persons *declared* free on January 1, 1863. Tens of thousands of slaves, in the lower Mississippi valley and elsewhere, would gain their freedom between January 1863 and the end of the war, but fate dictated that many more would await liberation until Confederate surrender.

It has sometimes been posited that the Emancipation Proclamation actually freed no slaves when issued, since it applied only to Confederate-held areas while excluding Union-controlled territory. But this was not the case. In those parts of the lower Mississippi valley under Federal military control but wherein no substantive steps toward state restoration had taken place, such as eastern Arkansas, northern Mississippi, and northeastern Louisiana, the proclamation – in addition to further securing the legal freedom of persons already emancipated under the confiscation acts – actually freed persons who belonged to loyal slaveholders or whose legal status, for whatever reason, was still in doubt. These freed persons would live under constant threat of recapture, and many of them would indeed suffer reenslavement. But the proclamation freed no small number of slaves in parts of the lower Mississippi valley that Federal forces occupied on January 1, 1863.

Lincoln also excluded areas of the lower Mississippi valley – all of Tennessee and southern Louisiana – where substantive efforts toward state restoration had been made but that did not meet the criteria for exclusion. No creditable congressional elections had occurred in west and central Tennessee, and those areas were nowhere near being represented in Congress on January 1, while east Tennessee remained almost entirely under Confederate authority. A stronger case for exclusion could be made for southern Louisiana, where congressional elections had garnered more than a majority of the districts' voters. The requirement that a majority of a *state's* qualified voters participate in the election, omitting any allowance for *parts* of states, may well have been an oversight on Lincoln's part, but the two claimants, Flanders and Hahn, had not been seated in Congress by January 1, as required. To be sure, these were technicalities, and Lincoln no doubt made the exclusion on the grounds that the "respectable citizens of Louisiana" had complied with the spirit if not the letter of the law. This would not be the last time Lincoln granted Louisiana special dispensation in hopes of facilitating its restoration. But subsequent events would force Lincoln and Republicans to confront the possibility of Louisiana and Tennessee being restored to the Union, after the proclamation had been issued, with slavery legally in place.

Even though the Emancipation Proclamation did not abolish slavery and excluded parts of the lower Mississippi valley, thousands of slaves had already gained their freedom under the confiscation acts. To be sure, slaveholders in those areas of Tennessee and southern Louisiana that were already under Federal control when the 1862 Act was passed, and who had taken the oath of allegiance within the specified time period, could claim exemption from both the confiscation acts and the proclamation. But for most Republicans, such legal niceties had become meaningless. All slaveholders were rebels and should lose their slaves. If nothing else, a significant part of the excluded section of Louisiana – the Lafourche region west of New Orleans – had come under Federal control only *after* the passage of the second act, and after the expiration of the sixty-day grace period to resume loyalty that dated from Lincoln's July 25 cease-and-desist proclamation. Yet even this rationale was superfluous for emancipation's proponents, who had long since concluded that all slaves in areas under Federal control, including areas excluded from the proclamation, had been freed.

Moreover, a viable system of free labor under Federal military auspices was beginning to take root, especially in southern Louisiana. The success of free labor was not inevitable, and it depended on the presence of Federal authority, but the longer that presence was maintained, the less were the chances of slavery's defenders revitalizing their institution. Lincoln always insisted that he would countenance the return to slavery of no slave liberated during the war. But, in a larger sense, the men and women whom Federal authorities no longer treated as slaves had crossed an irreversible psychological barrier. Having tasted freedom, they would never again think of *themselves* as slaves. Countless observers remarked upon this phenomenon, which former slaveholders either were slow to grasp or refused to acknowledge. As one Federal officer in Louisiana explained later in 1863, the planters and overseers "do not sufficiently appreciate, or regard, the change that has taken place, especially in respect to this institution of slavery."[15]

Such intransigence would reflect the mindset of almost every former slaveholder for years to come. Delusion, resentment, anger, and similar emotions suffuse their letters, diaries, and plantation journals. No doubt, many former slaveholders failed to appreciate the changes that had taken place, but the officer had also identified an irrefutable truth. No matter how severely slavery had been damaged or how many persons had been emancipated, most slaveholders considered slavery to be very much alive. The proclamation had only *declared* the slaves free. The vast majority of the more than one million slaves in the lower Mississippi valley would remain in bondage until the war ended. The proclamation could not abolish slavery as an institution, moreover, and it said nothing about how slavery would factor into state restoration. Indeed, the conjoining of abolition and state restoration after January 1, 1863, would prove to be among the war's most difficult challenges. It would first be undertaken in the lower Mississippi valley.

* * *

When Lincoln altered the course of US history by issuing the Emancipation Proclamation, he also replaced *limited* with *universal* military emancipation in the insurgent states. He had declared all slaves in rebellious areas to be free. In late 1862, Lincoln actively advocated the holding of congressional elections – in three of the states of the lower Mississippi valley in particular – as an alternative to universal emancipation. Lincoln's actions in this respect can be interpreted as a willingness to allow the seceded states back into the Union with slavery still intact, if such a policy would hasten the restoration of the Union. It can also be read, however, as an attempt to offer the seceded states every opportunity to return to the Union before he imposed universal emancipation on them. Lincoln had done everything he could, he would later be able to claim, before playing his last card. The Confederates had left him no choice. Yet this strategy would itself have repercussions. After Lincoln issued the proclamation, proslavery Unionists in Louisiana and Tennessee would seize upon its exemptions – and its fundamental limitations – in attempting to restore their states to the Union while preserving slavery. Only in hindsight were they deluded.

Even before Lincoln issued the final proclamation, northern observers had already begun to anticipate the difficulty of translating emancipation into

---

[15] *Freedom: WGFL-LS*, 454–56 (doc. 94; quotation, 455).

lawful abolition. "The language of the proclamation itself, indeed, does not abrogate State laws, but merely suspends them in reference to certain persons and for a certain cause," remarked an editorial in November – although the proclamation did not even suspend the slave codes in the seceded states. "The President does not proclaim that the rebel States shall, after January 1, 1863, be forever free, but that the slaves in such States at that time shall be freed; thus leaving open the question what shall be the powers of such States hereafter in reference to slaves who may be in any way introduced." Consequently, the piece continued, "this act is an executive and not a legislative one, and it makes of itself no change in the Constitution, and its authority expires with the lifetime of such emancipated slaves." In short, the proclamation would free slaves but not abolish slavery, and it would no longer be operative once the war ended. Having identified this essential problem, the editorial assured its readers that the necessary measures would follow. "Of course, if carried out, its influence would be lasting, and would bring great legislative changes in its train." The historical record is replete with references to the proclamation as a military necessity, and with pronouncements that slavery would never survive the war. Less well understood – at the time and since – was how to secure the end of slavery as a legal institution. As contemporaries would discover, and as historians have probably failed to appreciate fully, achieving those "great legislative changes" would prove to be a monumental task.[16]

---

[16] "Editor's Table," *Harper's New Monthly Magazine*, vol. 25, no. 150 (November 1862): 843–48 (quotation, 846).

PART II

From Military Emancipation to State Abolition, 1863

5

"The Return of the Seceded States to This Union as Slave States"

On January 1, 1863, the Civil War began anew. Although Union military forces had been emancipating slaves almost from the start of the conflict, Federal policy now shifted from limited to universal military emancipation, with exceptions, in the rebellious states. Moreover, in renewing the military campaigns against Vicksburg and Port Hudson, Federal forces now included black servicemen. Nowhere in the South did this change have more important consequences for the war and the destruction of slavery than in the lower Mississippi valley. By April, neither effort to secure control of the Mississippi River was anywhere near success, but the freeing of slaves and the overall attack on slavery intensified.

Even as slaves were gaining freedom under the Emancipation Proclamation, many observers demonstrated confusion over what the proclamation would do. Northerners slowly came to appreciate the essential distinction between military emancipation and constitutional abolition. Yet it remained unclear how the proclamation would affect the process of state restoration. In early 1863, northern antislavery advocates began to address this issue in earnest. By the spring, they had identified the potential problem, as one leading Republican expressed it, of "the return of the seceded States to this Union as slave States." Consequently, Republicans began to rally around the concept – as a matter of policy – that no rebellious state would be restored to the Union without abolishing slavery. They also began to rely – as the underlying rationale for this position – on Article Four, Section Four, of the US Constitution, which required the Federal government to guarantee to the states "a republican form of government."

This new course became all the more imperative, since the proclamation also reconfigured the southern Unionist coalitions, especially in the Federally occupied parts of the lower Mississippi valley. Lincoln's emancipation policy split Unionists in Tennessee and Louisiana into proslavery and antislavery factions that would vie for control of the state restoration process. "Conservative" Unionists hoped to restore their states to the Union under the states' antebellum, proslavery constitutions, while antislavery Unionists undertook to secure restoration on a free-state basis. Even as universal military emancipation was being implemented in the seceded states, the challenge of translating military emancipation into constitutional abolition was beginning to take shape in the lower Mississippi valley.

I

"[I]t can not be too often repeated that this war must be decided not on the banks of the Potomac, but on the banks of the Mississippi," affirmed *Harper's Weekly* in early 1863. "So long as the rebels hold any portion of the great river it will avail us little to beat their armies in Virginia." Confederates could fight the war to a draw in the east for twenty more years, but once Federal forces had gained control of the Mississippi, "the hopes of a national existence for the Confederacy [are] gone," it insisted. "The possession of the Mississippi River is the key to victory in the war." True, but this was easier said than done. After failing to take Vicksburg the previous fall, General Ulysses S. Grant devoted the early months of 1863 to finding some way of circumventing Vicksburg's batteries and gaining the high ground on the east bank of the Mississippi. Union troops continued to free slaves in the surrounding countryside, while slaveholders fled to the interior. But as weeks passed and the campaign went nowhere, frustration grew. By March, Grant was rethinking the whole thing.[1]

Meanwhile, Union operations at Port Hudson proceeded even more slowly, partly owing to the change in command in the Department of the Gulf, as General Nathaniel P. Banks replaced Benjamin F. Butler. Born in 1816 near Boston, Banks rose from humble origins to become a successful attorney and leading Massachusetts politician. He won election to Congress as a Democrat in 1852 but later switched to the new Republican Party and in 1856 became its first Speaker of the House. Banks was elected governor of Massachusetts in 1857 and had been considered an 1860 presidential contender. Once hostilities started, Lincoln commissioned him as a major general of volunteers. Dashingly handsome, confident to a fault, and given to overstatement, Banks would exert immeasurable influence over Louisiana affairs as military commander and Lincoln's political pointman. Although his antislavery credentials were solid, a conservative quality infused his administration, and critics thought him too accommodating of slaveholders and other rebels. Still, he was a welcome contrast to the quarrelsome Butler, and for all of his faults, Banks would oversee Louisiana's 1864 abolition of slavery.[2]

---

[1] *Harper's Weekly*, January 10, 1863, 18; Hess, *Civil War in the West*, 125–26, 134–42; Winters, *Civil War in Louisiana*, 174–85; Ballard, *Vicksburg*, 156–64, 171–90; Dimond and Hattaway, *Letters from Forest Place*, 305. See also Kate Stone's March 1863 journal entries in Anderson, *Brokenburn*. By early April, the Stone family finally left for Texas with their slaves.

[2] Banks has received considerable scholarly attention, including biographies and studies of wartime Reconstruction in Louisiana. The most recent biography is Hollandsworth, *Pretense of Glory*. For a contemporary assessment of the many challenges Banks faced, see "Slaves in Louisiana," *Harper's Weekly*, February 21, 1863, 114.

But Banks's main objective right then was Port Hudson, which Confederates had been fortifying since August. Banks hoped to utilize the network of waterways near the confluence of the Mississippi and Red Rivers so as to invest Port Hudson and force its surrender without having to make a deadly, frontal assault. Several attempts in early 1863 to achieve that goal were repulsed, and by early April, Banks, like Grant, had little to show for his efforts.[3]

Early 1863 also witnessed the enrollment of black men into the Union armed forces in the lower Mississippi valley. The enlisting of former slaves as soldiers had been one of the main points of dispute between Butler and his subordinate, General John W. Phelps. Despite his original opposition to black enlistment, Butler eventually changed his mind and enrolled the Louisiana "Native Guard" into the Federal service, although this unit consisted of free men of color and not former slaves.[4] The Emancipation Proclamation settled debate on this issue, and Lincoln, despite initial reservations over black men's military capacity, now endorsed black recruitment wholeheartedly. In a series of letters in early 1863, he privately urged commanders to employ black troops or commended them for having done so, previewing the argument, which he soon began making publicly, that black troops were integral to the Union war effort. "The colored population is the great *available* and yet *unavailed of*, force for restoring the Union," he remarked to Andrew Johnson. "The bare sight of fifty thousand armed, and drilled black soldiers on the banks of the Mississippi, would end the rebellion at once. And who doubts that we can present that sight, if we but take hold in earnest?"[5]

Lincoln might have been excused for such hyperbole, but in order to take hold of this force, Secretary of War Edwin M. Stanton delegated officials throughout the occupied South to organize black regiments. General Lorenzo Thomas, the Adjutant General of the War Department, was directed in late March to foster recruiting efforts in the lower Mississippi valley, a mission that assumed heightened significance as the Vicksburg campaign attracted ever-larger numbers of fugitives. Throughout April and May, Thomas organized black regiments, which now bore the designation US Colored Troops (USCT), and established procedures for selecting white officers to command them. He

---

[3] Hess, *Civil War in the West*, 168–70; Ballard, *Vicksburg*, 164–70; Winters, *Civil War in Louisiana*, 206–9, 212–14; Taylor, *Louisiana Reconstructed*, 18–21; *OR*, ser. 1, vol. 15, 590, and ser. 3, vol. 3, 101–3.

[4] The Butler–Phelps feud is examined in every general history of black soldiers during the Civil War. For a good overview, see *Freedom: BME*, 41–44, and the accompanying documents. See also Hollandsworth, *Louisiana Native Guards*, chaps. 1–2. The "Native Guard," it will be recalled, originally offered its services to Louisiana Confederate Governor Thomas O. Moore, who recognized the unit but never deployed it. After the Federal capture of New Orleans, the men of the Native Guard volunteered their services to Butler, who initially declined their offer.

[5] *CWL*, 6: 149–50. For similar letters, see *CWL*, 6: 48–49, 56, 158. Cimprich, "Military Governor Johnson and Tennessee Blacks," 464–65.

also spoke to large assemblies of white troops to overcome opposition to the new policy. These endeavors marked a key turning point in black enlistment, from piecemeal initiatives to what has been called "a systematic, centrally coordinated recruitment policy." Despite various challenges – including opposition to black soldiers within the Union army and northern society, recruitment practices that amounted to impressment, systematic discrimination on pay and other matters, and the refusal of Confederates to recognize black men as soldiers – the Federal government was now fully committed to the deployment of black servicemen.[6]

With black enlistment now an established policy, the lower Mississippi valley proved central to the black military experience in the South as a whole. Of the nearly 180,000 black men who served in the Union army, almost 68,000, or nearly 38 percent, were officially credited to the states of the lower Mississippi valley, representing 68 percent of the 98,600 black troops recruited in the eleven rebellious states. Of the aggregate black male population of military age (eighteen to forty-five) in the lower Mississippi valley, 28 percent served in the Union army. The state with the lowest proportion was Mississippi, at 21 percent. (The number reached double digits for no other seceded state.) Only the border states of Delaware, Maryland, Kentucky, and Missouri individually and collectively had percentages comparable to or higher than those of the lower Mississippi valley, although the absolute number of black troops in those states was less than half that of the lower Mississippi valley. Louisiana boasted the highest number of black soldiers of any state, with just over 24,000. The mere sight of 50,000 black soldiers on the banks of the Mississippi was not enough to end the war, but the nearly 68,000 black soldiers from the valley were crucial to the Union cause.[7]

II

"Americans in early 1863 could already sense that military emancipation was not the same as constitutional emancipation," Michael Vorenberg has written in his study of the Thirteenth Amendment. Antislavery advocates now confronted the reality that the Emancipation Proclamation had freed slaves – and then mostly in theory – but had not abolished slavery, which still existed under the laws and constitutions of the insurgent states. The North fought to preserve the Union and uphold the Constitution, Lincoln and others had insisted since the war started and would continue to insist until it ended. The proclamation

---

[6] *Freedom: BME*, 9–10 (quotation); Hess, *Civil War in the West*, 142–44; Christ, "They Will Be Armed"; *CWL*, 8: 1–2.

[7] *Freedom: BME*, 12. The numbers of black recruits, by state, and their percentage of the black male population of military age: Arkansas, 5,526 (24 percent); Louisiana, 24,052 (31 percent); Mississippi, 17,869 (21 percent); and Tennessee, 20,133 (39 percent).

was a means of achieving those goals. "The problem, simply put," Vorenberg further notes, "was that unionists were now supposed to fight two seemingly incompatible wars: one against slavery, and one for a Constitution that supported slavery."[8]

Ever since Lincoln had announced the preliminary proclamation, much confusion surrounded what the final proclamation would actually do. Many commentators, including both advocates and critics of Lincoln's emancipation policy, declared that the proclamation had "abolished" slavery in the areas where it applied. Even those who correctly understood the proclamation's shortcomings made this mistake. The trope that "slavery would never survive the war," or that the Federal military presence alone effectually destroyed slavery, had already taken hold. Even observers who distinguished between emancipation and abolition equated the two. "In what we have to say we shall use the terms Emancipation and Abolition as being of like signification," the Rev. N. H. Eggleston noted in an October 1862 essay comparing emancipation in the West Indies and the United States. "For, although they are in themselves distinct, and neither necessarily implies the other, yet, as a practical matter, relating to us at the present time, we think they are inseparably combined." Whether the slaves were emancipated by military means or an act of Congress, he added, "we cannot doubt that the abolition of slavery, as an institution, will quickly follow."[9]

Nonetheless, slavery's opponents eventually came to appreciate this crucial distinction and its political implications. Emancipation would have to be made *universal* and grounded in law. It is tempting to assume in hindsight that antislavery advocates would have moved swiftly to put forward an amendment to the US Constitution abolishing slavery. Because Lincoln had freed the slaves as a military measure, an amendment would secure this freedom and make it universal. Yet this was not the case. The proclamation had been issued during the "short" congressional session, which would adjourn in early March. It would have been impossible to secure such a monumental measure in a mere two months' time. Americans were also still coming to terms with the proclamation and would have had no enthusiasm for contemplating a constitutional amendment. But perhaps most importantly, as Vorenberg also argues, there existed little support for abolishing slavery by amending the Federal constitution. Most Americans held that document to be the near-sacred work of the Founders, beyond substantive revision. They often spoke of having "reverence" for the Constitution or of "the genius of our institutions" in denying the need for change. Few people at the time would have embraced

---

[8] Vorenberg, *Final Freedom*, 33, 34.
[9] Rev. N. H. Eggleston, "Emancipation," *New Englander and Yale Review*, vol. 21, no. 4 (October 1862): 783–84. See also the editorial entitled "Slavery Practically Abolished," *Harper's Weekly*, October 4, 1862, 626.

the idea of amending the Constitution to carry out *any* kind of major social or political reform – let alone ending slavery. They adhered to this position well after the proclamation.[10]

This thinking led in different directions. A small number of radical observers, contending that the Constitution was an antislavery document, insisted that the Federal government was already empowered to legislate an end to slavery. To require an amendment, they argued, was to admit the Constitution's proslavery character. Others maintained that slavery, as a local institution, had ceased to exist legally the moment the rebellious states violated the Constitution, and that the Federal government possessed the authority to intervene in their internal affairs. Moderate Republicans rejected these claims. Subscribing to the principle of Federal noninterference with slavery in the states, they countered that the states themselves would assume responsibility for ending slavery once the rebellion had been defeated. Some observers seemed to presuppose that white Southerners would experience an epiphany and end slavery voluntarily, others that slavery would somehow magically disappear. All things considered, a Federal abolition amendment might well have been the *last* thing on Unionists' minds immediately after the proclamation.[11]

Various factors contributed to Northerners' awakening to the difference between military emancipation and constitutional abolition, and to the need to secure the latter. The growing animus in the North against the white South for the war, illustrated by the change from a war of conciliation to one of conquest, heightened the attack on slavery. The military advantages to be gained from black enlistment – and the need to secure freedom for black soldiers and their families – further contributed to this shift. Slavery in the border states, which were exempted from the Emancipation Proclamation but experienced military emancipation, likewise underscored the need for constitutional abolition, as did the debate over admitting West Virginia. The ambiguous status of former slaves in areas of the seceded states excluded

---

[10] Opposition to amending the Constitution, even after the Emancipation Proclamation, is central to Vorenberg's *Final Freedom*, but see esp. 5–6, 23–35, 41–46. In 1856, before his election to Congress, Ohio Radical Republican James M. Ashley had advocated the abolition of "the crime of American slavery" by amending the US Constitution, a proposal that Leonard Richards describes as "clearly fanciful." Richards, *Who Freed the Slaves?*, 5. Rebecca E. Zeitlow's study of Ashley, *Forgotten Emancipator*, excludes this session of Congress – as well as the rest of the period between the issuing of the proclamation and the convening of the Thirty-Eighth Congress in December 1863 – entirely. Other scholars have observed Americans' general aversion to amending the Constitution before the war.

[11] On these points, for example, see Hon. F. P. Stanton, "The Consequences of the Rebellion," *Continental Monthly*, vol. 3, no. 1 (January 1863): 26–39; Rev. Leonard Bacon, "Reply to Professor Parker's Letters, in the Boston Post, to Rev. Leonard Bacon, D.D.," *New Englander*, vol. 83 (April 1863): 191–258, esp. 253–56.

from the proclamation also contributed. All of these factors elucidated the need for constitutional abolition.[12]

Another crucial factor was the debate – which events in the lower Mississippi valley would profoundly influence – over how to restore the seceded states to the Union. The question of state restoration had received considerable discussion since the secession crisis and had generated any number of theories, but the push for military emancipation had largely disguised it. However, the Emancipation Proclamation now made unavoidable the question of how universal emancipation would affect state restoration. Since the proclamation did not abolish slavery, how might the restoration of the seceded states on a free-state basis be secured, and how would abolition be conjoined to state restoration? Determining the process of state restoration was not a new problem in 1863, but the proclamation greatly complicated it. The debate over this problem was still amorphous at this point, and it included states other than those of the lower Mississippi valley. Nonetheless, the contest over state restoration in the lower Mississippi valley – Louisiana and Tennessee in particular – and the possibility of slavery surviving the war would help to crystallize the problem of transforming military emancipation into constitutional abolition.[13]

Two matters in early 1863 arising from political conditions in the lower Mississippi valley illustrated congressional Republicans' turn toward linking emancipation and state restoration. The first involved the seating of Michael Hahn and Benjamin F. Flanders, whose elections in December had gained southern Louisiana exclusion from the Emancipation Proclamation. The second entailed legislation authorizing congressional elections in Union-held Louisiana and Tennessee for representatives to the Thirty-Eighth Congress, scheduled to convene a year hence.[14]

In a mid-December resolution endorsing the preliminary Emancipation Proclamation, passed largely by Republican votes, the House had endorsed

---

[12] Vorenberg, *Final Freedom*, 36–38.
[13] As scholars such as James Oakes, Rebecca E. Zietlow, and Leonard L. Richards have well established, antislavery advocates before the war had forwarded any number of theories justifying Federal action against slavery in the states in the event of civil war, thereby circumventing the problem of the Federal consensus. However, these theories were by definition of no use under peacetime conditions. But more importantly, they were wholly inadequate for addressing the specific conditions that now existed as a result of the war, in particular the concrete problem of organizing loyal governments in the seceded states and restoring those states to the Union (presumably, while also securing the abolition of slavery), which, Lincoln and most Republicans had argued from the beginning, was the whole point of the war. The Federal government could free slaves and perhaps even invalidate state laws regarding slavery in the course of suppressing rebellion, but it still could not abolish slavery in the states. Such power, moreover, left unresolved how the insurgent states would be restored to the Union on a free-state basis.
[14] Belz, *Reconstructing the Union*, 110–15, 117–22.

Lincoln's emancipation policy and the exclusions from it on the basis of congressional representation. In debating whether to seat the Louisiana claimants, the representatives addressed myriad issues – constitutional and partisan, theoretical and practical. They expounded upon the nature of government and loyalty and quibbled over the wording of Lincoln's proclamations and Military Governor George Shepley's election directive. They also deliberated over the property rights of loyal slaveholders in the excluded areas and whether the elections reflected genuine Unionism.[15] The House eventually voted overwhelmingly to seat Hahn and Flanders, while at the same time denying claimants from Virginia, North Carolina, and Tennessee. The bill authorizing congressional elections in Louisiana and Tennessee easily passed in the House near the end of the session but was defeated in the Senate. In debating the Louisiana cases, congressional Republicans expressed no special concern that they might be offering recognition to the state's existing, proslavery constitution, or that they might be establishing a dangerous precedent regarding state restoration. They would later express grave concern over these issues. For now, however, they were willing to sanction the exclusions from Lincoln's emancipation policy.[16]

Yet the debates over these two issues – and the incipient discussion in the North over the political consequences of emancipation – reflected the growing Republican consensus that no slave state would be restored to the Union. They also revealed an emerging theoretical basis for this position that moderate Republicans – the mass of the party – could accept. Eschewing "territorialization," congressional Republicans began to emphasize the constitutional provision enjoining the Federal government to guarantee to the states a "republican form of government." This principle empowered Congress to establish conditions by which the rebellious states – never having left the Union but having subverted their relations to it – would be restored to the Union. Republicans would need time to work out the details, but the minimal conditions would eventually include political proscriptions against leading Confederates, repudiation of rebel debts, and new state constitutions that provided for abolition. Whereas the "Federal consensus" prohibited the Federal government from interfering with slavery in the states, Congress could require the rebellious states to take concrete steps toward eliminating slavery before resuming their former status in the Union. Radicals would continue to promote "territorialization," and Republicans and Democrats would debate for the rest of the war the meaning of "republican" government and whether

---

[15] For the debate over Hahn and Flanders, see *CG*, 37th Cong., 3rd Sess., 831–37 (February 9), 855–66 (February 10), 1010–16 (February 16), 1030–36 (February 17; including final vote).

[16] For the main activity, including the final votes, on the bill authorizing congressional elections in Louisiana and Tennessee, see *CG*, 37th Cong., 3rd Sess., 1483–84 (March 2; House), 1523–25 (March 3; Senate).

slavery was compatible with it. But whichever rationale for Reconstruction legislation they endorsed, or however they disagreed on other aspects of state restoration, Republicans were coming to demand that no seceded state could be readmitted to the Union with slavery.[17]

A bill introduced by New York Senate Republican Ira Harris in mid-February illustrated both the shift in Republican thinking and some of the issues still to be worked out. Harris had previously sponsored Reconstruction legislation predicated on territorialization, but the new bill employed the "republican form of government" formula. Employing the phrase in its very title, the measure included a proviso that "no law whereby any person has heretofore been held to labor or service in [a seceded] State shall be recognized or enforced by any court or officer in such State." The bill also required all laws governing trial and punishment for white persons to extend to "all persons whatsoever," thus moving toward the principle that would be known as equality before the law. It further mandated the writing of new state constitutions – in a process that would be limited to genuine Unionists – that would prohibit former Confederates from voting or holding state office, repudiate Confederate debts, and recognize and guarantee the freedom of all formerly enslaved persons "who shall be declared free by any act of Congress."

The Senate eventually voted to table Harris's bill, which raised numerous difficulties. Although it did not expressly mandate that the rebellious states abolish slavery, the bill required them, as a condition for readmission to the Union, to provide constitutional sanction to wartime emancipation. It also offered a template for future Reconstruction legislation. Motivated partly by affairs in the lower Mississippi valley, congressional Republicans were coming to link emancipation with state restoration under the "republican form of government" clause. But this was only the start.[18]

III

While Northerners were assessing the meaning of the Emancipation Proclamation for state restoration, the proclamation drove a wedge into southern Unionism. Nowhere else did this development have more important

---

[17] Belz, *Reconstructing the Union*, 121–25. Some abolitionists had argued before the war that the "republican form of government" clause enabled Congress to prohibit new slave states in the Union, but this was a minority position. Northern congressmen opposed to admitting Missouri as a slave state had also used the idea. Sinha, *The Slave's Cause*, 187–88. See also, Zietlow, "Ideological Origins." For an earlier, extended discussion of the clause during the war, though one that did not call for abolition as a condition for state restoration, see Hon. Timothy Farrar, "State Rights," *New Englander and Yale Review*, vol. 21, no. 4 (October 1862): 695–724, esp. 705–11.

[18] CG, 37th Cong., 3rd Sess., Senate Bill 538, esp. sections 1, 2, 7; Belz, *Reconstructing the Union*, 122–25; Wilson, *History of the Antislavery Measures*, 338–39.

consequences than in the lower Mississippi valley, as Unionists in Louisiana and Tennessee split into free-state and proslavery factions. Even as the Federal government moved toward universal military emancipation during 1862, an essential part of the political calculus in both states was the determination of slaveholders and other members of the antebellum establishment to salvage slavery. Having barely secured exemptions from the proclamation, they would redouble their efforts to preserve slavery for nearly the next two years. Federal military personnel were forbidden to remand fugitive slaves under any circumstances, and thousands of slaves had already gained their practical freedom. Given the extent to which the war had undermined slavery, salvaging it would not be easy. Still, slaveholders were not about to abandon hope for slavery's resuscitation before they had exhausted every possible means. Only in hindsight does slavery's destruction appear inevitable and its survival delusional. The contest between proslavery and free-state Unionists must be understood from the vantage point that abolition, having not yet become a condition of state restoration, was not a foregone conclusion, no matter how gravely slavery had been wounded.

In Louisiana, talk of abolishing slavery had been muted before the proclamation but afterward came to the fore. The amorphous movement that Butler had formed into the "Union Association" included a wide range of views, but its members had more or less cooperated in holding the congressional elections that allowed for southern Louisiana's exclusion from the proclamation. By early 1863, however, the movement began to splinter into the constituent factions that would characterize Louisiana Unionist politics for the remainder of the war: the proslavery "conservative Unionists," and the antislavery "free-state" association, which itself would divide into "moderate" and "radical" factions. In essence, there would be two principal organizations – conservative Unionist and free state – but three factions, since the latter included moderates and radicals. The two free-state factions would work together through mid-1863, but relations between them thereafter would become increasingly strained. As the conservative Unionists' relevance lessened into 1864, the differences among free-state Unionists became more pronounced.[19]

Conservative Unionism in Louisiana rested on the three pillars of the *ancièn régime*. It included influential attorneys and jurists such as Christian Roselius,

---

[19] Taylor, *Louisiana Reconstructed*, 21–22. This three-faction framework is central to all works on wartime Reconstruction in Louisiana. But because scholars have tended to focus on the conflict between moderate and radical free-state Unionists, especially over black political and legal rights, they have failed to appreciate fully the importance of the conservative Unionists to wartime Reconstruction. One exception is McCrary, *Abraham Lincoln and Reconstruction*. Similarly, while scholars have understood the significance of proslavery (or conservative) Unionists in the border states, Kentucky especially, they have underestimated their importance in the Union-occupied South, the lower Mississippi valley in particular.

Joseph A. Rozier, J. Q. A. Fellows, and Edmund Abell. It also included members of the New Orleans mercantile and financial community that sustained the slave economy. But the core of conservative Unionism consisted of the sugar planters, obsessed as they were with labor and racial control. If the lawyers and businessmen did not state their aim to be the preservation of slavery, the planters were more candid about their intentions. Insisting that sugar could not be made in Louisiana without involuntary labor, and that black people would never work without the threat of corporal punishment, they were determined to reestablish the antebellum status quo. This goal was not as unrealistic at the time as it would later appear. "[I]t is now obvious that this faction had no chance of success," Joe Gray Taylor has observed. "But what is obvious today was not so obvious in early 1863, and these Conservative Unionists would do what they could to prevent the reorganization of the state on any basis other than a return to prewar conditions."[20]

The conservative Unionists never formally spelled out their argument in a single manifesto, but their position emerged through the pages of the *New Orleans Daily True Delta*. Published for many years by Dr. Hugh Kennedy, the Belfast-born, conservative Democrat who after the war would serve briefly as mayor of New Orleans, the journal encapsulated conservative-Unionist thinking on slavery and state restoration. In contrast to Republicans, conservative Unionists distinguished, as did northern War Democrats, between slavery and disunion, and between a war to preserve the Union and one to abolish slavery. Conservative Unionists rarely if ever explicitly stated their goal to be the preservation of slavery. They sometimes avoided mentioning slavery at all, preferring the euphemism "domestic institution" (especially the nonplanter elements), and they often claimed agnosticism on its morality. At times they criticized slavery, but more for the political harm it had caused the nation (for which northern abolitionists bore more responsibility), and they maintained that the master–slave relationship was essentially benign. Unlike almost all Republicans and even some northern Democrats, conservative Unionists had no moral reservations about slavery – often deeming it a positive good – in discussing state restoration.

In relentlessly castigating abolitionist "fanaticism," the ultimate goal of which, they charged, was "Negro equality," conservative Unionists left no doubt where they stood on abolition. They also issued the obligatory pronouncements on black racial inferiority and dire warnings of the catastrophe that would inevitably follow slavery's end. Moreover, in contending that only the loyal people could decide upon slavery in the states, conservative Unionists rejected the notion that Congress could impose abolition as a condition for a seceded state's "return" to a Union it had never left. The fate of slavery in the

---

[20] Taylor, *Louisiana Reconstructed*, 22.

seceded states, they maintained, could only be determined *after* those states had been restored to the Union. To do otherwise would deprive the (loyal) people of the right to regulate their own domestic institutions, thus violating one of the essential features of "republican" government. Abjuring secession, they argued that the sole objective of the war must be to restore the US Constitution "as it is," by which they meant prior to secession, when slavery enjoyed – as they saw it – constitutional protection. They called for the speedy restoration of civilian government, and they insisted – once that goal had been achieved – that the seceded states be restored to all of their former rights under the Constitution.

All of this added up to restoring the seceded states to the Union with slavery legally intact. "The Abolition party, forgetting the origin of the war, and sedulous to have their own complicity in producing it excluded from popular observation and patriotic criticism," read one articulation of their philosophy, "now is rapidly wheeling into line and occupying the ground that no reconstruction of this government and nation ... shall be permitted in this great democratic republic unless through such form of the abolition of slavery as they shall prescribe." It continued: "In a word, the Federal compact is a deception, the constitution a snare, liberty itself is a delusion, unless as they choose to recognize and interpret them." In Union-occupied Louisiana, "we are farcically assured [that] all our rights and franchises as citizens of the United States are to be scrupulously respected and maintained," insisted another, "for no men are either allowed to hold places of trust who do not avow themselves the enemies of slavery and slave owners, or are regarded with a particle of favor or even consideration by the national government." In arguing that secession and slavery could be separated, and that the seceded states retained all of their rights under the Constitution, the conservatives repudiated the Republican position that those states could only be restored to the Union once slavery had been destroyed.[21]

---

[21] This explication of conservative-Unionist thinking is based on a reading of the *New Orleans Daily True Delta*, especially for 1863. On January 1, 1864, Kennedy sold the paper to the free-state moderate, Michael Hahn, and the periodical's outlook changed at that point. See in particular the following articles or editorials (all 1863): "Distresses of Philanthropy," February 12; "Who Are the Friends of the Institution?" March 21; "The Antagonism of Races," March 22; "A Northern Mistake," April 4; "Loyalty and Loyal Citizens," April 19; "The Actual State of Affairs," May 17; "The Question Briefly Put," May 19; "Nursing the War," May 30; "Refusing Admittance," July 4; "What Is Wanted Here," August 2; "Wake Up, Louisiana!" August 4; "Anonymous Patriotism," August 7; "Our Civil Administration," August 8; "The Absorbing Issue," August 9 (first quotation); "Construction or Destruction," August 18 (second quotation); "Let Us Look at the Coming Time," August 21; "The Infamous Constitution," August 26; "What Is Government?" September 5; "Organizing Civil Government," September 9; "The Union and the Constitution," September 23; "Important Intelligence," October 25; "Perplexities of Politics," December 18; "The Message," December 20.

If the conservative Unionists' ultimate goal was to restore Louisiana with slavery, the more immediate objective of the planters was to secure Federal assistance in reestablishing control over their laborers. In February, some sixty influential planters held a meeting in New Orleans, organized by E. E. Malhiot and Thomas Cottman, the latter of whom had signed Louisiana's secession ordinance, for the purpose of influencing the military's labor policy. Hoping to benefit from Banks's supposedly more accommodationist outlook, they petitioned him and other Federal officials for assistance in reestablishing order on the plantations. "The main idea was to keep things together as well as possible until the return of the *old state* of things would restore them to power," observed a northern correspondent, "and relieve them of the interference of the Federal Government." Planters also held meetings in the countryside for the same purpose. "We ask such power & authority as will enable us to preserve order & compel the negroes to work so as to make the crops necessary for the support of our families & of the negroes themselves," read the petition of a group of Terrebonne Parish planters. Such authority was essential to prevent chaos, they insisted. "But by a prompt & decided course, requiring obedience & work from our Slaves the Govt. may save the country & especially the poor negroes from Such dire calamities." The reference to "our slaves" was no proto-Freudian slip, and planters would sound this theme repeatedly in the coming years.[22]

By contrast, the members of both free-state factions – having generally occupied positions on the periphery of the antebellum establishment – were committed to abolishing slavery, though from here the differences between them were subtle. While endorsing abolition, the moderates wanted to decouple it from racial equality, which they opposed. They attempted to make abolition more palatable to the public by arguing that military emancipation had already made slavery's demise a fait accompli, and that any effort to resuscitate slavery would stir up a hornet's nest. Insisting that the consequences of abolition only be addressed after the state's restoration to the Union, they wanted white loyalists to be in charge of all questions relating to black freedom. The moderates eventually came under the leadership of Michael Hahn. Nathaniel Banks did not involve himself initially in free-state affairs, but he later became closely identified with Hahn and the moderates. Lincoln also tended to favor the moderates, although factional disputes in Louisiana and elsewhere drove him to distraction.

The free-state radicals were a small but eclectic group. They did not advocate equality before the law or black suffrage, but some of them were at least sympathetic to those objectives. In addition to Benjamin F. Flanders, the

---

[22] "Important from Louisiana," *New York Times*, March 5, 1863, 2; *Freedom: WGFL-LS*, 408–10 (quotation); Rodrigue, *Reconstruction in the Cane Fields*, 38–40; McCrary, *Abraham Lincoln and Reconstruction*, chap. 3, esp. 115–22.

radical leadership included Dr. A. P. Dostie and Thomas J. Durant. The latter was a northern-born attorney who had settled in New Orleans on his own as a teenager in the 1830s. A long-time Democrat and supporter of Stephen A. Douglas for president in 1860, he ran unsuccessfully as a cooperationist for Louisiana's secession convention. Although he had previously complained to Lincoln of the disruptions caused by the Union army, Durant came to embrace abolition and would eventually advocate racial equality. A disciple of the French utopian socialist Charles Fourier, Durant would play an integral role in the free-state movement, but as his disenchantment with the conservative drift of Reconstruction under Hahn and Banks grew, he became increasingly obstructionist. The radical faction also included several European émigrés who had fled the revolutions of 1848, such as the Belgian scientist and social reformer Jean-Charles Houzeau, who espoused a radical egalitarianism – and who, though white, never corrected the mistaken notion that he was a free man of color. It also included various Treasury department officials, who, operating out of the New Orleans Custom House, benefitted from the patronage of radical Salmon P. Chase.[23]

The radicals also drew support from the New Orleans free people of color. Although excluded from formal politics, they had long practiced an informal version. Among the most economically and culturally advanced of the free-black populations of all the southern states, the New Orleans free people of color traditionally consisted of an Afro-Creole elite and an Afro-Anglo rank and file. The Afro-Creoles customarily spoke French or were bilingual, and they were generally lighter complexioned, well educated, and wealthier, with some even owning slaves. The Afro-Anglos generally spoke English, were of darker complexion, and practiced trades or were manual laborers. With Union occupation, both groups were now at liberty to condemn slavery, but the former, led by Paul Trévigne, Louis Charles Roudanez, and Rodolphe Lucien Desdunes, tended to focus on preserving their privileged status within a three-tiered racial order, while the latter advocated universal racial equality. Even so, Roudanez and Desdunes had started up in September 1862 the French-language newspaper, *L'Union*, which linked slavery and racial prejudice. Despite lingering tensions among the free people of color, and later between them and the former slaves, the common foe of white supremacy would induce these distinctive black constituencies to overcome their differences in the name of racial unity and uplift.[24]

---

[23] On the Louisiana radicals, especially in early 1863, see Taylor, *Louisiana Reconstructed*, 23–32; Harris, *With Charity for All*, 114–17; McCrary, *Abraham Lincoln and Reconstruction*, 125–30; Houzeau, *My Passage at the New Orleans* Tribune. On Durant: Tregle, "Thomas J. Durant."

[24] There is a voluminous scholarly literature on the New Orleans free people of color before and during the Civil War, but essential studies remain Berlin, *Slaves without Masters*, and Blassingame, *Black New Orleans*. See also Rankin, "Origins of Black Leadership." An

In early 1863, the differences between the free-state factions remained latent. Not for another year would the fissure between them widen to a chasm. With the conservative Unionists a viable force and slavery very much alive, their main concern was preventing Louisiana's restoration as a slave state. In late February, with Flanders and Hahn still in Washington, the free-state leadership, under Durant's guidance, outlined a plan for Louisiana's political reorganization. It proposed holding an election for delegates to a state convention that would write a free-state constitution before elections for a state government and Congress. Toward that end, the free-state organization would oversee a registry of loyal voters, with loyalty defined as one's never having voluntarily supported the Confederacy. The election of delegates would thus be limited to a loyalist core, with each parish's representation at the convention determined by the size of its white population only. Although the proposal did not allow for black participation, the apportionment provision would favor the Unionist element in New Orleans and negate the disproportionate influence that rural slaveholders had traditionally enjoyed under Louisiana's antebellum constitutions, which had generally based representation on total population.

While in Washington, Flanders and Hahn consulted often with Lincoln, who came to trust these two long-time residents of New Orleans and unconditional Unionists as leaders of Louisiana's free-state movement. He indicated his approval, through Hahn, of the convention proposal. At a Unionist meeting in early April, Durant read a letter from Hahn conveying Lincoln's support for the proposal and his intention to instruct Banks and Military Governor Shepley to provide all necessary assistance in implementing it. By mid-April, even as Banks was occupied at Port Hudson and Grant at Vicksburg, the Louisiana free-state initiative seemed to be up and running.[25]

IV

In Tennessee, Unionist politics reflected the traditional divisions that dated from the antebellum era as well as individual loyalties since secession. Although few Unionists initially supported emancipation, the Emancipation Proclamation still rendered the question of slavery unavoidable. The Union victory at Stones River in early January seemed to augur the liberation of east Tennessee that Military Governor Andrew Johnson considered essential to the state's restoration. Despite Tennessee's exclusion from the proclamation,

---

excellent analysis of the antebellum intellectual background of wartime radicalism is Bell, *Revolution, Romanticism, and the Afro-Creole Protest Tradition*, esp. 222–39 on *L'Union* in late 1862 and early 1863.

[25] McCrary, *Abraham Lincoln and Reconstruction*, 127–28; Cox, *Lincoln and Black Freedom*, 49–50.

Lincoln's emancipation policy placed the state's Unionists, who had argued all along that Unionism was the best way to secure slavery, in a difficult position. How could proslavery Unionists look for protection from – and in turn support – an administration openly committed to the destruction of slavery? Congressional deliberations that showed increasing support for linking abolition and state restoration also did not bode well. Assuring Lincoln in mid-January that Tennessee's exclusion from the proclamation "will be worth much to us," Johnson nonetheless went on to observe that the proclamation "has disappointed and disarmed many who were complaining and denouncing it as unjust and unwise."[26]

Although many Unionists eventually came to the conclusion that slavery must go, the process by which Tennessee Unionism split into free-state and proslavery factions was slower and more uneven than in Louisiana. Unconditional Unionism had always rested more easily with slavery in the upper than in the lower South. Congressman Emerson Etheridge, former governor William B. Campbell, and Thomas A. R. Nelson – respectively of west, central, and east Tennessee – led the group that hoped to preserve slavery. Benjamin C. Truman and Edwin Paschal, founder and editor, respectively, of the *Nashville Press*, established in May 1863, originally supported Johnson and Lincoln before later turning against them. Conversely, the former staunchly proslavery Unionist William G. Brownlow, having suffered harsh treatment by Confederates, converted to antislavery and became a leader of the free-state faction. Samuel C. Mercer, although only having arrived in Tennessee the previous year to start up the pro-administration *Nashville Daily Union*, vociferously advocated abolition, as did James B. Bingham, editor of the Memphis *Bulletin* and a close ally of Johnson. Only later in the war would congressman Horace Maynard embrace antislavery. As late as July 1863, he advocated returning liberated slaves to bondage in return for an end to the rebellion.[27]

Johnson's own conversion would also take time. Not until mid-1863 – with Lincoln pressing for a commitment to abolition in some form, and himself facing an insurgency from proslavery Unionists – did Johnson finally decide to stake his political future on antislavery. In a series of well-received speeches in northern cities during March and April, as part of an extended trip to Washington to confer with Lincoln, he gave strong indications of moving in that direction, castigating rebels and associating slavery with secession. Yet he also evinced little sympathy for the slaves or black people in general. "Before I would see this Government destroyed I would see every negro back in Africa,

---

[26] *CWL*, 6: 48, 53; *OR*, ser. 1, vol. 20, pt. 2, 317.
[27] Cimprich, *Slavery's End in Tennessee*, 101–3; Trefousse, *Andrew Johnson*, 165–70; Harris, *With Charity for All*, 105–6; Cimprich, "Military Governor Johnson and Tennessee Blacks," 462–63; Atkins, "Failure of Restoration," 304–7. On Mercer, Bingham, Truman, and Paschal: *PAJ*, 6: 62, 326–27; on Thomas A. R. Nelson: Alexander, *Political Reconstruction in Tennessee*, 40–42.

disintegrated and blotted out of space," he announced in Indianapolis. For Johnson and many other Tennessee Unionists, abolition was less about the immorality of slavery or justice for the former slaves than about retribution against slaveholding rebels for the catastrophe they had wrought.[28]

* * *

In mid-June 1863, as the Union siege of Vicksburg dragged on, George S. Boutwell, the US Senator from Massachusetts and leading Radical Republican, addressed the National Union League Association in Washington, DC. Speaking on a range of topics, including Reconstruction in Louisiana, Boutwell called attention to the "possible difficulty" of "the return of the seceded States to this Union as slave States." He had looked "with interest towards Louisiana, at the indications there made that the loyal people of that State are about to frame a new constitution and ask for admission into the Union." Boutwell made no mention of proslavery Unionists, in Louisiana or elsewhere, but the threat was understood. "The policy of allowing these eleven seceded States to return to the Union with the institution of slavery upon them," he contended, "is to receive into the Union the cause of all our woes. I do not desire to see the return of these States to the Union, unless they return with republican forms of government." Boutwell went on to articulate the Republican consensus that slavery and republican government were incompatible, and that the seceded states could only be returned to the Union on a free-state basis. To do otherwise would be a "calamity," he continued, and anyone willing to "countenance the reconstruction of the Union with slavery existing in these States" would bear responsibility "not only for the civil wars, but for the servile wars, which inevitably must follow." Boutwell wanted peace and reunion, but only once freedom had been secured to all persons. "Until we have such a Union, there can be no peace."[29]

Boutwell's was actually a highly partisan address, and he condemned northern Democrats for supporting the nightmare scenario he had pictured. For the remainder of the war, Republicans and Democrats would disagree over Lincoln's emancipation policy and its consequences for Reconstruction. Northern antislavery advocates were establishing the position that slavery would have to be abolished as a condition for state restoration, even as the Emancipation Proclamation split Unionists in Louisiana and Tennessee into contending factions that would struggle for control over the process of organizing new state governments. Much to his chagrin, Lincoln would be forced to intervene in this factional warfare. Slavery's advocates in both states, who, as Boutwell warned, did not lack for northern allies, had begun to mount a rear-guard defense of their institution.

---

[28] Trefousse, *Andrew Johnson*, 166; *PAJ*, 6: 148–59 (quotation, 156).
[29] Boutwell, "Power of the Government to Suppress the Rebellion," 222–24.

6

"Repugnant to the Spirit of the Age"

As was so often the case in the lower Mississippi valley during the Civil War, political and military developments moved in tandem. The Confederate surrenders in July 1863 at Vicksburg and Port Hudson, along with the Union victory at Gettysburg, irrevocably altered the course of the war, even if the outcome was still far from certain. Union operations on the Mississippi River also generated the first significant combat experience in the war for black soldiers, who proved their mettle at Port Hudson and Milliken's Bend. Even as the military campaign for the river approached its dénouement, the struggle between rival Unionist factions in the lower Mississippi valley also escalated. In Tennessee, the attempt to hold a pan-Unionist convention in early July only succeeded in precipitating the less-than-amicable split between proslavery and antislavery factions. In Louisiana, where conservative and free-state Unionists had already gone their separate ways, both groups put forward state restoration plans that forced Lincoln, not for the last time, to choose sides in an intrastate squabble. As a result, he now stood firmly behind the free-state initiative. Conservatives in neither state were going away, but with an essential element of the Union's overall military strategy having been achieved by mid-1863, political success against slavery seemed sure to follow.

I

Having failed for months to circumvent Vicksburg's batteries, General Ulysses S. Grant had decided by late March on a new plan. He would trek his men south along the west bank of the Mississippi River and cross below the city while Admiral David Porter's gunboats and transports would run the batteries. Two daring bolts on April 16 and April 22 placed the Union navy below Vicksburg with minimal losses, as Grant continued to move his army south. Meanwhile, "Grierson's Raid" – an audacious foray from La Grange, Tennessee, to Baton Rouge, between mid-April and early May, by Colonel Benjamin Grierson and 1,700 cavalry troops – created a major diversion behind Confederate lines. Eventually crossing the river about thirty miles below Vicksburg, Grant and his troops were positioned by the end of April on the east side of the Mississippi. Grant at this point considered but decided against moving further south and linking up with Banks to take Port Hudson before proceeding against Vicksburg.[1] Capitalizing on an ineffective Confederate response, Grant won a series of five hard-fought battles over the next three weeks – Port Gibson on May 1, Raymond on May 12, Jackson on May 14 (the third state capital of the region to fall), Champion Hill on May 16, and Big Black River Bridge on May 17 – before investing Vicksburg from the east. Approaching Vicksburg on May 18, Grant hoped to seize the city without having to resort to a siege. A hurriedly assembled assault on May 19 was repulsed, as were two separate attacks on May 22 with heavy losses. Grant now dug in.[2]

Meanwhile, the Port Hudson campaign also devolved into a siege. In late March, General Nathaniel Banks prepared to renew his operations against Port Hudson by first securing the lower Red River valley via Bayou Teche. Slogging his way north toward the Red River in April, Banks freed many slaves along Bayou Teche whom Confederates had impressed to build defensive works. By May 7, Federal forces controlled Alexandria, which the Confederates had abandoned several days earlier. (As part of this operation, Federal forces occupied the town of Opelousas, to which the Confederate state government had fled in 1862 after the Federals took Baton Rouge. Louisiana's Confederate state government now relocated to Shreveport.) On May 12, Banks received a communication from Grant requesting Banks's assistance against Vicksburg. Realizing that the anticipated help from Grant against Port Hudson was not in the offing, Banks decided to move against Port Hudson on his own, and he began transporting his army down the Red River. By May 22, the day of Grant's second assault at Vicksburg, Banks's men were investing Port Hudson. As had Grant at Vicksburg, Banks wanted to take Port Hudson without resorting to a siege, but a poorly planned and executed assault on May 27 was repulsed with heavy casualties. By late May, both Port Hudson and Vicksburg were essentially besieged – although a second assault against Port Hudson on June 14 also ended in defeat and heavy losses.[3]

The May 27 attack included two regiments of the Louisiana Native Guard, the black unit that Benjamin Butler had organized the previous year, marking the first major combat experience of black soldiers in the Civil War. One

---

[1] Hess, *Civil War in the West*, 134–39, 145–51; Ballard, *Vicksburg*, 191–203, 211–20. On Grierson's raid, see Dinges and Leckie, *A Just and Righteous Cause*; Smith, *Real Horse Soldiers*.

[2] Grant, *Memoirs*, 1: 321; Ballard, *Vicksburg*, chaps. 8–10, 325–26, 332–51; Hess, *Civil War in the West*, 151–52; Smith, *Champion Hill*; Smith, "'A Victory Could Hardly Have Been More Complete'"; *OR*, ser. 1, vol. 24, pt. 3, 888, 890. For a detailed examination of the attacks of May 19 and 22, see Woodworth and Grear, *The Vicksburg Assaults*.

[3] Frazier, *Blood on the Bayou*; Winters, *Civil War in Louisiana*, chap. 15, 242–61; Hess, *Civil War in the West*, 170–72; Taylor, *Destruction and Reconstruction*, chap. 9.

regiment consisted of free men of color, the other largely of former slaves. Enduring various disadvantages and thrown against one of the strongest parts of the Confederate defenses, the roughly thousand men of the Native Guard fought bravely before being driven back and suffering a staggering one-third casualties. Under a flag of truce, Union burial parties removed only the bodies of the white soldiers. The circumstances surrounding this indignity would be much disputed, but the remains of some of the first black soldiers to die fighting for the Union during the Civil War would lay unburied, rotting, until Port Hudson surrendered six weeks later.[4]

The next notable black combat action resulted not in indignity but atrocity, this time on June 7 at Milliken's Bend, Louisiana. The Confederate raid on this post – along with simultaneous attacks at Lake Providence and Young's Point, Louisiana – had been timed to take advantage of the reassignment of Federal troops to Grant at Vicksburg. The 1,400 defenders of Milliken's Bend belonged almost entirely to the recently organized "African Brigade." The brief but bitter engagement included hand-to-hand combat and the use of bayonets and rifle butts. The overpowered Union forces were nearly driven into the river but for the timely arrival of Federal gunboats that halted the Confederate attack.[5] Though a relatively minor engagement, Milliken's Bend had important repercussions. Black soldiers had again fought and died bravely, and had again suffered horrific losses. But this time they were also the victims of deliberate atrocities, as many of them were murdered as they lay wounded, while others were captured and reenslaved. Grant later acknowledged that the black soldiers at Milliken's Bend had been poorly trained and equipped, but that their conduct had been "most gallant" and that "with good officers they will make good troops." Many Northerners came to the same conclusion. The savage fighting at Milliken's Bend – along with the earlier assault at Port Hudson and the subsequent one at Fortress Wagner, South Carolina, involving the Fifty-Fourth Massachusetts Infantry – would galvanize northern support for enlisting black men into the Union army, and for allowing them to exercise one of the essential duties of citizenship by fighting and dying for their country.[6]

---

[4] There are many scholarly accounts of the Native Guard at Port Hudson, especially in the assault of May 27, including Hollandsworth, *Louisiana Native Guards*, 50–58; Quarles, *Negro in the Civil War*, 215–20; Cornish, *Sable Arm*, 142–43.

[5] *Freedom: BME*, 532–34 (doc. 211). Milliken's Bend has also received much scholarly attention. Every study of the black military experience during the Civil War discusses it. For Union Adjutant General Lorenzo Thomas's report of the battle, see *Freedom: BME*, 530–32 (doc. 210). For Confederate General Richard Taylor's account, see *Destruction and Reconstruction*, 134–36.

[6] *OR*, ser. 1, vol. 24, pt. 2, 446 (quotation), 462–66, esp. 466; Ballard, *Grant at Vicksburg*, 66–77.

II

As the military campaigns on the river were unfolding, the contests between proslavery and antislavery factions over state restoration in Tennessee and Louisiana were also reaching important turning points. The two sides in Tennessee continued a pretense of cooperation, although, with the divide among them increasingly evident, the charade would not last. Meanwhile, Military Governor Andrew Johnson's insistence that state reorganization could not begin until east Tennessee had been liberated – an objective that appeared in no way imminent – was also challenged, as was his entire administration.

Despite Confederate control of east Tennessee, proslavery Unionists elsewhere in the state now mounted a political challenge to Johnson, who had only recently embraced Lincoln's military emancipation policy. Growing impatient over the lack of progress on state restoration, Tennessee Unionists of various persuasions pushed for a state convention to work toward organizing a new government. In late May, Johnson returned from his extended trip to Washington and was immediately met with requests to call a convention. Johnson hesitated to endorse the move, but it received backing from a wide spectrum of Unionists, including central and west Tennessee slaveholders, east Tennessee exiles, and Memphis residents concerned with rehabilitating the city's reputation and reviving commerce. Despite Johnson's opposition, a call went out in June, endorsed by prominent Tennessee Unionists such as Horace Maynard and William G. Brownlow, for a state convention to meet in early July in Nashville. Its purpose would be "to maintain the State Government in connection with the Federal Union as it stood prior to the rebellion and the war."

Johnson could hardly block such an initiative, and on July 1 more than 200 delegates from 43 counties converged on Nashville. Johnson supporters were in attendance, lest proslavery Unionists seize control of state restoration. No sooner had the convention met than the conservatives' objectives became clear. They immediately proposed elections – to be held in August, before east Tennessee could possibly be liberated – for a state government and members of Congress under the antebellum constitution. Given the growing support for emancipation among Unionists, the conservatives clearly hoped to get Johnson out of the way and restore Tennessee as soon as possible. Johnson's allies and the east Tennessee delegates, though not supporters of abolition, opposed the conservatives' proposal, using Johnson's argument that no statewide election could take place without east Tennessee.[7]

Debate extended over several days, during which the news of Union victories at Gettysburg and Vicksburg arrived. The convention deliberated over

---

[7] Previous two paragraphs: *PAJ*, 6: 288–89 (quotation); Harris, *With Charity for All*, 106–8.

various matters relating to state reorganization, including the officials to be elected, the propriety of electing a legislature without also electing a civilian governor, and the very need for a military governor. The last point was a not-so-subtle criticism of Johnson. Although most of the debate did not involve slavery, Johnson, as the representative of Lincoln's emancipation policy, provided much of the subtext. "Gov. Johnson undoubtedly ha[s] the power to arrest this whole Convention and send the members to the Penitentiary," contended John Lellyett, a Johnson critic who also opposed "any action on the part of the Convention which had a tendency to cast its moral influence in favor of a Military Government." Lellyett then offered a resolution approving of Johnson's policy, as announced in his early 1862 address to the people of Tennessee upon being named military governor – well *before* the Emancipation Proclamation. Lellyett's resolution also pledged to support "all constitutional and lawful measures ... tending to the restoration of Tennessee to her former position in the Federal Union." There was no mistaking the implication that much of what Johnson *had* done as military governor was unconstitutional and unlawful. The resolution was defeated.[8]

Only at length did the convention compromise on a series of resolutions. The first declared all measures enacted by the state legislature since secession and in furtherance of rebellion to be "unauthorized, the work of usurpation, and therefore void." The convention called for the state legislature to meet in Nashville in early October, and for Johnson to organize legislative elections for August 1 or as soon as possible thereafter. The resolutions said nothing about gubernatorial or congressional elections, which the conservatives had advocated. While the resolutions mentioned neither slavery nor emancipation, they affirmed that "the overthrow by treason of the civil powers of the State has demanded the exercise of the power granted to the Federal government to guarantee to every State a republican form of government." The convention also approved Johnson's appointment as military governor and his course of action in that capacity, and it pledged to him its "hearty co-operation and support" of any measures necessary for Tennessee's restoration.[9]

The convention marked a setback for the conservatives, who had hoped to sideline Johnson and begin restoring Tennessee under the antebellum constitution. Although the meaning of "republican" government would still be much debated, antislavery advocates had already staked out the position that it was incompatible with slavery. Paradoxically, Johnson's main concern was liberating not the slaves but east Tennessee from Confederate rule. Until that goal had been achieved, he could use the military situation to thwart any conservative attempt at state restoration. Although Johnson ultimately refused to authorize

---

[8] *Nashville Daily Union*, July 1–8, 1863 (quotations, July 7).
[9] *PAJ*, 6: 288–89; Harris, *With Charity for All*, 107–8; Trefousse, *Andrew Johnson*, 170; Cimprich, *Slavery's End in Tennessee*, 102.

even the legislative elections that the convention had endorsed, he could not prevent the conservatives from organizing a gubernatorial election or continuing to push for statewide elections. Johnson had fended off this conservative-Unionist counterattack. And even though Tennessee's restoration would remain stalled for the rest of the year, political warfare with conservative Unionists would force him and his allies to embrace more firmly immediate abolition in Tennessee.

III

In Louisiana, the line separating conservative and free-state Unionists had become pronounced by the spring, and both sides would solicit Lincoln's intervention. By mid-April, Lincoln had endorsed the free-state proposal of creating a registry of loyal voters and holding a convention to write a free-state constitution. Later that month, Nathaniel Banks briefly returned to New Orleans from the Port Hudson campaign and issued orders that significantly revamped his conciliatory policy toward Confederates and boosted the morale of the free-state group. Buoyed by such support, Thomas J. Durant and other free-state leaders spent the next few weeks planning for the proposed convention.[10]

At a May 21 meeting in New Orleans, free-state Unionists formally approved a plan that called for a registration of loyal voters and an election for delegates to a state convention to be held in New Orleans. The convention would frame "a new constitution adapted to the change of circumstances and conditions produced by the rebellion," the meeting's resolutions read, and it would organize a civilian government. The plan included a loyalty oath mandating future allegiance to the United States and requiring persons to "solemnly repudiate" any previous allegiance to the Confederacy. This provision reflected a softening of the radicals' previous position, which required the "iron-clad" oath (no past voluntary support for the rebellion) in determining loyalty. The entire state reorganization process was limited to "loyal free white male citizens," and the apportioning of delegates was restricted to the state's white population. The plan also requested Military Governor George Shepley's assistance in its implementation.[11]

Shepley agreed to the free-state proposal and pledged to help register voters, though he claimed no authority, without approval from Washington, to sanction elections or a convention. He especially worried lest the initiative appear to be driven by the military and not the people themselves. In late May, Shepley forwarded the free-state proposal, along with his correspondence with the organization, to Secretary of War Stanton, requesting instructions. "As the

---

[10] McCrary, *Abraham Lincoln and Reconstruction*, 128–29; Harris, *With Charity for All*, 116.
[11] OR, ser. 3, vol. 3, 231–34.

State of Louisiana will probably be the first of the seceded States to re-establish a State government under the Constitution of the United States," he wrote to Stanton, "the question as to the mode of accomplishment of this result becomes one of great importance." In mid-June, before receiving a response, Shepley appointed Durant state attorney general and commissioner of registration and authorized him to begin registering voters. When Shepley received no response from Stanton by July, he decided to go to Washington. His extended absence from the state would adversely affect the entire initiative, but for now the free-state forces appeared to be in control of Louisiana's reorganization.[12]

This is how the conservative Unionists read the situation. By this time, the Louisiana planters and their allies had been maneuvering for control of the restoration process for months. The military's support of the free-state movement did not help their cause. A May 1 meeting in New Orleans had authorized a commission of seven planters to travel to Washington and to present to Lincoln "the condition of the loyal planters of the State of Louisiana, and to request of him Such action and assistance, as while restoring the State to the Union, will as far as possible, secure the prosperity of the loyal people therein." Eventually, a delegation of three planters – E. E. Malhiot, Thomas Cottman, and Bradish Johnson – met with Lincoln in late May or early June. The petition they presented to him much more explicitly articulated their goals than had their previous instructions. The delegation sought, as the petition expressed it, "a full recognition of all the rights of the State, as they existed previous to the passage of an act of secession, upon the principle of the existence of the State Constitution unimpaired, and no legal act having transpired that could in any way deprive them of the advantages conferred by that Constitution." In other words, because the 1861 Louisiana secession convention had enacted a new constitution after the state seceded, the planters advocated a reversion to the state's 1852 constitution. "Under this constitution," the petition continued, "the State wishes to return to its full allegiance, in the enjoyment of all rights and privileges exercised by the other states under the Federal Constitution." Toward that end, the petition requested that Lincoln direct the military governor to order an election for early November for all state and Federal offices.[13]

In hindsight, the conservatives' proposal appears hopeless. Given all that had happened since the start of the war, Louisiana's return to the situation that had existed prior to secession might have seemed impossible. As countless observers remarked at the time, slavery would never survive the war, and the insurgent states would have to acknowledge that reality before resuming their

---

[12] *OR*, ser. 3, vol. 3, 231 (Shepley to Stanton), 234–35 (Shepley to free-state leaders).
[13] Louisiana Planters to Abraham Lincoln, May 1, 1863, ALP; *CWL*, 6: 287–88 (petition); McCrary, *Abraham Lincoln and Reconstruction*, 131–32.

place in the Union. Lincoln might have accepted what the conservative Unionists were offering before the Emancipation Proclamation; after it, a return to the status quo ante was no longer possible. Yet legally speaking, there was nothing at this point to preclude any seceded state from being restored to the Union once its citizenry had renounced secession. If Republicans were now demanding that the seceded states abolish slavery as a condition for restoration to the Union, no law as yet required those states to do so. Congress could refuse to seat members-elect from formerly seceded states, but that was about all the Federal government could do, absent Reconstruction legislation, to prevent these states from being restored to the Union. In this sense, northern War Democrats – and even southern conservative Unionists – stood on firmer legal ground than did Republicans who insisted on abolition. The war was undermining slavery, but the planters were correct to argue that slavery in the states continued to enjoy legal sanction. They said it in dealing with their slaves, and they were saying it in dealing with the president.

Lincoln delayed responding to the planters. At around the same time he met with them, he received a letter from Michael Hahn, written about a week after the planters' May 1 meeting. Hahn briefed Lincoln on recent developments and requested his assistance. "We are making an effort at the organization of a loyal state government," Hahn informed the president. Banks and Shepley were aiding this effort, he observed, "but instructions from you would help us materially," and he asked Lincoln to write to both men in support of it, adding, "if you deem proper write me a letter on the same subject which I can show to the people." Hahn wanted to dispel rumors, circulating in New Orleans, that Lincoln opposed the free-state initiative. "No time should be lost in this matter, as we are very anxious that Louisiana should be the first of the seceded States to return to the Union," Hahn noted, "and it is not necessary for me to state to you the advantages to the cause of the Union and your administration which would inevitably flow from a restoration of our State to the Union."[14]

Despite Hahn's sense of urgency, no record exists of a response. Several weeks later, in early June, Hahn tried again. Lincoln undoubtedly received Hahn's second letter *after* he had met with the planters but *before* his June 19 response to them. Although Lincoln was receiving information from other Louisiana sources, and had probably already seen the free-state convention proposal that Shepley had forwarded to Stanton, it may well have been Hahn's June letter that persuaded Lincoln finally to reply to the planters. "The Union people of this State," Hahn wrote, "are all in favor of a re-organization of a loyal state government." In case Lincoln had not already figured it out for himself, Hahn boiled the situation down to its essentials. "The only question on which they are divided is as to whether a new Constitution should be made, or the old

---

[14] Michael Hahn to Lincoln, May 9, 1863, ALP; Harris, *With Charity for All*, 117.

Constitution of 1852 adhered to," he observed. "Those in favor of a Convention and a new Constitution are the more radical or free-soil Union men, and expect to succeed in making a free-soil Constitution," he added. "Others, whose interests are in the institution of slavery and who desire to preserve that institution are strongly opposed to a new Constitution and are satisfied with the Constitution of 1852." It was as simple as that: Would Louisiana organize a new government under its proslavery constitution or write a free-state constitution first?[15]

If Lincoln harbored any doubts about how to respond to the planters, Hahn's letter would have put them to rest. In his response to the planters, Lincoln firmly but diplomatically declined the request that he endorse their state restoration proposal. Since receiving it, he explained, he had obtained "reliable information," probably referring to Hahn but perhaps also to Shepley and other informants, "that a respectable portion of the Louisiana people desire to amend their State constitution, and contemplate holding a convention for that object. This fact alone, as it seems to me, is a sufficient reason why the general government should not give the committal you seek, to the existing State constitution." Lincoln's refusal to support the planters may not have amounted to an explicit endorsement of the free-state movement, but his language – citing the plan to amend (actually rewrite) the constitution, clearly to abolish slavery, and refusing to endorse "the existing State constitution" – left little doubt where he stood. With the Vicksburg and Port Hudson campaigns in mind, Lincoln perhaps tried to soften the blow by invoking military necessity. "[W]hile I do not perceive how such committal [to the current state constitution] could facilitate our military operations in Louisiana," he observed, "I really apprehend it might be so used as to embarrass them." Indeed, what would it look like for Lincoln to sanction Louisiana's existing constitution just as Union forces were about to establish control of the Mississippi River?

In rejecting the planters' petition, Lincoln invoked military necessity. Yet he also decided against using conciliatory language that Secretary of State William H. Seward had suggested. "If the military force of the rebellion were already out of the way, so that the people of Louisiana could now practically enter upon the enjoyment of their rights under the present State and National Constitutions," Lincoln wrote in a draft response, employing language from Seward that he ultimately did not use, "your request would stand before me in a different aspect." Lincoln probably rejected this text because, upon further reflection, he realized that military necessity was not the reason he was denying the request. In effect, even "if the military force of the rebellion were out of the way" – that is, if Union forces controlled the entire Mississippi River – that would *still* not

---

[15] Michael Hahn to Lincoln, June 6, 1863, ALP; McCrary, *Abraham Lincoln and Reconstruction*, 132.

have placed the planters' request "in a different aspect." The military situation had nothing to do with it. Lincoln could not grant their request for the simple reason that he had no intention of endorsing Louisiana's existing constitution. He would not allow even for the possibility of restoring Louisiana to the Union as a slave state, especially with a movement afoot to abolish slavery there.

Having discarded this conciliatory language, Lincoln reassured the planters that there remained "abundant time" for organizing a November election. "The people of Louisiana shall not lack an oppertunity of a fair election for both Federal and State officers by want of anything within my power to give them," he wrote. Yet even here Lincoln prevaricated. Whether sufficient time existed to organize elections for November, what Lincoln left unsaid was that he would permit no reorganization of Louisiana's government other than on a free-state basis. Presented with contrasting proposals for Louisiana's restoration to the Union, Lincoln rejected the one based on "the principle of the existence of the State Constitution unimpaired," and he endorsed, however implicitly, the one predicated on "a new constitution adapted to the change of circumstances and conditions produced by the rebellion." In short, as *Harper's Weekly* tartly observed, Lincoln had rebuffed the overtures of "Mr. Cottman and his two friends, who recently asked the President to re-establish slavery in Louisiana." The Emancipation Proclamation had not abolished slavery, but free-state Unionists in Louisiana were making progress in translating military emancipation into constitutional abolition. Lincoln's endorsement of this initiative did not end the conservatives' campaign to preserve slavery. But by mid-1863, just as the sieges at Vicksburg and Port Hudson were culminating, the prospects for abolishing slavery in Louisiana looked promising.[16]

IV

Meanwhile, the sieges on the Mississippi River, which began in late May, lasted for six long weeks until Vicksburg surrendered on July 4. Port Hudson – the last Confederate stronghold on the river but now rendered useless – followed five days later. The conditions endured at both sites would become the stuff of legend. With Federal control of the Mississippi River secured, the Confederacy had been split in two, and an essential element of the Anaconda Plan had at last been achieved. The slaves of Second Creek, Mississippi, had also been vindicated, and the Father of the Waters, in Lincoln's famous words, hereafter flowed "unvexed to the sea."[17]

---

[16] *CWL*, 6: 287–89. Lincoln also required prodding by one of the members of the delegation to respond to their petition. Cottman to Lincoln, June 18, 1863, ALP. Harris, *With Charity for All*, 116–17.

[17] *CWL*, 6: 409. On the Vicksburg siege and surrender: Ballard, *Vicksburg*, chaps. 12, 13; Ballard, *Grant at Vicksburg*; Hess, *Civil War in the West*, 152–59. On Port Hudson, see Winters, *Civil War in Louisiana*, 261–83; Hess, *Civil War in the West*, 171–74.

The surrender of Port Hudson also meant that the remains of the black soldiers fallen in the assault of May 27 could finally be laid to rest. Among the corpses that had been decomposing in the searing Louisiana heat was that of André Cailloux, whose story was representative of the times. Born a slave in rural southern Louisiana in 1825, Cailloux was removed to New Orleans with his enslaved parents at age five, although his mother was subsequently sold. He was trained as a cigar maker, and his owner permitted him to "hire out" – a common practice with urban slaves. Although an Afro-Creole and bi-lingual, Cailloux took great pride in his dark complexion. He enjoyed relatively privileged status, as had his father, and he was manumitted in 1846 at age twenty-one. He eventually acquired property and became a respected member of the free black community. In 1849, he purchased his mother, but she may have died before he could emancipate her. Cailloux married a woman who had also been manumitted, and by the start of the war they had raised three children in addition to the adopted son she bore a former master. Cailloux helped found the Native Guard under the Confederacy and was elected a lieutenant, but he raised a company under Benjamin Butler's reorganization of the unit and became its captain. Charismatic, self-assured, and a superb horseman, Cailloux exhibited natural leadership qualities, and he believed that he and his comrades, despite the discrimination and hostility they faced, had everything to prove by fighting for the United States.[18]

Cailloux was one of the few men to survive Nathaniel Banks's purge of black officers from the Native Guard. Having fought for the right to fight for his country, Cailloux died for it in that May 27 assault. A Confederate shell struck him in the head as he led his men forward, but not before a bullet had shattered his left arm. Confederates who searched the battlefield that night came across his body and found his officer's commission in his pocket. Those from New Orleans evidently recognized him, though only a finger ring identified his remains by the time they were recovered. His death aggrieved the New Orleans black community, which celebrated him as a martyr to freedom. The northern press also took up Cailloux's story, making him what one scholar calls "the first national black military hero of the Civil War."[19]

Cailloux's remains were transported to New Orleans via steamer, attended by some of the wounded men of his regiment. Arriving in the city on July 25, his body lay in state for four days at a black mutual-aid society of which Cailloux had been a leading member. Cailloux's funeral on July 29, an elaborate ceremony, elicited a massive outpouring by the New Orleans black community. It was the largest public event held in the city since the burial of the first Louisiana Confederate officer killed in the war. Officiating was Father Claude Paschal Maistre, a Roman Catholic priest. Born in France in 1820 and

---

[18] This account of Cailloux is based on Ochs, *A Black Patriot and a White Priest*.
[19] Ochs, *A Black Patriot and a White Priest*, 163.

ordained in 1844, Maistre had immigrated to the United States in 1850 and arrived seven years later in New Orleans, where he ministered to the city's free black community. Although no other New Orleans priest would likely have officiated, the choice of Maistre by Cailloux's widow was deliberate.

Maistre had always been a maverick, finding trouble almost everywhere he went. He had evidently expressed antislavery sentiment before the war, but the Union occupation of New Orleans prompted his conversion to abolition and even racial equality, putting him at odds with the Roman Catholic hierarchy in Louisiana. The Archbishop of New Orleans was Jean-Marie Odin, also a native of France and a firm though not zealous supporter of the Confederacy. As Maistre became more outspoken in his views, he drew the ire of the city's white Catholics and of Odin himself. By May 1863, Odin had suspended Maistre and placed his parish under censure, prohibiting Catholics from having any dealings with him. Maistre defied Odin and continued his work, and the Catholics who attended Cailloux's funeral did so in defiance of Church authority. Although Cailloux had served as a Church layman, it remains unclear whether he and Maistre ever met, but they were linked by their commitment to the ideals of freedom and equality that Cailloux's public funeral was designed to promote. Maistre facilitated the emerging alliance between the Afro-Creoles – and the larger New Orleans free black community – and white, radical Unionists. He continued to mix religion and politics, operating a schismatic parish until 1870, when he finally submitted to Church authority – but only after Odin had died and been replaced, and after the ideals for which Cailloux and others had given their lives had been incorporated into the nation's political creed.

* * *

On July 25, 1863, the very day André Cailloux's body arrived in New Orleans, the "Union Association of New Orleans" held a meeting in which it approved of Lincoln's course of action with the Louisiana planters. The members of the organization had been made aware, "with surprise and indignation," as the assembly's resolutions stated, of the attempt by "certain gentlemen, claiming to represent the planting interest of Louisiana," to induce Lincoln and the Federal government "to fetter once more the Freemen of this State, by putting in force a Constitution, the principles of which are utterly at variance with the sentiments of a large majority of the Loyal People, and repugnant to the Spirit of the Age." They had also learned, "with the liveliest feelings of satisfaction," of Lincoln's "noble utterances ... in rebuke of the self-constituted, slavery-preserving delegation," and of his approval of the efforts of "the truly loyal" to secure a constitution "based upon the principle of 'Freedom to all.'" They further resolved to "deprecate all efforts" to organize a state government "under the Constitution in force prior to the outbreak of the present Rebellion," and to oppose, "by all legitimate means, every measure having for its object the recognition of slavery in any Constitution that may hereafter be formed." In essence, the free-state Unionists were celebrating what they saw as their victory over the conservative Unionists, and they intended to follow through on it.[20]

By mid-1863, the Union had secured control of the Mississippi River, while free-state Unionists in Louisiana and Tennessee appeared to be gaining the upper hand in the contest over state restoration. In the weeks ahead, Little Rock would fall to Union military forces, allowing restoration efforts in Arkansas to begin in earnest. Nonetheless, proslavery Unionism remained a viable political force in Louisiana and Tennessee, and slavery enjoyed legal sanction in all of the seceded states. Slavery may have been disintegrating, but the onus still rested firmly on its opponents to end it.

---

[20] [Resolutions], Union Association of New Orleans, July 25, 1863, forwarded in James E. Tewell to Lincoln, July 31, 1863, ALP.

7

"The Greatest Question Ever Presented to Practical Statesmanship"

Following the Federal conquest of Vicksburg and Port Hudson, the destruction of slavery in the lower Mississippi valley made headway yet also encountered troubling undercurrents. While Federal military forces were consolidating their hold over the Mississippi River, state restoration – now on a free-state basis – was revitalized in Arkansas and received a major boost in mid-September with the capture of Little Rock. Despite this progress, the hopes that Union military success had raised for free-state initiatives in Tennessee and Louisiana began to dampen. In Tennessee, conservative Unionists conducted a gubernatorial election in August that both Military Governor Andrew Johnson and Abraham Lincoln refused to recognize. By late summer, Johnson had declared for immediate abolition and began to move haltingly toward holding state and congressional elections – until the Union defeat at Chickamauga again put Tennessee's reorganization on hold. In Louisiana, where Lincoln had rebuffed the conservatives in late June, the free-state cause subsequently became bogged down. Lincoln's failure to issue clear instructions as to who was in charge of the free-state constitutional convention initiative exacerbated what were probably unrealistic expectations for how quickly it could be completed. By contrast, conservative Unionists formulated plans to hold congressional elections in November and send representatives to Congress. If free-state Unionists in Louisiana and Tennessee seemed to have gained the upper hand, conservatives showed no signs of capitulating.

In a process that already began before Vicksburg and Gettysburg but accelerated afterward, northern antislavery advocates demonstrated an increasing awareness – partly owing to events in the lower Mississippi valley – of the problem of restoring the rebellious states to the Union while securing the abolition of slavery. In exploring the question of state restoration, some northern commentators countered the widely held belief – to which many scholars still subscribe – that slavery's end was fated. They instead raised the very real possibility of the seceded states returning to the Union while revitalizing or reestablishing slavery. This ramping up of the northern debate over state restoration intersected with the heightened contest between rival Unionist factions in the lower Mississippi valley, establishing the framework within which the issue would be disputed for the remainder of the war.

I

Now that they controlled the entire Mississippi River, Federal military forces turned their attention to securing and administering conquered enemy territory. The large numbers of fugitive slaves who descended on Vicksburg – and on Natchez once that city was occupied in mid-July – complicated the task of providing relief to the starving civilian population. Able-bodied former slaves were employed as military laborers or enlisted as soldiers, while others were put to work on leased plantations or sheltered in refugee camps. Black men now enlisted by the thousands, even though they were relegated to fatigue duty. By early August, Lincoln sent General Lorenzo Thomas back to the lower Mississippi valley to resume his organizing efforts. Lincoln further amplified his support for black military service, beginning to describe it as essential to the Union war effort and the meaning of the war.

Meanwhile, northern merchants and speculators pushed for a revival of trade along the river, which many people believed was necessary to revitalizing Unionism. These considerations had to be weighed against military conditions, as Confederate raids would continue to disrupt life on the Mississippi. Many observers believed that the loss of Vicksburg had dealt the Confederacy a decisive blow and that Unionism in the surrounding area might be cultivated. In Natchez, where support for secession had been restrained, much socializing now took place between the elite and Federal officers. Planters readily resumed their allegiance in hopes of reestablishing control over their former slaves, and they came to new arrangements with their workers – though without conceding slavery's demise.[1]

II

The fall of Vicksburg also revived restoration efforts in Arkansas that had stood dormant for months. The prospects for Arkansas's restoration as a free-state improved dramatically with the conversion of Confederate general Edward W. Gantt to emancipation. A large slaveholder from southwestern Arkansas, Gantt had been elected to Congress in 1860 but never took his seat. He commanded Confederate forces at New Madrid, Missouri, before his June 1863 capture, whereupon he renounced the rebellion and took the loyalty oath. Gantt met with Lincoln in mid-July, and the two men discussed Arkansas's restoration at length. Gantt stressed that the people of the state

---

[1] Previous two paragraphs: Currie, *Enclave*, chaps. 1–3; Hess, *Civil War in the West*, 161–67, 199–208; *Freedom: BME*, 171; *Freedom: WGFL-LS*, 635; *CWL*, 6: 374–75, 406–10; Smith, *Mississippi in the Civil War*, 128–29; Powell and Wayne, "Self-Interest and the Decline of Confederate Nationalism," 30, 35–36; Fanny E. Conner to [Lemuel P. Conner], July 11, 1863, Conner Family Papers, LSU. On Federal relief efforts at Vicksburg, see Manning, *Troubled Refuge*, 134–40.

were tired of war and eager to return to the Union. Lincoln pledged leniency toward former Confederates and support for a loyal government once Little Rock had capitulated, but he insisted that the Emancipation Proclamation would be enforced. After their meeting, Gantt advised that a Unionist newspaper be established in Arkansas and that upcoming Confederate congressional elections be suppressed. Organizing a Unionist convention, he added, would allow the state to "secede from Davis & come home!"[2]

Later that month, Lincoln received word that William K. Sebastian, one of Arkansas's US Senators when it seceded, was willing to resume his seat, and that he enjoyed the support, as a Federal official in Memphis observed, of the "leading men of the State." Born in 1812 and raised and educated in Tennessee, he moved in the mid-1830s to Helena, where he gained admission to the Arkansas bar and became a successful attorney and planter and a leading Democrat. He held various offices, including associate justice of the state Supreme Court and president of the state senate, before being appointed to the US Senate in 1848 to fill a vacancy. Sebastian served in this body until his expulsion in July 1861 for supporting secession. Initially returning to Helena, he resumed planting and practicing law before relocating to Memphis after the Union occupation of it and eastern Arkansas.[3]

Further encouraged over restoring Arkansas as a free state, Lincoln wrote to friend and Illinois political ally General Stephen A. Hurlbut, the Union commander in Memphis, strongly supporting the idea. The Senate would decide on seating Sebastian, Lincoln conceded, but he hoped to link Arkansas's readmission to the abolition of slavery. Insisting that the Emancipation Proclamation applied to Arkansas and would not be retracted, Lincoln was willing to accept gradual abolition for the state, so long as it began immediately. This matter especially concerned him because Missouri Unionists were then considering a gradual abolition proposal that would not *begin* until 1870, a delay that Lincoln feared would allow slavery's defenders to overturn the measure. Any abolition plan "should begin at once," Lincoln insisted. Were Sebastian to endorse such a plan for Arkansas, "a single individual will have scarcely done the world so great a service." Lincoln would have agreed to just about any abolition proposal that began immediately, his secretary John Hay observed. "It deeply interests him now," Hay noted, referring to both the Sebastian initiative and the larger question of

---

[2] E. W. Gantt to [Lincoln], July 15, 1863, ALP; *Freedom: L&L-1865*, 307–8; Finley, "'This Dreadful Whirlpool' of Civil War," 53–72.

[3] B[enjamin] W. Sharp to Lincoln, July 20, 1863, ALP (quotation); *PAJ*, 6: 279n; *OR*, ser. 1, vol. 17, pt. 2, 865–66; Harris, *With Charity for All*, 83–86; Moneyhon, *Impact of the Civil War and Reconstruction on Arkansas*, 77, 157–58; Cowen, "Reorganization of Federal Arkansas," 37; *Biographical Dictionary of the U.S. Congress*, 1786. See also *CWL*, 6: 358–59; DeBlack, *With Fire and Sword*, 88–91.

state restoration. "He considers it the greatest question ever presented to practical statesmanship."[4]

The question was evidently too great for Sebastian's statesmanship. He took no action on Lincoln's suggestion, and the initiative died. "I have seen Mr. Sebastian and shown him your letter," Hurlbut informed Lincoln in early September. "I doubt if Sebastian has nerve enough, to accept the necessities of the times." Any disappointment Lincoln might have felt would have been tempered by his having avoided the difficulty of reconciling military emancipation with gradual abolition, or with his long-held principle of flexibility and state autonomy in ending slavery. As was the case with Lincoln's gradual abolition proposal in December 1862, his suggestion created the potential incongruity of persons in rebellious states, having been *declared* free by the proclamation, remaining enslaved – for who knows how long – under a state gradual abolition plan. Despite going nowhere, the Sebastian dalliance had allowed Lincoln to reaffirm his insistence on linking abolition to state restoration.[5]

By the time Lincoln read Hurlbut's letter, Union forces had captured Little Rock. Following the conquest of Vicksburg, military authorities again turned their attention to Arkansas. General Frederick Steele, now back in command at Helena, set out on August 10 and, overcoming stiff resistance, had by September 10 taken the last of the four state capitals of the lower Mississippi valley. At about the same time, Federal forces operating out of the Indian Territory captured Fort Smith, on Arkansas's western border.[6] Most of Arkansas was now ostensibly under Union control. Although this control in many places was tenuous, Federal military success rejuvenated Unionism in Arkansas and bolstered hopes for the state's restoration. Public meetings were held in places under Federal authority, and northern newspaper reports and other accounts attested to white Arkansans' restored allegiance. Prominent residents also wrote directly to Lincoln to convey that message. Charles P. Bertrand, the acting mayor of Little Rock, called on Lincoln to proclaim a general amnesty, assuring him in October "that Arkansas, ere long, will be numbered among the loyal States of the Federal Union."[7]

After Little's Rock's capture, Gantt returned to the state and assisted in these efforts. He issued a long address in early October recounting the many misdeeds of Confederate authorities and imploring the state's citizens

---

[4] Lincoln to Hurlbut, July 31, 1863, ALP; Burlingame and Ettlinger, *Inside Lincoln's White House*, 68–69.
[5] Hurlbut to Lincoln, September 8, 1863, ALP.
[6] Moneyhon, *Impact of the Civil War and Reconstruction on Arkansas*, 127–28; DeBlack, *With Fire and Sword*, 91–103. See also: *OR*, ser. 1, vol. 22, pt. 1, 468–544, esp. 472–88.
[7] C. P. Bertrand to A. Lincoln, October 19, 1863, ALP; C. C. Bliss to A. Lincoln, November 9, 1863, ALP; Harris, *With Charity for All*, 126–27; Cowen, "Reorganization of Federal Arkansas," 33–34.

to resume their loyalty. While expressing the conventional wisdom that the war had destroyed slavery, he also forwarded the unorthodox contention that slavery, having achieved its historical objective, should be discarded. "[N]egro slavery has accomplished its mission here. A great mission it had," he avowed. "A new and fertile country had been discovered, and must be made useful. The necessities of mankind pressed for its speedy development. Negro slavery was the instrument to effect this. It alone could open up the fertile and miasmatic regions of the South, solving the problem of their utility, which no theorist could have reached." With that objective achieved, slavery's existence "had become incompatible with the existence of the Government." Gantt acknowledged his mistake in thinking that slavery would outlast the Union, not vice versa. "The Government was stronger than slavery," he now admitted. Gantt contributed to reorganization efforts during the fall before returning to Washington, where he further advocated free-state Unionism. He would later become one of the first high-ranking Confederates to receive a pardon under Lincoln's December 1863 Amnesty and Reconstruction proclamation.[8]

III

If freedom was advancing in Arkansas, slavery refused to retreat in Tennessee, as conservative Unionists continued their efforts to seize control of state restoration from Andrew Johnson. Undaunted by the refusal of the Nashville Unionist meeting in July to endorse their proposal for a gubernatorial election, the conservatives nominated William B. Campbell for governor anyway, and they proceeded to organize an election. They secured endorsements from leading newspapers, lending their plan the patina of credibility. The election took place on August 6, though only in certain parts of west and central Tennessee. In what one scholar has called a "farcical contest," Campbell received some 2,500 votes, and his supporters declared him the winner.[9]

Johnson ignored the election result. But perhaps recognizing the potential threat, he shifted further in the ensuing weeks toward integrating abolition – even immediate – into state restoration. In a series of addresses and other communications, Johnson offered a vigorous defense of emancipation, and, acknowledging frustration over the state's delayed reorganization, he promised to hold elections as soon as possible. In Nashville in late August, for

---

[8] Gantt, *Address of Hon. E. W. Gantt*, 19–20; S. A. Hurlbut to [Lincoln], December 29, 1863, ALP; Harris, *With Charity for All*, 127. Gantt reiterated these themes and warned against the growing sentiment for territorialization in the North in an early November address before the Union Club at Little Rock. *New York Times*, December 4, 1863. For northern skepticism over how representative Gantt's support for emancipation was of white Southerners in general, see "General Gantt's Letter," *Harper's Weekly*, November 28, 1863, 755.

[9] Harris, *With Charity for All*, 108–9 (quotation); Trefousse, *Andrew Johnson*, 170.

instance, he called slavery "a cancer on our society" that demanded complete extirpation. Johnson "was for immediate emancipation, if he could get it," the newspaper account of his speech observed, "if this could not be obtained he was for gradual emancipation; but emancipation at all events."[10]

Within days of this address, the Union cause received a major lift in early September when Federal forces occupied Knoxville and Chattanooga. The liberation of east Tennessee, an essential step toward the state's restoration, seemed imminent. "All Tennessee is now clear of armed insurrectionists," Lincoln wrote to Johnson, perhaps counting his chickens. He urged Johnson to lose not a moment in organizing a loyal government. "The re-inauguration must not be such as to give control of the State, and it's representation in Congress, to the enemies of the Union, driving it's friends there into political exile," Lincoln warned. "Let the reconstruction be the work of such men only as can be trusted for the Union. Exclude all others, and trust that your government, so organized, will be recognized here, as being the one of republican form, to be guaranteed to the state." Lincoln hardly had to define "republican" government – but he did so anyway. "I see that you have declared in favor of emancipation in Tennessee, for which, may God bless you," he commended Johnson. "Get emancipation into your new State government – Constitution – and there will be no such word as fail for your case." What mattered most to Lincoln, aside from military victory, was a free-state constitution.[11]

Johnson responded by reassuring Lincoln of his stance on immediate abolition. "I have taken decided ground for Emancipation for immediate emancipation from gradual emancipation," he explained. "Now is the time for settlement of this question." Johnson also appeared ready to advance Tennessee's reorganization with all deliberate speed. Writing from Nashville on September 8, Charles A. Dana, the Assistant Secretary of War who frequently briefed Stanton, reported that Johnson was preparing to order congressional and state elections for early October – only a month hence. "Slavery he says is destroyed in fact," Dana noted, "but must be abolished legally." Johnson was "thoroughly in favor of immediate emancipation" and planned to "recommend it emphatically to the Legislature when it assembles." He was also certain that the large majority of white Tennesseans favored emancipation, "their only doubt being about the subsequent status of the negro," and that "the Legislature will provide for emancipation, either immediately or at an early day." Of course, "the subsequent status of the negro" would remain the all-consuming issue for decades to come.[12]

---

[10] *PAJ*, 6: 334–39, 344–45 (Nashville).
[11] Hess, *Civil War in the West*, 187–90; *CWL*, 6: 440–41.
[12] *CWL*, 6: 187, 468–69; *PAJ*, 6: 377–80; *OR*, ser. 1, vol. 30, pt. 1, 182–83.

Meanwhile, the two west Tennessee representatives on the State Central Committee, which the Unionist convention had appointed in July, issued an address in September urging local Unionists to petition Johnson to order legislative elections. Once convened, the legislature could authorize gubernatorial and congressional elections and elect US Senators. While mentioning neither slavery nor conservative Unionists, the address warned that radical plans such as territorialization might require the state to meet "perhaps insurmountable" conditions for readmission, in addition to abolishing slavery. "Procrastination will be dangerous, possibly fatal," it advised. The address, which was co-authored by a close Johnson ally and could not have been issued without his approval, reflected the growing commitment of free-state Unionists to immediate abolition, even if they clearly opposed racial equality.[13]

Almost as suddenly as the prospects for Tennessee's restoration had brightened, however, they again dimmed – this time with the Union debacle at Chickamauga, in northern Georgia, on September 19–20. The result compelled Johnson to postpone the October elections, which, though not officially announced, had been widely anticipated. Despite the setback, Johnson remained convinced that slavery in Tennessee was doomed. In the reorganization of the state government, he informed General Hurlbut, the Federal commander in Memphis, in early October, "the Slavery question should be settled in this state definitely," while slavery should "no longer constitute an institution established by law." As a practical matter, Johnson considered emancipation as already having taken place; the only issue, he added, reiterating views he had previously expressed to Dana, was the former slaves' legal status. "As soon as we can have anything like a fair & full reflection of popular sentiment it should lead either in the election of a Legislature or a convention," Johnson insisted. "This is a point to be maturely considered."[14]

Conservative Unionists contended that there had already been enough mature consideration on state restoration. They wanted action. They had been pressuring Lincoln to recognize Campbell's election as governor, and with Johnson again putting off elections, they redoubled those efforts. They also condemned any attempt to settle the slavery question before the organizing of a civil government and the restoration of the state to the Union had been completed. Such a policy, they argued, would effectually deprive the state's citizens of deciding on the matter. "We, of course, regard the question of African slavery in Tennessee as one to be referred exclusively to the consideration and decision of the people of this State," insisted the Nashville *Press*. "For those who have an interest in the *future* of Tennessee, this slavery question, and the *negro* question that lies behind it, have an import of transcendent value,

---

[13] "Reconstruction. Political Progress in Tennessee," *New York Times*, September 27, 1863, 6.
[14] *PAJ*, 6: 402–3; Hess, *Civil War in the West*, 190–92.

that demands for their adjustment, the utmost degree of forethought, deliberation, and the spirit of compromise." After calling for deliberation and compromise, the editorial went on to rebuke "transient adventurers" and "slap-dash innovators" for forcing abolition on the state.[15]

Whatever their underlying rationale, the conservatives' charges of stalling at least appeared plausible. Despite Johnson's having informed Charles Dana in early September of his intent to hold elections in early October, more than ten days had passed by the time of the Chickamauga defeat without his having issued an election proclamation. It seems highly unlikely, given conditions in Tennessee, that he could have organized statewide elections so soon. Lincoln probably wished that Johnson would move more quickly with elections, though he was aware of the risks. Johnson had always maintained that state reorganization could not take place until east Tennessee had been secured. Now that his commitment to abolition had significantly upped the ante, he could not risk elections until he was dead sure of the result.

The conservatives continued to press their case. In late September, congressman Emerson Etheridge penned a long letter to Lincoln condemning Johnson's abuse of power as military governor and advocating the recognition of William B. Campbell as the state's civilian governor. "The election of Gen. Campbell has been, in all things, in conformity with the Constitution and laws of Tennessee," Etheridge claimed. Despite Johnson's obstructionism, the vote had gone overwhelmingly (unanimously, Etheridge seemed to suggest) for Campbell, as did public opinion. "[N]early every Union citizen" wanted Campbell installed as governor, Etheridge assured Lincoln, although Campbell would not take office without Lincoln's approval. "Could the Union men of the State be assured that the Federal Government would recognize the validity of said elections, Gen. Campbell would consent to assume the Executive office of the State." Loyal Tennesseans "have confidence in his honor, his honesty, and his courage," Etheridge continued, adding – in a clear slap at Johnson – that Campbell was too honorable "to use power, however conferred, for the gratification of personal or political hate." Because no gubernatorial election was scheduled for another two years, Etheridge concluded, refusal to recognize Campbell would leave "our people the victims of that anarchy, which may, to a great extent, be avoided." Lincoln evidently ignored the letter, since no record of a reply exists. The implications of Lincoln's rejection of the Tennessee conservatives' election stratagem could not be denied.[16]

"The revolution that has been effected in Tennessee is not only political, but moral," wrote the *New York Times* in mid-September – just before the Union

---

[15] *Nashville Daily Union*, September 15, 1863, reprinting and commenting on a recent, undated article from the *Nashville Press*.

[16] Etheridge to Lincoln, September 28, 1863, ALP.

defeat at Chickamauga. "There is a change not only of facts, but of ideas." The paper admitted that "Anti-Slaveryism" had yet to take "any firm foothold in either Middle or West Tennessee." Still, "the people are ready and anxious to accept the Union restored," it insisted, "and are willing to see the fate of Slavery left to determination by natural causes." Slavery's "ultimate extinction in all the States," it concluded, was "merely a matter of time." Considerable evidence supported this contention, yet partisans on either side in Tennessee had much reason to dispute it.[17]

IV

Lincoln's rebuffing of the Tennessee conservatives was less explicit than had been his dismissal of the Louisiana conservatives back in June. Yet such progress as free-state Unionists in Louisiana were able to make with state restoration masked underlying difficulties that eventually came to light. Thomas J. Durant, as de facto free-state leader and state attorney general, assumed charge over registering loyal voters, while Military Governor George F. Shepley had left for Washington in July to confer with Lincoln and Stanton. In Shepley's absence, Durant appealed to Nathaniel P. Banks for assistance with the voter registration, but Banks declined, focused as he was on organizing an expedition into Texas. The free-state group faced various other challenges, in addition to registering voters, that would have been formidable even with military assistance. Without it they were crippling.[18]

Lincoln also sent mixed messages. He again endorsed the free-state Unionists without expressly ordering military authorities to assist them. Following an early-August meeting with Shepley, Lincoln characteristically offered Banks suggestions rather than directives. "While I very well know what I would be glad for Louisiana to do, it is quite a different thing for me to assume direction of the matter," he contended, though he quickly added what he hoped to see done. "I would be glad for her to make a new Constitution recognizing the emancipation proclamation, and adopting emancipation in those parts of the state to which the proclamation does not apply." Lincoln again approved the free-state plan to register loyal voters and hold a constitutional convention, but he also acknowledged the opposition of proslavery Unionists. "As an anti-slavery man I have a motive to desire emancipation, which pro-slavery men do not have," he noted, "but even they have strong enough reason to thus place themselves again under the shield of the Union; and to thus perpetually hedge against the recurrence of the scene through which we are now passing." Having previously pledged to the conservatives the opportunity to conduct congressional elections, Lincoln now pressed the

---

[17] "Observations in Tennessee," *New York Times*, September 18, 1863, 4.
[18] McCrary, *Abraham Lincoln and Reconstruction*, 159–64, 166–69, 181.

free-state group to complete its work before Congress convened. "If these views can be of any advantage in giving shape, and impetus, to action there," Lincoln suggested, "I shall be glad for you to use them prudently for that object." He advised Banks to confer with influential citizens of the state, including Durant, Michael Hahn, and Benjamin F. Flanders, each of whom received a copy of the letter.[19]

This was an ambitious timetable. Although progress had been made in Louisiana's restoration during the previous fifteen months, Lincoln now proposed writing a new constitution and holding congressional elections by the time Congress met in early December, a mere four months hence. Succumbing to typical overstatement, Banks assured Lincoln in early September that these objectives could be accomplished. "I shall not only execute your orders," he crowed, but "I cordially concur in your views," adding that "there will be no serious difficulty in the restoration of this state to the Union." Banks may have indicated his understanding of Lincoln's intentions and his determination to execute Lincoln's "orders." Yet Lincoln had issued no express orders to Banks, and neither had he conferred upon Banks the authority to carry them out. At least this is what Banks later claimed when the plan fell through.[20]

Whereas Lincoln had not issued direct orders, Secretary of War Stanton later did – not to Banks but to Shepley. Stanton's orders, issued on August 24 at Lincoln's behest, authorized and directed Shepley to implement the free-state plan for reconstructing Louisiana. Shepley was to undertake a voter registration – as soon as possible "after the people are relieved from the presence of the rebel troops and included within the lines occupied by the armies of the United States" – that would include only citizens who had voluntarily sworn allegiance to the United States for the purpose of organizing a loyal state government. Shepley was then to conduct an election for delegates to a convention that would write a new constitution, establish a civilian government, and enact "all needful ordinances and laws." The orders included a formula for apportioning delegates that failed to include the qualifier "white," but this omission was no doubt intended to limit the representation of slaveholding areas and not to introduce black suffrage. To all intents and purposes, Lincoln had charged Shepley, not Banks, with implementing the free-state restoration plan.[21]

These orders appeared straightforward, but carrying them out was another matter. Since much of Louisiana remained under Confederate authority, determining when the people of the state would be "relieved from the presence of the rebel troops" – assuming they even wanted to be – would be difficult. Also, Shepley – who, unlike Johnson in Tennessee, was not a resident of the

---

[19] CWL, 6: 364–66.
[20] Banks to Lincoln, September 5, 1863, ALP.
[21] OR, ser. 3, vol. 3, 711–12; McCrary, *Abraham Lincoln and Reconstruction*, 164–65; Harris, *With Charity for All*, 118.

state – envisioned the military governor as subordinate to the military department commander, and, despite Stanton's directive, he took virtually no action without approval from superiors. Compounding this passivity, Shepley did not return to Louisiana until mid-September, an absence of more than two months, during which time the registration stagnated. By the end of the summer, little progress had been made in registering voters beyond New Orleans.[22]

For their part, the conservatives soldiered on with their own campaign for state restoration. Undeterred by Lincoln's rejection of their petition, they met in New Orleans throughout the summer to discuss strategy. Like their Tennessee counterparts, they hatched a plan to hold state and congressional elections in early November, which would have been scheduled under Louisiana's antebellum constitution, in hopes of forcing Lincoln to recognize their work. In early September, just as Banks was assuring Lincoln of Louisiana's free-state reorganization, J. Q. A. Fellows, a New Orleans attorney and leading conservative, proposed to Lincoln that he appoint a "Civil Governor *protem*" who would be empowered to organize November elections for a state government. "The party composing the so-called Union Associations here," Fellows insisted, meaning the free-state group, "is growing less every day & never had many men of influence connected with it, in this community. Their course is very detrimental to the course of the Union."[23]

Lincoln did not respond to Fellows's request, but Louisiana's conservative Unionists met in New Orleans on September 18–19 to formulate their election proposal. They appointed a committee to request Shepley's assistance in organizing state elections in November. Although their overture did not specifically mention congressional elections, Shepley declined on the technicality that no election could be ordered until the state had been redistricted in accordance with the 1860 Federal census, as directed by law. Undaunted, the conservatives established an executive committee that was authorized with securing "as speedily and effectively as possible the reestablishment of a civil government in Louisiana on the basis of the constitution and laws as they stood" prior to secession. In addition to Fellows and other New Orleans delegates, the committee included the planters William J. Minor, E. E. Malhiot, Thomas Cottman, and Andrew McCollam, each of whom had been involved with conservative Unionism since its inception. During the next several weeks, they continued to work toward the November elections. By late summer, free-state Unionists, who enjoyed Lincoln's support, seemed to be foundering, while the conservatives, despite Lincoln's opposition, were moving ahead.[24]

---

[22] McCrary, *Abraham Lincoln and Reconstruction*, 162.
[23] J. Q. A. Fellows to Lincoln, September 5, 1863, ALP; McCrary, *Abraham Lincoln and Reconstruction*, 174–75; Taylor, *Louisiana Reconstructed*, 22.
[24] McCrary, *Abraham Lincoln and Reconstruction*, 175.

V

The political contests in the lower Mississippi valley fueled the growing debate among Northerners, antislavery advocates especially, over state restoration, or Reconstruction. "[T]he return of the seceded states to the Union," noted the influential social reformer Orestes A. Brownson, "is a question that will severely tax American statesmanship, – far more severely than the military suppression of the rebellion has taxed American generalship." Many Northerners believed that the end was nigh, their hopes raised by the recent military victories and growing Confederate discontent. The debate over Reconstruction would ratchet up during the fall, as Congress prepared to convene, and continue throughout the congressional session and indeed for the remainder of the war. Whereas antislavery Northerners in early 1863 had first begun to consider the implications of the Emancipation Proclamation for state restoration, the period following Vicksburg and Gettysburg saw them fully immersed in deliberations over how to restore the seceded states to the Union while securing the end of slavery.[25]

Northern commentators both shaped and reflected public opinion on Reconstruction through various means, including speeches and public addresses, extended essays in mainstream periodicals, and newspaper pieces. In making their arguments, they focused on neither the lower Mississippi valley nor proslavery Unionists, and they expressed almost as much concern over the reenslaving of persons already freed as they did over slavery surviving as an institution. Still, they often invoked the states of the lower Mississippi valley in their analyses. Perhaps more importantly, they teased out the underlying problem that conservative Unionism in those states represented: the possibility of the seceded states returning to the Union under their proslavery constitutions. The contest over state reorganization in the lower Mississippi valley was not the sole factor in alerting antislavery Northerners to the threat of slavery surviving the war, but it was a crucial one. Scholars are familiar with the debate over Reconstruction at this point in the war, but they have less fully appreciated Northerners' trepidation over the rebellious states returning to the Union without abolishing slavery. They have perhaps too readily accepted the view that slavery's demise would inevitably follow northern military victory, or they have incorrectly assumed that a Federal abolition amendment was readily in the offing.[26]

Although Republicans and other antislavery advocates disagreed over various aspects of Reconstruction, virtually all of them equated the defeat of the

---

[25] Brownson, "Return of the Rebellious States," in *Works of Orestes A. Brownson*, 17: 448–77. See also Gienapp and Gienapp, *Civil War Diary of Gideon Welles*, 278 (August 19, 1863).

[26] For an overview of the northern debate over Reconstruction during the second half of 1863, which includes points of emphasis different from those presented here, see Belz, *Reconstructing the Union*, 128–43.

rebellion with the destruction of slavery. The problem, as Michael Vorenberg has observed, "was one of means, not ends." Some moderate and almost all conservative Republicans, subscribing to the view that the states had never left the Union and had retained their rights under the Constitution, expressed reservations over the Federal government explicitly mandating that the seceded states abolish slavery as a condition for restoration. While largely accepting the "republican form of government" clause as the rationale for Reconstruction, they nonetheless cautioned against Reconstruction measures that might upset traditional notions of federalism. Insisting that slavery would never survive the war and that the slaveholders would never regain their previous power and influence, they almost assumed that the seceded states would see the errors of their ways and abolish slavery on their own. Forcing them to adopt this course, if anything, would be counterproductive. Whether the rebellious states "will have the power under their constitutions to establish slavery hereafter is a question to be hereafter considered," noted *Harper's Weekly* before reassuring its readers "that they are not likely to try the experiment."[27]

Other commentators, including most moderate and virtually all Radical Republicans, insisted on an explicit abolition requirement. Without one, they warned, slavery could be revitalized and the slaveholders restored to power. Given its awesome political, social, and economic influence, slavery, no matter how badly damaged, was never going to wither away. The fact that Lincoln had as yet announced no official Reconstruction policy – in addition to reports that his Cabinet was divided over Reconstruction, with "radicals" Salmon P. Chase and Edwin M. Stanton squared off against "conservatives" William H. Seward and Montgomery Blair – also contributed to concerns that slavery might survive the war. So did the apprehension that Lincoln might modify or rescind the Emancipation Proclamation as part of a peace initiative or negotiated settlement, or that the Union might achieve military victory before abolition had become established policy. "If the Rebellion should suddenly collapse, democrats, copperheads & Seward would insist upon

---

[27] Vorenberg, *Final Freedom*, 42; "The National and State Governments," *Harper's Weekly*, September 19, 1863, 594. For other articulations of these views during the summer and fall of 1863 in the *New York Times*, see "Peace and Reconstruction," July 19, 4; "The Question of Reconstruction," August 13, 4; "Union and Reconstruction. Their Mode and Condition," August 25, 4; "The Disappearance of Slavery and Its Consequences," September 18, 4; "The Administration and the War," November 14, 1 (the text of an address by Henry J. Raymond on November 6 in Wilmington, Del.); "'Masterly Inactivity' the True Civil Policy Toward Slavery," November 27. Additional articles include "The Policy of the Government," and "How To Do It," *Harper's Weekly*, August 15, 514, 515; "The Policy of the Administration Towards the Rebels," *New York Herald*, September 3, 4; "The State Plan of Government," *Harrisburg (PA) Weekly Patriot and Union*, November 5, 2; "Slavery after the Rebellion," *The Living Age*, vol. 78, no. 1008 (September 26): 614–15.

amnesty & the Union & 'no questions asked about Slavery,'" Charles Sumner complained following Gettysburg. If Lee's army had been destroyed, he continued, expressing the commonly held view that the Union had squandered a golden opportunity to end the rebellion after the battle, "that question would have been upon us."[28]

Among the first systematic attempts to address the problem of state restoration following Gettysburg and Vicksburg was an essay entitled "The Return of the Rebellious States to the Union," by William Whiting, a general solicitor within the War Department. Originally delivered as an open letter to the Union League of Philadelphia in late July, the piece was published in pamphlet form and reprinted widely in the northern press, igniting a firestorm of commentary. Whiting's insistence on treating the seceded states as "conquered districts" probably attracted the most attention, but the possibility of those states returning to the Union after military defeat and reestablishing slavery was his central concern, and it underpinned the entire discourse.

Were former Confederates to be shown leniency following Union victory, as many people were proposing, they would quickly regain control of the state governments, elect members to Congress and insist they be seated, and demand the restoration of their "former privileges and immunities as citizens of the United States." They would also revive laws "making slavery the cornerstone of their local government," Whiting contended, evoking a familiar phrase, "and they may make slavery perpetual, in violation of the laws of the United States and the proclamation of the President."

Lest this scenario seemed far-fetched, Whiting offered the reminder that persons "representing themselves as Union men" from the occupied South, including Louisiana, "are now knocking at the door of Congress for admission into the Union." They must not be admitted "without proper safeguards," he advised. "Do not allow old States, with their Constitutions still unaltered, to resume State powers." All of Whiting's theorizing was intended to prevent this sole outcome. "Now, if the rebellious States shall attempt to return to the Union with constitutions guaranteeing the perpetuity of slavery, – if the laws of these States shall be again revived and put in force against free blacks and slaves," he cautioned, "we shall at once have reinstated in the Union, in all its force and wickedness, that very curse which has brought on the war and all its terrible train of sufferings." The slaveholders were fighting for the perpetuation of slavery, Whiting insisted. "Shall we hand over to them, at the end of the war, just what they have been fighting for?" he asked rhetorically. "If you concede

[28] Palmer, *Selected Letters of Charles Sumner*, 2: 184 (quotation), 186. For disagreement between Welles and Chase on Reconstruction, see the entries for August 12, 13, 19, and 22, 1863, in Gienapp and Gienapp, *Civil War Diary of Gideon Welles*, 271–74, 277–78, 280–83. Throughout the summer and fall, the *New York Herald* reported repeatedly on Cabinet dissension over Reconstruction, though as a staunchly Democratic paper, it would have been expected to highlight Republicans' difficulties.

State rights to your enemies," he continued, "what security can you have that traitors will not pass State laws which will render the position of the blacks intolerable; *or reduce them all to slavery?*" Requiring the seceded states to adopt free-state constitutions was the only way to avoid this eventuality. Tellingly, Whiting addressed no other issue pertaining to state restoration than the fate of slavery.[29]

The Maine jurist Woodbury Davis, a founding member of the Republican Party, echoed these themes in an essay entitled "Political Problems and Conditions of Peace," published in *The Atlantic Monthly* in August. Davis's main concern was also preventing slavery from surviving the war. He recognized the crucial distinction between military emancipation and abolition, and he insisted that the Federal government prosecute the war "until Slavery is abolished, *and forever prohibited,* within all the Rebel States." Because the Emancipation Proclamation had not abolished slavery, the seceded states *must* be required to abolish slavery as a condition for readmission to the Union. "It would be worse than madness," he warned, to allow the states back into the Union under "their present constitutions upholding Slavery." In order to prevent the states from ever subsequently reestablishing slavery, Davis added, the Federal government must also demand "the *perpetual prohibition* of Slavery within the Rebel States."

Paradoxically, having accentuated the possibility of slavery surviving the war, Davis downplayed the threat of conservative Unionism in the seceded states. "There is no evidence that loyal persons in the Rebel States claim or desire to uphold the existence of those States, under their present constitutions, with the system of Slavery," he asserted. Yet this was precisely what proslavery Unionists in Tennessee and Louisiana were trying to do. Despite this oversight, Davis went on to dismantle the conservatives' *raison d'être.* "It is their misfortune to reside in States that have revolted," he insisted. Their loyalty did not spare their states from being considered "enemies" of the national authority; neither did it "prevent *their own* condition from being determined by that of their States." As slaveholders, they bore "in part" responsibility for the rebellion of their states. "The theory, therefore, that such loyal men constitute loyal States, still existing, in distinction from the States that have rebelled, is utterly groundless."[30]

Few Americans at the time spoke with more moral authority on slavery than did Charles Sumner, the US Senator from Massachusetts and leading Radical Republican. In October, Sumner offered his first systematic treatment of the question of Reconstruction in an essay entitled "Our Domestic Relations," which appeared in *The Atlantic Monthly* and drew widespread discussion in

---

[29] Whiting, *Return of the Rebellious States to the Union,* 3–4, 5–6, 14–15. (Italics in original.)
[30] Woodbury Davis, "Political Problems and Conditions of Peace," *The Atlantic Monthly,* vol. 12, no. 7 (August 1863): 253–59 (quotations, 253, 254, 255, 256, 259).

the North. (Originally published anonymously, it was strongly suspected to be the work of Sumner.) In a disquisition deeply rooted in constitutional history and theory, Sumner examined the various justifications for Reconstruction legislation and explored the practical issues that state restoration entailed. His central points were that slavery, as a local institution, had ceased to exist legally the moment a state had engaged in rebellion; that the rebellious states, once defeated, would come under the direct authority of Congress; that only Congress – not the president – could set the conditions for their return to the Union; and that those conditions must include, among other things, the abolition of slavery. Only near the end of the essay did Sumner turn to the problem of slavery being preserved and revitalized. While he framed the issue in terms of the reenslaving of persons who had already gained their freedom, rather than the survival of slavery as a legal institution, his main concern was that "the freedmen will be rescued from hands that threaten to cast them back into Slavery."

Without mentioning restoration efforts in Louisiana or Tennessee, Sumner pointed to copious evidence of "what the restored State governments will do." Conservatives on the floor of Congress were already openly embracing "the horrid menace of reënslavement," and some newspapers were endorsing the idea. "That is to say, no matter what may be done for Emancipation, whether by Proclamation of the President, or by Congress even, the State, on resuming its place in the Union, will, in the exercise of its sovereign power, reënslave every colored person within its jurisdiction," Sumner warned. "The brutal pretension thus flamingly advanced, to reënslave those who have been set free, puts us all on our guard," he continued. "There must be no chance or loop-hole for such an intolerable, Heaven-defying iniquity." Even as he declared slavery already legally dead in the rebellious states, Sumner invoked the specter of reenslavement in advocating that those states be prohibited ever to resuscitate it. Significantly, Sumner – as was true of Whiting and Davis – did not so much as hint at a Federal abolition amendment. Congress must require the *states* to abolish slavery.[31]

---

[31] [Charles Sumner], "Our Domestic Relations; Or, How To Treat the Rebel States," *The Atlantic Monthly*, vol. 12, no. 72 (October 1863): 507–29, esp. 527–28. Sumner had already composed the essay by late August. Palmer, *Selected Letters of Charles Sumner*, 2: 188. In a letter from late-July 1863, the British Member of Parliament and radical reformer John Bright had written to Sumner on Reconstruction in a letter Sumner forwarded to Lincoln: "Would it be possible to declare that, in accordance with the [Emancipation] Proclamation, Slavery was legally at an end & that anything in the Constitution & laws of the states which legalized & enacted Slavery must be repealed & abolished to give them a right to their ancient position in the Republic?" Bright asked. "Unless something definite & resolute is done," he continued, "you may have the states repealing their ordinances of Secession, & announcing their old position in the nation, & electing members to Congress &c and then beginning a fight with the central Govt. in the Supreme Court as to the legality of the Proclamation, & insisting on the retention of

One commentator who broached the idea of Federal abolition was Orestes A. Brownson, who also explored many of the foregoing themes in an essay entitled "Return of the Rebellious States," published in October. Yet even Brownson's main point was that Congress must not readmit the seceded states until they had abolished slavery. Brownson castigated the "so-called 'conservative Republicans'" and "copperhead Democrats," who, maintaining that the seceded states had never left the Union, advocated their return "with their old state constitutions still in full life and vigor." These persons, proclaiming to uphold the Union but "really in sympathy with the rebels," were "more intent on preserving slavery than on saving the nation." Brownson acknowledged the genuine Unionists in the seceded states, but, like Woodbury Davis, he countered that they did not represent their states. Neither should any members-elect from these states be seated in Congress. "These states, though they might have fewer slaves, would all be slaveholding states as much as they were before the outbreak of the civil war, and would be even more tenacious of remaining such." Although Congress, not having considered the matter thoroughly, had previously seated "very respectable gentleman from Virginia, Tennessee, and Louisiana," it had established no inviolable precedent. These states, Brownson insisted, had "no more right to representation in congress than Timbuctoo, Dahomey, or Senegambia."

Brownson also emphasized the distinction between military emancipation and abolition and highlighted its implications. The Emancipation Proclamation "abolishes slavery nowhere, and could not do it. There is a wide difference between emancipating slaves actually held in bondage and abolishing slavery." Thus, any rebellious state could abandon the Confederacy, return to the Union under its proslavery constitution, and remand emancipated persons to slavery – all in defiance of Federal authority. "A state may

> Slavery. The Govt. would be powerless under such circumstances – all the base pro-slavery party in the North would unite with the South & possibly your next Presidential election may be made to turn on this vital question, & your whole nation may be dishonored for ever by the repudiation of the Proclamation which the existing Administration has failed to sustain." Palmer, *Selected Letters of Charles Sumner*, 2: 187–88n. It is worth noting that some of Bright's language sounds similar to language Lincoln would use in his letter of November 1863 to Nathaniel Banks, discussed in Chapter 9, warning of Louisiana possibly being restored to the Union as a slave state.
>
> Sumner's essay prompted a flurry of commentary, including from Montgomery Blair, Lincoln's postmaster general. In a blistering public address in early October, largely in response to Sumner and widely reprinted, Blair castigated what he called the "revolutionary schemes of the ultra abolitionists," juxtaposing them to "the policy of the President." Despite his vitriol, Blair reaffirmed his commitment to universal emancipation on the basis of restoring "Republican Governments" in the seceded states. As the frank but civil exchange between Blair and Sumner also demonstrated, the essential difference between them was not over emancipation but over how best to secure it under the Constitution. [Blair], *Speech of the Hon. Montgomery Blair*; Palmer, *Selected Letters of Charles Sumner*, 2: 204–5; Vorenberg, *Final Freedom*, 41–42.

declare any portion of its population slaves that it chooses, so long as slavery is held to be not repugnant to the constitution of the United States, or inconsistent with a republican form of government." Brownson likewise repeatedly denied that slavery's demise was inevitable. "Let us not be deceived by the vain talk that slavery is dead, that the system is so shaken that it cannot survive, and that we need trouble ourselves no more about it," he contended, in one of several such passages in the essay. "It will not die, but revive in more than its former ferocity," if the policy of northern conservatives were followed. "That policy suppresses the rebellion indeed, but leaves slavery unabolished, and the slave interest as powerful as ever, and even more virulent. On that policy slavery is not dead nor likely to die."

Indeed, because nothing under the current constitutional framework barred any state from either introducing or reestablishing slavery in the future, Brownson reasoned, the only way to prohibit slavery forever throughout the United States would be to amend the Federal Constitution. Yet Brownson, like so many others of his time, preferred "to leave the constitution as it was left by our fathers." Neither could such a change be made without the consent of the seceded states after they had been readmitted. Until then, the proponents of abolition had to rely on the principle "that no state be admitted into the Union whose constitution does not exclude slavery." This method did not provide "absolute security," Brownson admitted, "but it will probably prove practically sufficient." In any event, "it is all that can be obtained even from the loyal states in their present temper." Few antislavery advocates would have found this a satisfying answer, but Brownson had identified a key conundrum they had yet to resolve.[32]

The debate trundled on, but the "temper" of the free states was already showing signs of shifting. As Michael Vorenberg has observed, abolitionists launched petition drives in 1863, especially during the second half of the year, and often with northern women as the driving force, urging Congress to make emancipation universal. Abolitionists had been petitioning for Federal antislavery action since the start of the war, and Congress had responded with various piece-meal measures, such as the confiscation acts, largely predicated on military necessity. What was needed now was some sweeping, comprehensive

---

[32] Brownson, "Return of the Rebellious States," in *Works of Orestes A. Brownson*, vol. 17 (quotations, 448, 455, 460, 461, 467, 471–74). For other essays published during the fall of 1863 (and into 1864) that addressed many of these issues, see [The Hon. F. P. Stanton], "The Restoration of the Union," *The Continental Monthly*, vol. 4, no. 4 (October 1863): 444–51; [Henry Everett Russell], "Reconstruction," *The Continental Monthly*, vol. 4, no. 6 (December 1863): 684–89; [Francis Wayland, Jr.], "Letter to a Peace Democrat. Addressed to Andrew Jackson Brown," *The Atlantic Monthly*, vol. 12, no. 74 (December 1863): 776–89; [Stephen Pearl Andrews], "The Great American Crisis," *The Continental Monthly*, vol. 4, no. 6 (December 1863): 658–70 (pt. 1), vol. 5, no. 1 (January 1864): 87–99 (pt. 2), esp. 96–99, and vol. 5, no. 3 (March 1864): 300–17 (pt. 3).

measure. As had often been true of abolitionist thought before the war, these petitions were usually vague on precisely *how* to achieve this goal. Some expressly called for an abolition amendment to the US Constitution, others for legislative emancipation, and still others prescribing no specific means at all. As Orestes Brownson demonstrated, most Americans, even antislavery advocates, were still only beginning to come to terms by mid-1863 with the idea of amending the US Constitution as a means of enacting social or political reform. They still largely assumed that the *states* would abolish slavery. Nonetheless, if antislavery advocates had reached no consensus on a constitutional amendment, popular support was growing for Federal action against slavery. Of equal significance, as Vorenberg also notes, a small but important number of War Democrats were starting to advocate, for various constitutional, ideological, and partisan reasons, a Federal abolition amendment. Such a measure confronted countless challenges, and at this point it was no more than an idea, but it was no longer as inconceivable as it had once been.[33]

Because many Northerners, even antislavery advocates, remained dubious of a Federal abolition amendment, they continued to face the problem of securing the return of the seceded states to the Union on a free-state basis while upholding traditional notions of federalism. As this sampling of the debate over state restoration shows, there were emerging points of consensus. It would be an overstatement to say that the contest over state restoration in the lower Mississippi valley – or the threat of conservative Unionism – was the sole factor in awakening Northerners to the possibility of slavery surviving the war, but this awakening cannot be understood without it. Moreover, as the northern debate over state restoration further dovetailed with the efforts of conservative Unionists in Tennessee and Louisiana to preserve their states' proslavery constitutions, the momentum behind a Federal abolition amendment would continue to build.

* * *

In his early-August letter to Nathaniel Banks endorsing the free-state convention plan, Lincoln also offered one of his first substantive statements since issuing the Emancipation Proclamation on the South's emerging labor system. "I think it would not be objectionable for [Louisiana] to adopt some practical system by which the two races could gradually live themselves out of their old relation to each other, and both come out better prepared for the new," he remarked. "After all, the power, or element, of 'contract' may be sufficient for this probationary period; and, by it's simplicity, and flexibility, may be the better." Lincoln no doubt had in mind Federally sponsored wartime free labor in the Union-occupied South, especially Louisiana, which had provoked much

---

[33] Vorenberg, *Final Freedom*, 36–40, 43–46.

harsh criticism. But he was also addressing the larger issues to which the end of slavery as a labor system would give rise. Although Lincoln believed at this point that the two sides – white and black, former master and former slave – would reach mutually agreeable arrangements based on the free-labor principle of the freedom of contract, he also realized that both parties would require a "probationary period" in adjusting to the new circumstances. During the next two years, Lincoln would come to question this viewpoint, especially whether the free-labor idea of a mutuality of interests infused the relationship between capital and labor, and whether it provided an adequate model for the postemancipation South.

Lincoln's comments presupposed the ultimate destruction of slavery, but much evidence showed this outcome to be far from certain. Indeed, (former) masters and (former) slaves on the plantations of the lower Mississippi valley were battling over the contours of the new social order even as it remained unclear whether "their old relation to each other" had ever died.

8

"The Name of 'Slavery'"

Insofar as slavery was a legal institution grounded in property rights, its destruction was essentially a political question, one that had become inseparable from state restoration and would be decided by the states and the Federal government. As a labor system, set of social relations, and way of life, by contrast, slavery would be destroyed on farms and plantations in the countryside, and in the innumerable conflicts between slaves, slaveholders, Federal officials, and other parties. The disintegration of slavery and the construction of systems of voluntary labor to replace it were both integral to the process of translating military emancipation into constitutional abolition. Federal military and civilian authorities assumed primary responsibility for substantiating the freedom of former slaves even as wartime free labor exposed the limits of military emancipation. In many respects, the conflict between planters and former slaves on the plantations of the lower Mississippi valley – mediated by Federal authority – replicated the political contest between free-state and conservative Unionists over state restoration.

The struggle over labor in the lower Mississippi valley unfolded within two separate agricultural systems. The sugar region of southern Louisiana and the cotton country to the north offered many contrasts during the war, owing to how each was conquered, the divided military command structure over them, and their differing crop regimes. Yet Federal officials in both areas confronted the same interconnected problems of fostering Unionism, providing relief to fugitive slaves, implementing new labor arrangements, and reviving the plantation economy. They improvised labor policies for the 1863 agricultural season that prohibited the worst features of slavery but in other respects were voluntary in name only. The results satisfied almost no one.

In southern Louisiana, which Federal forces had captured relatively quickly, many sugar planters began by early 1863 to organize politically and to work collectively to reestablish control over labor and preserve slavery. By no means were they conceding defeat. The cotton area, by contrast, was too expansive and too politically splintered for the planters to organize into a single movement. In any event, the Vicksburg campaign convulsed the entire region south of Memphis, and many cotton planters simply took flight with their slaves into the Confederate interior. Federal authorities instituted a leasing program for these abandoned and confiscated cotton plantations, while resident planters who remained on their estates were compelled to reach new arrangements with their workers under Federal auspices.

Much as the fall of Vicksburg raised the stakes in the political contest over state restoration, conflict intensified during the second half of 1863 over modes of life and labor that would replace slavery on the region's plantations. As slavery continued to collapse throughout the lower Mississippi valley, the efforts of Federal officials to revitalize plantation agriculture ran headlong into the former slaveholders' and former slaves' contrasting notions of labor, and of almost everything else, as they engaged one another on a new basis. The 1863 harvest buttressed sugar planters' traditional claim that sugar could not be made in Louisiana with voluntary labor. Yet some planters also gave the first indications of what would become an increasingly divided mind. They might be willing to abandon "the name of 'slavery,'" as one of them conceded, to retain the substance. In the cotton country, resident planters were equally determined to maintain the racial dominance and labor control that inhered in slavery – by whatever name it went – even as they accommodated themselves to the new order.

I

In southern Louisiana, which fell within the purview of the military Department of the Gulf, sugar planters hoped to preserve slavery even as they enlisted Federal authority in attempting to regain control over their workers for the new agricultural year. Following the chaotic fall 1862 harvest, planters made the necessary arrangements to operate their estates without acknowledging the loss of their right to property in slaves or slavery's very existence. They held meetings in New Orleans in early 1863 to discuss their plight, hoping to capitalize on General Nathaniel P. Banks's attempt to cultivate Unionism and repair the damage of his predecessor, Benjamin F. Butler.

Despite his accommodationist approach, Banks was not about to grant the planters carte blanche. In late January, he established the broad outlines of labor policy for the new year and authorized the Sequestration Commission – the military agency charged with administering plantation affairs in southern Louisiana – to devise specific regulations. Banks's system would be predicated on the assumption that all persons capable of self-support must "maintain themselves by labor" but that "labor is entitled to some equitable proportion of the crops it produces." Toward those ends, Banks instructed the commission, after it had conferred with the various parties involved, to establish "a yearly system of negro labor" that would provide the laborers with basic necessities, proper treatment, and "just compensation." Once labor arrangements had been accepted, the instructions continued, "all the conditions of continuous and faithful service, respectful deportment, correct discipline and perfect subordination, shall be enforced on the part of the negroes by the officers of the Government." Events would show these terms to be open to any number of interpretations. "This may not be the best," Banks admitted, "but it is now the only practicable system."[1]

One week later, in early February, the Sequestration Commission issued labor regulations in the form of a standardized contract and accompanying directive. The contract – which was between the Federal government and individual planters, *not* between planters and laborers – provided that army provost marshals will "induce the Slaves to return to the Plantations where they belong" and "require them, and those remaining on the Plantations to work diligently and faithfully" for the entire year. Without explicitly prohibiting corporal punishment, the regulations required the laborers to exhibit respectful deportment and perfect subordination while enjoining the planters to "treat them properly." In addition to food and clothing, the workers would collectively receive a one-twentieth share of the crop, or individuals would receive monthly wages of between $1 and $3 (depending on sex and occupation). These rates were far below the $10 of the previous year and what soldiers or military laborers currently received. The contract referred to planters as "employers" but to laborers as "the Slaves," who were expressly deemed not party to the contract. The laborers' presence on the plantation would constitute "proof of their assent," but the employer's acceptance of the contract did not imply "the surrender of any right of property in the slave." Banks defended the program as an attempt to restore plantation operations "upon a system compatible with the laws and spirit of the age," and he directed military personnel to make that objective generally known.[2]

Banks's program envisioned black plantation workers and white planters relating to one another as labor and capital rather than as master and slave. It also reflected the northern free-labor notion that labor and capital shared a mutuality of interests and were not locked in immutable class warfare. Yet over the ensuing months, these assumptions proved deficient, as the parties contested every aspect of plantation life and labor, with Federal military officials playing the role, not always objectively, of arbiter. Despite the supposition that antebellum work routines would serve as a template for labor arrangements, the reality was that everything was now up for grabs. In a larger sense, disputes over the particulars of plantation routine signaled the contrasting outlooks of laborers and planters. Rejecting slavery's legal existence and southern Louisiana's exemption from the Emancipation Proclamation, laborers considered themselves *former* slaves, whereas planters

---

[1] *Freedom: WGFL-LS*, 355, 414–15 (doc. 81). On the early period of Banks's administration: McCrary, *Abraham Lincoln and Reconstruction*, chap. 3; Rodrigue, *Reconstruction in the Cane Fields*, 38–43; *Freedom: WGFL-LS*, 354.
[2] *Freedom: WGFL-LS*, 355, 419–21 (doc. 84).

were intent on maintaining the old relations. Moreover, as Stephanie McCurry argues, Federal labor policy betrayed officials' obsession with the former slaves' domestic relations and with marriage and traditional patriarchalism as the antidote to the dependency on government support that they feared would result from emancipation. Yet this thinking was itself undermined, McCurry further contends, by the wholesale conscription of young men into the Union army – especially as the Vicksburg-Port Hudson campaigns intensified – and the resulting preponderance of women, children, and the elderly on many plantations.[3]

No sooner had Banks outlined his program than planters objected to any compromising of their old authority or right to slave property. Describing themselves as "loyal citizens and planters," a committee of planters in St. James Parish insisted that southern Louisiana had been excluded from the Emancipation Proclamation and that slavery still existed there. The planters acknowledged that "slavery is abolished" in areas where the proclamation applied, but they contended that slavery in their region "is expressly maintained as if the proclamation had not been issued." Banks's "voluntary system of labor" might be appropriate "for those portions of Louisiana where slavery is no longer permitted under the President's proclamation," they admitted, but its enforcement in areas "where slavery is maintained, would be an attempt to reconcile things which, in their nature, are utterly incompatible." Such enforcement would also amount "to an actual and immediate emancipation of all slaves of the State of Louisiana," since "voluntary or free labor cannot be governed by the same rules as forced labor, without changing entirely the status of the slaves." The planters put forward their own solution to the problem of labor disruption. Recognizing the Federal prohibition against military personnel returning fugitive slaves to their owners, they proposed that the civil authorities be permitted to organize "police guards and patrols" in accordance with local ordinances. Under this system, "the Slaves could . . . be made to return to and labor steadily on the plantations of their owners." This goal could be achieved peaceably, the planters added, so long as Banks's strictures against vagrancy and idleness were enforced and Federal military personnel were forbidden "to encourage or assist slaves to leave their masters." The reference to "slaves" and "masters" was no oversight.[4]

The St. James committee leveled but one of many critiques of Banks's policy. Laborers on the plantations, along with their advocates in New Orleans, Washington, and the North, rejected its draconian elements. Although it

---

[3] Rodrigue, *Reconstruction in the Cane Fields*, 40–42 (and the sources cited therein); *Freedom: WGFL-LS*, 354–60, 401–58 (docs. 74–95); McCurry, *Women's War*, 92–104.

[4] *Freedom: WGFL-LS*, 421–23 (doc. 85). At about the same time, a delegation of planters in nearby Terrebonne Parish forwarded a similar proposal, suggesting that the civil authorities be granted "the authority formerly held under the laws of the state to Arrest and imprison" fugitive slaves (423n).

eliminated slavery's worst attributes, these critics contended, it was still ersatz slavery. Laborers were to be treated "properly" and receive "equitable" compensation, but Banks's program could hardly be described as a "voluntary system of labor." Yet had the regulations been more solicitous of labor, the planters still had a point. How could they be expected to work their plantations with voluntary labor if Lincoln had expressly excluded them from the Emancipation Proclamation? Also, Banks may have been pushing the boundaries of freedom as far as he could, given the political and legal limitations he faced, but his regulations expressly refrained from invalidating the planters' right to property in slaves. Indeed, the planters could have made an even stronger case, since nowhere had the proclamation, as they mistakenly noted, "abolished" slavery. Even in those parts of Louisiana where the proclamation applied, slavery still legally existed. Moreover, although they did not mention it, those St. James planters who had taken the oath of allegiance were also excluded from the 1862 Confiscation Act, since their area had already been under Federal military control when that act was passed.

Not all planters in southern Louisiana could claim to be loyal. Because so many had fled to the Confederate interior, the Federal government assumed control of dozens of estates, many of which it leased to private individuals, including Northerners. These lessees adhered to different ideas about labor, but they were often imbued with the racialistic attitudes endemic to nineteenth-century American society. Even when they were not, they still confronted the challenge of supervising laborers whose ideas of freedom extended beyond returning to the same old work routines for paltry compensation. "I cannot go ahead with the work on this place unless I can controul the labor I pay for," complained one northern lessee. Although espousing the virtues of "voluntary" labor, Federal officials often resorted to various forms of coercion in dealing with – in their view – recalcitrant workers. "No plantation can be successfully worked unless the overseer has full control of the laborers," a Federal supervisor of plantations insisted, employing language the slaveholders would have appreciated, "and most perfect obedience must be exacted from them or all attempts at Cultivations will prove a failure."[5]

Intent on preserving slavery, the planters of southern Louisiana initially agreed to Nathaniel Banks's labor policy only because they had no choice, even though it weighed far more heavily in their interests than in the laborers'. Neither did Banks challenge the planters' claim to property in their slaves. That being said, the planters had begun by mid-1863 to make concessions to their workers and to come to terms with the new labor arrangements. On virtually every specific matter of plantation routine, they were compelled to bargain for the services of persons whom they still considered their property. Moreover, even when Federal officials blatantly favored planters in adjudicating disputes,

---

[5] *Freedom: WGFL-LS*, 358–60, 405–7 (doc. 77), 447–53 (doc. 93; quotation, 453).

the very act of appealing to Federal authority compromised their authority as slaveholders. Only at their peril did planters ignore the spirit of independence their laborers now exhibited. When they did, as one officer reported in June, "the consequence is, trouble, immediately – and the negroes band together, and lay down their own rules, as to when, and how long they will work &c &c. and the Overseer loses all control over them." By contrast, those planters "who seem to have recognized this feeling, and who have caused it to be respected – at least, in a measure," the same official added, "have had less negroes leave them, and have much better crops than the average."[6]

II

The situation that sugar planters found so disconcerting in 1863 compared favorably to affairs in the cotton-producing areas of the lower Mississippi valley, which largely fell under the authority of the Federal military Department of the Tennessee and was coterminous with the Army of the Tennessee under General Ulysses S. Grant. The appointment of Colonel John Eaton as Superintendent of Freedmen for the department and the establishment of contraband camps the previous fall had brought a measure of stability to the region. But implementation of the Emancipation Proclamation and renewal of the Vicksburg campaign during the winter and spring disrupted plantations as far south as Natchez and brought thousands more fugitive slaves into Union lines. "This country is in a deplorable state. The outrages of the Yankees and Negroes are enough to frighten one to death," lamented Kate Stone. "The country seems possessed by demons, black and white." Even as military operations liberated more slaves, the planters' abandonment of their estates brought thousands of acres of farmland under Federal control, presenting both opportunities and challenges for reviving the plantation economy while reconstituting the former slaves' working lives.[7]

Numerous proposals to achieve those objectives were forwarded to Secretary of War Edwin M. Stanton, who instructed Adjutant General Lorenzo Thomas, as part of the latter's mission to recruit black soldiers and organize black regiments in the lower Mississippi valley during the spring, to devise a means of employment for the able-bodied and support for persons deemed unfit for productive labor or military service. Thomas readily embraced the idea of linking black military service, Union loyalty, and revival

---

[6] *Freedom: WGFL-LS*, 357, 454–56 (doc. 94; quotations, 455–56). For a northern assessment of the progress of free labor in southern Louisiana by mid-1863, see "Symptoms of Caving-In," *Harper's Weekly*, June 6, 1863, 354.

[7] Anderson, *Brokenburn*, 184 (March 22, 1863); Fanny E. Conner to [Lemuel P. Conner], June 20–21, 1863, Conner Family Papers, LSU. On the unsettled state of affairs in the cotton-producing areas of the lower Mississippi valley during 1863, especially as a result of the Vicksburg campaign, see [Eaton], *Report of the General Superintendent*, 3–12.

of the plantation economy throughout the lower Mississippi valley. He was also driven, as were so many others of this era, by fears that the former slaves would become permanently dependent on government support. By mid-April, some two weeks after arriving there, he had formulated a plan, which he forwarded to Stanton.[8]

In essence, Thomas proposed leasing abandoned plantations, mostly on the west side of the Mississippi River, to "persons of proper character and qualifications" – presumably Northerners and southern Unionists. These persons might also enter into agreements with local planters of demonstrable loyalty. Thomas's plan combined elements of voluntary and involuntary labor. Former slaves would be relocated from contraband camps to the plantations and employed on a wage-labor basis, receiving monthly wages of $7 for men and $5 for women. Children between the ages of twelve and fifteen received less, and those younger than twelve were exempt from field labor. Lessees were required to provide laborers with food, housing, and clothing, the last of which would be deducted from the laborers' wages, at cost. The laborers were to be treated "humanely," and corporal punishment was prohibited. Military authorities were to supply any lessee, upon application, with "as many negroes ... as he may desire." This provision effectually denied laborers the choice of employer, although Thomas also prohibited the involuntary separation of families. Once hired, the laborers would remain to complete the crop. Lessees assumed responsibility for all matters relating to plantation management, leaving the laborers with little say over their working lives. Plantations not leased out would be operated by superintendents "for the exclusive benefit of the government," or "upon such terms as, in their judgment, shall be best adapted to the welfare of the negroes, taking care that, in all plans adopted, the negroes shall be self-sustaining, and not become a charge upon the Government." Thomas did not allow for former slaves to work the plantations independently.

Women, children, and men unfit for military service would constitute the main plantation workforces, whereas able-bodied men would be conscripted either as military laborers or soldiers. One of the main responsibilities of the black regiments would be to guard the leased and operating plantations against Confederate attack. "The negro Regiments could give protection to these plantations, and also operate effectively against the guerillas," Thomas explained. "This would be particularly advantageous on the Mississippi River, as the negroes, being acquainted with the peculiar country lining its banks, would know when to act effectively. They could also garrison positions, and thus additional regiments could be sent to the front." Thus, as Amy Murrell Taylor has observed, Thomas's plan "essentially reenvisioned the

---

[8] For Stanton's order to Thomas, see *OR*, ser. 3, vol. 3, 100–1. See also *Freedom: WGFL-LS*, 630, 677–80 (doc. 158).

antebellum plantation as something more akin to a fortified village." Similarly, the black women working on these plantations would play a vital role in the Union war effort, occupying conquered "enemy" territory, providing a buffer between the Confederate interior and the river, and reducing the number of persons requiring government support.[9]

Thomas admitted that the safety of persons on leased plantations could not be guaranteed, but he expressed confidence "that the military organization of the negroes will afford all the protection necessary." He had already submitted his plan to Grant, he informed Stanton, who approved it. Also, "several gentlemen of Capital have already applied for lands to cultivate," he noted, "and but for the lateness of the season . . . I would have no doubt of its success." With this plan, "it is hoped to accomplish much in demonstrating that the freed Negro may be profitably employed by enterprising men," Thomas noted. "I shall give immediate publicity through the plan in the hope of inducing persons of enterprize & capital to come here and engage in the matter." Likewise, the New York attorney George B. Field, an associate of Stanton and one of three "commissioners" chosen to oversee the program, predicted that it "may be easily extended so as to embrace the whole region between Memphis & New Orleans, thereby furnishing complete protection to the commerce of the Mississippi Valley, besides furnishing the black population, Now idle, with immediate employment that shall render them self sustaining."[10]

Despite these lofty ambitions, the reality of operating cotton plantations in the lower Mississippi valley in 1863 was even further removed from the ideal than it was in southern Louisiana. As was true of Banks's program, Thomas's plan was an extemporaneous response to an immediate crisis. It would have been difficult to implement under the best of circumstances, let alone amidst one of the war's largest military operations. Several dozen plantations would be leased in southeastern Arkansas and northeastern Louisiana, but the crop season was commencing weeks behind schedule, as Thomas had indicated. Meanwhile, the Vicksburg campaign provoked Confederate raids and guerilla activity, destabilizing the countryside and sending former slaves scurrying back to Federal military lines for protection. The contraband camp at Helena became so overcrowded that Federal officials began relocating hundreds of

---

[9] Taylor, *Embattled Freedom*, 112–16 (quotation, 114). This is also an important theme in McCurry, *Women's War*, chap. 2; Manning, *Troubled Refuge*; and Glymph, *The Women's Fight*.

[10] For Thomas's leasing plan, see *Freedom: WGFL-LS*, 630–33, 699–702 (doc. 162). For Thomas's plans for black enlistment, see *Freedom: BME*, 487–89 (doc. 194). *Freedom: WGFL-LS*, 630, 680–84 (doc. 159; Field). For optimistic northern commentary on the initiative, see "The Mission of the Adjutant General," *The Living Age*, vol. 77, no. 994 (June 20, 1863): 556–57.

indigent former slaves to St. Louis and points further north. Some 5,000 former slaves were dependent on government support in Memphis alone.

The experiences of former slaves on the plantations also left much to be desired. The cruelest practices of slavery had ended, only to be replaced by a truncated freedom. Predictably, many freed persons were forced onto plantations against their will, and work forces were cobbled together in accordance with the lessees' interests and not the laborers'. The plantations were organized largely on the old gang system, and many lessees hired managers who had been overseers before the war.[11] As in southern Louisiana, northern lessees were not always imbued with new ideas about labor. "I regret to state that in no case have I found a strict compliance with the terms of their contracts on the part of Lessees of plantations, and in too many an utter disregard of even the commonest principles of humanity and the rights of individuals, in their treatment of the contrabands," reported a Federal inspector of leased plantations later that year. "Generally the negro has been treated by those employing him, as a mere brute, from whom the greatest amount of labor should be gained at the least possible expense." Lessees routinely gouged employees for clothing and other items, provided grossly deficient rations and housing, and often failed to pay wages. "The report does not half show the hardships and ill treatment the free negroes are subjected to," added the inspector's superior, General John P. Hawkins, in forwarding the report to the War Department, "and if better policy for them cannot be introduced, and humanity, is [as?] a matter of consideration we had better call back their former masters and let them take charge of them."[12]

If northern lessees were likened to slaveholders, reenslavement remained a grim reality for former slaves, as shown by a series of Confederate raids in June against government plantations. Taking advantage of Federal troop reassignments to bolster Grant's forces outside Vicksburg, the raids were intended to sow terror and confusion behind Federal lines. Confederate raiders burned buildings, destroyed crops and farm implements, killed or commandeered animals, and murdered former slaves. In one infamous raid at Goodrich's Landing, Louisiana, Confederates inflicted widespread devastation and captured some 1,200 former slaves before Union gunboats drove them off. Federal officers attested that former slaves had been burned alive in their cabins, while children were found "skulking in the canebreak pierced with wounds" and women had been "shot down in the most inhuman manner." The attacks belied Federal officials' faith in the ability of black troops alone to defend the leased plantations, which some now deemed more trouble than they

---

[11] *Freedom: WGFL-LS*, 39n, 631–37, 699 (doc. 161), 709–11 (doc. 166), 711–12 (doc. 167), 714–15 (doc. 169); Cimprich, *Slavery's End in Tennessee*, 48–49, 66–67; Christ, "'They Will Be Armed'"; Moneyhon, "From Slave to Free Labor."

[12] *Freedom: WGFL-LS*, 635 (quotation), 728–35 (doc. 177; quotations, 729, 735).

were worth. "I would recommend that this leasing of property on the River be stopped," Admiral David Porter complained to Navy Secretary Gideon Welles. "It leads to a great deal of injustice in the first place, offers strong temptation to the Rebels to infest the river, and is a great expense to the Government for which it will get no return." Even before the Goodrich's Landing raid, Grant had expressed reservations about the system, and he concluded that leasing plantations so near Vicksburg had been a bad idea. The program continued, but not as its advocates had intended.[13]

Some local planters remained on their estates and took their chances with Federal military authorities. "So many are getting letters of protection from the general at [Milliken's Bend]," observed Kate Stone. "Aunt Laura, formerly so bitter against the Yankees, is now urging Mamma to go in to Omega and get letters protecting us." Having already sent most of their slaves to the interior, the Stone family eventually fled to Texas. Planters also found that the loyalty oath provided no guarantee against Federal interference. Mary Duncan, the member of a prominent Natchez-area family who boasted of important northern connections, complained directly to Secretary of War Stanton that Federal officials had impressed her male laborers, whose freedom she claimed to have recognized, and had seized her cotton – violating the "protection papers" she had received from General Grant and Admiral Porter. "I have seen FOR MYSELF that Unionist & rebel both fare alike," she insisted, "for cotton & negro labor *must* be had, & the political views of the lawful owners are unheeded – where plunder is to be obtained." How someone who had acknowledged her slaves' freedom continued as a "lawful owner" remained unclear. An investigation failed to substantiate Duncan's claims, but few planters, no matter how locally prominent, possessed the resources to get a hearing from Washington.[14]

Under such circumstances, the master–slave relationship further disintegrated, as slaveholders discovered that the authority they once wielded over their slaves had vanished. "Mr. Valentine came over last evening in very low spirits indeed," Kate Stone again remarked in one of many such observations during this period. "He says his Negroes will not even pretend to work and are very impudent, and he thinks they will all go off in a body the next time the Yankees come on his place." As in southern Louisiana and elsewhere, many slaves realized that they did not have to flee to the Yankees to secure freedom. To all intents and purposes, they were already free. "Charles is very divided in

---

[13] *Freedom: WGFL-LS*, 634, 712–14 (doc. 168; quotations); *OR*, ser. 1, vol. 24, pt. 2, 466, 516–18. Scholars have long understood reenslavement as a frequent occurrence in the process of wartime emancipation, but the practice as systematic Confederate policy is explored in Oakes, *Freedom National*, chap. 11.

[14] Anderson, *Brokenburn*, 178 (March 12, 1863); *Freedom: WGFL-LS*, 633, 707–9 (doc. 165; quotation); Powell and Wayne, "Self-Interest and the Decline of Confederate Nationalism."

his feelings. He wishes to go with his children, but cannot bear to leave 'Master,'" noted Elizabeth Frances Conner of the Natchez District, in commenting on her family's slaves. "He cried like a child this evening when he came to talk to me about it. I told him if he preferred to go he might do so." If such episodes illustrated the genuine affection that sometimes bound master and slave, Conner all but admitted her impotence as a slave mistress.[15]

These episodes also hinted at the former slaves' broader conceptualizations of freedom, a topic on which John Eaton offered his observations in a late-April report. In response to the interrogatory "What of their notions of liberty," some former slaves "need instruction" or "[d]on't seem to realize that labor is attendant on liberty." Others, by contrast, demonstrated what Eaton considered "[g]enerally correct" ideas. Likewise, some former slaves' notions of freedom could be described as "Indefinite; anticipate having it as the result of the war," whereas others evinced no ambiguity whatsoever. "A slander to say their notion of liberty is idleness," as Eaton put it. "Their notions of liberty have no more to do with their love of ease in the black than in the white race." Eaton was an empathetic observer, despite his occasionally patronizing assumptions, but the now-former slaveholders would have begged to differ. "I am truly sorry to hear of Mr. McMurran's loss at Riverside," remarked Lemuel P. Conner, husband of Elizabeth Frances Conner, in response to the news, only days before the fall of Vicksburg, that his in-law's slaves had absconded. "Tis just what may be expected when negroes have the opportunity," he continued. "There is something magical about the word 'Freedom,' which the poor deluded creatures cannot resist." Delusion was indeed at work here.[16]

III

As the 1863 fall harvest, or "rolling season," approached in the Louisiana sugar region, no observer familiar with antebellum plantation routines would have recognized conditions there. Whether working for their former owners or new employers, laborers continued to object to the draconian elements of Federal labor policy and to any attempt to reinstitute the old routines. Such experiences, however familiar they were becoming, reinforced the planters' long-held belief that voluntary labor was incompatible with sugar cultivation in Louisiana. Operating under various environmental limitations, including a shorter growing season than sugarcane requires and an abbreviated harvest season, planters insisted that they needed control over labor, especially the ability to inflict corporal punishment. Amidst a disastrous rolling season,

---

[15] Anderson, *Brokenburn*, 175 (March 5, 1863), and generally 169–86 (March 2–24, 1863); Fanny E. Conner to [Lemuel P. Conner], June 16, 1863, Conner Family Papers, LSU.

[16] *Freedom: WGFL-LS*, 693 (quotations); Lemuel P. Conner to [Frances E. Conner], June 28, 1863, Conner Family Papers, LSU.

William J. Minor calculated that it would take a full month longer to harvest his crop under the present system than it had "before the negroes got to think themselves free." Consequently, "it settles the question in the negative," he surmised, of whether "sugar [can] be made in Louisiana ... by free labour." As they totaled up their losses, other planters came to the same conclusion.[17]

Much as they were determined to restore Louisiana as a slave state, planters were set on reestablishing authority over their "slaves." In testimony before the American Freedmen's Inquiry Commission (AFIC) – an agency created to investigate the conditions of former slaves in the Union-occupied South – Union General James S. Wadsworth, a War Department special inspector, described this pervasive mindset. He reported a conversation with "a proslavery and secession planter" in Louisiana who fully anticipated slavery being restored "in some form" once the Union army had left. The laborers had become "greatly demoralized" and would resist the reimposition of antebellum forms of discipline, the planter admitted, but they would eventually be "returned to slavery." While insisting that such opinions were typical of the "proslavery men," Wadsworth also detected another phenomenon at work – what he called "a disposition to restore slavery, under another name." Although fully committed to preserving slavery, some planters were beginning to contemplate the challenge of labor control in a world without it. "We are ready to give up the name of 'slavery,' we care nothing about the name," Wadsworth quoted another slaveholder, "but we must have a certain control over these men." Using Federal labor policy in Louisiana as a blueprint, state authorities might institute a new form of servitude by replacing *chattel* slaves (personal, moveable property) with "*adscripti glebæ*" – laborers legally bound to the soil. "You are Emancipationists, you are Abolitionists; and you leave these people *adscripti glebæ*; and we will just go on with your system," is how Wadsworth conjured up such reasoning. Whereas some slaveholders had resolved to preserve slavery itself, others would forsake "the name of 'slavery'" to regain control over labor.[18]

Even as planters in southern Louisiana were attempting to revive mastery, they also repudiated the customary duties and obligations that had grounded the ideological defense of slavery. Many of them, for instance, began

---

[17] Plantation Diary 36, November 14, 1863, Minor Family Papers, LSU. For the 1863 harvest in general, see Rodrigue, *Reconstruction in the Cane Fields*, 42–43, 46–47, and sources cited therein; *Freedom: WGFL-LS*, 456–58 (doc. 95), 463–69 (doc. 100), 471–75 (docs. 102, 103), 492–511 (doc. 107), esp. 494–95; Hepworth, *Whip, Hoe, and Sword*, 50–51.

[18] *Freedom: WGFL-LS*, 492–511 (doc. 107), esp. 497, 508–9. In March 1863, Secretary of War Stanton appointed three well-known northern reformers – Samuel Gridley Howe, James McKaye, and Robert Dale Owen – as commissioners to the AFIC. The commission would issue various preliminary and supplementary reports in addition to a final one in 1864. For an excellent analysis of the commission, see Reidy, *Illusions of Emancipation*, 251–65.

systematically driving away nonproducers from their estates, forcing the Federal government to support them. The point of such practices was to create difficulties for Federal authorities, but planters were also renouncing an essential element of their identity. Ironically, this behavior was partly shaped by Federal policy itself. Anticipating a directive from Washington, Nathaniel Banks in mid-July had ordered the transfer of abandoned and confiscated plantations to the Treasury Department. The lessees and agents of government-run plantations responded by "sifting out" nonproducers and turning them over to the military for support, retaining only productive workers. To make matters worse, the continued recruitment and conscription of able-bodied men into the military disrupted plantation routine as the rolling season approached. Banks tried to rectify the situation, but resident planters continued to complain about the interference in their affairs. Watching helplessly as their ablest workers were dragooned into the army, they also took to driving off nonproducers.[19]

Banks described the situation in mid-October to Union General-in-Chief Henry Halleck. "Those who have leased [plantations], prefer in working them, the able bodied men and women to the disabled and infirm," he observed. "They are daily sifting them out placing the helpless, on plantations . . . that are and have been uncultivated," while "it is expected the military authorities are to support them." Confederates exacerbated the problem by running valuable slaves into Texas and leaving the rest behind. "The lessors of Government plantations, and the enemy turn over to us, all their helpless men women children," Banks explained, whereas "we" – meaning the War Department – "turn over, very gladly, all plantation property to the Treasury Department." This raised the obvious question: "Does the support of the infirm and poor negroes, go with the property to which they naturally belong or is it a charge upon the army as military expenses, and fastened upon the war Department?" After consulting with Secretary of War Stanton, Halleck authorized Banks in late October to issue the necessary regulations to provide for nonproducers and to prohibit the practice of sifting out nonproducers from operating plantations and consigning them to government assistance. The War Department subsequently suspended the conscription of plantation laborers, helping to stabilize the labor situation as the fall harvest was commencing. Nonetheless, the first rolling season conducted entirely under Federal auspices only intensified the planters' determination to counteract the disruptions that emancipation and wartime free labor had caused.[20]

---

[19] *Freedom: WGFL-LS*, 360–63, 461–63 (doc. 98); *Freedom: BME*, 157–58 (doc. 55); *OR*, ser. 1, vol. 26, pt. 1, 704, 740–41, 803. Banks's directive did not apply to plantations worked by resident owners. In October, the War Department ordered this policy for the entire occupied South. For the War Department's order, see *OR*, ser. 3, vol. 3, 872–73.

[20] *Freedom: WGFL-LS*, 469–71 (doc. 101).

Indeed, with the sugar country in a state of flux, events on the adjoining Terrebonne Parish estates of Hope Farm and Aragon – owned respectively by the brothers William A. and John Bisland – for 1863 epitomized the contest over the emerging order. What began as a dispute over the workers' compensation revealed deeper disagreements over a range of issues regarding plantation routine before descending into an all-out test of wills between former slaveholders and former slaves. Although ending without clear resolution, the episode illustrated the transformations that had upended the sugar region during the 1863 crop season – and that would plague the start of the new one.

Both Bislands had been serving as Confederate officers when the Federals arrived in Terrebonne in late 1862, and they had arranged in early 1863 to lease their estates in absentia to John P. Van Bergen, a native of New York, for half the year's profits. By mid-May 1863, Union military authorities had cancelled the leases, suspecting that Van Bergen intended not to work the places but to keep them intact until the Bislands returned. Federal authorities thereafter paid little attention to the two estates, and the nearly 300 residents worked both of them on their own account, providing for themselves and eventually producing significant crops of sugar and molasses.[21]

Sometime in mid-September 1863, a few weeks before the rolling season was to begin, one S. E. Pierce arrived on the scene. He informed the residents that he was now leasing both plantations from the Federal government and would pay the laborers collectively a one-twentieth share of the crop, as stipulated under Banks's regulations. The laborers' portion seems not to have been made entirely clear, however, since many of them believed they were to receive a *one-third* share, splitting the crop equally with Pierce and the Federal government. The misunderstanding would later lead to hard feelings. The residents made it clear, as they previously had with Van Bergen, that under no circumstances would they work "in the same manner as we had been doing in rebel times," as one of them put it, or "as we used to do under our Master." They also offered differing opinions on the treatment they received from Pierce. None alleged cruelty or physical abuse, but many attested to inadequate rations and clothing for the workers and none at all for the dependents. "I have not been treated well by Mr Pierce," one former slave typically noted. "I do not mean by that, that he has abused or punished me or the rest. I mean to say he has not given me and the rest enough to eat since he came here."

Once the harvest had been completed, the various parties involved – members of the Bisland family, their former slaves, Pierce, and even Van Bergen – vied for disposition of the crop. In mid-December, two former slaves, Herry Locket and Henry Jones, traveled to New Orleans and pleaded

---

[21] All facts and quotations from this episode regarding the Bisland estates are from *Freedom: WGFL-LS*, 482–91 (doc. 106A-C). I have silently changed capitalization and punctuation in some cases to improve readability. See also Eiss, "Share in the Land," esp. 63–66.

their case before Treasury Department officials. The residents had worked the places on their own for most of the year, the two men argued, whereas Pierce had only arrived in early October (actually September). Pierce had provided food and clothing to the workers only, leaving the rest to furnish themselves, and he intended to pay them collectively a mere one-twentieth share of the crop. "We respectfully ask . . . that we be paid more than 1/20 of the Crop," Locket and Jones requested, "as it has been by our own exertions, that any crop at all has been made." Upon hearing the complaint, Capt. Samuel W. Cozzens, the Treasury Department Superintendent of Plantations for Louisiana, ordered that Pierce pay the residents of both places, for the entire year retroactive to February, sums amounting to $10 per month for male hands, $8 for females, and $2.50 for nonproducers "in lieu of proper clothing which should have been furnished them." Cozzens also ordered William H. Wilder, a Treasury Department inspector, to investigate the matter further.

Although the historical record remains silent on the final settlement for the 1863 crop, it documents the Bislands' difficulties in reestablishing authority over their former slaves for the new year. In late December 1863, Fannie A. Bisland, wife of John Bisland, arranged to lease out Aragon plantation for 1864, and William Bisland's father-in-law made similar arrangements for Hope Farm. Yet Fannie Bisland's attempt to hire a new overseer, or even to reside on Aragon, met with determined resistance. In mid-January, she informed a relative of "the *rebellion* on the place about Mr. Grey's (the overseer) coming there." Upon Grey's arrival days earlier, Bisland already suspected something was amiss. "I told him I thought he would have a good deal of trouble before he could bring them straight," she noted, "but never dreaming of the trouble he did have." As Grey made his way onto the plantation, "the bell commenced ringing furiously," and soon "every man, woman and child on the plantation had collected around the overseer's house." Before Grey had even reached the house, "one of the men seized the bridle and told him he should not set foot in that house, that the quarter belonged to them and no d----- white man should live there."

Grey tried to speak with the Aragon residents, Bisland continued, "but they shut him up immediately and told him they did not want to hear a word from him." He should not come onto the place, they insisted, according to Bisland, "unless he could show a written order from Gen. Banks and if Gen. Banks himself said that he was to come there, he should not live down there but must live at the house with *Mrs. Bisland*." The residents added, for good measure, that "Mrs. Bisland had no right to come there and give orders, &c&c." They "said too much for me to begin to tell you what they did'nt say," Bisland further noted. "One man told [Grey] if he went to live in that house they would burn powder and lead round it all night." Deciding that discretion was the better part of valor, Grey moved on to Hope Farm, but the residents there were equally set on barring him from the premises. "This shows a concerted movement between the two places," Bisland concluded, perhaps stating the obvious.

Even the presence of a Union soldier failed to quell the disturbance, and Bisland was left hoping that a squad of soldiers from nearly Thibodaux might restore order. "If a severe example is set in this instance; something may be done," she observed. "If not all the white people will have to leave and give the parish up to the negroes." The episode may have strengthened Bisland's resolve to reestablish her authority, but she effectively conceded defeat by admitting that she could do nothing without Federal assistance. "I am more determined than ever to take charge down there since this affair, and if the government will support me in it I will do so," she asserted. "Mr. Grey says he is going there if they kill him in the attempt. The whole parish is interested in putting this down." Federal military authorities in New Orleans needed to be informed of the episode, Bisland insisted, since the former slaves in the area had made "similar threats on several places; that no overseer or white man shall come on the places."

Despite their determination to regain the upper hand, neither Grey nor Bisland succeeded. Several days after the mid-January "rebellion," Samuel Cozzens ordered a further investigation "into the difficulty existing between Mrs. Bisland, and the negroes on the Plantations." No record of a subsequent investigation exists, but by April 1864 the matter had not been resolved. Fannie Bisland had evidently given up and turned Aragon over to the same relative who was leasing out Hope Farm. If the world according to Bisland and her ilk had been turned upside-down, their former bondspeople were determined that it would never be restored.

IV

In the cotton country, the conquest of Vicksburg and Port Hudson brought an end to the major disruptions that the military campaigns had caused, but stability came slowly, and much discontent manifested itself over General Lorenzo Thomas's plantation leasing program and the efforts to establish new labor arrangements. Large numbers of former slaves continued to stream into Union lines, overwhelming Federal officials. Along the Mississippi River, for miles above and below Vicksburg, what one army surgeon referred to as "numerous family contraband camps" sprang up around Union military posts. Residents of the camps were often left to provide for themselves, and conditions were dire. Greatly alarmed by the situation upon his return to the lower Mississippi valley in August, Thomas ordered women, children, and elderly men who were still on their home plantations to remain there, effectually compelling persons whom the Emancipation Proclamation had freed to remain with their former owners. He also "encouraged" those who had already left to return, so long as their former owners regarded them as free and agreed to compensate them for any labor they performed.[22]

Getting the planters to regard their laborers as free was the main problem. Even so, Thomas sounded the theme – widespread by mid-1863 – that slavery would never survive the war. He had conversed with a number of planters, including "several strong union men at Natchez," Thomas informed Secretary of War Stanton in August, all of whom were of the opinion "that slavery has received its death blow, and cannot again exist in regions passed over by our armies." The planters were "perfectly willing to hire the negroes and adopt any policy the Government may dictate," he added. "Many citizens of Mississippi, Louisiana and Arkansas are desirous that their States should resume their position in the Union with laws providing for the emancipation of slaves in a limited number of years." Such sentiments were constantly increasing, Thomas assured Stanton, "even among those who were strong advocates of secession." By the fall, Thomas was also proclaiming his leasing program "a complete success" and a model to be expanded. "I purpose to continue the same system for the next year, but of necessity on a much more enlarged scale, as our forces now cover and protect a much larger extent of country on the Mississippi River," he wrote in mid-October to Stanton. "Northern Union men will be invited to come here and engage in the work, until we make if possible the whole negro population self supporting."[23]

Yet considerable evidence belied this upbeat appraisal. "The System of leasing out Plantations is a bad one," countered Admiral David Porter. "No one can tell except those who have seen it, what evils it has led to. It has benefitted no one, and has been the means of having many of the Plantations destroyed." The lessees were "greedy adventures" intent on making a quick killing. "They treat the Negroes brutally, and chastise them worse than their former masters did." Porter had seen the scenario numerous times: the lessee enters into an arrangement with the owner to work the place; before long, the lessee takes control "and elbows the owner out," whereupon the dispossessed owner joins a guerrilla band, determined to "come back and burn the Plantation kill half the Negroes and carries of[f] the rest in irons to Texas." This narrative applied to "more than half" of such transactions, Porter contended. "The banks of the Mississippi have been made scenes of ruin and desolation owing to the Plantation [leasing] system." Other observers, including Colonel John Eaton, agreed.[24]

---

[22] *Freedom: WGFL-LS*, 637–38, 719–20 (doc. 172; Thomas's order), 746–49 (doc. 182).
[23] *Freedom: WGFL-LS*, 308–310 (doc. 110), 638, 739–42 (doc. 180).
[24] *Freedom: WGFL-LS*, 639–40, 742–45 (doc. 181), 746–49 (doc. 182; Porter), 757–63 (doc. 185). On the havoc and suffering caused by Confederate raids throughout the lower Mississippi valley during 1863, especially among formerly enslaved women and children, see Glymph, *The Women's Fight*, 241–50.

Neither had the resident planters reconciled themselves to new labor arrangements to the extent Thomas claimed. General James S. Wadsworth, who extensively toured the lower Mississippi valley during the fall, found the cotton lords just as determined to preserve slavery as were the sugar barons of southern Louisiana. Many "old Masters," he noted, "had not accepted the Proclamation as a finality & entertained a lingering hope that they would be able to restore the old system if not in form in substance." Only when the former slaves were convinced that their freedom was secure and that their former masters were prepared to acknowledge their new status would stability return to the plantations. "So long as [the employer] occupies the ambiguous position of paying wages to his laborers, but not fully recognizing the completeness of their freedom," Wadsworth insisted, "he must suffer all the, to him, great annoyances & vexations of a change from the old system without reaping any of the benefits which history throughout the world has accorded to freedom." Indeed, so long as "the whites cling to the idea that they can reestablish Slavery & throw impediments in the way of the new System," Wadsworth concluded, the revival of plantation operations "will be considerably retarded."[25]

As 1863 drew to a close, acrimony worsened between planters, both residents and lessees, and laborers who received little upon the settling of accounts. Borrowing terminology from the previous year, one Northerner described "a general stampede" from the plantations of laborers upset with their meager earnings. Planters bemoaned the lack of labor control and saw some form of involuntary labor as the solution, while former slaves objected to work routines and compensation that differed little from what they had known as slaves. Their advocates pushed for changes. Colonel John Eaton proposed that northern freed people's aid societies and other benevolent organizations sponsor plantations on which former slaves would be employed as independent cultivators of small plots of land. After a fall tour of the lower Mississippi valley, James E. Yeatman, president of the Western Sanitary Commission, likewise urged overhauling the plantation-leasing system. In a highly publicized proposal, he called for limiting lessees to tracts of 200 acres, so as to promote leasing by former slaves, and for paying laborers on leased estates monthly wages of $15–$25 for men and $12–$20 for women. Laborers would be responsible for their own provisions, but lessees would provide schools.[26]

These criticisms had some effect. By late 1863, as the Treasury Department assumed responsibility for administering government-controlled plantations,

[25] *Freedom: WGFL-LS*, 757–63 (doc. 185), esp. 761–62. This document is a mid-December report Wadsworth submitted directly to Lorenzo Thomas following his tour of the lower Mississippi valley. Wadsworth offered an even more critical assessment of the leasing program in his early 1864 testimony before the AFIC: *Freedom: WGFL-LS*, 492–511 (doc. 107).

[26] *Freedom: WGFL-LS*, 639–41.

Treasury secretary Salmon P. Chase ordered revisions to Lorenzo Thomas's leasing system. After consulting with Yeatman and others, Chase in late December directed William P. Mellen – the Treasury Department supervising agent responsible for the northern extent of the lower Mississippi valley – to draft regulations for government-run plantations for the coming year. Chase's instructions took note of the various critiques of Thomas's leasing program and were designed to protect the former slaves' welfare. All persons involved in leasing plantations, Chase insisted, must be "honest, conscientious, competent men, earnestly desirous for the amelioration and elevation of the freedmen, and ready to make sacrifice of comfort and pecuniary gain for the sake of doing good." The lessees should be required to pay regular wages, preferably weekly but at least monthly, which "should be sufficiently liberal to induce laborers to *desire* the employment." The laborers would be parties to labor contracts, Chase further directed, and the practice of compelling them to work on places involuntarily was to be "discontinued and broken up."

Chase also encouraged black access to land. He advocated leasing entire plantations, whenever possible, "to associations or partnerships of the laborers themselves," and making parcels of land available to individuals or small groups. The owners of abandoned and confiscated estates, meanwhile, should be discouraged from returning and instead encouraged to sell the land in forty-acre lots to the former slaves. "I am not at present authorized to speak for the President," Chase demurred, "but I am very confident he would relieve the plantations of any proprietor remaining or coming to remain within our lines, and desirous to sell it, in this manner, from the effects of the confiscation acts." In essence, Chase hoped to use the threat of confiscation in order to initiate a voluntary dismantling of the plantation system, suggesting, however elliptically, that he had Lincoln's support. Although no evidence exists that Lincoln endorsed Chase's proposal, he was by this point undoubtedly becoming more solicitous of the former slaves' welfare.[27]

* * *

In October 1863, General John P. Hawkins, the Union commander for northeastern Louisiana, who had served out west before the war, wrote to the prominent northern abolitionist Gerritt Smith. In critiquing the plantation-leasing system, Hawkins also offered thoughts on the prospects of free labor in the lower Mississippi valley. "There is a greater gold mine here than was ever known in California or Pikes Peak," he wrote. "The lands to be occupied are all along the Miss. River from Memphis to New Orleans, up the White and Arkansas Rivers and probably Red River." Hawkins envisioned dramatic transformations for this area. "The ownership of the soil here will change during and after the war," he confidently predicted. "Slavery will be done away

[27] *Freedom: WGFL-LS*, 641, 763–66 (doc. 186).

with, and the labor education of the slave holder will prove of no use to him. Free labor will be an annoyance to him and if he can sell his lands and get rid of the trouble he will do it." Eventually, the plantation system based on involuntary labor would be replaced by homesteads operating under free labor. "Which is best for our country," Hawkins asked rhetorically, "that the lands shall be held in small farms or in immense tracts[?]"[28]

Little of what Hawkins foresaw would come to fruition. Slavery would indeed "be done away with," but the plantation system would largely survive. Far from prompting the planters to sell their lands, the "trouble" or "annoyance" of free labor would embolden them to hold onto those lands all the more desperately. With slavery gone, many planters would eventually sell their estates, as scholars who have examined "planter persistence" have demonstrated, but few would do so willingly, and not before they had done everything in their power to retain them.

Yet as Hawkins had correctly anticipated, "the labor education of the slave holder" would prove totally incompatible with the new reality. Widespread dislocation and disorganization had replaced the order and discipline – rooted in violence – that had once characterized the plantation system of the lower Mississippi valley. The contours of a new labor system were slowly becoming apparent, and the central issues in reconstituting the plantation regime were being addressed, if to the satisfaction of no one. Each in their own way, former slaveholders and former slaves made their opinions known on the state of affairs and on what needed to be done. Federal officials, though hardly of one voice, tried as best they could to arbitrate the resulting disputes even as they put forward their own visions of the new order. Of the many challenges this new order faced, perhaps the most intractable was the slaveholders' determination to reestablish control over labor and to preserve slavery. By the close of the 1863 crop year, the destruction of slavery – as both a legal institution and a labor system – had made considerable progress, but it would continue to face ferocious opposition and the immense weight of history.

[28] *Freedom: WGFL-LS*, 742–45 (doc. 181; quotations, 744). I have made minor changes in spelling and punctuation.

9

"Repudiating the Emancipation Proclamation and Reestablishing Slavery"

By late 1863, the campaign against slavery in the lower Mississippi valley was achieving critical mass. In the months following the Federal capture of Little Rock in September, Arkansas Unionists made greater progress in organizing a new government – on a free-state basis – than they had in the previous two years. In Tennessee, victory at Lookout Mountain in late November finally established Federal control of east Tennessee and likewise paved the way for the state's reorganization. Although the free-state movement appeared to have stalled in Louisiana, where conservative Unionists were plowing forward with their plan to hold congressional elections in early November and send members-elect to Congress, an exasperated Lincoln countered by placing General Nathaniel P. Banks unequivocally in charge of the state. Fearing the possible organization of a state government "repudiating the Emancipation Proclamation and reestablishing slavery," Lincoln named Banks "master" in hopes of revitalizing the free-state initiative. Meanwhile, the Louisiana free-state radicals – allying with the New Orleans free people of color and beginning to embrace black suffrage – were gaining ascendancy over their moderate rivals within the free-state movement.

As Congress convened in early December, Tennessee conservative Unionist Emerson Etheridge – the acting Clerk of the US House of Representatives – led a conservative scheme to seize control of the organization of the House. The "Etheridge Plot" came to naught, but it previewed the political battles to come, as Congress prepared to consider Reconstruction legislation and an amendment to the Federal Constitution abolishing slavery. The commencement of the Thirty-Eighth Congress also witnessed the unveiling of Lincoln's "ten-percent" plan. The proposal was Lincoln's attempt, as a matter of policy, to conjoin the abolition of slavery to state restoration. Despite its limitations, the initiative reflected the shift that had occurred in northern antislavery thought, which, though still divided over means, had concluded that the seceded states must abolish slavery as a condition for restoration to the Union. By year's end, both military victory and the destruction of slavery seemed within reach.

I

With the Federal capture of Little Rock in September, along with the conversion of Edward Gantt and other prominent Confederates to free-state Unionism, unconditional Unionists such as Isaac Murphy seized the initiative. In late October, Unionists representing twenty of the state's fifty-five counties met at Fort Smith and began planning Arkansas's restoration. They called for a constitutional convention, to meet in early January in Little Rock, that would abolish slavery and create a loyal state government. They also scheduled elections for convention delegates for late November and nominated Col. James M. Johnson, a Huntsville physician, for Congress. Johnson, along with his brother Frank and Isaac Murphy, had been driven into exile after Arkansas seceded, and James Johnson had subsequently organized and commanded an Arkansas Federal infantry regiment. For the next several weeks, Unionists met to nominate or select delegates to the convention. Despite the risks, elections were said to have taken place in twenty-eight counties. James Johnson was declared elected to Congress, and in December Isaac Murphy was endorsed for governor. "There is no difficulty in bringing Arkansas in to the Union with Slavery abolished if it is desired," General Stephen A. Hurlbut, the Federal commander at Memphis, somewhat overconfidently reported to Lincoln.[1]

The free-state cause received further aid from the many slaveholders of the Arkansas River valley who, in response to the Federal presence, fled with their slaves to Texas. "[T]he immense immigration of planters & others flocking there to save their slaves," one eyewitness reported, had left "the lukewarm, and disloyal," that is, Unionists, in possession of the area. While the flight of so many slaveholders from the state certainly empowered the antislavery forces, proslavery Unionism in fact had had no chance of success by the fall of 1863 in Arkansas. With Republicans unequivocally committed to ending slavery, it was too late to initiate a political movement, akin to those in Louisiana and Tennessee, to restore Arkansas to the Union as a slave state. Since working with Federal authorities was not an option, slaveholders who wanted to preserve slavery had no choice but to decamp for Texas and hope for the best. Arkansas was thus the one state of the lower Mississippi valley that experienced wartime Reconstruction but no meaningful attempt to preserve slavery.[2]

Meanwhile, Tennessee's restoration stagnated following the Union's September reversal at Chickamauga. The delay frustrated free-state Unionists and emboldened their proslavery rivals, who added to their charges against

---

[1] Hurlbut to Lincoln, November 10, 1863, ALP; G. L. Miller to Steele, December 10, 1863, and W. N. Hood to Steele, December 30, 1863, Steele Papers, Stanford; Harris, *With Charity for All*, 127–28; Smith, *Courage of a Southern Unionist*, 50; DeBlack, *With Fire and Sword*, 105; Cowen, "Reorganization of Federal Arkansas," 38–40.

[2] Monroe, McIntosh, and Crist, *Papers of Jefferson Davis*, 10: 129; Oakes, *Freedom National*, 460.

Johnson the improbable one that he was colluding with northern abolitionists to end slavery in Tennessee in exchange for the 1864 Republican presidential nomination. In late October, Lincoln invited Johnson to Washington for consultations. The invitation presented Johnson with an opportunity to influence the planned Reconstruction initiative that Lincoln was then known to be contemplating. Yet Johnson declined on the grounds that Tennessee affairs required his presence. He instead forwarded his views through Postmaster General Montgomery Blair, an old ally and kindred spirit. While reaffirming his support for abolition, Johnson cautioned against territorialization and other radical approaches to Reconstruction. Johnson also reiterated his belief that slavery was already dead, but more for the purpose of defending state sovereignty. "The institution of slavery is gone," he insisted, "& there is no good reason now for destroying the states to bring about the destruction of slavery."[3]

Even as Johnson penned these words, military fortunes in Tennessee were about to turn yet again. In mid-October, Ulysses Grant assumed command at Chattanooga, and within weeks he had resuscitated Union hopes there. General William T. Sherman and his troops arrived a month later, and in the Battle of Lookout Mountain of November 23–25, including the Union assault up Missionary Ridge, Grant forced the Confederates again back into northern Georgia, this time for good. Days later, Confederates were repulsed at Knoxville and retreated into southwestern Virginia. By early December, east Tennessee was finally in Union hands. "[T]he insurgent force is retreating from East Tennessee," read Lincoln's formal announcement, "under circumstances rendering it probable that the Union forces can not hereafter be dislodged from that important position." Lincoln applauded this development "of high national consequence." Although Confederates continued to hamper Unionists and threaten the state for another year, the liberation of east Tennessee, which Johnson had maintained was essential to the state's restoration, had at last been achieved.[4]

II

While state restoration proceeded, however unevenly, in Arkansas and Tennessee, the contest between conservative and free-state Unionists in Louisiana escalated. By mid-September, as Military Governor George Shepley returned from his extended trip to Washington, both Unionist groups developed their competing plans for Louisiana's reorganization. Conservatives

---

[3] *PAJ*, 6: 448n, 492 (quotation); *CWL*, 6: 498; Harris, *With Charity for All*, 111–12; Hess, *Civil War in the West*, 189–94.

[4] Hess, *Civil War in the West*, 193–98; *CWL*, 7: 35. See also *OR*, ser. 1, vol. 30, pt. 4, 404. Armstead Robinson, in *Bitter Fruits of Bondage* (chap. 10), sees the Confederate debacle at Missionary Ridge as the *dénouement* of the Confederacy at large.

advanced theirs to hold state and congressional elections in early November. Throughout the summer, free-state Unionists struggled to conduct a registry of loyal voters, pursuant to holding a constitutional convention that would abolish slavery. Not the least of their difficulties was the lack of support from Nathaniel Banks, preoccupied as he was with a proposed incursion into Texas. By late summer, the registry had ground to a halt. In early October, Durant wrote directly to Lincoln. Responding to a copy he had seen of Lincoln's early-August letter to Banks, in which Lincoln had endorsed the constitutional convention and registry of voters, and had expressed hope that Louisiana might be reconstructed by the opening of Congress, Durant spelled out the difficulties in working toward those goals. "[I]t is not possible," he informed Lincoln, "to have the work completed by the next session of Congress."

Durant summarized the struggle over slavery in Louisiana during the previous fifteen months. In the summer of 1862, loyal slaveholders might have been amenable to establishing a loyal government "under a guarantee of the permanent safety of the slave system." Although that opportunity had been lost, those same slaveholders nonetheless "look for the withdrawal of the [Emancipation] Proclamation" and intend "that the persons freed by the Proclamation shall be made slaves again." The proclamation was "purely a military measure," Durant reminded Lincoln. "It emancipates certain slaves. It does not abolish slavery." The exclusion of areas from the proclamation, moreover, "inspires [slavery's] friends with hope, that it may be reestablished" throughout the state. "We, in Louisiana, are now so situated that we must choose between the systems of Slavery and freedom," he contended. "To put the matter at rest we must abolish the principle of property in man by a constitutional enactment."

Much progress was being made toward that end, Durant continued, but he got to the heart of the matter. "By your letter to General Banks, you appear to think that a Registration of voters is going on under my superintendence, with the view of bringing on the election of delegates to a constitutional convention," he informed Lincoln, "but such is not the case." Much of Louisiana remained under Confederate authority, Federal control was too weak in many places to make a registration viable, and Federal officials were not providing the necessary assistance. Durant also reminded Lincoln that Louisiana, having gained one House seat under the 1860 Federal census, had not been reapportioned, and that until the legislature, which did not then exist, redistricted the state, or Congress authorized elections, the state could send no representatives to Congress. "It is not likely that any serious evil may result from the absence, for a time, from the House of Representatives, of members from Louisiana," Durant assured the president, who – aware of what the conservatives were up to – might have begged to differ. "In the mean time all can devote their energies to a more important object, that of reorganizing a state Government on the basis of freedom." In essence, Louisiana would not write a new constitution, establish a free-state government, or elect members to Congress by December, as Lincoln had hoped.[5]

It is difficult to know what might have angered Lincoln more: that the free-state plan was going nowhere; that the military was not assisting the free-state forces; or that Louisiana would not send members-elect to Congress. Even as Lincoln read Durant's letter, northern Democrats – along with proslavery Unionists in Louisiana, Tennessee, and elsewhere – were scheming to control the organizing of Congress. In early October, before he received Durant's letter, Lincoln had met with Michael Hahn, who, as a leading free-state moderate, blamed the lack of progress on Durant and the radicals. Later that month, by which point Lincoln had read Durant's letter, he met with Benjamin Flanders, the Treasury Department official who also went to Washington to brief Lincoln, and who, as an ally of Durant, pointed the finger at Banks. Lincoln's exasperation was evident. He now insisted, according to Flanders, that "the necessity for immediate action was so great that he would recognize and sustain a state government organized by any part of the state we then had control of," and he instructed Flanders "to say so on his return to Louisiana."[6]

Lincoln reiterated these views in an uncharacteristically blunt letter of early November to Banks. Three months earlier, he reminded Banks, he had approved of Durant's registry plan, of which Shepley had informed him at the time. Now, he learned that nothing was being done. Though admitting that this situation "disappoints me bitterly," Lincoln did not blame Banks, but he urged all parties "to lose no more time." Shepley had instructions from the War Department, Lincoln affirmed, referring to Stanton's August directive. "I wish him – these gentlemen and others co-operating – without waiting for more territory, to go to work and give me a tangible nucleus which the remainder of the State may rally around as fast as it can, and which I can at once recognize and sustain as the true State government," Lincoln insisted. "And in that work I wish you, and all under your command, to give them a hearty sympathy and support."

Shepley's instructions were predicated on the military working in conjunction with "the loyal element," by which Lincoln meant the advocates of both abolition *and* reunion. "Time is important," Lincoln emphasized, with the convening of Congress obviously in mind. "There is danger, even now, that the adverse element seeks insidiously to pre-occupy the ground." Lincoln harbored no illusions about what this "adverse element" would do. "If a few professedly loyal men shall draw the disloyal about them, and colorably set up a State government, repudiating the emancipation proclamation, and re-establishing slavery, I can not recognize or sustain their work. I should fall powerless in the attempt. This government, in such an attitude," Lincoln

---

[5] Thomas J. Durant to Lincoln, October 1, 1863, ALP.
[6] McCrary, *Abraham Lincoln and Reconstruction*, 173; Harris, *With Charity for All*, 118.

continued, employing familiar language, "would be a house divided against itself." Addressing the consequences of emancipation, Lincoln added that were a new state government, working in conjunction with the Federal government, "and consistently with general freedom," to enact "a reasonable temporary arrangement, in relation to the landless and homeless freed people," he would not object to it. However, "my word is out to be *for* and not *against* them on the question of their permanent freedom."[7]

It is tempting to interpret Lincoln's words as hyperbole, intended to goad Banks into action. The idea of a rebellious state returning to the Union with slavery intact, nearly a year after the Emancipation Proclamation had been issued, strains credulity. Yet this is precisely the problem certain antislavery advocates had been addressing for months, and it is precisely what conservative Unionists were attempting to do. At this point there was nothing to prevent, as a matter of law or policy, the rebellious states from repudiating the proclamation and reestablishing slavery, as Lincoln feared. Lincoln clearly had the conservative Unionists in mind in warning Banks of "a few professedly loyal men" setting up a proslavery government. Other than winning the war, the restoration of the insurgent states to the Union on a free-state basis – and preventing the return of those states with slavery – had become for Lincoln and Republicans the essential objective.

Focused as he was on military operations against Texas, Banks would not read Lincoln's letter until early December. Coincidentally, only days after Durant had written to Lincoln in early October, Shepley finally authorized a registration of voters in Union-occupied Louisiana. Later that month, Durant informed Banks that he was renewing the registration in the rural parishes. Banks might have derived some satisfaction from this information, except that Durant also addressed the rumor, then circulating in New Orleans, that Banks was assisting the conservative Unionists with *their* election. Having been alerted to the matter earlier by Durant and other free-state Unionists, Shepley had also written to Banks about the rumor. Banks responded immediately in separate letters to both men, disavowing any previous knowledge of the conservative Unionist election and denying he had assisted it in any way. While emphasizing that the conservative initiative reinforced the need to reconstruct Louisiana on a free-state basis as quickly as possible, Banks added that no election would revive Unionist sentiment in the state "that does not bind in some degree the leading men of the different political parties."[8]

---

[7] *CWL*, 7: 1–2.
[8] For Shepley's call for registration and the exchange between Durant, Shepley, and Banks: *New Orleans Bee*, October 12, 1863. See also McCrary, *Abraham Lincoln and Reconstruction*, 174, 176–77; Hollandsworth, *Pretense of Glory*, chap. 10.

Banks's belief that a free-state government might win over Louisiana's "leading men," including its planters, was an attempt to square the circle. Although lacking Federal sanction, the conservatives moved ahead. On October 21, more than a dozen of them – including attorneys J. Q. A. Fellows and A. P. Field, publisher Hugh Kennedy, former US and Confederate Postmaster James L. Riddell, and planter Thomas Cottman – met in New Orleans to discuss their election plan. Fellows also updated them on the plot to control Congress. Their ultimate goal, according to the northern correspondent in attendance, was "nothing less than an attempt to set the old State machine, with all its vilianous laws and edicts, in full operation." The attendees considered themselves "the only really unconditional Union men, because they are willing to accept the Union with slavery." This endeavor was "only the entering wedge," the correspondent insisted. Although "Rebels at heart," but also recognizing that the Confederacy was doomed, they now wanted to restore the "Union as it was," after having done everything they could to destroy it, "with slavery in all its pristine glory." Days later, the group published an address urging the voters to participate in the election and assuring them that Federal authorities would approve the results. The address also charged free-state Unionists with conspiring to territorialize Louisiana even as it invited them to participate in the election.[9]

Shepley at last quashed the elections in New Orleans. In several rural parishes, however, congressional (not state) elections were held on November 2. A conservative Unionist meeting several days later in New Orleans proclaimed A. P. Field and Thomas Cottman elected to the seats previously held by Benjamin Flanders and Michael Hahn, and it declared Joshua Baker, another conservative, elected to a third seat. Although Durant, in his capacity as state attorney general, denied the validity of their claims, Field and Cottman went to Washington and would be provisionally seated at the December convening of Congress. All three claimants would eventually be denied seats on the grounds that Louisiana could not enjoy congressional representation without having been reapportioned. Congress denied the claimants on a technicality, but the larger meaning of their defeat was clear. Lincoln had previously rejected the conservatives' petition to restore Louisiana under its antebellum constitution, and congressional Republicans would do much the same. The political campaign to preserve slavery was proving as fruitless as the one on Louisiana's plantations, but conservatives were far from done.[10]

---

[9] "Important Developments. Louisiana Desires to Return to the Union," *New York Herald*, November 3, 1863, 10 (reprinting item from the *New York Tribune* of November 2, 1863); McCrary, *Abraham Lincoln and Reconstruction*, 177–78.

[10] McCrary, *Abraham Lincoln and Reconstruction*, 178–80; Harris, *With Charity for All*, 119; Belz, "Etheridge Conspiracy of 1863," 556, 561–62.

III

While Louisiana conservatives were suffering another setback, the rift between free-state moderates and radicals widened. This division had so far remained latent, as both free-state factions focused on abolishing slavery. But the issue of black legal and political rights – and especially the inclusion of free black men in the voter registry – now came to the fore. Having followed closely the events of the previous year and a half, the New Orleans free black population began more assertively to demand racial equality. In June 1863, the free-state group had allied itself with *L'Union*, the French-language newspaper owned and operated by free men of color, with assistance from the white radical Jean-Charles Houzeau, and in July the paper went bilingual. Although the free people of color – and especially the Afro-Creoles – tended initially to focus on equal rights for themselves and not the former slaves, they eventually came to embrace universalist language. Indeed, owing to the efforts of the free people of color, nowhere else in the Union-occupied South did black suffrage become linked to state restoration more quickly or with more profound consequences for Reconstruction than in Louisiana.[11]

Although the free-state split would not fully manifest itself for some time, the fall of 1863 marked the emergence of black suffrage in free-state politics. At a large, interracial rally in New Orleans on November 5, only days after the conservatives' congressional election, a number of speakers, including several free black leaders, forcefully advocated black suffrage. Among them was P. B. S. Pinchback, who was destined to play a pivotal role in postwar Reconstruction politics in Louisiana and would serve as the first black governor in US history. Soon thereafter, a group of free black men petitioned Shepley to include free-born men of color, though evidently excluding former slaves, in the voter registry. Later that month, Benjamin Flanders returned to New Orleans. Armed with marching orders from the president for prompt action, free-state Unionists called on Shepley to set a date for the constitutional convention, suggesting late January. Shepley at first responded to neither request, being even more hesitant to act now that black suffrage was part of the equation. Speaking before another Unionist rally in early December, Durant implicitly endorsed limited black suffrage, insisting that free-born black people were entitled to full and equal citizenship rights. Just as free-state Unionists seemed poised to gain the upper hand over their conservative rivals, questions surrounding the consequences of emancipation had arisen

---

[11] Houzeau, *My Passage at the New Orleans Tribune*, 75. Every modern study of wartime Reconstruction in Louisiana emphasizes the split between free-state Unionists over black suffrage. There is also a considerable scholarly literature on the wartime political mobilization of the New Orleans free people of color, but see especially Bell, *Revolution, Romanticism, and the Afro-Creole Protest Tradition*, chap. 7.

potentially to divide them, while Durant himself seemed to be moving in a more radical direction.[12]

If Banks were displeased with these developments, he was mortified to receive in early December Lincoln's letter of a month earlier, admonishing him for the lack of progress in Louisiana. Banks managed not to fire off an intemperate reply. But he was clearly taken aback by Lincoln's allegations, and he offered an indignant though respectful response. "You will judge my surprise, leniently I hope, when I learned by your letter of the 5th of Nov. that you attached responsibility to my actions in regard to the execution of your wishes," Banks observed. "I assure you it is not so understood here. I do not so understand it." All Federal officials in Louisiana had been given to understand, by special instructions from Washington, that responsibility for state reorganization rested exclusively with Military Governor Shepley. Likewise, when the conservative Unionists' "unauthorized election" was made known, along with the rumor that he himself had given it his approval, Banks explained, both Shepley and Durant had officially notified him that Shepley alone was in charge of Louisiana's organization. Banks had nothing to do with it. "I have had neither authority, influence or recognition as an officer entrusted with this duty," he insisted. "My suggestions are respectfully, but silently received by the Governor and his associates."

Under the circumstances, Banks asked, how could *he* be held responsible for the results. "Had the organization of a *free* state in Louisiana been committed to me under general instructions only, it would have been complete before this day," he asserted. This goal could be accomplished in sixty days, "even in *thirty* days, if necessary," Banks added, employing his usual overstatement. But it required someone who possessed the necessary authority, could harmonize the various interests involved, and was committed "to the creation of a FREE STATE," Banks reasoned. "I do not suppose I have the qualifications for this duty; certain I am that I have not the authority," he demurred. "How then can I be held responsible for the failure to satisfy your expectations?" Banks's defense reflected considerable sophistry. Yet Lincoln had in fact only provided Banks with *suggestions*, not orders, and he had by no means put Banks unequivocally in charge in Louisiana. However disingenuous his argument, Banks had a point.[13]

Lincoln may have understood as much in his reply of December 24, which remains among the most important documents on his handling of wartime Reconstruction. Lincoln attempted to assuage Banks's bruised ego by arrogating responsibility for the Louisiana situation. He now unequivocally placed Banks in charge of reconstructing the state, using the term "master" four times in a relatively short communication. "I deeply regret to have said or done

---

[12] McCrary, *Abraham Lincoln and Reconstruction*, 182–85.
[13] *CWL*, 7: 90–91.

anything which could give you pain or uneasiness," Lincoln wrote. "I have all the while intended you to be *master*, as well in regard to re-organizing a State government for Louisiana, as in regard to the military matters of the Department." This is why all of his letters on Reconstruction in Louisiana, Lincoln explained, had been addressed directly to Banks. "My error has been that it did not occur to me that Gov. Shepley or any one else would set up a claim to act independently of you; and hence I said nothing expressly on the point." Among Lincoln's faults, it has often been noted, was a tendency to offer suggestions when direct orders were needed. Lincoln had done this with Banks, who could claim that he had not received clear authority. Thus, Lincoln, who never took public matters personally, had to accept the blame.

"I now tell you that in every dispute, with whomsoever, you are master," Lincoln informed Banks, who could not get this wrong. Shepley was "to *assist*" Banks and not to thwart or act independently of him. Shepley had received direct instructions merely to spare Banks "detail labor" and "not to supersede" Banks's authority. "This, in it's liability to be misconstrued, it now seems was an error in us. But it is past." In absolving Banks for previous misunderstandings, Lincoln placed responsibility for reorganizing a free-state government for Louisiana firmly upon his shoulders. "I now distinctly tell you that you are master of all, and that I wish you to take the case as you find it, and give us a free-state re-organization of Louisiana, in the shortest time possible." Military considerations must take priority over political ones, and Banks was not "to throw away available work already done for re-construction." Neither did Lincoln intend "that war is to be made upon Gov. Shepley, or upon any one else, unless it be found that they will not co-operate with you." In all such cases, Lincoln again assured his general, "you are master while you remain in command of the Department."[14]

Thirteen months after refusing to place Louisiana's reorganization under "our military and quasi-military, authorities," Lincoln was doing just that. But nearly a year after issuing the Emancipation Proclamation, and six months after denying the conservative-Unionist petition to restore Louisiana as a slave state, Lincoln had to acknowledge that the free-state cause in Louisiana had stalled. Instead, it was the *proslavery* Unionists who were sending members-elect to Congress. Lincoln and congressional Republicans could block the restoration of seceded states with slavery, but that was not same thing as abolishing slavery in them.

Lincoln's making Banks "master of all" in Louisiana arguably reflected an attempt to steer the free-state movement on a more moderate course, concerned as he was with the radicals' evident support for black suffrage and their apparent ascendency within the movement. In mid-December, Lincoln met with conservative Unionists Thomas Cottman and James Riddell. Perhaps hoping to preempt black suffrage, the two conservatives suggested that Louisiana's citizens

---

[14] *CWL*, 7: 89–90.

might accept abolition in return for a speedy restoration without black suffrage. They also recommended electing a state government under Louisiana's antebellum constitution and Lincoln's Reconstruction proclamation, which, announced a week earlier, made no mention of black political or legal rights after slavery. Such a proposal was especially imperative since Congress was expected to take up Reconstruction legislation, and since a movement was already afoot for an amendment to the Federal Constitution abolishing slavery. Either of these initiatives could possibly include black suffrage.[15]

Yet the notion that Lincoln was deflecting calls for black civil rights by turning Louisiana affairs over to the more conservative Banks must be measured against Lincoln's stated purpose to bring free-state Unionists *together* to abolish slavery. The last thing he wanted to do was to intervene in factional quarrels. "The strongest wish I have, not already publicly expressed, is that in Louisiana and elsewhere, all sincere Union men would stoutly eschew cliqueism, and, each yielding something in minor matters, all work together," Lincoln wrote to Cottman after their meeting, emphasizing the need to reconstruct Louisiana on a free-state basis. If anything, it was Banks who would take Louisiana's reorganization down a more conservative path, arguably against Lincoln's own wishes. Nonetheless, having put Banks in charge in Louisiana, Lincoln would become increasingly identified with Banks's handiwork.[16]

IV

Along with these events, an episode that would reach a *dénouement* at the opening of Congress in early December had also been developing. It involved the scheme – orchestrated by Emerson Etheridge, the disaffected Tennessee conservative Unionist who had become a bitter administration opponent – to seize control of the US House of Representatives upon the organizing of the Thirty-Eighth Congress. The "Etheridge Plot" had its origins in the reversals Republicans had suffered in the fall 1862 congressional elections. It entailed an attempt by Etheridge, as incumbent Clerk of the House, to fashion a coalition of northern Democrats, border-state Unionists, and several members-elect from the Union-occupied South – including the Louisiana claimants elected in November – to gain control of the House by invalidating on technicalities the credentials of several Republican and Unionist representatives.[17]

A former Whig, Etheridge had remained an unconditional Unionist during the secession crisis and had even been considered for the Cabinet. But by late

---

[15] McCrary, *Abraham Lincoln and Reconstruction*, 194–204; Vorenberg, *Final Freedom*, 48–53.
[16] *CWL*, 7: 66–67.
[17] Belz, "Etheridge Conspiracy of 1863." Unless otherwise indicated, the narrative and quotations presented here rely on this source.

1863 he had become an implacable administration foe. Owing to his allegiance and influence as a southern Unionist, Etheridge was elected Clerk of the House in July 1861, when the Thirty-Seventh Congress convened in special session. He continued to serve in that capacity, and under House rules he remained acting Clerk as the next Congress organized. Having backed the administration early in the war, he played a key role in convincing Lincoln to exclude Tennessee from the Emancipation Proclamation. But as Republicans embraced an emancipationist war, he broke with the administration, eventually becoming a leading Tennessee conservative Unionist.

It remains unclear how closely Etheridge, House Democratic leader Samuel S. "Sunset" Cox of Ohio, and other conservatives had coordinated their efforts to control the organization of the House. There had been talk of putting forward Frank Blair – of the prominent Maryland and Missouri family and brother of Lincoln's postmaster general – as Speaker. But Cox also began to envision a Democratically controlled House with himself in that role. Given the Republican electoral losses in 1862, along with the results in the border states and parts of the Union-occupied South in 1863, the pro- and anti-administration forces in the new House would be closely divided. The legal basis for the plan, paradoxically, was a loophole in a law Congress had passed at the very end of the Thirty-Seventh Congress, in March 1863, governing the organization of the next Congress. Although intended to preclude seating members-elect of dubious loyalty, or who had been elected under questionable circumstances, from the seceded states, the law instructed the Clerk of the House to place the names of members-elect on the House roll. This oversight made Etheridge, as one observer noted, "master of the position."

Any collusion between Etheridge and Cox remained nebulous, but as the two men communicated throughout the summer of 1863, an understanding emerged. Lincoln's rejection of Etheridge's late-September appeal to recognize William Campbell's election as governor of Tennessee was probably the last straw. Etheridge began writing to northern Democratic leaders on the credentials of congressional members-elect. He informed Cox during the fall of his intentions regarding the organization of Congress, and he indicated to Louisiana conservatives, as they planned congressional elections, that he would include on the House roll the names of any claimants. Were "the conservative majority" of the new House to elect the Speaker, remarked the Democratic *New York Herald* in late October, it would establish, "in that one act, the conservative policy of the President as the policy of Congress, and convince the rebellious States that the war is and will be prosecuted for the Union, and not for the abolition of slavery as the condition precedent to the readmission of the seceded States."[18]

---

[18] "The Speaker of the New Congress – The Duty of the Conservatives," *New York Herald*, October 31, 1863, 6.

As this and other commentary demonstrated, the Etheridge-Cox plot by this point had become an open secret. "It is a scheme as deep laid and as damnable as that by which the slave party sought to fasten slavery upon Kansas," insisted the northern correspondent who had attended the October meeting of Louisiana's conservative Unionists, and who warned of "a repetition of the Kansas frauds." By late October, Lincoln had been fully apprised of the plot, which no doubt influenced his caustic letter of early November to Nathaniel Banks. In the weeks before Congress convened, anticipation intensified. As rumors swirled of a potential coup, the administration and leading Republicans in Congress and the North discussed various countermeasures, including forcibly removing Etheridge from Congress if necessary.[19]

But things unraveled almost immediately. When Congress opened on December 7, with Lincoln's secretaries John Hay and John G. Nicolay in attendance, Etheridge left off the roll the names of sixteen Unionist or Republican members-elect, while including those of Thomas Cottman, A. P. Field, and Joshua Baker from Louisiana, elected a month earlier. Etheridge defiantly rejected an initial Republican attempt to have the excluded names read, but he then appeared to back down, ruling a second motion to be in order, over Democratic protests, and allowing the matter to go to a vote. Etheridge had seemed to lose his nerve at the critical juncture, according to John Hay. The names initially left off the roll were included, and the Republicans elected Schuyler Colfax as Speaker and went on to organize the House. The "coup," such as it was, had been averted.[20]

Still, it was a close call. Republicans had carried the crucial motion by a majority of twenty votes, which included five northern Democrats, six border-state Unionists, and A. P. Field himself. A flipping of those votes would have reversed the result. If the coalition that Etheridge, Cox, and other conservatives had envisioned held together, the organization of the House along Republican lines could have been blocked. What might have happened next is a matter of speculation. The northern claimants in question, whose elections were beyond doubt, could not have been excluded indefinitely. At the very least, the plot represented an attempt to assemble a conservative coalition at the first congressional session – and upon the convening of the first new Congress – since Republicans had linked state restoration to the abolition of slavery. This objective had yet to become law, however, and with Congress

---

[19] "Important Developments. Louisiana Desires to Return to the Union," *New York Herald*, November 3, 1863, 10 (reprinting item from the *New York Tribune* of November 2, 1863). For other northern commentary on the plot: [Stephen Pearl Andrews], "The Great American Crisis," *The Continental Monthly*, vol. 5, no. 1 (January 1864): 87–99 (pt. 2), esp. 97–98.

[20] Burlingame and Ettlinger, *Inside Lincoln's White House*, 121 (December 9, 1863). See also McCrary, *Abraham Lincoln and Reconstruction*, 178–80.

about to return to the question of Reconstruction, many conservatives saw this moment as the last chance to restore "the Union as it was." They had failed.

Antislavery Northerners also viewed the Etheridge plot as further evidence of the campaign to preserve slavery. Lambasting what it called "the so-called delegation from Louisiana" in a postmortem on the episode, *Harper's Weekly* summarized the two prevailing views on Reconstruction. The first held that the loyal people of the seceded states were entitled to representation in Congress "without regard to the social institutions which they favor for their respective States," while the second insisted that "no State shall be readmitted to the Union until it shall have purged its borders of slavery." The journal further demanded that Congress seat no southern claimants who had not been duly and legitimately elected. "[S]ome semi-rebels in Louisiana appear to be anxious to save some of their property from the wreck by sending certain persons to Washington as members of Congress," it warned, having previously sent their sons to the Confederate army and their "best speakers" to the Confederate Congress. It advised that the matter of Reconstruction be postponed until the rebellion had been suppressed. This echoed similar commentary from the same journal of a week earlier. "The time has not arrived for attempts to reconstitute State Governments even in Tennessee or Louisiana; and the chances are that, if premature experiments of the kind are made, the rebel sympathizers in those States will contrive to turn them to the advantage of the traitors." This was the very scenario many antislavery advocates feared, even if they disagreed on the solution. "[I]t will probably devolve upon the Thirty-eighth Congress to determine the conditions upon which this reconstruction and this restoration can be effected," the journal concluded. "But not just now."[21]

V

The Etheridge plot, in fact, foreshadowed a tumultuous legislative session. Before its July 1864 adjournment, Congress would address various matters relating to emancipation and state restoration, including Lincoln's ten-percent plan, a Reconstruction bill, and – perhaps most momentously, though it hardly

---

[21] *Harper's Weekly*, December 12, 1863, 786, and December 19, 1863, 802. Even as the Etheridge plot was going down to defeat, border-state and northern conservatives met in Cincinnati in early December, constituting themselves as the "Conservative Union National Committee." Including, among others, William B. Campbell of Tennessee, Garrett Davis, Thomas E. Bramlette, and Leslie Combs of Kentucky, and the old Jacksonian Amos Kendall, the group put forward the name of former Union General George B. McClellan for president in 1864. They met again in Philadelphia on December 24 and reaffirmed the nomination, also naming William Campbell for vice president. *Wisconsin Daily Patriot* (Madison, WI), December 7, 1863, 2; *The Crisis* (Columbus, OH), December 9, 1863, 368; *New York Herald*, December 25, 1863, 1; *Weekly Patriot and Union* (Harrisburg, PA), December 31, 1863, 1.

seemed so at first – a Federal abolition amendment prohibiting slavery throughout the nation. By late 1863, almost all Republicans maintained that military victory, state restoration, and the end of slavery were inseparable. Likewise, for the remainder of the war, the Federal abolition amendment, Reconstruction legislation, and events in the lower Mississippi valley would resonate as the notes of a discordant musical chord.

In his letter of late December making Nathaniel Banks "master" in Louisiana, Lincoln did not mention his Reconstruction initiative. The Proclamation of Amnesty and Reconstruction was announced on December 8 as part of the Annual Message to Congress. Given recent Union military success, along with frustration over state reorganization in Louisiana and Tennessee and the failure of Congress to enact Reconstruction legislation, some presidential initiative on Reconstruction was clearly in the offing. Lincoln's drafting of a plan during the fall was well known, and the opening of Congress saw much anticipation over what he would recommend.[22]

Insofar as the ten-percent plan represented a new departure concerning Reconstruction, it was *not* because Lincoln was finally turning his attention to this topic, as is often believed. Lincoln had been thinking about Reconstruction since before the war started. Rather, by recommending to Congress that the rebellious states be required to abolish slavery before resuming their place in the Union, Lincoln was attempting to craft a formal policy that incorporated abolition into the process of state restoration. As an executive matter, this was unprecedented – though the plan's abolition requirement was more implied than expressly stated. The plan would have profound repercussions for the lower Mississippi valley. Lincoln designed it very much with Louisiana in mind, but it would also stimulate restoration efforts in Arkansas and Tennessee. Only Mississippi remained impervious to wartime restoration.

As its title indicates, Lincoln's plan was based on the executive power under the Constitution to grant pardon or amnesty. Lincoln would pardon any person, "with restoration of all rights of property, except as to slaves," who, having participated "directly or by implication" in the rebellion, subsequently swore henceforth to uphold the Constitution and to abide by all wartime measures concerning slavery. Certain classes of persons were excluded, mostly high-ranking Confederate officials. For each seceded state, once a number of persons equivalent to one-tenth of the votes cast in the 1860 presidential election had taken the oath, then those persons who had taken the oath, and who had been qualified voters in the state before secession, "and excluding all others," could "re-establish a State government." This government "shall be republican," and, so long as it was "in no wise contravening said oath," it would be recognized "as the true government of the State." The states were enjoined

---

[22] Burlingame and Ettlinger, *Inside Lincoln's White House*, 121 (December 9, 1863); *CWL*, 7: 36–53 (Annual Message), esp. 50–53, and 53–56 (Proclamation).

to confer no political or legal rights on the former slaves. Lincoln would accept "any provision" the state government may adopt, "in relation to the freed people of such State, which shall recognize and declare their permanent freedom, provide for their education, and may yet be consistent, as a temporary arrangement, with their present condition as a laboring, landless, and homeless class." He imposed no other conditions regarding the former slaves. Lincoln indicated his flexibility on Reconstruction by allowing that Congress would decide on seating members-elect from the seceded states, and by affirming that his plan precluded no others.

Lincoln elaborated on his plan in the text of the Annual Message. In requiring individuals to accept wartime antislavery measures as a condition for pardon, he offered a strident defense of his emancipation policy. He reiterated his familiar refrains that the Emancipation Proclamation would not be modified or retracted and that no person freed during the war would be reenslaved, but he acknowledged the authority of Congress or the Supreme Court to modify or void the provision of the oath mandating acceptance of emancipation. In requiring loyalty of only one-tenth of a state's voters, Lincoln hoped to provide "a rallying point" – or what he had called "a tangible nucleus" in his November letter to Banks – to potential southern Unionists. His permitting any "temporary arrangement" in the South's labor system was made "with the view of possibly modifying the confusion and destitution which must, at best, attend all classes by a total revolution of labor throughout whole States." Although Lincoln had previously approved of apprenticeship, which would bind former slaves to work for a set number of years or until reaching a certain age, he now insisted that labor arrangements be "reasonable" and "temporary." He recognized that white southerners might more readily abandon the rebellion "if, to this extent, this vital matter be left to themselves," but he conceded no abridgement of the "power of the national Executive to prevent an abuse." Lincoln thus granted white Unionists much latitude – but not a free hand – in reconfiguring the region's social landscape.

Lincoln's plan initially earned praise from both moderate and Radical Republicans. In the ensuing months, however, the plan would receive increasing criticism, and scholars have often noted its shortcomings. Its failure to address black political or legal rights after slavery would attract much attention. Southern Unionists could establish new governments and write free-state constitutions, but without black suffrage those governments could never gain broad support. The plan also failed to call for a Federal abolition amendment, as some of Lincoln's advisers had recommended, or to employ Federal authority in any other way. The states would remain in charge of eliminating slavery. By providing the seceded states with no guidelines on how to achieve this goal, Lincoln left them free to enact gradual abolition plans that could take decades to complete, while also entitling them to the Federal compensation he had previously offered. It thus reflected traditional thinking on federalism and slavery.²³

But perhaps the plan's greatest shortcoming, one that historians tend to overlook, was its inability to require the rebellious states *explicitly* to abolish slavery. Instead, it called for them – by "in no wise contravening" the individual oath of allegiance – to comply with wartime antislavery measures. However, because the Emancipation Proclamation freed slaves but did not abolish slavery, as many contemporaries noted, the ten-percent plan likewise did not – and *could* not – expressly require the seceded states to abolish slavery as a condition of restoration. Here, Lincoln was assuming, as did many people, that freeing slaves and abolishing slavery were one and the same, or that the one would inevitably lead to the other. But neither of those suppositions was true. The seceded states could comply with the Emancipation Proclamation and ten-percent plan and still not abolish slavery. The Federal government lacked the authority under the Constitution to regulate slavery in the states. The president could emancipate slaves as a military measure to suppress rebellion, and Congress could enact legislation – presumably – requiring the seceded states to abolish slavery as a condition for restoration to the Union. But the president could not require the states to abolish slavery. Republicans had long since agreed that the seceded states must end slavery as a condition for restoration, even if they still disagreed over how precisely the states would do this. As Republicans would argue in the coming months, Lincoln's plan might actually allow those states to return to the Union with slavery in place.

Antislavery advocates began making this point almost immediately. Orestes A. Brownson identified what he believed were its numerous deficiencies, including its failure to provide sufficient safeguards for eradicating slavery. "The executive plan does not appear ... to give any adequate security even for the ultimate abolition of slavery," he contended. "It will, if the states are restored, and still hold their slaves even temporarily, be easy for them to alter their constitutions, prescribed by the executive, and make slavery perpetual. When once recognized as states they are competent to do it." Upon readmission, the rebellious states would again be free to govern their internal affairs, "and in ten or a dozen years slavery, in all the states, may be reëstablished as firmly as ever, perhaps more firmly than ever." Kentucky had already become "the grand slave mart of the Union," and soon after the war it would be able "to restock a large portion of the South." Despite wartime antislavery measures, Brownson concluded, there remained "plenty of nest-eggs for slavery."²⁴

---

[23] Palmer, *Selected Letters of Charles Sumner*, 2: 216–17; Burlingame and Ettlinger, *Inside Lincoln's White House*, 121–22 (December 9, 1863).

[24] Brownson, "The President's Message and Proclamation" [from *Brownson's Quarterly Review* of January 1864], and *Works of Orestes A. Brownson*, 17: 510–36 (quotations, 521–22).

The ten-percent plan did not redefine the war to the same degree as the Emancipation Proclamation. If anything, it obfuscated the crucial distinction – which antislavery advocates had been at pains to elucidate – between military emancipation and constitutional abolition. The plan would not end calls for retracting the proclamation; neither did it preclude the possibility of Confederates suing for peace on the basis of keeping slavery. Despite these limitations, it was still transformative. It now equated loyalty with support for Federal wartime emancipation measures, and it established the abolition of slavery – however implicitly and imperfectly – as a condition of state restoration. "[T]here can be no doubt that we are put under bonds of honor by the President's proclamation," opined a northern periodical. "If the destruction of slavery is to be a consequence of the war, shall we regret it? If it be needful to the successful prosecution of the war, shall any one oppose it? Is it out of the question to be constitutional, without putting the slaveholders back precisely where they were before they began the rebellion?" Northern Democrats – or, "the opposition" – may have been amenable to a peace that allowed slavery to continue, it added, "but it becomes more and more certain that the people, instructed by the experience of the past three years, will never consent to any plan of adjustment that does not include emancipation." Noting the "great strides" that public opinion had recently made "in the direction of freedom," the *New York Times* expressed a similar sentiment. "[A]nd now comes the Proclamation of the President to clinch the nail by declaring that the Union is to be reconstructed on the basis of general emancipation," it observed. "The public mind was ripe for this transcendently important measure."[25]

The ten-percent plan's limitations could also be misleading. White loyalists would enjoy exclusive control over state reorganization, and the states were under no obligation to address the consequences of emancipation. Yet just as Lincoln had believed that he could not issue the Emancipation Proclamation until he had exhausted all other possibilities, he also thought it premature to address emancipation's consequences before slavery itself had been eliminated. Lincoln was trying to unite all free-state Unionists around the single – and essential – goal of abolishing slavery, while sidestepping the divisive issue of black legal and political rights. Before the war, Lincoln and other centrist Republicans had tried to separate the end of slavery from racial equality (while also distinguishing between slavery in the states and its extension into the territories), whereas abolitionists

---

[25] "The President's Message," *The North American Review*, vol. 98, no. 202 (January 1864): 234–60 (quotation, 259); "President Lincoln's Plan for Reconstruction," *New York Times*, December 13, 1863, 5. See also "The President's Message," *Harper's Weekly*, December 26, 1863, 818.

countered that slavery and racial inequality were inseparable. Now, the key question for Lincoln and others like him was not whether abolition would lead to racial equality, but whether the seceded states would be required to abolish slavery at all. The ten-percent plan was Lincoln's attempt to ensure that they would be. But as his Republican critics would note, especially with reference to wartime Reconstruction in the lower Mississippi valley, it might fail to do even that.

* * *

Upon convening in December 1863, Congress undertook another major initiative: Various proposals were introduced that eventuated in an amendment to the Federal Constitution prohibiting slavery everywhere in the United States. The amendment, the success of which was hardly a foregone conclusion, would require two full years to be ratified – longer than the time between the start of the war and the Emancipation Proclamation. The groundwork for the amendment had been established in 1861 when Federal soldiers began emancipating slaves in Virginia, but it was also a strike into uncharted territory, overturning notions about the Constitution and slavery that dated to the origins of the republic. The Emancipation Proclamation brought Federal wartime emancipation measures to their logical conclusion by freeing all slaves in rebellious areas. Yet the proclamation could not end slavery as an institution. Antislavery advocates still faced the monumental task of translating military emancipation into constitutional abolition, a task that required political methods.

Many Americans believed by mid-1863 that slavery would never survive the war. Yet generations of Americans had also believed that only the states could abolish slavery, a view to which most Northerners adhered through the first two years of the war. Events in the lower Mississippi valley had revealed the myriad difficulties of translating military emancipation into constitutional abolition, not least of which was the possibility of conservative Unionists organizing new governments that would preserve slavery. By year's end, Lincoln and Republicans had fended off these challenges, but they could not do so indefinitely. The Federal abolition amendment ended the phase of the war – and of American history – in which regulating slavery was largely considered a state matter, but elements of this mindset would survive. Indeed, the amendment was originally thought of not as a stand-alone measure but as a complement to Federal legislation that would require the seceded states to abolish slavery as a condition for restoration to the Union. As developments relating to the lower Mississippi valley in 1864 would demonstrate, the abolition of slavery would proceed along two distinct but interrelated paths – state *and* Federal. The latter would supplement, not replace, the former.

Emancipation in the Lower Mississippi Valley

Figure 4 According to the original caption, this illustration is said to depict fugitive slaves who had previously belonged to Confederate President Jefferson Davis entering Federal lines at Chickasaw Bayou, Mississippi, probably sometime in late 1862 or early 1863. By this point in the war, formerly enslaved persons were arriving at Union lines *en masse* and were being emancipated under the confiscation acts or, after January 1, 1863, the Emancipation Proclamation. This illustration, the caption further notes, "might serve as well for a hundred similar scenes" wherever Federal military forces gained Confederate territory. *Getty Images*

Figure 5 This often-misidentified photograph, which probably dates from 1863, shows formerly enslaved persons who had secured refuge – and freedom – with Federal troops at what had previously been a female academy in Baton Rouge, Louisiana. (Note the soldiers in the background.) The preponderance of women is quite likely the result of the young men having been enrolled into the military. *Getty Images*

Union Officers Who Implemented Military Emancipation

Figure 6 Essentially apolitical before the war (though personally averse to slavery), Union General Ulysses S. Grant quickly embraced military emancipation upon entering Tennessee in early 1862, and he eventually became a strong proponent of black military enlistment. Victories in the lower Mississippi valley, at Vicksburg and Chattanooga in particular, would springboard Grant to command of all of the Union armies. *Getty Images*

Figure 7 Appointed by Ulysses S. Grant to oversee freed people's affairs in the Department of the Tennessee in 1862, Col. John Eaton became one of the former slaves' most forceful advocates and defenders in the Federal military establishment. He played an integral role in the transition from slavery to freedom in the lower Mississippi valley, focusing especially on educational initiatives for the freed people. Eaton served briefly in the Freedmen's Bureau after the war, and he devoted the rest of his long career to education. *Library of Congress*

Figure 8 As commander of Union forces in Arkansas in 1862, General Samuel R. Curtis went well beyond Federal policy, as it stood at the time, in emancipating enslaved persons throughout the Arkansas Delta, including issuing "free papers" to all fugitive slaves who escaped to Union lines. He was replaced in late 1862 by General Frederick Steele. *Library of Congress*

Figure 9 Appointed to command of Federal forces in Arkansas in late 1862, General Frederick Steele was a less enthusiastic supporter of military emancipation, and was more accommodating of former Confederates, than his predecessor, Samuel R. Curtis. Nonetheless, Steele – like his Louisiana counterpart, Nathaniel P. Banks – would oversee the creation of Arkansas's free-state constitution and Unionist government in 1864. *Library of Congress*

Figure 10 Although an influential Massachusetts Democratic state legislator who endorsed proslavery candidates before the war, General Benjamin F. Butler was the originator of Federal "contraband" policy in Virginia in 1861. A "political general," Butler was named commander of the Department of the Gulf (southern Louisiana) in early 1862, and he, along with Navy Flag Officer David Farragut, captured New Orleans that spring. Butler's uncompromising Unionism and harsh measures against Confederates – along with allegations of corruption – earned him white New Orleanians' undying hatred, and he was replaced in late 1862 by Nathaniel P. Banks. *Library of Congress*

Figure 11 A nationally prominent Massachusetts Republican who served as Speaker of the House in Congress and as Governor before the war, Nathaniel P. Banks was also a Union "political general" who replaced Benjamin F. Butler as commander of the Department of the Gulf in late 1862. Lincoln made Banks "master" of Louisiana's political affairs in late 1863, and Banks would steward the creation of the state's free-state constitution and government in 1864. His draconian labor policies, however, along with the failure of Louisiana's Unionist government to provide for black civil rights, elicited much criticism. Banks led the Union's disastrous Red River campaign in Louisiana during the spring of 1864. *Library of Congress*

Federal Military Authority in the Lower Mississippi Valley

Figure 12 Union army Adjutant General Lorenzo Thomas addresses a large crowd of freed people, including a number of black Union soldiers, in Louisiana in 1863. Thomas traveled extensively throughout the lower Mississippi valley between 1863 and 1865 recruiting and organizing black regiments, urging white Union soldiers to accept black enlistment, and fostering free-labor initiatives. As shown here, Thomas also spoke to the freed people about the possibilities and responsibilities of freedom, a message the freed people would hear repeatedly from Federal officials in the coming years. *Getty Images*

Figure 13 Union General Nathaniel Banks conducts a meeting with Louisiana planters at the St. Charles Hotel in New Orleans, probably in early 1863. As military commander for southern Louisiana, Banks attempted to reconcile the fundamentally conflicting interests of former slaves and former slaveholders, especially concerning life and labor on the plantations. Although the repressive features of Banks's labor policies generated much criticism from the freed people and their advocates, Louisiana sugar and cotton planters also found much to dislike about military-sponsored "free labor." Many of these planters would form the core of conservative Unionism, with the goal of restoring Louisiana to the Union as a slave state. *Getty Images*

National Political Leaders

Figure 14 Once Abraham Lincoln had issued the Emancipation Proclamation, his greatest fear – other than not winning the war – was the restoration of the rebellious states to the Union without abolishing slavery. Lincoln facilitated the creation of free-state governments in Arkansas, Louisiana, and Tennessee (and Virginia), and he played a key role in securing congressional passage of the Thirteenth Amendment. Yet his failure to reach accord with congressional Republicans on Reconstruction legislation – accentuated by his veto of the Wade-Davis bill in 1864 – left no policy in place for restoring the seceded states to the Union or for addressing the consequences of emancipation by the time the war ended – and upon his untimely death. *Library of Congress*

Figure 15 A US Representative and Radical Republican from Ohio, James M. Ashley was an early supporter of emancipation who steered the Thirteenth Amendment through the House. He also devoted much effort – ultimately futile – to enacting Reconstruction legislation during the war, and he in fact saw the amendment and such legislation as interconnected. *Library of Congress*

Figure 16 A US Representative and Radical Republican from Maryland, Henry Winter Davis was a staunch critic of Lincoln's Reconstruction policy for what he saw as its failure to secure the abolition of slavery. He co-sponsored (with Ohio US Senator Benjamin F. Wade) the Wade-Davis bill, which would have required the rebellious states to write free-state constitutions as a condition for readmission, and he co-authored the vitriolic Wade-Davis Manifesto after Lincoln vetoed the bill in July 1864. Davis saw the Thirteenth Amendment, which he supported, as inadequate for addressing the myriad issues of state restoration, and he doubted whether a sufficient number of *loyal* states would ratify it. *Library of Congress*

Leading Free-State Southern Unionists

Figure 17 Andrew Johnson's disastrous presidency has overshadowed his laudable record as Military Governor of Tennessee from 1862 to 1865. Although he hated slavery and despised the planter elite, whom he held responsible for the war, Johnson endorsed the successful petition to Lincoln in late 1862 to exclude Tennessee from the Emancipation Proclamation. Yet he eventually became a strong supporter of emancipation and of black military enlistment. He also oversaw the abolition of slavery in Tennessee in early 1865 – though opposing black political and legal equality – before ascending to vice president. *Library of Congress*

Figure 18 An East Tennessee Unionist known for his vitriolic rhetoric as a newspaper publisher, Methodist minister, and former Whig politician, William G. "Parson" Brownlow supported slavery at the start of the war but eventually converted to abolition. Along with his rival, Democrat Andrew Johnson, Brownlow led Tennessee's free-state loyalists, and he won election as governor in early 1865. *Library of Congress.*

Figure 19 Born in Virginia in 1799, Isaac Murphy was a small slaveholder and educator from northwest Arkansas. He intrepidly opposed disunion, and, as a delegate at Arkansas's 1861 secession convention, he ultimately cast the lone vote against secession. Forced into exile, Murphy later returned to Arkansas to organize loyalists, and he was elected the state's first free-state governor in 1864. *Courtesy Shiloh Museum of Ozark History/Peter Harkins Collection (S-90-194-40)*

Figure 20 Along with Isaac Murphy, William M. Fishback led Arkansas free-state Unionists. Born and raised in Virginia, he moved to Illinois in the late 1850s, becoming personally acquainted with Abraham Lincoln, before settling in Arkansas prior to the war. Fishback originally opposed secession but voted in favor of it as a delegate at the 1861 secession convention before later reverting to Unionism. Although widely seen as an opportunist of dubious loyalty, Fishback was elected to the US Senate by the state's Unionist government in 1864 but was not seated. He later served as Governor of Arkansas. *Courtesy Arkansas State Archives (PHC3019)*

Figure 21 An Arkansas slaveholder and Confederate general, Edward W. Gantt abandoned the Confederacy and converted to free-state Unionism after his capture in 1863. He conferred frequently with Lincoln thereafter, and he was instrumental in abolishing slavery in Arkansas and in organizing the state's Unionist government under Lincoln's ten-percent plan. *Courtesy Butler Center for Arkansas Studies, The Paul Dolle Civil War Collection (BC.MSS.03.18), Central Arkansas Library System*

Figure 22 A German-born immigrant who settled in New Orleans with his family as a youth, Michael Hahn was a Democrat before the war but stridently opposed secession. Remaining in the city, he became an influential Unionist following the Federal occupation of southern Louisiana in 1862 and was elected to Congress that December. As a leading free-state moderate who opposed black political and legal equality, Hahn (with Nathaniel P. Banks's backing) was elected Louisiana's first free-state governor in 1864. He resigned in early 1865 upon his election to the US Senate, but he was ultimately not seated. Like almost all free-state moderates, Hahn came to support black suffrage, and he was injured in the New Orleans riot of July 1866. *Getty Images*

Figure 23 A Rapides Parish planter and former slaveholder, J. Madison Wells had led Unionists in central Louisiana during the early phase of the war before making his way to New Orleans and becoming involved in Unionist politics. Wells came to support the abolition of slavery, although he initially opposed black political and legal equality. Elected Lieutenant-Governor in 1864, he became Governor in early 1865 when Michael Hahn resigned after winning election to the US Senate. After the war, Wells at first allied with conservatives and former Confederates and supported Andrew Johnson's Reconstruction policy, but he eventually broke with them and sided with Louisiana Republicans, even endorsing black suffrage. Wells's support for reconvening the 1864 constitutional convention contributed to the New Orleans riot of July 1866. *Library of Congress*

Figure 24 This illustration from *Frank Leslie's Illustrated Newspaper* depicts the inauguration of Michael Hahn as Unionist Governor of Louisiana in March 1864 in New Orleans (the capital of Unionist Louisiana during the war). Creation of the loyalist government was largely overseen by General Nathaniel P. Banks, whom Lincoln had placed in charge of Louisiana's Reconstruction. At the time, Federal forces controlled less than half of Louisiana's territory and slavery remained to be formally abolished in the state. Many people would question the legitimacy of this government. Although Louisiana's 1864 constitution would abolish slavery, and the state's ratification of the Thirteenth Amendment would be counted, Congress would not recognize Louisiana's reconstructed government, and Louisiana would come under Radical Reconstruction in 1867. *Library of Congress*

Leading Conservative Unionists

Figure 25 A former Whig and Tennessee Governor before the war, William B. Campbell was a proslavery Unionist from middle Tennessee whose supposed election as civilian governor in 1863 failed to win recognition from Lincoln. He was considered a possible running-mate to George B. McClellan in the 1864 presidential election but declined to have his name put forward, owing to the ascendance of Peace Democrats. *Courtesy Tennessee State Museum and Tennessee Historical Society Collection (1.860)*

Figure 26 A nationally prominent Tennessee proslavery Unionist and Congressman, Emerson Etheridge served as Clerk of the US House of Representatives for the Thirty-Seventh Congress (1861–1863). He originally supported the Lincoln administration but broke with it over Union emancipation policy and became an outspoken critic. He also helped to coordinate the failed "Etheridge Plot," which attempted to control the organizing of the closely divided Thirty-Eighth Congress in December 1863. He would be briefly incarcerated after the war for his continued criticism of Tennessee's free-state government and constitution. *Library of Congress*

Figure 27 Christian Roselius was a German-born immigrant who became an influential New Orleans attorney before the war and a leading Louisiana conservative Unionist during it. Recognized for his brilliant legal mind, he strongly opposed disunion (though he acceded to Confederate authority after Louisiana seceded), but he also rejected approaches to Reconstruction that required the abolition of slavery. Although Roselius readily took the oath of allegiance following the Federal capture of New Orleans in 1862 (before the Emancipation Proclamation had been issued), he protested against having to take subsequent oaths that included support for emancipation. *Images of the Civil War and Reconstruction, Tulane University Special Collections*

Postwar Scenes

Figure 28 William H. Grey emerged as an influential African American political and religious leader in Arkansas near the end of the war. Born free in Washington, DC, in 1829, he moved west with his family before settling in St. Louis just before the war. By 1865, Grey had relocated to Helena, and he delivered the keynote address at the political convention held in Little Rock in late 1865 that advocated black political and legal equality. He became a leading black political figure in Arkansas during Reconstruction. *Courtesy Arkansas State Archives (PS02.1)*

Figure 29 This depiction of black Union soldiers being mustered out of the service and reuniting with family members and other loved ones at Little Rock, Arkansas, in the spring of 1866 was representative of similar scenes that took place throughout the South in the year or so after the war. The presence of black soldiers in the Union army of occupation enraged many white Southerners, and black soldiers would make up nearly a third of the confirmed fatalities in the Memphis massacre of May 1866. *Library of Congress*

Figure 30 This image from *Harper's Weekly* portrays the violence that engulfed Memphis, Tennessee, between May 1 and 3, 1866. While the illustration depicts the wanton and deliberate shootings of African Americans and conveys the impression of arson, it does not show the other forms of violence – aggravated assault and battery, robbery and theft, destruction of property, and rape and sexual assault – that the city's black population endured. This episode would prove to be only one of many race "riots" or massacres during Reconstruction, but as the first it shocked the nation. No perpetrator of the violence at Memphis – or at New Orleans nearly three months later – was so much as charged with a crime. *Getty Images*

Figure 31 This illustration – one in a series from the August 25, 1866, issue of *Harper's Weekly* depicting various scenes from the New Orleans riot of July 30 – shows the struggle over the US flag between black processioners, including many Civil War veterans, and a white mob in the moments before violence erupted. White New Orleanians, led by the city's police force, were determined to stop the reconvening of Louisiana's 1864 constitutional convention, which was planning to implement black suffrage and bar former Confederates from office. The Memphis and New Orleans "riots" together profoundly turned northern public opinion against Andrew Johnson's Reconstruction policy and led to Radical Reconstruction. *Getty Images*

PART III

Abolition: State and Federal, 1864

10

"Slavery Is Incompatible with a Republican Form of Government"

The events of 1863 demonstrated the difficulties of moving from military emancipation to the constitutional abolition of slavery. Republicans and their northern supporters had come to agree that the seceded states must abolish slavery as a condition of restoration to the Union, but converting that objective into reality was another matter. The period between the opening of Congress in December 1863 and the US Senate's approval in April 1864 of an amendment to the Federal Constitution abolishing slavery witnessed the first substantive attempts by congressional Republicans, following the Emancipation Proclamation, to conjoin state restoration and the abolition of slavery as a matter of law. This initiative produced subtle yet critical differences in the various Republican approaches. Meanwhile, the abolition of slavery via a constitutional amendment – which was not nearly as inevitable as it appears in hindsight – emerged out of a cluster of proposals for securing wartime emancipation and organizing loyal governments in the seceded states. Many contemporaries viewed abolishing slavery through the state constitutions – under Federal oversight, as part of the process of organizing new state governments – to be a more practical and secure means of ending slavery than amending the US Constitution, which had not been done since the era of the Founders. Even the most radical of abolitionists before the war had assumed that the states, not the Federal government, would abolish slavery. By early 1864, Republicans had long since achieved consensus on linking abolition and state reorganization but not on a Federal constitutional amendment.

As the congressional session began, Republicans were prepared to cooperate with Lincoln in crafting Reconstruction legislation. This legislation would work in conjunction with the Federal abolition amendment, which was not originally designed as a stand-alone measure for abolishing slavery. As political reorganization on a free-state basis unfolded in Tennessee, Arkansas, and Louisiana, however, congressional misgivings over Lincoln's Reconstruction policy became evident. Lincoln and congressional Republicans were united on winning the war and ending slavery, but Henry Winter Davis of Maryland, a leading Radical in the House of Representatives, put forward a Reconstruction bill that he envisioned as an alternative to both Lincoln's plan and the abolition amendment.

Although the US Senate, enjoying an overwhelming Republican majority, easily passed the amendment in April, Republicans still considered legislation on state restoration equally essential to ending slavery.

I

"Congress is tranquil – beyond all precedent," Charles Sumner, the US Senator from Massachusetts and one of the towering figures of the antislavery movement, remarked to the abolitionist Thomas Wentworth Higginson several days after Congress convened. "Never before since I have been here have the signs of a quiet session been so positive. The battle of 'ideas' was fought in the last Congress," he added. "It remains now only to assure the victory, & this we shall do." As events would show, Sumner's assertion that the battle of ideas had already been thrashed out could not have been more wrong.[1]

In fact, once they had derailed the Etheridge plot, congressional Republicans moved promptly to address state restoration and emancipation. Although facing a significantly reduced majority in the new Congress, they overwhelmingly supported Lincoln's ten-percent plan; and while many of them doubted the success of an abolition amendment, they were fully committed to destroying slavery. The House of Representatives immediately established, with near Republican unanimity, "the Select Committee on the Rebellious States," which included a balance of moderates and Radicals. Although chaired by Henry Winter Davis, who was destined to become a major opponent of Lincoln's plan, the committee was originally intended to work with Lincoln. Most congressional Republicans assumed that the plan required legislation to become operative. In early 1864, even as state restoration initiatives in Tennessee, Arkansas, and Louisiana were gathering steam, Lincoln and congressional Republicans were largely in accord.[2]

Of the various measures introduced at the start of the session addressing state restoration, the most important was a bill by Representative James M. Ashley of Ohio, another leading Radical who at about the same time also proposed a constitutional amendment abolishing slavery. Ashley conceptualized the two measures in tandem, as part of what Michael Vorenberg has called "a two-pronged program of reconstruction – a constitutional amendment to secure emancipation, and a reconstruction statute to enforce it." Ashley's bill, which was evidently drafted in consultation with Secretary of War Edwin M. Stanton, War Department solicitor William Whiting, and perhaps

---

[1] Palmer, *Selected Letters of Charles Sumner*, 2: 213.
[2] Belz, *Reconstructing the Union*, 168–76; Oakes, *Freedom National*, 430–45; Benedict, *Compromise of Principle*, 73–77. For a concise overview of Davis's background, see Richards, *Who Freed the Slaves?*, 137–44.

Lincoln himself, was the first substantive congressional response to the ten-percent plan, and it served as an important predecessor to the better-known Wade–Davis bill.[3]

Despite important differences between Ashley's bill and Lincoln's plan, the former was generally understood to supplement the latter. Indeed, as Rebecca E. Zietlow has noted, Ashley's bill marked an important ideological shift by its author, who now abandoned territorialization as the basis for Reconstruction and replaced it with the more palatable (for most Republicans) "republican form of government" guarantee. Employing this principle, Ashley's new bill required the seceded states to end slavery as a condition for restoration to the Union. "Slavery is incompatible with a Republican form of government," the bill's preamble declared. "[T]he existence of slavery in the insurrectionary States has caused and maintained the rebellion therein," it continued, "and the Emancipation of said slaves and a constitutional guarantee of their perpetual freedom is essential to the permanent restoration of State governments, Republican in form." Toward that end, the bill envisioned the main tasks of Reconstruction as writing new constitutions that would abolish slavery and establish loyal governments in the seceded states. By requiring the states themselves to abolish slavery, though under Federal oversight, Ashley's bill adhered to traditional notions of federalism and slavery. How the state constitutions came to be written and implemented, and how they addressed the consequences of abolition, produced important differences between Ashley's and Lincoln's plans, but these differences were considered manageable.[4]

Ashley's bill directed the president to establish an interim military government in each seceded state under Federal control, which was intended to be temporary and to facilitate the establishment of civilian government. The "Provisional Military Governor," appointed by the president, assumed responsibility for civil administration and for enforcing the law and all presidential proclamations until a state government could be organized. The bill sanctioned the freedom of all enslaved persons liberated by wartime Federal antislavery measures. It also provided "that all laws, judicial decisions, or usages which recognize or sustain slavery," or which excluded black testimony in courts of law, denied black people the right to trial by jury, or punished

---

[3] Vorenberg, *Final Freedom*, 48–54, on the link between Ashley's bill and the constitutional amendment (quotations, 49, 51). In quoting Vorenberg, I have collapsed together two separate passages that speak to the same issue. Rebecca E. Zietlow also emphasizes the link for Ashley between his Reconstruction bill and a Federal abolition amendment, although Ashley did not subscribe to the Federal consensus and believed the Federal government already possessed the authority to regulate slavery in the states. *Forgotten Emancipator*, 109–12. Benedict, *Compromise of Principle*, 73–74, on consultation with Stanton, Whiting, and perhaps Lincoln.

[4] Zietlow, *Forgotten Emancipator*, 111; Belz, *Reconstructing the Union*, 179–80 (quotation, 179).

persons who taught black people to read or write, "shall be utterly void." The bill thus moved significantly toward equality before the law, and it criminalized any attempt to deprive a former slave of his or her freedom or to arrest any former slave for failure to pay a debt.

The bill outlined the process of establishing loyal governments in greater detail than did Lincoln's plan. Once the people of a Federally occupied state "signified to the Governor a desire to return to their obedience to the Constitution," the provisional governor would order an enrollment of all adult male citizens. Ashley's bill, like Lincoln's plan, thus allowed for Reconstruction to begin before the war ended. When this enrollment equaled 10 percent of the 1860 vote, the provisional governor would order an election for delegates to a constitutional convention. All persons were required to take Lincoln's oath, supporting emancipation and pledging future allegiance, to vote for or to serve as a convention delegate. However, the bill also barred from the convention process persons who voluntarily bore arms against the United States or who held civil or military office under Confederate authority. This provision, much stricter than Lincoln's voting requirement, was tantamount to the "ironclad oath," and it ensured that only genuine loyalists would participate in wartime Reconstruction. By mandating the enrollment of "all loyal male citizens," without the qualifier "white," moreover, and by guaranteeing that "every male citizen of the United States," with the exception of former Confederates, "shall be entitled to vote" for convention delegates, the bill further secured loyalist control of the new governments – by allowing for black involvement – even as it paved the way for black suffrage.

Ashley imposed stricter requirements on the new constitutions than did Lincoln. The constitutions had to be "Republican and not repugnant" to either the US Constitution or the Emancipation Proclamation. They were required to recognize and guarantee the freedom of all persons liberated under Federal military emancipation, to abolish slavery immediately and permanently, and to prohibit leading former Confederates from voting and holding office. No person who had held civil or military office under Confederate authority could vote in any state election or hold any state office until pardoned by the legislature. The bill did not explicitly require the constitutions to include black suffrage, but the black suffrage mandate in the elections for convention delegates indicated that they were expected to do so. Ashley's bill thus included sterner punishments against former Confederates and stronger guarantees of the former slaves' legal and political rights than did Lincoln's plan.

Finally, the new constitution would go to the voters, including black men and excluding former Confederates, for approval, and a state government would be elected. The president would then issue a proclamation "declaring the government formed to be the constitutional government of the state," and US Senators and Representatives would be elected and "entitled to appear" in Congress. Should the new constitution fail to meet the bill's provisions, the state would remain under military government and subject to Federal oversight until the people of the state produced an acceptable one. In theory, Ashley's bill allowed for the possibility of a state remaining indefinitely under military control, but the political revolution it was intended to spawn would presumably prevent such an eventuality. Oddly, Ashley's bill was designed to complement and not challenge Lincoln's plan, but it gave white southern Unionists who opposed black civil rights greater incentive to proceed under Lincoln's plan. The bill was immediately referred to the House select committee on the rebellious states, on which Ashley served.[5]

Although Ashley's bill was intended to work in conjunction with a proposed Federal abolition amendment, congressional Republicans were far from agreeing in early 1864 that amending the Constitution offered the best means for abolishing slavery in the United States. A grassroots campaign had swept the North in 1863, garnering more than a million signatures, to petition Congress for a comprehensive Federal antislavery measure. Early in the current session, Republicans responded by introducing a number of bills toward that end. Still, such an objective faced seemingly insurmountable obstacles. In addition to many Americans' aversion to amending the Constitution in principle, let alone to abolish slavery, there remained the practical problem of securing state ratification. With a total of thirty-five states in early 1864, the eleven seceded states alone could block ratification. "From the nature of the case such an amendment cannot be consummated at once. Time must intervene, with opportunities of opposition," Charles Sumner would warn in comments supporting the amendment. "Even under the most favorable circumstances it is impossible to say when it can become part of the Constitution. Too tardily, I fear, for all the good that is sought. Therefore I am not content with this measure alone. It postpones till to-morrow what ought to be done to-day." Because the only way to ratify the amendment would be to require approval by the seceded states as a condition for readmission, Reconstruction legislation was essential. "The amendment of the Constitution meets my hearty approval," Henry Winter Davis later declared in support of his own Reconstruction measure, while noting the impossibility of getting the necessary states to ratify the amendment, "but it is not a remedy for the evils we must deal with."[6]

---

[5] Belz, *Reconstructing the Union*, 178–85, on which my summary of the bill relies, including quotations from the text. See *CG*, 38th Cong., 1st Sess., 681 (December 21, 1863) for introduction of the bill, and *House Journal*, 38th Cong., 1st Sess., 87 (December 21, 1863) for referral to committee.

[6] Vorenberg, *Final Freedom*, 36–40, on the petition drive; Oakes, *Freedom National*, 430–31, 437; [Sumner], *No Property in Man*, 18; *CG*, 38th Cong., 1st Sess., appendix, 84 (March 22, 1864; Davis). For an excellent overview of the Thirteenth Amendment, see Foner, *The Second Founding*, chap. 1.

Under the circumstances, congressional Republicans showed little urgency on an abolition amendment. The various proposals from both houses of Congress, including Ashley's, were referred to the Senate Judiciary Committee, chaired by Lyman Trumbull of Illinois, which took the lead on the matter. In drafting the amendment, Trumbull's committee ultimately rejected proposals that addressed the consequences of emancipation – such as one by Charles Sumner that would have made all persons "equal before the law" in addition to abolishing slavery – in favor of a narrower measure that was thought to reflect republican simplicity. Borrowing the language of the Northwest Ordinance of 1787 and invoking the Founders, the amendment declared that "neither slavery nor involuntary servitude, except as a punishment for crime, whereof the party shall have been duly convicted, shall exist within the United States, or any place subject to their jurisdiction." It also empowered Congress to enforce the article "by appropriate legislation." Much debate ensued, at the time and since, over how to construe this language. Radicals hoped for an expansive reading, especially of the enforcement provision, whereas most Republicans, and the few Democratic supporters, were more concerned with eliminating slavery as a source of conflict among white Americans than with securing a meaningful freedom for black Americans. For a host of reasons, congressional debate on the amendment would not begin until well into March.[7]

Historians have devoted little attention to the curious omission, given the significance with which it was freighted, of the word "abolish" or its variants in the text of the amendment. Employing the imperative, the amendment decreed that slavery "shall" not exist anywhere in the United States. While this wording affirmed that the Federal government would enjoin the states or any territory from having slavery, it also reflected the idea of the amendment as a supplement to state abolition. Federal authority would ensure that the seceded states abolish slavery as a condition for restoration to the Union. As Michael Vorenberg has shown, debate over the enforcement clause focused on the possibility of the defeated rebellious states refusing to comply with this requirement. In such instances, Federal power would be employed to prevent any state from continuing to have slavery or from refusing to abolish it. The amendment thus articulated the abstract principle of prohibiting slavery in the states. But it also rested on the assumption that the seceded states would abolish slavery as part of the restoration process, and it guaranteed that no state, having abolished slavery, would ever reintroduce it. Almost by definition, the amendment thus functioned as a *complement* to state abolition, which

---

[7] Vorenberg, *Final Freedom*, 51–60, and 71–79 on Democratic support for the amendment; Oakes, *Freedom National*, 438–45; Foner, *The Second Founding*, 28–32; *CG*, 38th Cong., 1st Sess., 553 (February 10, 1864).

would be mandated by Reconstruction legislation, rather than as an independent measure to abolish slavery through Federal power.[8]

II

Most observers expected the differences between the ten-percent plan and Ashley's Reconstruction bill to be reconciled, and the prospects of Lincoln and congressional Republicans agreeing on Reconstruction legislation initially appeared promising. By mid-February 1864, however, this understanding was breaking down, and discord over state reorganization in Louisiana and Arkansas was growing.[9] In contrast to the circumstances of a year earlier, when Congress had seated Benjamin F. Flanders and Michael Hahn in order to *exempt* southern Louisiana from the Emancipation Proclamation, election cases in these two states demonstrated congressional doubts over Lincoln's Reconstruction policy.

In late January, Congress considered the three Louisiana claimants elected in November under conservative-Unionist auspices. Their claims had nothing to do with the ten-percent plan or the government Banks was organizing, but those matters became unavoidable. The brief debate focused on Louisiana's reapportionment under the 1860 census, Military Governor George Shepley's suppressing of the elections, and the previous seating of Flanders and Hahn. It also addressed whether small Unionist minorities in the seceded states, working under Federal military authorities, could form legitimate governments – the very raison d'être of Lincoln's plan. Even moderate Republicans expressed reservations on this matter. Henry Winter Davis then submitted a resolution contending that there existed "no legal authority to hold any election" in Louisiana, and that any attempt to hold an election was "a usurpation of sovereign authority" and had been "properly forbidden" by the US military.

---

[8] Vorenberg, *Final Freedom*, 50, 67–68, 114, 132–33. Although neither James M. Ashley's Reconstruction bill nor his version of the amendment would ultimately be adopted, congressional Republicans would pursue both objectives in tandem – at least until early 1865, when the amendment would take precedence over Reconstruction legislation.

[9] As early as mid-January, for instance, Thaddeus Stevens of Pennsylvania, a leading Radical Republican in the House, submitted his own Reconstruction bill that made not the slightest pretense of complementing Lincoln's plan but instead was predicated on territorialization. Maintaining that only Congress possessed "sufficient power permanently to change or annul [the municipal laws and domestic institutions]" of the seceded states, the bill provided that "all laws and parts of laws which permit slavery shall be, and are hereby abolished" in all territory "conquered and subdued" by Federal arms, and that "slavery shall never again be established within said territory." No state would be readmitted, moreover, until its people "shall, by its organic law, forever prohibit slavery." The bill went nowhere, but it reflected early misgivings among some congressional Republicans over Lincoln's policy. Belz, *Reconstructing the Union*, 193–94; H.R. [US House of Representatives bill] 118, 38th Cong., 1st Sess. (January 11, 1864).

Davis's motion, though ruled out of order, spoke more to the conservative Unionists' sham election than to the current Louisiana situation, and the three claimants, as expected, were not seated. But the debate and Davis's resolution portended deep disagreement over Louisiana.[10]

The Arkansas election case was more complicated, since it directly involved the free-state government Unionists were then organizing, but it revealed similar concerns. It entailed James M. Johnson, the unconditional Unionist elected to Congress in November, following the Federal capture of Little Rock. Immediately after the adjourning of a January convention in Little Rock that had written a free-state constitution and had scheduled for mid-March a referendum on it and state and congressional elections, Johnson was dispatched to Washington to claim his seat in Congress. When the House initially took up his case in mid-February, debate focused not on the merits of his claim but on whether his credentials should even be received and referred to committee. Congress had routinely adopted this course on previous occasions and had done so in the Louisiana cases. By this point, however, congressional Republicans were receiving letters from free-state radicals in Louisiana complaining about Nathaniel Banks, and they were themselves following Louisiana affairs. They did not like what they saw. Henry Winter Davis once again took the lead, moving that the case be tabled and not even referred to committee. "[I]t is not a mere question of election law, which would be involved," he argued, "but a question of the recognition or refusal to recognize the organization of a State government in Arkansas." Davis was correct that no government currently existed in Arkansas that was recognized by the United States, but Unionists there had been organizing a free-state government for months, and Johnson's election had resulted from their efforts.

The House therefore debated – in addition to such philosophical questions as the essential nature of governments and constitutions – the merits of the Arkansas and Louisiana governments then being organized and the authority under which this was being done. There was considerable sentiment to receive the credentials, since it was evident that Johnson – whose Unionism was beyond reproach – would not be seated anyway. Eventually, Davis's motion to table was defeated, and the case was referred to the House committee on elections. Johnson ultimately would not be seated, but the whole matter again indicated serious Republican misgivings over the Louisiana and Arkansas governments then being organized. Indeed, even before it had been resolved, Henry Winter Davis, in conjunction with Benjamin F. Wade, US Senator from Ohio, had already proposed an alternative to Lincoln's Reconstruction policy – the Wade–Davis bill. Congressional debate on this bill would very much focus

---

[10] Belz, *Reconstructing the Union*, 195–96; *CG*, 38th Cong., 1st Sess., 411–15 (January 29, 1864); Benedict, *Compromise of Principle*, 76.

on the shortcomings of Lincoln's governments, especially over abolishing slavery, in the lower Mississippi valley.[11]

III

Although Lincoln and congressional Republicans were committed to winning the war and ending slavery, the Wade–Davis bill further underscored the growing differences between them – and among congressional Republicans – over Reconstruction. James M. Ashley had envisioned his Reconstruction bill and the abolition amendment as a legislative package, and he had intended his bill to work in conjunction with Lincoln's plan. But he had failed by mid-February to get his bill out of committee. Instead, Henry Winter Davis, as head of the House select committee on the rebellious states, had introduced his own measure as an alternative to both Ashley's bill and the amendment, and as the more effective means for addressing the twin problems of emancipation and state restoration. Davis's bill would undergo significant revision before Congress passed it as the session ended in early July, but its importance to wartime Reconstruction – especially in the lower Mississippi valley – cannot be overstated.[12]

Much overlap but also significant differences characterized Davis's and Ashley's bills. Predicated on the Constitution's republican-government clause, Davis's bill reaffirmed the power of Congress to require the rebellious states to abolish slavery as a condition for readmission to the Union. It also recognized the states as existing entities that had not left the Union and acknowledged the temporary nature of the provisional governments. Davis provided for a civilian rather than a military provisional governor and defined the provisional governor's duties more broadly than did Ashley, though both bills saw that official's main role as one of organizing a constitutional convention that would establish a loyal government and abolish slavery. Perhaps the most salient difference between the bills was that Davis's postponed state reorganization until the

---

[11] Belz, *Reconstructing the Union*, 195–97; Cowen, "Reorganization of Federal Arkansas," 39, 51–52; *CG*, 38th Cong., 1st Sess., 680–87 (February 19, 1864; Davis, 681–82, 685). Johnson seemed to think that his case would not be decided until the Arkansas constitutional referendum and election in mid-March, but no member of Congress seems to have suggested that course. J. M. Johnson to I. Murphy, February 8, 1864, Steele Papers, Stanford.

[12] On the failure of Ashley's bill and its replacement with Davis's, see Vorenberg, *Final Freedom*, 128–29; Zietlow, *Forgotten Emancipator*, 112–13. Zietlow also observes that Ashley saw his bill and the amendment as complementary, whereas Davis envisioned his own bill "as an alternative to the amendment, in case the amendment failed," and she suggests that it was the black suffrage provision that doomed Ashley's bill (113). In introducing his own bill (*CG*, 38th Cong., 1st Sess., appendix, 82–85), Davis elaborated at length on the weaknesses of both the amendment and Lincoln's ten-percent plan.

military conflict had ended and thus made no allowance for wartime Reconstruction.

The role of former Confederates and the status of the former slaves – two particularly divisive issues regarding state reorganization – also produced notable differences. Davis's bill, like Ashley's, did not attempt the legislative abolition of slavery, but it secured the freedom of all enslaved persons liberated during the war and emancipated those who had not been, declaring that "they and their posterity shall be forever free." Davis then went beyond Ashley's bill by guaranteeing that any person who "shall be restrained of liberty," under the pretense of any claim to service or labor, would be freed in Federal court on a writ of habeas corpus. The Davis bill further criminalized any attempt to reenslave or reduce to involuntary servitude any person freed by the act or by wartime antislavery measures, and it invalidated the enforcement of any law or usage "whereby any person was heretofore held in involuntary servitude" in the seceded states. The bill also initiated equality before the law by directing that "the laws for the trial and punishment of white persons shall extend to all persons."

While the emancipation provisions of Davis's bill were similar to or even stronger than those in Ashley's, Davis included the qualifier "white" in determining participation in the state reorganization process. By negating the black suffrage provision that was crucial to Ashley's bill, and that distinguished it from the ten-percent plan, Davis excluded black people from any role in Reconstruction. Perhaps owing to the fate of Davis's bill, in revised form, and the controversy over Lincoln's veto, its retreat from Ashley's endorsement of black suffrage is almost always overlooked. Yet even as it excluded black men from political power, Davis's bill also imposed stronger proscriptions on former Confederates. State reorganization would not begin until the rebellion had been militarily suppressed and the people of each seceded state, as determined by the provisional governor, had "sufficiently returned to their obedience to the Constitution and the laws of the United States." Reconstruction would thus be initiated by the provisional governor and not by the people themselves, and only after the military conflict was over. This provision arguably marked the most significant difference between Davis's bill and both Lincoln's and Ashley's plans, since it did not envision the creation of loyal southern governments during the war. Once the war had ended and the provisional governor had made the necessary determination of obedience, he would order an enrollment of "all white male citizens of the United States," each of whom would swear to uphold the US Constitution. Once this number had reached 10 percent of the 1860 vote, as in both Lincoln's and Ashley's proposals, the provisional governor would order an election for delegates to a convention that would establish a state government.

The Davis bill, like Ashley's, imposed the ironclad oath, prohibiting any person who held office under Confederate authority or who voluntarily bore arms against the United States from participating in the convention process. However, while Davis's bill also specified, as did Ashley's, that the new constitutions must bar any former Confederate civil or military official from voting for or serving as a state legislator or governor, it *excluded* Ashley's proviso allowing the state legislature to lift this proscription. Indeed, Davis included no mechanism for politically rehabilitating former Confederates (though the state constitutions could presumably address this issue). Davis's bill likewise included a provision, entirely absent from Ashley's, specifying that every person "who shall hereafter" hold any civil or military office under Confederate authority "is hereby declared not to be a citizen of the United States." Whereas Lincoln's plan called for future loyalty and forgave past acts, and whereas Ashley's bill punished past acts but permitted future political rehabilitation, Davis's bill punished past acts while making no provision for later dispensation, and it punished continued disloyalty after its enactment by stripping Confederates of their US citizenship.

The rest of the reorganization process in Davis's bill essentially resembled Ashley's. The new state constitution, in addition to punishing former Confederates, would be required to prohibit involuntary servitude "forever" and to guarantee "the freedom of all persons," but the bill mandated no explicit constitutional guarantee of black legal or political rights. Oddly, while both bills provided for some form of equality before the law during the state reorganization process, and Ashley's even called for black suffrage, neither one expressly required the new constitutions to incorporate this principle. The constitution would have to gain voter approval, again limited to white loyalists, and a state government would be elected. Once the constitution was approved, the president, with congressional assent, would declare the new government to be the duly constituted one, after which US Senators and Representatives would be elected. Were the constitution not to comport with the act, the provisional governor would dissolve the convention, and – only after the president had made the necessary determination of loyalty – the whole process would begin again.[13]

The exclusion of black suffrage from Davis's bill was not considered exceptional. Radical Republicans – let alone all Republicans – were not yet united in early 1864 on the measure, which was considered too divisive, especially when abolition itself had yet to be achieved. The issue was already causing a rift among Louisiana free-state Unionists, and the defeat at this time of black suffrage in legislation organizing a territorial government for Montana did not augur well for implementing it in the seceded states. Increasing congressional doubts over state restoration in Louisiana and Arkansas, moreover, did not amount to opposition to Lincoln's Reconstruction policy. As committed as

---

[13] H.R. 244, 38th Cong., 1st Sess. (February 15, 1864); Belz, *Reconstructing the Union*, 198–208; Richards, *Who Freed the Slaves?*, 146–48.

congressional Republicans were to abolishing slavery, they were genuinely apprehensive over the legitimacy of new constitutions and governments in the seceded states created without the sanction of law. They were equally dubious over the allegiance of those states' white populations. "There is no rebel State held now by the United States enough of whose population adheres to the Union to be intrusted with the government of the State," Davis maintained, in support of his bill. But with preparations being made for the spring 1864 military campaign, and with General Ulysses S. Grant about to assume command of all Union armies, Northerners were hopeful of victory. Having introduced his Reconstruction bill in mid-February, but with so much other congressional business pending, Davis did not attempt to move forward with it until mid-April, as the governments in Arkansas and Louisiana took shape.[14]

IV

By mid-March, the Senate prepared to debate the Federal abolition amendment. In the three months since its introduction into Congress, northern society deliberated on the amendment as well as on the larger principle – which was relatively new at this point in American history – of amending the Constitution as a means of social reform. Although the amendment had gained considerable traction among the public, a number of Republicans, both Radicals and moderates, expressed doubts, fearing, especially in a presidential election year, the charge of racial equality. A few Democrats supported the measure, but the majority unalterably opposed it. Many abolitionists, black and white, and the northern black community were less vested in the amendment at first than they would be a year later. They hardly opposed it, but they bemoaned its failure to address issues they considered inseparable from abolition: equality before the law, voting rights, and economic independence.[15]

Once congressional debate commenced, Republicans had to balance the potential partisan advantage the amendment might give them in an election year against the need for Democratic support, in the House in particular, to secure a two-thirds majority. The debate was shaped as much by legal and constitutional theory as by overt partisanship. It was also unprecedentedly frank on the question of slavery. Whereas other issues, such as states' rights, had always camouflaged previous debate, lawmakers now spoke expressly about slavery and its role in the war. Republicans castigated the

---

[14] *CG*, 38th Cong., 1st Sess., appendix, 83 (March 22, 1864; Davis). The provision in Davis's original bill requiring only 10 percent of the voters to swear allegiance would be revised to 50 percent in the final version. On the Montana bill, and on congressional sentiment in early 1864 on Reconstruction, especially the Wade—Davis bill, see Benedict, *Compromise of Principle*, 70–83, 77–79.

[15] Vorenberg, *Final Freedom*, chap. 3.

"Slave Power" for corrupting the antislavery origins of the Constitution or averred that the Founders had been wrong to think that slavery would eventually die out. The war was a tragic consequence of this error, which the amendment would rectify, even if doing so meant rethinking the Constitution. Democrats blamed abolitionist fanaticism, aided and abetted by the Republicans, for inflaming the public mind and driving the South to secede, or they simply alleged that Republicans had planned abolition all along. Ignoring the question of slavery's morality, Democrats employed, according to James Oakes, the "twin pillars of proslavery thought": the inviolability of property rights and the innate inferiority of black people. At the same time, as Michael Vorenberg has observed, both sides worked harder at "describing their opponents' transgressions" than in examining how the amendment would work.[16]

Senate debate on the amendment – which took place during the last week of March and first week of April – was highly partisan but also veered toward the political center. Republicans emphasized the amendment's limitations and elided the issue of racial equality. Democrats employed their familiar race-baiting strategy but largely avoided the inflammatory rhetoric that would later characterize House debate. They steered clear, for instance, of the recently coined term "miscegenation." The few proamendment Democrats were also critical to formulating a broadly conceived amending power. They thereby contradicted decades of party orthodoxy, and of American thought, which held that the Constitution, as the work of the Founders, could not be substantively amended.[17]

Oddly, the Senate devoted little attention to how the states would eliminate slavery or to the enforcement clause, despite the avowed intentions of former slaveholders – in the lower Mississippi valley in particular – to replace slavery without using the term. Also missing were the previous year's difficulties in organizing governments in Louisiana and Tennessee, especially the conservative-Unionist threat to preserve slavery, or the current reorganization efforts in the lower Mississippi valley. The concrete questions relating to state restoration had no appreciable impact on Senate debate on the amendment. However, political reorganization in Louisiana and Arkansas was being discussed in other contexts, such as the seating of members-elect from those states. Moreover, with debate still pending on the Wade–Davis bill, and with most Republicans still linking the amendment to Reconstruction legislation, there was little reason to delve into Reconstruction during debate on the amendment. Indeed, for all of the amendment's shortcomings, its simple elegance and unencumbered language cut through the clumsy verbiage of

---

[16] Vorenberg, *Final Freedom*, 89–96 (quotation, 95); Oakes, *Freedom National*, 437–56 (quotation, 450).
[17] Vorenberg, *Final Freedom*, 96–112.

legislative attempts, such as Ashley's and Davis's bills, to secure emancipation and prohibit slavery in the future. But that very simplicity and limited scope also precluded it from addressing the knotty questions surrounding state restoration and the consequences of emancipation. If state restoration and the fate of slavery had been converging since late 1862, Senate debate on the amendment provided the first indication that the abolition of slavery might come to supersede state restoration as a northern political objective.

* * *

On April 8, 1864, the Senate approved – thirty-eight to six, with five absences – the constitutional amendment abolishing slavery. All Republicans voted in favor, as did several border-state Democrats and Unionists and three northern Democrats. Republican unanimity made the amendment seem a partisan issue, but border-state and northern Democrats, though few in number, were evenly divided. Debate would not take place for nearly two months in the House, where the amendment faced a much steeper challenge. "The issue is at last openly joined," observed *Harper's Weekly* after the Senate vote. "If the House fail to concur by the necessary two-thirds vote, the Congressional elections of next autumn will turn upon the question of the Constitutional Amendment, and the vote of this spring shows what the result will be."[18]

The Senate vote hinted at a paradox. Reconstruction legislation – which congressional Republicans had been considering for two full years, and which was initially seen as an essential complement to the abolition amendment once that measure had been introduced into Congress – would not be enacted before the end of the war. By contrast, the abolition amendment – originally thought to have little chance of success – would win congressional approval before the war ended, leap-frogging over state-level abolition. In the states of the lower Mississippi valley save Mississippi, the abolition of slavery – though initiated by the executive branch rather than the legislative – would be carried out much as Republicans and other antislavery advocates had always intended, by *state* means, whereas slavery would end in the other rebellious states – except Virginia, which also abolished slavery by state action – under Federal dictate after the war. Owing to events over the next year, future generations would come to see Federal abolition as the original goal and state abolition as the exception. Yet most Americans at the time would have considered Federal abolition to be exceptional and state abolition the norm.

---

[18] "The Amendment to the Constitution," *Harper's Weekly*, April 23, 1864, 258.

11

Of Foul Combinations and the Common Object

Congressional action on Reconstruction in early 1864 both shaped and was shaped by Unionist politics in the lower Mississippi valley. Spurred on by Abraham Lincoln's ten-percent plan, Tennessee, Arkansas, and Louisiana each took a distinctive path toward organizing loyal governments and abolishing slavery. All three also witnessed heightened intra-Unionist conflict on these matters. Tennessee and Arkansas – examined in this chapter – offered a study in contrasts akin to the tortoise and the hare. In Tennessee, where various constituencies pressured Military Governor Andrew Johnson to commence state reorganization, Johnson responded by authorizing local rather than state elections and by prescribing a loyalty oath that generated fierce opposition. Enjoying some initial success, Johnson's election plan was soon beset by what an ally referred to as "foul combination[s]," hampering further progress.[1]

Arkansas Unionists, meanwhile, plowed forward by crafting a free-state constitution in January 1864 that by mid-March had won popular approval. The speed of the process caused considerable confusion, however, and the whole initiative exuded a ramshackle quality. Neither did the absence of conflict over abolishing slavery preclude Unionists from splitting into "radical" and "conservative" factions over further democratic reforms. By mid-April, Arkansas had formally ended slavery – achieving what Lincoln called "the common object" – and a new government prepared to assume power. But its foundations were as soft as its organization had been speedy. Arkansas Unionists had written a free-state constitution consistent with Lincoln's guidelines, but the new government would encounter determined resistance in asserting its authority, especially in enforcing the constitution's emancipation provisions.

I

In late December 1863, with east Tennessee finally secure, Andrew Johnson traveled to Washington to confer with Abraham Lincoln. Reiterating his

---

[1] Lincoln's plan also spawned Unionist efforts in Florida, Alabama, and North Carolina in early 1864, but they were of little consequence. Meanwhile, Virginia's loyal government also arranged for a constitutional convention that would abolish slavery.

long-held view that no state elections could take place until Unionists controlled the entire state, Johnson proposed holding local elections that would serve as an initial step toward reestablishing a state government. This approach was not in keeping with Lincoln's proclamation, but Lincoln as usual deferred to Johnson on state matters. Johnson remained wary of an unholy alliance between conservative Unionists and former Confederates that might seize control of any new government. His opponents countered that he was obsessed with holding onto power and exacting vengeance against them. They also employed racial demagoguery by alleging – all evidence to the contrary – that Johnson advocated racial equality in addition to abolishing slavery.

Meanwhile, Johnson's own supporters – in petitions directly to him and in a series of mass meetings in Memphis, Nashville, and elsewhere – called for state reorganization under Lincoln's ten-percent plan, hoping to forestall the more radical measures, such as James M. Ashley's Reconstruction bill, then before Congress. Black Tennesseans likewise mobilized, often in defiance of state and local laws prohibiting them from assembling in public. They held marches, parades, and other demonstrations to demand the abolition of slavery and equal rights. Led by soldiers, ministers, businessmen, and other leaders, and representing churches, schools, fraternal organizations, and other institutions, these events celebrated the progress already made toward freedom while rejecting methods of Reconstruction, including Lincoln's, that left black people with no voice.[2]

Johnson could hardly ignore these overtures. Returning to Tennessee in mid-January, he began to indicate that state reorganization would soon commence. "I am satisfied that a convention should be called which will put the state at once upon its legs [and] for ever settle the slavery question," he wrote to congressman Horace Maynard. "Public sentiment is becoming stronger every day for a restoration of the Government." At a Nashville Unionist meeting on January 21, Johnson proposed, as he had with Lincoln, first holding local elections. In determining who would participate in them, he pledged "a hard oath – a tight oath," stricter than Lincoln's "exceedingly lenient" one. With local officials installed, a state convention would be held that would revise – not rewrite – the existing constitution to abolish slavery and organize a state government. Amending the constitution by means of a convention was essential, even though the state constitution did not expressly allow for a convention, since doing so through the legislative process was impossible without an existing state government. Johnson also feared that proslavery Unionists might try to preserve slavery by utilizing a state constitutional

---

[2] Previous two paragraphs: *PAJ*, 6: 528 (petition); Trefousse, *Andrew Johnson*, 170–72; Cimprich, *Slavery's End in Tennessee*, 104; LeForge, "State Colored Conventions of Tennessee," 231–32; Harris, *With Charity for All*, 212–13.

provision prohibiting the legislature to emancipate slaves without their owners' consent. Amending the constitution via a convention might generate "a little croaking dissatisfaction," Johnson admitted, but "sometimes we may do irregular things for the sake of returning to law and order." As a dyed-in-the-wool Jacksonian, Johnson maintained that a convention represented the true voice of the people. "Who dare say the people shall not assemble in convention?" Johnson also castigated the slaveholders whom he held responsible for the rebellion, insisting that their "social power must be destroyed," even as he endorsed "a white man's government." Hoping that "the negro will be transferred to Mexico, or some other country congenial to his nature," he contended, as he often did, that abolition "will free more white men than it will black men." For Johnson, abolishing slavery and preserving white supremacy were inseparable.[3]

Several days later, on January 26, Johnson issued a proclamation announcing his plan. He authorized elections on March 5 for county and local officials that would include only white men who had taken a prescribed oath and who met the state's voting requirements. Johnson's oath went beyond Lincoln's, requiring voters to swear henceforth to uphold the US Constitution and "defend it against the assaults of all its enemies." Voters also had to swear to "ardently desire" the suppression of the rebellion, the "success" of Federal armies, "and the defeat of all those who oppose them," and to "heartily aid and assist all loyal people in the accomplishment of these results." Whereas Lincoln's oath required Confederates to resume their allegiance and cease participating in the rebellion, and to support emancipation, Johnson's required them to contribute actively to suppressing it. Johnson's oath made no mention of wartime antislavery measures, but it required support of all laws and proclamations made in upholding the US Constitution. These elections would serve as "an initiatory step," Johnson pledged, toward the state's reorganization. "All other steps will be taken, looking to the election of the other officers, Federal and State, as soon as practicable."[4]

Predictably, Johnson's "Damnesty oath" provoked howls of protest from persons who, having taken Lincoln's oath, understandably believed that they

---

[3] *PAJ*, 6: 548–51, 557 (Maynard), 574–90 (Nashville); Cimprich, *Slavery's End in Tennessee*, 105; Trefousse, *Andrew Johnson*, 171–72. Under Tennessee's constitution, an amendment required passage by two consecutive legislative assemblies and approval in a popular referendum. This provision, not uncommon in nineteenth-century state constitutions, would have been difficult to meet even under the best of circumstances. Although the state constitution did not expressly allow for a constitutional convention, it included a provision declaring that "[a]ll power is inherent in the people, and ... they have at all times an inalienable and indefeasible right to alter, reform or abolish the government in such a manner as they think proper." Cimprich, "Military Governor Johnson and Tennessee Blacks," 66.

[4] *PAJ*, 6: 594–96; Trefousse, *Andrew Johnson*, 172–73.

had already been pardoned. "I had supposed that upon taking Mr. Lincoln's oath persons otherwise qualified under the Constitution of Tennessee, would be completely qualified, without doing anything more to exercise the privilege of voting," Edwin H. Ewing, former congressman and editor of a conservative Nashville newspaper, complained to Johnson. "Then, I would ask, will it be necessary also, before a person is allowed to vote, that he should take the oath prescribed by you? If this be so," Ewing continued, "then the taking of Mr. Lincoln's oath does not restore one who has been in rebellion to all of his civil personal rights, one of which is the right of voting." Others appealed directly to Lincoln. Their logic may have been sound, but Lincoln was not buying it. He refused to intervene and supported Johnson. Responding to one petitioner that "no conflict" existed between the two oaths, Lincoln affirmed that Johnson's "is entirely satisfactory to me," adding that no one who had been pardoned under Lincoln's oath, "and who intends to observe the same in good faith, should have any objection to taking that prescribed by Governor Johnson as a test of loyalty."[5]

Lincoln undoubtedly felt he had to support Johnson, and his ten-percent plan had left room for other modes of Reconstruction. But there was no denying that Lincoln had specified that all who had taken his oath were qualified to participate in state reorganization. Johnson's oath was both divisive and counterproductive. It alienated conservative Unionists and former Confederates who might have accepted Lincoln's emancipation policy, in return for pardon, even as it gave political cover to emancipation's opponents by deflecting attention away from emancipation to Johnson's oath. Conservative Unionists who hoped to preserve slavery, for instance, could claim that they opposed Lincoln's Reconstruction program *not* because it required support for emancipation but because of the severity of Johnson's oath. Still, although Johnson may have antagonized potential white allies, to whom Lincoln had offered wide latitude in defining black freedom, neither Lincoln nor Johnson was willing to risk proslavery Unionists gaining control of a reorganized government.

Johnson's oath undoubtedly contributed to the uneven election results. Many individuals refused to take the oath and were barred from voting. As had happened in 1862, moreover, Confederates also partially disrupted the elections. Voting was light in parts of central and west Tennessee. "[S]ome of our Union men shrank Back and Left me almost alone," remarked a Johnson supporter at Clarksville, where a mere eighty-four votes were cast. "Our men of wealth are almost all southern sympathizers." Memphis and Nashville, though, reported hotly contested campaigns. "So far as I have been able to learn the Election was a Complete success," observed Union General Alvan C. Gillem,

---

[5] *PAJ*, 6: xliii ("Damnesty"), 600–1 (Ewing); *CWL*, 7: 209–10; Harris, *With Charity for All*, 214–15; Trefousse, *Andrew Johnson*, 173–74; Atkins, "Failure of Restoration," 309–10.

also Johnson's adjutant general. "Ed Ewing & Co through their mouth peice the 'Press' did everything in their power to prevent the *People* from voting. So far they have failed." Gillem overstated the matter, but 40,000–50,000 votes were cast statewide, and some two-thirds of Tennessee's eighty-four counties elected officials. "I hope we shall have a convention called Ere Long when the people will meet and fix the status of our state," remarked the same Johnson supporter in Clarksville. "[Y]our most bitter opponents in this section are your old Democratic friends (the Leaders)," he added. "[W]ith the masses you have a hold. I think the Skies are Brightening and Ere 12 months we shall have peace."[6]

Johnson found the results encouraging. "Indications on the part of the people were much better than I anticipated in regard to the emancipation of Slavery," he assured Lincoln in early April. "As Soon as practicable there must be a Convention, which I believe will Settle the Slavery question definitely and finely." Johnson also explicitly endorsed for the first time the Federal abolition amendment, which the Senate was just then about to pass. "[T]he Sooner it is done, the better." State restoration in Tennessee seemed finally to be gaining momentum.[7]

II

Perhaps sensing that public opinion in Tennessee was shifting toward abolition, and still angered by Johnson's oath, some conservative Unionists, especially in east Tennessee, again attempted to circumvent his authority, this time by calling a convention of their own. In early April, the conservative Thomas A. R. Nelson, who had presided over a convention of east Tennessee Unionists at Greenville in June 1861, called for that body to reconvene on April 12 at Knoxville. The original Greenville convention had not tried to prevent Tennessee from seceding but instead had hoped to form a separate state of East Tennessee that would remain neutral in the coming conflict. Johnson was aware of the proposed Knoxville convention and inquired of William G. "Parson" Brownlow whether to attend it. But it was probably the advice of James R. Hood, another ally, who cautioned, "it is important to forestall indesreet men at Knoxville," that convinced Johnson to attend.[8]

The Knoxville convention, though dominated by genuine Unionists, featured acrimonious debate. The conservative majority objected to Lincoln's ten-percent plan, especially its implementation by Johnson, and charged that any new state constitution would allow Johnson to perpetuate his power by disfranchising his opponents, as his oath had demonstrated. They also

---

[6] *PAJ*, 6: 638–39, 643–45; Harris, *With Charity for All*, 215.
[7] *PAJ*, 6: 658–60, 663–64 (Lincoln).
[8] *PAJ*, 6: 663–64; Harris, *With Charity for All*, 215–16.

condemned Lincoln's emancipation policy and called for Tennessee's continued exemption from the Emancipation Proclamation, although some were amendable to gradual, compensated abolition. When Johnson's supporters countered by putting forward resolutions supporting emancipation, black enlistment, and Lincoln's reelection, rancorous debate ensued. A vitriolic speech by Johnson – denouncing the rebellion and slavery though conspicuously avoiding the question of a state constitutional convention – received prolonged applause. Still, it could not mask the divisions among *east* Tennessee Unionists, the very persons without whom Johnson had long insisted the state's reorganization could not begin. After four days, the delegates gave up trying to reach agreement and adjourned.[9]

Knoxville hardly boded well for a state convention that would address the contentious issues of abolition and state reorganization. Once the convention adjourned, Johnson and his supporters immediately held their own mass meeting on April 16 in Knoxville, designed to galvanize support for the proposed state convention. Brownlow, Johnson, and others delivered addresses, with Johnson again defending a convention as the will of the people and emphasizing that slavery was effectually defunct but remained to be ended legally. "This thing called Slavery is lying dead; we can't hold on to it any longer," he insisted. "Then call the Convention and recognize the fact as it exists," he added, and "legalize freedom." The attendees agreed. Yet they just as vehemently affirmed the Federal and state governments as "*the Governments of the free white man.*"[10]

By this point, officials who had been elected in March were beginning to take office and reestablish local government. Johnson issued a supplemental proclamation in early April authorizing local elections in communities that had been unable in March to conduct them. During April and May, these officials also assumed office. Johnson's plan of reconstructing Tennessee at the local level first, working toward a convention that would abolish slavery and organize a state government, seemed to be moving forward. At the same time, however, Confederate sentiment was too widespread and the military situation too precarious to allow for a statewide election, while conservative Unionists were still a viable threat. Although east Tennessee was under Union control, the devastation and civilian suffering in the region hampered political reorganization efforts. Under the circumstances, Johnson had no choice but to postpone calling for the state convention that was supposed to have followed the local elections "as soon as practicable" – a decision that outraged Johnson's opponents, frustrated his supporters, and disappointed Lincoln.[11]

---

[9] *PAJ*, 6: 670–73; Harris, *With Charity for All*, 215; Cimprich, *Slavery's End in Tennessee*, 105–6; Trefousse, *Andrew Johnson*, 174.

[10] *PAJ*, 6: 673–79; Harris, *With Charity for All*, 216–17; Trefousse, *Andrew Johnson*, 174.

[11] *PAJ*, 6: 658–59; Harris, *With Charity for All*, 217.

Johnson would not have found reassuring a letter he received in late April from the Memphis Unionist James B. Bingham. "I am opposed to any more elections, State or Municipal, until we have one for the election of members of a State Convention, and I am in favor of putting that off for several months," Bingham advised. "With very few exceptions, the men now in possession of our municipal government are unprincipled, disloyal and even dishonest," he continued. "If you permit another farce of a municipal election, *before the election for* members to a State Convention, the effect will be all injurious to *our* Side, because in the small vote usual in a municipal election, they will probably be able to triumph, which will give them strength in the State election to follow." Bingham recommended that Johnson appoint genuine Unionists to office rather than allow candidates of questionable loyalty to be elected. "By appointing our officers, we break up the foul combination, put better men in their places, and have all the advantage for our own side." Johnson could not disagree. But after more than two full years as military governor, he faced increasing calls to restore civilian government even as he staved off attempts by "foul combinations" to thwart his administration. Such was not what Johnson had had in mind back in December when he proposed his local election plan to Lincoln.[12]

III

Events in Arkansas outpaced this halting progress in Tennessee. The ten-percent plan may have had no more galvanizing an effect than in Arkansas, where abolition and state reorganization, despite having previously lagged behind Louisiana and Tennessee, occurred with lightning speed. Yet there remained a superficial quality to the whole enterprise. Although abolishing slavery proved to be less divisive among Arkansas Unionists than in Louisiana or Tennessee, state reorganization still produced factionalism. "Unionism" in Arkansas had sprung from many different sources, which did not always work well together, even though the chances of preserving slavery had long since expired. Following Federal military gains of the fall, Unionists planned for a constitutional convention in January in Little Rock. Lincoln had not reappointed a military governor after John S. Phelps resigned in early 1863, so General Frederick Steele, a West Point graduate and the Arkansas military commander, assumed oversight of the initiative. Like his Louisiana counterpart Nathaniel P. Banks, Steele boasted firm antislavery credentials, but a decidedly conservative tone – as with Banks – infused his administration.[13]

---

[12] *PAJ*, 6: 680–82.

[13] John B. Steele to [Frederick Steele], January 14, 1864, Steele Papers, Stanford; Moneyhon, *Impact of the Civil War and Reconstruction on Arkansas*, 159; Harris, *With Charity for All*, 197; Cowen, "Reorganization of Federal Arkansas," 39–41.

Lincoln's ten-percent plan inspired Arkansas Unionists with optimism for a speedy state restoration. A large Unionist meeting in Little Rock in late December, in anticipation of the convention, approved a series of resolutions that included support for emancipation. It also appointed a delegation – led by former Confederate general Edward W. Gantt – to consult with Lincoln and gain his support for the convention initiative. Steele at first believed that matters were perhaps moving *too* quickly, since much of the Arkansas countryside had yet to be pacified, but he soon saw the value of a loyal state government. Toward that end, and no doubt taking his cue from Lincoln, he employed a conciliatory policy toward Confederates, expressing a willingness to work with anyone who resumed allegiance and agreed to emancipation.[14]

Dispatching a delegation to Washington was not without ulterior motive, given that Unionist factionalism had already emerged. The split involved not abolition per se but rather the best method for restoring Arkansas to the Union and the *kind* of state to be restored. In addition to Gantt, the leaders of the "radical" faction included Isaac Murphy, a small slaveholder from northwest Arkansas and the lone holdout against disunion at the 1861 secession convention; William M. Fishback, a Fort Smith attorney who had originally voted against secession at the convention but changed his vote in the name of unity; James M. Johnson, who had recently been elected to Congress; and Elisha Baxter, whom Confederates had almost prosecuted for treason. While this group included slaveholders and others who had initially supported secession, its members evinced a clear animus toward the antebellum elite. They pledged that the upcoming convention, in addition to abolishing slavery, would implement a host of democratic reforms, thereby ending the thrall to which slavery had subjected all white Arkansans.[15]

The "conservative" faction consisted of planters, businessmen, and professionals who identified with the old elite. Among its leaders were Cincinnatus Vann Meador, a Little Rock newspaper editor; Charles Bertrand, a Little Rock businessman who had served as interim mayor; and Anthony A. C. Rogers, a Pine Bluff planter. Harboring no illusions about preserving slavery, they hoped to forestall the radical reform program. They advocated the appointment of a military governor rather than holding a convention, and they argued – not implausibly – that conditions in Arkansas were too unsettled to organize a new government. The conservatives were clearly in the minority among Arkansas Unionists, and although many of them had supported secession, they anticipated that Steele's conciliatory policy would allow them a role in shaping the state's reorganization. Even before reaching Washington,

---

[14] Steele to Maj. Genl. N. Kimball, March 23, 1864, Steele Papers, Stanford; Harris, *With Charity for All*, 197, 199; Moneyhon, *Impact of the Civil War and Reconstruction on Arkansas*, 159, 161; Cowen, "Reorganization of Federal Arkansas," 45–46.

[15] Moneyhon, *Impact of the Civil War and Reconstruction on Arkansas*, 159–60.

Edward Gantt had to deny rumors, then rife in Little Rock, that the delegation sought to replace Steele with Gantt as military governor. "I suppose that the secessionists in Little Rock would use Meador or some such creature to start such report," Gantt reassured Steele. "I have only to say, that it is *utterly false*, and that *I will resist any such effort coming from any source*, with whatever influence I may possess."[16]

Overcoming these differences, Arkansas Unionists assembled in convention on January 4 in Little Rock. Questions over the validity of various delegates' credentials delayed the proceedings for a week, but once the convention got down to work, some forty-five delegates – representing twenty-three of the state's fifty-seven counties – conducted business for the next two weeks. Many delegates had been selected by highly irregular methods, but they all swore to Lincoln's oath, including more than a dozen former slaveholders. Although the convention had not yet received approval from Washington, Steele assured the delegates that Lincoln would sanction their work. The convention immediately proceeded to craft a new constitution abolishing slavery; it also declared null and void all acts of the secession convention and invalidated Arkansas's Confederate debt. On January 15, the convention approved a provision for the immediate "abolishment of slavery," though only after defeating a proposed amendment by Thomas M. Jacks of Philips County, who would later be elected to Congress but not seated, postponing abolition until 1885. The measure received prolonged discussion before going down to defeat. On January 19, the convention approved the new constitution unanimously and issued an address to the people of the state. "Slavery is forever prohibited," the address proclaimed. "This resolution, as to slavery, is because of the now almost universal belief that peace, made on any other plan, would be of short duration, and for that reason not worth the trouble of accomplishing."[17]

The radical majority also implemented its democratic reforms, making a host of state-level offices elective, including judges, and allowing a simple legislative majority to override the gubernatorial veto. In addition to abolishing slavery, the convention authorized black education and apprenticeship, both of which the ten-percent plan advocated, but it bestowed no legal or political rights on the former slaves, explicitly limiting suffrage to "white male citizens of the United States." Before adjourning on January 23, the convention

---

[16] Gantt to Steele, January 7, 1864, Steele Papers, Stanford; Moneyhon, *Impact of the Civil War and Reconstruction on Arkansas*, 160–61; Smith, *Courage of a Southern Unionist*, 55. During the following weeks, New York congressman John Steele reassured his brother Frederick several times of the support he enjoyed in Congress and in Lincoln's administration.

[17] *Journal of the Convention of Delegates of the People of Arkansas*, 22, 31–35; Harris, *With Charity for All*, 199–200; Moneyhon, *Impact of the Civil War and Reconstruction on Arkansas*, 161–62; Smith, *Courage of a Southern Unionist*, 51–53; DeBlack, *With Fire and Sword*, 105–6; Cowen, "Reorganization of Federal Arkansas," 42–45.

established a provisional government, with Isaac Murphy as governor, and it legalized the election of James M. Johnson to Congress, sending him to Washington with a copy of the new constitution. The convention also established March 14 as the date for a referendum on the constitution and elections for state officials and other members of Congress.[18]

But the conservatives had not quite conceded slavery's demise. Thomas M. Jacks, who had earlier called for delaying abolition, seized the opportunity of the final vote on the constitution to lodge a "protest," reiterating the need to move slowly. "I recognize the President's emancipation proclamation as a finality, as regards the theoretical abolishment of slavery in all the rebellious States," Jacks noted. Acknowledging "theoretical emancipation as a fixed fact," he nonetheless insisted that "to reduce theory to practice often requires no inconsiderable time," and he deemed emancipation "one of the theories most difficult to put into practicable shape." Jacks may have correctly posited that the "status of the negro can not be practically fixed either by a swoop of the executive pen, or by hasty legislation," but he also ignored the slaves' role in making emancipation a "fixed fact." Jacks would have preferred that the convention simply abide by Federal antislavery measures, an action that would have comported with the ten-percent plan, "and that we should have left ourselves untrammeled by hasty legislation." Even so, Jacks affirmed his support for the new constitution and the eventual end of slavery. "While I ask time for slavery practically to die, I do not insist that it shall not die," he insisted. The suffering slavery had caused the nation – by which Jacks presumably meant white Americans and not the slaves – justified its condemnation, "but its conviction is not its execution." Claiming that he wanted "time for slavery practically to die," and that he saw "no possibility of immediate practical emancipation," Jacks asked of the convention "that we 'make haste slowly.'" But since the convention had not obliged, "my wish is, that you may be right." At the moment of slavery's "execution" in Arkansas, its defenders were left hoping for an eleventh-hour reprieve.[19]

IV

Whereas the convention had worked with notable efficacy, the weeks following would be confused and contentious. Steele – whose brother John was a Democratic congressman from upstate New York and a frequent correspondent – had to balance military and civilian affairs while coordinating

---

[18] Moneyhon, *Impact of the Civil War and Reconstruction on Arkansas*, 161–62; Cowen, "Reorganization of Federal Arkansas," 45; Harris, *With Charity for All*, 199–200. Technically, the convention set the election to take place over three days, March 14–16, but March 14 was the date on which the election effectively took place and to which all parties referred.

[19] *Journal of the Convention of Delegates of the People of Arkansas*, 43–44.

between Washington and Little Rock and mediating between Arkansas's Unionist factions. Soon after the convention, provisional governor Murphy responded to an earlier inquiry in which Steele had asked whether Murphy approved of his "conciliatory policy" or found it "disheartening to the really Union men." Murphy reassured Steele that his policy of "war against all the enemies of our Government," as Murphy put it, was not disheartening, but this endorsement conveniently avoided the issue of former rebels who wanted to resume their allegiance and participate in Reconstruction. The initially amicable relations between Steele and the Murphy-Fishback faction would become increasingly strained in the ensuing months, as the political and military situation in Arkansas worsened.[20]

Even as the Arkansas convention was assembling in early January, Lincoln ordered General Nathan Kimball to Arkansas to distribute amnesty books and oath forms among the population, and he instructed Steele to lend Kimball the necessary assistance. Two weeks later, as the Arkansas convention was ending, Lincoln met with the state's delegation, headed by Gantt, that had been appointed in December. They would confer on several occasions during the week of January 20–27. Lincoln was pleased by the progress in Arkansas, especially upon receiving the delegation's assurance that the new constitution would abolish slavery. On January 20, before word of the convention's results had reached Washington, and after consulting with the delegation, Lincoln instructed Steele to assist in organizing a state gubernatorial election, to take place on March 28. This date – Lincoln and the delegation had no way of knowing – was two weeks after the date already set by the convention. Lincoln's letter to Steele also included detailed instructions for conducting the election, which would take place under the state's antebellum constitution and laws, with the proviso that the constitution would already have been "so modified" as to prohibit slavery. Following another meeting two days later, Lincoln announced that he would appoint no military governor for Arkansas, and that Steele would oversee the reorganization. The members of the delegation, in turn, expressed themselves "fully satisfied" with Lincoln's action. "[Y]ou are now called upon to act in a new sphere – not quite Military," Steele's brother advised him.[21]

Several days later, news of the Arkansas convention reached Washington. On January 27, with the delegation preparing to return to Little Rock, Lincoln wrote again to Steele. Realizing that the work of the convention, though "having the same general object" as his earlier instructions, "may clash somewhat with my programme," Lincoln instructed Steele to work with Gantt, upon

---

[20] Murphy to Steel [sic], January 22, 1864, Steele Papers, Stanford.
[21] *CWL*, 7: 108–9, 141–42, 144; John B. Steele to [Frederick Steele], January 26, 1864, Steele Papers, Stanford; Cowen, "Reorganization of Federal Arkansas," 41, 45–46; Harris, *With Charity for All*, 201–2.

the latter's return to Arkansas, "to harmonize the two plans into one, and then put it through with all possible vigor." Lincoln disavowed any interest in how the two plans were reconciled – save that the new constitution abolish slavery. That was all he cared about. "Be sure to retain the free State constitutional provision in some unquestionable form," Lincoln advised Steele, "and you and he can fix the rest." Days later, having read particulars of the Arkansas convention, Lincoln approved the convention's work and urged Steele to assist it as best as he could. With Arkansas on the cusp of abolishing slavery, Lincoln wanted to prevent bickering among Unionists. "Of all things, avoid if possible, a dividing into cliques among the friends of the common object," he warned. "Be firm and resolute against such as you can perceive would make confusion and division."[22]

Although Steele had received Lincoln's instructions to "harmonize" the competing plans by early February, correspondence between Washington and Little Rock during the next two weeks revealed the difficulty of achieving that objective. Given the irregularity of communications and the unsettled conditions in Arkansas, confusion over the election date was understandable. Yet opponents of the convention movement were also likely attempting to thwart the entire free-state project. Members of Congress were clearly aware of the situation, and it no doubt contributed to their action in the Arkansas election case and to their growing dissatisfaction with Lincoln's Reconstruction policy. A mid-February letter to William Fishback revealed Lincoln's own growing impatience. Ever since he had learned of the convention's plan, Lincoln noted, he had been trying to yield to it, but to no avail. "I have sent two letters to Gen. Steele, and three or four despatches to you and others, saying that he – Gen. Steele – must be made master, but that it will probably be best for him to merely help the convention on it's own plan." Lincoln had made Steele "master" in Arkansas, as with Banks in Louisiana, but for the purpose of *assisting* and not directing local Unionists. "Some single mind must be master, else there will be no agreement in anything, & Gen. Steele, commanding the Military, and being on the ground, is the best man to be that master," Lincoln explained. "This discord must be silenced." Perhaps prompted by Lincoln's annoyance, Steele finally managed to reconcile the two plans and set the election for March 14, an action that Lincoln immediately approved.[23]

---

[22] *CWL*, 7: 154–55, 161; Johnson to Murphy, February 8, 1864, Steele Papers, Stanford; Moneyhon, *Impact of the Civil War and Reconstruction on Arkansas*, 162; Cowen, "Reorganization of Federal Arkansas," 46–47; Harris, *With Charity for All*, 200–1.

[23] Steele to Lincoln, February 2, 1864, and General Orders No. 2, Headquarters Department of Arkansas, February 2, 1864, both in Steele Papers, Stanford; *CWL*, 7: 173–74, 185–86, 189–90 (quotation), 190–91, 199; Moneyhon, *Impact of the Civil War and Reconstruction on Arkansas*, 162; Cowen, "Reorganization of Federal Arkansas," 47; Harris, *With Charity for All*, 201.

The plans had been harmonized, but the discord continued, especially between military officials and local Unionists. When Lincoln considered sending General Daniel L. Sickles to Little Rock in late February to investigate matters, Unionist leaders rushed to assure Lincoln no investigation was needed. "Everything is working well," Murphy insisted. "General Steele is doing everything that can be done." No one wanted an investigation, especially with Congress scrutinizing Arkansas affairs.[24] Despite these tensions, Steele endeavored to ensure the election's success. There was little of a traditional campaign. Isaac Murphy faced no challenger for governor. Some candidates were nominated at Unionist meetings; others put forward their own names. Most of the campaign amounted to the candidates questioning one another's past loyalty, especially former conditional Unionists. Yet no one challenged the new free-state constitution. Although Confederate authorities, who still controlled the southwestern third of the state, were determined to prevent persons from taking the loyalty oath and to disrupt the election, Steele remained confident. "The civil Dept will soon be off my hands," he informed General-in-Chief Henry Halleck. "It is believed that there will be votes enough cast in the Dist of Little Rock to bring the State back." Steele even put off assisting Nathaniel Banks's preparations for the military Red River campaign in Louisiana in order to facilitate the Arkansas election.[25]

On February 29, Steele issued a proclamation urging the people of Arkansas to participate in the mid-March election. "Peace has been so far restored in our midst as to enable you to institute proceedings for the restoration of the civil government," he announced. A new constitution, "based upon the principles of freedom," had been drawn up, and "every facility will be afforded for the expression of your sentiments, uninfluenced by any consideration save those which affect your own interests and those of your posterity," Steele assured the people. "If you will now institute a government of your own," he predicted, "quiet and security will soon be restored to your entire borders," disunionists will resume their former allegiance, "and peace will prevail throughout the land." Steele noted that 5,400 votes were needed to validate the election under the ten-percent plan, and that "no interference from any quarter will be allowed to prevent the free expression of the loyal men of the State." He forwarded a copy of the proclamation to Lincoln, who heartily approved it. As the election approached, Lincoln encouraged Murphy and Fishback to

---

[24] *OR*, ser. 1, vol. 34, pt. 2, 427; *OR*, ser. 3, vol. 4, 127–28 (Murphy to Lincoln); *CWL*, 7: 208–9; Bertrand to Lincoln, February 20, 1864, and John B. Steele to [Frederick R. Steele], February 12, 1864, both in Steele Papers, Stanford; Moneyhon, *Impact of the Civil War and Reconstruction on Arkansas*, 163; Cowen, "Reorganization of Federal Arkansas," 47–48.

[25] [Steele] to Halleck, February 25, 1864, [Steele] to Banks, February 28, 1864, and Steele to Banks (copy), March 7, 1864, all in Steele Papers, Stanford; Harris, *With Charity for All*, 202; Cowen, "Reorganization of Federal Arkansas," 48.

work for its success. "Do your best to get out the largest vote possible," he advised, "and, of course, as much of it as possible on the right side."[26]

The referendum on the constitution, along with the election of a new state government and representatives to Congress, took place on March 14 – nine days after Tennessee's local elections. Large crowds and heavy turnout were reported at many places, despite, according to Murphy, "immense efforts" by Confederate guerillas to hinder the election and threats "to hang every one, that went to the polls." The election was far more successful than Unionists had anticipated, the total vote more than twice the number required by the ten-percent plan. The constitution won approval by a vote of 12,179 to 226, and Isaac Murphy, running uncontested, was elected governor. Other officers of the executive branch were also elected, as were state circuit court and Supreme Court justices and local officials. "The Legislature is radical to the core and almost to a man," William Fishback informed Steele. Two congressmen were elected, including Thomas M. Jacks, who had urged postponing abolition until 1885, and the conservative Unionist Anthony A. C. Rogers. "Returns sufficient have been received to make it sure that the election is a success," Steele telegraphed Lincoln. "It is probable that ten thousand votes have been cast, and but very few, so far as heard from, against the Constitution. I believe every man elected will support your administration."[27]

The vote was also historic. West Virginia had been admitted as a new state in 1863 with the proviso that it abolish slavery. The "Restored Government" of Virginia was currently holding a convention to write a free-state constitution, and Maryland was in the process of organizing one. But Arkansas held the distinction of being the first seceded state to adopt the immediate abolition of slavery via a constitution that required voter approval. Arkansas was also the first state to abolish slavery outright during the war, and the first state to do so at all since New York had ended slavery in 1827. Six months after the capture of Little Rock, Arkansas had elected a new government and approved a free-state constitution. Tennessee had achieved neither objective after two full years, and Louisiana had yet to abolish slavery. "Arkansas has given a larger vote for the Union than even Louisiana, and is also ahead of her in the adoption of a Free State Constitution," the *New York Times* observed after the election. "Though the latest reduced 'Confederate' State, it is yet the first of any to reconstitute itself on a Free State basis. It has been admirably prompt both in deciding and executing." As the new government prepared

---

[26] "Proclamation. To the People of Arkansas," February 29, 1864, Steele Papers, Stanford; *CWL*, 7: 221–22, 239–40.

[27] *CWL*, 7: 253 (Murphy); Fishback to Steele, April 11, 1864, and Steele to Lincoln, March 18, 1864, both in Steele Papers, Stanford; Moneyhon, *Impact of the Civil War and Reconstruction on Arkansas*, 163–64; Cowen, "Reorganization of Federal Arkansas," 48–50; Harris, *With Charity for All*, 203.

for its April inauguration, the speed with which affairs had changed in Arkansas had been startling.[28]

Still, the election also revealed the lengths to which Confederates would go to derail the free-state project and the difficulty the new government would have in establishing its authority. Federal control, which ostensibly extended over two-thirds of the state, was fragile, and Confederates easily outnumbered Unionists in many areas. On March 23, governor-elect Isaac Murphy issued a proclamation encouraging the people of southwestern Arkansas to elect officials under the new constitution as soon as they could safely do so. But that would not happen until after the war.[29]

Indeed, communications that Murphy sent to Lincoln after the election included no small measure of distress. "The people are full of enthusiasm but much alarm," Murphy telegraphed on March 17. "Will you give them assurance of the energetic protection of the government – praise be to God!" Several days later he sounded a similar theme. "Should the army leave the line of the Arkansas [River] unprotected terror would prevail the state," he informed Lincoln. "The swamps & mountains are full of armed rebels waiting for the movement of the army to pounce upon unprotected points," he continued. "As it is, the risk is great. All may be lost that has been gained by the election." Lincoln promised to protect the new government, "but can act with no better intentions than have always done." A month later, after he had been inaugurated and the new state legislature had convened, Murphy again requested aid. "The country north & south of the Arkansas River is full of guerillas." One member of the legislature had reportedly been killed en route to Little Rock. "If reinforcements are not sent soon," Murphy warned, "we are in great danger." Lincoln's "common object" had been achieved in Arkansas, but these were not good omens.[30]

---

[28] "The Restoration of Arkansas," *New York Times*, March 21, 1864, 4. Between February 13 and April 11, a constitutional convention – consisting of a total of seventeen delegates – was held in Alexandria, Virginia, under the authority of the Restored Government of Virginia. On March 10, the convention voted to abolish slavery. On April 4, it rejected a resolution to submit the constitution to the voters, and it voted on April 7 to adopt the constitution, declaring it to be in force. Bearss, "Virginia Constitutional Convention (1864)."

[29] Smith, *Courage of a Southern Unionist*, 56, 59–62.

[30] *CWL*, 7: 253, 318. On general conditions in Arkansas at this time, see DeBlack, *With Fire and Sword*, 107–8. On Murphy's victory as affirmation of his stalwart Unionism during the secession crisis, see *Harper's Weekly*, April 2, 1864.

12

"The Jewel of Liberty"

State reorganization efforts in Tennessee and Arkansas in early 1864, however convoluted, paled against those in Louisiana. After Abraham Lincoln changed course in the state by making General Nathaniel P. Banks "master" of the situation, Banks devised a plan that both conflicted with Lincoln's own policy and turned upside-down the free-state proposal to hold a constitutional convention before electing a new government. Lincoln's directive to Banks to organize a free-state government as soon as possible further weakened the conservative Unionists, but Banks's endorsing of Michael Hahn and the moderates – in part to forestall black suffrage – also precipitated the decisive split between free-state radicals and moderates. By early March, Hahn headed a Unionist government. As preparations were being made for a constitutional convention that would abolish slavery, Lincoln "privately" suggested to Hahn that the new constitution include limited black suffrage so as to preserve "the jewel of liberty." It was the first time – but not the last – that Lincoln expressed support for black voting rights in relation to Louisiana.

I

By late 1863, Louisiana's free-state radicals, working with the New Orleans free black community, had begun to gain the upper hand over their moderate rivals and were moving toward black suffrage – despite Lincoln's having strengthened the moderates' position by putting Banks in charge of the state's reorganization. Under the radical Thomas J. Durant, free-state Unionists had been planning to hold a constitutional convention for months. Their voter registration had stalled, but they still believed they were acting with Lincoln's blessing, and they had petitioned Military Governor George Shepley to authorize a January election for convention delegates. Having been upbraided by Lincoln in November for the lack of progress in Louisiana, however, and alarmed by the growing support for black suffrage, Banks had other ideas. On December 30, even before receiving Lincoln's letter making him master in Louisiana, he outlined to Lincoln his plan for the state's reorganization.

Banks proposed organizing a loyal government *before* holding a constitutional convention that would abolish slavery. A new government would thus be elected under the existing, proslavery constitution, except that the provisions of the constitution recognizing slavery would be declared, Banks insisted, "*inoperative and void.*" Only then would a constitutional convention be held. This approach directly contradicted the free-state plan, which Lincoln had previously endorsed, and aligned more closely with that of the conservative Unionists. Nonetheless, it offered a safer and more feasible method for ending slavery, Banks contended, than the current free-state plan. The citizens' "self-respect, their *Amour proper*," he believed, would allow them to vote more readily for a new government than for a state convention to abolish slavery. "Offer them a Government without slavery, and they will gladly accept it as a necessity resulting from the war." His plan could be implemented promptly and would ensure success, he believed, and it could even be adopted in other states. "I would unhesitatingly stake my life upon the issue," Banks declared, with his customary hyperbole. The current free-state plan, by contrast, "does not seem to promise results so speedy or certain," and it would still take months to complete. This was a suggestion only, Banks assured Lincoln, and he pledged to "cordially sustain any policy you may indicate."[1]

What Banks conveniently left unsaid was that his plan would exclude black men, who were pushing for voting rights. This was hardly accidental. Banks's plan would also preclude unconditional Unionists from writing a new constitution that would disfranchise former Confederates. Under both Lincoln's and Banks's proposals, anyone who took Lincoln's oath – and who already enjoyed the right to vote – could participate in Reconstruction. Lincoln's plan would not necessarily have prohibited southern loyalists from imposing restrictions on former Confederates' political rights under a new constitution – and many of them intended on doing just that. But Banks's plan would allow former Confederates to establish a foothold in a new government, thereby preempting the political revolution that various interests were hoping to foster. However inadvertently, Banks highlighted one of the key differences between the ten-percent plan and congressional Reconstruction legislation.

On January 8, before receiving a response from Lincoln on his election proposal, but after receiving Lincoln's December letter making him master, Banks informed Durant of his intention to order an election for state officers and Congress. A flabbergasted Durant protested that preparations were being made for the planned election of convention delegates on January 25 (though the convention had never been announced), and he reminded Banks that no congressional election could be held without congressional authority and until the legislature had redistricted the state. Brushing aside these points, Banks countered that Durant's convention plan had already taken too long and was still far from complete. Several days later, on January 11, he issued a proclamation setting an election on February 22 for, among other officials,

---

[1] *CWL*, 7: 124–25n.

governor, lieutenant-governor, secretary of state, treasurer, and attorney general. Upon their installation on March 4, these officials would constitute the state government under the current constitution, with the exception that all laws and constitutional provisions pertaining to slavery would be "declared inoperative and void." Persons who had taken Lincoln's oath and who were otherwise qualified to vote could participate in the election, and the voter registration already undertaken was "confirmed and approved." Also, in order to "harmonize" the state constitution "with the spirit of the age," an election would take place on April 4 for delegates to a constitutional convention. Banks took Durant's advice on one point by excluding congressional elections.

"The fundamental law of the State is martial law," Banks infelicitously announced. Although he had intended in this statement to affirm that the military would accede to civil authority as soon as possible, he went on to proclaim, no less imperiously, that "[w]hen the national existence is at stake and the liberties of the people in peril, faction is treason." Opponents of Lincoln's Louisiana government would use these words to good effect in the coming months. In forwarding a copy of the proclamation to Lincoln, Banks acknowledged receipt of Lincoln's "master" letter, which, he noted, "give[s] me all the authority I can desire," adding that legislative and judicial elections would not take place until the fall. "I am confident that it will receive a very general support of all classes of people," he confidently predicted about the upcoming election, "and a strength at the Polls that will surprise as well as gratify the friends of the government elsewhere." Banks closed with the gratuitous charge that Durant and the free-state radicals would try to obstruct this initiative, insisting that they would fail. He also assured Lincoln that "every possible effort will be made to harmonize all interests and to have all classes justly represented" in the election. Banks thus intended to include in the reorganization process the very persons – members of the antebellum elite – whom radicals in Louisiana and Washington wanted excluded.[2]

This is how free-state radical Benjamin F. Flanders saw the matter. "The Free State men are bitterly disappointed by the course of Gen Banks in ordering an election for State Officers and in his not ordering an election for a Convention," he complained to Lincoln days after Banks's announcement. The free-state leadership had previously petitioned Banks instead to hold an election for convention delegates on February 22, and Flanders now asked Lincoln to direct Banks to hold such an election. Flanders then spelled out the dangers of following Banks's plan. "We are threatened with a division into Free State men and 'Copperhead' interest," he explained, "all the men who denounced your proclamations will unite and draw the proslavery men into a party with the hope of electing men who will bring back slavery and fasten it

---

[2] *OR*, ser. 3, vol. 4, 22–23; Banks to Lincoln, January 11, 1864, ALP; *CWL*, 7: 125n; McCrary, *Abraham Lincoln and Reconstruction*, 205–7.

upon us for years." Lincoln might have recognized this warning as the very one he had made back in November to Banks: slavery might be preserved in Louisiana. Flanders acknowledged that Banks required the voters to take Lincoln's oath supporting emancipation. However, he reminded Lincoln, "you have not abolished Slavery but only emancipated slaves in a portion of the State" – putting his finger on the central problem of state restoration since January 1863. "There is nothing to prevent the continuance of this as a Slave State if the pro slavery party get control."[3]

As another consequence of Banks's announcement, Durant resigned as state attorney general and as commissioner of registration. He also indicated his intention not to participate in the election, marking the start of his alienation from Louisiana's reorganization and his shift toward an oppositional, even obstructionist, stance. The other radical leaders now faced the question of whether to adhere to their convention plan and boycott the election, convinced as they were that they enjoyed the rank-and-file's support. Only after much deliberation did they decide to participate, scheduling a nominating convention for February 1 to select candidates. But this decision raised the question of whether to cooperate with Banks in the election or oppose him. The radical leadership blamed him for their difficulties with the voter registration, and they were certain he had bamboozled Lincoln into placing him in charge in Louisiana. Now fully involved in Louisiana affairs, Banks backed Michael Hahn – the German-born moderate who had briefly served in Congress a year earlier, and who opposed black suffrage – for governor. The question of whether to cooperate with or oppose Banks proved even more divisive. While several leading radicals endorsed what was becoming the Banks–Hahn faction, the rest remained deeply suspicious of Banks.

Hahn enjoyed several advantages over the radicals, in addition to Banks's and the military's support. He had purchased a newspaper, the former conservative-Unionist *Daily True Delta*, and he could communicate directly with the city's large German population. Also, it was no longer Durant and the radicals but rather Banks – and therefore Hahn – who enjoyed Lincoln's backing. In the lead-up to the convention, the radical leadership proposed a compromise to Banks, suggesting that the elections for state officials and convention delegates be held simultaneously. Banks had even indicated this possibility in his original outline to Lincoln. Presumably, the radicals would not oppose Hahn in exchange for an early convention date. After conferring with Hahn, however, Banks rejected the idea. The state election would take place first, much to the radicals' consternation.[4]

---

[3] Flanders to [Lincoln], January 16, 1864, ALP.
[4] Previous two paragraphs: McCrary, *Abraham Lincoln and Reconstruction*, 207–14.

II

By late January, Banks received Lincoln's approval of his reorganization plan, upon which he had already embarked. "Your confidence in the practicability of constructing a free state-government, speedily, for Louisiana, and your zeal to accomplish it, are very gratifying," Lincoln wrote. Yet aware of Banks's propensity for braggadocio, he also offered a word of caution. "It is a connection, than in which, the words '*can*' and '*will*' were never more precious." Lincoln clearly doubted Banks's assurance of a readily organized free-state government. But he urged Banks to move ahead "with all possible dispatch" and to use his own discretion "in all matters." Banks was also to inform all Federal officials to provide him their "full, and zealous co-operation."[5]

Even before receiving this letter, Banks updated Lincoln on progress in Louisiana. "All parties participate in the selection of candidates, and a very handsome vote will be given," he assured Lincoln – although at this point no candidates had actually been chosen. "Not a word is heard from any one in favor of a restoration of slavery, and no objection is made to the free state basis upon which the election is based." Neither of these claims was true. The indications were "very strong," Banks continued, that Hahn would be elected governor, and Louisiana would soon send a full delegation to both houses of Congress, "composed not only of loyal men but earnest supporters of your administration." These results shall have been achieved, Banks allowed himself to boast, within ninety days of receiving Lincoln's instructions to organize a free-state government.

But Banks also identified a problem. Certain "of the most conservative men" hesitated to take Lincoln's oath as a condition for voting in the election, including the prominent attorneys Christian Roselius and Joseph Adolphus Rozier, who objected on the grounds that they had already taken a loyalty oath to vote in the December 1862 congressional elections and had otherwise proven their loyalty. Roselius and Rozier had indeed been staunch Unionists, refusing to vote for secession at the 1861 convention and only acceding to Confederate authority after the state seceded. They took particular exception, Banks explained, "to the clauses referring to the laws of congress &c. relating to slavery and the confiscation of property." Evidently anticipating that they might be called upon to litigate future cases relating to property confiscation, especially slaves, they feared that swearing to abide by all antislavery measures might "forbid this exercise of their professional privileges." Banks went on to argue that the oath in the ten-percent plan, as he understood it, had been intended to apply to states where no previous elections had been held. He also suggested that allowing individuals to vote who had previously taken the oath – even an oath that did not include emancipation – would bolster the

[5] *CWL*, 7: 123–24.

overall vote without altering the outcome. Banks was looking to maximize voter turnout, even allowing individuals who did not swear to support emancipation to participate, while ensuring a Hahn victory.[6]

Roselius had previously written to Lincoln on the matter, offering a more forthright rationale of the conservatives' motives. While certain that state reorganization and a constitutional convention "will be carried into effect with entire success," he called Lincoln's attention to one feature of the oath that "may possibly create a disturbing element." Roselius suggested that the oath in the ten-percent plan should be limited to individuals who had not previously resumed their allegiance. Observing that more than 7,000 "good and loyal men" had voted in the December 1862 elections, he insisted that it would "be exacting too much from them now" to compel them to take the new oath. He did not specify how this requirement was too exacting. Many unconditional southern Unionists objected to having to take Lincoln's oath in order to participate in Reconstruction, but they did so anyway. Roselius was conveniently forgetting that previous oaths had not required support for emancipation. Indeed, many persons in Louisiana had taken the oath prior to January 1, 1863, for the express purpose of *preventing* emancipation. The whole point of the ten-percent plan, including its loyalty oath, had been to incorporate emancipation into the process of state restoration. Roselius was essentially equating apples to oranges.[7]

Lincoln did not respond to Roselius. However, in contrast to his support for Andrew Johnson's "Damnesty" oath, he agreed to Banks's suggestion to exercise leniency for voting. Individuals who fit the very specific circumstances Banks described would *not* be required to take the oath supporting emancipation. Responding to Banks in late January, Lincoln quoted passages from the ten-percent plan and his Annual Message – pasting printed clippings from both onto his letter – stipulating that other approaches to Reconstruction might be accepted. "These things were put into these documents on purpose that some conformity to circumstances should be admissible," he noted, adding that when he had instructed Banks that "available labor already done should not be thrown away," he had in mind "the very class of cases you now mention." Banks was therefore free to adopt any criteria that would limit voting to "unquestionably loyal free-state men and none others." But perhaps exasperated over this lawyerly quibbling, clearly intended to avoid emancipation, Lincoln concluded: "And yet I do wish they would all take the oath." In Tennessee and Louisiana, Lincoln supported his man on the ground: in the former to exclude persons of dubious loyalty, and in the latter to include them.[8]

---

[6] Banks to Lincoln, January 22, 1864, ALP; *CWL*, 7: 162n.
[7] Roselius to Lincoln, January 12, 1864, ALP.
[8] *CWL*, 7: 161–62.

Louisiana was an exceptional situation. Many persons who had opposed secession before the state seceded, only later to have supported the Confederacy, had subsequently resumed their allegiance before the Emancipation Proclamation had been issued. Lincoln may also have agreed with Banks that the gambit of allowing certain individuals who had not sworn to accept emancipation to vote in the election – so as to increase turnout and meet the ten-percent threshold – was worth the risk. Moreover, Lincoln did not issue a carte blanche pass to all persons who had previously sworn loyalty but rather gave Banks discretion to allow certain individuals in specific instances to vote. Still, the problem was that while Roselius, Rozier, and others like them were "unquestionably loyal," they were not unquestionably "free-state men," as evidenced by their objection to Lincoln's oath, whatever sophistry they used to justify it.

Lincoln's decision also enabled conservative Unionists to sidestep, if only temporarily, their own dilemma. For most of them, restoring Louisiana to the Union as a slave state was the goal, but the ten-percent plan required support for emancipation to participate in Reconstruction. Banks's plan of electing a state government before revising the constitution, however, offered conservatives an opportunity to participate in that government and possibly to shape the constitution-writing process. Lincoln's decision, likewise, allowed certain of them to avoid having to swear to support emancipation in order to participate in Louisiana's reorganization. To be sure, Lincoln required the seceded states – though implicitly – to abolish slavery before being readmitted. Congress was also working on Reconstruction legislation and a Federal abolition amendment, so the risk in allowing certain individuals to vote might have seemed minimal. Still, the ten-percent plan had no standing at law, and there was no telling what might happen with Reconstruction legislation and the amendment. Conservative Unionists by no means supported a free-state restoration, but Lincoln and Banks believed they needed leading citizens to participate in the reorganization process to give it legitimacy. This would later become one of the essential difficulties – though over black civil rights – of Radical Reconstruction.

III

As free-state Unionists prepared for the February 1 nominating convention, the Banks–Hahn moderates, enjoying Lincoln's support, gained new adherents, including the unconditional Unionist J. Madison Wells. A Whig planter and former slaveholder from Rapides Parish, and the leader of a group of Red River exiles who had conducted partisan activities before making their way to New Orleans, Wells was destined to play a major role in Louisiana affairs over the next two years. The moderates also welcomed individuals from the city and surrounding areas whose loyalties – let alone views on emancipation – were dubious, and the radicals suspected a scheme to pack the convention. Although excluded from the process, the free men of color pressed their claims for black suffrage. At a mass meeting on January 5, with white radicals endorsing black suffrage with property or literacy requirements, a petition was framed calling for voting rights for free-born black men. A subsequent meeting two weeks later selected two free men of color, Jean Baptiste Roudanez and Arnold Bertonneau, respectively an engineer and a wine merchant, to present the petition to Lincoln and Congress. Durant wrote a letter of introduction for them, assuring Lincoln that "both of these gentlemen are men of high respectability, and of devoted loyalty to our country," who, "being unable to obtain a favorable hearing from those in authority in this quarter," Durant added, in a dig impossible for Lincoln to miss, "deem themselves justified . . . in appealing for relief to the Representatives of the nation."[9]

For Lincoln and others whose main concern was maintaining unity among "unquestionably loyal free-state men," the free-state nominating convention went about as badly as possible, precipitating the factional split that had been so long in the making. The meeting at Lyceum Hall was clearly packed with Hahn supporters, many of questionable fidelity to emancipation, and it opened with the predictable dispute over credentials. After two tumultuous hours, settling nothing, the radicals departed and reconvened at the organization's headquarters, though the question then became whether they had bolted or been expelled. The moderates nominated Hahn for governor and the radicals chose Flanders, who had not originally been a candidate but agreed to run. The two free-state Unionists who had represented Louisiana in Congress a year earlier now faced each other in the governor's race. For lieutenant governor, both sides selected J. Madison Wells, whose political views were not well known but who was expected to attract rural voters. By evening's end, a single free-state movement, though not without internal tensions, had fractured into rival organizations.[10]

The conservative Unionists met days later to name their candidates. Christian Roselius unexpectedly declined the gubernatorial nomination, which then went to J. Q. A. Fellows, another leading New Orleans attorney. Fellows had previously proposed to Lincoln almost the very same plan – holding a state election under Louisiana's 1852 constitution, although without suspending its slavery provisions – upon which the current contest was being conducted. The attorney Joseph Adolphus Rozier was nominated for attorney general. Any hope for victory the conservatives might have entertained as

---

[9] "Petition of the Free Colored Citizens of Louisiana," *The Liberator*, April 1, 1864; Durant to Lincoln, February 10, 1864, ALP; McCrary, *Abraham Lincoln and Reconstruction*, 208–9, 215–18, 229–32; Harris, *With Charity for All*, 174.

[10] McCrary, *Abraham Lincoln and Reconstruction*, 218–20; Taylor, *Louisiana Reconstructed*, 27–28; Harris, *With Charity for All*, 174.

a result of the free-state divorce would be undone by the refusal of many of their supporters to take Lincoln's oath, especially among those who, as Roselius had previously noted, had already sworn allegiance.

At the convention, Roselius and Rozier delivered addresses that articulated the by-now familiar tenets of conservative Unionism. Since neither Louisiana nor any other seceded state had left the Union, Roselius contended, these states retained their rights under the Federal Constitution. Individuals would suffer the consequences of treason, but the states continued to enjoy their "qualified sovereignty." Studiously avoiding the term "slavery," Roselius instead referred euphemistically to "certain domestic institutions," which, he conceded, might well have received "their death blow" under "the law of nations" – although this notion contradicted the claim that the seceded states remained in the Union. But his essential point was that the Constitution prohibited the Federal government to interfere with the states in regulating their own domestic institutions. The Federal government was "supreme and independent with regard to the enumerated powers delegated to it," he maintained, but it was "utterly powerless as to the domestic policy and institutions of the States." The Constitution therefore conferred upon the Federal government no authority to compel so-called seceded states to abolish slavery as a condition for returning to a Union they had never left.

Sounding similar themes, Joseph Rozier was also more forthright – if not in explicitly defending slavery, then in condemning wartime emancipation and the free-state initiative. The Unionist movement, after overcoming initial difficulties, had been proceeding "*swimmingly*," Rozier insisted, until disrupted by the introduction of "Abolition resolutions" by a small minority of outsiders who were "agitating a delicate subject of *no practical importance during the existence* of this war." No sooner had these agitators divided the Unionist movement than they began squabbling among themselves. Rozier castigated the attempt to organize a state government that did not represent all of the (white) people of Louisiana, and to decide on the question of slavery before the state had been restored to the Union. "How can you radically change the organic law at this time, without a representation on the part of the majority of the people of Louisiana – giving them an opportunity of coming under Federal rule?" he asked. "As you have asked my opinion about slavery, I would say, do not agitate this question or any other which would throw the people in commotion." Better to focus now on suppressing the rebellion, Rozier insisted, and leave the state constitution alone. "In the course of time, *as soon as this war is over*, you can alter or change it as a real majority of the people may ask for."

In criticizing Lincoln's ten-percent plan, Rozier condemned what he mistakenly referred to as the "iron-clad oath" – by which he meant not the actual iron-clad oath, which required never having voluntarily assisted the rebellion, but rather Lincoln's oath, which mandated *future* loyalty and compliance with wartime emancipation. It violated republican government, he charged, to require a person – as a condition for voting or participating in a state constitutional convention – "to support the proclamations of the President of the United States, and all his future proclamations, on the question of slavery." No oath to uphold the Constitution could contain provisions that transcended that document itself. Wartime emancipation had been an unmitigated disaster, he went on, and no provisions had been made for the consequences of abolition. Political and legal equality was out of the question. "The white population of the Southern States will never put a slave upon the same footing of equality with them." Insofar as slavery had to be eliminated, Rozier advocated that it be done "gradually" and "in times of peace," so as to be *for the benefit of all concerned*." Like others of his ilk, Rozier urged a return to the principles of the Founders on the Union and the Constitution and avoidance of the divisive question of slavery. "Having contended for what I think are the only real and true Union doctrines, as laid down by Madison and Jefferson, I would say, let this slave question – total abolition – be ignored; in this canvass discard it, and think alone of sustaining the military authorities here and elsewhere," he insisted. "Let us maintain the constitution and the supremacy of the laws of the United States."[11]

With the nominating conventions now complete, the gubernatorial contest featured three candidates: Hahn, the free-state moderate; Flanders, the free-state radical; and Fellows, the conservative Unionist. Soon after the conventions, Banks issued an order encouraging the citizens of Louisiana to take the oath of allegiance and to participate in the election. "Indifference will be treated as a crime, and faction as treason," he again pontificated. Despite this call for unity, Hahn and the moderates, confident of success, rebuffed a proposed compromise that the radical leaders had endorsed, and the divide hardened. The campaign was lively, if brief, and the moderates brought their formidable advantages to bear. Banks invalidated a provision of the state constitution prohibiting men in military uniform from voting, since a small number of white Louisianans served in the Union army. He also issued orders ostensibly intended to facilitate voting but that also provided opportunities for electoral fraud – this in a state not known for honest elections. No en masse voting by Union soldiers or other systematic irregularities occurred, but the

---

[11] *New Orleans Daily True Delta*, February 7 (Roselius), and February 9, 1864 (Rozier); Taylor, *Louisiana Reconstructed*, 28; McCrary, *Abraham Lincoln and Reconstruction*, 223. The two men's comments were sufficiently veiled so as to mislead some observers. The New Orleans correspondent to the *New York Times* remarked that the "Conservative" party "is *suspected* of squinting toward the possible return of Slavery in Louisiana," adding that "[e]ven the Conservative party is *ostensibly* for the abolition of Slavery throughout Louisiana." Despite the qualifiers, the first clause was a gross understatement and the second entirely incorrect. "Department of the Gulf," *New York Times*, April 5, 1864 (byline dated March 25, 1864), 9.

campaign was clearly the work of the "military and quasi-military, authorities" that Lincoln had previously warned against.[12]

Although firmly committed to abolition, Hahn and the moderates resorted to racial demagoguery, equating the radicals' support for black suffrage with "social" equality. They supplemented this tactic with a class-oriented appeal to (white) "workingmen," small business owners, and yeoman farmers, while castigating the planters and other representatives of the antebellum establishment. As a Hahn victory became apparent, the bandwagon started rolling, and a number of radicals, realizing that a vote for Flanders was as good as a vote for Fellows, switched to Hahn. The conservative Unionists, for their part, remained crippled by a loyalty oath that nullified their raison d'être. They barely mounted a campaign, though some expressed qualified support for compensated emancipation.[13]

The election on February 22, which took place before those in Tennessee and Arkansas, resulted in a decisive moderate victory. With 6,183 votes to Fellows's 2,996 and Flanders's 2,232, Hahn received an outright majority in a three-way race. Turnout amounted to one-fourth of the statewide antebellum vote, and it approximated prewar levels for the occupied areas. J. Madison Wells, nominated by both free-state factions, was overwhelmingly elected lieutenant governor. Although nearly half of the slightly more than 11,400 votes were cast in New Orleans, the total, as in Arkansas, more than doubled the number necessary under the ten-percent plan.[14]

The election "was conducted with great spirit and propriety," Banks informed Lincoln, adding that no "unfairness or undue influence" marred the result. In the end, all voters had taken Lincoln's oath, since Lincoln's instructions regarding exemptions had arrived late. "There is no sounder basis for a State government, in this country than is presented by this population," Banks boasted. "The convention for Revision of the constitution will confirm the absolute extinction of slavery upon which the election has proceeded and to which every voter has assented," he further insisted. "The change that has occurred in this state since Jan. 1863 is without parelell in history," Banks continued, as usual overstating matters. "It has been far greater than could have been anticipated with reason." Tellingly, Banks devoted most of his letter to reassuring Lincoln that the election accurately represented Louisiana society. He mentioned Hahn's victory almost as an afterthought, virtually

---

[12] *OR*, ser. 1, vol. 34, pt. 2, 227–31 (quotation, 231); Taylor, *Louisiana Reconstructed*, 28–29; McCrary, *Abraham Lincoln and Reconstruction*, 221–23, 234–35.

[13] Taylor, *Louisiana Reconstructed*, 28–29; Shugg, *Origins of Class Struggle in Louisiana*, 198–99; Harris, *With Charity for All*, 175–76; McCrary, *Abraham Lincoln and Reconstruction*, 203–5, 220–29, 234–35.

[14] Election returns and analysis: McCrary, *Abraham Lincoln and Reconstruction*, 235–36, 240–41; Taylor, *Louisiana Reconstructed*, 29–30, 179–81.

taking it for granted, and he confidently predicted that more than 20,000 votes would be cast on the constitution.[15]

Durant and the radicals offered a different take, redoubling their letter-writing campaign to Lincoln, congressional Republicans, and other party leaders protesting events in Louisiana. "I desire respectfully to submit to you," Durant wrote to Lincoln, "that this election does not restore Louisiana to the Union." He pointedly reminded Lincoln of his previous approval of the free-state constitutional convention proposal before reversing himself and handing Louisiana affairs to Banks. The election had been for executive officials only and had made no provision for the legislature or judiciary, "giving us therefore but the fragment of a Government." Banks also illegally allowed soldiers to vote, Durant charged, and his other voter registration measures were unconstitutional. Durant beseeched Lincoln not to recognize the Louisiana government but rather to assist the state's "loyal and legal citizens" in organizing a constitutional convention free from military interference or control. "What sort of a State is this which we have reestablished," Durant asked in a follow-up letter, using Lincoln's own language against him, "where one man, not a citizen of the state, and having none but military power, is entire Master of its civil destiny, calling a Convention at his will to modify or abolish its government."[16]

Durant made valid points – even if he overlooked Lincoln's qualifier that Reconstruction need not follow the ten-percent plan to the letter, and even though Durant had once advocated repudiating the state constitution that he claimed Banks had violated. But Lincoln was not about to reject his own handiwork, and Hahn and other officials were installed on March 4 as the new civilian government. In his inaugural address, Hahn denied "that the sovereign people of this State had ever seceded from the Union," and he urged Louisiana's citizens to support the new government, though admitting that for now "civil government must necessarily harmonize with military administration." The Union must prevail over "State rights," he further insisted, especially when those rights included a "sectional institution, founded on a great moral, social and political evil, and inconsistent with the principles of free government."

"The institution of slavery is opposed alike to the rights of one race and the interests of the other," Hahn continued; "it is the cause of the present unholy attempt to break up our government." He regarded "its universal and immediate extinction as a public and private blessing." Hahn applauded the efforts toward establishing a new labor system, recognizing that they had not been without difficulty, and he pledged that the state legislature would meet – after the constitutional convention – to address the issue. "[T]he absorbing

---

[15] Banks to Lincoln, February 25, 1864, ALP.
[16] Durant to Lincoln, February 26 and 28, 1864, ALP.

labor question will at once demand [the legislature's] most serious attention," Hahn assured his constituents. "Proper legislation ... will enable the people to profit by the new life that is being infused into our social system; and in presence of the change no man of observation, enterprise and enlightenment need have a discouraging apprehension." Hahn also issued an unambiguous warning. "No person able to work will be allowed ... to be a burden on the community," he intoned; "the condition of man is to earn his bread by the sweat of his brow, and useless, unproductive drones must comply with the law of our being or remove from among us." Hahn hardly needed to identify who these "drones" were, and he said nothing about black political or legal rights.[17]

A week after the new government assumed office, the free-black delegation of Jean Baptiste Roudanez and Arnold Bertonneau, appointed in January, met with Lincoln to deliver the black suffrage petition. While in Washington, they had previously conferred with Charles Sumner and Representative William D. Kelley of Pennsylvania, both antislavery stalwarts, who convinced them to expand their petition to include former slaves as well as the free-born. In his meeting with Roudanez and Bertonneau, Lincoln expressed his personal support for limited black suffrage but demurred that he could only publicly endorse it as "necessary to the readmission of Louisiana as a State in the Union." Nonetheless, he promised to refer the matter to the leaders of the upcoming convention. After their visit to Washington, Roudanez and Bertonneau continued on a tour of the North, where they met with prominent antislavery figures, including Frederick Douglass, William Lloyd Garrison, and Massachusetts governor John Andrew, and publicly advocated black suffrage and equal rights.[18]

Although Lincoln could not give the endorsement the two men sought, he was deeply impressed by the meeting, and he kept his word to refer the matter. Soon after the interview, he wrote to Hahn in what would become a much-debated document on his racial thought. In a letter marked "*Private*," Lincoln congratulated Hahn "on having fixed your name in history as the first-free-state Governor of Louisiana." Referring to the upcoming convention, "which, among other things, will probably define the elective franchise," Lincoln went on to "barely suggest," for Hahn's "private consideration, whether some of the colored people may not be let in – as, for instance, the very intelligent, and especially those who have fought gallantly in our ranks." Black voters, Lincoln

---

[17] Hahn, *Inaugural Address of Michael Hahn*; Tregle, "Thomas J. Durant," 504.
[18] *OR*, ser. 3, vol. 4, pt. 1, 170–72; *New Orleans Era*, March 16, 1864 (quotation), as cited in Cox, *Lincoln and Black Freedom*, 95; Hollandsworth, *Louisiana Native Guards*, 94–96; McCrary, *Abraham Lincoln and Reconstruction*, 255; McPherson, *Negro's Civil War*, 281–84; Harris, *With Charity for All*, 183; Bell, *Revolution, Romanticism, and the Afro-Creole Protest Tradition*, 251–52. *The Liberator*, April 1, 1864, includes the original petition framed in New Orleans on January 5 and the memorial Roudanez and Bertonneau presented to Lincoln, dated March 10.

continued, "would probably help, in some trying time to come, to keep the jewel of liberty within the family of freedom." He closed this brief but remarkable communication by reiterating that "this is only a suggestion" and was made "not to the public, but to you alone."[19]

Whatever racial assumptions were embedded in his language or in how he framed the issue, Lincoln had embraced black suffrage in principle. To be sure, he subscribed to the widely prevalent notion that black voters must pass a literacy or intelligence test. Neither did he want his views publicized, marking the letter "private" in an age when such letters were customarily circulated and even published. Lincoln had also put black suffrage forward as a "suggestion," no doubt realizing that the convention was unlikely to adopt it. Even so, Hahn could not miss the significance of this suggestion, since Lincoln often used this method to indicate he supported something. By linking military service to voting rights, moreover, Lincoln nullified for thousands of black men any property or literacy requirement. Lincoln was acknowledging that the postwar settlement could well be contentious, and that black support would be essential to "keep the jewel of liberty in the family of freedom." Fully expecting the convention to reject his "suggestion," he was plausibly laying the foundation for a more expansive understanding of black freedom in the foreseeable future. A year later Lincoln would go public.

IV

The installation of a free-state government in Louisiana did not resolve the issue of whether this government represented the will of "the people." Banks insisted that it did, but various other interests – free people of color, former slaves, free-state radicals, and conservatives, though for different reasons – begged to differ, as did a growing number of congressional Republicans. Although Hahn was now civilian governor, Lincoln also appointed him military governor to replace the ineffectual George Shepley. Hahn used this authority to appoint city officials and to prepare for the election of convention delegates. This election – which Banks, not Hahn, had moved up from April 4 to March 28 – revived the radicals' dilemma over whether to participate. Durant at first intended to run as a delegate before deciding against, and he convinced Flanders and other radical leaders to follow suit. Yet some radicals disagreed, hoping to shape the new constitution, and they entered into an arrangement with certain conservative Unionists. This strange-bedfellows alliance of breakaway radicals and conservatives – or both ends against the middle – dubbed itself the "Free State Citizens' Ticket," with the former

---

[19] *CWL*, 7: 243.

challenging moderates in some districts and the latter in others. There was again talk of a free-state *rapprochement*, to no avail.[20]

The campaign for delegates generated nowhere near the interest of the state election, even though the convention was about to make history by abolishing slavery in Louisiana. Indeed, crafting a new constitution was arguably more important than electing a new administration under the existing, now-obsolete constitution. With conservative Unionists in disarray and most radicals boycotting the election, the moderates were poised to capture the vast majority of seats. Banks's order apportioning delegates on the basis of the white population – instead of total population, as per the 1852 constitution – further undermined the conservatives' position. J. Q. A. Fellows condemned a convention "in which but eleven out of fifty four [actually forty-eight] parishes in the State can be represented, and the election districts so jerrymanded as to secure a majority to the powers that be." Banks himself was mostly absent, involved in the Red River campaign that was designed to bring a large swath of Louisiana under Federal control in time for the election. His absence contributed to the desultory campaign, but the main problem was apathy, with the result a foregone conclusion.[21]

The election was a landslide for the Hahn forces, the Frankensteinesque Free State Citizens' Ticket standing no chance. Turnout, however, disappointed proponents of the new government. Although the unsettled conditions prevented a definitive count, only some 6,000–6,500 votes were cast, nowhere near the 20,000 Banks had predicted. In theory, 152 delegates were to have been elected, representing the entire state, but this would obviously never happen with much of Louisiana under Confederate control. Ultimately, ninety-eight delegates would participate in the convention, sixty-three of whom hailed from New Orleans. The disproportionate influence of the city, which in 1860 represented 25 percent of Louisiana's total population and 42 percent of its white population, had traditionally provoked political conflict before the war, a problem now exacerbated by the apportioning of convention delegates by the white population. Only four members of the New Orleans delegation were not affiliated with Hahn, along with a handful of the remaining thirty-five delegates from the rest of the state. Christian Roselius won election but would resign almost immediately, as the convention organized, over a decision to require the delegates to take a loyalty oath even if they had already done so. The convention would clearly be a Hahn–Banks–New Orleans operation.

There was much complaining about the quality of the convention delegates. No doubt, the radical-conservative boycott left out many talented individuals who might have made vital contributions. Scholars have debated the

---

[20] *CWL*, 7: 248; McCrary, *Abraham Lincoln and Reconstruction*, 238–42.
[21] Fellows to Hon. Jacob Collamer, March 4, 1864, ALP; Taylor, *Louisiana Reconstructed*, 48–49; McCrary, *Abraham Lincoln and Reconstruction*, 242–43.

socioeconomic backgrounds of the delegates, but, as Peyton McCrary has demonstrated, the convention was an "overwhelmingly middle-class body," essentially consisting of various professionals and the *petit bourgeoisie*, along with a few members of the working classes. Although a handful of representatives of the antebellum elite participated, the convention marked an overturning of the *ancièn régime*. Only days after it assembled on April 6 in New Orleans, however, came news of the Union military debacle at Mansfield, Louisiana. The failure of the Red River campaign would cast a pall over the convention before its work had even begun.[22]

* * *

Lincoln's intention that the ten-percent plan serve as a "rallying point" for southern Unionists in organizing free-state governments achieved only partial success in the lower Mississippi valley. The plan revitalized the state reorganization process in Tennessee, Arkansas, and Louisiana even as it exacerbated conflict among Unionists. The split among Louisiana Unionists – between free-state and conservative Unionists, and among the free-state forces themselves – became the most pronounced. Lincoln's intervention in Louisiana secured the triumph of the free-state Unionists but also precipitated the rupture among radicals and moderates – the very thing Lincoln had been at pains to avoid. Lincoln was above all determined to secure the abolition of slavery in restoring the rebellious states to the Union, even if it meant separating abolition from the endlessly more divisive issue of black civil rights. Yet he was also coming to realize – as the advocates of black suffrage in Louisiana, Congress, and elsewhere had been arguing, and as his letter to Hahn indicated – that defending the "jewel of liberty" might require a more expansive approach to the consequences of abolition.

---

[22] Preceding two paragraphs: *OR*, ser. 3, vol. 4, 170–72; Taylor, *Louisiana Reconstructed*, 43–45; McCrary, *Abraham Lincoln and Reconstruction*, 244–53 (quotation, 245).

13

"The Virus of Slavery Is As Virulent As It Ever Was"

As the free-state cause gained momentum in Arkansas, Tennessee, and Louisiana during the first half of 1864, slavery withered and new labor arrangements took firmer root throughout the Union-occupied lower Mississippi valley. Although the divided military command structure dictated that the sugar and cotton sections would still be administered separately, they shared much in common. In southern Louisiana, Federal officials implemented labor regulations that consolidated and extended the gains former slaves had made since the start of the occupation. In the cotton areas, a measure of stability had barely begun by mid-1864 to replace the chaos and dislocation of the previous year, and administrative uncertainty compounded the problem.

Conflict between planters and laborers continued to permeate every aspect of life and labor in both crop regions. Despite the limitations of wartime free labor, former slaves grew more confident in challenging the planters' authority, a process that Federal officials largely facilitated and encouraged. For their part, former slaveholders in both sections tried to hold the line, insisting that their slaves belonged to them and that they would restore the old status quo once Federal military authority was removed. "The virus of slavery," observed James McKaye of the American Freedmen's Inquiry Commission (AFIC), "is as virulent ... as it ever was." This mindset notwithstanding, former slaveholders increasingly acknowledged that slavery might well be defunct and that they should perhaps prepare for the consequences.

As free-state organization remained nebulous through mid-1864, Federal military authorities also continued to assume primary responsibility for substantiating the freedom of former slaves, especially with regard to their working lives and the care and maintenance of persons incapable of productive labor. Wartime free labor, despite much progress, further demonstrated the limitations of military emancipation and the need for formal abolition. By mid-year, Arkansas had abolished slavery, thus crossing a crucial threshold, while Louisiana prepared to follow suit and Tennessee was moving toward that end. Yet if military emancipation was being translated into constitutional abolition in much of the region, constitutional abolition itself depended on Federal military victory.

I

As the 1864 crop season commenced in southern Louisiana, General Nathaniel Banks drew up labor regulations that were inflected by conflict over previous policy and by the state reorganization process. Having suspended the slavery provisions of Louisiana's 1852 constitution in January 1864, Banks in early February issued labor guidelines that attempted to reconcile the conflicting interests of planters and laborers while grafting voluntary labor onto the plantation regime. Although designed as a "continuation of the system" from the previous year, the regulations marked a significant break from previous policy and a dramatic improvement in the former slaves' status. Still, they did not lack a degree of compulsion. They eliminated references to "slaves" or "fugitives from service or labor," ensured that families would be kept intact, and allowed laborers to choose their own employers. But once laborers had chosen their employers, they were required to fulfill their contracts and could not leave the plantation except under certain conditions. Employees would provide "respectful, honest, faithful labor," with work designated a "public duty" and "idleness and vagrancy a crime." Any laborer violating the contract would be put to work on the public roads without pay, and wages and rations would be deducted in cases of illness, actual or feigned. The "universal law of labor will be enforced upon just terms," Banks decreed.

Toward that end, monthly wages for "first class" male workers, a mere $2 in 1863, were increased to $8, with the rates ranging down to $3 for a "fourth class hand." Planters and workers could agree to share wage arrangements in which the latter collectively received a one-fourteenth share of the proceeds of the crop. This proportion marked an increase from one-twentieth of the previous year. The laborers received a lien on the crop. Employers were required to provide medical care, clothing, rations, fuel, and housing to workers and dependents, and to furnish workers with garden plots of up to one acre each. Employers were also encouraged to offer "perquisites for extra labor" and "land for share cultivation." The sick or disabled were to be "provided for upon the plantations to which they belong," and schools and a "Free Labor Bank" would be established. The workday was set at ten hours in summer and nine in winter. Sunday work would be avoided and considered "extra labor" when necessary and compensated accordingly. "Flogging and other cruel or unusual punishments" were prohibited. The sale of intoxicating drinks to laborers was severely restricted, as was the possession of firearms "or dangerous weapons." Banks continued the prohibition against military recruitment on plantations, and soldiers were banned from visiting plantations without permission. The order was silent on slavery itself or on the former slaves' legal status.

Banks also instituted the practice of withholding one-half of the monthly wage until year's end, to ensure that planters would have dependable labor for the entire crop season. Familiar in the North, where "at-will" employment was a relatively recent innovation, and suited to the needs of an agricultural economy, this practice was destined to become one of the defining features of free labor in the sugar country. Laborers would object to the practice after the war, and employers would resort to full monthly payment as a way of attracting labor. But for now, Banks strongly discouraged the practice of full payment. "The last year's experience shows that the Planter and the Negro comprehend the Revolution," Banks insisted, indulging in wishful thinking. In administering the system, Banks invested army provost marshals "with plenary powers upon all matters connected with labor," and he warned all employers "that undue influence used to move the [Provost] Marshal from his just balance between the parties representing labor and capital, will result in immediate change of officers, and thus defeat that regular and stable system upon which the interests of all parties depend."[1]

These regulations applied specifically to plantations worked by their owners. For abandoned and confiscated plantations that the Federal government leased out or operated directly, Capt. Samuel W. Cozzens, the Treasury Department's superintendent of plantations for southern Louisiana, formulated supplemental regulations. Although applying mainly to northern lessees or managers, Cozzens's regulations imposed far greater restrictions on laborers than on employers. The entire document focused almost exclusively on governing the "hands" and placed few obligations on their supervisors. Employers enjoyed wide discretion in disciplining workers, including docking their wages for innocuous transgressions. Cozzens may have assumed that Northerners required less guidance in managing free workers than did former slaveholders. But he also relegated laborers on government or leased plantations to the status of wage workers, who would enjoy few opportunities for independent production or alternatives to plantation employment.[2]

Although employers and laborers had little to negotiate under Federal regulations, former slaves relished the chance to deal with former owners as putative equals. Planters told of difficulties with their employees – in what would become an annual ritual – in settling accounts for the completed year and contracting for the new one. With laborers free to choose employers, if not to negotiate most terms of employment, many planters colluded in order not to compete for labor. They also complained of having to provide for workers as well as for dependents and other nonproducers. They again took to driving them away, or to charging them for or denying altogether the necessities they

---

[1] *Freedom: WGFL-LS*, 365–66, 512–17 (doc. 109); Rodrigue, *Reconstruction in the Cane Fields*, 44–45; *OR*, ser. 1, vol. 34, pt. 2, 227–31. For an example of a favorable reading of Banks's labor policy in the North, crediting Banks with having "totally abolished slavery": "The Reconstruction of Society in Louisiana," *The Living Age*, vol. 81, no. 1035 (April 2, 1864): 38–40.

[2] *Freedom: WGFL-LS*, 366, 368, 527–28 (doc. 113), 528–29 (doc. 114), 537–39 (doc. 118).

were supposed to provide. Yet if former slaves also pushed against what they saw as at best a quasi-freedom, planters likewise objected to a system in which they were expected to fulfill their traditional responsibilities for their workers' welfare while being denied the authority over labor that they deemed essential to running their plantations. Despite Banks's attempt to spell out both parties' duties in the revised guidelines, conflict infused every aspect of plantation operations during the spring planting season, as planters and former slaves evinced opposing understandings of the "revolution" through which they were passing. Displaying greater confidence and becoming more assertive, former slaves availed themselves at every turn of what one Federal officer called the "right to demand the protection of the Government."[3]

Planters in southern Louisiana continued to put forward the argument that black people's inability to work without compulsion made slavery necessary. They also reaffirmed their claim that sugar cultivation in Louisiana required coercive labor, since free workers would never subject themselves to the regimen of the sugar plantation. At the same time, the planters also further recalibrated their rhetoric in a process that had begun the previous year. As it became increasingly apparent in 1864 that Louisiana would abolish slavery, they focused less on the legal preservation of slavery than on labor as an abstract problem. Whereas southern slaveholders had customarily defended slavery as both a means toward the end of labor (and racial) control *and* as an end in itself, sugar planters increasingly insisted that the whole point of slavery had been to secure dependable labor. If they could achieve that objective by other means, some now argued, then so be it. The sugar planters therefore descended, individually and collectively, into an even deeper psychosis, bracing themselves for the worst while hoping for the best. "[T]he planters see that Slavery is dead but the spirit yet lives," observed Col. George H. Hanks, Superintendent of Negro Labor in southern Louisiana, in early 1864 testimony before the AFIC. "[T]hey are even more rampant to enslave the negroes than ever before." However unwittingly, Hanks encapsulated the planters' mindset: slavery was dead, yet it still lived. "[T]he disposition of the planters toward their own hired slaves is by no means friendly," he continued, "they submit to the terms dictated by Government because obliged so to do" and "accept the idea of freedom under compulsion."[4]

The planters' determination to nullify emancipation pervaded the AFIC's final report, issued in May 1864, and its various supplemental reports. In one such supplement, *The Mastership and Its Fruits: The Emancipated Slave Face to Face with His Old Master*, commissioner James McKaye focused on the Louisiana sugar region. McKaye examined "the intrinsic nature of the

---

[3] Rodrigue, *Reconstruction in the Cane Fields*, 46–49; *Freedom: WGFL-LS*, 367–69, 511–12 (doc. 108), 517–21 (doc. 110; quotation, 519), 521–25 (doc. 111), 535–37 (docs. 116, 117).
[4] *Freedom: WGFL-LS*, 517–21 (doc. 110; quotation, 520).

antagonisms that stand in the way of the successful introduction of the free labor system" in the region "and of the political reconstruction based upon it." While noting the many difficulties of implementing a new labor system, McKaye underscored the former slaveholders' intransigent opposition to emancipation. "The difficulty is not with the emancipated slave," he insisted, "but with the old master, still enthralled by his old infatuation."

"Of all portions of the slave region to which the Commission have had access," McKaye observed, "the valley of the lower Mississippi affords the most interesting field for the observation and study of the slave system, as well as of the great changes which, at the present moment, slave society everywhere is undergoing." In contrast to other parts of the South, where slave society was "in a state of total disruption," McKaye noted, "here are found all the elements of that society still in existence; but in a state of revolution and transformation." In this region, "facing the broad river on either side, still stand the great white mansion of the planter; by its side, just without its shadow, the long rows of cabins called the negro quarters," he continued. "In many instances the old master still occupies the mansion, and the negroes their old quarters; but under circumstances and in relations quite new, strange, and full of anxiety to both." In other Union-held areas, "the emancipated could only be seen as fugitives, and the old masters not at all," whereas "in such portions of the valley of the Lower Mississippi as are within our military lines, and especially in the river region of Louisiana, many of them still stand face to face in the presence of the great revolution, and of the trials to which it summons both."

Of the many challenges that free labor faced on Louisiana's sugar plantations, McKaye contended, the main one was the planters' mindset. "The simple truth is, that the virus of slavery, the lust of ownership, in the hearts of these old masters, is as virulent and active to-day as it ever was," he insisted. "Many of them admit that the old form of slavery is for the present, broken up," but "they scoff at the idea of freedom for the negro, and repeat the old argument of his incapacity to take care of himself, or to entertain any higher motive for exertion than that of the whip." The old masters merely awaited the withdrawal of military authority "and the re-establishment of the civil power of the State," he contended, which was "to be controlled and used as hitherto for the maintenance of what, to them doubtless, appears the paramount object of all civil authority, of the State itself, some form of the slave system."

"Reunion, then, and the preservation of the essential life of the constitution, demand, not only the release of the slave population from their bonds and the degradation thereby imposed upon them," McKaye maintained, "but the deliverance of the master population also, wholly and forever, from their mastership, and from the fatal delusions and depravations that are inherent in it." The slaveholders as much as the slaves would need to be liberated from the thrall of mastership. "This is the primary necessity of any rational attempt to establish free labor and a better social order in the Slave States, the very first step towards any wise, or well-founded reconstruction." Toward that end, McKaye recommended securing the "personal freedom" of the former slaves beyond any possible doubt; guaranteeing to them all the rights of citizenship, including the vote; confiscation and redistribution of the plantation lands; and "some uniform system of supervision and guardianship for the emancipated population in the interim of their transition from slavery to freedom." The first two recommendations would later be adopted in the postwar constitutional amendments and in "Radical Reconstruction." Land redistribution would never be undertaken, but the last recommendation would be carried out with the establishment of the Freedmen's Bureau.

What McKaye and the AFIC called "the lust of ownership" – by which they meant not slaveholding for its own sake but rather the command over labor that slavery entailed – was as strong as ever and would last for years, even decades. Only at great length would the former slaveholders of southern Louisiana and the South become reconciled to abolition, and many of them never did. Still, some planters were coming to understand – in their actions if not their rhetoric – that a new social order was taking shape, however slowly, and that "the mastership" was giving way. Almost despite themselves, the planters were awakening to the reality that they now had to bargain for their workers' services and could no longer simply resort to compulsion. The behavior if not the *mentalité* was changing.[5]

Under the slave regime, as Richard Follett has shown, sugar planters had customarily incentivized plantation routine and "paid" their slaves for extra work, especially during the harvest. But this was different. Payment was no longer a function of the planters' beneficence but rather of the relations that now existed between the two sides, however unequal in terms of resources and power they may have been. Planters and laborers now engaged one another as buyers and sellers of the laborers' productive capacity, which had once belonged to the planters, along with every other aspect of the slaves' existence. This new relationship did not yet enjoy the sanction of law, but the Federal government was firmly committed to it, and governments in three states of the region were moving toward that end. "[U]ntil the new order of things shall be better understood by the employer and the employed, and the free-labor system be more completely established, there will be a necessity for some kind of Government supervision and protectorate for the benefit of both parties," McKaye concluded, quoting Nathaniel Banks. "But this is not specially incident to the new system of negro labor. It is only by Governmental supervision and assistance that the labor of any race has been fostered and established."[6]

---

[5] *Freedom: WGFL-LS*, 529–34 (doc. 115). See also McKaye, *Mastership and Its Fruits*, 3, 4, 22, 26, 29, 33–34, 36, 38.
[6] Follett, *The Sugar Masters*.

II

Much of James McKaye's description of southern Louisiana, especially the planters' death-grip on slavery, also applied to the cotton-producing areas of the lower Mississippi valley. In places that had been directly affected by the Vicksburg campaign, or where the Union military presence was sporadic, conditions were too unsettled into 1864 to undertake plantation operations. In areas that had undergone less disruption and where many owners remained on their estates, by contrast, or that had experienced some version of free labor in 1863, Federal officials implemented regulations that tried to correct for previous difficulties. By mid-1864, the free-labor experiment on the lower Mississippi valley's cotton plantations could boast of much progress, but it proved no more satisfying to the various parties than in the sugar region.

In accordance with Treasury secretary Salmon P. Chase's directions, William P. Mellen, a departmental supervising agent, drew up regulations for abandoned and confiscated plantations in this section of the lower Mississippi valley. Incorporating criticism of General Lorenzo Thomas's 1863 leasing system, Mellen intended to allow former slaves greater access to land while mandating higher wages and providing stronger safeguards. His regulations, issued from Memphis in January 1864, directed that plantations be leased "to good and loyal citizens" who swore allegiance and accepted emancipation. Preference would be shown to lessees "wishing small tracts of land," obviously meaning former slaves. Mellen forbade any lessee to rent more than one plantation but placed no limit on the amount of acreage leased. "Freedman's Home Farms" would be established "at convenient locations" and operated under Treasury superintendents, who would oversee all aspects of leasing plantations and employing laborers on them. The Home Farms would function as employment centers, where former slaves would be registered and employers could apply for workers, and they would serve as homes for persons incapable of self-support. Families could not be broken up, and lessees employing parents would also have to accept their children and other dependents.

Monthly wages, half of which could be withheld until the end of the year, ranged from $25 to $15 for men and $18 to $10 for women, with the reserved portion being forfeited, and split between the government and lessee, whenever a laborer failed to fulfill the contract. Lessees were required to provide housing and one acre of land per family of four, but laborers would pay 10 percent above cost for clothing and food. In lieu of monthly wages, the parties could arrange for laborers to receive a share of the profits. Able-bodied persons unable or unwilling to find employment would be put to work on the Home Farms, receiving rations and clothing but no wages. The "use of the lash, paddle and all other cruel modes of punishment" were prohibited. Treasury officials were authorized – whenever the lessee "overtasks his laborers, or otherwise abuses them, or violates his agreement" – to void the contract and assume control of the plantation, or to release the laborers from the contract while ensuring them any back pay. A tax on cotton and other products on leased plantations would support nonworkers. Former slaves over the age of twelve were required to work, and schools would be established that children aged six to twelve were required to attend. Persons "living together as husband and wife" were to be legally married, and all marriages, births, and deaths would be recorded. In forwarding the regulations to Chase, Mellen predicted that "we can make the whole system self-sustaining," later adding that his program, unlike Lorenzo Thomas's, would secure "the improvement of the freedmen in his new relation."[7]

However well-conceived, Mellen's plan immediately encountered difficulties. Lessees who had already entered into arrangements for the new year, and resident planters who intended to use the regulations to operate their estates, protested against the lucrative wage rates, the taxation system to support nonproducers, and the limit of a 10-percent markup over cost on necessities. Echoing these complaints, Lorenzo Thomas deemed the new regulations "beautiful in theory, but utterly impracticable."[8] Though hardly an objective critic, Thomas was not far off the mark, as the regulations ran up against other harsh realities. Despite Mellen's good-faith effort to provide for nonproducers, the transfer of abandoned plantations to the Treasury Department, while the War Department continued to care for refugees and the indigent, created a bureaucratic nightmare and resulted in much recrimination. Mellen's regulations "were so unsatisfactory to persons who had gone down intending to lease and plant," insisted Col. John Eaton, the military General Superintendent of Freedmen for most of the cotton region, that these individuals "were all abandoning the business and going home." Eaton further objected to placing civilians in charge of plantations located in an active war zone without adequate military protection.[9]

These misgivings were soon borne out. When Union military forces deployed inland for a February expedition against Meridian, Confederates launched a series of raids along the Mississippi. In almost a replay of the previous year's Vicksburg campaign, plantations were attacked and burned, livestock and provisions destroyed, and residents killed or reenslaved. "Panics and stampedes have been of continual occurrence" as a result of "guerrilla

---

[7] *Freedom: WGFL-LS*, 641–42, 774–78 (doc. 188). See also [Eaton], *Report of the General Superintendent*, 68–72. In Arkansas, Home Farms were established at Helena (on the plantation of Confederate General Gideon Pillow), Little Rock, and Pine Bluff. Moneyhon, *Impact of the Civil War and Reconstruction on Arkansas*, 145.

[8] *Freedom: WGFL-LS*, 778–80 (doc. 189), 783–84 (doc. 191); *OR*, ser. 3, vol. 4, 235 (Thomas).

[9] *Freedom: WGFL-LS*, 642, 798–802 (doc. 197; quotation, 800). For Eaton's assessment of plantation and freed people's affairs in the cotton sections of the lower Mississippi valley for 1864, see *Grant, Lincoln, and the Freedmen*, chap. 12.

atrocities," Eaton observed. "People and planters have fled for their lives, often leaving dead and captives behind them." Much of the work of the present crop season – and of the long-term project of implementing a new labor system – was lost. "I would further remark that if such Military protection had been placed upon the Mississippi River as was promised in January, I could have leased every Plantation along the river in my district," reported a Treasury official at Skipwith's Landing, Mississippi. "The absence of protection on the river has had a most disastrous influence upon many of these Negroes, and is rapidly working thier ruin. They collect in abandoned camps in large numbers and make a precarious living by chopping a little wood stealing Cotton, corn, mules &c on the abandoned Plantations," he continued. "A demoralized camp of this kind exists upon the river opposite Skipwith's Landing. Several hundred negroes were living there in filth and disease, with all manner of booty stolen from the surrounding country."[10]

The raids cast a pall over plantation operations. General Thomas redoubled his criticism of the Treasury's leasing program, contending that the "military authorities must have command of the negroes." In late February, Lincoln reversed the earlier transfer of abandoned plantations along the Mississippi to the Treasury Department, directing Thomas to "take hold of and be master of the contraband and leasing business." After less than two months, the Mellen-Treasury plan was being shelved. "Mr Mellen's system is doubtless well intended," Lincoln observed in his instructions to Thomas, "but from what I hear I fear that if persisted in it would fall dead within it's own entangling details."[11]

Claiming that his regulations had the support of lessees and "large numbers of owners of plantations," Mellen now remonstrated to Secretary Chase. Although Washington officials refused to intervene, Mellen prevailed upon Thomas not to scrap the Treasury plan entirely. Instead, the two men agreed that Thomas would issue regulations similar to Banks's in southern Louisiana but largely retaining Mellen's rules. They would also preserve, as Mellen later informed Chase, "the contracts made with lessees and owners except as to compensation[,] classification [of laborers] and police Regulations." In other words, the essential framework of Mellen's plan would be kept in place, including labor contracts that had already been entered into, but wage rates would be adjusted – that is, lowered – and the military was back in charge. In early March, Thomas issued new regulations governing the leasing of plantations and the employment of former slaves in the cotton-producing section of the lower Mississippi valley.

---

[10] [Eaton], *Report of the General Superintendent*, 53; *Freedom: WGFL-LS*, 642–43, 794–98 (doc. 196; quotations, 795).

[11] *Freedom: WGFL-LS*, 643–44, 798–802 (doc. 197), esp. 800–1; *CWL*, 7: 212.

Thomas's new labor rules bore the unmistakable imprint of army policy. Indeed, they were explicitly based on Banks's order for southern Louisiana, issued a month earlier, and repeated much of it verbatim – including the sections in which Banks was clearly referring to Louisiana's political reorganization. Thomas left many Treasury regulations in force, but the military resumed responsibility for overall administration of the system. Contracts already agreed to for leasing abandoned plantations and employing "freedmen" were left in effect. Instead of adopting Banks's rigid wage structure, Thomas set "minimum wages" at $10 per month for men and $7 for women (half withheld), which were closer to 1863 levels, while also leaving employers and laborers free to negotiate their own terms. Employers were now responsible for the laborers' food and clothing, though a subsequent revision required laborers to purchase the latter, in addition to other basic necessities. All of Banks's strictures regarding the behavior of employers and laborers were carried over, as were the prohibitions against military recruitment and the presence of soldiers on plantations. The enforcing of contracts and law enforcement in general became the duties of provost marshals rather than Treasury agents, but the latter would still perform routine administrative tasks. Military authorities and the representatives of northern benevolent organizations assumed control of the Home Farms. Although wage labor would not have the same staying power in the cotton region as in the sugar region after the war, Thomas's wage system would prevail, with minor revisions, in much of the lower Mississippi valley for the rest of the war.[12]

Thomas's regulations and Federal military oversight of the plantation-leasing system provided a measure of stability, but they could not overcome the challenges of replacing a coercive labor system with a voluntary one amidst a war-ravaged landscape. Neither could they reconcile the conflicting interests of employers and laborers. Try as it might, the military was unable to provide the security necessary to conduct plantation operations and on which many employers counted. Confederate guerrillas and regulars continued to carry out raids, especially in the interior and against plantations located at a distance from towns or army posts. Northern lessees and resident planters attempting in good faith to work their estates under free-labor arrangements were forced to abandon the effort, determining that the profits to be made by producing cotton at wartime prices were not worth the risk to life and limb. Former slaves were understandably hesitant, even with the promise of high wages, to leave the relative safety of towns, home farms, or military posts for the dangers of

---

[12] Previous two paragraphs: *Freedom: WGFL-LS*, 643, 798–802, 802–8 (docs. 197, 198); [Eaton], *Report of the General Superintendent*, 14–17. On the contest between Mellen and Thomas for control of plantation affairs, see Gerteis, *From Contraband to Freedman*, chap. 8.

employment on government-sponsored plantations that Confederates were hell-bent on destroying.[13]

The resulting labor shortage exacerbated the planters' woes and redounded to the laborers' benefit. "Planters have not enough freedmen to cultivate what they have planted; and as the competition for hands increases, wages for their work go up, and actually settle the troublesome question of what wages shall be paid," observed one provost marshal. Employers – especially the lessees – complained of having been misled, as one of them observed, "by the promise of an abundant supply of labor." They also took exception when military authorities refused to assist them in inducing – in other words, forcing – laborers to accept their offers. "That he could not compel them to go with me, but that I was at liberty to take them if I could persuade them to go," is how one frustrated lessee described his encounter with Eaton. "The result of my interview was, that I got no hands, but got abuse," he added. "After a weeks delay and the sacrifice of time and *money*, I got a few hands, some of them sick, while the camps and home-farms are full of able-bodied persons, who do not average one day's work in three."[14]

Once employers and laborers came to terms and plantation operations commenced, there still remained the matter of overhauling plantation regimen. As in southern Louisiana and the entire Union-occupied South, every aspect of life and labor on the lower Mississippi valley's cotton plantations had to be redefined and therefore became a potential flashpoint. Notwithstanding Thomas's attempt to delineate the responsibilities of employers and workers, or the efforts of provost marshals and other officials to act as independent arbiters, neither party seemed to think that the other properly understood the new arrangements.

No sooner had Thomas's regulations replaced Mellen's than laborers predictably objected to what they saw as the unilateral lowering of their wages. "On no consultation with them, or consent of theirs, that promise [of $25 per month] was broken by authority above that of the Freedmen Department," Eaton observed. "They awoke one day to find that the employers' part of the contract was broken, but *their's* kept whole." They consequently refused to work or left the plantations altogether for the camps and settlements that Northerners deplored as "demoralizing." M. D. Landon, a northern lessee at Helena, Arkansas, gave up trying to work under Thomas's guidelines. They "would do to govern slaves," he insisted. He instead reverted to the Treasury

---

[13] *Freedom: WGFL-LS*, 644, 834–42 (doc. 209). On attacks in northeastern Louisiana by Confederate guerilas and jayhawkers, some of whom donned Union military uniforms, see Winters, *Civil War in Louisiana*, 322–23. See also *OR*, ser. 1, vol. 34, pt. 2, 967.

[14] *Freedom: WGFL-LS*, 644, 824–26 (doc. 206), 838; [Eaton], *Report of the General Superintendent*, 31. For complaints of Arkansas planters, see Moneyhon, *Impact of the Civil War and Reconstruction on Arkansas*, 146; [Eaton], *Report of the General Superintendent*, 33–34.

Department program, which "the pr[a]ctical anti-slavery planter" found preferable. "I can not use them and get labor, cheerful and happy labor from the people," he continued, referring to Thomas's regulations, which "keep the negro still a slave in practice – a slave in responsibility – a slave in advancement." Laborers refused to work under them. "They say 'We used to work so in Secesh times.' This is the strongest argument against it."[15]

Objecting to anything that resembled their previous working lives, former slaves were determined to have a say over the new arrangements. "The Freedmen regulated the matter to suit themselves," a Federal official observed in one instance, "and quit work when they thought they had done as much as they ought." Many employers, both northern lessees and resident owners, complained that workers did not provide the ten hours of honest, steady labor that Thomas's regulations called for. The laborers' "old slave habits, so slow and shiftless, often antagonize with the quick, active blood of the new Yankee planters," Eaton noted. On many plantations, Eaton further reported, former slaves complained "of rough, or profane, or obscene, or insulting usage, while blows and kicks have been not infrequently administered on some." As AFIC commissioner James McKaye had contended, planters had the greater difficult internalizing the new rules. "The complaints demanding most attention were those of abuse made by Freedmen," reported one of Eaton's subordinate officers. "Planters had often to be reminded, that they were not working slaves, and that abuses of this kind could not be tolerated."[16]

Since the slaves' very existence had consisted of unrelenting toil, punctuated by brutal punishment, distinguishing the old work routines from the new was as essential as it was difficult. It soon became an article of faith among former slaveholders that former slaves, having associated slavery with work, would define "freedom" as the absence of work. The only way to prevent them from descending into idleness, indolence, and vice, planters reasoned, was corporal punishment. "Some old planters, not yet clear of the old notions," Eaton explained, claimed that such former practices as "severity of manner, or profanity," were still necessary, and the old planters "try to practise them." In Arkansas, where slavery had been abolished as of March 1864, the old modes of thought and behavior died hard. "A few planters of the old *regime* have in good faith embraced the new order of things," reported a superintendent of freedmen in that state. "But the great majority of them acquiesce only through compulsion; and, as they hope their subjugation will be but temporary, they are at pains to retain their former slaves as near them and

---

[15] *Freedom: WGFL-LS*, 826–29 (doc. 207; quotation, 827). See also [Eaton], *Report of the General Superintendent*, 30–31, 34–35, 48; *Freedom: WGFL-LS*, 643–44, 790–91 (doc. 194); Moneyhon, *Impact of the Civil War and Reconstruction on Arkansas*, 145–48.

[16] [Eaton], *Report of the General Superintendent*, 30, 45, 63, and 53–54 on former overseers in general; *Freedom: WGFL-LS*, 645.

as much within their knowledge as possible." The Northerners who were supposed to have brought new ideas regarding labor were instead sometimes infected with the old ones. They were not above "the use of a club," as Eaton's subordinate put it, in disciplining laborers.[17]

"The complaints arising between planter and laborer are endless," Eaton observed in his report for 1864. "The laborer is accused as lazy, as vicious, as impudent, as thievish or a liar, as quarrelsome, as a breeder of discontent," he noted. "The planter is accused of keeping false time, overcharging for goods, giving short rations, refusing to feed dependents, neglecting the sick, severity, insults and blows." Such were the growing pains of a new social order, which at this point only Federal power could mediate. "The presence of military authority, in the person of a military Provost Marshal, is needed every week, on every plantation, both by planter and laborer; and the bare presence of such authority would accomplish most of the required results," Eaton insisted. "Not only is the necessity evident to an observer, but felt and asserted, with *entire unanimity*, by both black and white."[18]

* * *

In June 1864, Col. Samuel Thomas, the Provost Marshal of Freedmen in the Department of the Tennessee and one of Eaton's main adjutants, forwarded the results of an extended investigation into conditions in the vicinity of the Natchez District. His report offered a window onto the progress of free labor on the lower Mississippi valley's cotton plantations as a whole, and on some of the South's wealthiest lands. Even as he documented the many challenges that the new labor system faced, including the conflicting assumptions of planters and laborers over what the new system should look like, Thomas nonetheless tried to provide a positive assessment of the progress that had been made. Yet this assessment was itself predicated on a constricted vision of success. "That the laborer is going to receive a large amount of money for his year's work is not claimed by any one," Thomas admitted. In any event, the goal should be "to place his labor on an equal footing with white labor, and neither endow him with a fortune, nor open up his road to jump at once to ease or affluence, that he does not know how to use or enjoy." Paying the laborer "his" just due and providing laws to "let him work his way up" were the key objectives, he contended, not "starting out each freedman with a competency for the rest of his life." The former slaves "must labor for the food they eat, and the clothes they wear," Thomas pontificated. "Capital does now, and will for some time to come carry on great enterprises," he added, "and a large portion of the human family, both white and black, must labor for this capital at regulated wages, without any direct interest in the result of the enterprise."

---

[17] [Eaton], *Report of the General Superintendent*, 30, 65–66; *Freedom: WGFL-LS*, 645.
[18] [Eaton], *Report of the General Superintendent*, 54–55.

Generations of slaves and former slaves of the lower Mississippi valley, living and deceased, had already participated in a "great enterprise" – one of world-historical proportions. They had transformed the region's natural landscape into some of the most productive and valuable agricultural land in the nation. They had done so without receiving wages or enjoying any other compensation, and while enduring brutal oppression. Now, the former slaves were embarking upon another great enterprise: the destruction of slavery. Among the many challenges they faced was Thomas's assumption, which he shared with many other Northerners and almost all former slaveholders, that the former slaves must be disabused of the notion that freedom meant not having to work. The former slaves knew better than anyone that this was malarkey. The issues they now confronted were how to gain control over their working lives and secure the fruits of their labor. They had made great strides, and slavery seemed mortally wounded. But the virus of slavery remained as virulent as ever. Insofar as slavery *was* doomed, moreover, the system that would replace it was only beginning to emerge. Former slaves could overlook the patronizing assumptions on which the northern preaching of the gospel of free labor rested. But in the years to come, they would object to a form of social relations that allowed them no meaningful alternative to plantation employment, or that mandated their subordination to capital "without any direct interest in the result of the enterprise."[19]

[19] *Freedom: WGFL-LS*, 834–42 (doc. 209). For positive northern commentary on free labor in the cotton sections of the lower Mississippi valley during the spring of 1864, see "The Freedmen," *Harper's Weekly*, May 14, 1864, 306.

14

"No Longer Slaves but Freedmen"

During the spring and summer of 1864, the destruction of slavery in the lower Mississippi valley achieved another milestone, with the writing of a free-state constitution for Louisiana, but it also encountered setbacks. The failure of the Federal Red River campaign – the last major military operation of the war in the lower Mississippi valley – generated political reverberations while underscoring the region's decreased military significance. Whereas the valley had been central to the course of the war prior to the fall of Vicksburg, the Red River debacle offered irrefutable proof that the war's military outcome would be decided elsewhere.

But not the political outcome. Despite the military disaster, the constitutional convention organized by General Nathaniel P. Banks and the new Louisiana government produced a document that, pending popular approval in September, would formally abolish slavery. Yet the last-gasp attempt that the convention evoked from conservative Unionists to prevent abolition revealed the depth of proslavery sentiment among them. The convention also laid bare the opposition of the large majority of free-state Unionists to black suffrage or to any meaningful advance toward racial equality. In Arkansas, the legislature similarly declined to address abolition's consequences, despite urging by Governor Isaac Murphy to confer minimal legal rights on the former slaves. Hardly a racial egalitarian, Murphy simply pointed out an unavoidable truth. "The slaves are still among us," he reminded the legislature, "no longer slaves but freedmen." In Tennessee, Military Governor Andrew Johnson's June nomination as Abraham Lincoln's running-mate by the Republican-Union national convention in Baltimore underscored the lack of progress in organizing a free-state government after more than two years. By August, these things hardly seemed to matter. With the Union war effort at a virtual standstill, Lincoln appeared destined to lose the election.

I

The Federal Red River campaign of the spring of 1864 was among the most poorly conceived and executed campaigns of the entire war. Ostensibly under the command of Nathaniel P. Banks, it was intended to destroy the Confederate army in western Louisiana, capture Louisiana's Confederate capital of Shreveport while bringing much of Louisiana under Federal control, establish a Federal presence in east Texas, and seize thousands of bales of cotton. Meanwhile, Federal forces under General Frederick Steele would clear Confederates from southwestern Arkansas while also threatening Shreveport. However, the campaign was of dubious strategic value – with some observers arguing that Galveston or Mobile should take priority in the west – and operationally complicated. It also suffered various logistical difficulties, and state restoration efforts in Arkansas and Louisiana compromised military decisions. Banks did not bear sole responsibility for the fiasco, but he made critical mistakes. Of the several failures he suffered as military commander during the war, perhaps none was of greater consequence than the Red River campaign.[1]

Banks delayed the start of the campaign until after the March 4 installation of Louisiana's government. Retracing his steps from a year earlier during the Port Hudson campaign, he advanced toward Alexandria via Bayou Teche and the Atchafalaya River. By March 25, Banks had reached Alexandria, where he remained for more than a week to consolidate his position and organize elections for delegates from the area to the constitutional convention about to meet in New Orleans. The elections took place on April 1 but attracted little turnout. Low water on the Red River also prevented Federal gunboats from surmounting the rapids at Alexandria until early April. The Federal presence once again sparked the flight of slaves from the surrounding plantations, while rebel slaveholders abandoned dependent slaves and hauled their valuable ones off to Texas.[2]

When Banks embarked in early April for Shreveport, he unwisely chose a route that diverged from the Red River, forfeiting the protection of Federal gunboats. Although Confederate General Richard Taylor and his superior, General Edmund Kirby Smith, commander of the Confederate Trans-Mississippi Department, disagreed on how best to challenge Banks, Taylor decided to attack at Mansfield on April 8. The surprised Union forces were routed, and although they regrouped and held at Pleasant Hill the next day, the two engagements effectually ended the Union advance. Banks pulled back to Alexandria, but not until mid-May were his engineers able to dam the low water on the river, allowing the Federal gunboats to descend the rapids and Banks to resume his retreat. Union soldiers took out their frustration by laying waste the countryside, including what Confederates called "carrying off negroes" – in other words, freeing slaves. After looting and burning

---

[1] [Steele] to Banks, February 28, 1864, and Steele to Banks (copy), March 7, 1864, Steele Papers, Stanford; Winters, *Civil War in Louisiana*, 324–31; Hollandsworth, *Pretense of Glory*, 172–77; DeBlack, *With Fire and Sword*, 108–9.

[2] Winters, *Civil War in Louisiana*, 330–34; Hollandsworth, *Pretense of Glory*, 177–81; *OR*, ser. 1, vol. 34, pt. 1, 509, pt. 2, 494, 610–11.

Alexandria, they pillaged all the way back to the Mississippi, unconcerned with how destroying civilian property would win converts to the new Unionist government. By May 21, a campaign that William Tecumseh Sherman described as "one damn blunder from beginning to end" was over.[3]

Meanwhile, Frederick Steele's "Camden Expedition" fared no better. Setting out from Little Rock with 8,500 men on March 23, Steele intended to occupy Camden, on the Ouchita River in south-central Arkansas, where he would resupply before advancing on Shreveport. Dragging large supply trains over the war-ravaged landscape and encountering Confederate resistance, Steele only arrived at Camden on April 15. Finding no supplies, he sent foraging parties into the countryside while awaiting word from Banks, who by this point had already abandoned his offensive. On April 18, Confederate cavalry attacked a Federal wagon train at Poison Spring and massacred dozens of men of the First Kansas Colored Infantry, many of them scalped by Confederates and their Indian allies after being wounded. Another slaughter took place a week later at Marks' Mill, where a large number of "negroes and Arkansas refugees," a Federal officer reported, "were inhumanly butchered by the enemy." Steele decided to abandon the campaign, having suffered some 2,500 casualties, and in early May the Federals lurched back into Little Rock. The expedition marked the only substantive opportunity during the war – however fleeting – for slaves in southwestern Arkansas to gain their freedom.[4]

Aside from freeing more slaves, the Red River and Camden operations were indeed colossal blunders, failing to achieve their objectives while weakening the new governments in Louisiana and Arkansas. Partly in response to these defeats, Lincoln appointed General Edward R. S. Canby to command the newly created Military Division of West Mississippi, headquartered in New Orleans and encompassing Banks's and Steele's commands. With the Union war effort now focused on Ulysses S. Grant in Virginia and Sherman in Georgia, the defeats demonstrated the reduced strategic significance of the lower

---

[3] Winters, *Civil War in Louisiana*, 317–24, 334–80; Hollandsworth, *Pretense of Glory*, 181–99, 197–203; Joiner, *One Damn Blunder from Beginning to End*. Despite the Confederate success, Taylor and Kirby Smith would fall out over the Federals' escape, with Taylor insisting that Kirby Smith had prevented him from destroying Banks's army. Taylor continued to criticize his superior until Kirby Smith relieved him of command in early June, 1864. For Taylor's account of the campaign: *Destruction and Reconstruction*, chaps. 10, 11.

[4] *OR*, ser. 1, vol. 34, pt. 1, 714–15 (quotation); DeBlack, *With Fire and Sword*, 108–17; Poe, "Contours of Emancipation," 123–24; Burkhardt, *Confederate Rage*, chap. 9; Urwin, "'We Cannot Treat Negroes,'" 132–52. As Urwin notes, while some reports may have exaggerated the number of black fatalities at Poison Spring, the First Kansas's highly disproportionate ratio of 117 deaths against 65 wounded indicates that many of the black dead were killed after having surrendered or being wounded. For a reminiscence that arrives at the same conclusions about casualties, see Petty, *History of the Third Missouri Cavalry*, 81–82. On the First Kansas, see Spurgeon, *Soldiers in the Army of Freedom*, chaps. 12, 13.

Mississippi valley. Yet the upper Red River valley, which could claim to have been unvanquished during the war, was destined to become one of the South's most violent places during postwar Reconstruction.[5]

If these events had not dispirited Unionists enough, mid-April also witnessed the infamous Fort Pillow massacre in west Tennessee. Perpetrated by Confederate forces under Nathan Bedford Forrest after the fort surrendered, it resulted in the deaths of some 300 Union troops, two-thirds of whom were black, and the large majority of whom were butchered as they lay wounded or after having surrendered. The few black soldiers who survived were treated not as prisoners-of-war but as recaptured property, along with about forty black women and children sheltering in the fort. However horrific, the slaughter at Fort Pillow – and at Poison Spring and Marks' Mill – violated Confederate policy only to the extent that captured black "soldiers" were to be remanded to state authorities and dealt with as slaves engaged in insurrection – in effect, to receive a death sentence, though ostensibly carried out under due process of law.[6]

II

The news from the Red River was also a setback for the constitutional convention that gathered in early April in New Orleans. The convention would endure other challenges. If there had been a slap-dash quality to the Arkansas convention, which completed its work in a mere two weeks, Louisiana's sat for almost four full months. Absenteeism was a constant problem, and the convention debated trivial or moot questions at length. The convention's raison d'être had always been the abolition of slavery; the only real question was how far it would go toward racial equality. This issue had hardly arisen in Arkansas but was unavoidable in Louisiana. Black suffrage in particular was expected to generate almost as much conflict as abolition itself. Congress and northern society were watching Louisiana affairs carefully, and Lincoln had recently endorsed, albeit privately, limited black suffrage, a position that Banks indicated he now supported. For all of its problems, the

---

[5] Palmer, *Selected Letters of Charles Sumner*, 2: 239; John B. Steele to [Frederick R. Steele], May 14, 1864, Steele Papers, Stanford; Hollandsworth, *Pretense of Glory*, 204–6; Moneyhon, *Impact of the Civil War and Reconstruction on Arkansas*, 128. On the political implications of removing Steele, see Harris, *With Charity for All*, 314, n. 33. There is a significant body of work on violence along the Red River during Reconstruction. But see especially Fairclough, *The Revolution That Failed*.

[6] There is a large scholarly literature on the Fort Pillow massacre and Forrest's role in it. Recent accounts include Burkhardt, *Confederate Rage*, chap. 8; Castel, "Fort Pillow Massacre," 89–103; Hess, *Civil War in the West*, 234–35; and Cimprich, *Slavery's End in Tennessee*, 92–96. For documents on the massacre and an overview of Confederate policy on black prisoners of war, see *Freedom: BME*, 539–48 (doc. 214A-C), 567–70.

convention produced a document, however short-lived it proved to be, that abolished slavery, but most of the delegates also showed themselves to be almost as firmly committed to white supremacy as to abolition.[7]

Although overwhelmingly associated with the Banks–Hahn faction, the delegates held a broad range of views. As Peyton McCrary has shown, issues directly related to race – abolition, suffrage, and education – gave rise to three distinct voting blocs among the eighty or so delegates who amassed measurable voting records. The liberal bloc included some twenty delegates who voted consistently for measures furthering racial equality. A middling group of approximately forty moderates endorsed abolition and even black education to varying degrees but opposed black suffrage, although a subset of twenty of these delegates ultimately agreed to authorize the state legislature to enact it. Finally, some twenty conservatives consistently opposed almost all measures regarding black freedom, including thirteen holdouts who voted against abolition. The leader of this faction was Edmund Abell, a prominent New Orleans attorney who after the war would serve as a state district judge.[8]

Abell assumed this role because the attorney Christian Roselius resigned his seat after not being elected convention president, and over the decision to require the delegates to swear to Lincoln's loyalty oath affirming to support emancipation. Several committees addressed issues relating to abolition, including an emancipation committee; a legislative committee, which dealt with suffrage; and a public education committee. By late April, the emancipation committee presented majority and minority reports. The former included five sections, each of which addressed a specific aspect of abolition. Section one borrowed the familiar language of the Northwest Ordinance and the abolition amendment before Congress, save that it explicitly declared slavery to be abolished rather than merely stating it "shall" not exist. Section two forbade the legislature ever to make any law "recognizing the right of property in man," thereby knocking out the central pillar of the ideological defense of slavery. Section three invalidated and abolished all "legislation and jurisprudence on the subject of slavery." Sections four and five moved the state toward equality before the law by prohibiting racial discrimination in the penal code and apprenticeship laws for minors.[9]

The minority report was a different story. Essentially the work of Edmund Abell, it employed the familiar tenets of the proslavery argument: the sanctity of slaveholders' property rights, black peoples' incapacity for freedom, the failure of the emancipation experiment in the North, and the public welfare of

---

[7] Taylor, *Louisiana Reconstructed*, 48–50; McCrary, *Abraham Lincoln and Reconstruction*, 254–56; Harris, *With Charity for All*, 183–84.

[8] McCrary, *Abraham Lincoln and Reconstruction*, 258; Ross, *Great New Orleans Kidnapping Case*, chap. 9, esp. 187.

[9] *Debates in the Convention*, 3–27, 96; McCrary, *Abraham Lincoln and Reconstruction*, 258–60.

the slave states. "[T]he adoption of the majority report," it concluded, "would be unconstitutional, in violation of the first principles of right, and unjust to the loyal owner" (although the report made no distinction between loyal and disloyal slaveholders); "ruinous, demoralizing and destructive to the best interests of the slave; [and] dishonorable and dangerous to the safety of the State." It recommended the "indefinite postponement" of abolition until the state legislature, in conjunction with Congress, compensated loyal slaveholders "for their slaves" and arranged to remove all emancipated persons from the state. It further urged that the state "take possession of all unclaimed slaves, and hire or employ them to the best advantage," with the proceeds of their labor going to the state treasury.[10]

The convention devoted most of the period May 2–11 to debating abolition. Abell led the conservatives, repeatedly sounding themes in the minority report. Although the convention resoundingly rejected the minority's compensated emancipation proposal, Abell and the conservatives continued to resuscitate it as the convention considered the committee's majority report. Abell inevitably veered into a defense of slavery, claiming at one point that he had "never seen a negro whipped in cruelty, and only two or three for the purpose of correction." The conservatives also employed various parliamentary maneuvers to disrupt the proceedings, including proposing amendments to each section of the majority report, prompting convention president Edward H. Durrell to allege "an intention on the part of the minority to prevent the majority from doing business." An undaunted Abell introduced an amendment prohibiting the legislature from ever "authorizing free negroes to vote." It carried overwhelming, sixty-eight to fifteen, demonstrating the firm opposition of even most free-state delegates to black suffrage.[11]

After a week of such obstructionism, frustration was setting in among the free-state delegates. The convention hosted an overwhelmingly antislavery majority yet seemed to be going nowhere. If the conservatives intended to offer amendments to every section of the emancipation committee's report, exploiting divisions among the free-state delegates, the convention might possibly grind to a halt. "We have been here five weeks, and what have we done? We have listened to debates upon every subject but that which we are called upon to perform," complained George A. Fosdick, a member of the liberal faction and chairman of the legislative committee. "I now begin to think that Louisiana is not a free but a pro-slavery State." The problem, of course, was that Louisiana *was* a slave state. The solution, therefore, would be to

---

[10] *Debates in the Convention*, 97–98.
[11] *Debates in the Convention*, 192–97 (Abell, 195), 205–8 (Durrell, 207), 210–18 (black suffrage, 210); McCrary, *Abraham Lincoln and Reconstruction*, 260–61. The anti-black suffrage measure was rendered moot by subsequent events.

streamline the report, even if doing so meant sacrificing the provisions calling for equality before the law, and zero-in on Lincoln's "common object."[12]

On May 11, a day of much drama, the convention decided, in a series of disputatious votes, to eliminate the third, fourth, and fifth sections, and all amendments thereto, of the majority report. The report had been stripped down to its first two sections, abolishing slavery and prohibiting any laws recognizing property in man, while the provisions addressing the *consequences* of abolition were being dropped. Even as the convention moved toward final adoption of the report, the conservatives continued to stall, introducing new measures and resorting to other delaying tactics, to no avail. The final vote on the two sections, which again featured conservative attempts to lodge protests and otherwise block the proceedings, was seventy-two to thirteen in favor. "The first and second sections of the majority report of the Committee on Emancipation have passed their third reading and are now a part and parcel of the law of the State of Louisiana," Durrell announced, to thunderous applause. "The Ordinance of Emancipation without compensation was finally adopted today," Michael Hahn immediately telegraphed Lincoln, "& is now the law of the State." The two sections would become the first two articles, right after the preamble, of the new constitution.[13]

The free-state forces could take pride in their achievement, having secured the constitutional abolition of slavery. Yet some of them – along with the free-state radicals and the free people of color – could not help but feel dismayed. A convention created for the specific purpose of abolishing slavery had needed weeks to achieve that goal, and it had been forced to abandon provisions securing equality before the law. The conservatives, to be sure, had done everything in their power to thwart the proceedings, but what some observers found especially galling were the claims of loyalty by erstwhile defenders of slavery. Although several conservatives insisted that they opposed not abolition but the uncompensated loss of property, their comments rested on the assumption that slavery could still be divorced from the rebellion – that there were still loyal slaveholders. Nonetheless, it should have come as no surprise that slavery would only go down after a bitter fight to the death.[14]

With abolition accomplished, the convention turned to suffrage and education, both of which further underscored the antislavery delegates' tepid commitment to black civil rights. The legislative committee's report, while expressly restricting the vote to white men, offered a compromise by empowering the legislature to grant voting rights to "such other persons, citizens of the United States," who served in the military, paid taxes, or demonstrated

---

[12] *Debates in the Convention*, 218–21 (quotations, 220–21), including similar comments by the German attorney Ernest J. Wenck and the Polish immigrant Joseph Gorlinski.
[13] *Debates in the Convention*, 221–24; Hahn to Lincoln, May 11, 1864, ALP.
[14] McCrary, *Abraham Lincoln and Reconstruction*, 261–62.

"intellectual fitness." Putting aside the still-unresolved question of whether black people were citizens, a legislature consisting exclusively of white Southerners was never going to implement such a measure, however euphemistically worded, and it was overwhelmingly defeated. However, pressure was brought to bear on the middling delegates for the next month to reconsider the issue. The free people of color, though with no official voice, relentlessly pushed for it, while Hahn and Banks arm-twisted wavering delegates. On June 23, as the result of what may have been a deliberate ploy, the limited black suffrage proposal was reintroduced and brought to a vote. After some confusion and protestations, it carried by a vote of forty-eight to thirty-two. Black suffrage had been achieved, but only as pure symbolism.[15]

Public education for black children proved only slightly less vexing, though it enjoyed greater support than black suffrage. Louisiana had established a public education system before the war that was of limited scope outside New Orleans and prohibited free black children. Banks had hoped to incorporate the schools created under Federal auspices into the state system. Education had long been essential to northern reformers' vision of the southern postemancipation social order, as it had been to the former slaves, and Lincoln had included it in the ten-percent plan. The public education committee originally recommended free universal public education on a segregated basis, though with no distinction in the funding sources. A conservative alternative restricting education to white children was easily defeated before a compromise providing for separate schools and separate funding won approval. In a somewhat surprising move, however, the convention subsequently enacted a provision – more radical than even the committee's original proposal – mandating neither segregated schools nor separate funding systems. "The Legislature shall provide for the education of all children in the State," it simply stated, "by maintenance of free public schools by taxation or otherwise." Yet this provision lacked any real enforcement mechanism, and racially integrated public education would prove as illusory under Louisiana's 1864 constitution as black voting rights.[16]

Aside from mandating that "[a]ll able-bodied men in the State" be enrolled in the militia, the constitution included no other provisions regarding black freedom. It contained no bill of rights (although it protected some basic liberties), no prohibition against discriminatory legislation, no guarantee of

---

[15] *Debates in the Convention*, 146, 450; McCrary, *Abraham Lincoln and Reconstruction*, 262–63; Taylor, *Louisiana Reconstructed*, 47–48; Harris, *With Charity for All*, 184. The original report also proposed basing legislative apportionment, always a contentious issue in Louisiana before the war, on the number of voters rather than on either the white or total population, while also recommending a literacy requirement for *white* men. This proposal was also defeated.

[16] *Debates in the Convention*, 474–76, 601; McCrary, *Abraham Lincoln and Reconstruction*, 264–65.

equality before the law, and no affirmation of black people as citizens. By contrast, it included no apprenticeship provision or other "temporary arrangement," in Lincoln's words, that would have bound former slaves to the plantations. The new constitution accomplished the main goal of abolishing slavery, but it failed to address black freedom in any substantive way. The radicals and free people of color were deeply disappointed.

As the convention moved toward final approval of the constitution, the conservatives fought to the bitter end. Edmund Abell again castigated abolition – calling it "the most vital stroke at the life of the nation" – on behalf of loyal slaveholders. "By this unfortunate act you virtually say to the loyal men of the fourteen slave States, that the reward or *penalty* of loyalty is to be despoiled of their property against their will and without compensation," he insisted, "and no one is so simple as to suppose that the loyal men of those States will lay down their arms to be robbed of that property they have acquired under the guarantee of the parent government." Slavery, for Abell, was essentially a matter of property rights.[17]

In rejecting immediatism and calling instead for gradual abolition and compensation for loyal slaveholders, the conservative attorney Antonio Mendiverri likewise articulated key elements of the proslavery argument. Condemning slavery as "the veritable worm that is gnawing the vitals and destroying the happiness of our people," Mendiverri nonetheless countered that "reason, conscience, humanity, civilization, [and] the interests of the slaves themselves" militated against immediate abolition. "Pronounce immediate abolition, the negro will be free; ignorant of the true signification of the word 'liberty,' he will interpret for another word 'license.' Liberty, according to his comprehension, would be idleness, idleness would become misery, and misery degenerate into crime." Immediate abolition would do the former slaves more harm than good, Mendiverri contended, exchanging a form of slavery that "affords protection, food and clothing" for one that "destroys by cold and hunger," and reducing its supposed beneficiaries to an enslavement of "dire misery" that was "a thousand times worse" than legal slavery. No proslavery theorist ever crystallized the argument better.

Instead, Mendiverri continued, postpone abolition for ten years and compensate loyal slaveholders, so as to avoid "having destroyed any individual interest or right of property." He also proposed ameliorative measures to eliminate some of slavery's worse abuses: prohibit the slave trade; provide the slaves elementary education and confer upon them certain legal protections, including the recognition of marriages and families; and codify punishment, "without leaving it to the discretion of the masters and slaves" (as though the latter ever enjoyed such discretion). "Let labor be decreed as the fundamental law, and prosecute idleness and vagrancy to the utmost limit,"

---

[17] *Debates in the Convention*, 602 (quotation), 606–7.

Mendiverri intoned. By this point in the war, as Eugene D. Genovese has shown, some southern divines were expressing such reformist views, but Mendiverri was doing so before a convention that was on the verge of abolishing slavery.[18]

The final vote on the constitution was sixty-seven to sixteen. "The constitution of Louisiana is adopted as a whole, in Convention, this 22d of July, 1864," Durrell proclaimed, again to wild applause. The convention devoted its last days to various logistical matters, including declaring null and void Louisiana's secession ordinance, which had been "brought about in the interest of slavery," and endorsing the Federal abolition amendment. On July 25, Governor Hahn addressed the convention. "I am satisfied that the constitution that you have made will not only meet with a warm response and an overwhelming approval from the loyal people of Louisiana," he declared, "but that it will come up to the expectations of all loyal men all over this great country." To become operative, the constitution required voter approval in a referendum, to be held in early September. In one of its last acts, the convention authorized its president to call the body back into session "for any cause," or, should the constitution fail to win approval, to take any measures necessary to organize a loyal government. Although the constitution would win approval, the provision allowing the convention to reassemble would have tragic consequences after the war. Its work completed, the convention adjourned, and Michael Hahn left for Washington to present the document to Lincoln.[19]

Nathaniel Banks immediately informed Lincoln of the result. Proud of his handiwork, he described the new constitution, with the obligatory hyperbole, as "one of the best ever penned." In addition to abolishing slavery immediately "without condition or compensation," it authorized the legislature to enact black suffrage, required all able-bodied men to serve in the state militia, and provided free public education for "*all* children without restriction as to color." Banks could also not help but exaggerate, claiming that black people were now placed "upon an equal footing with the whites before the law" and that black suffrage "may be regarded as secure." Neither could he keep from deprecating the radicals' "open and unreasoning hostility" to the free-state initiative. He urged Lincoln to assist "with all available means" in the upcoming vote on the constitution. "The controversy will be violent, because this State forms *this* pivot upon which the great civil struggle of the year will turn," Banks lectured Lincoln. "It ought not to be imperiled for want of support."[20]

"I have just seen the new Constitution adopted by the Convention of Louisiana; and I am anxious that it shall be ratified by the people," Lincoln responded in early August. Nearing upon the very nadir of his presidency,

---

[18] *Debates in the Convention*, 603–6; Genovese, *A Consuming Fire*, 12–33, 51–61.
[19] *Debates in the Convention*, 607, 620, 623, 628–29.
[20] Banks to Lincoln, July 25, 1864, ALP; Hollandsworth, *Pretense of Glory*, 209.

Lincoln desperately needed good news, and Louisiana's constitution, along with Arkansas's (and Maryland's), provided some. He also took up Banks's call to political arms. "I will thank you to let the civil officers in Louisiana, holding under me, know that this [ratification of the constitution], is my wish, and to let me know at once who of them openly declare for the constitution, and who of them, if any, decline to so declare." By the time the vote took place a month later, the entire trajectory of the war had changed.[21]

III

By mid-April, soon after the Louisiana convention convened, and despite the ongoing Camden calamity that would significantly compromise its authority, the new Arkansas government led by Isaac Murphy prepared to take office. In theory, all but southwestern Arkansas had been secured, but in reality Federal control was tenuous, as evidenced by the legislature's failure, upon convening on April 11, to achieve a quorum for a full week. Union control of Little Rock was never threatened, but Confederate guerillas wreaked havoc in the countryside, and Unionism, so carefully cultivated in recent months, suffered accordingly. By mid-summer, tensions between the Unionist factions intensified, Congress refused to seat the state's members-elect, military–civilian relations bottomed out, and Steele's inaction demoralized the civilian population. Neither did the legislature address the consequences of abolition. Reconstruction in Arkansas seemed to be in disarray.

Yet there had been reason for cautious optimism upon Murphy's April 18 inauguration as governor. Speaking outside the state capitol before a racially integrated audience of some 15,000 persons, he devoted about a quarter of his inaugural address to slavery, defending Federal emancipation policy as a means of suppressing the rebellion while largely ignoring emancipation's consequences. The rebellion had been undertaken to perpetuate slavery, he contended, which, as "hostile to democratic institutions," the Federal government had the right to destroy. Like many southern Unionists, Murphy was more concerned with how abolition would affect the white population than the former slaves. Individuals (meaning slaveholders) had suffered from abolition, he allowed, but the public at large would benefit, "and the prosperity of our nationality and the government of the people [would] be rendered more secure, and an increased degree of prosperity and happiness obtained for the masses of humanity."[22]

Although Murphy's inaugural address did not mention the former slaves' legal and political status, his official message to the legislature, delivered two days earlier, spoke to that issue. Yet he marked the former slaves more as

---

[21] CWL, 7: 486–87.
[22] *Journal of the Convention of Delegates of the People of Arkansas*, 30–35.

bystanders than as makers of their own destiny, illustrating the condescension so common to white reformers of the age. Slavery in Arkansas was dead and buried "too deep ever to be resurrected," Murphy insisted, but abolition imposed "a great responsibility" on the white population to exert the necessary guidance, direction, and control over the former slaves. "The slaves are still among us, no longer slaves but freedmen," he observed, "with all the rights of freemen." He quickly added: "except political rights, or the right to take part in the government of the State or of the United States." This right would never be permitted. "The colored race having no choice in the Government," Murphy assured the legislators, "the white race must govern and legislate for them."

That being said, Murphy went on to suggest, ever so delicately, that these rights should include testifying in court – possibly against white persons. "The colored freeman should be as fully protected in all his rights of life, liberty, character, and property as the white freeman," he acknowledged. "He should also be compelled to perform his contracts, whether with the white man or the colored, by legislation suitable to his condition, and to effect this object some change in the law of evidence may be necessary." *Some change in the law of evidence* meant black testimony, which would not be popular with white Arkansans. The former slaves should also be provided education "suitable to their condition," along with "some protective legislation" legitimizing their marriages and family relations. But that was it. Murphy advocated nothing close to racial equality, and he made little allowance for black autonomy or self-determination. Although he deemed this subject "of great social importance" and called for the legislature's "earnest consideration," the legislature would take no action.[23]

Despite legislative inertia on emancipation, Arkansas Unionists still hoped to secure congressional recognition of their government. While considering the seating of James M. Johnson in February, the US House of Representatives had questioned whether a loyal government existed in Arkansas. But that was before ratification of the free-state constitution, the election of two more congressmen, and installation of the Murphy government. In early May, even as Steele's troops were trudging back into Little Rock, the legislature prepared to elect US Senators. The selection of William M. Fishback and Elisha Baxter, however, further aggravated the factional rift between Arkansas Unionists. Baxter's Unionism was beyond doubt, but Fishback's was not. As a former resident of Illinois whose acquaintance with Lincoln was supposed to have been a plus, Fishback had in fact exhibited highly questionable loyalty during the secession crisis and after, and conservatives pounced on his election to castigate the entire radical faction. When Arkansas House Speaker and conservative Horace B. Allis refused to sign Fishback's election certificate, the House replaced Allis with a speaker who signed it, prompting Allis to

---

[23] *Journal of the Convention of Delegates of the People of Arkansas*, 17–29, esp. 18–19.

head to Washington to defeat Fishback's seating. The Murphy–Fishback faction, in turn, lobbied in Washington against the conservatives, especially congressman-elect Anthony A. C. Rogers and former House Speaker Allis. Lincoln worried lest this factional bickering jeopardize congressional recognition of the new government, and the seating of Fishback and Baxter would indeed become entangled in the controversy over the Wade–Davis bill and the contest between Lincoln and Congress over Reconstruction.[24]

For the rest of the spring and into the summer, the situation in Arkansas worsened. Following the Camden debacle, Steele hesitated to take any initiative, while Confederates operated openly in remote areas. One Federal officer reported to Lincoln in early June that the military setback had "caused some depression of union sentiment" in Arkansas, "so that the country seems to have generated into bushwhackers." But for the defeat of Banks and Steele, Murphy added, "the state would have had the means to sustain herself." Instead, the Camden disaster "resulted in the reoccupation of the state by the Rebels – and the flight or murder of most of the Loyal voters who had taken part in the election." When Steele refused his pleadings to act, Murphy begged Lincoln for assistance. "The rebels take the country, and now the Union element are leaving at the average of 100 per day, broken-hearted and hopeless, whilst the rebels are enjoying security from both sides, and enjoying the property of the refugees, favored and petted by Federal commanders, the representatives of your Excellency," Murphy alleged. "These things are hard to bear. You will excuse me; I write from feeling."[25]

Lincoln instructed Steele to defend the Arkansas government, even after Congress refused to seat the state's members-elect. But Murphy still had little influence with Steele. The situation helped neither the state government nor Unionism in general. When Murphy subsequently discovered that the War Department in late July had revoked his authority to appoint officers for

---

[24] *Journal of the Convention of Delegates of the People of Arkansas*, 35; *CWL*, 7: 334–35; Moneyhon, *Impact of the Civil War and Reconstruction on Arkansas*, 164; DeBlack, *With Fire and Sword*, 106–7; Cowen, "Reorganization of Federal Arkansas," 50–51; Harris, *With Charity for All*, 206. Steele, whose relations with Murphy were already strained, tried to remain above the fray. Fishback did not help his own cause by referring, in a speech before the legislature, to C. P. Meador, a conservative newspaper editor and fierce opponent of his election, as a "Pimp" for Steele's staff. Neither was Steele assuaged by Fishback's explanation that he had heard Steele himself make the comment "on several occasions," or that "the remark is so generally known" that Fishback "did not dream of giving offense to your staff." Steele's staff, no doubt in a foul humor over the Camden failure, took offense, with one member attempting to assault Fishback. Fishback to Steele, May 3, 1864, Steele Papers, Stanford.

[25] General Christopher C. Andrews to Lincoln, June 5, 1864, and Murphy to Lincoln, July 23, 1864, both in ALP; *OR*, ser. 3, vol. 4, 463; Moneyhon, *Impact of the Civil War and Reconstruction on Arkansas*, 165–66; DeBlack, *With Fire and Sword*, 117–22; Harris, *With Charity for All*, 205.

Arkansas regiments, his frustration boiled over. "This seems to me to be both a hardship and an indignity," he protested to Lincoln in early August. "For God's sake Mr President and I say it out of the anguish of my despair do not allow unnecessary obstacles to be thrown in the path of the State organization at this critical time, for I fear that if these things continue Arkansas will be so lost that she can only be reclaimed as a barren wilderness." The War Department order "will shake [the people's] confidence in the stability and permanence of the present state government," Murphy further warned, and he asked Lincoln to reverse it. But no doubt with weightier issues on his mind, Lincoln did not reply. Arkansas had abolished slavery and instituted a loyal government, but its restoration to the Union as a free-state would have to await the outcome of the presidential election and the next meeting of Congress.[26]

IV

The Republican – or Union – ticket in the election would now include a Tennessean, Andrew Johnson, as the vice presidential candidate. By mid-1864, Johnson had been stewarding Tennessee's political reorganization for more than two full years. Although progress was being made, the initiative – especially compared to those in Arkansas and Louisiana – seemed to be in the doldrums. Also, while the nomination made a great deal of sense, the one thing no one seems to have considered was the possibility of Johnson actually becoming president. Only in hindsight would the catastrophe of his nomination become clear.[27]

News of the nomination was greeted in Nashville with much jubilation. In an address on June 9, the day after the National Union convention adjourned in Baltimore, Johnson (who did not attend) affirmed his commitment to abolition while sounding familiar themes: slavery had given rise to an "arrogant aristocracy" that had subjugated the South's white population as well as the slaves; the "spirit of the rebellion" had been intent on perpetuating both slavery and the principle of aristocracy; and ending slavery would liberate more white people than slaves. The slaveholders who had instigated the rebellion "must be punished and impoverished." Yet even as he proclaimed "slavery is dead," Johnson issued a warning. "There is an element in our midst who are for perpetuating the institution of slavery." Johnson no doubt had in mind proslavery Unionists and former Confederates, whose loyalties were suspect. "A fellow who takes the oath merely to save his property, and denies the validity of the oath is a perjured man, and not to be trusted." Consequently,

---

[26] Murphy to Lincoln, August 6, 1864, ALP; Ed T. Wood to Steele, June 3, 1864, Steele Papers, Stanford; Moneyhon, *Impact of the Civil War and Reconstruction on Arkansas*, 165–66.

[27] Trefousse, *Andrew Johnson*, 176–80.

"in calling a convention to restore the State," Johnson asked rhetorically, "who shall restore, and re-establish it?" The answer was obvious: only unconditional Unionists who unequivocally supported emancipation could now be entrusted with the responsibility of state reorganization.[28]

Indeed, Johnson's nomination further complicated Reconstruction in Tennessee, where free-state Unionists now had less than a year, assuming Republican-Union presidential victory, to organize a new government and abolish slavery before Johnson's removal from the scene. Conservative Unionists still presented a formidable opposition, and their contention that Johnson had delayed state reorganization so as to hold onto power assumed greater salience in light of the new deadline. They had been clamoring for Tennessee's reorganization for months since Lincoln issued the ten-percent plan (and long before that), and there was little chance that a state reorganization under their auspices would comply with Lincoln's abolition requirement. Neither did conservative criticism of Federal emancipation policy following Johnson's nomination bode well for abolition in Tennessee. The Federal abolition amendment, which the Republican-Union platform endorsed, seemed to obviate state-level abolition – although the seceded states would need to ratify it and therefore had to be reconstructed. But at this point, the success of the Union war effort, the Lincoln-Johnson ticket, or the amendment was far from certain.[29]

Nothing better epitomized the turbulent situation in Tennessee during the summer of 1864 than Nathan Bedford Forrest's August raid against Memphis, a culmination of the bedlam he had wrought during the preceding months. Although devoid of strategic value, the raid embarrassed and demoralized Unionists while rejuvenating Confederates. It also demonstrated the challenges of pursuing political objectives in a war zone. The Memphis raid occurred only two days before Lincoln instructed his Cabinet to sign the "blind" memorandum, indicating that he expected to lose the election. By late August, it appeared as though all that had been endured in hopes of preserving the Union and abolishing slavery had been for naught.[30]

---

[28] *PAJ*, 6: 723–28.
[29] Trefousse, *Andrew Johnson*, 180–81; Cimprich, "Military Governor Johnson and Tennessee Blacks," 466–67; Atkins, "Failure of Restoration," 310.
[30] Hess, *Civil War in the West*, 233–38; *OR*, ser. 1, vol. 38, pt. 4, 480.

15

"So Long As a Spark of Vitality Remains in the Institution of Slavery"

Even as the free-state governments in Louisiana and Arkansas were taking shape, congressional Republicans drew upon them in grappling with emancipation and Reconstruction. From March through the end of the first session of the Thirty-Eighth Congress in early July, Republicans again attempted to enact Reconstruction legislation – this time with the Wade–Davis bill. In debating the bill, especially in the House of Representatives, northern Democrats exhibited much ideological overlap with southern conservative Unionists. Republicans welcomed the opportunity to label their Democratic opponents as slavery's lackeys, but they also targeted the shortcomings of Abraham Lincoln's ten-percent plan and his reconstructed governments. By the time the House passed the bill in early May, congressional Republicans had articulated their very real concerns that former Confederates – following the path laid out by southern conservative Unionists, and aided by their northern Democratic enablers – might gain control of hastily reorganized governments and restore the rebellious states to the Union while preserving slavery. "Too well I know the vitality of slavery with its infinite capacity of propagation, and how little slavery it takes to make a slave State with all the cruel pretentions of slavery," Charles Sumner warned. Although Republicans did not focus exclusively on the states of the lower Mississippi valley in making this argument, they drew much of their political ammunition from them.[1]

Other national developments intersected with wartime Reconstruction in the region during the summer of 1864. The Republican-Union national convention met in early June and nominated Lincoln for reelection while endorsing the Federal abolition amendment. Having now become a partisan matter, the amendment failed in mid-June to receive the necessary two-thirds majority in the House. The US Senate's refusal to seat Arkansas's claimants also dealt Lincoln's Reconstruction policy a setback. As the session ended, the Senate finally passed the Wade–Davis bill, but Lincoln's "pocket" veto of the bill and his proclamation justifying this action prompted the bill's cosponsors to

---

[1] [Sumner], *No Property in Man*, 18–19. Although Sumner made this remark in speaking on the abolition amendment and not on the Wade–Davis bill, he nonetheless spoke to the Republican fear of slavery surviving the war.

respond in early August with their acerbic "manifesto," which seemed to signal open warfare between Lincoln and Radical Republicans. The manifesto's rancorous language, paradoxically, camouflaged the substantive points – which antislavery advocates had been making for some time, which wartime Reconstruction in the lower Mississippi valley had helped to bring to the fore, and which historians have often missed – that neither the Emancipation Proclamation nor the ten-percent plan abolished slavery, and that slavery might therefore survive northern military victory. By late August, however, the faltering Union war effort and Lincoln's sinking reelection prospects obviated that issue.

I

By late March 1864, after a delay of several weeks, Maryland Representative and leading Radical Henry Winter Davis, chairman of the House select committee on the rebellious states, reported his Reconstruction bill out of committee. It substituted for that of fellow committee member James M. Ashley of Ohio. Both bills bore similarities to the ten-percent plan, although Davis saw his bill as an alternative to it. The two bills would have initially required 10 percent of the voting population to swear allegiance before commencing state reorganization. Unlike Lincoln, however, they restricted participation in that process to individuals who could take the "ironclad" oath. Both bills sanctioned the emancipation of all slaves in the seceded states and required those states to prohibit involuntary servitude before being restored to the Union. One critical difference between them was that Ashley's required black suffrage, whereas Davis's limited the vote to white men. Davis believed, as did other Radical Republicans in early 1864, that black suffrage would never get through Congress.[2]

The Wade–Davis bill, cosponsored by US Senator Benjamin F. Wade of Ohio, sparked bitterly partisan debate. Republicans and northern Democrats disagreed over many specific provisions of the bill, but the main point of contention was the fate of slavery. House debate – which took place intermittently between late March and early May – in many respects echoed the arguments of free-state and conservative Unionists in Louisiana and Tennessee. Whereas Republicans held that slavery and secession were inseparable and that slavery was incompatible with "republican" government, northern Democrats countered that slavery and the Union could still coexist, and they urged the insurgent states to resume their former relations with the Union – with slavery legally intact if necessary. Conservative-Unionist claims to loyalty,

---

[2] On Davis substituting his bill for Ashley's, see Vorenberg, *Final Freedom*, 128–29; Richards, *Who Freed the Slaves?*, 146–47; Zietlow, *Forgotten Emancipator*, 113. See also: Belz, *Reconstructing the Union*, 200–2.

along with increasing Confederate discontent, lent plausibility to northern Democratic charges that Republicans were obsessed with waging an abolitionist war. Congressional debate on the Wade–Davis bill thus reflected deeply contrasting visions of a reconstructed Union.[3]

Democrats embedded their criticism of Republican Reconstruction proposals within what they contended was a litany of transgressions in conducting the war. Republicans had foisted an abolitionist war on the country; imposed conscription, onerous taxation, and property confiscation (especially on loyal slaveholders); suppressed dissent and civil liberties; espoused racial and even "social" equality; prosecuted a war of subjugation rather than conciliation; aspired to control the reconstructed states' electoral votes in the upcoming presidential election; and were determined to obliterate state and local government and consolidate power in a "centralizing" Federal government under Republican auspices. Democrats had made these arguments throughout the war, but their arguments assumed greater salience in the Wade–Davis debate. They were no doubt partaking of the "paranoid style," and virtually every one of their denunciations of Republican Reconstruction policy degenerated into a racialist screed. Yet their racial hyperbole and charges of a grand tyrannical conspiracy – which they equated with the rebellion itself in subverting the Constitution – often masked legitimate arguments. While Democrats objected to many specific provisions of the ten-percent plan and the Wade–Davis bill (often blurring the two), the Republican insistence on abolition lay at the core of their critique. It also provided common ground for War and Peace Democrats.[4]

---

[3] As Michael Vorenberg observes, congressional debate has always been inherently partisan, "marking political territory," but it has also reflected ideological positions and prevailing attitudes in society. I would add that while personal correspondence, diary or journal entries, or similar kinds of evidence may reveal legislators' inner thoughts, the floor of Congress has functioned as the institutional mechanism through which their views found expression. Notwithstanding the limitations of democratic government in the mid-nineteenth-century United States, what the members of Congress said in formal debate generally represented (figuratively and literally) the spectrum of public opinion. Vorenberg, *Final Freedom*, 90.

[4] This overview of the northern Democratic critique of Republican policy during the Wade–Davis debate is based on the following addresses by House Democrats: *CG*, 38th Cong., 1st Sess., 1737–39 (April 4, 1864; James C. Allen of Illinois), 1981–85 (April 29; Augustus C. Baldwin of Michigan), 2039–41 (May 2; Charles Denison of Pennsylvania), 2043–45 (May 2; Meyer Strouse of Pennsylvania), 2045–49 (May 2; James A. Cravens of Indiana), 2067–69 (May 3; Francis Kernan of New York), 2071–74 (May 3; Nehemiah Perry of New Jersey), 2074–78 (May 3; Fernando Wood of New York), 2095–102 (May 4; Samuel S. Cox of Ohio), 2105–7 (May 4; George H. Pendleton of Ohio). Important scholarly works that examine Northern Democrats or devote considerable attention to them during the Civil War and Reconstruction era include Baker, *Affairs of Party*, 344–52; Silbey, *Respectable Minority*, 70–88; Weber, *Copperheads*, 64–71; Wood, *Black Scare*, 19–29; Smith, *No Party Now* and *The Stormy Present*, chap. 7; and Neely, *The Union Divided* and *Lincoln and the Democrats*.

In criticizing Republican approaches to Reconstruction, Democrats pinpointed three particular issues. First, working from Lincoln's own position that the seceded states could not leave the Union, Democrats objected to imposing conditions on them – especially the abolition of slavery – for restoration to it. *Individuals* had engaged in rebellion, but the states' constitutions and laws, including those pertaining to slavery, were still operative, and their domestic institutions remained intact. For Congress to require a state to abolish slavery in order to be restored to a Union it had never left was constitutionally unsound and logically absurd. Second, Democrats denied that slavery was incompatible with "republican" government, by which they simply meant one in which the people were sovereign. Neither did the republican government guarantee extend beyond minimal Federal oversight. So long as their governments were "republican," the states could regulate their domestic institutions as they saw fit. Finally, Democrats condemned a loyalty oath that made acceptance of Federal emancipation measures a condition for participation in state reorganization. (On this point, they often conflated the iron-clad oath and Lincoln's more lenient oath.) "The truth is, a test oath to require citizens to support [the President's] policy as to slaves is not an oath of allegiance to republican government, but to the Republican party," insisted Samuel S. Cox of Ohio. "It is an oath of fealty to Abraham Lincoln."[5]

What all of this added up to, northern Democrats charged, was that the (white) people of the seceded states were being denied their constitutional right to self-government, including the right to decide whether to have slavery. Where is the authority under the Constitution, George H. Pendleton of Ohio asked, for the Federal government to decide "whether there shall or shall not be slavery or involuntary servitude within [the State's] limits?" Under the Constitution as it stood at the time, this was not an unfair question. Northern Democrats insisted that they were not defending slavery but rather the right of the people in the states to determine its fate. "We do not like slavery," Samuel S. Cox of Ohio pronounced. "For one, I say again as I have said before, let it die, if die it must, not by the rough usages of war, not by the starvation, miscegenation, or extirpation of the black race, not by the strangulation of State and popular sovereignty," Cox explained, "but by the voluntary and legal action of the States when they are in a condition freely to express their choice." Unlike northern Democrats who claimed to hate slavery, Republicans no longer employed the conditional "if" in deliberating whether slavery must die. As northern Democrats demonstrated in the Wade–Davis debate, southern conservative Unionists had powerful allies in Congress and northern society at large.[6]

---

[5] *CG*, 38th Cong., 1st Sess., 2097 (May 4, 1864; Cox).
[6] *CG*, 38th Cong., 1st Sess., 2096 (May 4, 1864; Cox), 2106 (May 4; Pendleton). See also *CG*, 38th Cong., 1st Sess., 1739 (April 19, 1864; Allen), 2039 (May 2; Denison), 2044 (May 2; Strouse), 2068–69 (May 3; Kernan), 2074 (May 3; Wood). All biographical information on members of Congress derives from the *Biographical Directory of Congress*.

II

By contrast, Republican commentary on the Wade–Davis bill reflected tensions between congressional Republicans and Lincoln – and among the former themselves – over state restoration and emancipation. Already ongoing for two years, these tensions greatly intensified with the organization of Arkansas's and Louisiana's governments under the ten-percent plan. That being said, no Republican expressed the slightest doubt over slavery as the root cause of the rebellion and the need to abolish it, or over congressional authority under the "republican government" guarantee to require abolition as a condition for restoration. Despite their many differences, Republicans agreed on this much.

Congressional Republicans went to considerable lengths to cast northern Democrats as apologists for slavery, but they also emphasized the shortcomings of the ten-percent plan. Commentary on the plan, at the time and since, has traditionally focused on the undemocratic nature of the governments to be established, the "leniency" toward former Confederates, and the failure to provide for black civil rights. However, Republicans expressed even greater concern – which scholars have almost always overlooked – over the possibility of slavery surviving the war. Owing to the limitations of the ten-percent plan for securing abolition, along with northern Democrats' position on state restoration, Republicans warned that the seceded states might well be restored to the Union without ending slavery. They thereby gave sanction to the fears that antislavery advocates had been voicing since the Emancipation Proclamation. Tempting though it may be to dismiss these warnings as hyperbole or fear-mongering, employed for political effect, they can only be ignored at the risk of taking the abolition of slavery for granted, something no contemporary would have dared to do.

In supporting the Wade–Davis bill, Republicans accentuated the inadequacies of both the ten-percent plan and the Federal abolition amendment. Henry Winter Davis, the bill's cosponsor, endorsed the amendment but emphasized its impracticality. The eleven seceded states themselves could block ratification, Davis observed, but three-fourths of the *loyal* states might also fail to ratify it. Whereas the amendment failed to provide for the political reorganization of the seceded states, the ten-percent plan likewise failed to secure abolition. "How does it [the ten-percent plan] accomplish the final removal of slavery? How does it accomplish the reorganization of the government on the basis of universal freedom?" Davis asked rhetorically. "The only prescription is that the government shall not *contravene* the provisions of that proclamation [the Emancipation Proclamation]."

"But what is the proclamation which the new governments must not contravene?" Davis again asked, driving the point home. "That certain negroes shall be free, and that certain other negroes shall remain slaves." Indeed, no Federal antislavery measure emancipated all slaves in the seceded states, let alone abolished slavery. "The proclamation therefore recognizes the existence of slavery. It does just exactly what all the constitutions of the rebel States prior to the rebellion did. It recognizes the existence of slavery, and they recognize the existence of slavery; and, therefore, the old constitutions might be restored to-morrow without *contravening* the proclamation of freedom." The seceded states could comply with the Emancipation Proclamation and the ten-percent plan and yet *still* not relinquish slavery. Davis had isolated the ten-percent plan's essential flaw, one more fatal than its failure to address black political and legal rights. It could only require the new state constitutions to comport with Federal wartime antislavery measures. But since these measures freed slaves but did not abolish slavery, the ten-percent plan left slavery legally intact. The only way to establish loyal governments in the seceded states based on free-state constitutions was through congressional legislation. Davis would sound these themes repeatedly in the coming months.[7]

Other Republicans underscored the failure of the ten-percent plan to abolish slavery. Michigan's Fernando Cortez Beaman contended that the plan does not "require or suggest the adoption of any constitutional provision abolishing slavery." (The ten-percent plan arguably *suggested* free-state constitutions but did not require them.) Military emancipation and constitutional abolition, he noted, were two very different things. "Conceding the legality and sufficiency of the executive proclamations for liberating the slave, I fail to perceive that any one of them has vacated the constitution or laws under which the institution of slavery is protected and sustained." Consequently, once 10 percent of the voters had established a loyal government under Lincoln's plan, there was nothing to prevent that government from preserving or reestablishing slavery. With the domestic slave trade still operating, the border states could help to revive slavery. "When Arkansas shall have been restored, though all of her late slaves shall have been emancipated, commerce will be left free and unrestrained; and what legal principle shall prevent her people from buying and holding in bondage all the slaves in Kentucky and Tennessee?" The Wade–Davis bill was essential, Beaman insisted, to prevent "the resuscitation of slavery."[8]

Republicans relentlessly raised the specter of slavery's revitalization in a restored Union. "[I]t may be said slavery and the nation may continue to

---

[7] *CG*, 38th Cong., 1st Sess., appendix, 84 (March 22, 1864).

[8] *CG*, 38th Cong., 1st Sess., 1245, 1246 (March 22, 1864; Beaman). For other Republicans or Unionists who spoke to the weaknesses of either the abolition amendment or the ten-percent plan in advocating the Wade–Davis bill, see 1739–43 (April 19; Nathaniel B. Smithers of Delaware), 1767–71 (April 20; John M. Broomall of Pennsylvania), 2011–14 (May 2; John W. Longyear of Michigan), 2036–39 (May 2; Ignatius Donnelly of Minnesota), 2102–5 (May 4; George S. Boutwell of Massachusetts). Despite enacting a host of wartime antislavery measures, ironically, Congress never prohibited the interstate slave trade.

exist in unison," intoned Ignatius Donnelly of Minnesota, who was destined for a legendary career as a Gilded-Age reformer. Yet "there is no safety for this nation so long as a spark of vitality remains in the institution of slavery." To be sure, some congressional Republicans gave voice to the trope, as did a few Democrats, that slavery would never survive the war. But no Republican considered abolition a fait accompli. "While I want to see every rebel State brought back into the Union," maintained Jesse O. Norton of Illinois, "yet I would make it a condition precedent to their readmission to all these rights and privileges, that they come knocking at our doors with a free constitution in their hands, whereby the shackles are knocked from off the limbs of every slave within their limits." Although wartime Reconstruction in Arkansas and Louisiana had made great strides, Republicans nonetheless expressed misgivings that political reorganization in those states might yet go awry, with potentially dire implications for the other rebellious states. "No stronger illustration of the necessity and propriety of immediate action need be given," insisted John W. Longyear of Michigan, "than the case of Tennessee, Louisiana, and Arkansas."[9]

In positing their postwar scenarios, Republicans often ignored the distinction between conservative Unionists and former Confederates, but they still cautioned that the conservatives, working with northern Democrats, might pave the way for a restored Union with slavery. "These are no times for what are falsely called *conservative* men," contended Thomas Williams of Pennsylvania. "If these States are in the Union, with all their rights and privileges unimpaired, they may return to-morrow, even without submission, after being conquered in the field, to conquer their conquerors in the councils of the nation." Then, Williams warned, the former Confederate "will come back into your Halls. The northern Democrat will rush into his arms. The two elements, like kindred drops, by an attraction a good deal stronger than that of miscegenation, will melt incontinently into one." The slave power and northern Democrats will renew their "old bargain," he observed. "The proclamation of freedom will be revoked; your acts of Congress repealed; your debt repudiated unless you will assume theirs; and yourselves, perhaps, ejected from these Halls." Lest he sounded paranoid, Williams reminded his colleagues of the recent Etheridge plot. "And the effect will be," he predicted, "that for all your great expenditures and all your bloody sacrifices, you will have won back, not *peace*, but a master – the 'old master,' in negro phraseology – who governed you before – as turbulent, as vindictive, and as ferocious as ever."[10]

However, the most sustained elaboration of these Republican fears came from James M. Ashley, a member of the select committee who supported the

---

[9] *CG*, 38th Cong., 1st Sess., 1766 (April 20, 1864; Norton), 2012 (April 30; Longyear), 2037 (May 2; Donnelly). See also 2081 (May 3; Kelley), 2102 (May 4; Boutwell).

[10] *CG*, 38th Cong., 1st Sess., 1976 (April 29, 1864).

Wade–Davis bill even though it had replaced his own Reconstruction measure. Although Ashley offered his remarks in late March, relatively early in the debate (but *after* Arkansas had abolished slavery), he foregrounded much of the Republican commentary that followed. While addressing myriad issues pertinent to state restoration, Ashley called special attention to the possibilities of former Confederates gaining control of hastily reorganized governments in the seceded states under the ten-percent plan, and of those states being restored to the Union with proslavery constitutions. He thus anticipated much of the congressional Republican criticism of the ten-percent plan and of Lincoln's reconstructed governments.

Ashley postulated what might happen, with the presidential election on the horizon, were the president or military authorities to organize governments – based on small minorities "claiming to be loyal" – in the occupied seceded states without congressional authority. Were these states' electoral votes to be counted, the election might be thrown into the House of Representatives, or "a proslavery President" might be elected. Considering "our present unguarded and loose manner of reorganizing the rebel States," Ashley argued, such an outcome was not unthinkable. A president sympathetic to slavery, "with the entire military power of the country, and one tenth of the local population of the rebel States, professing to be loyal," would enable the seceded states to "reestablish slavery and old slave State governments in every rebel State, and thus bring back many of the traitors to the vacant seats here." Once the proslavery interests had gained the presidency and a House majority, they would "reinstate the old order of things": assume the Confederate debt, reenslave persons freed during the war, and restore confiscated estates to their owners. In effect, the rebellious states could "revive the old State constitutions, and obtain their recognition by the executive branch of Government, as the constitutional government of these States without the consent of Congress." However fantastical a scenario, Ashley contended, the history of the slave power before war, aided and abetted by northern Democrats, showed it to be possible.

Ashley drew heavily on the current situation in Louisiana. He roundly condemned the free-state project under Nathaniel Banks, who, he claimed, had much to answer for. Banks had employed military authority in an "unwarrantable and indefensible assumption of civil authority in that State"; had acted "in defiance of the well-known wishes of the only organization known to the country, or recognized by the unconditional Union men of Louisiana" – that is, the free-state radicals; had called an election for state officers "under the old State organization and pro-slavery constitution"; and had "pander[ed] to rebels and slaveholders." Ashley made much of Banks's unfortunate phrase, in his January 11 proclamation ordering state elections, that "the fundamental law of the state is martial law," and he castigated Banks's decision to elect a new government under the antebellum constitution before holding a constitutional convention. Michael Hahn's election as governor he considered a "farce."

With Louisiana's constitutional convention soon to meet, Ashley continued, any number of things could go wrong. State officers who had already been installed might "refuse to submit to or recognize the validity of any new State constitution adopted by the convention." Any legislators or members of Congress elected before the approval of a new constitution could likewise "disregard the action of that convention and remain under the old constitution." Were Congress to recognize the Hahn government, "such recognition will legally reestablish the old State constitution and slave code of Louisiana," while "the officers of this assumed State government" would be able to "defeat the adoption of a free State constitution." Or suppose that the convention should produce another proslavery constitution, "and the openly disloyal and pro-slavery conservative elements claiming to be loyal are permitted to vote for it." With Lincoln's blessing, Ashley charged, Banks had provided a blueprint for former Confederates, "uniting with the conservative faction opposed to a free State," to return to power and revive slavery.

The only way to avert the doomsday scenario Ashley conjured up was for the seceded states to craft free-state constitutions under congressional authority prior to organizing new governments and seeking readmission. Thus, the Wade–Davis bill, although flawed, was necessary to prevent the creation of ramshackle governments in the rebellious states. Otherwise, "[p]rofessed loyalists and open-throated rebels, who have been guilty of every crime, will conspire together to crush the free State men," Ashley warned. "The amnesty oath will be taken by thousands, who will at once strike hands with perjurers, robbers, and murderers to destroy the men who have, from the first, been faithful to the Constitution and the Union." With the war over, "the wily enemy will attempt to regain by diplomacy much that he has lost by an appeal to arms," and slavery might be saved. "Therein," Ashley concluded, "lies our danger."[11]

Although these phantasms never materialized, Republicans had every reason to fear them. The apprehensions they generated – however irrational in hindsight – were very real at the time, and they motivated Republicans to extinguish any "spark of vitality" that remained in the institution of slavery. Arkansas had already abolished slavery when Ashley spoke, but the ultimate destruction of slavery could hardly be considered a foregone conclusion, as the efforts of what Ashley called the "pro-slavery conservative elements claiming

---

[11] *CG*, 38th Cong., 1st Sess., 1354–59 (March 30, 1864). Early in this speech, Illinois Democrat William J. Allen, in an attempt to pin Ashley down on whether the rebellious states were in or out of the Union, interrupted Ashley by asking whether he would "allow a loyal State to come in with slavery?" "Never," Ashley replied (1354–55). The challenge, of course, was translating that sentiment into law. Rebecca E. Zietlow, in *Forgotten Emancipator* (112), identifies Ashley's speech as being in defense of his own Reconstruction bill. However, by late March, Henry Winter Davis's bill had already come to replace Ashley's, and Ashley was speaking in defense of the Wade–Davis bill.

to be loyal" in Louisiana and Tennessee were demonstrating. Wartime Reconstruction in the lower Mississippi valley had exposed the dangers that attended the restoration of the seceded states following the Emancipation Proclamation. The ten-percent plan had attempted to address this problem, but, as congressional Republicans insisted, it did not suffice.

By early May, after several weeks of intermittent deliberation on his bill, punctuated by a week of intense debate, Davis reported two amendments. The first increased the loyalty threshold to commence state reorganization from 10 to 50 percent. Both Republicans and Democrats had criticized this provision of the various Reconstruction measures. The second change lessened the political proscription against former Confederates by prohibiting from the reorganization process only high-ranking military and civilian officials, "so that the exclusion merely operates on persons of dangerous political influence," as Davis noted. The higher threshold to start the reorganization process allowed for greater leniency in the later stages. The status of the Louisiana and Arkansas governments remained unclear. Davis's revised bill essentially passed along party lines and went to the Senate, which, for several reasons, did not take it up until late June. By early May 1864, the House had passed Reconstruction legislation but not the abolition amendment, whereas the Senate had passed the amendment but not Reconstruction legislation.[12]

Scholars have often noted the failure of the ten-percent plan to provide for racial equality. Yet as congressional Republicans insisted during the Wade–Davis debate, the plan also allowed for the possible restoration of the seceded states without abolishing slavery. The very outcome that Lincoln had hoped to prevent could actually *result from* his Reconstruction policy. Neither was James M. Ashley's warning about a "pro-slavery President" mere hyperbole, given the overlap between the arguments of northern Democrats and southern conservative Unionists. Although both groups claimed to defend the right of the people of the states to choose whether to have slavery, along with the property rights of loyal slaveholders, they both also borrowed liberally from the canon of proslavery thought. This Republicans could not abide.

By the time the House passed the Wade–Davis bill in early May, the Union military campaigns in Virginia and Georgia were commencing. As they ramped up in the ensuing weeks, conflict over Reconstruction – driven by a series of episodes in which the states of the lower Mississippi valley, however indirectly, once again came into play – likewise intensified. It would reach a crescendo in early August over the Wade–Davis bill.

---

[12] *CG*, 38th Cong., 1st Sess., 2107 (May 4, 1864); H.R. 244, 38th Cong., 1st Sess. (April 29; amendment by Stevens); Belz, *Reconstructing the Union*, 210–13, 218n. For the votes, see *CG*, 38th Cong., 1st Sess., 1207–8 (May 4, 1864). See also: H.R. 244, 38th Cong., 1st Sess., as amended on May 5, 1864.

III

The first episode involved the Republican-Union convention that assembled in Baltimore in early June to nominate a presidential ticket. The convention projected party unity on the war and emancipation, but the divisive question of Reconstruction was unavoidable. Lincoln had fended off his various challengers to gain the nomination, and the party platform endorsed the abolition amendment while conspicuously evading racial equality. However, the seating of delegates from the Union-occupied South set off a brief but intense debate, as Louisiana, Arkansas, and Tennessee, along with Virginia and South Carolina, sent delegations. Florida sent rival ones.[13]

Some delegates objected that seating these delegations might set a precedent, as James M. Ashley had warned, and as Maine congressman James G. Blaine later observed, for "recognizing the right of States in rebellion to participate in the Electoral College." Even if this were unlikely to happen, "[t]he admission of the delegations from Tennessee, Arkansas, and Louisiana was a question of no less interest," Blaine continued. "It involved the effect of the rebellion upon the relation of rebelling States to the Union. Could they have a voice in public affairs without specific measures of restoration, or were the acts of secession a nullity without influence upon their legal status?" Whether the seceded states were in or out of the Union had been the issue from day one (with emancipation having greatly complicated it), and it had cropped up again. An impassioned address by Horace Maynard of Tennessee persuaded the convention to seat nearly all of the delegations. The choice of Andrew Johnson as vice president also seemed to endorse the view that the seceded states had remained in the Union, but this minor skirmish only further highlighted the need for Reconstruction legislation.[14]

With the House of Representatives preparing to take up the abolition amendment in mid-June, the Baltimore convention also transformed the amendment into a partisan matter. Bipartisan support had remained a possibility after the Senate passed the amendment in mid-April, despite Democratic opposition, but the convention made the amendment, as Michael Vorenberg notes, "a Republican symbol and a test of party loyalty, representing not merely the issue of black freedom but the candidacy of Abraham Lincoln." House debate was consequently far more overtly partisan than the Senate, and House Democratic leaders demanded strict party discipline. House debate also departed markedly from the Senate on race, as House Democrats abandoned the restraint that Senate Democrats had exercised. The

---

[13] Burlingame and Ettlinger, *Inside Lincoln's White House*, 199 (June 5, 1864); McCrary, *Abraham Lincoln and Reconstruction*, 272–73; Vorenberg, *Final Freedom*, 121–27.

[14] Blaine, *Twenty Years of Congress*, 1: 518–19; Burlingame and Ettlinger, *Inside Lincoln's White House*, 200 (June 6, 1864), 349; *New York Herald*, June 9, 1864; Belz, *Reconstructing the Union*, 213–15; Smith, *No Party Now*, 102–7.

brief period since House passage of the Wade–Davis bill had witnessed a ratcheting-up of Democrats' racialist language, which now included unabashed use of the term "miscegenation." Republicans tried to deflect the charge of supporting racial equality by putting forward an extremely narrow understanding of black freedom, and by arguing – much evidence to the contrary – that the amendment's enforcement clause would probably not be needed.[15]

Republicans had maintained for two years that state restoration and abolition were inseparable. Yet House Republicans now had "an important tactical reason," as Michael Vorenberg further observes, for keeping the amendment and the Wade–Davis bill separate, and for preventing debate on the former from becoming a "replay" of the latter. Were the two measures to be linked, Republicans would have to confront the question of the seceded states' participation in the ratification process. Because the Wade–Davis bill postponed state restoration until the war was over, and because the eleven seceded states could prevent ratification of the amendment, the bill, ironically, created the possibility of ratification of the amendment being delayed indefinitely. House Republicans solved this problem by ignoring the question of state ratification as much as possible, and by dodging the issue when Democrats pressed them on it. House debate on the amendment thus further contributed to the process by which abolition came to supersede state restoration.[16]

Despite unanimous Republican support, the amendment failed to secure a two-thirds majority. Only four Democrats voted in favor. The amendment's supporters were stuck between embracing abolition as a party matter in an election year and needing opposition votes. The defeat left the Wade–Davis bill as the sole legislative measure on emancipation and Reconstruction still before Congress. Paradoxically, whereas House debate on the amendment further indicated that abolition might now eclipse state restoration, the amendment's defeat also reaffirmed the link between the two. "Reconstruction is impossible so long as Slavery exists in the land," lamented the *New York Times* after the amendment's House defeat. "The institution, in instigating the rebellion, has committed an inexplicable crime, and the people are fixed in their determination that it shall die the death." Yet if reunion could not take place so long as slavery still existed, then neither could the abolition amendment be ratified – assuming it even got through Congress – until the rebellious states had been reconstructed.[17]

---

[15] Vorenberg, *Final Freedom*, 115–36 (quotation, 127); Oakes, *Freedom National*, 437–54. Richards, *Who Freed the Slaves?*, chap. 5, also emphasizes House Democrats' opposition to the amendment as a matter of party allegiance.
[16] Vorenberg, *Final Freedom*, 129–30.
[17] Vorenberg, *Final Freedom*, 136–40; "Rejection of the Anti-Slavery Constitutional Amendment," *New York Times*, June 17, 1864, 4.

More fuel was thrown on the Reconstruction fire as Congress considered the Arkansas claimants. Three House representatives were claiming seats, but the Senate took the lead in taking up the cases of Elisha Baxter and William M. Fishback, whom the legislature had recently elected. Fishback, as predicted, immediately sparked protests. "Nothing has been done yet by Congress touching the recognition of the state of Arkansas," representative-elect Anthony A. C. Rogers reported in early June to General Frederick Steele. "I think we should have had no trouble if Fishback had not been elected. Radicals and Democrats alike denounce him. His election has cast a shadow over the whole thing, & I now fear the worst consequences."[18]

Rogers was not a disinterested observer, and the problem went beyond Fishback, but he was not far off the mark. The presentation of the claimants' credentials in mid-June – along with the introduction of a resolution recognizing the Arkansas government – set off a long and spirited debate that focused mostly on Fishback's loyalty. But in also addressing whether the Murphy government was "republican" and genuinely representative, the debate turned once again to Lincoln's Reconstruction policy, providing yet another opportunity for the airing of grievances. The matter was referred to the Senate Judiciary Committee, chaired by Lyman Trumbull, which in late June unanimously recommended against the claimants. "The committee have come to the conclusion that there was no Legislature which elected these two gentlemen," Trumbull explained. "We thought the body which sent these gentlemen here was not the Legislature of the State of Arkansas." The ensuing debate – in which Republicans disagreed over whether even to decide the case, with the Wade–Davis bill pending – revealed the Arkansas government's shallow support. Although several senators questioned the process that had generated Arkansas's constitution, none expressed concern that rejecting the government might allow a revival of slavery. Indeed, the word "slavery" did not come up in the deliberation, perhaps reflecting Republicans' confidence that they would enact the Wade–Davis bill.[19]

On June 29, with the session winding down, the Senate overwhelmingly approved the committee's report, denying Baxter and Fishback seats. Although several Republicans voted against the report, the large majority of Senate Republicans clearly opposed the Arkansas government. After the vote, a disappointed Fishback visited Lincoln, who assured him, according to Fishback, that "he intends to protect us, irrespective of Congress." Lincoln also instructed General Steele in Little Rock to lend the new state government "the same support and protection that you would if the members had been

---

[18] Rogers to Steele, June 4, 1864, Steele Papers, Stanford.
[19] *CG*, 38th Cong., 1st Sess., 2895–907 (June 13, 1864; referral, 2906), 3360–68 (June 29; Trumbull quotation, 3365); Harris, *With Charity for All*, 206–8; Butler and Wolff, *United States Senate Election*, 117–20.

admitted." However, Edward W. Gantt, the former Confederate general who had become the public face of a reconstructed Arkansas, read more ominous repercussions into the Senate's decision. "We are thunderstruck to find you in favor of driving us away," he wrote in a public letter to Charles Sumner, who played a leading role in the case, "and throwing the victory at last to a handful of Copperheads in Arkansas who hope still to retain Slavery."[20]

IV

Not until July 1, in the session's final, hectic days, did the Senate take up the Wade–Davis bill, which had languished for weeks, much to Benjamin F. Wade's frustration. The Senate had been attending to other business, including the Arkansas case. Insofar as the Wade–Davis bill was an alternative to the amendment, the amendment's failure in the House made enactment of the bill all-the-more imperative; but insofar as the bill and the amendment were elements of a legislative package, the failure of the amendment in the House rendered Senate passage of the bill moot until Congress met again. Despite the efforts of its sponsors to bring the bill forward, the amendment's mid-June failure in the House may have contributed to Senate Republicans' lack of urgency on the bill. Only after the failure of a last-minute attempt to amend the bill – which included complicated parliamentary maneuvering and almost no formal debate – did the Senate on July 2 finally approve the House version in a close vote. The bill then went to Lincoln, but the manner of its passage left some Republicans dubious of its fate.[21]

Republicans nonetheless expected Lincoln to sign the bill. He had said little about it, ignoring congressional commentary on his Reconstruction policy. Because the bill had passed at the end of the session, Lincoln could "pocket" veto it by not signing it. On July 4, just before the session's noon adjournment, Lincoln was in an office in the Capitol building signing bills. When word circulated that he might not sign this one, several leading congressional Republicans, including Senator Zachariah Chandler of Michigan, visited him and, according to Lincoln's secretary John Hay, implored him to sign.

---

[20] *CG*, 38th Cong., 1st Sess., 3362 (June 29, 1864); Fishback to [Steele], June 29, 1864, Steele Papers, Stanford; *CWL*, 7: 418; "Secession and Readmission," *New York Times*, June 3, 1864 (Gantt); Cowen, "Reorganization of Federal Arkansas," 52–55. Gantt's letter was dated June 1, but Sumner's opposition had already been well established. Also on June 29, the House tabled further consideration of the Arkansas claimants James M. Johnson, T. M. Jacks, and Anthony A. C. Rogers. However, this action did not deny them seats but rather put off the question until the next session of Congress. Belz, *Reconstructing the Union*, 220n; *CG*, 38th Cong., 1st Sess., 3394 (June 29, 1864; motion to table); *Journal of the U.S. Senate*, 38th Cong., 1st Sess., 677 (June 29, 1864; vote).

[21] *CG*, 38th Cong., 1st Sess., 3364 (June 29, 1864); Belz, *Reconstructing the Union*, 216–23; McCrary, *Abraham Lincoln and Reconstruction*, 274–77.

Chandler acknowledged the bill's shortcomings but emphasized its "prohibiting slavery in the reconstructed states."

"That is the point on which I doubt the authority of Congress to act," Lincoln responded. Chandler countered that Lincoln himself had done this with the Emancipation Proclamation (though he had freed slaves, not prohibited slavery). "I conceive that I may in an emergency do things on military grounds which cannot be done constitutionally by Congress," Lincoln insisted. Admitting that he could not "controvert" Lincoln's argument, Chandler gave up and left. "I do not see how any of us now can deny and contradict all we have always said," Lincoln continued, now to Hay, "that congress has no constitutional power over slavery in the states." Lincoln further objected to the bill's "fatal admission," according to Hay, that the seceded states had left the Union – although the bill did no such thing. It was to obviate what Lincoln called this "merely metaphysical question" that he had supported "the movement for an amendment to the Constitution abolishing slavery." As Louis Masur has suggested, Lincoln may have been so obsessed with the question of whether the seceded states were in or out of the Union "that he saw it even when it was not present." Moreover, because the role of the seceded states in ratifying the amendment remained unsettled, as did the whole matter of Reconstruction, Lincoln's solution of a constitutional amendment to abolish slavery – which was hardly a certainty – would not solve the far from "metaphysical question" of how to secure the restoration of the seceded states without slavery.[22]

Lincoln further elaborated upon his thinking in a formal proclamation explaining the veto, issued in part to assuage radical annoyance (which was also sparked by his acceptance of Treasury secretary Salmon P. Chase's resignation). Here, Lincoln articulated several familiar ideas. He refused to be "inflexibly committed," as he had previously said, "to any single plan of reconstruction." He again denied "a constitutional competency in Congress to abolish slavery in States," although he endorsed the abolition amendment. (It is difficult to know whether Lincoln was genuinely mistaken on this point or deliberately obfuscated the issue, since the bill did not abolish slavery in the states.) Neither was he about to abandon the reconstructed governments in Arkansas and Louisiana, allowing them to be "set aside and held for nought." Despite these reservations, Lincoln declared himself "fully satisfied with the system for restoration contained in the Bill," and he pledged to assist the loyal people of any seceded state who wished to organize under its provisions. This claim was disingenuous, since Lincoln promised to execute a bill he had refused to sign into law, and since few southern Unionists were likely to take him up on his offer. As Lincoln had already stated and would reiterate in the

---

[22] Burlingame and Ettlinger, *Inside Lincoln's White House*, 217–19 (July 4, 1864); Masur, *Lincoln's Hundred Days*, 112; Belz, *Reconstructing the Union*, 223–27.

ensuing months, he acknowledged a congressional role in Reconstruction, but he was not about to discard work that had already been done.[23]

Critics of Lincoln's Reconstruction policy were not buying it. Although some Republicans admitted to having handled the Wade–Davis matter poorly, the pocket veto and unorthodox proclamation inflamed radical anger. In early August, the bill's cosponsors issued their famous "manifesto," which, while ostensibly responding to Lincoln's action on the bill, gave vent to frustration over his entire handling of Reconstruction. The authors accused Lincoln of "dictatorial usurpation," and they denounced his defense of "those shadows of Governments" in Louisiana and Arkansas, labeling them "creatures of his will" and "mere oligarchies." Those governments had been "imposed on the people by military orders under the forms of election, at which generals, provost-marshals, soldiers and camp-followers were the chief actors, assisted by a handful of resident citizens, and urged on to premature action by private letters from the President." They also accused Lincoln of manipulating the presidential election through control of the electoral votes of reconstructed states, which he held "at the discretion of his personal ambition," and they castigated his willingness to implement the bill, if called upon, without the sanction of law. "[T]he authority of Congress is paramount and must be respected," the authors proclaimed, suggesting that the president restrict himself to enforcing the law "and leave political reorganization to Congress."[24]

The intemperate manifesto backfired and gained Lincoln greater public support. Northern Democrats and Lincoln's radical detractors made strange bedfellows, and Wade and Davis, as one scholar has observed, "sounded like Copperheads." Yet contemporaries who perused the document would have recognized the arguments that Republicans and other antislavery advocates had long been making about the challenges of restoring the seceded states to the Union without slavery. The vitriol of the Wade–Davis manifesto masked its substantive arguments. If northern Democrats, for all of their pomposity during the Wade–Davis debate, had leveled legitimate criticisms against Republican Reconstruction policy, Wade and Davis likewise scored legitimate points in challenging Lincoln's rationale for tanking their bill.[25]

The authors dismissed Lincoln's claim that the bill had been hurriedly passed, noting that it had been debated for months. The Senate passed the

---

[23] *CWL*, 7: 433–34; McCrary, *Abraham Lincoln and Reconstruction*, 276–77.
[24] Wade and Davis, "Protest of Senator Wade and H. Winter Davis, M.C."
[25] Weber, *Copperheads*, 157. Although providing an interpretation favorable to the Radicals, Trefousse's *Radical Republicans* (293–94) typically focuses on the language rather than the content of the manifesto. Vorenberg's *Final Freedom* (150–51) offers one of the few analyses that note the manifesto's substantive criticism of Lincoln's plan of Reconstruction. Richards, *Who Freed the Slaves?* (148), notes almost in passing the manifesto's critique that the ten-percent plan failed to provide for the abolition of slavery, but he does not develop this idea.

same version on July 2 that the House had approved two months earlier. Turning to the process by which new governments and constitutions were created for Louisiana and Arkansas, the authors again quoted Nathaniel Banks's declaration that "the fundamental law" in Louisiana was "martial law," and they lambasted "the farce called an election" that had created the Hahn government. The election had garnered less than 12,000 ballots, 4,000 of which they alleged were cast by soldiers or government employees, while Federal authority prevailed over a mere third of Louisiana's land area. The Arkansas government and constitution were no different, and "like ones may be organized in every Rebel State where the United States have a camp." Wade and Davis highlighted the unavoidable reality that Lincoln had essentially installed rump governments in Louisiana and Arkansas.

The authors also contested Lincoln's claim denying congressional authority to abolish slavery in the states. "But the bill nowhere proposes to abolish Slavery in States," they countered. Instead, it provided "that all *slaves* in the Rebel States should be *manumitted*." Lincoln himself had signed bills manumitting slaves in the seceded states, and he had claimed congressional authorization in emancipating slaves by proclamation. It was therefore "quite inconceivable," Wade and Davis argued, "that the President should think Congress could vest in him a discretion it could not exercise itself." Congress might not have possessed the power to abolish slavery, they allowed, but it could – as could the president – emancipate slaves in suppressing rebellion. Also, with the exception of the excluded parts of Virginia and Louisiana (and, they might have added, Tennessee), the bill applied only to geographical areas that the Emancipation Proclamation had covered. By giving the proclamation the sanction of law, it "perfected the work the President professed to be so anxious to accomplish."

"Slavery as an institution can be abolished only by a change of the Constitution of the United States or of the law of the State; and this is the principle of the bill," the authors contended, pinpointing the primary challenge of state restoration since January 1863. The bill "required the Constitution of the State to provide for that prohibition." As slavery's opponents had repeatedly advocated, Congress could – must – require the seceded states to prohibit slavery as a condition for restoration to the Union. Indeed, Wade and Davis contended, the president in his recent proclamation "does not venture to object to insisting on that condition." Lincoln, in fact, had not explicitly questioned Congress's authority to require the seceded states to prohibit slavery as a condition for restoration (only its authority to abolish slavery in states). "Nor will the country tolerate its abandonment." Yet in vetoing the bill, Lincoln "defeated the only provision imposing it" on the seceded states that Congress had passed, thereby striking what they called – ironically, given Lincoln's future historical reputation – a "great blow at emancipation."

Quoting Lincoln, the authors questioned the basis for his "sincerely hoping and expecting" that the abolition amendment would be adopted. Such sentiments were unrealistic, they suggested, in light of the amendment's recent defeat in the House, and "in the face of the political complexion of more than enough States to prevent the possibility of its adoption within any reasonable time." As Davis had previously noted, enough *loyal* states might not ratify the amendment. Because the role of the seceded states in the ratification process remained unclear, moreover, there was no telling when – or if – the amendment would ever be adopted. Had Lincoln wanted to secure universal emancipation as soon as possible, the authors asked rhetorically, why did he "not indulge his sincere hopes with so large an installment of the blessing as his approval of the bill would have secured[?]" Whatever the bill's shortcomings, this was not an unreasonable question.

The Wade–Davis bill had been designed, its sponsors insisted, to accomplish three goals: prevent the rebellion's leaders from returning to power, invalidate the Confederate debt, and prohibit "the continuance of slavery." By vetoing the bill, Lincoln had given the seceded states the opportunity to organize new governments and petition for restoration without meeting these conditions. The plan "is silent respecting the Rebel debt and the political exclusion of Rebel leaders," they contended, "leaving *Slavery* exactly where it was by law at the outbreak of the Rebellion," and adding "no guaranty even of the freedom of the slaves [the president] undertook to manumit." Lincoln's oath required compliance with Federal wartime antislavery measures, but it did not abolish slavery. Neither did it secure the freedom of slaves already freed (or declared free) or require the seceded states to adopt free-state constitutions. "It does not secure the abolition of Slavery, for the proclamation of freedom merely professed to free certain slaves while it recognized the institution," they maintained, again noting the central problem of the proclamation. "Every Constitution of the Rebel States at the outbreak of the Rebellion may be adopted without the change of a letter; for none of them contravene that Proclamation."

Even were the US Supreme Court to validate the Emancipation Proclamation, they continued, the proclamation "exacts no enactment by the State, either in law or Constitution, to add a State guaranty to the proclamation title; and the right of a slave to freedom is an open question before the State courts on the relative authority of the State law and the Proclamation." Indeed, there could be no question as to how southern jurisprudence would operate after the war with regard to persons whom the Emancipation Proclamation had freed or declared free. "What the State courts would say of the Proclamation," the authors again asked rhetorically, "who can doubt?" Moreover, nothing in the ten-percent plan could prevent the 90 percent of the population that had not participated in Reconstruction from later gaining control of any reorganized government and, once it had been recognized, reestablishing slavery. As congressional Republicans had warned for months, the South could lose the war and still preserve slavery. "Such are the fruits of this rash and fatal act of the President – a blow at the friends of his Administration, at the rights of humanity, and at the principles of republican government."

The Wade–Davis manifesto caused an initial stir, but it soon died down. Lincoln privately expressed uncharacteristic anger over the document, and it made him even more determined to secure voter approval of Louisiana's free-state constitution. Other matters quickly removed the manifesto from the headlines, and it proved to be but one of several challenges Lincoln faced that summer. The entire Wade–Davis episode has often been seen as demonstrating a breach between Lincoln and the Radical Republicans over Reconstruction, but in truth they were more united than divided. It has also been viewed as part of the Radical campaign to replace Lincoln as the Republican presidential candidate, but the dictates of party would induce Wade, Davis, and virtually every other Radical to endorse him. Much has also been made of the manifesto's vitriolic language, and rightly so, since the authors indeed sounded like Copperheads. But it also offered a sober critique of the ten-percent plan and the governments created under it, crystallizing the Republican fear that Lincoln's Reconstruction policy, despite its creator's intent, might allow for slavery's survival.[26]

* * *

As the first session of the Thirty-Eighth Congress adjourned, both the abolition amendment and the Wade–Davis bill had failed. The former fell victim to partisanship in the House, while the latter succumbed to Senate Republican infighting and to executive-legislative rivalry. Lincoln insisted that the Wade–Davis bill would have invalidated the free-state governments of Louisiana and Arkansas, whereas congressional Republicans countered that Lincoln's ten-percent plan, even following Union military victory, might allow the seceded states to be readmitted while preserving slavery. Both arguments had merit. The abolition of slavery by two rebellious states could not just be written off, yet no seceded state could be restored, as Ignatius Donnelly had warned, so long as slavery still exhibited a spark of vitality. By mid-1864, Lincoln's fears might have seemed more firmly grounded in reality than those of his Republican critics. The risk of discarding abolition that had already been

---

[26] Harris, *With Charity for All*, 190. For an example of mainstream northern commentary on the manifesto that focused on its intemperate language rather than on its substantive points, see "The Wade and Davis Manifest," *Harper's Weekly*, August 20, 1864, 530.

accomplished was arguably greater than that of slavery surviving Confederate military defeat. By almost all accounts, slavery appeared to be crumbling, and many contemporaries were convinced, assuming Federal military victory, that it would never survive the war. So long as the war were pushed "to its logical conclusion," one northern essayist typically wrote in July 1864, slavery was doomed. "War means now, consciously with many, unconsciously with most, but inevitably, abolition. Nothing can save slavery but peace."[27]

Yet this outcome appears certain only in hindsight. Other contemporaries – influenced at least in part by events in the lower Mississippi valley – expressed the fear that the insurgent states might return to the Union without abolishing slavery and that slavery might yet be preserved. Republicans and other antislavery advocates had been warning about this outcome since early 1863, and these warnings powerfully influenced Republican commentary in debating the Wade–Davis bill and in critiquing the ten-percent plan. They also formed the central theme – almost always overlooked – of the Wade–Davis manifesto. Neither were such fears simple paranoia. As Chandra Manning has argued, the historical record is replete with instances in which slavery came under attack during war only to survive and be revitalized afterward. Likewise, as the scholarship on the "second slavery" maintains, with some validity, New World slavery had been significantly weakened during the late eighteenth century but came back stronger than ever – at least in certain places – during the nineteenth. Slavery was not dead, not by a long shot. To make this argument, it is important to note, is not to deny the significance of the slaves' role in bringing slavery down – whether behind Union or Confederate lines. But it is to recognize the very real limits to what so-called "self-emancipation" could accomplish.[28]

Slavery *might* survive northern military victory, but without victory the point was moot, and by the summer of 1864, it was not Union but Confederate success that looked more promising. When Wade and Davis issued their manifesto in early August, the Union war effort had ground to a halt and Lincoln was entering upon the nadir of his presidency. Pressured by some of his own Republican allies, he considered issuing a public statement calling for reunion while saying nothing about slavery, an act so desperate and potentially inflammatory that he ultimately decided against it. Expecting to lose the election, he discussed a fantastical plan with Frederick Douglass to free

---

[27] "The Rebellion: Its Causes and Consequences," *North American Review*, vol. 99, no. 204 (July 1864): 246–68 (quotations, 267–68).

[28] The possibility of slavery surviving the war is a central theme of Manning's *Troubled Refuge*, but see 13, 195–99, 236–38, and 281–83. For an effective overview of the "second slavery" literature, see Mathisen, "Second Slavery," especially the works cited at 694–96, n. 12–21.

as many slaves as possible before he was turned out of office. On August 23, he famously had his Cabinet endorse the "blind" memorandum, conceding defeat and pledging to try to save the Union before his successor's inauguration, "as he will have secured his election on such ground that he cannot possibly save it afterwards." As northern Democrats prepared in late August to nominate a challenger to Lincoln, the voters seemed poised to elect, in James M. Ashley's words, a "pro-slavery President."

16

"Freedom, Full, Broad and Unconditional"

Just as the skies seemed darkest, as historians have often noted, they suddenly brightened. The Federal capture of Mobile Bay, the Democrats' nomination of George B. McClellan for president and their platform labeling the war a failure (and the naming of Peace Democrat George Pendleton as McClellan's running-mate), and, most importantly, the fall of Atlanta – all between August 23 and September 2 – redefined the presidential campaign. Subsequent Union military success and Republican electoral gains during the fall, along with Maryland's approval in October of a free-state constitution, virtually secured Abraham Lincoln's reelection. Defeating Lincoln had been the Confederacy's last best hope, but that hope was fading.

In the lower Mississippi valley, Louisiana's free-state constitution received popular approval and became operative in early September, formally ending slavery in the state. Yet conflict over the consequences of emancipation showed no signs of abating. Neither did questions over the legitimacy of the Louisiana government. In Arkansas, the free-state initiative seemed to be regressing after so much early promise. The civilian government remained unable to establish its authority, and General Frederick Steele would ultimately be removed. In Tennessee, the long-delayed state reorganization was subsumed by the presidential election, as the two Unionist factions offered rival plans for participating in it. The political mobilization of black Tennesseans during the campaign, moreover, showed the consequences of abolition to be unavoidable. It also produced public remarks from Military Governor Andrew Johnson, which, in addition to proclaiming freedom in Tennessee to be "full, broad and unconditional," depicted Johnson in the unlikely role of the former slaves' deliverer from bondage.

Whereas Republicans had embraced the Federal abolition amendment at their national convention in June, they made a tactical retreat from it during the presidential campaign. They were responding to the full-throated racism that northern Democrats made central to their campaign, but the Democrats' racialized rhetoric also marked a crucial shift from defending slavery to instead defending white supremacy. Conservative Unionists had thus lost important allies. But more importantly, Lincoln's reelection sounded the Confederacy's death knell and ended any hope of restoring the seceded states to the Union with slavery.

I

By the time the vote on Louisiana's free-state constitution took place on September 5, Lincoln's reelection prospects had improved dramatically, but the campaign for the constitution remained desultory – the result a forgone conclusion. As expected, the new constitution was overwhelmingly approved, 6,836 to 1,566, and officially took effect. Slavery, which had existed in Louisiana since the early eighteenth century, was formally abolished, though enslaved persons living under Confederate authority, having in theory gained freedom a second time, would still await their liberation. The total of 8,400 votes on the constitution – including, Banks allowed, nearly 1,200 by soldiers – was disappointing. Banks alleged, on the basis of no evidence, that 15,000 votes would have been cast but for the radicals' obstructionism, and he as usual overstated the result. "History will record the fact that all the problems involved in the restoration of States and the reconstruction of government have been already solved in Louisiana with a due regard to the elevation of the black and the security of the white race," he assured Lincoln. "Your policy here will be adopted in other states and work out in the end the re-establishment of the Union." Abolishing slavery *was* a tremendous accomplishment, but history would prove Banks's prediction totally wrong.[1]

Scheduled along with the constitutional plebiscite were legislative and congressional elections. The five representatives elected to the Thirty-Eighth Congress, set to reconvene in December, were largely free-state moderates and unconditional Unionists, but their election reflected the unsettled conditions in Louisiana, and Congress eventually seated none of them. The legislature was also under moderate control, featuring many convention delegates. Convening in early October, it met in special session for the rest of 1864 and in regular session into the spring of 1865, but it would fail to address the consequences of abolition. Despite the US Senate's refusal to seat Arkansas's claimants, the legislature prioritized the election of senators, and it named R. King Cutler to a full term and Charles Smith, president pro tem of the state Senate, to the short term that would expire in March 1865, when the current Congress ended. The question of their seating in early 1865 would mark the major test of Lincoln's Louisiana government. Meanwhile, on election day in November, the legislature, at Hahn's behest, took the unorthodox step of selecting what Hahn assured Lincoln were "seven good Lincoln men" as presidential electors, since no popular vote had been held, but Congress would refuse to count Louisiana's electoral votes.[2]

---

[1] Lincoln to Banks, August 9, 1864, ALP; *CWL*, 7: 486–87n; Harris, *With Charity for All*, 190–91; McCrary, *Abraham Lincoln and Reconstruction*, 267–69; Hollandsworth, *Pretense of Glory*, 208–9.

[2] Hahn to Lincoln, November 11, 1864, ALP; Harris, *With Charity for All*, 192; Benedict, *Compromise of Principle*, 89; Taylor, *Louisiana Reconstructed*, 53–54; McCrary, *Abraham Lincoln and Reconstruction*, 269–70.

Hahn urged the new legislature, upon convening, to address black freedom. "The great duty of the Legislature will be to provide a system of laws applicable to the new condition of things," he announced. "Slavery can no more exist, nor can man ever again in Louisiana have or pretend to have property in man." Hahn called for equal education for black and white children, as authorized by the constitution, though without endorsing integrated schools, as well as laws regulating the new labor system. "The change from servile to compensated labor," he further noted, "requires careful, liberal and humane legislation, in order to secure the rights of those people who have not been accustomed to provide for and protect themselves." The current laws governing contracts and the "hiring of labor" had to be replaced. "[T]he subject is of the highest possible importance and should be dealt with in a spirit of enlightened liberality and humanity." Labor arrangements under Federal military auspices had provided a temporary solution, Hahn added, "but another system must be established ultimately, and the people cannot begin too soon to prepare."[3]

Hahn made no recommendation to the legislature on black suffrage and did not mention the issue. In November, however, he requested permission to make public Lincoln's private letter to him of the previous March, in which Lincoln had recommended that the Louisiana constitutional convention adopt limited black suffrage. No record exists of a response. Several days after Hahn wrote to Lincoln, Charles Smith introduced a bill to extend the vote to black veterans and to black men who met literacy or property requirements, as provided for by the constitution. The state Senate immediately and overwhelmingly rejected the bill, however, and by the end of the year the legislature had taken no action on education, labor, or any other issues defining black freedom.[4]

Meanwhile, the New Orleans black community continued to push for racial equality, black suffrage in particular, despite frustration over the failure of the new constitution to mandate black suffrage and the defeat of Smith's bill. The black community debated whether to petition the legislature for voting rights – and thereby recognize its legitimacy – or to boycott it and appeal directly to Congress. In this debate, the black press played a more vigorous role. In July, *L'Union* had ceased publication and soon reconstituted itself as the New Orleans *Tribune*, which took a harsher line against the new government. The journal remained under the proprietorship of Dr. Louis Charles Roudanez and Paul Trévigne, but it now included the white radical, Jean-Charles Houzeau, as managing editor. Houzeau had arrived in New Orleans in early 1863 and became active in radical circles. He wrote for *L'Union* before leaving for Philadelphia and

---

[3] *Official Journal of the Proceedings of the House of Representatives of the State of Louisiana*, 9–14; Harris, *With Charity for All*, 192.

[4] Hahn to Lincoln, November 11, 1864, ALP; Harris, *With Charity for All*, 192–93. On the black suffrage bill: Tunnell, *Crucible of Reconstruction*, 80–81; Taylor, *Louisiana Reconstructed*, 56–57; *Journal of the Senate of the State of Louisiana*, 58–59 (November 14–15, 1864).

thereafter served as the paper's "northern correspondent." Offered the editorship in October 1864, he returned to New Orleans to run the new paper.[5]

Aiming "to transform a local newspaper into a newspaper of national importance," Houzeau also intended to shift its mission from defending the interests of the free people of color to advocating racial unity and uplift for all black people. In particular, Houzeau hoped to overcome what he called "the alienation of the black slave from the free man of color." The latter "tended to separate their struggle from that of the Negroes; some believed that they would achieve their cause more quickly if they abandoned the black to his fate," he contended. "In their eyes, they were nearer to the white man; they were more advanced than the slave in all respects. They believed they might be granted what, in their opinion, the black man would never possess – civil equality." Until his tenure at the *Tribune* ended in 1868, Houzeau worked tirelessly to bridge this intraracial divide. He attacked all Reconstruction proposals that did not provide for unqualified black suffrage, equality before the law, and meaningful economic independence, and he evinced an uncompromising commitment to justice and equality.[6]

The campaign for equal rights and racial unity took a major step forward with the holding of a national black political convention in October 1864 in Syracuse, New York. Attended by nearly 150 black representatives from eighteen states, including several from Louisiana, the assembly established the National Equal Rights League, an organization committed, among other things, to lobbying Congress for national black suffrage. A Louisiana chapter of the organization would hold a founding convention in New Orleans in January 1865, and the *Tribune* would become its official organ. The black community would remain divided over petitioning the legislature for voting rights, but the majority, supported by the *Tribune*, consistently opposed this strategy. The New Orleans free-black community *had* occupied a distinct status within antebellum society, especially the Afro-Creole elite, and vestiges of this "alienation" persisted for years to come. Yet the former slaves and former free people of color would eventually come together over the common foe of white supremacy.[7]

II

Approval of Louisiana's constitution also did little to quell the in-fighting among free-state radicals and moderates or to soften the radical critique of the new government. After the September election, Hahn and his allies

---

[5] Houzeau, *My Passage at the New Orleans* Tribune, 19–24; Tunnell, *Crucible of Reconstruction*, 79–83; Bell, *Revolution, Romanticism, and the Afro-Creole Protest Tradition*, 252–55; Ripley, *Slaves and Freedmen*, 178–80.

[6] Houzeau, *My Passage at the New Orleans* Tribune, 78–84 (quotations, 79, 81); McPherson, *Negro's Civil War*, 284–85.

[7] Tunnell, *Crucible of Reconstruction*, 82–83; Bell, *Revolution, Romanticism, and the Afro-Creole Protest Tradition*, 255–56.

besieged Lincoln to remove radicals in the Treasury Department, but Lincoln was loath to carry out a purge prior to the presidential election and with Congress expected to look closely at Louisiana affairs. Instead, Lincoln called upon Banks – who, following ratification of the constitution, had been granted a three-week leave of absence, during which he traveled North and met with Lincoln – to remain in Washington to lobby Congress on behalf of the Louisiana government. Banks's leave would be extended to continue this work, and he ultimately returned to Louisiana only after Lincoln's assassination. At the same time, Thomas J. Durant and other radicals continued throughout the fall to urge congressional Republicans to reject the Louisiana government.[8]

Even before leaving New Orleans, Banks attempted to drum up support for that government by publishing in the New Orleans newspapers in late September a lengthy public letter to US Senator James H. Lane of Kansas, a key supporter of Lincoln's Reconstruction policy. Widely reprinted in the northern press and later published in pamphlet form, the letter amounted to a vigorous response to the Wade–Davis manifesto, a withering attack on Thomas J. Durant (without naming him), and a sustained defense of the entire Louisiana initiative. Much of the document consisted of a point-by-point refutation of the Wade–Davis manifesto's key charges against the Louisiana constitution and government. But Banks also insisted, quite implausibly, that the state's reorganization had met "every material provision" of the Wade–Davis bill, and that "every substantial guarantee had been recognized and established."

Such a claim was dubious on its face, and it forced Banks into obfuscation and sophistry. He might have done better to point out that the new constitution abolished slavery, as the Wade–Davis bill required, and left it at that, especially since the lack of an explicit abolition provision – and the possibility of slavery surviving the war – had been the manifesto's central complaint. Banks even had to admit that the constitution did not meet the Wade–Davis bill's restrictions on former Confederates' voting rights. But he then insisted, incorrectly, that it made "all men equal before the law." Worse still, Banks made the ludicrous claim that Louisiana's reorganization – which attracted less than 10,000 votes in a state that had cast more than 50,000 votes in 1860 – had met the Wade–Davis requirement that 50 percent of a state's voting population swear allegiance.[9]

Durant's rejoinder – published in newspapers and as a pamphlet in late October, in the form of an open letter to Henry Winter Davis – made precisely

---

[8] Harris, *With Charity for All*, 191; Hollandsworth, *Pretense of Glory*, 213–18.
[9] Banks, *Letter from Major Gen. N. P. Banks*, 2, 4; McCrary, *Abraham Lincoln and Reconstruction*, 282–85. See also Banks's defense of his labor policies in Louisiana in *Emancipated Labor in Louisiana*, an address he delivered on two occasions in Boston in late October and early November 1864 and published in pamphlet form.

that point. Durant engaged Banks directly and explicitly, offering a detailed rebuttal of Banks's claims while reiterating the radicals' familiar criticisms of the Louisiana government. But the crux of his argument was that the organization of that government had conformed to neither the Wade–Davis bill nor the constitution and laws then in effect. Although Durant had the better case, it was not without difficulties. Durant easily dismantled Banks's claims that Louisiana's new government represented the state's electorate and enjoyed popular (white) support. Yet he conveniently ignored the fact that any such government would never have abolished slavery. Invoking once again Banks's order declaring martial law to be the "fundamental law" of Louisiana, Durant contended that the entire convention had been conducted under military dictate. Perhaps. But here he sounded like the conservative Unionists at the convention. Durant correctly challenged Banks's assertion that the constitution provided for equality before the law, and he noted the difficulty in securing limited black suffrage, but he also overlooked Wade–Davis's failure to provide for black suffrage. In a larger sense, by the time Durant published his pamphlet, the whole complexion of the presidential election had changed, and his charge of "Executive dictation," with Lincoln's reelection all but assured, was hopelessly out of touch.[10]

Still, Durant and his allies were determined to present their case to Congress. Three weeks after the publication of Durant's pamphlet, by which point Lincoln had won reelection, they penned a formal protest, calling upon Congress not to seat the state's members-elect or to count its electoral votes – and, by implication, not to recognize the Hahn government. Signed by thirty leading New Orleans radicals, including Durant, the memorial summarized political and military affairs in Louisiana since the secession crisis, including the state's reorganization under the ten-percent plan (which it did not mention), and it rehashed the radical case against the new government. "Now, your memorialists respectfully protest against all the elections, proclamations, orders, conventions, and legislatures, and all the acts and doings thereof, so far as it may be pretended that they have any civil force or legal effect whatever," the petition read. It concluded by calling for enactment of the Wade–Davis bill. Durant requested Henry Winter Davis to ensure its introduction before both houses of Congress. Davis was happy to oblige, and he introduced it just as Louisiana's claimants presented their credentials.[11]

By now, Lincoln could expect opposition to his Louisiana government from various quarters, but when it came from his own generals, his equanimity gave way to anger. With Banks on leave, his replacement, General Stephen Hurlbut, an old Illinois political associate of Lincoln, began interfering in civil affairs.

---

[10] [Durant], *Letter of Thomas J. Durant*, 2, 27.
[11] *Memorial of Citizens of Louisiana*; McCrary, *Abraham Lincoln and Reconstruction*, 287. See also *CG*, 38th Cong., 2nd Sess., 5 (December 7, 1864).

Hahn inevitably protested to Hurlbut's superior, General Edward R. S. Canby, who backed Hurlbut, prompting Hahn to appeal directly to Lincoln. As he had done a year earlier with Banks, Lincoln responded with an uncharacteristically acerbic letter, this time to Hurlbut. "Few things," he began, in a letter marked "*Private*" and written after the election, "have impressed me more painfully than what, for four or five months past, has appeared as bitter military opposition to the new State Government of Louisiana." Although abolition and its consequences had no bearing on the current dispute, Lincoln tellingly highlighted this aspect of the Louisiana project. "A very fair proportion of the people of Louisiana have inaugurated a new State Government, making an excellent new constitution – better for the poor black man than we have in Illinois," he insisted. "Every Unionist ought to wish the new government to succeed; and every disunionist must desire it to fail," Lincoln continued. "Every advocate of slavery naturally desires to see blasted, and crushed, the liberty promised the black man by the new constitution. But why Gen. Canby and Gen. Hurlbut should join on the same side is to me incomprehensible."[12]

Both generals were distressed by Lincoln's criticism (Hurlbut showed the letter to Canby), and each responded separately. "I recognize as thoroughly as any man the advance toward the right made by the adoption of the Free Constitution of Louisiana," Hurlbut reassured Lincoln, "and have done and shall do all in my power to vindicate its declaration of freedom, and to protect and prepare the Emancipated Bondsmen for their new status & condition." Canby responded less defensively, reminding Lincoln that honest differences of opinion should not subject officers to recrimination. As he often did after writing what were for him intemperate letters, Lincoln sent a conciliatory message to Canby that nonetheless defended the new government. "[I]t is a worthy object to again get Louisiana into proper practical relations with the nation," he insisted, "and we can never finish this, if we never begin it. Much good work is already done, and surely nothing can be gained by throwing it away." Lincoln would return to this formulation in defending his Louisiana government.[13]

III

Whatever Louisiana's difficulties, Arkansas's affairs looked shakier by the fall than they had earlier in the year, as the momentum behind the free-state initiative seemed to be petering out. Military inertia had settled over Arkansas following the Red River-Camden fiasco, and Steele showed little initiative. In October, the members of the Murphy administration requested his help in organizing special legislative elections in counties that had not

---

[12] *OR*, ser. 1, vol. 41, pt. 4, 413; Hahn to Lincoln, October 29, 1864, ALP; *CWL*, 8: 106–7; Harris, *With Charity for All*, 193–95.
[13] *CWL*, 8: 106–8, 163–65; Harris, *With Charity for All*, 195–96.

participated in the elections of the previous spring. "[W]ith some little military protection," they believed, Unionists in these areas "would now gladly send up representatives." Such a move would counter the Confederate legislature that was preparing to meet in southwestern Arkansas, "as if to rival thereby," they added, "the loyal civil government which we represent." Steele did not provide the requested aid, however, and no special election was held.[14]

But it was Steele's military failings that led to his undoing. From late September through late October, Confederate General Sterling Price conducted a major raid through Missouri and parts of Kansas and the Indian Territory. His forces also trampled through northern Arkansas and, though ultimately defeated, took refuge in southwestern Arkansas. The raid was a strategic failure, but Steele's inability to stop it led Canby to replace him in late November with General Joseph Reynolds. Relations between Steele and Arkansas Unionists had often been strained, but both factions had supported him. H. B. Allis, former Speaker of the Arkansas House, wrote to Lincoln in mid-October on Steele's behalf, as did former Little Rock mayor Charles P. Bertrand. Steele's brother, New York Democratic congressman John B. Steele (who lost his seat in the election), had assured him in mid-November that he still enjoyed support in Washington. A mass meeting in Little Rock in early December protested the removal, but to no avail. However dismayed over the situation, Lincoln was unwilling to countermand an order issued out of military necessity. Given Nathaniel Banks's extended leave from Louisiana, two of Lincoln's three pointmen in the lower Mississippi valley were no longer on the scene.[15]

Steele had been removed for military reasons, but there was no denying the dire political situation. In late November, just before Steele was relieved, Arkansas Secretary of State Robert J. T. White offered him an intended show of support that in fact detailed the government's shortcomings. "An impression seems to prevail in many parts of the country that the State of Arkansas is entirely overrun by guerillas, confining our civil and military controll of the State to a few military posts," White wrote. "It is also thought by many, unacquainted with the facts, that the present state organization of Arkansas is the result of outside and illegitimate influences and not a spontaneous movement of the Loyal citizens of the State – or at least not of a majority of those citizens." Because these impressions were "calculated to prejudice the interests of Arkansas, in both a civil and military point of view," White suggested that Steele "furnish the public with a vindication, so far as justified by the facts," to counter them. The new government may not have been the product

---

[14] Murphy et al. to Steele, October 20, 1864, Steele Papers, Stanford. The letter was also signed by the Arkansas Secretary of State, Attorney General, Treasurer, and Auditor, and by an H. [N.?] Hargrove.

[15] Allis to Lincoln, October 13, 1864, ALP; John B. Steele to Frederick Steele, November 21, 1864, and John B. Steele to [Frederick Steele], November 22, 1864, both in Steele Papers, Stanford; Moneyhon, *Impact of the Civil War and Reconstruction on Arkansas*, 166; DeBlack, *With Fire and Sword*, 122–31; Harris, *With Charity for All*, 209–10.

of "outside and illegitimate influences," but Henry Winter Davis himself could have provided no more damning indictment of Reconstruction in Arkansas.[16]

In supplying the requested "vindication," Steele acknowledged overseeing the state's political reorganization but denied having been the driving force behind it. Although originally dubious of the free-state initiative, he soon came to see it as "a spontaneous movement on the part of the people to establish a civil government." The loyal citizens had so long suffered under Confederate "military despotism" that they would have tolerated no Federal military interference. "The movement was initiated by them, and they had every opportunity of expressing their unbiased opinions at the polls," Steele contended, adding that the election had been entirely free from fraud. "So far as I could judge there never was a more honest election, and a very large majority of the loyal citizens of the State recorded their votes." There were "some guerillas in this state," Steele admitted, but he deemed them more "highway robbers" than partisans, and he downplayed other Confederate activity, including Price's raid. Steele was correct to assert that "at present the rebels hold no portion of this state," aside from the southwest, but the problem was not so much Confederate control as the new government's inability to establish its authority.[17]

Even before Steele's removal, Canby, in consultation with the Union high command, had already decided in mid-November upon a strategic consolidation of Arkansas units. The resulting abandonment of several posts sparked howls of protest from Unionists, who understandably felt betrayed. Governor Murphy dispatched an emissary to Washington to have the order countermanded. Charles P. Bertrand, among others, wrote directly to Lincoln. "Does [General Canby] mean to abandon the state?" he asked. "Do you know that this abandons one entire Congressional district and the whole of another, save two or three counties, and that two-thirds of the members and perhaps three-fourths of the Legislature, now in session here, are furnished from the district of country thus to be abandoned and given up?" The order was reversed in early 1865, but not before Arkansas's already demoralized Unionists lost further confidence in the new government, or before the government's already slim prospects for gaining congressional recognition had been further eroded.[18]

IV

Although Tennessee's reorganization had lagged behind Arkansas and Louisiana during the previous year, only Tennessee attempted to conduct a presidential election, which inevitably became enmeshed with state

---

[16] Robt. J. T. White to Steele, November 25, 1864, Steele Papers, Stanford.
[17] [Frederick Steele] to R. J. White, November 30, 1864 (copy), Steele Papers, Stanford.
[18] *OR*, ser. 1, vol. 41, pt. 4, 582, 836 (Bertrand); DeBlack, *With Fire and Sword*, 135–36; Moneyhon, *Impact of the Civil War and Reconstruction on Arkansas*, 166–67; Harris, *With Charity for All*, 210.

reorganization. Andrew Johnson's nomination as vice president exacerbated the split between conservative and free-state Unionists, as the two factions put forward competing election plans that resulted in the conservatives simultaneously protesting against and calling for Lincoln's intervention. Free-state Unionists made no progress toward abolition during the fall, and Tennessee's electoral votes were not counted, but the election marked the conservatives' last gasp.

Johnson took the occasion of accepting the vice presidential nomination – in a letter not published until July 20 – to reaffirm his commitment to the destruction of slavery. No restoration of the Union could take place until "the distracting element of slavery" had been eliminated, Johnson insisted. The authority of the Federal government was supreme, and no institution, "whether it be slavery or any other organized power," could eclipse it. Johnson restated his support for Lincoln's emancipation policy and the Federal abolition amendment, the latter of which "comes stamped with the authority of the people themselves, acting in accordance with the written rule of the supreme law of the land."[19]

Meanwhile, conservative Unionists seized upon the presidential election again to challenge Johnson's power. During the summer, they formally organized themselves into a "Conservative Union" Party and allied with the short-lived Conservative National Union Committee, an organization headquartered in New York City attempting to unite all Unionists who opposed an abolitionist war. The Tennessee conservatives proposed a presidential ticket of McClellan and William B. Campbell, the former governor and Tennessee Whig, whom they claimed in August 1863 had been elected governor. Although Campbell now refused to have his name put forward (owing in part to the ascendancy of the Peace Democrats), the conservatives pressed on. They renamed themselves the Constitutional Union Party, invoking the 1860 presidential race and favorite son John Bell, and they cobbled together a slate of ten presidential electors that included Campbell, Emerson Etheridge, and Thomas A. R. Nelson. They also unleashed a newspaper attack on Johnson and Lincoln, equating abolition with racial equality, and denied slavery's demise in Tennessee. Despite Federal military success and Lincoln's increased reelection prospects, they still hoped to overthrow Johnson and restore Tennessee as a slave state.[20]

Free-state Unionists also sought to link the election to state restoration. In early August, a group of Johnson supporters issued a call for a convention, to meet in Nashville a month hence, to formulate "some plan for the restoration of Tennessee to the rights and privileges to which her loyal population is

---

[19] *PAJ*, 7: 7–12; Trefousse, *Andrew Johnson*, 180, 182. In a speech near Gallatin soon thereafter, Johnson reiterated this theme but just as vehemently condemned "negro equality," which he considered "a doctrine as wicked and fallacious as it is imaginary and unfounded." *PAJ*, 7: 41–44.

[20] Harris, *With Charity for All*, 218–19; Cimprich, *Slavery's End in Tennessee*, 107–8.

entitled," and "to take such action as may be necessary" to enable the state to conduct a presidential election. Delegates from fifty counties gathered in early September, including a number of conservative Unionists under the impression that the convention was a genuinely bipartisan affair. When the conservatives proposed reorganizing the state government and holding the election under Tennessee's antebellum constitution, permitting voting on the basis of Lincoln's amnesty oath, their proposals were met with derision from Johnson "radicals," who were not feeling magnanimous following the Democratic national convention and recent fall of Atlanta. The conservatives predictably walked out, and the free-state delegates ran the convention. They resolved that Tennessee participate in the presidential election and called for a loyalty oath, as a requirement for voting, even more stringent than Johnson's "damnesty oath." They also endorsed Johnson as military governor and Lincoln's reelection and advocated abolition "by all suitable and proper amendments" to both the state and Federal constitutions.[21]

Even as the convention was in progress, Johnson on September 7 issued a proclamation outlining the restoration of Tennessee's civil government. Johnson would "appoint officers and establish tribunals," as he had previously done, "when and wherever the people shall give evidence that they are loyal, and desire a return of civil government." These officials would carry out their duties until regular elections could be held, and they would be guided by the laws and constitution "as compiled and published prior to the existing rebellion." All appointees had to subscribe to Johnson's "damnesty oath," moreover, which included the controversial phrases "ardently desire the suppression of the present insurrection" and "heartily aid and assist" in its suppression, and required compliance with all Federal measures – meaning emancipation – toward that end. With the election approaching, Johnson was jump-starting state reorganization.

Johnson's September 7 proclamation also effectively suspended Tennessee's slave code. "All cases, civil and criminal, coming before the judicial tribunals of this State, involving the rights of colored persons, shall be adjudicated, and disposed of as [those involving] free persons of color," it declared. This provision came nowhere near equality before the law, but it gave former slaves minimal legal rights, and it moved them a step closer to citizenship in light of the US Attorney General's November 1862 decision declaring free black people to be American citizens. A week later, Johnson ordered the enrollment of all able-bodied adult males, "white and colored," in the state militia. Black men from Tennessee had already been serving in the Federal military, but participation in the state militia was a traditional privilege of (male) citizenship to which they could now lay claim.[22]

[21] Harris, *With Charity for All*, 219–20 (quotations); Trefousse, *Andrew Johnson*, 181.
[22] *PAJ*, 7: 141–43 (proclamation), 159–61 (militia); Trefousse, *Andrew Johnson*, 183.

In late September, Johnson issued another proclamation, directing that Tennessee would conduct a presidential election. Based explicitly on the resolutions of the recent Nashville convention, it spelled out the procedures to be followed. The loyalty oath for voting would be the more stringent one the convention had endorsed. In addition to incorporating Johnson's oath, this one required a prospective voter to be "an active friend of the Government of the United States, and the enemy of the so-called Confederate States"; to "sincerely rejoice in the triumph" of Federal military forces "and in the defeat and overthrow" of those "of the so-called Confederate States"; and to "cordially oppose all armistices or negotiations for peace with rebels in arms." Recognizing the difficulties of organizing a statewide election on such short notice, Johnson allowed that persons "of known and established loyalty" who had failed to register would still be entitled to vote. After having put off restoring civilian government for so long, Johnson now authorized a statewide election in a mere five weeks. He was no doubt keen to reaffirm Tennessee's status in the Union, and he could hardly allow his home state to be sidelined in an election in which he was a candidate. Lincoln might also need Tennessee's electoral votes. Still, Johnson had again contravened Lincoln's amnesty policy on the grounds that conservative Unionists, in whose loyalty he placed no faith, must not be permitted to jeopardize Tennessee's reorganization as a free state.[23]

Tennessee's two Unionist factions had now offered competing election proposals. With their political nemesis behind the opposing one, the conservative Unionists protested directly to Lincoln. They drafted a petition – signed by their ten presidential electors, including Campbell, Nelson, Etheridge, and John Lellyett, the last of whom presented it personally to Lincoln in mid-October – that remonstrated "on behalf of the loyal people of our State" against Johnson's election proclamation. The petitioners emphasized the disparity between Lincoln's amnesty oath and the proclamation's, insisting that the latter violated Lincoln's policy and Tennessee's voting requirements, and alleging that it "is only calculated to keep legal and rightful voters from the polls." They took umbrage at the requirement that a voter "rejoice" in Confederate defeat, and thus take pleasure "over the scenes of blood, and of wounds, of anguish and death" that would include friends, family, and loved ones. They similarly objected to the language opposing any armistice or negotiated settlement, quoting in full Lincoln's own "To whom it may concern" memo of the previous July. In it, Lincoln had pledged that any proposal from Confederate authorities embracing "the restoration of peace, the integrity of the whole Union, and the abandonment of slavery" would be met "by liberal terms on other substantial and collateral points." Was the nation destined, they asked, to "unrelenting war to the bitter end?"

---

[23] *PAJ*, 7: 203–5; Harris, *With Charity for All*, 220–21; Trefousse, *Andrew Johnson*, 181–82.

But the main point was Johnson's attempt to rig the election by preventing his opponents from voting. "[W]e solemnly protest against the interference of the Military Governor with the freedom of the elective franchise in Tennessee," they wrote. "We deny his authority and yours, to alter, amend or annul any law of Tennessee." The recent convention "was a mere partisan meeting, having no authority, and not representing the loyal men of Tennessee." They requested that Lincoln revoke Johnson's proclamation, and "that all military interference shall be withdrawn so far as to allow the loyal men of Tennessee a full and free election." They also alleged that Johnson's election proclamation – which had only been issued *after* they had drawn up their own electoral slate – had been specifically designed to exclude them from the election.

Such an appeal was unlikely to gain Lincoln's approval, and it did not. According to Lellyett's account of his meeting with Lincoln, published several days later and widely reprinted in the Democratic press, Lincoln responded testily. "May I inquire how long it took you and the New-York politicians to concoct that paper?" he asked, no doubt referring to the Conservative National Union Committee. When informed that it had been "concocted" in Nashville, entirely by Tennesseans, Lincoln responded: "I expect to let the friends of George B. McClellan manage their side of this contest in their own way; and I will manage my side of it in my way." After a further brief exchange, with Lincoln indicating that he would provide additional commentary on the petition, the meeting ended. "The paper which I had the honor to present to the President is not the 'concoction of New York politicians,' however that might affect its merits," Lellyett later insisted. "It is the solemn voice of a once free and proud people, protesting against their own disfranchisement by the agent of Abraham Lincoln. It is the voice of those loyal men in Tennessee who have borne the reproach of a people they still loved, supporting the President in all lawful efforts to preserve the Union," he continued. "The reward of our loyalty is disfranchisement."

In providing the promised elaboration a week later, Lincoln once again found himself in the awkward position of having to support Johnson even though Johnson's plan clearly violated the ten-percent plan's voting requirement. Lincoln denied having had anything to do with Johnson's proclamation and foreswore any authority to sustain, revoke, or modify it. The president plays no role in the election in the states, Lincoln insisted, and there was no military reason for him to intervene. "In no proper sense can [the convention-Johnson election plan] be considered other than as an independent movement of at least a portion of the loyal people of Tennessee," he noted. "I do not perceive in the plan any menace of violence or coercion towards any one." Lincoln also suggested, somewhat disingenuously, that the petitioners "[d]o as you please on your own account peacefully and loyally, and Governor Johnson will not molest you." Getting to the crux of the matter, almost as an aside,

Lincoln added: "the conducting of a Presidential Election in Tennessee in strict accordance with the old code of the State is not now a possibility." Lincoln was well aware that preserving the "old code of the State" was precisely what the conservative Unionists were hoping to accomplish. Ultimately, Lincoln indicated, "another department of the Government," meaning Congress, would decide whether to count a state's electoral votes. "Except it be to give protection against violence, I decline to interfere in any way with any presidential election."

Determined to have the last word, three of the petitioners – including Campbell and Lellyett – composed a counterresponse that appeared soon after the election. "The argument on this subject is nearly exhausted," they insisted – though they then proceeded to keep it going. They charged Johnson with unleashing a "reign of terror" in Tennessee, and Lincoln with employing "a doctrine of despotism in 'irrepressible conflict' with the principles of public liberty." The Johnson-convention plan constituted an "independent movement" only insofar as it was "[m]anifestly independent of all lawful authority – independent of and at war with the federal Constitution." Federal soldiers had broken up McClellan meetings, and Johnson and his allies routinely referred to McClellan supporters as "rebels and traitors." At least once, they added, in a comment that spoke volumes, the streets "were paraded by an immense procession of negroes, bearing torches and transperencies, with such inscriptions on the latter as 'Lincoln and Johnson,' 'Liberty or Death.'"

The authors further castigated Lincoln's suggestion that they do as they please, "peacefully and loyally," and that Johnson would leave them alone. "If you mean that Governor Johnson will allow us to stay away from the polls without molestation, we trust there is some truth in your assurance," they observed sardonically. "But if you mean to suggest that we hold separate elections 'on our own account,' and to assure us that we shall not be molested but protected in such a 'movement,' we know by experience, and by the facts above set forth, that your assurance is a cruel mockery." Lincoln had not actually advised "separate" elections, but they pursued the point anyway. "We will not advise our citizens to put in jeopardy their lives in going through the farce you propose, of holding an election under the laws at one ballot-box, while Governor Johnson holds an election under his 'plan' at another." This would not be an election, they avowed, but an exercise in despotism. "There will be no election for President in Tennessee in 1864," the authors conceded, adding that they had no choice but to "announce that the McClellan Electoral Ticket in Tennessee is withdrawn."[24]

---

[24] Documents pertaining to this episode, and all quotations, are in *CWL*, 8: 58–72. See also Harris, *With Charity for All*, 221–22; Trefousse, *Andrew Johnson*, 184.

Even before said withdrawal, some conservatives had begun to reconsider their position. They had always claimed to support the war, but northern Copperheads allowed Johnson to portray them as disloyal. Their complaints against Johnson were not complete fabrications, but neither were Johnson's actions entirely unwarranted, since their criticism of the conduct of the war was sometimes indistinguishable from opposition to the war itself. As Lincoln's reelection became increasingly likely, some conservatives expressed the opinion, at least privately, that continued opposition only enabled Johnson and his allies to consolidate their position and was thus counterproductive. A few of them swallowed their pride and abandoned McClellan. "Every thing is right in this end of the State," William G. "Parson" Brownlow assured Johnson from Knoxville just before the election. "The McClelland party is a mere *faction*, led on by a set of sore-headed Union men, some of them old Democrats, but most of them old Whigs, who have a bad Union record. They have played out."[25]

V

As the conservative Unionist petition had indicated, black Tennesseans, although excluded from formal politics, intensified their campaign for equal rights. In marches, mass meetings, and other demonstrations, they called for black suffrage and the removal of all legal distinctions based on race. They also campaigned for the Lincoln–Johnson ticket, thereby equating – in their own minds and those of their white opponents – Republican victory with racial equality. The large majority of Tennessee's black leaders had been free before the war. Most were ministers or preachers, skilled laborers, and small shop owners or businessmen. Tennessee's black population did not experience the same "alienation" between former slaves and former free persons of color as did Louisiana's, but neither did Tennessee Unionism include white radicals who endorsed black suffrage. With few white allies to speak of, black Tennesseans were largely on their own. They nonetheless sent a delegation in October to the National Equal Rights League convention in Syracuse, where Ransom Harris of Nashville was elected to the national executive board, and in early 1865 they organized a state chapter.[26]

It was one such event – a black torchlight procession in Nashville on the evening of October 24 – that provided the setting for one of the most unusual addresses of Andrew Johnson's entire public career. Delivered at the capitol building, where the procession had ended and a large, overwhelmingly black crowd had gathered, Johnson's "Moses of the Colored Men" speech ventured

---

[25] PAJ, 7: 276; Harris, *With Charity for All*, 222–23; Atkins, "Failure of Restoration," 310–12.

[26] Cimprich, *Slavery's End in Tennessee*, 104, 107, 109–13; LeForge, "State Colored Conventions of Tennessee," 232–34.

into what for Johnson was uncharted territory. As the editors of Johnson's papers have observed, the address was "demagogic beyond his usual wont." But Johnson's expression of empathy for what slavery had done to black people stood out from just about everything he had ever said or ever would say on the question of race.[27]

Observing that Tennessee's exclusion from the Emancipation Proclamation had left many persons enslaved (without noting his own role therein), Johnson assured his listeners that "the hour has come when the last vestiges of [slavery] must be removed." He then made a proclamation of his own: "I, Andrew Johnson, do hereby proclaim freedom, full, broad and unconditional, to every man in Tennessee!" Johnson's pronouncement of universal freedom was notable, inasmuch as Tennessee had yet to abolish slavery, but so was his affirmation of black people's right to self-defense, since white mobs routinely attacked and molested public gatherings such as this one. More remarkable still, Johnson went on to condemn both black women's sexual exploitation under slavery and the slaveholders' moral depravity. "Colored men of Tennessee! This too shall cease!" he announced. "Your wives and daughters shall no longer be dragged into a concubinage, compared to which polygamy is a virtue, to satisfy the brutal lusts of slaveholders and overseers!" "Thank God! Thank God!" exclaimed Johnson's listeners, warming to his message. "And if the law protects you in the possession of your wives and children," he continued, "and if the law shields those whom you hold dear from the unlawful grasp of lust, will you endeavor to be true to yourselves, and shun, as it were death itself, the path of lewdness, crime and vice?" "We will! We will!" the crowd shouted back.

"Looking at this vast crowd of colored people," Johnson continued, "and reflecting through what a storm of persecution and obloquy they are compelled to pass, I am almost induced to wish that, as in the days of old, a Moses might arise who should lead them safely to their promised land of freedom and happiness." When several listeners called out, "You are our Moses," the crowd took up the refrain. "We want no Moses but you!" "Well then," Johnson replied, "humble and unworthy as I am, if no other better shall be found, I will indeed be your Moses, and lead you through the Red Sea of war and bondage, to a fairer future of liberty and peace." Andrew Johnson, champion of the common (white) man, had improbably vowed to guide the former slaves to the promised land of freedom. "Rebellion and slavery shall, by God's good help, no longer pollute our State," he added in closing. "Loyal men, whether white or black, shall alone control her destinies." The crowd roared its approval.[28]

Johnson had likely let the passions of the moment get the better of him, and subsequent events would prove this speech an aberration. The monumental

---

[27] *PAJ*, 7: l.
[28] *PAJ*, 7: 251–53; Trefousse, *Andrew Johnson*, 183–84.

struggles of his presidency would reveal his true colors. The speech, predictably, provoked strong reactions, for and against, and Tennessee's conservative press had a field day. Johnson had adhered to a strictly gendered reading of emancipation and to traditional, patriarchal assumptions about the family. And his address included no small measure of condescension. Yet rarely had Johnson ever condemned slavery in such explicitly moral terms or spoken so vehemently about what it did to black people. He had previously limited his criticism of slavery largely to its effects on white society. However anomalous, Johnson's "Moses" speech, along with his demonstrable personal bravery, his firm measures against "treason" and "traitors," and his embrace of immediate abolition, contributed to his estimable record as military governor, no matter how starkly it contrasted with his abysmal record as president.[29]

Within a fortnight of voicing these sentiments, Johnson had been elected Lincoln's vice president. Tennessee conducted a presidential election in accordance with the free-state Unionist plan. Some 35,000 votes were cast statewide, a mere quarter of the 1860 total, 5,000 of which went to McClellan. Roughly half of Lincoln's votes came from Unionist east Tennessee. The Lincoln–Johnson ticket easily won in Memphis and Nashville in a result marred by low turnout. One Johnson ally estimated that a mere one-third of eligible Memphis voters participated. "We begged them, for the sake of the commercial interests of Memphis, to join in with us and vote, but they would not," he reported. "We know that the next election – for members of a constitutional Convention – will require a much larger vote to make us successful."[30]

Black Tennesseans had needed no such prodding. In Nashville, where an unofficial election was held in which black men voted, all but one of nearly 3,500 votes went for Lincoln. Congress would refuse to count Tennessee's electoral votes, on the grounds that no legitimate election had taken place. But with the matter decided, free-state Unionists turned again to the long-delayed tasks of organizing a new government and abolishing slavery, both of which Johnson was determined to complete before becoming vice president.[31]

---

[29] However remarkable, the speech was not unique. Three weeks later, in mid-November, Johnson delivered a similar one. Though avoiding references to Moses and using less intemperate language, Johnson returned to the slaveholders' profligacy, the moral bankruptcy of slavery, and the harm done to black people. "Slavery is the hot bed of prostitution, polygamy, and concubinage. It has debauched and ruined countless thousands of our people, both white and black, broken down the marriage altar, and brought indescribable misery and suffering into innumerable families. These facts are seldom spoken of among ourselves, but they are nevertheless as notorious as they are shocking, and subversive of the very foundations of society." *PAJ*, 7: 281–83.

[30] *PAJ*, 7: 273–74.

[31] Harris, *With Charity for All*, 223; Cimprich, *Slavery's End in Tennessee*, 111–12.

VI

Following the Republican-Union convention in June, the lack of military success during the summer forced Republicans to downplay the Federal abolition amendment in their campaign rhetoric, a stance even the fall of Atlanta did not change. Even after Jefferson Davis declared in early October, in an attempt to boost Confederate morale, that the South would accept nothing less than independence, regardless of slavery (thereby handing to Lincoln on a silver platter the very thing he had sought for months), Republicans maintained their silence on the amendment. Northern Democrats also said little about slavery or the amendment, realizing, as Michael Vorenberg has noted, that appearing to defend slavery at this point was tantamount to "political suicide." Instead, they continued to castigate Republicans for the *consequences* of emancipation, stoking white Northerners' racial fears with talk of "miscegenation," for example, and vowing to preserve white supremacy.[32]

Democratic race baiting kept Republicans on their heels, but it also made Republicans more inclined to highlight their opponents' problems than to accentuate their own emancipation policy. Benefitting from warfare between War and Peace Democrats, and from the latter's influence within the party, Republicans redoubled the attack on Democrats' loyalty, holding all Democrats accountable for the sins of the Copperheads, and depicting northern Democrats as the long-time enablers of the "Slave Power." Republicans also avoided the amendment by emphasizing state abolition. A campaign publication compiling the most important antislavery statements of Lincoln's career, and affirming his commitment to emancipation, for instance, underscored *state* abolition as a condition for restoration, making no mention of Federal abolition. "[T]he president has *determined*," it read, "that in reorganizing or reconstructing local governments in rebellious districts, with a view to their readmission to the Union, slavery shall be for ever excluded therefrom in the constitutions of their respective States, and that freedom and justice shall be the corner-stone of the Union." As Vorenberg has concluded, "one of the most remarkable aspects of the 1864 political campaign was the disappearance rather than the dominance of the antislavery amendment."[33]

---

[32] *CWL*, 8: 1–2; Davis, *Jefferson Davis*, 6: 358–59; Vorenberg, *Final Freedom*, 165; Weber, *Copperheads*, 183–86. Every study of wartime northern politics or biography of Lincoln devotes considerable attention to the 1864 presidential election. Oakes, *Freedom National*, 470–76, tends to emphasize the Republicans' commitment to the abolition amendment during the campaign.

[33] [Whiting], *Opinions on "Slavery,"* 16; Vorenberg, *Final Freedom*, 141, 167–75 (quotation, 174). There were important exceptions to this generalization. Despite his own tough reelection campaign, as Rebecca E. Zietlow notes, James M. Ashley spoke openly in defense of the amendment, which he claimed to have written, and even of equality before the law. *Forgotten Emancipator*, 117–18. For examples of mainstream northern public

Lincoln was reelected overwhelmingly, winning 55 percent of the popular vote and a landslide in the Electoral College. Yet 45 percent of the electorate had voted for McClellan, fully aware that he would stop the war altogether or end Federal emancipation policy. Either path, Republicans insisted, led to defeat. Republicans won in 1864 by downplaying, not accentuating, abolition. To be sure, preserving the Union and destroying slavery had become inseparable for Republicans, and only by winning the election could they achieve those larger objectives. Lincoln's reelection all but assured Federal military victory and the ultimate destruction of slavery, but the election hardly served as a referendum on the amendment.

Despite Republican equivocating on the amendment, Federal abolition would now appear to have superseded state abolition – except that the amendment did not begin to address the myriad issues regarding state restoration. Neither had the role of the rebellious states in ratifying the amendment been determined. So long as the Union prosecuted the war to final victory, many contemporaries believed, the destruction of slavery was certain. Yet so long as state ratification of the amendment was still unsettled, as Henry Winter Davis insisted, and so long as Congress and the president continued to disagree on Reconstruction, this mission could not quite be considered accomplished. Freedom had yet to become, in Andrew Johnson's words, full, broad, and unconditional.

opinion embracing the amendment during the campaign, see Henry Everett Russell, "The Constitutional Amendment," *Continental Monthly*, vol. 6, no. 3 (September 1864): 315–26; "The Two Platforms," *Continental Monthly*, vol. 6, no. 5 (November 1864): 587–600; R. J. Walker, "Letter of Hon. R. J. Walker, in Favor of the Reelection of Abraham Lincoln," *Continental Monthly*, vol. 6, no. 6 (December 1864): 686–705. Another important exception was the highly publicized address of Charles Sumner, delivered at the Cooper Institute in New York City days before the election. Characterizing Lincoln's "to whom" letter as "unquestionably the best he ever wrote," Sumner considered a negotiated settlement with the Confederacy as surrender to the "Slave Power *out of the Union*," while the restoration of the rebellious states without eradicating slavery would be surrender to "the Slave Power *in the Union*." Yet even this address must be understood as a partisan attack, rather than support for the amendment, equating a vote for McClellan and Democrats with a vote for slavery. [Sumner], *Slavery and the Rebellion*, 20, 27.

17

"To Resolve Never Again to Be Reduced to Slavery"

By late summer 1864, Arkansas and Louisiana had abolished slavery while Tennessee and Mississippi had yet to do so. Although few slaves remained in the Federally occupied parts of these states by this point, slavery could never be declared dead in them until it had been formally abolished and Federal military victory had been secured. At the same time, slavery had been disintegrating throughout the lower Mississippi valley for more than two years, and for the rest of 1864 it continued its descent into oblivion. Whatever happened in the realm of formal politics, slavery was being undone on a daily basis by war, Federal authority, and the actions of the slaves themselves. If a society's institutional structure shapes individual experience, then both institutions and individual experience were integral to slavery's destruction.

Despite calls for action by governors Isaac Murphy of Arkansas and Michael Hahn of Louisiana, the legislatures of these states would fail by year's end to address abolition's consequences. Plantation affairs therefore remained under Federal authority in most of the lower Mississippi valley. Although Federal forces had originally brought military emancipation to the region, Abraham Lincoln's reconstructed governments were not yet ready to assume responsibility for defining the new social order following abolition. As all interested parties looked to the future, Federal officials insisted that the new labor system was progressing, while former slaveholders and former slaves, for different reasons, expressed their frustration with it. Tired of kowtowing to Federal authorities, former slaveholders – even those who claimed to have accepted the end of slavery – demonstrated their commitment to the old order and hostility to the new by continuing to insist that servile labor and corporal punishment remained essential to plantation operations. Former slaves challenged this outlook at every turn and contested the restrictions of Federal labor policy. They also pursued alternatives to plantation employment, especially the independent cultivation of land. Above all, they were resolved, as one Federal official observed, "never again to be reduced to slavery." Yet even after Lincoln's reelection had dashed all Confederate hope, former slaveholders along the Mississippi River were still trying to return freed persons to bondage – actions as desperate as they were deluded.

I

The contest between War and Treasury Department officials over the administration of plantation affairs appeared finally to have been resolved in mid-1864 when it was again thrown into question. In December 1863, legislation had been introduced into Congress – following the investigations of the American Freedmen's Inquiry Commission and other agencies into the former slaves' welfare – to create a Federal "bureau of emancipation" that would oversee the transition from slavery to freedom (marking the legislative origins of the Freedmen's Bureau). Although disagreement between congressional Republicans over housing the agency in the War or Treasury Department derailed the bill during the current session, Congress authorized the Treasury Department in July 1864 to assume responsibility for abandoned lands, including farms and plantations being worked under military supervision, and for "the employment and general welfare" of former slaves not already serving in the military. To complicate matters further, Lincoln accepted Treasury secretary Salmon P. Chase's resignation just as the department had been assigned this greatly expanded remit.[1]

The difficulties arising from these changes soon became evident. In late July, William P. Mellen – now the supervising agent for all of the Treasury Department's special agencies – essentially reissued his previous regulations (since suspended), which would govern plantation labor throughout the entire lower Mississippi valley. While retaining most of Nathaniel Banks's 1864 labor guidelines for the sugar region and Lorenzo Thomas's for the cotton country, Mellen's regulations called for higher monthly wages, ranging from $25 to $15 for men and $18 to $10 for women. (Banks's ranged between $8 and $3, without distinguishing between men and women; Thomas set "minimum wages" at $10 for men and $7 for women.) Half of the monthly wage would still be withheld until year's end, but the laborers were now responsible for their own clothing and provisions. Also, Treasury Department agents and superintendents, rather than army personnel, would administer the entire plantation labor system.[2]

Military authorities, led by Col. John Eaton, the General Superintendent of Freedmen in the Department of Mississippi and the State of Arkansas, once again protested. Eaton welcomed the higher wages but opposed both the mid-year altering of the terms of plantation employment and the replacing of military with civilian authority. He implored upon Treasury officials to

---

[1] *Freedom: WGFL-LS*, 371; H.R. 1, *House Journal*, 38th Cong., 1st Sess., 43 (December 14, 1863); *Statutes at Large*, 13: 375–78. There is a significant scholarly literature on the Freedmen's Bureau, but see especially Bentley, *History of the Freedmen's Bureau*; Cimbala and Miller, *Freedmen's Bureau and Reconstruction*; Farmer-Kaiser, *Freedwomen and the Freedmen's Bureau*; and White, *Freedmen's Bureau in Louisiana*.

[2] *Freedom: WGFL-LS*, 371, 539–43 (doc. 119).

suspend the proposed transfer. By late August, with the home of the Federal emancipation bureau still to be determined, the new Treasury secretary, William P. Fessenden, agreed to suspend the transfer until the department was "prepared in all respects to assume such control under the law." Under the circumstances, this amounted to an indefinite postponement.[3]

Meanwhile, freed people's and plantation affairs underwent their own reorganization in southern Louisiana. In August, Thomas W. Conway, an Irish immigrant and former army chaplain who later became the first head of the Freedmen's Bureau in Louisiana, was appointed the new superintendent of the Department of the Gulf's Bureau of Negro Labor. Renaming the agency the "Bureau of Free Labor," Conway undertook measures to protect the rights of plantation laborers, ensuring them their back wages and prohibiting employers from selling crops until they had paid their workers. Despite these reforms, Federal officials in Louisiana did not receive word of Fessenden's decision to suspend the transfer of plantation affairs to Treasury, and they assumed that it would take place as planned. Formal announcement of the transfer was delayed for various reasons (including Banks's leave of absence) until late October, when military authorities in southern Louisiana finally ordered Treasury officials – in particular Benjamin F. Flanders – to assume control over plantation labor and freed people's affairs.

The transition, which was not even supposed to occur, did not go smoothly. Flanders began to make preliminary arrangements for the 1865 crop season, but he and his subordinates were unprepared for their new responsibilities and lacked the necessary resources. Conway provided all of the assistance he could, but his superiors, Generals Stephen Hurlbut (as of late September) and Edward R. S. Canby, were eager to divest the military of these matters. Only in mid-December did officials in southern Louisiana learn of the transfer's suspension and the remanding of plantation matters to the War Department. Thus, throughout the fall of 1864, Treasury secretary Fessenden and other officials in Washington believed that the military had retained oversight of plantation affairs, whereas Federal authorities in Louisiana assumed that it now rested with Treasury.[4]

This administrative confusion made the challenge of implementing new labor relations on Louisiana's sugar plantations none the easier. Just getting the plantations up and running earlier in the year had hardly portended a successful crop, the testimonials of free labor's advocates notwithstanding. Planters and their employees continued to articulate conflicting understandings of "free labor," producing conflict over every aspect of plantation routine.

---

[3] *Freedom: WGFL-LS*, 371–72, 873–77 (doc. 222B; quotation, 874).
[4] Previous two paragraphs: *Freedom: WGFL-LS*, 370–72; Conway, *Report on the Condition of the Freedmen*, 8–9; Conway, *Annual Report of Thos. W. Conway*, 4, 8–9; Ripley, *Slaves and Freedmen*, 61–64.

Planters further demonstrated a divided mind – insisting that their plantations could not be worked without involuntary labor yet evincing in their behavior gradual accommodation to the new order. The abolition of slavery in Louisiana convinced them that controllable labor – including the ability to inflict corporal punishment – was more essential than ever. Even planters who reconciled themselves to emancipation rejected the principle that former slaves were their equals or that capital was equivalent to labor. "While the planters have attained to the conviction that the abolition of slavery is an accomplished fact," Benjamin F. Flanders observed, "not one of them is converted to the belief that free labor, can adequately replace the old System."[5]

Although Federal military control of southern Louisiana was secure, Confederate raids threatened to disrupt the fall harvest. Banks responded by lifting the prohibition against recruiting plantation laborers and by reauthorizing conscription. Resident planters predictably protested. They urged Banks to limit conscription to "vagrants" and to restore the ban against recruitment on plantations. Banks, in turn, backtracked, agreeing to exempt one-fifth of each planter's workers who were subject to the draft. He also allowed for conscripts deemed unfit for military service to return to their homes and ordered the furloughing of any new recruits who could be spared for the harvest. These measures left everyone dissatisfied. Laborers understandably objected to being conscripted into the service and separated from family members who depended on them for support. When military recruiters – mostly at planters' behest – began dragooning New Orleans free men of color into the service, the leaders of that community protested to Banks. A Treasury inspector charged that military recruiters concentrated mostly on leased plantations while exempting resident owners, many of whom were "Known to be rebel sympathizers." Despite this preferential treatment, a Federal military officer complained, resident planters continued to oppose the presence of recruiters on their plantations.[6]

Even as planters struggled to secure sufficient labor for the harvest, the prospects for the 1864 crop appeared increasingly dire. A number of them had turned to cultivating cotton during the spring as a temporary expedient (southern Louisiana's environment was not conducive to cotton cultivation),

---

[5] *Freedom: WGFL-LS*, 563–67 (doc. 130; quotation, 564). On the 1864 crop season, see Rodrigue, *Reconstruction in the Cane Fields*, 47–51. In addition to the works cited, this section on the Louisiana sugar region also relies on Gerteis, *From Contraband to Freedman*; Roland, *Louisiana Sugar Plantations during the American Civil War*; Scott, *Degrees of Freedom*; Messner, *Freedmen and the Ideology of Free Labor*; Ripley, *Slaves and Freedmen*; Tunnell, *Crucible of Reconstruction*; and Dawson, *Army Generals and Reconstruction*.

[6] *Freedom: BME*, 161–63, 165 (doc. 58C; free-black protest), 167–68 (doc. 60), 168–69 (doc. 61; military officer); *Freedom: WGFL-LS*, 369–70, 550–51n, 551–54 (doc. 124; Treasury official).

but the late-summer onset of the army worm ravaged the cotton crop throughout the lower Mississippi valley. Many planters simply abandoned their operations mid-year, leaving the workers destitute. Some who stuck it out ground the entire crop rather than hold the customary one-fourth in reserve for planting the next year's crop – "thereby rendering the plantations destitute of Cane Seed, and worthless to future Lessees," a Treasury Department official explained. The harvest was indeed abysmal. The output of some 10,000 hogsheads for 1864 was but a fraction of the average annual output of more than 300,000 hogsheads for the last five antebellum years, or of the 1861 record crop of almost 460,000 hogsheads, the last made entirely with slave labor. The bottoming out of the sugar industry was the result of multiple factors, especially the chaos and destruction of war, but few planters would have ascribed to coincidence the formal abolition of slavery and the worst sugar crop in the state's history.[7]

II

Such results begged the question, as sugar planter Andrew McCollam put it, "what is to be done?" Planters and former slaves (and their advocates) provided contrasting answers. McCollam, who had been a reluctant secessionist, affirmed that he would "willingly submit" to compensated labor if it would "produce obedience, honesty and faithful labor," but "twenty year's experience" had convinced him "that the negro has little, or no ambition to provide for the future." Consequently, "corporal punishment is the only means that will effect it," he contended. "Two thousand years experience, I may say has devised no other means." In mid-November, after the transfer of plantation labor to the Treasury Department had been announced, McCollam proposed to Benjamin Flanders the establishment of "a permanent Police" in each parish, "whose duty it shall be to visit the plantations from time to time, for the investigation of all complaints – inflicting such punishments as you may authorize for neglect of duty." McCollam assumed that the former slaves, not the planters, would need to be held to account and taught the "moral obligations" of a contract. "If you succeed in enforcing the contracts," he assured Flanders, "the planters will owe you much."[8]

These views were hardly exceptional. To the contrary, McCollam belonged to a group of planters who met with Flanders later in November to devise a modus operandi for the coming year (with both sides misapprehending that the Treasury Department now assumed responsibility for plantation labor). Insisting that Federal labor policy had been a failure, the planters formed

---

[7] *Freedom: WGFL-LS*, 370, 551–52 (quotation); Rodrigue, *Reconstruction in the Cane Fields*, 49–50.

[8] *Freedom: WGFL-LS*, 554–57 (doc. 125).

a committee "to draw up rules and regulations for the better administration of the plantations of Louisiana, and the management, payment, and feeding of the freed laborers." The committee would also suggest such changes to the Treasury Department's regulations (those drafted by William Mellen in late July) as the planters "deemed of vital importance to the agriculture of the State." Working from the assumption that "[t]he whole study, aim and object of the negro laborer now is, how to avoid work, and yet have a claim for wages, rations, clothes, etc.," the committee proposed "[s]ome mode of compelling laborers to perform ten hours faithful work." This goal could be achieved mostly through a graduated system of fines or deductions of wages or rations, "but in obstinate cases, it can only be done by corporeal punishment." The committee likewise called for "insolence, disobedience, improper behavior, or contempt of superiors" to be punished "as formerly," and it advised that other infractions "*should be severely punished,*" or should "*be punished by fine, imprisonment, and, in obstinate cases, by corporeal punishment.*" Laborers would also be forbidden to keep livestock without permission, to cultivate cotton or sugarcane on their own account, to be outside their quarters at night, or to "*leave the plantation for the purpose of visiting or trading*" without permission.

The proposals were no doubt a far cry from slavery. Express reference to "slaves" was replaced by the terminology "laborers, and others domesticated on plantations." Presumably, the truly horrific forms of corporal punishment would no longer be inflicted. The planters implicitly recognized some intermediary authority, however temporary, between themselves and their workers, something unimaginable under slavery. On the surface, the planters conceded a great deal. Yet the proposals also provided a clear window onto their vision of the labor system that would replace slavery, and they attested to the planters' unassailable beliefs: plantations could only be operated with compulsory labor; black people were incapable of working voluntarily; and planters and laborers could never engage each other as equals. Paradoxically, these proposals, however draconian, were perfectly in keeping with Louisiana's new constitution, which, aside from abolishing slavery, included no mandate for black civil rights or protections for plantation workers. Embedded within the proposals were assumptions about race and labor to which the planters – and the vast majority of white Southerners – subscribed. The planters may have been compelled to relinquish slavery, but they were not about to surrender the underlying principles on which it had been based.

This was how Conway saw the matter. The meeting, he remonstrated to Flanders, "demonstrates how intensely the Planters of this country hold the notion that *Capital* shall control *labor*." Invoking elements of northern free-labor thought, he insisted that "considerations of justice" were equally applicable to both parties. "Labor is as important as capital, if not more so," he contended. In Louisiana, however, "[m]ost of the Planters have a disposition to *grind* the negroes," he lamented. "They want to have 'all to say' in the premises; and they want things in the way that suits *them*." Months later, Conway penned an even more blistering critique of the planters' proposals, which, if implemented, "*would have brought the freedmen into bondage, in fact, if not in name.*" As previous observers had noted, the planters were willing to abandon the *name* of slavery for the substance. "It was by adhering as closely as possible to the old system that the planters appeared to expect success," Conway continued in his later account. "They lost sight of the fact, that though the freedmen are, as a general thing not learned, they possess sufficient intelligence and good sense to resolve never again to be reduced to slavery."

Flanders did not incorporate the planters' recommendations into his own proposal for 1865. Based on the principle, as he described it in an early-December report to Treasury secretary Fessenden, of "promot[ing] mutual satisfaction and Kindly feelings between the employer and the laborers," his plan was more solicitous of the laborers' interests than were the planters' proposals. Flanders claimed in his report – implausibly, based on what the planters had recommended – that the planters had "unanimously agreed that the system would be satisfactory, and that they believed it would redound to the benefit of all interested in the agricultural prosperity in this State." Flanders's plan was eventually rendered moot in mid-December, however, when Federal authorities in Louisiana at last received orders to postpone the transfer of plantation affairs to the Treasury Department. "I have been under wrong impressions, and have acted somewhat too hastily," Flanders admitted to Fessenden, though he reassured his superior that he anticipated no difficulty "in the Continuance of Military Control in the matter." Not until March would military authorities issue labor regulations for the new year.[9]

In the meantime, the coming crop season also prompted former slaves and their advocates to vent their own frustration with Federal labor policy in Louisiana. Throughout late 1864 and into early 1865, the New Orleans free black population, along with free-state radicals, castigated a state government that failed to adopt black suffrage and a labor system that, they charged, essentially reestablished slavery. They made their views known in mass meetings in New Orleans, Baton Rouge, and other towns, in a petition to Congress, and in the pages of the New Orleans *Tribune*. The paper had originally offered qualified support for Banks's 1864 labor regulations, acknowledging that temporary restrictions on labor were necessary, but by late summer it characterized them as a "total failure." This criticism became increasingly strident during the fall, and the *Tribune* derided Flanders's November meeting with the planters. It instead proposed the creation of permanent councils, composed of

---

[9] This account of the meeting between Flanders and the planters relies on Conway, *Freedmen of Louisiana*, 7–9, and *Freedom: WGFL-LS*, 372–73, 559–61 (doc. 128), 563–67 (doc. 130).

representatives chosen by the planters and by the laborers, to oversee plantation affairs.[10]

This proposal was not adopted, but former slaves themselves also espoused their desire for access to land as an essential component of freedom and genuine economic independence. They had already been collectively working abandoned estates on their own, and discontent with existing labor arrangements enhanced their aspirations for independent cultivation. "We the undersigned Colored People residing on Wood lawn Plantation ask your humble attention to our humble appeal that you will please give us the opportunity of working the Place among ourselves and you confer a great blessing and favor upon us." Thus read one typical petition in early 1865 from a group of more than two dozen freed men "and many others" in Terrebonne Parish to a Treasury official. The plantation in question, "Woodlawn," was one of many owned by the powerful Pugh family of Bayou Lafourche, one of whose members, Alexander Franklin Pugh, had sat on the planters' committee during the November meeting with Flanders. Although the plantation had not been "abandoned," strictly speaking, the former slaves had essentially been working it on their own and wanted to continue doing so.

Their request was evidently granted, as were several others. Woodlawn was one of several abandoned or inoperative plantations in Terrebonne and adjoining Lafourche parishes that by the spring were being worked by multiple "companies" of former slaves. Another Treasury official reported in early 1865 that former slaves expressed "a great desire to cultivate land on their own account, and without exception they promise diligence, good order, obedience to regulations, and the faithful care and return of the property entrusted to them." These former slaves faced numerous challenges, but, as an inspector reported in April, "they are well advanced in their work." Devoting most of their efforts to raising small crops of corn and cotton, but also to cultivating sugarcane, they forcefully belied any claims of black people's supposed aversion to voluntary labor.[11]

III

During these same months, free labor in the cotton-producing sections of the lower Mississippi valley also made halting progress while encountering various roadblocks. Considering the devastation the region had previously endured, plantation operations in 1864 had been considerably revitalized. The area largely avoided the bureaucratic confusion that plagued southern Louisiana (once Fessenden postponed the transfer to Treasury in August), and military authorities remained firmly in charge. Still, success in implementing new labor

---

[10] *Freedom: WGFL-LS*, 372–73; Ripley, *Slaves and Freedmen*, 73–74.
[11] *Freedom: WGFL-LS*, 572–73 (doc. 133; quotations), 573–74 (doc. 134), 617 (doc. 144).

relations remained elusive. Former slaves expressed growing dissatisfaction with plantation labor, while resident cotton planters voiced their disapproval of the new order. "I do not remember an instance, where I have been regaled by the planter with complaints of the worthlessness of his hands, in which an examination of his hands did not reveal a most thorough lack of confidence in the integrity, or want of respect for the capacity, of the planter," observed an army chaplain after inspecting conditions at Natchez, Vicksburg, and Helena. "No man," he insisted, "who sums up the result of his year's experience with the blacks in this too common formula – 'Damn the nigger,' should have the opportunity to get further experience of them."[12]

Despite the difficulties of spring planting, Col. John Eaton expressed confidence in the new arrangements. In July, he reported, only 10,000 of the more than 100,000 former slaves within his jurisdiction were receiving government support. Nearly a third of the persons drawing government aid, moreover, were the dependents of household heads who were expected to reimburse the government. More than 100,000 acres of cotton were under cultivation in Eaton's area. White plantation owners and lessees worked the bulk of it, but a small amount was being cultivated by former slaves. "Some Negroes are managing as high as 300 or 400 acres," he noted.[13]

The crop in the cotton country initially looked promising until the arrival in September of the army worm, along with poor weather. Facing financial ruin, many planters and lessees – who in the spring had complained of labor shortages – cut rations, refused to pay wages, and drove laborers and their dependents from the estates on flimsy pretexts. Military officials redoubled their vigilance, reminding planters of their contractual obligations "and informing them that they would be *compelled* to live up to their agreement," reported Col. Samuel Thomas, one of Eaton's main subordinates. "This had the desired effect, although some of the meaner sort still try to practise the old game." Many planters, in turn, complained of "the most *worthless* class of labor," in addition to other problems. "[A]lthough we are fully engaged in carrying out the free labor system," protested a group of some two dozen planters near Vicksburg that included several resident owners, "we have to make oath that we will conform to the emancipation proclamation every time we wish to obtain only a few Dollars worth of supplies." Such complaints, however legitimate, were unlikely to convince former slaves of their employers' commitment to free labor.[14]

Confederate raids and reenslavement continued to hamper plantation operations. Almost a thousand former slaves in the vicinities of Natchez,

---

[12] [Eaton], *Report of the General Superintendent*, 52, 57.
[13] *Freedom: WGFL-LS*, 647; Eaton, *Grant, Lincoln, and the Freedmen*, 133–34.
[14] [Eaton], *Report of the General Superintendent*, 35; *Freedom: WGFL-LS*, 645, 847–51 (doc. 213).

Vicksburg, and Helena, another Eaton subordinate estimated near the end of the year, had been captured and reenslaved. "The Blacks have been taken back into the interior of the States and resold into bondage," he observed. In one episode, according to the Superintendent of Freedmen at Natchez, no fewer than forty-four former slaves were taken from a single plantation "and have not been heard from since." Confederate raiders specifically targeted northern lessees, resident owners working under Federal auspices, and independent black cultivators. "I would have entered into a contract as Government Lessee but the danger from bands of Confederate souldiers and Guerrillas was so great that I dare not incur it," claimed a resident of Crittenden County, Arkansas, who had previously taken the oath of allegiance. Other Arkansas planters told of similar woes. The situation was not helped by the abortive attempt in late 1864 to reorganize the Federal command structure and to abandon several key posts in Arkansas.[15]

These experiences heightened the former slaves' determination to seek alternatives to plantation labor. One such alternative was employment in the many woodyards that sprouted along the Mississippi River, supplying fuel for steamboats and lumber for general military purposes. "[W]oodyard labor is one of the many features of this District," reported Col. Samuel Thomas from Vicksburg, "and should be one of the most important that Freedmen industry is applied to, owing to its manifest necessity in carrying on military operations." Woodyards were operated under military auspices, often near contraband camps, as well as by private contractors and by former slaves themselves. "A grand rush was thus made by all who could gather together the material necessary for such an enterprise," Thomas further noted. "The necessity for wood has compelled us to encourage wood-yards where, for the lack of sufficient forces at our control, we were unable to protect the rights of the people," Col. John Eaton observed in his year-end report. Administering the woodyards was not without its challenges, but many of them, especially those overseen by the military and receiving the necessary protection, became thriving centers of black initiative and self-support. The woodyards could employ 12,000 former slaves within his jurisdiction, Eaton believed, and he insisted that they remain under his authority. "Though it would add specially to the burdens of my officers in charge of the Freedmen," he acknowledged, "I am confident there are no others so favorably situated to adjust this entire interest."[16]

These woodyards were often located near the cities and towns that served as beacons for former slaves seeking to escape plantation life. Despite the claims of white Southerners and Federal officials that the cities bred idleness,

---

[15] [Eaton], *Report of the General Superintendent*, 49, 62; *Freedom: WGFL-LS*, 852–53 (doc. 214).

[16] [Eaton], *Report of the General Superintendent*, 23–27.

vagrancy, crime, and other vices, they provided employment for the skilled and unskilled, men and women alike. As their populations swelled, the cities indeed developed many problems, and conditions in them were often dreadful. But they provided havens to the family members and other dependents of black soldiers stationed nearby. "Freedmen's villages" or "regimental villages" fulfilled the same purpose. "Officers of regiments are co-operating with us, in locating the families of their men in a body, on vacant lands adjoining the city, where they can labor; and yet far enough from the regimental camps to prevent the demoralization attendant upon constant intercourse," explained Samuel Thomas. "It is the only true plan to dispose of the wives and children of our soldiers," he added. "It is an injustice to those who are fighting in our armies to expose their families to murder and reenslavement on distant plantations." John Eaton also noted the "regimental villages" that were established "for the wives of soldiers, out of town where each family could have a garden and all might cultivate Regimental Gardens."[17]

So as to impose some control over these burgeoning populations, or to stem migration to the cities, military officials implemented pass systems or similarly restrictive policies. Eaton claimed that the pass systems had been designed to "assure the blacks of their freedom before the law, the same as whites," but they were often racially discriminatory. Lacking documentation or proof of employment, many former slaves found themselves hustled off to contraband camps or hired out on nearby plantations. The pass systems provoked anger and resentment wherever they were instituted, especially when black people, including free persons of color and long-time residents, were indiscriminately evicted. In one notorious episode, a military officer at Natchez issued an expulsion order so sweeping – and so objectionable – that it received attention in Congress and resulted in the approving general's resignation. For the rest of the war, the cities and towns of the lower Mississippi valley were sites of conflict between former slaves seeking security and opportunity, military officials concerned with order and discipline, and planters and white Southerners obsessed with racial and labor control.[18]

IV

The pursuit of alternatives to plantation employment, however successful, was a temporary strategy. For most former slaves, the independent cultivation of land remained the long-term goal, providing what they considered the only real foundation for substantive freedom. Landholding signified the former

---

[17] [Eaton], *Report of the General Superintendent*, 21–22 (Thomas); *Freedom: WGFL-LS*, 648, 843–47 (doc. 212; Eaton, 845); Slap, "On Duty in Memphis."

[18] *Freedom: WGFL-LS*, 649; [Eaton], *Report of the General Superintendent*, 21–22 (quotation).

slaves' internalization of such notions as acquisitive individualism and propertied independence that infused nineteenth-century US society. Yet it also reflected the mindset of an essentially rural and agricultural people who subscribed to communal conceptions of property. These conceptions were grounded in the former slaves' common experience of bondage and oppression, and they were by-products of a communitarian ethos that had provided them psychological sustenance to endure such hardship. In aspiring to own land and other productive property, the former slaves were articulating the belief that *their* labor – and not the owner's legal title – had given the land its value and legitimized their claim to it. They therefore combined American ideals with their own past in conceptualizing freedom.[19]

With Confederate raids a constant threat, most black independent cultivation took place along the Mississippi or near cities, towns, or military posts. Former slaves leased land in small plots by individual families or in larger tracts by groups who worked the land collectively and shared the proceeds of the crop. Black-cultivated land in tracts ranging from 5 to 150 acres dotted the landscape between Vicksburg and Helena. At Young's Point, on the river opposite Vicksburg, what one Federal official dubbed "these five acre men" carved out a livelihood, while further upriver "the tracts of land occupied by the blacks are larger." Of more than fifty "small agriculturalists" in one neighborhood, this same official reported, "there is not one, whom I have seen, who has not made enough to keep him comfortably alive through the winter." These cases may not have been typical, but neither were they exceptional. "Many [former slaves] in the State have this year cultivated for themselves little patches, and even hundreds of acres," a Federal official in Arkansas similarly reported. He added that "tens of acres could be rented, as well as hundreds," save that "the great plantations of the old regime are scarce ever broken." Many other former slaves squatted on abandoned or unimproved acreage further inland from the Mississippi. Their willingness to risk reenslavement by inhabiting remote areas spoke volumes of the former slaves' determination to achieve propertied independence.[20]

---

[19] In addition to the sources cited, this discussion of black aspirations for land rests on the scholarly literature for the lower Mississippi valley and the South at large. Important older works that focused on the origins of sharecropping include Davis, *Good and Faithful Labor*; Ransom and Sutch, *One Kind of Freedom*; and Wayne, *Reshaping of Plantation Society*. Recent works on black understandings of property, family, and household life, and their implications for the black community, both before and after emancipation, include Penningroth, *Claims of Kinfolk*, and Holt, *Making Freedom Pay*. On the Mississippi Delta in particular, see Bercaw, *Gendered Freedoms*; Willis, *Forgotten Time*; Cobb, *Most Southern Place on Earth*. On collectively owned "heir land" in the black community after emancipation, see Nathans, *A Mind to Stay*.

[20] [Eaton], *Report of the General Superintendent*, 37–38, 49–50 ("five acre"), 73 (Arkansas); *Freedom: WGFL-LS*, 645–46, 873–77 (doc. 222B), 864n; Moneyhon, *Impact of the Civil War and Reconstruction on Arkansas*, 145–49, and "From Slave to Free Labor."

The former slaves' advocates proclaimed the advantages of independent cultivation over wage labor on the plantations. Much of John Eaton's year-end report for 1864 amounted to a call for black proprietorship, but he was not alone. "While the laborers on the large plantations have not essentially improved their condition, the colored lessees have improved theirs," reported the Chaplain of the Post at Helena. "All of the colored lessees have made more than a living, and will be ready to begin another year with capital that will enable them to work to better advantage than in the past." These independent black cultivators generally preferred subsistence or truck farming, supplemented by hunting, fishing, and other activities, while avoiding cotton production. Yet with prices so high, even small amounts of cotton could provide former slaves the capital necessary to purchase land, draft animals, and other resources. Many former slaves thus viewed small-scale cotton cultivation as an essential first step toward propertied independence. "I respectfully make application for permission from the General Comd,g to Ship to W. W. Orme, at Memphis Tenn, the following Cotton owned by Freedpeople (colored)," the Superintendent of Freedmen at Helena wrote in early 1865. He listed a total of thirty-four bales of cotton, in lots of three to ten, owned by some fifty former slaves, including at least twelve women, in groups numbering between two and seventeen. The application, which was approved, was one of several made at around the time on behalf of former slaves in the Helena area, which in turn were among hundreds of others from throughout the lower Mississippi valley.[21]

Among the most salient examples of black independent cultivation in the lower Mississippi valley was the settlement at Davis Bend, Mississippi, the distinct community south of Vicksburg that included the estates of Jefferson Davis, his brother Joseph E. Davis, and other prominent slaveholders. As a result of the Federal incursions of 1862, including a June raid that destroyed the Davis brothers' plantations, the previously tight-knit community lay in ruins. By early 1863, however, a number of slaves who had evaded the forced migration into the Mississippi interior with Joseph Davis were working the places on their own account. Impressed with the residents' initiative under trying circumstances, Admiral David Porter took the community under his wing and provided sustenance and protection amidst the Vicksburg campaign. After the fall of Vicksburg, many Davis Bend slaves who had been forced away returned, while ever-larger numbers of fugitive slaves sought refuge among them. Overcrowding and its attendant problems soon set in. Acting under orders from General Ulysses S. Grant to transform the Davis lands into a "negro paradise," Col. John Eaton assumed responsibility for the community,

---

[21] *Freedom: WGFL-LS*, 646, 861–64 (doc. 217; quotation, 862); 877–78 (doc. 223; petition); [Eaton], *Report of the General Superintendent*, 59–60. William W. Orme was the supervising agent of the Treasury Department's Second Special Agency.

which he turned over to his subordinate, Col. Samuel Thomas. By the end of 1863, Thomas had imposed a measure of order and stability over the area.[22]

For 1864, Thomas hoped to recast Davis Bend by leasing small plots of land to black cultivators, with the Federal government providing the necessary supplies on credit, along with military protection, and northern missionaries and other reformers offering guidance and stewardship. Thomas's leasing plan, however, was hampered by the bureaucratic wrangling between War and Treasury Department officials. In addition, General William T. Sherman's Meridian expedition of February brought in a large influx of refugees, as did the spring Red River campaign. Thomas hired out able-bodied freed persons to local planters and northern lessees, alleviating the overcrowding, but many were disgruntled over the lowering of their monthly wages that resulted from the suspending of Treasury official William P. Mellen's original program. To complicate matters further, Treasury Department officials leased large portions of Davis Bend lands to northern investors or returned them to ostensibly loyal owners, leaving much of the land initially intended for black cultivation under white control.[23]

Even so, Col. Thomas in late March secured a 500-acre tract of Jefferson Davis's plantation for use as a "home farm" for the indigent, and another 2,000 acres of Davis Bend land for exclusive black cultivation. The home farm would provide sustenance to almost a thousand former slaves in 1864, while some seventy black farmers worked plots of up to 150 acres each. In general, the former residents of Davis Bend fared better than the new arrivals. The agent of a northern freedmen's aid association reported in April that "the slaves of the Estate" on one Davis Bend plantation occupied "neat and comfortable houses" and were "generally well supplied," whereas the recent refugees – consisting largely of women, children, and the elderly, since the able-bodied men had been conscripted into the military – resided in "wretched shanties or sheds" that were "not fit to shelter cattle in during a storm." This same official feared that disease would ravage the community, and indeed sickness, especially smallpox, took a fearsome toll on old residents and new arrivals alike.[24]

Overcoming these and other difficulties, the Davis Bend residents fashioned an independent livelihood. "Two thousand acres are cultivated by negro lessees, supplied with material by the Government, and under the control of the Superintendent of Freedmen," Samuel Thomas reported in mid-1864. "These lessees are as far advanced with their work, are as industrious and have as good a prospect of succeeding as the white lessees around them."

---

[22] *Freedom: WGFL-LS*, 647–48, 746–49 (doc. 182); Hermann, *Pursuit of a Dream*, 46 (quotation). In addition to the cited material, this discussion of Davis Bend is based on Hermann, *Pursuit of a Dream*, chap. 2; Currie, *Enclave*, 83–107; and Ross, "Freed Soil, Freed Labor, Freed Men."

[23] *Freedom: WGFL-LS*, 811–13 (doc. 200); Hermann, *Pursuit of a Dream*, 49–50.

[24] *Freedom: WGFL-LS*, 821–24 (doc. 205).

Demonstrating far more drive than wage laborers, the black farmers eventually produced sufficient crops to get them through the winter of 1864–5, despite the losses caused by the army worm. Even the home farm residents were self-supporting. "The success of this enterprise has created quite a desire, on the part of the colored people in this city [Vicksburg] to go into such a colony next year," Thomas reported in late 1864. "The more intelligent part of the Negro population are beginning to see the immense advantages of such a scheme," he explained, "and are engaged in organizing a colony, which proposes to take at least one thousand acres, divide it on the plan adopted this year, build their houses, secure the land for one year certainly, and, if possible, a[s]sure vested title to it." The project "promises success," Thomas concluded, "and if carried out will be done by Negroes entirely, under the direction of the proper authorities."[25]

Thomas and the former slaves got their wish, and the Davis Bend experiment was significantly expanded for 1865. In early November 1864, Thomas and Eaton prevailed upon General Napoleon J. T. Dana, commander of the Department of Mississippi, to set aside the entire Davis Bend site for the "colonization, residence, and support of freedmen," and to prohibit any white person to reside there without military permission. Armed with the necessary authority, Capt. Gaylord B. Norton, the Superintendent of Freedmen at Davis Bend, in early 1865 established rules and regulations for the area. Jefferson Davis's estate was designated a "Government Farm," and the rest of the lands would be divided and worked by "companies" of between three and twenty-five laborers. Each company would elect a "head," who would conduct all business on its behalf, and land would be allocated based on the number of laborers in each company. All companies and their members would have to register, and each member would share in the company's expenses and profits. Several companies would be grouped into "colonies," under the supervision of a military Superintendent, "whose duty will be to see that every company in his colony work their ground in the proper manner," and to whose authority "all companies and people living within his colony will be subject." The Government Farm was reserved for the indigent and the employment of able-bodied individuals who did not belong to companies, and who would receive pay and rations. Refusal to work, neglect of duties, theft, vagrancy, and idleness were strictly prohibited, and "all crimes and disobedience of orders" would be punished "according to the nature of the offence."[26]

Not that such strictures were necessary. Davis Bend was soon a self-regulating community, much as it had been before the war. Nearly 200 companies would be organized for the 1865 crop season. The residents elected

---

[25] *Freedom: WGFL-LS*, 834–42 (doc. 209; quotation, 837); [Eaton], *Report of the General Superintendent*, 41.
[26] *OR*, ser. 1, vol. 41, pt. 4, 437–38; *Freedom: WGFL-LS*, 867–69 (doc. 220).

a "sheriff" for each plantation, organized a system of courts and tribunals that heard complaints and adjudicated cases, and established an education system overseen by a board of directors. Later in the year, after the war had ended, a number of black lessees forwarded a plan for ginning, baling, and marketing their own cotton outside of military authority. (Samuel Thomas would reject the proposal, resulting in a dispute that festered well into 1866.) Davis Bend had hardly been a typical community, either before or during the war. Yet it highlighted the challenges that former slaves had to overcome in gaining access to land while illustrating the communitarian spirit that imbued their strivings for propertied independence.

Davis Bend continued as an independent black cooperative into the Reconstruction era. Before his death in 1870, Joseph Davis sold his plantation to his former trusted slave, Benjamin Montgomery, who led the community. Yet Jefferson Davis relentlessly fought to regain control of the family's estates, including Joseph's. By the early 1880s, with the community struggling financially and Reconstruction having ended, Davis had succeeded, and the Davis Bend experiment came to an end. A few residents would remain, but most eventually left – individually, in small groups, or as part of the "Exodus" to Kansas. In the late 1880s, a significant number of residents and their descendants, under the leadership of Benjamin Montgomery's sons Isaiah and Thornton, abandoned Davis Bend and founded a settlement at Mound Bayou, in northwestern Mississippi, which would survive as an autonomous black community well into the twentieth century. It still exists today as an incorporated city.[27]

V

As the many refugees who flocked to Davis Bend demonstrated, enslaved persons in Confederate-held parts of the lower Mississippi valley and the western theater in general, having yet to gain their freedom, continued to force the issue. They were determined to liberate themselves and their loved ones and to bring the system of slavery down. The fugitives who streamed into areas under Federal control came from somewhere, and the historical record is replete with instances of slaves trekking tens if not hundreds of miles – enduring incredible hardship – to gain freedom. As they had done from the moment Union troops first arrived in 1862, the slaves fueled what Steven Hahn suggests was "the greatest slave rebellion in modern history." Risking brutal punishment and even death if caught, enslaved persons seeking freedom often undertook multiple attempts to achieve their goal. Some brought family members with them; others made the heart-rending decision to leave them

---

[27] Hermann, *Pursuit of a Dream*, chaps. 6–7. On Jefferson Davis's efforts to have his family's lands restored, see Cooper, *Jefferson Davis*, 572–73, 587, 603–4, 628–31.

behind. Even when they reached their destination, there were no guarantees that freedom was permanent, and reenslavement always remained a possibility. So too did death behind Union lines, as Jim Downs and other historians have demonstrated, from disease, exposure to the elements, malnutrition, and mistreatment. Yet the slaves in Confederate-held areas – having long-since been *declared* free – braved all of these dangers to make freedom a reality.[28]

The slaves who remained behind also further accelerated the destruction of slavery. Throughout the war, slaves in Confederate-held areas had, in whatever limited ways they could, challenged their masters' authority, thereby helping to undermine the master–slave relationship and slavery itself. As it became increasingly clear through the second half of 1864 that the rebellion was doomed and that Confederate authority was disintegrating, slavery collapsed further. Individual masters in many instances still exerted supreme power – including decisions of life and death – over their slaves. But with the public authority that was always essential to slavery crumbling, the slaves became increasingly bold, in ways both subtle and not-so-subtle, in defying that power. Some observers complained of slaves in Confederate-held areas virtually considering themselves free. The forced migration of thousands of slaves into the Confederate interior wreaked havoc in the receiving communities, weakening slavery even in areas that had remained relatively unscathed by war. So long as Confederate authority, however compromised, continued to exist, and so long as Confederate armies remained in the field, slavery's destruction could not be taken for granted. Yet the absence of slaves who had taken flight, never to return, along with the unavoidable signs of Confederate military defeat, corroded the master's authority over those slaves who remained.[29]

[28] Hahn, *Political Worlds of Slavery and Freedom*, chap. 2; Downs, *Sick from Freedom*. The recent work on various aspects of emancipation by Thavolia Glymph, Stephanie McCurry, Chandra Manning, Joseph P. Reidy, and Amy Murrell Taylor offers much evidence of enslaved persons – in the South at large but especially in the lower Mississippi valley – enduring harrowing experiences to gain freedom. Glymph, *The Women's Fight*, chaps. 3, 7; McCurry, *Women's War*, chap. 2; Manning, *Troubled Refuge*, chaps. 2–3; Reidy, *Illusions of Emancipation*; Taylor, *Embattled Freedom*, esp. chap. 4.

[29] Kate Stone's diary, for instance, provides copious evidence of the unraveling of slavery in northwestern Louisiana and Texas, where Stone, along with her family and their slaves, had taken refuge from mid-1863 through the end of the war. Even Stone's assurances to herself of the slaves' docility acknowledged the vulnerability of the regime. During a sojourn to Monroe, Louisiana, well behind Confederate lines, in September and October 1864, Stone observed: "The Paternal Government at Washington has done all in its power to incite a general insurrection throughout the South, in the hopes of thus getting rid of the women and children in one grand holocaust. We would be practically helpless should the Negroes rise, since there are so few men left at home. It is only because the Negroes do not want to kill us that we are still alive. The Negroes have behaved well, far better than anyone anticipated. They have not shown themselves revengeful, have been most biddable, and in many cases have been the only mainstay of their owners."

Still, there was no mistaking the opposition of former slaveholders in Union-held areas to emancipation or their determination to reestablish labor and racial control. If the abolition of slavery in Arkansas and Louisiana and its effective demise in Tennessee and Mississippi had failed to convince the large majority of planters that voluntary labor and plantation agriculture were compatible, then so too had northern lessees' different ideas about labor (if not race) and the grudging accommodation of some resident planters to the new order. Cotton planters did not operate under the same unforgiving environmental limitations as their sugar-planting brethren, but the geographical extent of the cotton-producing sections of the lower Mississippi valley precluded the planters there from unifying to the same degree as had the sugar planters in dealing with Federal authorities. Nonetheless, the cotton planters were as fixated on regaining control over labor, and as certain that former slaves would not work without compulsion, as were the planters of southern Louisiana – and everywhere else.

Perhaps the most striking evidence of this mindset were the reports in late 1864 of planters in the lower Mississippi valley moving into the interior with the intent of reenslaving their former slaves. These actions, by individual civilians, were distinct from those of Confederate raiders, and news of them drew the attention of General Edward R. S. Canby, commander of much of the lower Mississippi valley. In an early-December report to Secretary of War Edwin M. Stanton, on "the plantation system in the valley of the Mississippi in its relations to the military occupation and military operations," Canby regarded securing the plantations as "second [in importance] only to the measures that are necessary for the suppression of the rebellion." He expressed special concern over the many resident planters who had ostensibly consented to the new social order but whose goal was to preserve the old one. "A large part of the original planters who accepted the conditions imposed by the Government," Canby insisted, did so "with the expectation that our occupation of the country would be temporary, and that they would be able, in the end, to secure not only their plantations but their slaves." These planters, "disappointed in their expectations of seeing the valley reoccupied by the rebels, have left, or are preparing leave, for points within the rebel lines[,] taking the negroes with them for the purpose of reducing them again into a state of slavery."[30]

Even before receiving Stanton's response, which advised him to do everything in his power, short of compromising military operations, to protect the plantations, Canby in mid-December issued an order to address the problem. He had received information, "entitled to credit," his order read, "that many of

---

However unintentionally, Stone attested to what scholars have come to recognize as the slaves' *historical agency*. Anderson, *Brokenburn*, 297–98 (September 5, 1864).

[30] *Freedom: WGFL-LS*, 864–66 (doc. 218).

the original planters on and near the Mississippi River, who are now cultivating their plantations [under Federal auspices], are making arrangements to sell their property and move into the interior, taking the negroes with them," in order to reenslave them. Local commanders were therefore ordered "to exercise a careful supervision" over plantations within their jurisdictions. "[W]henever there is satisfactory evidence of intention on the part of any planter, either from disposition or under the constraint of the rebel authorities, to take the negroes now on their plantations beyond the control of the national authorities," for the purpose of reducing them to slavery, local commanders were directed to ensure that the persons so endangered were "brought to a place of safety within the national lines" and remanded to the care of the proper officials. Commanders were also enjoined to prevent the freed people from being defrauded of their wages and other compensation. Even were the reports exaggerated, they were not complete fabrication, and military authorities were being put on alert.[31]

By late 1864, Lincoln had won reelection, the Confederacy's demise was a foregone conclusion, several states had abolished slavery, and Congress was preparing to pass the abolition amendment. Yet former slaveholders in the lower Mississippi valley were attempting to hold onto their slaves and preserve what they could of the *ancièn régime*. Some of them acted from Confederate compulsion, but others did so, as Canby put it, "from disposition." This was a disposition to cling to slavery as though their lives depended on it, and to view slavery not as a "necessary evil" but as a divinely ordained institution and as the "cornerstone" of a civilization worth killing and dying for. However delusional these actions seem in hindsight, they demonstrate that some slaveholders at the time did not consider the end of slavery to be imminent. The former slaves may have been resolved "never again to be reduced to slavery," but former slaveholders were equally determined – somehow, some way – to salvage the principle of property in man. "The hands, from which the President's Proclamation has released them, are still clutching after them," observed one of John Eaton's subordinates. "Though the fury of the beast, which has had its appetite sharpened by a taste of blood, and been deprived of its prey, be subdued into cajolery and deceit; it still keeps its eye on its victim."[32]

---

[31] *OR*, ser. 1, vol. 41, pt. 4, 828.
[32] [Eaton], *Report of the General Superintendent*, 73. On the purchasing and selling of slaves, and the remanding of fugitives, in southwestern Arkansas, which remained under Confederate control until the war ended, see Poe, "Contours of Emancipation," 109–30, esp. 125.

PART IV

The Destruction of Slavery, 1865

18

"The Tyrants Rod Has Been Broken"

By the end of 1864, both the rebellion and slavery were entering into their death throes, yet the consequences of their demise remained far from certain. Fresh from his electoral victory, Abraham Lincoln in early December recommended that the House of Representatives pass the Federal abolition amendment now rather than waiting for another year. Lincoln and congressional Republicans also appeared ready to strike a deal over Reconstruction legislation, with the military suppression of the rebellion only a matter of time. However, the prospective compromise on Reconstruction had fallen apart by mid-January over black civil rights and Louisiana's reconstructed government. The struggle for racial equality in Louisiana, moreover, fueled criticism of a free-state government that was committed to white supremacy. It also solidified the alliance between the former free people of color, the former slaves, and the (white) free-state radicals.

In Tennessee, the catastrophic defeat in mid-December of one of the last Confederate military initiatives of the entire war – the Franklin–Nashville campaign – allowed free-state Unionists finally to move toward organizing a civilian government and abolishing slavery. By mid-January, a state convention in Nashville, although meeting under irregular circumstances and highly contentious, had effectively achieved those goals. "Thank God that the tyrants rod has been broken," Military Governor Andrew Johnson justifiably exclaimed to Lincoln. Yet an appeal by black petitioners to the convention for equality before the law and black suffrage fell on deaf ears, and Tennessee's new constitution – as was the case in Louisiana and Arkansas – guaranteed neither of these rights.

The one thing all Republicans agreed on was the abolition of slavery. By early 1865, Lincoln and Congress had been dealing with the question of state restoration for nearly three years and the Federal abolition amendment for just over one. Though hardly an afterthought when first introduced into Congress, the amendment had originally been envisioned not as a stand-alone measure but rather as part of a legislative package, combined with Reconstruction legislation, that would address the rebellion's many consequences. With Reconstruction legislation having stalled, however, the House of Representatives at the end of January passed the abolition amendment by the necessary two-thirds majority.

Paradoxically, the Republican failure to enact a Reconstruction bill – a matter that Federal military success in the lower Mississippi valley in early 1862 had initially forced Congress to address – would help to transform the amendment into the *pièce de résistance* of the destruction of slavery.

I

As the Thirty-Eighth Congress reconvened in early December 1864, Abraham Lincoln was in a commanding position. He had just won reelection, and the Confederacy's demise was imminent. Yet Republicans also faced an uphill fight in securing the fruits of victory. In addition to the Federal abolition amendment, which Lincoln wanted passed, Congress also had to deal with a Reconstruction bill, the seating of Louisiana's recently elected claimants, and the proposed Federal "bureau of emancipation." As Lincoln delivered what proved to be his last Annual Message, the "short" congressional session, which would adjourn in early March, included an ambitious legislative agenda. But Lincoln and congressional Republicans were generally expected to overcome their divisions on matters relating to Reconstruction.

"The war continues," Lincoln pronounced in the document's concluding section, insisting that the Union side was determined to achieve final victory. Turning to Reconstruction, he applauded ongoing initiatives in the lower Mississippi valley and elsewhere, though admitting that they had encountered difficulties. About 12,000 citizens "in each of the States of Arkansas and Louisiana have organized loyal State governments with free constitutions, and are earnestly struggling to maintain and administer them," he observed, adding that similar movements, "though less definite," in Missouri, Kentucky, and Tennessee "should not be overlooked." Lincoln then hinted that his Reconstruction policy might change once the fighting ended. Referring to the ten-percent plan, he noted that "the door has been, for a full year, open to all," but that "the time may come – probably will come – when public duty shall demand that it be closed; and that, in lieu, more rigorous measures than heretofore shall be adopted."

Although the meaning of "more rigorous measures" was destined to remain a mystery, owing to his later assassination, Lincoln made it crystal clear that he wanted the Federal abolition amendment passed during the current session. The recent elections had ensured that approval by the next House (not scheduled to convene until December 1865) was inevitable. Thus, he asked rhetorically, "may we not agree that the sooner the better?" Conveniently ignoring Republicans' avoidance of the amendment during the campaign, Lincoln contended that the election had expressed the popular will, which "is most clearly declared in favor of such constitutional amendment." Lincoln then closed his Annual Message with the familiar refrains that he would neither retract nor modify the Emancipation Proclamation, and that no person freed during the war would be reenslaved. Although Lincoln had comingled state restoration and the amendment as part of his discussion of Reconstruction, his comments further added to the thinking that the amendment was coming to supersede state restoration.[1]

Despite Lincoln's urging, Ohio Radical James M. Ashley, sponsor of the amendment in the House, decided for various reasons not to hold debate on the amendment until January. Instead, Ashley, as a member of Henry Winter Davis's select committee on the rebellious states, turned again to Reconstruction legislation. In mid-December, he put forward a bill that offered the possibility of compromise with Lincoln on the Louisiana government and on black suffrage and civil rights. Ashley's new bill invalidated all state laws regarding involuntary servitude under the provisional governments and immediately "emancipated and discharged therefrom" all persons held to such servitude, declaring "they and their posterity shall be forever free." The new constitutions must also prohibit involuntary servitude "forever" and guarantee the freedom of all persons in the state. To begin state reorganization, the bill required a majority of each state's adult male citizens to swear allegiance. But in calling for the enrollment of "all male citizens" of the United States as voters and jurors, and in providing that delegates to the state constitutional conventions "shall be elected by the loyal male citizens," Ashley's bill, by excluding the essential qualifier "white," mandated black suffrage. The bill also required racial equality in all laws pertaining to trial and punishment. In return for Lincoln's endorsement of these measures, Congress would recognize the Louisiana government, which provided for neither of them, and readmit that state to the Union.[2]

Although Ashley's latest bill had evidently been the product of an understanding between Lincoln and congressional Republicans, Lincoln still expressed reservations. When Nathaniel Banks, who continued to lobby Congress on behalf of the Louisiana government, visited with Lincoln on December 18, Lincoln informed him, according to John Hay, that he liked the bill "with the exception of one or two things which he thought rather calculated to conceal a feature which might be objectionable to some." The first was the enrollment of black men as voters and jurors. (Lincoln cagily indicated here not that *he* opposed this provision but that "some" might.) Evidently speaking from authority, Banks reassured Lincoln that the qualifier "white" would be restored, else the bill "would simply throw the Government into the

---

[1] *CWL*, 8: 148–52; Vorenberg, *Final Freedom*, 177–78.
[2] *CG*, 38th Cong., 2nd Sess., 52–53 (December 15, 1864; Davis), 53–54 (December 15; Ashley); *CG*, 38th Cong., 2nd Sess., H.R. 602 (December 15, 1864); Vorenberg, *Final Freedom*, 176–80; Masur, *Lincoln's Hundred Days*, 137; Belz, *Reconstructing the Union*, 251–52; Richards, *Who Freed the Slaves?*, chap. 6, 221–24.

hands of the blacks, as the white people under that arrangement would refuse to vote." Lincoln's second objection concerned the bill's emancipation provision, especially "the declaration that all persons heretofore held in slavery are declared free." Lincoln had always questioned Congress's authority to emancipate slaves, and he again objected to legislation that would have emancipated slaves in areas, such as Tennessee, to which the Emancipation Proclamation had not applied and in which slavery still legally existed. Lincoln did not oppose Congress's sanctioning the freedom of persons whom executive action had emancipated, but Ashley's bill would have applied to *all* slaves in the seceded states – including those whom the proclamation had excluded. This was unacceptable.[3]

Otherwise, Lincoln and Banks "spoke very favorably" of Ashley's bill, Hay continued. Indeed, aside from its emancipation and black suffrage provisions, Ashley's new bill equated to a revised Wade–Davis bill that recognized Louisiana's government. Banks allowed as much. "He regards [the bill] as merely concurring in the Presidents own action in the one important case of Louisiana and recommending an observance of the same policy in other cases," again according to Hay. Lincoln had already endorsed limited black suffrage, and he had objected to the Wade–Davis bill because it would have invalidated his Louisiana and Arkansas governments, which had already abolished slavery. Lincoln and Banks also acknowledged that the bill laid down no "cast iron policy" but instead allowed flexibility in readmitting the other seceded states, another of Lincoln's requirements. With the Ashley bill, Banks believed, Congress was asserting its role in Reconstruction, which it had every right to do. He therefore thought it best not "to make a fight" over the bill – aside from the two points at issue. Doing so might squander "the positive gain" of a congressional endorsement of Lincoln's policy by readmitting Louisiana, along with the state's vote in ratifying the abolition amendment.[4]

Soon after this meeting, on December 20, Ashley incorporated the two changes Lincoln had requested – or almost. For enrollment and voting, the qualifier "white" was restored, save that citizens "in the military or naval service of the United States" would also be included. Black veterans in the seceded states other than Louisiana would thus gain the right to vote. The bill likewise restricted freedom to persons "who have been declared free by any proclamation of the President," though it reaffirmed that "they and their posterity shall be forever free." Otherwise, it was the same bill. During the holiday recess, both the abolition amendment and the Reconstruction bill were hotly debated in northern political circles. The administration's campaign to

---

[3] Charles Sumner, for example, believed an "arrangement" had been reached between Lincoln and congressional Republicans on Reconstruction. Palmer, *Selected Letters of Charles Sumner*, 2: 258–59. Historians generally agree.
[4] Burlingame and Ettlinger, *Inside Lincoln's White House*, 252–54 (December 18).

secure votes for the amendment is well known, but Lincoln was only slightly less vexed over Louisiana. "The Presdt. is exerting every force to bring Congress to receive Louisiana under her Banks govt.," Charles Sumner wrote. Although deeply suspicious of that government, Sumner was willing to recognize it for a guarantee of black political and legal equality in the other seceded states. Henry Winter Davis also complained of administration arm-twisting on Louisiana, but when Congress reconvened in January, the fates of both the amendment and the Reconstruction bill were uncertain.[5]

There also remained the seating of Louisiana's members-elect. Congress had refused to seat the Arkansas claimants during the previous session, but Louisiana had since ratified its free-state constitution and elected members to both houses. Of the five House claimants, three, including A. P. Field, were thought to have legitimate chances. Field had previously claimed a seat as a result of the conservative Unionists' elections in November 1863, but he had been denied. Now, the Louisiana House claimants pledged to vote for the abolition amendment, something Banks undoubtedly used in his lobbying efforts. Charles Sumner even seemed to think that the state would provide its five votes for the amendment. In the Senate, R. King Cutler and Charles Smith were thought to have stronger cases than William Fishback and Elisha Baxter of Arkansas. Even as the Louisiana claimants presented their credentials, both houses received the memorial, drawn up in November by Thomas J. Durant and the Louisiana radicals, urging Congress to reject the state's government. In yet another sign of possible compromise, however, the cases were immediately referred to their respective house committees, thus avoiding a needless fight – at least at this point – over the government's legitimacy.[6]

II

Even as Congress deliberated on various matters pertaining to Reconstruction, political affairs remained unsettled in Arkansas and contentious in Louisiana. Confederate guerrilla activity proliferated in the former state, which still reeled from the abortive attempt in late 1864 to reorganize the Federal military command. With the Federal military, now under General Joseph Reynolds,

---

[5] *CG*, 38th Cong., 2nd Sess., H.R. 602, as amended (December 20, 1864); *CG*, 38th Cong., 2nd Sess., 53 (December 15, 1864; introduction of bill), 81 (December 20, 1864; committee reports); Palmer, *Selected Letters of Charles Sumner*, 2: 261–64; Belz, *Reconstructing the Union*, 254–58; McCrary, *Abraham Lincoln and Reconstruction*, 289–90; Benedict, *Compromise of Principle*, 90–91; Masur, *Lincoln's Hundred Days*, 138. For other Sumner commentary casting doubt on the Louisiana government, see Palmer, *Selected Letters of Charles Sumner*, 2: 269–75, 279.

[6] Butler and Wolff, *United States Senate Election*, 121–23; McCrary, *Abraham Lincoln and Reconstruction*, 298. On the Louisiana delegation's promise to support the amendment, see Palmer, *Selected Letters of Charles Sumner*, 2: 259.

furnishing limited assistance to Isaac Murphy's struggling government, the consequences of abolition were not high on the agenda when the legislature reconvened in early November. Just before adjourning in late December, the legislature elected William D. Snow to the US Senate to replace the controversial William M. Fishback, whom the Senate had refused to seat and whose term would end in March, when Congress adjourned. (Snow was elected to the Thirty-Ninth Congress, which would not meet until December 1865.) Snow's election was thought to improve the Arkansas government's chances of gaining congressional recognition.[7]

In Louisiana, by contrast, the various interested parties maintained their own spirited debate over abolition's consequences. Despite Banks's extended absence, "the Banks oligarchy" pushed for recognition of the Louisiana government, while the radicals, led by Thomas J. Durant, maintained their steadfast opposition. The New Orleans free black community remained divided over the distinct but interrelated questions of, first, whether to boycott the Louisiana government entirely, and, second, whether to petition the legislature for limited or unrestricted black suffrage.[8]

These tensions within the black community were reflected at the founding convention, held in New Orleans during January 9–14, of the Louisiana chapter of the National Equal Rights League (NERL). Following the NERL's formation in Syracuse the previous October, black leaders in New Orleans began planning for a state convention, with James H. Ingraham, who attended the Syracuse meeting, assuming a central role. Born a slave in Mississippi in 1833 but manumitted when still young, Ingraham had served as a lieutenant in the Louisiana Native Guards and participated in the May 1863 assault at Port Hudson. Although later promoted to captain and a survivor of Banks's purge of black officers, Ingraham resigned his commission in early 1864 to focus on the struggle for racial equality. The NERL in theory represented all of Union-held Louisiana, but in reality the roughly 100 convention delegates hailed overwhelmingly from New Orleans. The most important issue before the convention, over which Ingraham presided as president, was whether to petition the state legislature for the right to vote. Implicit in this question was whether to advocate universal or limited black suffrage, since Louisiana's constitution only allowed for enfranchising black men who met property or literacy requirements. Some delegates called for

---

[7] Moneyhon, *Impact of the Civil War and Reconstruction on Arkansas*, 168–69; DeBlack, *With Fire and Sword*, 107–8, 136–39; Harris, *With Charity for All*, 210–11; Butler and Wolff, *United States Senate Election*, 117–20; *Journal of the Convention of Delegates*, 264 (December 30, 1864).

[8] McCrary, *Abraham Lincoln and Reconstruction*, 293–96; Ripley, *Slaves and Freedmen*, 178; Tunnell, *Crucible of Reconstruction*, 81–83 (quotation, 81).

petitioning the legislature to enact universal (male) suffrage even though it lacked the power to do so.⁹

The opponents of petitioning the legislature held a clear majority, though the proponents made up a sizable minority. A special committee initially submitted a divided report in which the majority *supported* petitioning, arguing that the NERL should petition the state government before appealing to Congress. The convention vehemently debated the report, with Ingraham leading the opponents. At length, the convention rejected the committee report by a decisive majority, but the petitioners continued to press the issue. The convention adjourned without reaching a decision, and the local chapters continued the debate. The petition advocates eventually prevailed – in a manner of speaking. On February 17 – by which point the prospects for congressional recognition of Louisiana had lessened dramatically – a propetition supporter in the state Senate introduced a petition, with some 5,000 signatures, calling for black suffrage. The petition was accepted and referred to committee but would ultimately produce no action. Adding insult to injury, another senator immediately introduced a resolution thanking Nathaniel Banks, the man most responsible for the current government, "for the untiring devotion and friendly spirit he has evinced for the loyal people of Louisiana in his indefatigable efforts to counteract the wilful misrepresentations of our enemies, who have tried every means in their power to defeat the restoration of the Union, the recognition of our State and the admission of our Representatives and Senators in Congress." There was no mistaking Durant and the radicals as the resolution's intended targets.¹⁰

Whereas black suffrage revealed tensions within the black community, the social and economic consequences of emancipation helped to overcome the "alienation" between the free-black elite and the former slaves. Devoting itself to what one historian has called "the moral, educational, and industrial development of the black community," the Louisiana NERL tirelessly advocated for the former slaves' economic independence, and, through the New Orleans *Tribune*, relentlessly criticized Banks's plantation-labor system. In late 1864, the *Tribune* began encouraging influential members of the New Orleans black community to form associations that would purchase abandoned plantations for former slaves to work on a cooperative basis. In addition to profiting investors and instilling in the former slaves the virtues of voluntary labor, the

---

[9] Foner and Walker, *Proceedings of the Black State Conventions*, 2: 242–53; Houzeau, *My Passage at the New Orleans* Tribune, 96–97n; Tunnell, *Crucible of Reconstruction*, 74–75; Ripley, *Slaves and Freedmen*, 178–79; Hollandsworth, *Louisiana Native Guards*, 77–78; McCrary, *Abraham Lincoln and Reconstruction*, 296.

[10] Houzeau, *My Passage at the New Orleans* Tribune, 97, 99n; Tunnell, *Crucible of Reconstruction*, 82–83; *Official Journal of the Proceedings of the Senate and House of Representatives of the State of Louisiana and the Legislative Calendar*, 153–54 (February 17, 1865).

plan would foster racial unity and uplift. By late February 1865, the New Orleans Freedmen's Aid Association had formed. Instead of purchasing plantations outright, the organization would lease and sublet them to former slaves. It would also provide various forms of assistance while appealing to northern benevolent societies for financial support. Jean Baptiste Roudanez, publisher of the *Tribune*, Oscar J. Dunn, and other black leaders belonged to the organization, as did Durant and Benjamin F. Flanders. The organization successfully leased several plantations for 1865, but the experiment did not last beyond that year, as the fate of abandoned lands in the South became embroiled in the politics of postwar Reconstruction.[11]

Relations between the old free-black elite and former slaves may have oscillated between alienation and solidarity, but the black community bristled at the condescension of even the most well-meaning members – including individuals such as Thomas W. Conway, head of the military Bureau of Free Labor – of the Banks–Hahn establishment. Throughout the winter of 1864–65, relations between the black community and the Banks oligarchy deteriorated, as the latter presumed to lecture the former on what was in its best interests. Prior to the Louisiana NERL convention in January, Hahn, Conway, and other white officials urged petitioning the legislature, and they criticized the decision not to do so. Free black leaders (even petition supporters) rejected this criticism and the paternalism on which it rested. But there still remained the question of who spoke for the black community at large. Even as free-black leaders rejected white paternalism, they sometimes exhibited a condescension of their own, arguing that they bore special responsibility for the former slaves' welfare, and laying claim, however implicitly, to racial stewardship. Nonetheless, there was by now clearly more that united the two groups than divided them.[12]

Whatever complaints the black community had about the Louisiana government, the state's political landscape was profoundly altered in January with the election of Governor Michael Hahn to the US Senate and the ascension of J. Madison Wells to governor. Hahn replaced Charles Smith, who, along with R. King Cutler, had been elected to the Senate in October, but whose term would end in March. Hahn's status as senator-elect was provisional, but he would resign as governor in early March, when the Thirty-Ninth Congress came into being. (As with William D. Snow in Arkansas, Hahn had been elected to the next Congress before the current Senate had decided whether to seat Louisiana's claimants.) Hahn's resignation made Lieutenant-Governor Wells, the loyalist refugee from Rapides Parish, the new governor. Wells had opposed secession and endured much Confederate persecution, so his

---

[11] Blassingame, *Black New Orleans*, 56–58 (quotation); Ripley, *Slaves and Freedmen*, 178–79; Tunnell, *Crucible of Reconstruction*, 84–85.
[12] Tunnell, *Crucible of Reconstruction*, 81–91.

Unionist credentials were beyond dispute. He was also a former slaveholder who had come to support abolition. Nonetheless, Wells was far more conservative than Hahn. He had endorsed compensated abolition during the 1864 constitutional convention, and he firmly opposed black suffrage. With Banks absent from the state, Wells soon began replacing Hahn appointees with his own. He was already taking the state government in a much more conservative direction by the time the war ended in the spring and former Confederates began returning home.[13]

III

In Tennessee, where Lincoln's electoral victory ensured Andrew Johnson's imminent removal from the scene, free-state Unionists now had months to accomplish goals that had evaded them for nearly three years. For Johnson to step down as military governor without having completed the state reorganization would have been a personal and political embarrassment and could possibly have jeopardized the free-state initiative. Free-state Unionists therefore intended to lose no time before Johnson assumed the vice presidency. Days after the election, east Tennessee Unionists, including William G. "Parson" Brownlow, called for a "preliminary State convention," to meet in Nashville on December 19, to nominate delegates to a *subsequent* state convention that would organize a new government and abolish slavery. Having been caught off guard, Johnson and his allies issued their own call several days later for a convention, at the same time and place, "to restore the state of Tennessee to its once honored status in the great National Union." This was a much broader objective than the east Tennesseans had advocated, and it introduced potential conflict. But by late 1864, Johnson was determined to reconstruct Tennessee posthaste.[14]

Yet as so often had happened in Tennessee, military affairs intervened one final time. The Confederate Army of Tennessee's Franklin and Nashville campaign of the late fall – itself a by-product of General William T. Sherman's Atlanta campaign – was the last major Confederate military operation in the western theater. Having replaced General Joseph E. Johnston as commander of that army in mid-July, and having subsequently abandoned Atlanta in early September, General John Bell Hood unsuccessfully attempted

---

[13] *Official Journal of the Proceedings of the Senate and House of Representatives of the State of Louisiana and the Legislative Calendar,* 119–20 (January 9, 1865); Dawson, *Louisiana Governors,* 153–57.

[14] Cimprich, "Military Governor Johnson and Tennessee Blacks" (second convention announcement); *Nashville Daily Union,* November 29, 1864; *PAJ,* 7: xxxiv–xxxvii, 314–15, 369, 371; Harris, *With Charity for All,* 223–24; Bergeron, *Andrew Johnson's Civil War and Reconstruction,* 55; Atkins, "Failure of Restoration," 312–14; Temple, *Notable Men of Tennessee,* 409–12.

to disrupt Sherman's supply lines in northwest Georgia before deciding to march his nearly 40,000 men across northern Alabama into central Tennessee, threatening Nashville, where Union General George H. Thomas was in command. On November 30, the two forces meet in the bitter but indecisive Battle of Franklin, thirty miles south of Nashville. After delaying his counterattack for two weeks (much to the frustration of the Union high command), Thomas finally inflicted a crushing defeat on Hood in the Battle of Nashville on December 15-16, destroying the Confederate Army of Tennessee as a viable fighting force. "The effect of the great victory over Hoods army at Nashville is being seen & felt in every part of the State," Andrew Johnson commended Thomas as 1864 closed. "Its withering influence upon Rebels is more decided than anything which has transpired since the beginning of the Rebellion." The site of one of the Federal military's first major successes of the war, nearly three years earlier, and the first Confederate state capital to fall, also witnessed one of the Confederacy's last and most decisive defeats.[15]

Hood's campaign had forced a postponement of the state convention, but with the military situation finally secure, more than 500 delegates – nearly half from east Tennessee – assembled in convention on January 9 in Nashville. (Coincidently, both the Louisiana NERL convention and a Missouri convention to abolish slavery met concurrently with Tennessee's.) Predictably, the body immediately split over its very purpose. Samuel Milligan, a close friend and political associate of Johnson, and on whose behalf he no doubt spoke, proposed that the assembly reconstitute itself as a constitutional convention, and that the convention, rather than rewriting the entire constitution, draft amendments that would go to the voters for approval. Milligan's proposal was deeply contentious, with a significant minority opposing it. Although Johnson's impending inauguration as vice president made holding a second convention problematic, many delegates questioned the legitimacy of refashioning themselves as a constitutional convention.[16]

For three-plus days, the convention debated the issue before Johnson broke the impasse. In a fervent address on the evening of January 12, he urged the convention to adopt Milligan's proposal. Johnson once again defended the people's right to hold a constitutional convention, even if it was not strictly legal, and he insisted that "the shortest and simplest plan" of state reorganization would be best. He recommended amending the state constitution to abolish slavery and forever prohibit the legislature to revive it, else the Federal abolition amendment "will do it for you," he reminded the audience. "Let us take the credit of this work on ourselves." Johnson – the life-long

---

[15] Hess, *Civil War in the West*, 247–58; *PAJ*, 7: 371 (quotation).
[16] Harris, *With Charity for All*, 224; Cimprich, "Military Governor Johnson and Tennessee Blacks," 115; Bergeron, *Andrew Johnson's Civil War and Reconstruction*, 53–55; Alexander, *Political Reconstruction in Tennessee*, 18–30.

opponent of racial equality – then suggested, remarkably, equality in the state's criminal code. "Control and punish the negro, then, by the same laws that you have to punish white criminals." But he rejected black suffrage and advocated apprenticeship for the former slaves, which Lincoln no longer supported. Johnson also warned against the continuing threat of proslavery Unionism. "Now there are some Union men who are for putting off any action, with a lingering hope that something will turn up to save slavery." They thereby hoped "to put off the day of emancipation," he cautioned. "Now let us cut the cord which binds him to the negro, and relieve him of the negro, and the negro of him." Doing so "will go far to put down the rebellion," he insisted. Essentially ignoring congressional debate over the Louisiana and Arkansas governments, Johnson predicted ("I will wager my head – a bold bet," he dared) that completion of this agenda would secure Tennessee's readmission.[17]

Johnson's address created "a profound sensation," according to one newspaper account. "No speech has ever been made in the Capitol which created deeper feeling." The editors of Johnson's papers suggest that it may have been his greatest accomplishment as military governor. Johnson had indeed persuaded the convention to act as a constitutional body, but the delegates took a narrow view of state reorganization. The convention approved an amendment abolishing slavery "forever" and prohibiting the legislature to enact any law "recognizing the right of property in man," but it declined to incorporate racial equality into the penal code. (Neither did it adopt apprenticeship.) Appended to the amendment was a "Schedule" of provisions that invalidated the secession ordinance and all legislative measures following therefrom, and that approved Johnson's appointments as military governor and the reorganization process. One provision abrogated the clause in the state constitution prohibiting the legislature to emancipate slaves without their owners' consent. Another authorized the first legislature that met under the amended constitution to determine voting qualifications, but that was as close as the convention came to allowing black suffrage.[18]

In addition to these measures, the convention set February 22 for a plebiscite on the amendment and the appended "Schedule," and March 4 for gubernatorial and legislative elections. Voting would be limited to persons who met the very strict qualifications used in the presidential election, thus disfranchising virtually all former Confederates. The convention nominated "Parson" Brownlow for governor, and it drew up a "general ticket" of legislative candidates that the voters would accept or reject in its entirety. It also named a three-member committee to appeal to Lincoln to declare Tennessee no longer in

---

[17] *PAJ*, 7: 392–400 (quotations, 395–96).
[18] *PAJ*, 7: xxxvi–xxxvii, 487–91 (quotations, 487–88); Alexander, *Political Reconstruction in Tennessee*, 30–31.

rebellion. Lincoln sympathized when he met with the committee in early February, but he did not grant the request.[19]

Try as it might, the convention could not avoid the question of civil rights, as black Tennesseans were determined to make their voices heard on the issue. The state NERL presented a petition to the convention, signed by more than sixty "American citizens of African descent," including many veterans, calling for the abolition of slavery and for political and legal equality. Commending the measures already undertaken "for the good work of freedom," especially the Emancipation Proclamation, the petitioners urged the convention "to complete the work begun by the nation at large, and abolish the last vestige of slavery by the express words of your organic law." Otherwise, they warned, the reenslavement of individuals and the survival of slavery as an institution remained distinct possibilities. "Many masters in Tennessee whose slaves have left them will certainly make every effort to bring them back to bondage after the reorganization of the State government, unless slavery be expressly abolished by the Constitution." Condemning their enslavement "as one of the greatest crimes in all history," the petitioners claimed freedom "as our natural right," and they pressed the convention to "cut up by the roots the system of slavery, which is not only a wrong to us, but the source of all the evil which at present afflicts the State." The petitioners also advanced various arguments, principled and practical, advocating black suffrage and equality before the law. "This is not a Democratic Government," they concluded, "if a numerous, law-abiding, industrious, and useful class of citizens, born and bred on the soil, are to be treated as aliens and enemies, as an inferior, degraded class, who must have no voice in the Government, which they support, protect and defend, with all their heart, soul, mind, and body, both in peace and war."[20]

The convention did the petitioners the courtesy of receiving the document and debating the issues it raised. A few delegates supported black suffrage, mostly out of concern that former Confederates would otherwise gain control of the state, but with Johnson, Brownlow, and other leaders opposed, it stood no chance. The convention approved the provision – similar to Louisiana's – authorizing the legislature to enact black suffrage, but such an outcome was as likely in Tennessee as it was in Louisiana or any other southern state. This action did not bode well for black civil rights at the hands of even the most loyal of southern Unionists. Other than the right not to be enslaved, which was not nothing, black Tennesseans gained no new rights under the amended constitution.[21]

---

[19] *PAJ*, 7: 453–56; Harris, *With Charity for All*, 224–25; Bergeron, *Andrew Johnson's Civil War and Reconstruction*, 55–56.
[20] *Freedom: BME*, 811–16 (doc. 362); LeForge, "State Colored Conventions of Tennessee," 234.
[21] Cimprich, "Military Governor Johnson and Tennessee Blacks," 115; *Nashville Daily Union*, January 12–18, 1865; *Chicago Tribune*, January 18, 1865; *New York Tribune*, January 24, 1865.

"The convention composed of more than five hundred delegates from all parts of the State have unanimously adopted an amendment to the constitution forever abolishing Slavery in this State and denying the power of the Legislature passing any law creating property in man," Johnson jubilantly telegrammed Lincoln on January 13. "Thank God that the tyrants rod has been broken." The amendment would go to the voters on February 22, when, Johnson confidently predicted, "the state will be redeemed and the foul blot of Slavery erased from her escutcheon." Johnson went on to express the hope that Tennessee would be excluded or exempted from James M. Ashley's Reconstruction bill, which required equality before the law and perhaps limited black suffrage as conditions for state restoration. "All is now working well and if Tennessee is now let alone will soon resume all functions of a State according to the genius and theory of Government," he insisted.[22]

"Yours announcing ordinance of Emancipation rec'd," Lincoln responded the next day. "[T]hanks to the Convention & to you." Johnson hoped to transfer power directly to the new government in April, but Lincoln wanted him in Washington for the inauguration, necessitating a new military governor. On the evening of January 14, Johnson delivered an impromptu address commending the convention for its historic accomplishment. "Let no man, then, delude himself with the dream, the vague hope, that he still holds on to slavery," Johnson proclaimed. "I feel that God smiles on what you have done, and that it meets the approbation of the hosts that surround him. O how it contrasts with the shrieks, and cries, and wailings which the institution of slavery has brought on the land!" Later in January, Johnson issued a proclamation setting the elections for February and March, as the convention prescribed, and spelling out how they would be conducted. He also applauded the convention for submitting its work to "the loyal people," whom he urged "with one voice" to approve it. "Strike down at one blow the institution of slavery – remove the disturbing element from your midst, and by united action, restore the State to its ancient moorings again," Johnson intoned, "and you may confidently expect the speedy return of peace happiness and prosperity."[23]

Tennessee became the seventh state – and the third in the lower Mississippi valley – to abolish slavery during the war. (The Missouri convention also did so.) Whereas Arkansas had rewritten its constitution in two weeks and Louisiana had required more than three months, Tennessee completed its work in a matter of days. The Tennessee convention evinced an improvised – even slap-dash – quality, having been called into being by no governmental body that possessed the necessary authority. The whole affair had been highly

---

[22] *PAJ*, 7: 404.
[23] *PAJ*, 7: 406, 407–11 (convention; quotations, 409–10), 436–38 (election proclamation); Alexander, *Political Reconstruction in Tennessee*, 31–32.

irregular at best, a usurpation at worst. Yet the Tennessee convention, as with Arkansas's, could also have been considered a spontaneous movement of the loyal (white) people to organize a new government and abolish slavery. After three long years, military emancipation had finally been transformed into constitutional abolition in Tennessee. This was no small accomplishment, but it would largely be overshadowed by the monumental effort to secure House approval of the Federal abolition amendment. As Johnson had indicated, moreover, the other conditions Congress might impose on the seceded states remained an open question.

IV

Following the holiday recess, in fact, Congress devoted much of January to the abolition amendment and Reconstruction. By the time House debate on the amendment began in earnest in early January, the national mood had shifted significantly in its favor. The Confederate national government's move toward arming its slaves underscored the absurdity of further delay on Federal abolition. State action in Tennessee and Missouri, and the debate over racial equality in Louisiana, also bolstered the amendment. Petitions from citizen groups, legislatures, and state conventions flooded Congress. Even if the amendment were gaining momentum, however, rumors of a Confederate peace mission and possible negotiations undercut Democratic support for it, as did the claim that state abolition obviated the need for Federal action, or the charge that Republicans were promoting miscegenation. Concluding that the amendment lacked the necessary support, Ashley postponed the final vote – slated for January 13 – to the end of the month. A proposal that the Tennessee convention, then in progress, elect House members, who could then vote for the amendment, came to naught.[24]

Meanwhile, Congress again addressed Reconstruction legislation. On January 7, Ashley submitted two amendments to the previous version of his bill – as of December 20 – that significantly altered it. The first explicitly required the seceded states' new constitutions to guarantee to all persons "the equality of civil rights before the law," thereby providing a much stronger affirmation of this principle. The second change, more importantly, brought Louisiana and Arkansas under the bill's provisions, whereas the previous version had excluded them. Congress would recognize these states' existing governments, provided that both states complied with the bill's requirements. Now, a *majority* of their voting populations would have to swear the loyalty oath. The new version of the bill retained the qualifier "white" for enrolling voters, but it also included black veterans in the enrollment. The new constitutions, in addition to abolishing slavery, would have to disfranchise

---

[24] Vorenberg, *Final Freedom*, 185–98; *PAJ*, 7: 404–5.

Confederate officeholders, repudiate Confederate debts, and guarantee to all persons equality before the law. Thus, the Louisiana and Arkansas constitutions – and those of the other states that had abolished slavery – would have to be revised before the states could be readmitted. Ashley's new bill, in effect, would have invalidated the Louisiana and Arkansas governments.[25]

Republicans offered various amendments to the bill during the next several days, and floor debate on January 16–17 was acrimonious. Radicals criticized the bill's limited black suffrage provisions; moderates opposed forcing all of the seceded states, including Louisiana and Arkansas, into the same rigid plan. At length, action on the bill was postponed for two weeks, despite objections that the delay would effectively kill it. Many Republicans did not consider this an unwelcome development. Few wanted an open breach with Lincoln, who was sure to veto the bill anyway, and many Republicans – moderates and Radicals alike – were happy to shelve Reconstruction until the next Congress. (In fact, the matter would come up once more before Congress adjourned.) At this point, it had become abundantly clear that the abolition amendment, which united Republicans, enjoyed better odds than did Reconstruction legislation, which divided them. Indeed, the amendment had now come to be seen as more urgent.[26]

Although the "compromise" between Lincoln and congressional Republicans on Reconstruction seemed dead, the seating of Louisiana's claimants remained possible. Even Republicans who opposed the Ashley bill might have been willing to readmit Louisiana, since it had already abolished slavery and might lend critical support to the abolition amendment. During these weeks, Nathaniel Banks continued to lobby on behalf of the Louisiana government, testifying before the House elections committee in mid-December and the Senate Judiciary Committee in early January. In his Senate testimony, Banks repeated many of the claims he had made in his dispute with Thomas J. Durant of the previous fall, though he added the implausible one that three-quarters of the state's population was now under Federal authority. Lyman Trumbull, the committee chair, forwarded a copy of Banks's testimony to Lincoln, who, familiar with Banks's propensity for overstatement, offered a qualified endorsement of it. Tellingly, Lincoln concluded his response to Trumbull by paraphrasing himself in what was becoming his catchphrase defense of the Louisiana government: "Can

---

[25] CG, 38th Cong., 2nd Sess., H.R. 602, as amended on January 7, 1865; Belz, Reconstructing the Union, 258–60; McCrary, Abraham Lincoln and Reconstruction, 290–99; Masur, Lincoln's Hundred Days, 139. For the text of the bill, as amended, see CG, 38th Cong., 2nd Sess., 280–81 (January 16, 1865).

[26] Belz, Reconstructing the Union, 260–63; Benedict, Compromise of Principle, 91–92, 96–97; Masur, Lincoln's Hundred Days, 139–40; McCrary, Abraham Lincoln and Reconstruction, 291–92.

Louisiana be brought into proper practical relations with the Union, *sooner*, by *admitting* or by *rejecting* the proposed Senators?"[27]

The Senate committee rendered a mixed verdict. On January 11, it recommended that Louisiana's claimants not be seated until Congress had formally recognized a legitimate state government. But it then affirmed that the Hahn government "fairly represents a majority of the loyal voters of the State," and it proposed recognizing that government and calling for the state's readmission. With so much other business before Congress, however, the Smith–Cutler cases were put off until mid-February. If this result was disappointing, the House cases approached the tragicomic. On January 17, the House Committee on Elections recommended seating three of Louisiana's five claimants, including A. P. Field. At a Washington hotel on the evening of January 22, however, Field slashed at Pennsylvania Representative William D. Kelley with a pocket knife in a drunken altercation over comments Kelley had made on the House floor. Kelley's wound was minor, but the political damage was irreparable. Even the promised votes for the amendment could not salvage the Louisiana House cases.[28]

By late January 1865, the House returned to the abolition amendment. Since the postponement of the vote, the administration had brought tremendous pressure to bear on House Democrats – especially the "lame-ducks" who had lost their seats in the fall election – to support the amendment, and debate has continued ever since over Lincoln's role in securing passage. As the House assembled on January 31 for the much-anticipated vote, high-ranking officials were among the spectators that packed the galleries. In the preceding days, word again circulated that Confederate peace commissioners, including Vice President Alexander Stephens, were in or near Washington, prompting Democrats to renew their protests that abolition was an obstacle to peace. Lincoln famously assured Congress that no such officials were in the nation's capital or expected to be, conveniently ignoring that he had authorized Secretary of State William H. Seward to meet with the commissioners behind Union lines in Virginia (in talks that Lincoln himself would join). During the debate, Democrats offered last-ditch proposals – as had conservatives in Arkansas, Louisiana, and other states – for gradual, compensated abolition, but Republicans brushed them aside as irrelevant. The final vote, taken amidst great drama, was 119 to 56, with 8 absences – a two-thirds majority with two votes to spare. It took a moment for the magnitude of what had happened to sink in before the House exploded into unrestrained jubilation. Almost

---

[27] *CWL*, 8: 206–7; Butler and Wolff, *United States Senate Election*, 121–23; McCrary, *Abraham Lincoln and Reconstruction*, 293; Benedict, *Compromise of Principle*, 88–90.

[28] Butler and Wolff, *United States Senate Election*, 121–23; Belz, *Reconstructing the Union*, 268–70 (quotation); McCrary, *Abraham Lincoln and Reconstruction*, 298–99; Benedict, *Compromise of Principle*, 93; Masur, *Lincoln's Hundred Days*, 141–42.

unimaginably, an amendment to the Federal Constitution forever abolishing slavery throughout the United States was going to the states for ratification.[29]

So pleased was Lincoln with the result that he (unnecessarily) signed the congressional resolution sending the amendment to the states. Calling the amendment, in public remarks, "a very fitting if not an indispensable adjunct" to the end of the war, he cautioned that much work lay ahead in securing ratification. In order to restore the Union on a permanent basis, he insisted, "it was necessary that the original disturbing cause should, if possible, be rooted out." He had done all he could "to eradicate Slavery by issuing an emancipation proclamation," but the "proclamation falls far short of what the amendment will be when fully consummated." Lincoln then highlighted the essential distinction between military emancipation and constitutional abolition. "A question might be raised whether the proclamation was legally valid. It might be added that it only aided those who came into our lines and that it was inoperative as to those who did not give themselves up, or that it would have no effect upon the children of the slaves born hereafter," he explained. "In fact it would be urged that it did not meet the evil." But the amendment was "a King's cure for all the evils," he famously concluded. "It winds the whole thing up."[30]

The amendment, of course, did no such thing. It was as much a "first" as a "final" freedom, and it would raise as many questions as it answered in the years ahead. Yet Lincoln had correctly posited the qualitative difference between military emancipation and constitutional abolition. No matter how many slaves had gained their freedom or how much damage slavery had sustained during the war, the large majority of slaves in the seceded states would still be enslaved when the war ended, and who knew what would become of "the children of the slaves born hereafter." As Republicans and other antislavery advocates had been warning for the past two years, it was not inconceivable that slavery as an institution might survive the war and experience a revitalization. For everything the amendment failed to do, which was a lot, it precluded this single outcome. In this sense if in no other, it was indeed "a King's cure" for the evil of a slavery that refused to die.

* * *

House approval of the abolition amendment marked a milestone in US history – though not quite in the way history has remembered it. Lincoln and congressional Republicans had pondered the question of state restoration since the start of the war. The essential problem – especially after the Emancipation Proclamation – had been to prevent the seceded states from returning to the Union with slavery,

---

[29] Vorenberg, *Final Freedom*, 198–208. In *Forgotten Emancipator* (119–27), Rebecca E. Zietlow devotes almost all of her attention during this period, understandably, to James M. Ashley's role in securing House passage of the amendment, to the exclusion of Ashley's and other congressional Republicans' efforts to enact Reconstruction legislation before the session – and the war – ended.

[30] *CWL*, 8: 254–55.

as conservative Unionists in the lower Mississippi valley had tried to do. Upon the amendment's introduction into Congress in December 1863, congressional Republicans largely saw the amendment and Reconstruction legislation as complementary parts of an integrated package: Federal authority would ensure that the rebellious states abolish slavery as a condition for restoration to the Union. After Lincoln's reelection, however, the amendment came to be seen as an independent initiative. Whereas the challenge after the proclamation had been to conjoin state restoration and abolition, and whereas Reconstruction legislation was originally thought to enjoy better prospects than a Federal abolition amendment, the amendment had now become the priority, while Reconstruction legislation languished. Indeed, with Lincoln about to embark upon a second full term, and with the House having passed the amendment, the impetus behind a Reconstruction bill, already weak, essentially collapsed. As history would show, postponing Reconstruction legislation until the war was over proved to be a tragic miscalculation.

As the debates in Louisiana and Tennessee and in Congress in early 1865 demonstrated, the abolition of slavery was being undertaken without its consequences having been decided. Addressing those consequences could not be put off indefinitely. The hoped-for compromise between Lincoln and congressional Republicans over Reconstruction had foundered on the interrelated questions of the Louisiana government and black civil rights. Republicans may have worried less now about slavery's survival than they had previously, with congressional approval of the amendment secured. But with Union military victory all but certain, some very difficult decisions regarding the nature of the postwar governments in the seceded states and the status of the former slaves under them would have to be made.

"If this bill do not become a law," Henry Winter Davis warned in February, as Congress made one last attempt to enact a Reconstruction bill before adjourning, dire consequences would follow. "[W]hen Congress again meets [in December 1865], at our doors, clamorous and dictatorial, will be sixty-five Representatives from the States now in rebellion, and twenty-two Senators, *claiming* admission," Davis predicted, and "*entitled* to admission beyond the power of argument to resist it; for peace will have been restored, there will be no armed power but that of the United States; there will be quiet, and votes will be polled under the existing laws of the State." He asked rhetorically: "Are you ready to accept that consequence?" If not, then Lincoln's policy offered an unattractive alternative. "But suppose," Davis continued, "that the fruitful example of Louisiana shall spread like a mist over all the rest of the southern country, and that Representatives like what Louisiana has sent here, with such a backing of votes as she has given, shall appear here at the doors of this Hall; whose representatives are they?"[31]

---

[31] *CG*, 38th Cong., 2nd Sess., 969 (February 21, 1865); McCrary, *Abraham Lincoln and Reconstruction*, 292–93.

19

"This Cup of Liberty"

By the spring of 1865, slavery was being further driven into oblivion, while the rebellion to which it had given rise finally succumbed. Tennessee abolished slavery in February and soon thereafter elected a free-state government. Louisiana ratified the Federal abolition amendment in mid-February, and in April Tennessee and Arkansas followed suit. By late February, Andrew Johnson stepped down as military governor of Tennessee to become vice president during what was expected to be Abraham Lincoln's second term. Michael Hahn also resigned as governor of Louisiana in anticipation of representing that state in the US Senate.

Congress adjourned in early March without enacting Reconstruction legislation or deciding on Lincoln's reconstructed governments. Military success in the lower Mississippi valley in 1862 had spurred the first congressional action on Reconstruction and raised the issue of linking the fate of slavery to state restoration. Now, a Federal abolition amendment was going to the states for ratification while the region's reconstructed governments remained in limbo, and the war was nearing its end with no Reconstruction legislation in place. However, Congress managed to overcome months of gridlock – and to achieve momentary consensus with Lincoln on the postwar order – by creating the Freedmen's Bureau.

Lincoln gave further indications – in his Second Inaugural Address in early March, and a month later in his "last" speech – of his postwar policy toward the rebellious states and his expanded understanding of black freedom. The Second Inaugural famously called for "charity" toward the defeated South, but it also advocated justice for the former slaves. In his final address, delivered on the evening of April 11, Lincoln offered an extended defense of his Reconstruction policy and Louisiana government. But he also acknowledged criticism of his policy and that government's deficiencies. By invoking "this cup of liberty," moreover, which the former slaveholders would supposedly hold to the lips of their former slaves, Lincoln articulated his vision of a meaningful freedom for the former slaves. He also took the occasion to publicly endorse black suffrage – the first time a sitting president had ever done so. Within days, Lincoln would be removed from the historical stage.

Not until early June did Confederate military forces west of the Mississippi finally surrender. The advent of "postwar" Reconstruction inevitably inflected deliberations over Unionist governments of Tennessee, Arkansas, and Louisiana that were representative of neither their black populations nor the large majority of their white ones. In unveiling his own blueprint for Reconstruction in late May, President Andrew Johnson attempted to settle the debate over these governments and over black suffrage. While following his predecessor's lead on the former issue, he utterly rejected it on the latter.

I

Following Tennessee's constitutional convention in mid-January, the plebiscite on the amendments on February 22 and the election of a new government on March 4 generated an uninspired campaign. Predictably, the conservative Unionists denounced the entire process as a sham and insisted, not without cause, that the Nashville convention and its work were illegitimate. Some conservatives advocated voting against the amendments and gubernatorial candidate William G. "Parson" Brownlow, but most of them urged a total boycott. With former Confederates barred from the elections and conservatives eschewing them, free-state Unionists worried less about electoral victory than about turnout. Cognizant of congressional misgivings over Arkansas and Louisiana, their main objective was a vote that far surpassed Lincoln's ten-percent threshold.[1]

Yet the work of the convention remained a tough sell, even among Unionists. "I learn from home that the pro-slavery office-holders, both State and National, are creating a little fuss over our proceedings at Nashville," a west Tennessee ally informed Johnson. "They do not make much opposition to the proposed amendments" but instead criticized the legislative nominees, who "are thoroughly sound men on the nigger question, and that hurts." At a Memphis meeting intended to endorse the convention, another Johnson confidant reported, the participants "denounced the Nashville Convention proceedings and set aside its nominations." Two of the four nominees dumped from the ticket were subsequently restored, but the incident "has tended not a little to set back our party movements." Some Johnson supporters were even said to oppose the amendments.[2] Neither did the reports of widespread violence help the free-state campaign. "[T]he people are anxious to hold an election," read the petition from a group of west Tennesseans that included several legislative candidates. However, "it would be madness for them to attempt it in the present condition of things," they added. "[R]obberies and

---

[1] *PAJ*, 7: 459; Harris, *With Charity for All*, 226; Bergeron, *Andrew Johnson's Civil War and Reconstruction*, 57; Cimprich, *Slavery's End in Tennessee*, 116.

[2] *PAJ*, 7: 459, 464–65 (west Tennessee), 475–76 (Memphis).

Murders are common, and the union men are fast leaving the state." While assuring Johnson from Knoxville that "[t]he people are all right upon the action of the Convention, and will *Ratify* it," Parson Brownlow nonetheless acknowledged that parts of east Tennessee were "overrun with Rebel guerillas" who were "robbing and murdering" with impunity.[3]

Despite the confident prediction of a Johnson ally that 55,000 votes would be cast, the results of the February 22 ballot on the amendments were disappointing. The nearly 27,000 votes in favor of the amendments – and less than 100 against – were a resounding triumph for the abolition of slavery and easily met Lincoln's ten-percent mark. The turnout also more than doubled the constitutional plebiscites in Arkansas and Louisiana. But the total was less than the 35,000 votes cast in the 1864 presidential election and less than 20 percent of the 1860 presidential vote – even though Confederate efforts to disrupt the election were largely unsuccessful. Slavery had been formally abolished in Tennessee, but the vote on the new constitution hardly signified mass approval.[4]

Anxious to embark upon his triumphal journey to Washington, Johnson did not even await the completed returns before declaring the amendments operative and preparing for the state election. In a proclamation of February 25, nearing the end of his career as military governor, Johnson congratulated the people of Tennessee for the "speedy and permanent reorganization" of the state government, the defeat of the rebellion, and the eradication of slavery. "A new era dawns upon the people of Tennessee," he announced. Gone was the "reign of brute-force and personal violence," to be replaced "by reason, law, order, and reverence." By the people's "own solemn act, at the ballot-box, the shackles have been formally stricken from the limbs of more than 275,000 slaves in the State." Again, abolition had freed whites as much as blacks. "The unjust distinctions in society, fostered by an arrogant aristocracy, based upon human bondage, have been overthrown; and our whole social system reconstructed on the basis of honest industry and personal worth." His work done, Johnson left that same day for Washington, almost exactly three years after his appointment as military governor. The last of Lincoln's three lieutenants responsible for Reconstruction in the region – along with Frederick Steele in Arkansas and Nathaniel Banks in Louisiana – was no longer on the scene.[5]

---

[3] *PAJ*, 7: 460–61 (Brownlow), 470–71 (west Tennessee). Also see *PAJ*, 7: 441–42, 446–47, 448–50, 470.

[4] *PAJ*, 7: 481, 493 (vote prediction); Bergeron, *Andrew Johnson's Civil War and Reconstruction*, 57; Harris, *With Charity for All*, 227; Alexander, *Political Reconstruction in Tennessee*, 39. *PAJ*, 7: 491, n. 2, citing official tallies in the Tennessee State Library and Archives, reports two different but essentially similar results: 26,865 to 67, and 27,684 to 113. For a detailed analysis of the vote, see Alexander, *Political Reconstruction in Tennessee*, 36–48.

[5] *PAJ*, 7: 487–91.

The first state elections ever conducted in Tennessee under a free-state constitution, held on March 4, were devoid of drama. Again, the only substantive question was turnout, and, again, the results were less than encouraging. Running to all intents and purposes unopposed, Parson Brownlow was elected governor almost unanimously, and the "general" legislative ticket was strongly endorsed. Yet the 20,000 votes cast, a mere 14 percent of the 1860 total, failed to match even the turnout for the constitutional amendments. "[W]ithout excuse or apology," a Nashville editor complained, the voters had "obstinately absented themselves from the polls." As had been the case in Arkansas and Louisiana, this was an inauspicious start.[6]

II

Even as Tennessee's free-state government was being created, Louisiana's was still working toward congressional recognition. The legislature was meeting in regular session when the Federal abolition amendment went to the states for ratification, so it was in a position to act quickly on the matter. Despite A. P. Field's altercation with William D. Kelley in mid-January, some people still hoped that Louisiana's ratification of the amendment might salvage its readmission to the Union. Acting on Governor Michael Hahn's endorsement, the legislature on February 17 ratified the amendment overwhelmingly and with little fanfare, although several legislators quibbled about the Federal government depriving citizens of property without compensation. Louisiana became the second seceded state (following Virginia), the fourth slave state (not counting West Virginia), and the first state in the lower Mississippi valley to ratify the amendment. Once again, however, the legislature failed to enact legislation defining the former slaves' legal and political status.[7]

Having previously gained election to the US Senate, Hahn in late February officially informed the legislature of his resignation as governor, effective March 3. His farewell address applauded the accomplishments of the new state government, especially the abolition of slavery. "[E]very slave has been set free," he proclaimed, "and slavery will never more have an existence in fact or a sanction in law in the State of Louisiana." In truth, "every" slave had yet to be freed, since much of the state remained under Confederate authority. Hahn also praised the state's progress toward racial equality, boasting that the new constitution "has provided for [the former slaves'] complete equality before the

---

[6] *PAJ*, 7: 491. Again, the vote for Brownlow produced different but essentially similar results: either 23,352 or 19,053 for, and 35 against.

[7] Taylor, *Louisiana Reconstructed*, 56–57. McCrary, *Abraham Lincoln and Reconstruction*, 304, n. 80, says the vote in both houses in Louisiana was unanimous, although *Journal of the Senate of the State of Louisiana*, 153, seems to indicate one vote against in that house. Maryland and Missouri were the other slave states that had already ratified the amendment.

law, including the extension to them of the highest privilege of citizenship." The constitution, of course, did no such thing. Hahn acknowledged as much, noting that universal suffrage would be adopted "whenever it shall be deemed wise and timely." As he left office, Michael Hahn, like Andrew Johnson, took justifiable pride in his administration's accomplishments. He was, in Lincoln's words, "the first-free-state Governor of Louisiana," and he now anticipated becoming US Senator. He could hardly have foreseen that in three years the constitution would need to be scrapped in order to institute the very provisions – equality before the law and black suffrage – he claimed it included. With Hahn's resignation, J. Madison Wells became governor.[8]

III

The US House of Representatives passed the abolition amendment only after Lincoln denied rumors – falsely – that a Confederate peace commission had been allowed through Union lines in Virginia. With the amendment secured, Lincoln authorized Secretary of State William H. Seward to meet with the three-member commission, headed by Vice President Alexander H. Stephens, before he decided to join the talks himself. The secret conference at Hampton Roads, Virginia, on February 3 came to naught, and the surviving participants later disagreed over what they had discussed. Stephens would later claim that Lincoln, even at this late date, had revived the age-old idea of compensated emancipation in exchange for an end to the war. Soon after the meeting, in fact, Lincoln concocted a hare-brained scheme offering the slave states – and the states that had already abolished slavery – the sum of $400 million in Federal bonds. One-half would be payable on condition that the rebellion cease by April 1, and the remainder on condition that the abolition amendment become operative by July 1. Such a plan would have encountered any number of difficulties, and Lincoln, facing his Cabinet's unanimous opposition, dropped it. Yet the proposal underscored the essential problem that antislavery advocates had faced since January 1863: If emancipating slaves was not equivalent to abolishing slavery, then how could the seceded states be prevented from returning to the Union with slavery still legally in place? Lincoln's proposal – however fantastical – had been an attempt to end the war while securing ratification of the amendment.[9]

The problem of securing both state restoration on a free-state basis and ratification of the amendment further underscored the need for Reconstruction

---

[8] Hahn's address: *Journal of the Senate of the State of Louisiana*, 155–56.
[9] Much has been written on the Hampton Roads conference. For a good overview and analysis of the previous scholarship, see Escott, *What Shall We Do with the Negro?*, chap. 7. For a more recent analysis, see Conroy, *Our One Common Country*. For Lincoln's compensated emancipation proposal, see *CWL*, 8: 260–61.

legislation. Although James M. Ashley's much-revised bill appeared dead following the mid-January decision to postpone action on it, Ashley, Henry Winter Davis, and other Radical Republicans put together one final push to enact legislation before the session (and the war) ended. On February 20, Ashley intrepidly reported yet another version of his bill. It provided for the former slaves' political and legal equality in the seceded states while allowing for the eventual recognition of the Louisiana, Arkansas, and Tennessee governments. It also recognized the existing governments in the other seceded states once those governments repudiated their Confederate debts and ratified the abolition amendment, and once state officials accepted Federal authority and swore allegiance. Yet the debate, which took place February 20–22, along with various proposed amendments, showed House Republicans to be hopelessly divided, irrespective of Democratic opposition. A vote to table the matter killed what slim chance had remained of enacting Reconstruction legislation during the session. Congressional Republicans could at least take solace in not having forced upon Lincoln another bill he would have had to veto.[10]

The demise of Ashley's bill bolstered the determination of Charles Sumner and other Senate Radicals to defeat the seating of Louisiana claimants Charles Smith and R. King Cutler, and to block recognition of the Louisiana government. Their cases did not reach the Senate floor until late February. Although debate replicated much of the congressional deliberation on Reconstruction of the past three years, it was clear that black political and legal equality were the main sticking points. With the session winding down and critical business still pending (and tempers flaring), the Senate voted on February 27 to postpone action on the Louisiana question – and on the entire matter of Reconstruction – until the next Congress. Peyton McCrary's assertion that Sumner "had almost single-handedly prevented the Senate from approving Lincoln's reconstruction policy in Louisiana" has merit, but Sumner had had plenty of help. The Senate's action dismayed Lincoln, but because the Senate had postponed the issue and not rejected the Louisiana claimants outright, the result was a temporary setback rather than an irreversible defeat. It even worked to Lincoln's advantage, since Congress had handed Reconstruction over to him just as the war was about to end. Still, the failure of the executive and legislative branches to agree on a plan for restoring the seceded states to the Union before the war ended would have catastrophic consequences for American history.[11]

---

[10] *CG*, 38th Cong., 2nd Sess., 936 (February 20, 1865); Belz, *Reconstructing the Union*, 262–67; Masur, *Lincoln's Hundred Days*, 140–41; Richards, *Who Freed the Slaves?*, 223–24.

[11] McCrary, *Abraham Lincoln and Reconstruction*, 298–302 (quotation, 302); Belz, *Reconstructing the Union*, 267–72; Richards, *Who Freed the Slaves?*, 224–26; Butler and Wolff, *United States Senate Election*, 121–23; Harris, *With Charity for All*, 244–46. See *CG*, 38th Cong., 2nd Sess., 1129 (February 27, 1865), for the vote.

Despite this failure, Congress carried through on another measure that would have profound repercussions for postwar Reconstruction: establishment of the Bureau of Refugees, Freedmen, and Abandoned Lands. Situated within the War Department and designed to oversee the transition from slavery to freedom in the slave states, the "Freedmen's Bureau" assumed responsibility for "all subjects" relating to the former slaves. It was also authorized to take control of abandoned farms and plantations and to make the lands from them available to former slaves and white refugees for rental and eventual sale. The bureau grew directly out of the efforts of various governmental and private agencies to provide aid and relief to refugees and former slaves and to investigate conditions in contraband camps and other places of refuge. The administration of plantation affairs and wartime free labor, especially in the lower Mississippi valley, had likewise been crucial to its creation, as had the conflict between War and Treasury Department officials over these matters, and congressional Republicans had had to overcome their own differences over which executive department would house the agency. Lincoln signed the legislation creating the bureau, passed on the last day of the session (along with the Freedman's Bank), but took no action on it before his death. Responsibility for getting this unprecedented Federal agency up and running would fall to Andrew Johnson, who harbored a deep suspicion of Federal authority. Despite its broad mandate, the Freedmen's Bureau possessed no real political authority, but it would inevitably become embroiled in the politics of postwar Reconstruction.[12]

The adjournment of the Thirty-Eighth Congress also brought with it the end of Lincoln's first term and the start of his second. "With malice toward none; with charity for all" is how Lincoln famously opened the peroration of his Second Inaugural Address, delivered on March 4, 1865. Yet, if Lincoln was prepared to extend magnanimity to former Confederates, he also indicated in other language that the former slaves would participate in the national discussion on the postwar settlement. Lincoln wanted to "bind up the nation's wounds," but reconciliation would be but part of what he called "a just, and a lasting peace." Mercy, in other words, would not come at the expense of justice. In the weeks that followed, the Confederate project further disintegrated. By mid-March, the Confederacy had sold its soul – such as it was – by authorizing the arming of enslaved men. Federal forces commenced the campaign against Mobile, having captured the city's coastal defenses the previous fall, though Mobile itself was not occupied until after Lee's surrender at Appomattox. In the east, William T. Sherman pursued Joseph E. Johnston's ragtag force in North Carolina,

---

[12] On the origins and beginnings of the Freedmen's Bureau, see Bentley, *History of the Freedmen's Bureau*, chaps. 1–3.

while Grant pressed against the ever-thinning Confederate line at Petersburg. The end was nigh.[13]

IV

During the first week of April, the Tennessee legislature convened at Nashville and Parson Brownlow was inaugurated as the state's first free-state governor. His message to the legislature was notably restrained, given his reputation for vituperation. He characteristically castigated the rebellion but called for no specific proscriptions against former Confederates. He urged the legislature to ratify the Federal abolition amendment and "strike down the monster institution," especially since the state had already abolished slavery. In defining the new racial order, Brownlow offered the customary combination of paternalism, condescension, and defense of white supremacy, insisting that legislation was "necessary for the protection, government and control of the emancipated slaves among us," but he made no recommendations regarding their legal rights. He did not so much as mention black suffrage, even though the recent constitutional amendments had authorized the legislature to determine voting qualifications. "The subject has been considered by several of our sister States," he observed euphemistically, "whose reform was not any more loudly called for than with us." This hardly sounded like an endorsement of black voting rights. Bemoaning the denial of Tennessee's readmission to the Union, Brownlow urged the election of US Senators and Representatives, expressing confidence – not entirely justified, given recent events in Washington – that they would be seated.[14]

On April 7, the legislature made Tennessee the twentieth state – and the fifth slave state – to ratify the abolition amendment. A month later, it elected US Senators. In early June, it enacted a law expressly restricting the vote to white men while disfranchising almost all former Confederates but also allowing to vote any white man "known to be a Union man" who had been forced into Confederate service. The legislature emulated the other reconstructed states by taking no action on the former slaves' legal rights – despite receiving a petition from the state's black residents calling for the vote and the right to testify in court – before adjourning.[15]

---

[13] *CWL*, 8: 332–33. There is of course a considerable scholarly literature on Lincoln's Second Inaugural Address.

[14] Brownlow's address in *Senate Journal of the First Session of the General Assembly of the State of Tennessee*, 18–32, especially 19–22. For an analysis of the composition of the assembly, see Alexander, *Political Reconstruction in Tennessee*, 69–72.

[15] Harris, *With Charity for All*, 227–28; Alexander, *Political Reconstruction in Tennessee*, 72–78. On the voting law, see McPherson, *Political History of the United States During the Period of Reconstruction*, 27; LeForge, "State Colored Conventions of Tennessee," 235–36. An excerpt from the black petition to the legislature appears in the *Nashville Daily Union*,

In Arkansas, the government of Isaac Murphy limped along during the spring. In mid-February, Murphy called for a special legislative session in early April to act on the Federal abolition amendment. Scheduled for April 3, the legislature needed an entire week to reach a quorum. On April 12, it received Murphy's message (dated April 3) recommending ratification of the amendment, which he called "the great act that will consolidate the union of the States on the basis of equality, politically and socially; remove the cause of our troubles and bind together all the States in a Union of interest and affection, not hereafter to be broken." Who Murphy had in mind in affirming political and social equality as the basis of the Union remained unclear, but he undoubtedly did *not* mean the former slaves. Along with Andrew Johnson, Parson Brownlow, Michael Hahn, J. Madison Wells, and every other white Southerner of their ilk, Murphy considered anathema the idea that political or legal equality followed from abolition. They instead maintained that lawmaking bodies would need to codify only those specific civil rights that black people would enjoy once slavery had been abolished.[16]

On April 14, an ominous date in US history, the Arkansas legislature unanimously ratified the amendment. The three reconstructed states of the lower Mississippi valley had now approved it with no meaningful opposition. In addition to this action, the legislature also attempted to address, among other issues, the former slaves' legal status. Both houses passed different versions of a bill that would have granted the former slaves basic rights but came nowhere near equality before the law. The House Judiciary Committee's report affirmed the need to enact laws "as will assure to them the *rights* and *recognition* of human beings," adding that failure to do so "will be a shameful proof of the insincerity of our former acts, and the *omission of such an act* will stand as a libel (so far as we are concerned) upon the cause which we profess to advocate." The two houses, however, were unable to reconcile their differences before the session's April 22 adjournment. Louisiana, Tennessee, and Arkansas had thus abolished slavery and ratified the Federal amendment but had yet to address abolition's consequences.[17]

V

Reconstruction – and Louisiana in particular – occupied much of Lincoln's "last" public address. Delivered on the evening of April 11, and occasioned by Robert E. Lee's surrender at Appomattox two days earlier, it amounted to

---

August 10, 1865; two petitions are noted in *Senate Journal of the First Session of the General Assembly of the State of Tennessee*, 46 (April 14), 133 (May 17).

[16] Murphy's message: *Journal of the Convention of Delegates of the People of Arkansas*, 12–13 (April 12). This volume contains multiple paginations. Moneyhon, *Impact of the Civil War and Reconstruction on Arkansas*, 168–69; DeBlack, *With Fire and Sword*, 147–48.

[17] *Journal of the Convention of Delegates of the People of Arkansas*, 22–26 (April 13–14; action on the amendment), 33, 35–36 (quotation), 39–40, 43, 48 (April 15, 18–21; legislation); DeBlack, *With Fire and Sword*, 148.

a defense of the Louisiana government and Lincoln's Reconstruction policy. With the war barely over (although Confederate forces in the west would not surrender for several weeks), and with his audience anticipating a strong dose of triumphalism, Lincoln instead chose this moment to offer a disquisition on the postwar order. Lincoln was responding in part to comments he had received that very day from Salmon P. Chase, his former Treasury secretary and now the Chief Justice of the US Supreme Court, who advocated universal male suffrage in all of the seceded states, including Louisiana and Arkansas. The last words Abraham Lincoln addressed to the American people were in response to this and other criticism of the Louisiana government and its implications for postwar Reconstruction.[18]

After briefly applauding Union military success, Lincoln moved quickly to Reconstruction, a matter "fraught with great difficulty." Dismissing the question of whether the seceded states had left the Union as "a merely pernicious abstraction," he contended that those states were, as he had always said, "out of their proper practical relation with the Union." The "sole object" of Reconstruction therefore was to restore that relation. Just as Reconstruction was a practical problem, the Louisiana government offered concrete progress that, while imperfect, should not be discarded. Lincoln outlined the government's formation under the ten-percent plan, which, he emphasized, his Cabinet and Congress had strongly approved. He denied playing any major role in creating the government, save for communicating with local loyalists and appointing Nathanial Banks to oversee it. Lincoln pledged to support the government but added his famous Machiavellian qualifier: "But, as bad promises are better broken than kept, I shall treat this as a bad promise, and break it, whenever I shall be convinced that keeping it is adverse to the public interest." But he had yet to be so convinced.

That being said, Lincoln acknowledged the government's deficiencies. It was based on some 12,000 voters, whereas "fifty, thirty, or even twenty thousand" would have been preferable. "It is also unsatisfactory to some that the elective franchise is not given to the colored man." Lincoln responded to this criticism by issuing his famous endorsement of black suffrage, which, however limited and qualified, was unequivocal. "I would myself prefer that it were now conferred on the very intelligent, and on those who serve our cause as soldiers." Lincoln had now gone public with the private "suggestion" he had made to Michael Hahn just over a year earlier. Despite these shortcomings, the issue was not whether the Louisiana government was perfect but whether it would facilitate the state's restoration. "Can Louisiana be brought into proper

---

[18] *CWL*, 8: 399–405, including Chase's letter. On the circumstances surrounding the address and its contents, see Donald, *Lincoln*, 580–85; Burlingame, *Abraham Lincoln*, 2: 800–4; Harris, *With Charity for All*, 255–58; Foner, *Fiery Trial*, 330–32; Masur, *Lincoln's Last Speech*.

practical relation with the Union," he asked rhetorically, in what had become something of a mantra, "*sooner* by *sustaining*, or by *discarding* her new State Government?"

Lincoln heralded the progress of Reconstruction in Louisiana. About 12,000 citizens had abandoned the Confederacy and resumed their allegiance, had held elections and organized a government that ratified the abolition amendment, and had written a constitution that abolished slavery, provided for racially integrated public education, and authorized the state legislature to adopt black suffrage. Repudiating the Louisiana government would demoralize these citizens, who, "thus fully committed to the Union, and to perpetual freedom in the state," had sought recognition and assistance, while sustaining it would encourage them to "adhere to their work" and strive for "a complete success." Likewise, "the colored man too, in seeing all united for him," would be "inspired with vigilance, and energy, and daring, to the same end." Black men demanded the right to vote, but would not this goal be more speedily attained "by saving the already advanced steps toward it, than by running backward over them?" Lincoln then employed his awkward "fowl-egg" metaphor, which would be roundly disparaged. "Concede that the new government of Louisiana is only to what it should be as the egg is to the fowl, we shall sooner have the fowl by hatching the egg than by smashing it?" He again invoked his mantra: "Can Louisiana be brought into proper practical relation with the Union *sooner* by *sustaining* or by *discarding* her new State Government?"

Nearing the end of the address, Lincoln observed that most of what he had said about Louisiana applied to the other seceded states. While reaffirming that "no exclusive, and inflexible plan" would be imposed upon all of them, he also observed: "Important principles may, and must, be inflexible." Lincoln closed this "last" address by indicating that "some new announcement to the people of the South" would be forthcoming, but he never got to make it.

Lincoln's address reflected his divided mind on Reconstruction, oscillating between state restoration and the remaking of southern society, even as it demonstrated his commitment to black freedom. No sooner had hostilities effectively ended than he publicly endorsed black suffrage. Throughout his career, Lincoln had calibrated his policies on slavery and race to northern public opinion. Now, he was staking out a position – on the most volatile issue of the day – far in advance of popular sentiment. By simply mentioning in a public forum that black men desired the right to vote, Lincoln acknowledged that black people had an essential voice in the political debate on the postwar settlement. Similarly, although Lincoln did not address social or economic issues, he applauded Louisiana's new constitution for authorizing black education, and for *not* adopting apprenticeship, which he had previously supported.

In a larger sense, Lincoln warned that rejecting the Louisiana government would undermine the former slaves' aspirations for a meaningful freedom.

"This cup of liberty which these, your old masters, hold to your lips, we will dash from you," the nation would be saying to the former slaves, "and leave you to the chances of gathering the spilled and scattered contents in some vague and undefined when, where, and how." In this remarkable statement, Lincoln insisted that genuine freedom for the former slaves must not be postponed to some indeterminate point in the future. It must be pursued now. Generations of white Southerners and white Americans would later espouse patience in response to black aspirations for racial equality. Lincoln rejected this argument. His view of the South's "old masters" may have been unrealistic. No reconstructed government had thus far held up a "cup of liberty" from which black people would have dared to drink. Nonetheless, their imbibing of it, Lincoln insisted, could not be put off to "some vague and undefined when, where, and how."

Lincoln had come a long way. But whether he had come far enough for his radical critics – who had long since moved beyond limited black suffrage and were demanding equality before the law and universal suffrage – remained less certain. His last speech illustrates the tensions between a definition of Reconstruction that saw state restoration as the "sole object" and one that addressed the consequences of emancipation. As the reconstructed states of the lower Mississippi valley demonstrated, restoring the seceded states to their "proper practical relations" with the Union before those consequences had been sorted out was not really viable. Far from a "pernicious abstraction," the question of whether the seceded states had been in or out of the Union, so long as the status of the former slaves remained unresolved, was an eminently "practical" one. Advocates of racial equality had been asking it all along.

Reaction to the speech covered all points on the political spectrum. As historians have often noted, one person in the audience understood Lincoln's remarks perfectly. Deeply despondent over the Confederacy's demise, and already having organized a far-fetched conspiracy to kidnap the president, John Wilkes Booth now resolved that Lincoln had indeed made his last speech.[19]

VI

Among Abraham Lincoln's last official acts was to authorize Nathaniel Banks's return to Louisiana after an absence of seven months. Although no longer exercising command, Banks arrived in New Orleans on April 21 to find a dramatically transformed political landscape. Since succeeding Michael Hahn as governor in early March, J. Madison Wells had been replacing Hahn appointees in favor of conservative Unionists and ex-Confederates. He appointed Dr. Hugh Kennedy, former proprietor of a conservative newspaper,

---

[19] Kauffman, *American Brutus*, 210; Burlingame, *Abraham Lincoln*, 2: 803.

as mayor of New Orleans, whereupon Kennedy commenced filling the city police force with returning Confederate veterans. Wells also replaced state and city judges in favor of conservatives such as Edmund Abell, and he appointed planters and ex-Confederates to positions in the parishes. He wrote self-serving letters to now-president Andrew Johnson justifying his actions and requesting that he be appointed military governor, as Hahn had been, or that the military commander – that is, Banks – be ordered to cooperate with him. Wells also disingenuously alleged that the dispossessed members of the Banks–Hahn oligarchy "openly proclaim not only their purpose to overthrow my government of the State, but their belief that military support will be given them to accomplish that end."[20]

When Banks attempted to reverse his removals in early May, a furious Wells fired off a letter of protest to Johnson. Wells and Kennedy also went to Washington to take their case to Johnson personally, armed with a letter of introduction from US Marshal Cuthbert Bullitt, who had enjoyed an amicable relationship with Lincoln. In vouching for the Louisiana government in his last address, Lincoln may not have fully appreciated what Wells was doing, but with Johnson as president, the political winds had shifted. Johnson backed Wells, giving him full control in Louisiana. On May 17, Johnson also ordered a military reorganization that effectively stripped Banks of what little authority he had left. Banks and his allies attempted during the summer to regain control of a Louisiana government of their creation but that Wells and the conservatives had hijacked. But they were essentially powerless.[21]

Wells's course marked a convergence between wartime conservative Unionists and former Confederates in the interests of white supremacy. Although an unconditional Unionist who had supported abolition, Wells rejected anything that approached racial equality. With black suffrage and equality before the law gaining ground as conditions for state restoration, Wells was pinning his political fortunes on a conservative alliance, even if it meant consorting with former Confederate adversaries. Likewise, the former moderate and radical wings of the old free-state movement, although no love was lost between them, began to experience a convergence of their own. The radicals continued to cast Wells's actions as the logical outgrowth of the free-state government under the Banks–Hahn oligarchy. The only solution, they insisted, was black suffrage, an argument the moderates were finding hard to resist. By the time Johnson sustained Wells, the political battle lines in Louisiana were being redrawn. Former free-state moderates and radicals

---

[20] *PAJ*, 7: 648–50, 651–53 (quotation); McCrary, *Abraham Lincoln and Reconstruction*, 308–11; Hollandsworth, *Pretense of Glory*, 218–19; Taylor, *Louisiana Reconstructed*, 58.

[21] *PAJ*, 8: 33–34; McCrary, *Abraham Lincoln and Reconstruction*, 311–12; Hollandsworth, *Pretense of Glory*, 219–20; Winters, *Civil War in Louisiana*, 405.

were coming together over black suffrage, and the framework of a Republican party in Louisiana was taking shape.[22]

VII

In the weeks after Lee's surrender, Confederate authority slowly crumbled. On April 26, Confederate General Joseph E. Johnston capitulated to William Tecumseh Sherman at Raleigh, North Carolina. With the surrender of General Richard Taylor, commander of Confederate forces in Alabama, Mississippi, and east Louisiana, at Citronelle, Alabama, on May 4, all organized resistance east of the Mississippi River ended. Yet the demise of Confederate authority west of the Mississippi dragged on for another month. Since the fall of Vicksburg, the Confederate Trans-Mississippi Department – commanded by General Edmund Kirby Smith and headquartered at Shreveport – had functioned almost as its own independent entity. Kirby Smith rejected surrender terms in early May, and during the next several weeks – as entire Confederate units disbanded en masse – complicated discussions took place between Confederate military and civil authorities and between Confederate and Federal military authorities. Not until June 2 did Kirby Smith – having removed his headquarters to Galveston – sign articles of surrender for the Trans-Mississippi Department that were essentially the same as those Lee had accepted. Confederate authority now ceased to exist, although resistance continued in Texas into the summer. While certain parts of the lower Mississippi valley were among the first to surrender to Union forces in 1862, others were among the last to do so.[23]

In early June, Federal forces occupied Shreveport and fanned out into northwest Louisiana, southwest Arkansas, and east Texas. The Federal commander at Shreveport issued an order announcing enforcement of the Emancipation Proclamation but making no mention of Louisiana's free-state constitution. "There are no longer any slaves in the United States," the order declared – incorrectly, since persons were still legally enslaved in Kentucky and Delaware. Any attempt to impede the proclamation's enforcement would be construed as continued rebellion and suppressed. The order recommended "that the freedmen be employed under specific contracts at reasonable wages and kindly treated." They would not be encouraged to leave their former masters, "and they must learn that they can not be supported in idleness," it

---

[22] McCrary, *Abraham Lincoln and Reconstruction*, 309–10; Taylor, *Louisiana Reconstructed*, 58–62; Hollandsworth, *Pretense of Glory*, 220–21.

[23] *OR*, ser. 1, vol. 48, pt. 2, 600–3, 604–6; *PAJ*, 7: 669; Winters, *Civil War in Louisiana*, chaps. 24–25; Moneyhon, *Impact of the Civil War and Reconstruction on Arkansas*, chap. 6, 169–71; DeBlack, *With Fire and Sword*, 136–43; Hess, *Civil War in the West*, 291–301. See also *OR*, ser. 1, vol. 48, pt. 1, 189–90. On the post-Appomattox surrenders, see Silkenat, *Raising the White Flag*, chaps. 8, 9.

continued. "To be worthy of their freedom they must be industrious and honest," the commander lectured the former slaves, expressing a sentiment they would hear repeatedly over the coming months. "Their status will in no way be compromised by remaining at home and working for wages." Until the Freedmen's Bureau had been established, military officers were enjoined to enforce the order. Local commanders in other parts of the lower Mississippi valley that only now came under Federal control issued similar directives. Nearly two and a half years after it had been issued, the Emancipation Proclamation was finally being enforced.[24]

Of the states of the lower Mississippi valley, only Mississippi had experienced no wartime Reconstruction. Despite pockets of resistance and much discontent among the yeomanry, nothing amounting to organized political opposition to the rebellion ever developed in Jefferson Davis's home state. But even here the reality of defeat sank in. As early as mid-April, Armistead Burwell, a Vicksburg attorney and unconditional Unionist who had fled to St. Louis after Mississippi seceded, had issued a call for a state convention, to meet on June 5 in Jackson, which would, among other things, amend the state constitution to abolish slavery. Burwell urged each county to send delegates, but, given the overall circumstances, the response was slow. Following Richard Taylor's surrender in early May, Mississippi Governor Charles Clark called for a special session of the state legislature, to meet on May 18, to order a state convention that would repeal the ordinance of secession and address the consequences of Confederate defeat. There were now two separate movements for a Mississippi convention.[25]

Johnson endorsed neither plan, and he in fact prohibited any such unauthorized initiative in Mississippi or elsewhere. On May 21, he directed

---

[24] *OR*, ser. 1, vol. 48, pt. 2, 749; Winters, *Civil War in Louisiana*, 427; *Freedom: L&L-1865*, chap. 1.

[25] On Confederate discontent and Unionism in wartime Mississippi, see Bynum, *Free State of Jones*; Bettersworth, *Confederate Mississippi*, chap. 11; Harris, *Presidential Reconstruction in Mississippi*, chap. 1; Smith, *Mississippi in the Civil War*, chap. 7. On the convention plans, see Harris, *Presidential Reconstruction in Mississippi*, 14–17. In mid-May, Vicksburg loyalist Ira A. Batterton – a transplanted Northerner who had served in the Union army after the fall of Vicksburg, and who had subsequently started a newspaper there – advised Johnson to endorse the Burwell initiative. He questioned the loyalties of former Confederates who only resumed their Union allegiance *after* military defeat, and he cast doubt on the legitimacy of any actions they undertook. Since Mississippi had never left the Union, rescinding the ordinance of secession was meaningless, and any act of the insurgent government, "so far as relating to the so-called Confederacy," was null and void. The Burwell convention, by contrast, "originates with the people and none but men of well known loyalty will be its members," Batterton maintained. "Judge Burwell's proposed Convention is in no way connected with the present Governor or legislature." Batterton wrote to Johnson again the next day, warning that Clark intended to convene the legislature and urging that it not be permitted to meet, and complaining that the "military here are slow to act." *PAJ*, 8: 76–78.

General Edward R. S. Canby to order the commanding general in Mississippi not to "recognize any officer of the Confederate or State government" as possessing any authority "to exercise in any manner the function of their late offices." Canby further directed his subordinate to prevent, "by force, if necessary," any attempt by the legislatures of the insurrectionary states to assemble "for legislative purposes," and to arrest and imprison any legislators or other persons attempting to carry out these functions. In addition to suppressing the legislature, Federal authorities arrested and briefly imprisoned Governor Clark. No rebellious state that had not been "reconstructed" would be permitted to act until Johnson – unbound by congressional legislation – had unveiled his policy.[26]

In the weeks after ascending to the presidency, Johnson conferred with numerous groups and individuals and received much advice on Reconstruction. Until his mid-May intervention in the Wells–Banks dispute, he had given few hints of his policy toward the seceded states. But even that episode had occurred in a reconstructed state and did not necessarily signal his approach toward the others.[27] In late May, Johnson announced his Reconstruction policy in the form of two proclamations: the first provided for individuals who had participated in the rebellion to receive amnesty or pardon; and the second appointed a provisional governor for North Carolina and outlined the process for the seceded states to establish loyal governments. It would be difficult to overstate the significance of these proclamations to postwar Reconstruction and to subsequent US history. They would have important implications for the states of the lower Mississippi valley even though only Mississippi had not yet been reconstructed.

The amnesty proclamation closely resembled elements of Lincoln's ten-percent plan. It offered amnesty and pardon to all persons who had participated "directly or by implication" in the rebellion, with restoration of all property rights, "except as to slaves" (and excepting other specific circumstances), provided that said person swore an oath of allegiance and pledged to support all wartime laws and proclamations "with reference to the emancipation of slaves." The proclamation excluded fourteen classes of persons, including the Confederacy's political and military leadership and individuals who had committed various other offences in aiding the rebellion (such as mistreating Union prisoners of war). Also excluded were persons who had voluntarily aided the rebellion and who owned taxable property worth more than $20,000, a provision clearly aimed at the South's planter elite. Anyone excluded

---

[26] *OR*, ser. 1, vol. 48, pt. 2, 520–21; Harris, *Presidential Reconstruction in Mississippi*, 15–17; Smith, *Mississippi in the Civil War*, 46–47.

[27] Simpson, Graf, and Muldowny, *Advice after Appomattox*; Trefousse, *Andrew Johnson*, 196–216.

from the general amnesty could apply for special pardon to Johnson, who indicated that clemency would be "liberally extended."[28]

The second proclamation provided for establishing loyal governments in the seceded states and restoring them to the Union. Based, in addition to other rationale, on the "republican form of government" guarantee, and "for the purpose of enabling the loyal people of said State to organize a State government," the proclamation appointed a provisional governor for North Carolina, who was charged with organizing a state convention "for the purpose of altering or amending the [state] constitution." He was also authorized with all necessary powers to enable the loyal people "to restore said State to its constitutional relation to the Federal government," and to establish a "republican" government that would entitle the state to its rights under the US Constitution. Voting for delegates to the convention and serving as a delegate at it would be restricted to persons who had taken Johnson's loyalty oath and who currently met the state's voting requirements as of the date the state seceded. Either the convention or the legislature later to be elected would determine the qualifications for voting and holding office. The proclamation further ordered the military commander in the state to assist the provisional governor in implementing the foregoing measures, and it directed Johnson's Cabinet members to reestablish their Federal departments in the state.[29]

Johnson always maintained that he had followed Lincoln's lead in formulating his policy. Although he did not stipulate in the proclamation how the conventions were to amend their constitutions or dictate other terms, he indicated in other forums that they would have to renounce their ordinances of secession, repudiate their Confederate debts, and abolish slavery and ratify the Federal abolition amendment. Then, once new state governments had been organized and congressional elections held, the seceded states would presumably be restored to the Union and "Reconstruction," as Johnson understood it, would be over. As scholars have noted, various factors – political, racial, and even personal – influenced Johnson as he crafted his policy. The North Carolina proclamation served as the template for the subsequent appointments of provisional governors for the other unreconstructed states, including the appointment on June 13 of William L. Sharkey for Mississippi. By appointing provisional governors for the unreconstructed states and not the reconstructed ones, Johnson directly intervened in the debate – which, as Congress had demonstrated during the previous year and a half, was far from settled – over the legitimacy of the reconstructed governments. Many Northerners still had doubts about the Louisiana government, which the martyred Lincoln had used his "last" public words to defend, but Johnson brushed those doubts aside. As a result of the failure of Lincoln and congressional Republicans to

[28] *PAJ*, 8: 128–31.
[29] *PAJ*, 8: 136–38.

enact Reconstruction legislation before the war had ended, Andrew Johnson – not Abraham Lincoln – was now solely in charge of setting the terms by which the seceded states would be restored to the Union. Johnson, moreover, saw Congress's role in Reconstruction as little more than rubber-stamping his own actions.[30]

And then there was black suffrage. Johnson clearly intended to exclude black men from the state reorganization process. Whatever kind of political revolution he hoped to bring about in the South, the reconstructed governments under his policy would remain under white control and were unlikely to enact black suffrage or equality before the law. This should hardly have come as a surprise, but Johnson was again intervening in a matter that was far from over. He essentially preempted deliberation over black political and legal rights in the unreconstructed states and unilaterally closed off debate – in medias res – in the reconstructed ones. Owing in part to wartime Reconstruction in the lower Mississippi valley, the Pandora's box of black suffrage had long been open by the time the war ended. Johnson was trying to close it. Johnson may have believed that he was adhering to Lincoln's policy in recognizing the governments of Louisiana, Arkansas, and Tennessee, but he was ignoring the public endorsement of black suffrage in what was arguably Lincoln's last political will and testament.

* * *

In the early twentieth century, Carl Schurz, the German-born statesman, Union General, and leading Radical Republican, penned a trenchant and often-cited comparison of the Reconstruction policies of Abraham Lincoln and Andrew Johnson. Countering the commonly held belief that Johnson's policies were an extension of Lincoln's, Schurz argued that the two could not have been more different. Lincoln's were framed during armed hostilities and designed to undermine the Confederate war effort, whereas Johnson's were devised only after resistance to Federal authority had ceased. Lincoln's "sweet temper" would have sought a solution agreeable to all sides, in contrast to Johnson's essentially pugnacious disposition. Lincoln would never have given the resentful former slaveholders and embittered white South carte blanche in determining the postwar order, as did Johnson, who abandoned the former slaves "to the mercies of that master class" and to the "metaphysical abstraction" of states' rights. Schurz was no doubt influenced by – and contributed to – the cult of Lincoln as the Great Emancipator and savior of the Union that emerged in the decades after his assassination, even as the nation was forsaking its black

---

[30] On Johnson specifying requirements in other ways, see *PAJ*, 8: xxx, 9: xi–xiii. No attempt is made here to cite the voluminous literature on Andrew Johnson's Reconstruction policy. But an essential work remains Eric McKitrick's *Andrew Johnson and Reconstruction*.

citizens in the name of regional reconciliation. Yet his view has largely been accepted.

Schurz noted another important contrast. Soon after the war, "there was an effort of persons lately in rebellion to get possession of the reconstructed Southern State Governments for the purpose, in part, of using their power to save or restore as much of the system of slavery as could be saved or restored." This objective "was to be accomplished by the precipitate and unconditional readmission of the late rebel States to all their constitutional functions. This situation had not yet developed when Lincoln was assassinated," Schurz added. "He had not contemplated it when he put forth his plans of reconstructing Louisiana and other States."[31]

Here, Schurz is on shakier ground. Johnson, for all of his faults, did not offer the seceded states "unconditional readmission." He required them, if little else, to abolish slavery. More importantly, although Lincoln was denied the opportunity to address postwar Reconstruction, he had been keenly aware – how could he not have been? – of wartime efforts to restore the seceded states to the Union with slavery. Such efforts had set in bold relief the need to incorporate abolition into state restoration, as this book has argued, and thus to transform military emancipation into constitutional abolition. Contrary to Schurz, Lincoln framed his Reconstruction policy as a conscious and deliberate response to the attempts by proslavery Unionists in the lower Mississippi valley to organize loyal governments and rejoin the Union as slave states. Other than military defeat, this was Lincoln's greatest fear. Once the war ended, as was already evident in Louisiana by the spring of 1865, conservative Unionists and former Confederates would come together in hopes of controlling the postwar settlement. Lincoln and other Republicans had very much "contemplated" such an alliance during the war, and they were determined to prevent it. On this point, Schurz could not have been more wrong.

Ultimately, Lincoln, Johnson, and the large majority of Northerners came to see the preservation of the Union and the abolition of slavery as inseparable. Although Lincoln had continued to differentiate between abolition and the divisive questions surrounding its consequences, by the end of the war he was already envisioning the abolition of slavery as the first step, not the last, in defining the new order. For Johnson, the abolition of slavery marked not the beginning but the end.

---

[31] Schurz, *Reminiscences*, 3: 221–25.

20

"Establish Things as They Were Before the War"

As Federal forces were crushing the rebellion during the winter and spring of 1865, the new agricultural year commenced haltingly in the Union-occupied lower Mississippi valley. The administrative confusion and conflict of the previous year surrounding oversight of plantation and labor affairs carried over into the new year, and the matter was settled only in early March when Congress placed the Freedmen's Bureau with the War Department. Slavery no longer legally existed in Arkansas and Louisiana and was soon to be abolished in Tennessee, yet the continuing inability of these states' Unionist governments to define the new labor system left this matter in the hands of Federal authorities. Meanwhile, planters and laborers fumbled toward working arrangements for the new season. Although the sugar and cotton plantations of the lower Mississippi valley would follow very different trajectories in the years ahead, one essential trait they shared by the time the war ended – and would share for decades – was the determination of dispossessed slaveholders, as one of them unabashedly put it, to "establish things as they were befor[e] the war." Former masters and former slaves in both crop regions had struggled over the new labor arrangements, in certain instances, for nearly three years. But they had come nowhere close – even were this possible – to reconciling their differences.

With the war over, this challenge extended to the previously unconquered areas of the lower Mississippi valley. Despite wartime emancipation, the overwhelming majority of the region's slaves – as was true of the seceded states as a whole – remained in bondage when Confederates in the west finally capitulated. These slaves gained their freedom in the following months, as Federal military authorities – the army and the Freedmen's Bureau – assumed responsibility for instantiating the promise of the Emancipation Proclamation. The freed people now faced the full wrath of former slaveholders and white people in general, who, reaffirming everything they had ever said or done regarding slavery, vented their implacable opposition to the new order. If slavery were to be abolished, and for many white Southerners this was still a big "if," then the main goal, almost all of them agreed, would be to replace it with something that differed in name only.

I

Labor and plantation affairs in southern Louisiana remained unsettled as the new agricultural year began. All parties generally assumed that these matters would be transferred to the Treasury Department upon completion of the 1864 crop and the expiration in February of the previous year's labor regulations. William P. Mellen, supervisor of the Treasury Department's special agencies, prepared to reissue from New Orleans in early February the regulations he had originally drawn up back in July but that had subsequently been suspended. Having gained approval from General Edward R. S. Canby, the military commander for the lower Mississippi valley, for the transfer, Mellen updated his previous regulations and provided for their implementation throughout the entire Union-occupied valley. Although Mellen had assured Treasury secretary William P. Fessenden that he would assume no responsibility for plantation affairs "until you direct it to be done," the transfer from the military to the Treasury Department once again sparked protests. With Congress still debating the Freedmen's Bureau bill, Fessenden again ordered the transfer suspended.[1]

As planters and laborers in the sugar country attempted to find their way in commencing the first crop season since the formal abolition of slavery, the aftereffects of the disastrous 1864 crop were still being felt. The meager returns, combined with the preponderance of "share wage" arrangements (in which laborers received a share of the proceeds of the crop), left many former slaves with little to show at the year-end settlement. They were determined to secure better compensation and greater autonomy in their working lives, though Federal oversight in truth left them with few options. The planters, for their part, were more insistent than ever upon reestablishing control over labor, and they clamored for the substance of slavery if not the form. They especially resented the interrelated difficulties of settling up with their workers for the previous year while contracting for the new one. As distasteful as they found this process, planters would have to get used to it if they wanted to continue their operations.[2]

Not until March 11, some two months into the planting season, but by which point Congress had decided to place the Freedmen's Bureau in the War Department, did General Stephen Hurlbut, the military commander for southern Louisiana, issue regulations that superseded those of Treasury and would apply throughout the lower Mississippi valley. Hurlbut's regulations represented yet another good-faith attempt by Federal military authorities to

---

[1] *Freedom: WGFL-LS*, 374, 586–91 (doc. 137; Mellon, 587), 873–77 (doc. 222B). For plantation affairs in southern Louisiana in late 1864 and early 1865, see Ripley, *Slaves and Freedmen*, chap. 4; Rodrigue, *Reconstruction in the Cane Fields*, 49–57; Tunnell, *Crucible of Reconstruction*, chap. 3.

[2] Rodrigue, *Reconstruction in the Cane Fields*, 51–55.

reconcile the conflicting demands of planters and former slaves following the end of slavery. They were once again an improvised response to immediate circumstances rather than a carefully crafted blueprint for a new social order. Yet, in contrast to previous years, a civilian government was now in place that was supposed to have defined the new labor arrangements and the legal status of the former slaves. It had come nowhere near achieving those objectives. Military oversight of plantation labor in early 1865, however necessary, offered no better evidence of the fundamental weakness of Lincoln's Louisiana government.

Hurlbut overlooked criticism of Banks's 1864 labor regulations in retaining most of their essential features. "Voluntary" contracts between the parties were again required, subject to approval by Thomas W. Conway, Superintendent of Free Labor. Laborers were free to choose their employers, but they were then required to fulfill their contracts for the year or forfeit any back wages "and be otherwise punished as the nature of the case may require." Wages were set at between $10 and $5 per month, according to classification, paid quarterly (not monthly), one-half up front and the balance withheld until completion of the crop. Employers were required to provide laborers with basic necessities and schooling for children. Laborers also received use of garden plots of up to one acre, on which they were free to raise crops of their choosing, but they were prohibited to keep any animals other than domestic poultry. The workday was set at ten hours in summer and nine in winter, and the workweek ended at noon on Saturday, with customary night and weekend labor during the harvest compensated "as extra work." Laborers were ensured just treatment, "and any cruelty, inhumanity or neglect of duty" by their employers would be "summarily punished." In turn, laborers were required to "work faithfully," with the military enforcing the contracts if necessary. The government "will protect and sustain them against ill treatment," Hurlbut assured the former slaves, but it "cannot support those who are capable of earning an honest living by industry." A tax to fund the system was levied on planters of $2 per laborer per year and on laborers of $1 dollar each. A lien on the crop and on other plantation property would secure the laborers' back wages. Contracts already entered into before the regulations had been issued would be submitted to Conway for approval.[3]

Unsurprisingly, Hurlbut's regulations immediately incited objections from the laborers' advocates. In a series of editorials throughout March, the New Orleans *Tribune* repeatedly rebuked the new labor policy as thinly disguised slavery. Hurlbut was so incensed that he threatened to have the *Tribune*'s editor, Jean-Charles Houzeau, who was not an American citizen, run out of the country. The New Orleans free people of color, led by the irrepressible James H. Ingraham, also chimed in. At a mass meeting in mid-March, they approved

---

[3] *Freedom: WGFL-LS*, 591–94 (doc. 138; quotations), 876n.

resolutions condemning the regulations, later presenting them to Hurlbut and having them published in the *Tribune* and the northern abolitionist press. The free people of color had previously criticized the Louisiana government and Banks's labor policy, and they had intensified that criticism since the formation in January of the Louisiana National Equal Rights League. Hurlbut's regulations provided more grist for the mill while further solidifying the bonds between the free people of color and the freed people. In addition to condemning Hurlbut's regulations and the entire military-labor apparatus, the resolutions demanded the unfettered freedom of contract and the elimination of all restrictions on geographical mobility "on account of color," the abolition of the Bureau of Free Labor and Conway's removal, and the establishment of a "tribunal of Arbitrators" that would include former slaves and to which military decisions "on matter of labor" could be appealed. "[W]e denounce, to the world," the resolutions' authors proclaimed, "the attempts, and wishes of the former slaveowners to transform, the boon of Liberty, solemnly offered to the American Slaves into a disguised bondage."[4]

Defending his own policy as forcefully as Banks had defended his, Hurlbut responded to the petitioners in kind. He questioned their integrity, all but accusing them of making statements they knew to be false. He denied their right to speak for the former slaves, contending, not without merit, that "there was always and is now bitterness of feeling" between the two groups. He defended military authority to oversee labor arrangements. "Are you willing with your knowledge of Society here," he asked, "to have the military officers withdraw all control and leave these questions of Labor of Freedom [Freedmen] and of rights to such Civil authority as exists in this State[?]" This was not an unfair question, but neither would the supporters of Louisiana's government have appreciated it. The measures complained of were "temporary," Hurlbut continued, adding that "the effects of two centuries of wrong upon White and Black" could not be undone "in a day or a year." Rather than holding meetings and passing resolutions, Hurlbut intoned, his critics should "work faithfully and slowly to educate the public mind both of whites and blacks, for the future." For now, and until such time as "the Freedman can safely appeal to society and the Civil Courts for his rights when invaded," Hurlbut insisted, military authority was essential, and he would not accede to his critics' demands. "I shall not change a system adopted without facts and reasons satisfactory to my mind," he imperiously concluded.[5]

However valid the criticism of his policy, Hurlbut had a point. Withdrawing military power and leaving the former slaves to the mercies of a civil

---

[4] Houzeau, *My Passage at the New Orleans* Tribune, 103–6; *Freedom: WGFL-LS*, 375, 594–96 (doc. 139; quotations); Ripley, *Slaves and Freedmen*, chap. 4.

[5] *Freedom: WGFL-LS*, 375, 596–98 (doc. 139; quotations).

government under local white control would have been a disaster. All one had to do was ask the former slaveholders themselves. They did not even pretend to disguise their view of emancipation as a catastrophe, and they were not shy in offering solutions. In their private journals and correspondence, and in whatever public forums were available to them, they bemoaned the "demoralization" of labor that they insisted was an inevitable consequence of abolition. With slavery gone, they argued, the state government would need to find a substitute that ensured its essence.

This is how William J. Minor saw the matter. The owner of multiple sugar and cotton estates and hundreds of slaves in southern Louisiana and the Natchez District, Minor had been one of the antebellum South's wealthiest slaveholders. No fire-eating zealot, he claimed to have opposed disunion even after Louisiana seceded. He had taken the oath of allegiance after the fall of New Orleans and subsequently played a prominent role in conservative Unionism. Testifying in late April 1865 (by which point Confederate forces in the west had yet to surrender) before a Federal commission investigating corruption in Louisiana but that also looked into other matters, Minor provided a dismal account of conditions on the plantations. Drinking, gambling, idleness, blasphemy (and "religious fanaticism"), adultery, wife-beating, "running about," etc. – not to mention the breakdown of work routines and its devastating financial consequences – prevailed without the old forms of discipline. The only remedy for these difficulties, Minor insisted, would be "to take us back under the Constitution & establish things as they were, but perhaps under some other name." When asked by the commission whether this meant "[r]etaining the institution of slavery," he responded affirmatively. "I am the more inclined to think so because I was one of those who were altogether opposed to going out in the beginning. I have been anxious for a restoration under the Constitution from the first day of secession up to the present day." Minor entertained no doubt that such a restoration entailed preserving slavery. "My own opinion is that if slavery is completely abolished" – the "if" may have been the most important word in this sentence – "this county [country] will have ceased to have been a sugar growing country."

Minor went on to condemn Louisiana's free-state government, contending that the white population had boycotted its creation. However, were the local residents, with views similar to his own, to assume control of that government without Federal interference, Minor sounded a different tune. "In case the state should come into the Union & the old citizens recovered the control of the state Govt. – then the laws that they would pass, – if not interfered with by the General Govt. & fully executed, – would, in a great measure, remedy these evils of which we complain." It did not take much to imagine what such laws would look like. "But this is based upon the assumption that the old citizens get possession of the Govt., for otherwise we could not rely upon it at all; & I dont think that the laws passed by people who have jost come here, would remedy the evils of which we complain." Minor deplored the seceded states being "carried back by force" into the Union, but the real problem was their forcible return without some approximation of slavery. "I think that we must have a reconstruction under the Constitution, that we may send our represenativ & establish things as they were befor[e] the war," he insisted. The Confederacy was dead, the rebellion trampled, and slavery abolished in Louisiana, but establishing things as they were before the war was now the goal.[6]

Minor was hardly alone. Other planters said similar things before the commission and in other contexts, and they would continue for years to come. By the spring of 1865, Louisiana sugar planters had been operating for nearly three years under a labor system that denied them the control they had once wielded. The main lesson they had drawn from that experience was that the old order somehow had to be reestablished. Yet their testimony – offered in so many ways, and despite their own intentions – revealed how dramatically everything had changed. Whatever the limitations of their wartime experience, black people could no longer be bought and sold as chattel, punished brutally, or killed with impunity, and never again would they think of themselves as slaves. Former slaveholders now looked to Federal authority – their erstwhile adversary – for help in resurrecting their lost world. The best they could hope for – although this cannot be underestimated – would be to control the state government and enact laws that might restore a semblance of their former dominance. Gone was the personal authority – itself a creation of state power and sanctioned at law – they had once exerted over their slaves. The outlook of former slaveholders such as Minor, who resided in areas long under Federal control, did not bode well for the response to emancipation by their counterparts who were only now succumbing to Federal authority.[7]

II

"But a new season opens," Col. John Eaton wrote from Washington, DC, in late January 1865, to Treasury secretary Fessenden. "I am anxious that it should start with all the advantages of the past year's experience." Eaton was discussing the interrelated questions, still unresolved, of whether the Treasury Department would assume control over the plantation-labor system, and

---

[6] *Freedom: WGFL-LS*, 376, 599–607 (doc. 140; all quotations). On Minor's wartime Unionism, see Smith, *Mississippi in the Civil War*, 128.
[7] *Freedom: WGFL-LS*, 376–77, 607–11 (doc. 141), and 611–13 (doc. 142) for other planter testimony before the commission. On the sugar planters at the end of the war, see Rodrigue, *Reconstruction in the Cane Fields*, 59–60.

where the proposed Freedmen's Bureau would be situated. "I am aware Congress is agitating the whole subject," he added. By early 1865, the Union-occupied cotton sections of the lower Mississippi valley had completed the first full crop under free labor. Although the results had been mixed, Eaton and others believed that great progress had been made, and they insisted that *independent* black labor – as opposed to wage labor on the plantations – ought to be the long-term goal of Federal policy. Notwithstanding the determination of former slaveholders in the cotton country to salvage some vestige of slavery, the reality was that all operating cotton plantations in Union-held areas were working with some version of voluntary labor. The struggle was over the contours of the new order and not its existence. As the new crop year was getting underway, all parties, like it or not, were building on what Eaton called "all the advantages of the past year's experience."[8]

Congress's decision to locate the Freedmen's Bureau in the War Department, however, did not end administrative uncertainty; neither did Hurlbut's labor regulations, which were adopted in much of the lower Mississippi valley. Some planters, both residents and northern lessees, had already entered into agreements with laborers for the year under Mellen's guidelines, only to discover that Hurlbut's had obviated them. Others, wanting to get an early start to the season, had made contracts based on the previous year's regulations. However self-servingly, some planters avowed that having to enter into a second or even third agreement in the space of three months would further impede their plantation operations. "It was difficult to make the negroes understand, *why* it was necessary to make a new bargain when they understood that the first was to hold good for one year. & they considerd they were bounden by it," insisted a group of some two dozen planters near Natchez – including residents and lessees – in early April, requesting that the existing arrangements be upheld and Hurlbut's regulations suspended. "If a 3^d agreemt must be made its effects will be very deleterious to them, & hinder much in prosecuting plan^{tn} work at this hurried season – & many of them would not agree thereto." The planters had a valid point. This *was* confusing. But the main problem for most of them, or at least the residents, was less the *change* of government labor policy than the need for one in the first place.[9]

Just as many former slaveholding cotton planters were set upon reestablishing the old forms of authority, former slaves were equally resolved to achieve

---

[8] *Freedom: WGFL-LS*, 861–64 (doc. 217), 869–71 (doc. 221), 871–77 (doc. 222A-B; quotation, 872), 878 (doc. 224); Eaton, *Grant, Lincoln, and the Freedmen*, 220. On plantation affairs during this time in the cotton-growing sections of the Union-occupied lower Mississippi valley, see Gerteis, *From Contraband to Freedman*, 162–67; Moneyhon, *Impact of the Civil War and Reconstruction on Arkansas*, 150–51; Wayne, *Reshaping of Plantation Society*, 39–52.

[9] *Freedom: WGFL-LS*, 879–80 (doc. 225).

economic independence. The petition by a group of Mississippi former slaves to a Treasury Department official at Memphis in June 1865 encapsulated these aspirations and demonstrated the lengths to which their adherents were willing to go to realize them. The petitioners, including both men and women, identified themselves as "men of colour of African decent, who have been recognized by their late owners as free, under the proclamation of President Lincoln, and as freed-men are laboring for their own support and benefit, and that of their families." As hostilities were ending in Mississippi, they explained, they had managed to secure the remnants of the local cotton crop, which the Confederate national government had previously purchased. The cotton had been exposed to the elements for months, and what little the Confederate soldiers had not hauled off or destroyed was rotten and worthless. Nonetheless, "out of what was left by said Rebel Soldiers, or not burnt," their testimonial continued, "your petitioners picked by hand, & with arduous labour, separated from the decayed and decaying Cotton, conveyed to the nearest Gin, repacked, rebaled & repressed, to the extent of Twenty six (26) Bales Cotton." One can only imagine the tediousness of these tasks and the "arduous labor" they required. The petitioners were transmitting the fruits of that labor to the treasury official. In return, they "respectfully claim[ed] the most liberal compensation allowable under the circumstances, for their own benefit & to discharge obligations to others (independent of their late owner)," which they had incurred in salvaging the crop. As was so often the case, the historical record is silent on whether the petitioners received the desired compensation. Twenty-six bales of cotton was no small consideration to persons coming out of slavery with almost nothing to their names, and whose goal was to become self-supporting and independent.[10]

The conflicting objectives of planters and freed people has traditionally infused the scholarship on labor arrangements in the postbellum cotton South. The former slaves' aversion to returning to the old order and their desire for autonomy under the new were crucial to the various versions of sharecropping and tenancy that later emerged there. Although free labor on the cotton and sugar plantations of the lower Mississippi valley shared much in common by the end of the war, the postwar transition played out very differently in the two regions. Louisiana sugar plantations underwent considerable change after the war, yet by the spring of 1865 their main characteristics were well entrenched. A centralized plantation regimen featuring monthly wage labor, the gang system under close white supervision, and housing patterns that replicated the "slave quarters" of the antebellum era would largely survive the destruction of slavery and last well into the twentieth century. Employers and laborers would do battle over wage rates and the method of payment as well as over the specifics of work routines, but they did so within the parameters of this centralized regimen. The lower Mississippi valley's cotton plantations, by contrast, exhibited labor arrangements

[10] *Freedom: WGFL-LS*, 889–90 (doc. 230). See also *Freedom: WGFL-LS*, 881–87 (doc. 227).

as the war ended that proved to be transitory to other modes of organizing labor. By the early 1870s, these plantations would come to be defined by a decentralized regimen. Although the various permutations of sharecropping and tenancy that predominated on them continued to evolve over time, they were generally characterized by multiple black families and households dispersed over the estate, with each one working its own plot of land more or less independently. In only a few short years, then, and for decades thereafter, the cotton plantations would look dramatically different from their 1865 counterparts.

The sugar and cotton plantations of the lower Mississippi valley were thus set apart by divergent labor regimes under slavery as well as by the long-term consequences of their wartime experiences. The "rehearsal" for Reconstruction in the lower Mississippi would produce very different outcomes in the sugar and cotton regions. Yet for all of these differences, the two most salient features of the transition to free labor in both crop regions – as would be the case everywhere else – were the freed people's aspirations for autonomy and control over their productive lives, which shaped just about everything they did in the coming years, and the former slaveholders' determination to "establish things as they were befor[e] the war."

III

By war's end, the editors of the Freedmen and Southern Society Project (FSSP) have estimated, about half a million of the 3.5 million enslaved persons in the seceded states – or nearly 15 percent – were emancipated. Of this number, which includes soldiers, military laborers, and civilians, about 250,000 were from the lower Mississippi valley: 100,000 in southern Louisiana; 125,000 in Mississippi, Arkansas, and western Tennessee; and 25,000 in central and eastern Tennessee. The lower Mississippi valley therefore included a disproportionate number of slaves in the seceded states who experienced wartime liberation. Whereas the 1.16 million slaves of the lower Mississippi valley constituted a third of the 1860 slave population of the Confederate states, the region accounted for half of the persons in those states freed during the war.[11]

These figures represent the *minimum* number of slaves so liberated. Because they account for persons *living* at the end of the war, at least for civilians, these figures exclude the countless freed persons who perished after their liberation. (The numbers for soldiers are based largely on recruitment and therefore account for mortality.) Disease and death, as Jim Downs and other historians have shown, ravaged the former slave populations of the contraband camps and other settlements. Taking

---

[11] These numbers are based on the estimates in *Freedom: WGFL-LS*, 76–79, which includes the rationale for the estimates. The figures presented here pertain only to the seceded states and do not consider the 500,000 slaves in the border states.

mortality into account, a figure 20 percent higher than 500,000 is not inconceivable, meaning that perhaps 300,000 or more slaves in the lower Mississippi valley and 600,000 or more in the Confederate states may have gained their freedom during the war. Yet even these additions left between 800,000 and 850,000 persons in the lower Mississippi valley – or roughly between two-thirds and three-quarters of the prewar slave population – in bondage when the war ended.[12]

These thousands of "slaves" awaited their deliverance despite having been declared free more than two years earlier by the Emancipation Proclamation. They remained subjugated on farms and plantations in northern and western Louisiana, southwestern Arkansas, and eastern Mississippi. Slaveholders had also "refugeed" tens of thousands of slaves into the Confederate interior in what was itself among the largest forced migrations in US history. Slaves west of the Mississippi were taken to Texas, while those east of the river were dragged into eastern Mississippi and Alabama. Untold numbers of these slaves died from disease or other causes before returning home or experiencing freedom. Many slaves languished in remote areas and would not gain their freedom until well into the summer.[13]

---

[12] The figure for Mississippi, Arkansas, and west Tennessee provided in the previous paragraph includes approximately 50,000 soldiers *on duty* at the time the estimate was made (thus excluding soldiers from those states who had died); the figures for the other areas are based on the number of soldiers *recruited*. On slave mortality during the war, especially fugitive slaves, see Downs, *Sick from Freedom*. Downs attempts no estimate of the mortality of slaves during the war, noting that the figures do not exist to provide even rough estimates (see esp. 194, n. 6.). It stands to reason that while the disruption, shortages, and chaos of war dramatically affected all southern civilians, black and white, sickness and mortality would have had a much greater effect on fugitive slaves, many of whom reached Union lines only to subsequently perish, than on slaves who remained on their home plantations. Given the overwhelming evidence that Downs presents, it is hardly inconceivable to envision mortality rates of 10 percent among slaves who reached Union lines. For recent examinations of life in the contraband camps and other places of refuge, though making no attempt to estimate mortality among the former slaves in them, see Manning, *Troubled Refuge*, esp. 31–41, 106–39; Taylor, *Embattled Freedom*, esp. chap. 2. Sternhell, *Routes of War*, esp. chap. 3, examines civilian population movement in general during the war. On death among former slaves in contraband camps and as refugees in Arkansas, and on population decline in that state in general during the war, see Moneyhon, *Impact of the Civil War and Reconstruction on Arkansas*, 177–79. For similar observations for Mississippi, see Harris, *Presidential Reconstruction in Mississippi*, 26–27.

[13] On conditions from the end of the war through 1865 in southwest Arkansas, see Poe, "Contours of Emancipation." For Tennessee, see Cimprich, *Slavery's End in Tennessee*, 119–20; Ash, *Middle Tennessee Society Transformed*, chaps. 5–6; Alexander, *Political Reconstruction in Tennessee*, chap. 4. For southwest Louisiana, see Wade, "I Would Rather Be Among the Comanches," 45–64. For Mississippi, see Harris, *Presidential Reconstruction in Mississippi*, chap. 2.

As a vast scholarly literature has shown, and as the wartime dismantling of slavery in the lower Mississippi valley and elsewhere demonstrated, emancipation was as much a process that unfolded gradually as it was a distinct, identifiable moment after which the world would never look the same. The finality of Confederate military defeat notwithstanding, freedom came slowly to those parts of the South that had escaped wartime Union occupation. "There was no one grand moment when slaves and slaveholders all learned of emancipation," the FSSP editors have observed. That being said, what Eugene D. Genovese called the "moment of truth" – that precise instant when it dawned on both master and slave that the game was up – infuses the historical record. In thousands of individual encounters between men and women, black and white, what Genovese and Elizabeth Fox-Genovese subsequently described as the master class's "fatal self-deception" was finally exposed for the sham it had always been. Their slaves had not loved them after all, the slaveholders now discovered, and had no intention of remaining loyal. The ex-slaveholders did not take the news well. The "moment" of emancipation, such as it was, unleashed the full range of emotions within the human psyche – from unspeakable joy and elation to the depths of desolation and despair to blinding rage and hatred.[14]

During the previous three years, many masters and slaves of the lower Mississippi valley had already experienced the drama of emancipation, with both sides learning hard lessons and discovering inconvenient truths along the way. Now, their counterparts in the rest of the lower Mississippi valley and the South as whole experienced it for themselves. Whether known as "the day of Jubilo," "Juneteenth," or something else, the reckoning had come, as word of Confederate military defeat and slavery's demise spread throughout the previously unconquered parts of the lower Mississippi valley. Even in these areas, the war had significantly weakened slavery, but Confederate capitulation dealt it a crippling blow.

For every former slaveholder who was resigned to the freeing of his or her slaves, many others were not. Again, the historical record for this period is replete with former masters vowing never to reconcile themselves to what many contemporaries called "the new order of things." This intransigence often manifested itself in violence: savage beatings and whippings, sexual assault, and even murder. Just being forced off the plantation and told to fend for oneself was also a traumatic experience. Many masters and slaves had no doubt felt genuine affection for one another, while something amounting to paternalism had in certain instances existed between them. Yet these experiences affirm how deeply the master–slave relationship had been rooted in

---

[14] *Freedom: L&L-1865*, 75; Genovese, *Roll, Jordan, Roll*, 97–112 (quotation, 97); Genovese and Fox-Genovese, *Fatal Self-Deception*. Seminal works on this moment of emancipation include Litwack, *Been in the Storm So Long*, and Roark, *Masters without Slaves*.

violence. "The tying up of women by the thumbs, and the cruel punishment of all classes and ages of colored people is indulged in to the heart's content of these enlightened and humane whites," sardonically observed the Federal commander at Columbia, Louisiana.[15]

These attacks were part of the larger epidemic of mayhem that swept the southern countryside in the war's immediate aftermath. Essential to the narrative of postwar Reconstruction is how violence against former slaves – and the refusal of white civil authorities to do anything about it once they had regained power – helped to turn northern public opinion against Andrew Johnson's Reconstruction policy. The antebellum South had always been a violent place, and this violence, fueled by the white obsession with controlling a restive slave population, had intensified with the chaos and confusion of war. Now, white Southerners unleashed upon the former slaves a systematic campaign of terror – even if individual attacks were inflicted arbitrarily and capriciously – as thousands of embittered Confederate veterans, inured to violence, returned home, and as the freed people lost the elementary protection their masters had once afforded them.[16]

Although such violence reflected the visceral reaction to emancipation, many white residents of the lower Mississippi valley consciously connived to overturn emancipation and salvage slavery. However delusional in hindsight, the belief that slavery was not dead itself refused to die. Many people were taking Johnson's amnesty oath "simply to acquire political power to be used, in again reducing the people nearly to Slavery as possible," a Federal officer reported in July after touring northern Mississippi. By controlling the state government, "they hope to use it in the interest of the Planters, as against the free labor of the state," he continued, adding that "the number is by no means small who are hoping. & half *expecting* to get their slaves back – under the state government." Many persons were "studying the question of 'what to do with the negro,['] but always with a leaning back towards slavery." Such views were also widely expressed in the states that had abolished slavery. After being informed by the local bureau agent in August that a former slave whom he had previously prevented from leaving the plantation with his belongings was in fact free to do so, a former Arkansas slaveholder responded that he considered him "my property still, having seen no enactment of the Federal Congress, nor of our State Gov.^t authorizing anyone to demand him of me." Having claimed immunity from Federal and state antislavery measures, he

---

[15] *Freedom: L&L-1865*, 152–55 (doc. 25), 165–66 (doc. 31; quotation).

[16] On conditions in the lower Mississippi valley by the summer of 1865, especially with regard to ending slavery, see Taylor, *Louisiana Reconstructed*, 88–94; Moneyhon, *Impact of the Civil War and Reconstruction on Arkansas*, chap. 9; Harris, *Presidential Reconstruction in Mississippi*, 18–36, 79–82; Cimprich, *Slavery's End in Tennessee*, 118–26; Ash, *Middle Tennessee Society Transformed*, chap. 6; Wayne, *Reshaping of Plantation Society*, 39–45.

continued his disquisition: "When I am perfectly satisfied that the slaves have been emancipated by such authority as is regarded as constitutional by our higher courts of Law & Equity," he solemnly pronounced, "then, & not till then will I willingly by word or deed make any contract with a slave, nor regard them in any other light than as the property of those who have either purchased or raised them." This would-be legal scholar hastened to add that he had no intention of interfering with "the constitutional authorities of the U. States."[17]

Given such attitudes, it indeed fell to Federal authorities to make emancipation a reality. This monumental task was taken up first by the army but soon devolved onto the newly established Freedmen's Bureau, the controversies over which were destined to become an essential element of postwar Reconstruction. Little remained beyond the bureau's purview in overseeing the transition from slavery to freedom, but the large majority of bureau officials viewed as central to their mission the objective of inculcating both former slaves and former slaveholders with the principles of voluntary labor. Although they generally assumed that neither side properly understood how such a labor system worked, these officials also remained convinced, as the head of the Freedmen's Bureau for Mississippi observed, that the "interests of the Planters and the Freedmen lie parallel to each other." Consequently, he added: "They cannot become hostile unless prejudice makes them so."[18]

In trying to overcome this prejudice, the bureau's first and only commissioner was Major General O. O. Howard, who, despite an uneven war record, harbored a sincere concern for the former slaves. Howard appointed "assistant commissioners" to lead the bureau in the eleven seceded states and Washington, DC, choosing men with whom he had served during the war or who shared his outlook. Thomas W. Conway, despite having engendered criticism as head of the Bureau of Free Labor in Louisiana, stayed on to lead the bureau there. Col. Samuel Thomas, who had served as John Eaton's right-hand man in the lower Mississippi valley, administered the bureau in Mississippi. For Arkansas, General John W. Sprague, who had served with Howard in the war, was selected. For Tennessee, Howard chose General Clinton B. Fisk, a firm abolitionist before the war. John Eaton, who had been so deeply involved with the freed people during the war, headed the bureau's Washington branch and essentially assisted Howard in running the bureau. By mid-October, Conway was removed, a victim of Andrew Johnson's war on the

---

[17] *Freedom: L&L-1865*, 74, 77, 110–28 (doc. 14; Mississippi quotation, 116), 144–45 (doc. 21; Arkansas); *Freedom: WGFL-LS*, 843 (doc. 211). For the continuation of proslavery ideas in Mississippi through 1865, and the refusal of white society to accommodate itself to emancipation, see Harris, *Presidential Reconstruction in Mississippi*, chaps. 4–7; Ash, *A Year in the South: 1865*, 143–56, 219–33.

[18] For a succinct overview of the Freedmen's Bureau, especially for the immediate postwar period, see *Freedom: L&L-1865*, 170–97 (Mississippi quotation, 180).

bureau; the other assistant commissioners served into 1866. Even in the lower Mississippi valley, where the rudimentary framework for the bureau was already in place, the agency never received the resources consistent with its vast responsibilities. By August 1865, a mere ninety-seven agents manned the district or field offices of the four states of the region (twenty-four in Arkansas; thirteen in Louisiana; forty-nine in Mississippi; and eleven in Tennessee). By December, the number had increased to about 150, but this figure still left each agent responsible for an average area of more than 1,000 square miles.[19]

Despite the often-heroic efforts of these officials, even former slaveholders who reconciled themselves to the new order generally envisioned labor and race relations that resembled slavery as closely as possible. Whether the issue was the hours and pace of work, discipline and corporal punishment, the former slaves' freedom of movement, their personal behavior and deportment, or just about anything else, the former slaveholders were intent on maintaining their old prerogatives. They seemed genuinely unable to comprehend, a Mississippi Freedmen's Bureau agent noted, that they no longer possessed the "Divine right" to whip their former slaves. In Louisiana, a group of former slaveholders unabashedly petitioned Federal authorities "to have the control of the labor system put in their own hands that they may reinstate the former regulations existing before the war." Getting former masters to acknowledge slavery's legal demise was one thing, persuading them to abandon old practices and habits was another.[20]

Among the most telling of the former slaveholders' various stratagems for complying with the letter but not the spirit of the law involved their use of the phrases "as they have always done" or "as heretofore" in defining the former slaves' new obligations and duties. Although ostensibly applicable to both parties, such language was clearly intended for only one. From their initial interactions with former slaves, informing them that they were free, to the contracts they signed with them, usually without bureau

---

[19] On Howard and the assistant commissioners, see US Congress, House of Representatives, *Freedmen's Bureau*, 2–3; McFeely, *Yankee Stepfather*, chaps. 4–5; Bentley, *History of the Freedmen's Bureau*, 56–61, 70–71. On the number of bureau officials in the states of the lower Mississippi valley, see *Freedom: L&L-1865*, 174–76; US Congress, House of Representatives, *Freedmen's Bureau*, 28–32, 38; Project Files, Freedmen and Southern Society Project, University of Maryland. Thanks to my former FSSP colleague Steven F. Miller for providing information on the number of agents from the project's files. On the Freedmen's Bureau in general in the states of the lower Mississippi valley, see Bell, "'Une Chimère'"; Cimprich, *Slavery's End in Tennessee*, 124–29; Harris, *Presidential Reconstruction in Mississippi*, 82–103; Finley, *From Slavery to Uncertain Freedom*, esp. chap. 2; Finley, "Personnel of the Freedmen's Bureau in Arkansas"; McCrary, *Abraham Lincoln and Reconstruction*, 322–30; Moneyhon, *Impact of the Civil War and Reconstruction on Arkansas*, 210–19; Rodrigue, "The Freedmen's Bureau and Wage Labor"; Tunnell, *Edge of the Sword*, chaps. 6–8; White, *Freedmen's Bureau in Louisiana*.

[20] *Freedom: L&L-1865*, 84, for both quotations, and on the problem of corporal punishment in general.

approval, to the enforcement of those contracts, former slaveholders routinely employed language signifying their intent to maintain the old modes of control. By promising to "compensate" them as they had always done, they hoped to bamboozle former slaves into consenting to other facets of plantation life, especially those pertaining to discipline and authority. "The very common feeling of the planters was that it was quite desirable that the Freed men should remain on the plantations, where they had lived – but *most* desirable that they should remain '*as they always had done*,'" observed a Federal officer in Mississippi. "This common, & evidently favorite form of expression, was plainly designed to cover the idea in most cases, that the people were to be kept subject to a control nearly as absolute as the former, but established by agreement of parties." Planters who used this expression without offering "*distinctive compensation* for labor," he went on, "simply felt compelled to cover their hostility to emancipation by such adroitly coined phraseology, while they meant by it as nearly nothing as possible." Other employers did not even bother with such sophistry. One Louisiana freedwoman entered into an agreement with her former owner that required her to conduct herself as when she "*was owned by him as a* SLAVE" while limiting her compensation to what she had received "*while she was the* SLAVE *of the employer*."[21]

Former slaveholders who only now confronted emancipation contested it every step of the way. Black people in some remote areas continued to live as "slaves," their "owners" withholding word of their deliverance. Planters were more committed than ever to regaining labor and racial control, and the contours of the new order were still undetermined. Yet owing to the resolve of the former slaves, backed by Federal authority, there was no regressing. By the fall of 1865, nearly all of the more than three-quarters of a million persons in the lower Mississippi valley who were still enslaved when the war ended had gained their freedom. Nonetheless, just as erstwhile conservative Unionists and ex-Confederates were converging to prevent black suffrage, former slaveholders who had experienced wartime free labor and those who had not were also joining forces, intent on preserving mastery.

IV

Henry Adams – the one less known to US history – was born a slave in 1843 in Georgia. Originally named Henry Houston, he and his family were taken in 1850 to De Soto Parish, in northwestern Louisiana near Shreveport, when he became Henry Adams. After his master died in 1858, Adams became the property of a teenage girl, Nancy Emily Adams, but he and his father were

---

[21] *Freedom: L&L-1865*, 110–28 (doc. 14; quotations, 110–11), 321.

hired out to a planter named Ferguson near Logansport, in De Soto. They worked there for the remainder of the antebellum period and during the war, although Adams's mother belonged to a different owner and lived separately from them. While still a slave, Adams had married a woman named Malinda, who bore him four children, but she and the children belonged to another owner, who at some point had taken them into Texas.[22]

Perhaps because he had been hired out as a slave, Adams had accumulated modest property and was considered "a rich negro" exiting slavery. He enlisted in the army in 1866 and served for three years, learning to read and write. He later immersed himself in the politics of Radical Reconstruction in northwestern Louisiana. By the mid-1870s, with Reconstruction increasingly under attack, Adams was promoting black emigration to Liberia, and he helped to organize the Colonization Council, which petitioned for Federal assistance in that endeavor. When "Kansas fever" swept parts of the lower Mississippi valley in the late 1870s, Adams and other emigrationists shifted their focus to that initiative. Although never moving to Kansas himself, Adams testified in 1880 before a US Senate committee investigating black emigrationist sentiment in the South. His testimony provided much of the information on his incredible life before he disappeared in the mid-1880s from the historical record.

Adams's testimony – recounting his and his fellow freed people's harrowing experiences in the months after gaining freedom – reads like the story of postwar emancipation in microcosm. "[T]he white men read a paper to all of us colored people, telling us that we were all free, and that we colored people could go where we pleased and manage our own affairs, and could work for who we pleased," Adams recalled of the moment he learned that he no was longer human property. W. M. C. Carrods, "the boss man" who managed Ferguson's plantation, advised Adams and the other former slaves to remain on the place and work for him, since "the bad white men was mad with all the negroes, because they were free, and they would kill you all for fun." By staying and signing labor contracts, Carrods insisted, the former slaves would enjoy the protection of their former masters, "and by that we may be able to protect you from the bad white men, and keep them from killing you all so much."

Despite much cajoling from Carrods, Adams refused to sign a contract, which he deemed a ruse to ensnare him and his fellow freed people. Neither would he carry the pass that Carrods insisted was necessary to prevent white men from beating or killing any black person found on the public road. "I said if I cannot do like a white man I am not free," Adams riposted. "You says we must carry a pass to keep the white men from killing us, or whipping us, so I think still we are all slaves, and I will sign no paper." Indeed, Adams realized

---

[22] The information on Adams is from his congressional testimony in US Congress, Senate, *Report and Testimony of the Select Committee*, pt. 2, 190–92. See also Hahn, *Nation Under Our Feet*, chap. 7; Painter, *Exodusters*, chaps. 6–8.

that no mere scrap of paper would offer black lives, bodies, or property any meaningful protection. "I might sign to be killed," Adams continued, "and I believe that the white people is trying to fool us to see if we are fools enough to go off to work for ourselves, and then everywhere they see one of us they will kill us and take all of our money away what we work for, and everything that we may have." Only at length did Carrods convince most of the sixty former slaves on the place to sign the contract – claiming that "the Yankees" required them to do so – though Adams and a few others held out. Despite the agreement, Carrods provided them with meager compensation – and sometimes none – for their work. "We split rails three or four weeks," Adams recalled, "and got not a cent for that."

Matters only worsened. In September, Adams told Carrods he planned to visit Shreveport for a few days, although he again refused to carry a pass. He had gotten but a few miles from home before a group of white men confronted him. When one of them asked him to whom he belonged, Adams replied: "I told him no one." This led to a beating, along with threats to kill him "and every other negro who told them that they did not belong to any one." Only after one of the marauders vouched for Adams as a "good nigger" did the beating stop, and Adams was allowed to continue on to Shreveport. Upon returning, Adams inquired of Carrods's wife Frances whether "the boss" was home. She responded by berating Adams and demanding that he and the other freed people continue to call her and her husband "mistress" and "master" or leave. "[W]e will have no nigger here on our place who cannot say mistress and master; and you shall, for you all are not free yet, and will not be until Congress sits, for General Butler cannot free any one, and you shall call every white lady misses, and every white man boss, master." Adding injury to insult, Frances Carrods later that week viciously assaulted Adams's younger sister, and the next day Carrods himself "whipped her nearly to death." Because the contract – for all that was worth – had specified that Carrods "was to hit no one any more," a number people on the place decided to leave.

Days later, Adams followed suit, heading for Shreveport with several other men and boys. The travelers were soon set upon by a posse of forty or fifty armed white men, who shot at them and stole all of their possessions and money, including Adams's horse and $150 in gold, swearing that "they were going to kill every nigger they found leaving their masters." Adams later retrieved his horse through Carrods's intersession. He took to peddling during the fall, although he was required to carry a pass in accordance with the laws and ordinances the states and local communities were enacting under Andrew Johnson's Reconstruction policy. Adams was accosted several times while conducting business. In one instance, a crowd of white men, under the pretext of searching for pistols, robbed him of $250 worth of goods and money, "and the law would do nothing about it." That same day, Adams was shot at by the same crowd of men, who also broke up black churches and attacked and robbed any black people whom they found trying to leave their former masters. The simple act of leaving the plantation constituted "running away," as it had formerly. The white people, Adams explained, "killed many hundreds of my race when they were running away to get freedom."

"After they told us we were free – even then they would not let us live as man and wife together," Adams continued. "And when we would run away to be free from slavery, the white people would not let us come on their places to see our mothers, wives, sisters, or fathers. We was made to leave the place, or made to go back and live as slaves." Adams claimed personal knowledge of more than 2,000 formerly enslaved persons in the Shreveport-Logansport area alone having been murdered, "trying to get away, after the white people told us we were free, which was in 1865."

21

"The Institution of Slavery Having Been Destroyed"

For the delegates who descended on Jackson, Mississippi, in mid-August 1865 for the state's Reconstruction convention, neither the vague language nor passive voice was accidental. Both were deliberate, the products of intense – and what many Northerners considered absurd – debate. "Slavery *having been* destroyed." If one of the central conundrums of Reconstruction was the attempt to reconcile such fundamental American traditions as government by the consent of the governed with the reality that the seceded states – or at least the large majority of their white populations – had been coerced back into the Union, those states now had to pretend that they were voluntarily abolishing slavery. Of course, they were doing no such thing. Most of the delegates recognized that they had no choice but to abolish slavery if they had any hope of being "readmitted" to the Union and regaining self-rule. Having gambled all on a desperate bid for independence, and having lost, they now faced the consequences.

Mississippi was the last seceded state of the lower Mississippi valley – but the first unreconstructed state – to abolish slavery and undertake political reorganization. The Mississippi convention was the offspring of President Andrew Johnson's Reconstruction policy, which the nation was debating even as it was being implemented. While each of the three reconstructed states of the lower Mississippi valley demonstrated its own characteristics in confronting the challenges of postwar Reconstruction, one feature they all shared – along with Mississippi and the other rebellious states – was the exclusion of their black populations from this process. This exclusion, however, did not prevent the southern states' black populations from putting forward their own aspirations for freedom, as exemplified by the black convention in early August in Nashville, Tennessee, one of many such conventions held throughout the nation in the months after the war.

If abolishing slavery was the central issue the Mississippi convention had to address, embedded within it was a cluster of distinct questions the delegates tried to disentangle. Had not slavery already been "abolished," or had it been "destroyed," and thus practically but not formally abolished? How could the delegates abolish something that essentially no longer existed? And then, who (or what) had abolished or destroyed it? How could the delegates vote to adopt a free-state constitution if they had already sworn a loyalty oath affirming that slavery had been abolished? On and on it went. For two and a half days the delegates deliberated before finally deciding that slavery, *having already been destroyed*, would not "hereafter" exist in Mississippi. Despite their petulance, and however implicitly, the delegates were debating a substantive point, one historians themselves have come to appreciate: who freed the slaves?

Amidst all of this talk, several delegates identified the essential difference between freeing slaves and abolishing slavery. The Emancipation Proclamation, it turns out, had not abolished slavery, and so the delegates, far from confirming a fait accompli, were exploring uncharted territory. Just as many white Southerners bragged openly about restoring slavery once Federal troops had left, the Mississippi delegates deliberated over the idea that slavery still existed. If this were true, then why should they abolish it, at least without getting something in return? This argument may have been more about the postwar settlement than about revitalizing slavery, but it once again illustrated the pitfalls of abolishing slavery under the Federal Constitution.

I

The war was finally over. But as Confederate forces surrendered in the west, as Federal military authority extended over the rebellious states, and as the remaining slaves gained their freedom (except in Delaware and Kentucky), the nation confronted the challenges of the postwar settlement. Few contemporaries could have anticipated how long this project would take, how difficult and contentious it would be, and how tragic its failure would be for the nation. Just establishing law and order, providing relief to the destitute, and destroying the last vestiges of slavery initially took precedence. Little with regard to political Reconstruction could be done until some semblance of "normality" had been achieved, although this objective itself required functioning civilian governments. The end of hostilities did not alter daily life as dramatically in wartime occupied areas as it did in unoccupied ones, but Confederate capitulation marked a distinct break even for persons long under Federal authority. Organizing loyal governments and ending slavery in the unreconstructed states was a given, yet modification of the reconstructed ones was also necessary. Much of the territory of these latter states remained under Confederate control when the war ended, and their white populations would have to be won over or brought to heel. This task was made no easier by the return of thousands of embittered Confederate veterans, convinced that their cause had been a righteous one.

Andrew Johnson outlined his policy toward the unreconstructed states, as noted, in two proclamations of late May 1865: the first providing for amnesty and pardon for former Confederates, the second appointing provisional governors for the seceded states and outlining the procedures by which those states would organize loyal governments. Among various other objectives, Johnson hoped to precipitate a political revolution in the South by replacing the antebellum and Confederate leadership with genuine Unionists. He also sought to prevent the chaos and disorder that many white people feared would follow from emancipation now that the former slaves no longer fell under their masters' control. Johnson excluded high-ranking Confederates and the planter elite from the general amnesty and pardon, but he allowed for them to apply for special pardons. The applications were supposed to be made to the provisional governors, who would then transmit (and recommend) them to the president, but hundreds – perhaps thousands – of applicants appealed directly to Johnson, many of them personally. Having threatened the leaders of the rebellion with political annihilation, Johnson essentially let them off the hook by issuing thousands of special pardons in the coming months. For a host of reasons, Johnson's policy of "self-Reconstruction" would ultimately fail, and, as historians have often noted, Johnson was often his own worst enemy. But no one had reason to believe in the summer of 1865 that this failure was inevitable.[1]

Of the four states of the lower Mississippi valley, only in Mississippi did Johnson appoint a provisional governor, William L. Sharkey. As a planter, former slaveholder, and prominent Whig attorney who had served as Chief Justice of the state Supreme Court before the war, Sharkey was not quite representative of the Unionists Johnson hoped to bring to the fore. Although of humble, east-Tennessee origins, he considered himself a patrician, and he personified what has been called "persistent Whiggery" after the war. Sharkey had fervently opposed disunion, and following secession he devoted himself to his Hinds county plantation and law practice, offering the rebellion no assistance or support. Confederate authorities suspected his loyalties and at one point even had him arrested, but he was not prosecuted. Following the fall of Vicksburg, Sharkey quickly took the oath of allegiance. Loyalists in the Natchez-Vicksburg area tried to persuade him to lead a Unionist movement, but no such initiative ever developed in Mississippi.[2]

Before his removal by Federal authorities in May (and before Johnson issued his proclamations), Confederate Mississippi governor Charles Clark had appointed Sharkey and fellow Unionist William Yerger as commissioners to consult with Johnson on Mississippi's restoration. The two men met with Johnson on June 8 – but as private citizens only. They described conditions

---

[1] Overviews of Presidential Reconstruction that focus on southern politics include Perman, *Reunion without Compromise*, and Carter, *When the War Was Over*. On Johnson, see McKitrick, *Andrew Johnson and Reconstruction*; Summers, *Ordeal of the Reunion*, chaps. 3–4.

[2] Carter, *When the War Was Over*, 26, 43–45; Harris, *Presidential Reconstruction in Mississippi*, 11–14; Harris, *With Charity for All*, 160–61; Smith, *Mississippi in the Civil War*, 48–49; Hall, "William L. Sharkey and Reconstruction."

in the state and made recommendations, assuring Johnson that his Reconstruction policy would meet with approval. Johnson made it clear, according to Yerger's later account, that no rebellious state would be readmitted to the Union without abolishing slavery. Sharkey and Yerger evidently gave Johnson the necessary assurance, and on June 13 Johnson appointed Sharkey provisional governor. The "commissioners" returned home, and on July 1 Sharkey issued a proclamation directing that a state convention meet in Jackson on August 14 and that elections for delegates be held a week earlier.[3]

Resisting advice from his ex-Whig supporters to purge the state government of Democrats, the pragmatic Sharkey realized that the immediate priority was to relieve Mississippi from Federal oversight. This objective would require, in addition to complying with Johnson's dictate on abolition, conferring minimal legal rights on the former slaves. Sharkey's appointment received widespread approval in the state, even from former secessionists, who, for good reason, had feared much worse. Although seventy years old, and, according to one scholar, "an aging veteran of an earlier political era," Sharkey moved expeditiously with the state reorganization process. Mississippi would be the only unreconstructed state to hold a convention during the summer and the first to abolish slavery – although it did not set a good example.[4]

The three reconstructed states of the lower Mississippi valley also confronted the challenges of postwar readjustment. In Tennessee, the return of Confederate veterans posed a special quandary for Johnson, who was bending over backward to rehabilitate former Confederates who then went on to vilify the very government and constitution he had helped create. The former conservative Unionists also continued their opposition to the new order. "There are men here, calling themselves *Union men*, who are seeking to overthrow the present State Government, and clamor for another election under the *old State Constitution*, asking that the *amended* Constitution be set aside and the elections with it," Governor William G. Brownlow informed Johnson in mid-June. "They are writing in the [Nashville] 'Dispatch,' *revolutionary* and *seditious* articles, calling on Rebels to assert their rights at the polls," he continued. "They ought to be imprisoned." After announcing their candidacies for congressional elections, scheduled for early August, conservative Unionists Emerson Etheridge and William B. Campbell continued to question the legitimacy of the recent constitutional convention. After Brownlow instructed military authorities to arrest candidates attempting to

---

[3] Harris, *Presidential Reconstruction in Mississippi*, 40–44. In an address at the state convention, Yerger recounted the mission to Washington and his meeting with Johnson. *Journal of the Proceedings and Debates in the Constitutional Convention of the State of Mississippi*, 145–47; Richardson, *Messages and Papers*, 7: 3512–14. For Sharkey's convention call, see *Mississippi Convention Journal*, 3–9.

[4] Harris, *Presidential Reconstruction in Mississippi*, 43–47; Carter, *When the War Was Over*, 43–45 (quotation, 45).

undermine the constitution, Etheridge was duly arrested and incarcerated until after the election. Campbell only escaped a similar fate when he publicly proclaimed to uphold the constitution and foreswore any attempt to restore slavery. But many private citizens continued to express open support for this objective.[5]

In Arkansas, Governor Isaac Murphy extended his conciliatory policy to the residents of southwest Arkansas by issuing in early May – while the area was still under Confederate authority – a proclamation urging them to resume their loyalty. "We have all done wrong," Murphy intoned. "No one can say that his heart is altogether clean, and his hands pure. Then as we wish to be forgiven, let us forgive those who have sinned against us, and ours." Murphy also retained many former Confederate local officeholders. A mid-June public meeting in Washington, the seat of the Confederate state government, called upon citizens to support the free-state constitution and government, as did Confederate Governor Harris Flanagin, and a large July Fourth celebration in Little Rock conspicuously avoided any reference to the late unpleasantness. Despite these attempts at reconciliation, some men's hands were cleaner than others', and some had more to be forgiven for. Secession and war had engendered much bitterness in this deeply divided state, and there remained the factional divide between free-state and conservative Unionists. Whereas the two wartime Unionist factions still had much in common, conservative Unionists and former Confederates were coming to share an even stronger antipathy toward the Murphy administration. Former Confederates appealed to Johnson to replace Murphy with a provisional governor, to no avail. Despite their previous differences, wartime conservatives and former Confederates eventually joined forces during the summer in organizing a "Conservative" Party.[6]

Conservative local officeholders made life difficult for Murphy "Unionists." Murphy, in turn, requested in early July that all recommendations he had made to Johnson for special pardons be withdrawn and that Johnson issue none to Arkansas former Confederates, though he almost immediately reversed himself. Murphy also continued to support a state "amnesty" law, enacted during the war, that disfranchised individuals who fought for the Confederacy after the loyal state government had been installed. Edward W. Gantt likewise recommended that Johnson issue "as few pardons as possible" until each applicant had been properly vetted. "Many bad men

---

[5] *PAJ*, 8: 199–200, 236, 430–31; Cimprich, *Slavery's End in Tennessee*, 118–23. On Tennessee's congressional elections in August, Alexander, *Political Reconstruction in Tennessee*, chap. 6 (87–90 on Etheridge's arrest). Etheridge wrote a long letter in mid-July to Johnson in his defense. *PAJ*, 8: 394–403.

[6] Smith, *Courage of a Southern Unionist*, 64–67; *PAJ*, 8: 373–74, 392. Henry M. Rector, governor during the secession crisis and the first Confederate governor of Arkansas, applied for and received a pardon in 1865. *PAJ*, 8: 337.

might thus be thrown upon us & control the elections in the fall," he warned. Despite their internal differences, Murphy Unionists vastly outnumbered conservatives. With many former Confederates barred from voting, moreover, Murphy felt secure enough by mid-August to order congressional elections for early October.[7]

If Brownlow threw his opponents in prison and Murphy tried to conciliate his, Louisiana governor J. Madison Wells defected to the other side. After Johnson sustained him in his dispute with Nathaniel Banks in May, Wells consolidated his power, replacing officials in New Orleans and the parishes with returning Confederates. He enjoyed the full support, at Johnson's behest, of military commander General Edward R. S. Canby. In June, he authorized areas that had been under Confederate control when the war ended – nearly two-thirds of the state – to hold local elections. New Orleans mayor Hugh Kennedy also continued to replace wartime Unionists with former Confederates in city positions, especially the police force. At a large conservative rally in New Orleans in mid-June, presided over by Confederate veterans, and before which he was introduced by the conservative Unionist J. Q. A. Fellows, Wells spoke warmly of Johnson's Reconstruction policy and castigated black suffrage. Wells had clearly abandoned his former free-state allies and was pinning his political fortunes on the emerging alliance between wartime conservative Unionists and former Confederates.[8]

Wells's shift – which would not be his last – reflected his almost cynical opportunism, but it was also indicative of the larger reconfiguration of the political fault lines in Louisiana resulting from the end of the war and the all-encompassing issue of black suffrage. Even as Wells tightened his grip on power, free-state Unionists continued to hope that Johnson might change his course. In June, the radicals, along with the free-black leadership, established the "Friends of Universal Suffrage," which later that month proposed conducting a voter registration for "citizens of color" and holding an alternate election. Set to take place simultaneously with the anticipated fall congressional elections, the alternate election would select an at-large representative whom Congress would recognize as a territorial delegate. This strategy adhered to the radicals' position that Louisiana had reverted to territorial status and its reconstructed government was illegitimate.

By contrast, the free-state moderates, still under the leadership of Michael Hahn and Nathaniel Banks, formed the National Union Republican Club, which also included black members and endorsed black suffrage. The members of this group, however, recognized the legitimacy of the current state

---

[7] Smith, *Courage of a Southern Unionist*, 67–76; Moneyhon, *Impact of the Civil War and Reconstruction on Arkansas*, 190–94; *PAJ*, 8: 313–14 (quotation), 351, 356–57, 429.

[8] McCrary, *Abraham Lincoln and Reconstruction*, 314–19; Taylor, *Louisiana Reconstructed*, 58–62.

government, which they had essentially created but which Wells and his ex-Confederate allies had stolen. Henry Clay Warmoth was elected president of the organization. Arriving in New Orleans in early 1864 as a Union army officer, Warmoth served as judge on the provost court before resigning from the service near the end of that year, whereupon he remained in New Orleans and used his connections to begin a lucrative law practice. Only with the end of the war did Warmoth take up his political calling, but he was destined to become a renowned figure in the annals of Reconstruction Louisiana.

By accepting an invitation to become the Friends of Universal Suffrage's Corresponding Secretary, the ambitious Warmoth facilitated the prospective fusion of the two free-state groups under the "Republican" banner. In early July, the Friends petitioned Wells for a statewide voter registration that would include "all loyal citizens, without distinction of color or origin," but Wells rejected the idea. A similar appeal to Johnson did not even elicit a response. Thomas W. Conway, who had headed the military's plantation labor system during the war and now led the Freedmen's Bureau in Louisiana, also fostered the free-state reunion. Conway supported black suffrage, and, despite the conservative proclivities of some of his officers in the field, he used the bureau to challenge the planters' campaign to reestablish labor control. But the free-state alliance, however obvious, was slow to emerge. Not until the Friends of Universal Suffrage held their convention in New Orleans in September, when Wells also announced that state and congressional elections would be held in November, did the two groups overcome their differences and affect a rapprochement. But it would be an uneasy one.[9]

II

At the same time, black Southerners – formerly enslaved and formerly free, in Union-occupied areas and in previously unoccupied ones, and in the lower Mississippi valley and the other states – were mobilizing. For some, this mobilization was as simple as walking off the plantation to prove they were free – though they often risked their lives in doing so – or to seek employment elsewhere, if only on another plantation. For others, it involved locating family members and other loved ones separated long ago under slavery or more recently during the war. For others still, it meant quitting the countryside for towns or cities. Such mobilization meant the basic freedom to come and go that had been denied to black people under slavery. When Federal military authorities, in the interest of establishing order and often in cooperation with

---

[9] The preceding paragraphs: McCrary, *Abraham Lincoln and Reconstruction*, 316–30; *PAJ*, 8: 393–94 (quotations). On the circumstances surrounding formation of the Friends of Universal Suffrage, and on petitioning Wells and Johnson, see *Proceedings of the Convention of the Republican Party*, 1–6.

civilian officials, attempted to stem this movement by instituting pass systems and similar measures, the resulting outcry prompted the War Department in late July to prohibit all racially discriminatory restrictions on physical mobility. This action established individual movement as an essential element of freedom, and it constituted, the editors of the Freedmen and Southern Society Project have written, "an early expression of the principle of equality before the law."[10]

This mobilization had a deeper purpose. For black people, it meant formulating and striving collectively to realize a substantive definition of freedom. This definition included, among other things, access to land and other productive property; control over their working lives and the fruits of their labor; legal marriages and autonomous families and households; churches, schools, and other institutions and education for their children; organized self-defense and protection of their communities from violence; entry to the legal system and the courts; the equal protection of the law and an end to all forms of legal discrimination based on race; and, ultimately, political power and to the right to vote. Black people, in short, were aspiring to a nonracial conception of citizenship and to the benefits of American freedom. So far, nothing being done in the former slave states took cognizance of these aspirations or allowed black people any input in the postwar settlement. Exclusion from formal politics, however, did not prevent them from attempting to shape the postemancipation order.[11]

Among the most salient manifestations of this mobilization in the immediate postwar period was the black convention movement. Building on the free-black convention tradition of the antebellum era, as well as on the various northern state conventions held during the war and the creation of the National Equal Rights League (NERL) the previous October in Syracuse, the convention movement during the next two years would pave the way for the black politics of Radical Reconstruction. In the lower Mississippi valley, the founding convention of the Louisiana NERL had already met in early 1865 in New Orleans; the Tennessee NERL had also been organized before the war ended; and a state convention would be held in Little Rock, Arkansas, in late November and early December. No statewide convention took place in Mississippi, but numerous local meetings were held, including one at Port Gibson in November in response to the Mississippi black code. (Conventions also met in 1865 in both Carolinas, Virginia, Washington, DC, and many northern states.)[12]

---

[10] *Freedom: L&L-1865*, 31 (quotation), 259. The classic account of the tumultuous immediate postwar period is Litwack, *Been in the Storm So Long*.

[11] A large literature on black politics exists, even focusing on the immediate postwar period. The best overview is Hahn, *Nation Under Our Feet*. For an excellent local study of the Natchez area, see Behrend, *Reconstructing Democracy*, esp. chap. 2.

[12] Foner and Walker, *Proceedings of the Black National and State Conventions*, xx–xxiii.

The Tennessee convention of August 7–10 in Nashville was one of the first black conventions held in the postwar South. (Virginia's met only days earlier.) The seventy-nine delegates represented twenty-two of Tennessee's eighty-four counties, perhaps reflecting continuing disorder in the state. Seventeen delegates hailed from the Nashville area, and twenty-six represented six of the state's USCT regiments. The convention named several "honorary" delegates. Many – and very likely the large majority – of the delegates had been free before the war and belonged to the free-black elite. Correspondents from New York and Cincinnati, in addition to local ones, covered the proceedings.[13]

The convention forcefully expressed black people's claim to political and legal equality and to the rights and privileges of American freedom and citizenship. Sergeant H. J. Maxwell, a soldier-delegate, affirmed the right to life, liberty, and the pursuit of happiness as "the rallying theme of the Convention." Having fought for their country, he continued, black men now demanded "two more boxes, beside the cartridge box – the ballot-box and the jury box." Other speakers called for these rights based on principle, precedent (black men had voted in Tennessee before the state's 1835 constitution restricted the vote to white men), and political necessity. The nation had turned to its black population during the war, observed the Rev. James Lynch of Baltimore, an honorary delegate, and "the question of political power in this country will soon present another necessity which will give us the ballot-box." General Clinton B. Fisk, the head of the Tennessee Freedmen's Bureau who accepted an invitation to address the convention, spoke to black people's broader aspirations for freedom. Fisk pledged the bureau's resources to protect families, secure homesteads, institute free labor, ensure equal protection of the law, and provide education. He proposed the establishment of a black "normal" school for teacher training (the historically black college Fisk University would be named for him). He also endorsed black suffrage. Perhaps engaging in wishful thinking, Fisk contended that Andrew Johnson would make good on his "Moses" speech (excerpts from which he read) by supporting it as well.[14]

In an address to "the White Citizens" of Tennessee, which was actually directed to the legislature, the convention echoed the recent petition by "the colored people of the State" to that body for the rights to vote and to testify in court, insisting that their adoption was "only a question of time." The address rejected racially discriminatory literacy or property qualifications for voting, pointedly observing that many black men in Tennessee – including two of the

---

[13] *Proceedings of the State Convention of Colored Men*, 7–11. A number of the delegates appear on John Cimprich's list of identifiable black political leaders in Tennessee around the end of the war in *Slavery's End in Tennessee*, 111–12. LeForge, "State Colored Conventions of Tennessee," 236–38.

[14] *Proceedings of the State Convention of Colored Men*, 6–7, 12–16 (Fisk).

delegates – had been "intelligent enough" to vote for Andrew Jackson. It denied that political and legal equality would lead to "social equality," countering that the races would voluntarily remain separate. "You have the right to select your company. We have the right to choose our associates." The address concluded by calling attention to "our numbers," reminding the legislature that black people made up a quarter of the state's population and that this was "a very important fact for politicians to consider."[15]

The convention combined assertions to equal rights and citizenship with exhortations to racial self-reliance and unity. "There is a gulf between the whites and us, because of intelligence on their part and illiteracy upon ours," a corresponding address to black Tennesseans acknowledged. "Neither politicians nor Congress can bridge this chasm, nor can it be done by any save ourselves, than by our own exertions in the direction of education, uprightness, the acquiring of wealth and industry." The address chided – "not in anger, but in kindness" – black men who dealt in "spirituous liquors," and it scolded former slaves who believed that freedom meant "the privilege to roam about the country as common idlers and rowdies, without any fixed habitation or apparent means of support." Black men and women were encouraged to regularize their marriages and to set "virtuous examples" for their children. Otherwise, "our enemies will use your neglect or refusal as a weapon to prove that we are incapable of exercising political and civil rights." Personal virtue would validate black people's capacity for civic equality. "Above all things let us have due respect for the laws of the land, for the most conclusive evidence that a person is properly qualified to exercise the rights of citizenship is his willing adherence to law and order." The address closed by bemoaning "the many petty differences ... between ourselves" and lamenting "any contentions among colored men at this particular time." It urged black people "in every portion of the State where those contentions may exist, in the name of all that is dear to man, to forget and forgive the past."[16]

The convention also pursued black aspirations for freedom through a more concrete agenda. It created a Central Committee to coordinate efforts toward the convention's goals after it adjourned. It appointed a committee on agriculture to report on the amount of land under black cultivation and the crops produced on it. It encouraged the creation of county-level committees to "look after the interests of our people throughout the State." These local committees would also inform the Freedmen's Bureau or the Central Committee of any "grievances," and they would assist the bureau and benevolent societies in establishing schools. The convention authorized the Central Committee to undertake a census of the state's black population: enumerating persons and their occupations, property owned and taxes paid, children and adults

---

[15] *Proceedings of the State Convention of Colored Men*, 21–22.
[16] *Proceedings of the State Convention of Colored Men*, 23–27.

attending school, and black-owned churches, and accumulating "all such other information . . . as showing our progress." The convention ordered the publication of its proceedings, and it established Abraham Lincoln's birthday and January 1 "as days of jubilee for the colored people of Tennessee, to be by them celebrated through all time."[17]

In a preface to the published proceedings that it had authorized, the Central Committee defended the convention against its white critics. While exhibiting the supplication and deference essential to nineteenth-century racial etiquette, the committee responded to the convention's detractors in kind, deeming it "a waste of time to try by *words* to convince them of their error," and vowing instead to "try and convince them by our *conduct*." No special strength of character was needed "to oppose colored people having an equal chance with other people," the committee charged, "and then burlesque their proceedings and laugh at their ignorance." The committee minced no words in asking: "Where is the whiskey-drinking common blackguard that can't do that?" Invoking the Biblical injunction that "the poor, ignorant and unfortunate" deserve "care and kindness" from their more fortunate brethren, the committee further posed the questions: "who made us black or colored? who made us degraded and ignorant?" These were both profoundly metaphysical and deeply political questions. The Central Committee again recommended the creation of local and county-level committees to continue the work of the convention. "Go to work, friends, and let us hear from you." As the historical record has shown, there would be a lot to say. This was only the start.[18]

III

On the very day the Nashville convention assembled, August 7, Mississippi held its election for delegates to a very different convention, one that would "reconstruct" the state and facilitate its restoration to the Union. When the convention met a week later, it hardly augured the smooth reunification of the nation for which many Americans were hoping. In his convention proclamation after being named Provisional Governor, William L. Sharkey had admitted that many white Mississippians refused to acknowledge the Emancipation Proclamation or the end of slavery. While allowing in theory for a future legal challenge to emancipation, he insisted that the proclamation be obeyed, and he urged the state's white residents to accept the result of the war so as to aid Mississippi's restoration to the Union[19]

---

[17] *Proceedings of the State Convention of Colored Men*, 18–20.
[18] *Proceedings of the State Convention of Colored Men*, iii–iv.
[19] Harris, *Presidential Reconstruction in Mississippi*, 44–47; Drake, "Mississippi Reconstruction Convention." Sharkey's proclamation: *Mississippi Convention Journal*, 3–9, esp. 6–7.

The five weeks between Sharkey's convention proclamation and the election left no room for a meaningful campaign. Former Whigs and conditional Unionists were more motivated to take the oath of allegiance and vote than were secessionist Democrats, many of whom, defeated and demoralized, largely shunned the restoration process. Some candidates explicitly opposed uncompensated abolition, contending that future legal challenges to wartime emancipation might provide grounds for compensation. Turnout for the election was light. In a pattern repeated in other rebellious states, voters repudiated fire-eating secessionism but not the Confederacy or the antebellum establishment. The overwhelming majority of delegates were former Whigs, conditional Unionists, or other moderates. Seven had served at the 1861 secession convention, six having voted against secession. Thirteen delegates excluded from Johnson's general amnesty would participate in the convention without having received a special pardon.[20]

Convening on August 14, the convention ultimately met for ten days. The delegates did themselves no favors with northern public opinion by considering memorials calling for the removal of black troops from the state and for the release of Jefferson Davis and Confederate governor Charles Clark. The convention elected J. Shall Yerger, brother of William Yerger and himself a firm wartime Unionist, as president. A Committee on the State Constitution would handle the abolition of slavery. On August 15, Johnson wired Sharkey with recommendations for the convention – something he had not previously done with the provisional governors. In addition to abolishing slavery and forever prohibiting property in man in the state constitution and to ratifying the Federal abolition amendment, Johnson advised, the convention should extend the vote to black men who met a literacy or property requirement. This concession, which would place "the Southern states in reference to free persons of color upon the same basis with the Free States," had nothing to do with principle, Johnson essentially acknowledged, but was designed instead to foil the Radical Republicans, "who are wild upon negro franchise." Johnson's Machiavellian canard made sense, but it also assumed greater foresight than the delegates would demonstrate.[21]

Several days later, on August 20, by which point the convention was mired in the abolition debate, Sharkey replied that the convention would probably leave black suffrage, black testimony in court, and the Federal abolition amendment to the state legislature. The convention was about to approve an amendment to the state constitution abolishing slavery, Sharkey assured Johnson, and authorizing the legislature to enact laws necessary to protect

---

[20] Harris, *Presidential Reconstruction in Mississippi*, 46–51. Carter, *When the War Was Over*, on the election results in the seceded states in general.
[21] *Mississippi Convention Journal*, 8–22; *PAJ*, 8: 599–600; Harris, *Presidential Reconstruction in Mississippi*, 51–52.

both the freed people and the state from "any Evils that may arise from their sudden emancipation." But Sharkey then went on to accuse the Freedmen's Bureau of stirring up the former slaves, and he informed Johnson – in a measure that would itself provoke much northern criticism – of the call he had issued for volunteer militia companies "to suppress crime which is becoming alarming." As though this were not enough, Sharkey asked Johnson to lift martial law, restore the writ of habeas corpus, and return the state arms to his authority. He also suggested the reorganization of the state militia.[22]

Johnson should have been angered by such effrontery, but he was not. Expressing himself "much gratified" at the work of the convention, he referred Sharkey to the military commander to keep the peace (though Sharkey was already embroiled in jurisdictional disputes with Federal military authorities), mildly suggested that the militia not be organized until "farther advances" had been made in state reorganization, and pledged to withdraw military authority and restore habeas corpus as soon as possible. Having expressly instructed the convention to ratify the Federal abolition amendment, Johnson essentially sanctioned its refusal to do so, blithely noting that the convention could "recommend" its adoption by the legislature. Johnson again voiced greater concern over "the extreme men in the North" than over former rebels – "hence the importance of being prompt and circumspect in all that is being done," he advised. "The proceedings in Mississippi will exert a powerful influence on the other States which are to act afterwards." If Johnson intended to discourage further resistance to Federal authority, he had a strange way of doing so.[23]

IV

The Mississippi convention would indeed "exert a powerful influence" on the other states, but not for its "prompt and circumspect" action on slavery. While the convention abolished slavery, it signaled the extent to which the rebellious states would have to be dragged, kicking and screaming, into meeting that requirement. The two and a half days of debate took up more than a quarter of the convention's meeting time, and even more of its substantive working time. As scholars have often noted, the southern Reconstruction conventions, in particular their tedious squabbling over abolition (along with widespread violence against the freed people), generated some of the first serious misgivings in the North over Johnson's Reconstruction policy. Yet, if the Mississippi convention foreshadowed much of what was to come, its dillydallying also masked an important point. Slavery may have been "dead, dead, *dead*," as one of the delegates insisted. But in their caviling over how precisely to word the

---

[22] *PAJ*, 8: 627–28. See also "Important Proclamation," *Meridian Daily Clarion*, August 25, 1865.
[23] *PAJ*, 8: 635.

state amendment abolishing slavery, the delegates anticipated – however inadvertently, and in their own warped way – the modern scholarly debate over who freed the slaves.

On August 17, the convention's fourth day, the Committee on the Constitution proposed an amendment to the state constitution. Embracing the unencumbered language of the Federal abolition amendment, it declared that "neither slavery nor involuntary servitude," except as punishment for crime, "shall hereafter exist in this State." It refrained from using the word "abolish" or from prohibiting the principle of "property in man." The amendment also mandated that the state legislature, "as the public welfare may require, shall provide by law for the protection of the person and property of the freedmen of the State, and guard them and the State against any evils that may arise from their sudden emancipation." The second part of the amendment would remain largely intact, but the first would provoke serious disagreement and undergo modification. When debate commenced the next day, Hugh A. Barr offered a substitute to the first part of the amendment. "Slavery having been abolished in this State by the action of the Government of the United States," it read, "it is therefore hereby declared and ordained, that hereafter there shall be neither slavery nor involuntary servitude in this State," except for crime. The rest of the amendment remained the same.[24]

In debating Barr's substitute, the delegates largely subscribed to the idea that slavery had already been "abolished" and that the Federal government was forcing the state to recognize a fait accompli. The key question, then, was how to recognize that fact. Should the amendment implicitly acknowledge that slavery had been destroyed, without saying who had destroyed it, and simply declare that it shall not "hereafter" exist? Or was an explicit affirmation needed that Mississippi, far from abolishing slavery voluntarily, was being compelled to formalize what the Federal government itself had already done? Honesty, self-respect, and *honor* – that most vital of Southern-white values – demanded an express acknowledgment, the advocates of the latter position contended, of this coercion. In countering this argument, William Yerger bemoaned what he called the "ceaseless wrangling over an immaterial issue." But many delegates hardly considered the issue immaterial, as George L. Potter, a Yale-educated attorney and Unionist Whig, demonstrated. Potter forcefully advocated for an explicit affirmation that Mississippi's arm was being twisted. "Gentleman say, that slavery is dead," he intoned. "But if it be dead, how was it destroyed?" No state convention had met during the last four years, no ordinance had been passed, and no "action of the people of Mississippi" had been taken, Potter contended, ending slavery. "Who claims, then sir, to have abolished it?" If slavery were indeed dead in Mississippi, Potter insisted, then "no man can

---

[24] *Mississippi Convention Journal*, 29–30 (amendment), 44 (Barr substitute).

deny, as a historical fact, that that extinction has been produced by the action of the Federal authorities."[25]

After much debate, Barr's substitute was tabled, as were various other proposals attributing the end of slavery to Federal action. George Potter then offered his own measure. Employing a long, discursive preamble, it made not the slightest pretense toward abolishing slavery, even as a matter of coercion. Rather, it placed the entire blame for destroying slavery on Federal authority while offering the most begrudging concession to that authority. In addition to questioning the legitimacy of all Federal wartime antislavery measures, it castigated the Federal government for reneging on compensated abolition, and it condemned Federal power for enforcing emancipation "against children of tender years, and other innocent persons, as well as against those implicated in the recent rebellion." The people of Mississippi, though reserving all of their rights, would "at present" submit to Federal authority and treat the former slaves "as if free," but they would only "continue so to regard and treat them until the said alledged acts and proclamations are annulled by the proper tribunals, or are otherwise lawfully vacated." Meanwhile, the legislature would enact all necessary laws to regulate the "colored population."[26]

In a long address defending his proposal, Potter argued that because Mississippi had never left the Union and retained all of its rights under the Federal Constitution, Congress had no authority to impose conditions in restoring it to the Union. Potter questioned the legality of the Emancipation Proclamation, and he urged Mississippi not to abolish slavery until the courts had decided on the proclamation's legality and until the matter of compensation had been resolved. Were the courts to declare emancipation valid, then the Federal government, having essentially abolished slavery, would have to assume responsibility for the "large pauper population" it had created. Ultimately, for Potter, the real danger was the northern Republicans, who would not be satisfied with abolition but were also set on imposing racial equality and military rule on the South. Although Potter's proposal was decisively defeated, nearly a third of the delegates voted in favor, thereby endorsing a measure that openly refused to abolish slavery and deemed wartime emancipation illegal.[27]

The next day, August 19, Robert S. Hudson offered a compromise between the previous proposals. Devoid of any language referring to the wartime destruction or abolition of slavery, Hudson's measure incorporated the original amendment's neutral wording that "neither slavery nor involuntary

---

[25] *Mississippi Convention Journal*, 44–45 (Yerger), 46–48 (Barr), 48–52 (Potter; quotations, 49, 50). On Potter, see Harris, *Presidential Reconstruction in Mississippi*, 53.

[26] *Mississippi Convention Journal*, 53 (vote to table), 55–56 (Potter).

[27] *Mississippi Convention Journal*, 56–70, esp. 59–60 (quotation, 61), 70–71 (vote); Harris, *Presidential Reconstruction in Mississippi*, 53. There is some incorrect pagination in this section of the convention journal.

servitude ... shall hereafter exist" in Mississippi. It also retained the provision authorizing the legislature to enact the necessary laws defining black freedom. However, it included the proviso that this amendment, and all legislation following therefrom, would be "suspended and inoperative" until Mississippi had been restored to the Union and a civilian government established. The convention would abolish slavery, in other words, but on condition that Congress impose no other requirements in readmitting Mississippi to the Union. Hudson's compromise also reserved the right "to compensation from the United States for the loss of any slave." Debate over Hudson's proposal dragged on for the next day and a half, consuming what proved to be the remainder of the convention's deliberation on abolition.[28]

In debating the Hudson substitute, the delegates expounded upon many topics relating to the war, slavery, and emancipation. The oath in Johnson's amnesty proclamation – and whether swearing to it enjoined the delegates to vote for a free-state constitution – received particular attention. The advocates of the original amendment (and thus the opponents of Hudson's measure) contended that adopting a free-state constitution, "unencumbered by any preambles – unencumbered by any proviso – unencumbered by any extraneous language," as Amos R. Johnston put it, was the surest way to restore self-government to the state. Because slavery was practicably abolished, they argued, it did not matter who had destroyed it or how. "I do not care who killed Cock Robin, or by what means," observed Richard Cooper, "or in what manner, slavery has been abolished; but I concede it as a fact." What mattered most was controlling the postemancipation order. Supporters of the original amendment also warned that the Hudson substitute – as an example of continuing southern intransigence – would play right into the Radical Republicans' hands in their plan to impose black suffrage and racial equality on the South. It would likewise alienate Andrew Johnson and the "conservative men of the North," Richard Cooper again noted, whose support was essential. Several delegates contended that the convention was not actually abolishing slavery – since Federal authorities had already done that – but merely ensuring that it would not "hereafter" exist. They likewise maintained that broaching the topic of compensation was unnecessary and counterproductive; the original amendment did not forfeit this claim, and such language might prejudice future action on it.[29]

The advocates of Hudson's substitute also emphasized state sovereignty in determining the postwar settlement, but they more strongly rejected Federal authority and demanded firmer protections against Federal interference. "Finding that the Convention is resolved to re-abolish slavery; to do that

---

[28] *Mississippi Convention Journal*, 71–72.
[29] *Mississippi Convention Journal*, 85–96 (Johnston; quotation, 89), 96–102 (John W. C. Watson), 109–10 (Cooper; both quotations, 110), 126–27 (Simonton).

which the Federal army and bayonet, and the President, and Congress could not legally do," Robert Hudson observed in defending his own measure, "I propose by the proviso offered, that while we make the concession, we make its effect and operation dependent upon the Congress, who can secure to us the pleasing reality of civil authority and civil liberty." In supporting the Hudson substitute, William T. Martin cited as proof of northern malevolence the Federal abolition amendment's broad enforcement provision. "I am not willing," he announced, "to trust to the fanatics of the North to frame for us a code that is to govern the freedmen of the State of Mississippi." Thomas A. Marshall rejected the Federal government's power to impose conditions on any state within the Union. "It is not whether the negro shall be free – but whether we shall be slaves," he intoned, exhibiting not the slightest hint of irony. The Federal government has "no right whatever to dictate to us, any amendment of our State Constitution," Marshall added, and he refused "to yield a principle so essential to freedom, and the dignity and honor of the State."[30]

In making their arguments, several supporters of the Hudson substitute intuited the difference between military emancipation and constitutional abolition, although they drew the wrong conclusions from it. "While I admit that slavery, in point of *fact*, is abolished, I cannot admit, but deny, that in *law* it is abolished," Robert Hudson insisted. Having drawn this correct distinction, he mistakenly concluded that only slaves who "were actually captured and held by the military of the United States, during the war," were free, "but no others." Similarly observing that "there may be a legal slavery still," Edmund J. Goode also allowed that persons who had gained their freedom during the war were unequivocally free, but, he added, "those persons who remained in slavery, at the end of the war, are legally slave." These delegates incorrectly argued that persons whom the Emancipation Proclamation had *declared* free, but who were still enslaved when the war ended, remained enslaved. But they were correct on the crucial point, almost despite themselves, that slavery still legally existed in Mississippi. Robert M. Brown also distinguished between the proclamation and constitutional abolition, but for the purpose of arguing that the delegates – having already sworn to uphold the proclamation, which had "abolished" slavery – could vote in good conscience *against* a free-state constitution.[31]

It fell to George Potter to articulate – and to explore the political significance of – the difference between military emancipation and constitutional abolition. Taking this argument much further than he had previously, he identified the key weakness of the Emancipation Proclamation while putting forward a perfectly logical – if now hopelessly outdated – argument for conditional

---

[30] *Mississippi Convention Journal*, 71–85 (Hudson; quotation, 71), 136–40 (Martin; quotation, 138), 226–31 (Marshall; quotation, 230).
[31] *Mississippi Convention Journal*, 75 (Hudson), 104–5 (Brown), 118 (Goode).

abolition. He also tore a page right out of the southern conservative Unionists' playbook, and pinpointed what had long been antislavery advocates' central conundrum: the Emancipation Proclamation freed slaves but did not abolish slavery. The objections to Hudson's proviso were based on "erroneous views," Potter insisted, regarding both the proclamation and the state abolition amendment.

"[I]s it true that President Lincoln attempted to declare *the institution* of slavery abolished in the State of Mississippi in the sense in which gentlemen speak of it?" Potter asked rhetorically. "In other words, did he attempt to overturn the fundamental law on which slavery rested in Mississippi? Was he dealing with the institution, and the laws made in support of it; or was he dealing with individual slaves?" The answers to these questions were obvious. Every slave who had been liberated on January 1, 1863, could have been removed from the state, Potter continued, "but in so doing you would not abolish slavery as an institution in Mississippi." Neither did the proclamation abolish slavery in the border states. "I have a full legal right to go to Kentucky, buy slaves there as property, and bring them here and hold them as slaves in Mississippi," Potter insisted. "Do gentlemen deny this as a legal proposition? Do they claim that the President in declaring that *persons* held as slaves, were free, overthrew our laws and the provisions of the Constitution of the State?" The president of course had done no such thing. "There is a distinction, broad and palpable, between the act of freeing certain persons, and an act overthrowing or annulling the fundamental law and policy of the State in which those persons may happen at the time to be."

It followed that the state amendment did not merely confirm a prior abolition of slavery. Instead, the amendment "goes beyond the [Emancipation Proclamation]," Potter contended, "it proposes to abolish, utterly and forever ... hereafter, the holding of slaves, as property in Mississippi." This was entirely different. "I wish gentlemen, to consider the difference between these two things, when they come to vote upon the [Hudson] proviso," he urged. "If I take a right view of that proclamation, it declared free only the persons, held as slaves, in certain parts of the South, on the first of January, 1863," Potter continued. "If I take a right view of the amendment, it declares that slavery shall not exist here in any form; that our citizens shall not bring slaves into the State, and hold them here." Delegates who had taken Johnson's amnesty oath were therefore not obligated to adopt a free-state constitution, since that oath compelled them to uphold the Emancipation Proclamation but not to abolish slavery. Potter again postulated that the Supreme Court might invalidate the proclamation, and he concluded by insisting that the convention's concession on abolition made Hudson's proviso – providing for Mississippi's prompt readmission to the Union – all the more necessary.[32]

---

[32] *Mississippi Convention Journal*, 128–36, esp. 133–35 (quotations, 128, 133–34).

Since January 1863, antislavery advocates had been warning that the rebellious states could comply with all Federal emancipation measures and still not abolish slavery in their constitutions. Now, with the war decisively at an end, duly elected representatives of the southern (white) people were making the same point. These were not proslavery radicals, moreover, but political moderates. To be sure, Potter's objective was less to salvage slavery than, as he noted, to "place the Radicals in a political predicament." The convention was offering Republicans the abolition of slavery – which it need not do, Potter argued – in return for control over the postemancipation settlement. As the historical record has shown, there existed at this point not the slightest hope of preserving slavery. Still, Potter and his allies were not the only white Southerners talking about reviving slavery once Federal oversight ended. Such talk was not mere hyperbole, and it had consequences.

Although Potter's was a minority position, William Yerger, one of the co-commissioners who had met with Andrew Johnson, went to great lengths to refute it. Admitting "astonishment" at some of the views expressed, and castigating certain delegates – clearly Potter and his allies – for indulging in "dreamy, abstract revery" rather than facing "stubborn facts," Yerger provided a detailed account of his and William Sharkey's meeting with Johnson. His point was clear: Johnson wanted slavery abolished, and if the convention did not abide, there were far worse alternatives in the offing. Yerger took issue with Potter's suggestion that slavery could still be revitalized, emphasizing that this was precisely the reason Johnson had insisted on abolition as a condition for readmission. Abolishing slavery would also undermine the Radicals' central contention that white Southerners did not, "in good faith, intend to give up the institution of slavery," and that they would "attempt to re-establish the institution of slavery, and insist upon its maintenance," once Federal authority had been removed.

Why alienate potential allies such as Johnson and northern conservatives, Yerger asked, in clinging to the false hope that slavery might yet be salvaged. Any attempt to perpetuate slavery would be construed as continuation of the rebellion. Was the South ready once again to take up arms? With slavery gone, the challenge now was for the state to define the new social order on its own terms. The Hudson substitute, Yerger warned, would provoke a backlash that neither Johnson nor northern conservatives would be able to withstand. It would be read as the act of "a defeated people" who "still defy the Government, and undertake to dictate the terms of restoration to political rights they have forfeited by rebellion." The one question Yerger did not address was whether to include language, as many delegates wanted, declaring that slavery had effectively been destroyed or "abolished" during the war and ascribing responsibility. But that was not really his main concern.[33]

---

[33] *Mississippi Convention Journal*, 140–64 (quotations, 141, 152, 161, 162).

With debate on it exhausted, the Hudson substitute was tabled. James T. Harrison, chair of the Committee on the Constitution, then offered an amendment, in the form of a brief preamble, to the original abolition amendment. It simply read: "The institution of slavery having been destroyed in the State of Mississippi." As something of a compromise, this revision provided the affirmative statement that slavery had already been destroyed in the state while allowing the delegates to claim that they had not "abolished" it but had merely decreed that it would not hereafter exist. By couching this provision in the passive voice, the delegates dodged the question of who, exactly, had destroyed slavery. Despite the delegates' truculence, there remained an ambiguity to this measure that could be considered historically correct. Slavery had been destroyed in Mississippi, although the delegates – as would be the case with later generations of scholars – could not agree on how and by whom. Just as the Federal abolition amendment mandated that slavery "shall" not exist, the state amendment declared that slavery had already been destroyed and would never "hereafter" exist.

Harrison's addendum was quickly accepted, and the convention also approved the revised amendment by a vote of eighty-seven to eleven. "The institution of slavery having been destroyed in the State of Mississippi, neither slavery nor involuntary servitude, otherwise than in the punishment of crimes, whereof the party shall have been duly convicted, shall hereafter exist in this State," it read, "and the Legislature, at its next session, and thereafter, as the public welfare may require, shall provide by law for the protection and security of the persons and property of the freedmen of the State, and guard them and the State against any evils that may arise from their sudden emancipation." The measure did not prohibit the principle of "property in man," and the topic never came up in debate. George Potter and Robert Hudson voted against. On August 21, 1865, Mississippi became the first unreconstructed state to abolish slavery.[34]

In addressing other matters relating to Reconstruction, the convention did not inspire confidence. It declared the ordinance of secession null and void, but only after much debate and after narrowly rejecting an alternative merely declaring it "repealed and abrogated." The convention failed to repudiate Mississippi's Confederate debt, ignored Johnson's instructions to ratify the Federal abolition amendment, and refused to consider Johnson's limited black suffrage recommendation. (Johnson made the suggestion to no other state.) The convention invalidated all state laws enacted since secession that conflicted with the US Constitution or aided the rebellion. It scheduled congressional, state, and local elections for early October, with the inauguration of the new government to take place soon thereafter. In a close vote, the convention

---

[34] *Mississippi Convention Journal*, 164–65 (previous two paragraphs); Harris, *Presidential Reconstruction in Mississippi*, 53–54.

declared these measures effective immediately, deeming a popular referendum "not practical or expedient ... under the circumstances." This was true, but some observers wondered whether the convention dare put abolition to the voters.[35]

After the convention adjourned, William Sharkey informed Johnson of the results. While devoting far more attention to the idleness and disorderliness of the former slaves, the demoralizing effect of black soldiers, and the mismanagement of the Freedmen's Bureau, Sharkey hailed the convention's limited accomplishments. Slavery had been abolished. "The negro is protected in his rights of persons and property," Sharkey added. "Possibly [the legislature] may allow the negro to testify." This was hardly a ringing endorsement of black testimony in court, though Sharkey believed sentiment for this right was growing. Black suffrage was a nonstarter, even though Sharkey had read Johnson's recommendation to the convention, and "it gave satisfaction." Sharkey doubted that Mississippi would accept the Federal abolition amendment because of the enforcement section, and he again called for the state militia to be reorganized. Sharkey assured Johnson of white Mississippians' loyalty but plainly spoke of widespread hostility to Federal authority. Nonetheless, the people of Mississippi were "now entitled to the consideration of the Government," he contended, and deserved "to be treated as though the rebellion had ended." Johnson was of course pleased with this state of affairs and saw it as an endorsement of his policy.[36]

Although the Mississippi delegates were aware that Northerners were scrutinizing everything they did, this first test of Johnson's Reconstruction program did not go well. Despite their best intentions, the delegates could not help but get bogged down in tedious debates that most other Americans considered silly – or worse – but that to them involved substantive issues. They had tried to reconcile what they thought the victors wanted with their own most dearly held beliefs. Again, these were not the radicals but the moderates. These debates sometimes reflected political divisions that predated the war, but they also emanated from a mindset that held as wrong neither slavery nor the attempt to construct an independent republic with slavery as its "cornerstone." The other state conventions produced much of the same. They all quibbled over the secession ordinances and nitpicked over abolition. Only North Carolina dispatched slavery relatively quickly. They all eventually adopted variations of "slavery having been destroyed" – except South Carolina, which alone attributed abolition to Federal action. None ratified

---

[35] Harris, *Presidential Reconstruction in Mississippi*, 54–60; *Mississippi Convention Journal*, 174–226 (secession ordinance; quotation, 174), 234–47 (state laws), 248 (ratification), 265–66 (debt).

[36] *PAJ*, 8: 666–67; Harris, *Presidential Reconstruction in Mississippi*, 58.

"SLAVERY HAVING BEEN DESTROYED" 435

the Federal abolition amendment. With the delegates carping over abolition, equality before the law and black suffrage were irrelevant.[37]

Northerners found the opposition to abolition troubling enough, but perhaps more disconcerting were the motives of those who supported it. The Radical Republican Carl Schurz – who was then touring the South, and who later spoke with several Mississippi delegates and convention observers – reported that the delegates had voted for abolition largely "to secure readmission." The action of the convention "with regard to the abolition of slavery is very incomplete in itself," he continued, "and must necessarily be amplified by laws to be passed by the Legislature to be worth anything." Worse still, the state's white population even more strongly opposed abolition. A few "enlightened men" were trying to bring the white citizenry around to the new order. "But so far they have not been able to modify or control the brutal instincts of the masses; nor have they shown much courage in boldly facing them." Were these men to gain election to the legislature, Schurz concluded, there might be hope. "But if the people succeed in securing a true representation, we must look for bad results."[38]

* * *

In his convention address supporting abolition, William Yerger drank deeply from the well of proslavery thought. Slavery "was generally of a character benignant to the negro," he contended. Far from creating "fiendish passions," it had "cultivated kindly affections between the master and slave." Despite the incidental wrongs committed under it, which were attendant upon "every industrial regulation" known to organized society, "in its moral and social influences, [slavery] tended to cultivate kind feelings on the part of the white man and the slave." The events of the war had confirmed this view. "All over the country, wherever the armies of the United States have penetrated," Yerger continued, "our people relied confidently on the loyalty and fidelity and kindness of their slaves" – even with the menfolk away at the front. "History does not show in any wars which have taken place for what is termed 'the freedom of mankind,' a people who, while accepting the freedom offered to them, have remained more true and loyal to their masters than our slaves have been to us." Generations of white Southerners would tell themselves the same story, which became central to the larger narrative of a "Lost Cause." Before the war, the slaves had

---

[37] Carter, *When the War Was Over*, 61–86, on the southern state conventions. See also Perman, *Reunion without Compromise*, 81–95; Foner, *Reconstruction*, 185–97.
[38] Simpson, Graf, and Muldowny, *Advice after Appomattox*, 106–17, esp. 107–8.

been happy and contented; during it they had remained loyal. Only when the war was over did they accept the freedom "offered to them." Yet for all of their pedantry over the institution of slavery having been destroyed in Mississippi, the one thing Yerger and the other delegates did not take into account – could not even imagine – was that the slaves might have had something to do with it.[39]

[39] *Mississippi Convention Journal*, 160. There is a voluminous scholarly literature on "the Lost Cause," but for one insightful study of the idea's resonance in Mississippi, see Goleman, *Your Heritage Will Still Remain*.

22

"Americans in America, One and Indivisible"

As the Federal abolition amendment lurched toward ratification during the fall of 1865, and as President Andrew Johnson's Reconstruction policy bore its poisonous fruit, contrasting visions of "the new order of things" continued to evolve – and to clash – in the states of the lower Mississippi valley. Although it was the last of the four states of the region to abolish slavery, Mississippi became the first former slave state to define the place of the freed people in southern society, leapfrogging over the reconstructed states and providing an example that the other rebellious states, to varying degrees, would emulate. The Mississippi "black code" augured the "reconstruction" of white supremacy and the maintenance of the plantation regime in a world without slavery. At the same time, the black populations of the lower Mississippi valley – and their white allies in Louisiana – put forward a very different vision of the postemancipation order, one rooted in nonracial citizenship, the equal protection of the laws, and universal (male) suffrage. Black people were "Americans in America, One and Indivisible," proclaimed William H. Grey before the Arkansas black convention that gathered in late November.

Although the three reconstructed states of the lower Mississippi valley had developed an identity distinct from that of the other rebellious states (save Virginia) during the war, this distinctiveness, already receding when hostilities ended, faded even further during the fall. Their Unionist governments never having received congressional recognition, Arkansas, Louisiana, and Tennessee participated in certain aspects of Johnson's Reconstruction program, and Northerners – Republicans in particular – tended to lump them together with the other seceded states. Owing largely to wartime Reconstruction in the lower Mississippi valley, the battle lines for postwar Reconstruction had already been drawn by the time Congress convened in December and the Federal abolition amendment was declared operative. By late 1865, one chapter of US history was closing and another was just beginning.

I

With twenty-three states – including Louisiana, Arkansas, and Tennessee – having ratified the Federal abolition amendment by late summer 1865, another four of the thirty-six states in the Union were needed to reach twenty-seven.

The question had never been settled as to whether the eleven rebellious states would be included in the number needed to ratify. Andrew Johnson had hoped to obviate this question – and to have "Reconstruction" completed by the convening of the Thirty-Ninth Congress in December – by requiring the state conventions to abolish slavery and ratify the amendment. Mississippi's failure to ratify the amendment had already thrown a monkey wrench into the works, and the other unreconstructed states would not begin holding their conventions until late September. Johnson therefore pressed forward during the fall with "self-Reconstruction," as the state conventions met, elections were held, and new state governments were organized. In the lower Mississippi valley, Mississippi, as the sole unreconstructed state, would hold congressional and state elections on October 2, and the legislature would convene two weeks later. Tennessee had already held congressional elections in August, and on October 9 Arkansas would follow suit.

Because so much of Louisiana had been under Confederate control when the war ended, and to consolidate his own position, Governor J. Madison Wells on September 21 called for state and congressional elections in early November and for the legislature to meet soon thereafter. Wells's action further reconfigured Louisiana's political landscape. Wartime conservative Unionists and a revived Democratic Party – both opposing black suffrage – endorsed Wells's "reelection" as governor and soon united under the "Conservative" banner. The former free-state factions, meanwhile, were slowly transmogrifying into the Louisiana Republican Party. With the Friends of Universal Suffrage already committed to black suffrage, the moderates found opposition to it no longer tenable. Convinced that everything he had worked for in Louisiana was unraveling, Nathaniel Banks finally resigned from the service in early September and returned to Massachusetts, where he immediately won election to Congress. Joining Michael Hahn, Henry Clay Warmoth now emerged as a leading moderate. Having previously called for a "voluntary" election and the registration of voters irrespective of color, the Friends planned a state nominating convention in New Orleans in late September and an election for delegates on September 16. The convention would be dominated numerically by the New Orleans contingent, which was fairly evenly integrated along racial lines, whereas the rest of the delegates were overwhelmingly white. Although the free-state moderates had continued to resist a formal alliance, Wells's election announcement only a few days before the convention precipitated the creation of the Louisiana Republican Party.[1]

---

[1] *Proceedings of the Convention of the Republican Party*, 8–12; McCrary, *Abraham Lincoln and Reconstruction*, 330–32, 335–36; Taylor, *Louisiana Reconstructed*, 70–77; Hollandsworth, *Pretense of Glory*, 223–25; Houzeau, *My Passage at the New Orleans Tribune*, 110–14. Houzeau collapses together the mid-September election for delegates and the "voluntary" election of early November.

Convening on September 25 and meeting for four days, the convention evinced lingering tensions over wartime Reconstruction but firmly supported black political and legal equality. Elected convention president, Thomas Durant sounded familiar radical themes by endorsing black (or "universal") suffrage, rejecting the 1864 constitution and state government as illegitimate, and urging the convention to appeal to Congress. The convention voted to reconstitute the Friends of Universal Suffrage as the state Republican Party, but only after intense debate, since the national Republican Party had not yet adopted black suffrage. Warmoth submitted resolutions supporting the proposal while further denouncing the state government and insisting that Louisiana not yet be readmitted. Warmoth also contended that only Congress (working with the president) could authorize a new government, condemned any attempt to replace slavery with "a system of serfdom, or forced labor in any shape," and endorsed "universal suffrage, liberty and the equality of all men before the law." These resolutions only won approval when another one was added urging the Republican Party to hold a national convention, "without distinction of race or color, to adopt a national platform on the basis of universal suffrage." But the Republican Party of Louisiana had been born.[2]

Despite these difficulties, the convention offered a forceful defense of legal and political equality without regard to race. "The people of African descent are now free, and as free as all other men," proclaimed a formal address to the people of the state. "This truth must be recognized and carried out in all its legitimate consequences." The address noted various instances in Louisiana's past in which free black people (at least in theory) had been considered equal before the law. "Every free man, a native of the United States, or naturalized, is a citizen according to the highest legal authorities," it insisted. "Every emancipated slave, therefore, has obtained with his freedom the title of a citizen of the United States." The address reiterated the radical position that no government, "legally speaking, now exists in Louisiana." The convention also declined to nominate candidates or to participate in the upcoming state and congressional elections. It instead endorsed the "voluntary" election to choose a territorial delegate who would represent "the republicans of Louisiana" in Congress.[3]

Before the convention adjourned, Henry Clay Warmoth put forward a highly unorthodox proposal: that the convention draft a new state constitution that would be presented to the voters "at the next election," preparatory to Louisiana's readmission to the Union. Warmoth's half-baked scheme was tabled, but it would not be the last time – tragically – that Louisiana Republicans attempted by means of a constitutional convention to outflank

---

[2] *Proceedings of the Convention of the Republican Party*, 14–17; McCrary, *Abraham Lincoln and Reconstruction*, 332–33; Warmoth, *War, Politics and Reconstruction*, 43–45; Houzeau, *My Passage at the New Orleans Tribune*, 114–16.

[3] *Proceedings of the Convention of the Republican Party*, 18–21.

Andrew Johnson's Reconstruction policy and replace the current state government. After Thomas Durant declined the nomination as Louisiana's territorial delegate in the November voluntary election (having pledged to accept "no office, honor, or emolument" in connection with the campaign for universal suffrage, so as to be "entirely untrammelled with personal interest in the matter"), the convention overwhelmingly nominated Warmoth.[4]

In addition to being the first interracial political assembly held in the South during Reconstruction, the convention gave Louisiana the distinction of having founded the first Republican Party in the seceded states and of being the first southern Republican Party to endorse black suffrage. The convention, however, essentially repudiated the constitution and state government that Abraham Lincoln had applauded in his last speech. It also celebrated the abolition of slavery in Louisiana even as it rejected the document that had accomplished that goal. Louisiana Republicans consequently found themselves at a political dead end. The Unionist government, which the free-state radicals had never recognized, had been usurped by former Confederates, aided and abetted by a governor previously affiliated with the free-state movement. The approaching elections portended the Conservatives' consolidation of power just as black freedom was finally to be defined. Although the Wells–Conservative marriage would not last, Louisiana Republicans – as had the radicals before them – would have to look to Congress.

II

The southern elections conducted during the fall of 1865 were characterized – in addition to low turnout – by the voters' preference for former Whigs or conditional Unionists. Each state demonstrated its own characteristics, and wartime Unionism was more prevalent in the upper than in the lower South. Yet even as they rejected the outright secessionists of 1860–61, the voters generally elected candidates who had opposed secession until their states seceded but then subsequently supported the Confederacy. Emboldened by Johnson's increasingly prosouthern rhetoric, moreover, these former "reluctant secessionists" began to speak more assertively of their "rights" than they had immediately after the war.[5]

In Arkansas, Governor Isaac Murphy's hopes of increasing the state's chances for readmission by holding congressional elections resulted in disappointment. Violence against the freed people and white Unionists continued to roil the state. Having forged a "Conservative" Party, Democrats and

---

[4] *Proceedings of the Convention of the Republican Party*, 21–31; Warmoth, *War, Politics and Reconstruction*, 45.

[5] Foner, *Reconstruction*, 185–97; Carter, *When the War Was Over*, 94 (state elections), 229–31 (congressional elections).

conservative Unionists conducted a vigorous campaign, despite the state's 1864 "amnesty" law that disfranchised many of their supporters. Conservatives employed overtly racialist rhetoric, accusing Unionists of promoting racial equality and presenting themselves as paladins of white supremacy. They even suggested that slavery might be restored. Election day in early October was peaceful, but turnout – less than 7,000 votes – was far smaller than that of the previous year for the new constitution and government. Who won was irrelevant, since such results were not going to help Arkansas's case for readmission. The whole thing dispirited Unionists and energized Conservatives, who received another boost in December when the state Supreme Court invalidated the 1864 disfranchising law.[6]

The Mississippi election, also in early October, similarly reflected political moderation. The only substantive issue of the campaign had been allowing black testimony in court, and this issue only arose in late September when William Sharkey, hoping to shut down the Freedmen's Bureau courts, ordered the state courts to admit such testimony. The two main gubernatorial candidates, Ephraim S. Fisher and Benjamin G. Humphreys, were both ex-Whig jurists who had initially opposed session and differed only in their subsequent support for the rebellion. Humphreys, boasting the stronger war record, was easily elected governor. The state's entire delegation to the US House of Representatives were former Whigs who had opposed disunion prior to secession, and former Whigs won solid majorities in both houses of the legislature (though not as large as in the Reconstruction convention). Such results marked a notable retreat from fire-eating secessionism, but they still represented allegiance to the old order.[7]

Humphreys was inaugurated on October 16, when the legislature also convened. Johnson did not relieve Sharkey as provisional governor until late December, however, retaining him in an advisory capacity. In an inaugural address long on constitutional history and theory but short on specific recommendations, Humphreys urged his state to acknowledge abolition's consequences, including recognizing the former slaves' legal rights, while unequivocally defending racial subordination. It would be "hypocritical and unprofitable" to claim that Mississippi had abolished slavery "willingly," Humphreys admitted, but it had done so "in good faith." Now, "the highest responsibilities and duties" of racial "guardianship" had devolved upon the state's white population. Several hundred thousand former slaves, "unfitted for political equality with the white race," had been "turned loose upon society," and so the state "must deal justly with them and protect them in all their rights of persons and property." The freed people must also be assisted in achieving "the highest degree of elevation in the scale of civilization to which they are

---

[6] Moneyhon, *Impact of the Civil War and Reconstruction on Arkansas*, 190–96.
[7] Harris, *Presidential Reconstruction in Mississippi*, 104–16; *PAJ*, 9: 288–89.

capable," Humphreys continued, "but they cannot be admitted to political or social equality with the white race." Neither could it be forgotten "that ours is and shall ever be a government of white men," he insisted. "The purity and progress of both races require that caste must be maintained, and intermarriage between the races be forbidden."

"To work is the law of God, and is the only certain protection against pauperism and crimes of both races," Humphreys pontificated. "The negro is peculiarly adapted to the cultivation of the great staples of the South," he further intoned, and should be "encouraged" to engage in productive labor "by assurances of protection against the avarice, cupidity and injustice of his employer." Humphreys offered no guidance on how to achieve this objective. "He is free to choose his labor, and to make his own bargain," Humphreys allowed. "But he should be required to choose some employment that will insure the maintenance of himself and family." By the same token, employers needed assurances of "continuous labor" and guarantees that laborers would fulfill their contracts. No planter could conduct operations "unless the laborer is compelled to comply with his contract, remaining and performing his proper amount of labor day after day, and week after week, through the whole year," Humphreys insisted. "[A]nd if he attempts to escape, he should be returned to his employer, and forced to work until the time for which he has contracted has expired." *Compelled to comply. Attempts to escape. Forced to work.* This did not sound like the language of voluntary labor. "By such a system of labor, the welfare and happiness of the African may be secured, the agricultural and commercial prosperity of the State sustained, and our homes again become the abode of prosperity."[8]

The Mississippi legislature was eager to put Humphreys's proscriptions into place. The main point of contention would be how far to go to "protect" the former slaves "in all their rights of persons and property." The legislature created a special joint committee to recommend the laws necessary to fulfill these goals, and by early November, legislative action on black freedom in Mississippi began in earnest.[9]

III

The "black codes" of Mississippi and the other ex-Confederate states marked a key turning point in the course of Presidential Reconstruction. Even putting aside the question of the codes' actual enforcement, the Mississippi code – being the first – reflected white Southerners' unadulterated vision of a slave society without slavery. Northern reaction to the Mississippi code would force

---

[8] *New York Times*, October 28, 1865.
[9] Harris, *Presidential Reconstruction in Mississippi*, 123.

the other states to modulate their versions, at least to a degree, but Mississippi led the foray into terra incognita.[10]

In responding to what almost all white Southerners saw as a mounting crisis, the Mississippi legislators drew upon various precedents. These included the antebellum laws governing free people of color in the southern states; the legal codes of the northern states, which also imposed various forms of racial segregation and discrimination, in addition to prohibiting vagrancy and other forms of "vice"; and the more stringent measures of the Freedmen's Bureau, especially regarding relief. The War Department had already prohibited pass systems and other racially discriminatory limitations on physical mobility, but military rule would presumably soon be lifted. By the fall of 1865, moreover, white Southerners were expressing grave anxiety over the freed people's refusal – fostered by hopes of gaining the promised "forty acres and a mule" – to sign labor contracts for the coming year. The summer had yielded the first indications of what would become the "Christmas Insurrection Scare" of 1865: the widespread fear that the former slaves would rise up at year's end, either to seize what had been promised them or to wreak vengeance against their former oppressors. The political moderates may have been in charge, but the attitudes that informed the Mississippi black code, as William C. Harris has observed, "were not tempered by moderation."[11]

Since the end of the war, white Southerners had talked about little else than how to regain control over their former slaves. As the Mississippi legislature prepared to address this problem, two distinct approaches were evident. The "radicals" argued for firm measures in regulating the former slaves, limiting their rights to those free black people had previously enjoyed or restricting those rights even further. The "moderates," by contrast, would confer elementary rights on the former slaves and acknowledge their legal identity and its protection at law. Whereas the two groups were operating from contrasting motives, they shared an unflinching commitment to white supremacy and the plantation system. To that end, the Mississippi black code included an apprenticeship act, an act revising the state penal code, a vagrancy act, and a "civil rights" act (along with a supplemental civil rights act). However draconian these statutes may have been, their real tragedy, as Dan T. Carter argues, was that they were essentially the work of the moderates, not the radicals, and thus were the *best* the white South had to offer at the time. The other states may have calibrated their codes in response to northern criticism of Mississippi's, but Carter's generalization holds true for Mississippi as well.[12]

---

[10] Carter, *When the War Was Over*, chap. 6.
[11] Harris, *Presidential Reconstruction in Mississippi*, 124 (quotation), 128–30. On the Christmas Insurrection Scare: *Freedom: L&L-1865*, chap. 9, especially the chapter essay, 796–808; Hahn, "'Extravagant Expectations' of Freedom"; Carter, "Anatomy of Fear."
[12] The Mississippi code can be found in US Congress, Senate, *Letter of the Secretary of War*, 190–97; Harris, *Presidential Reconstruction in Mississippi*, 121–23, 130–40; Carter, *When the War Was Over*, 231.

The apprenticeship act, which was ostensibly designed "to protect the interest" of orphans and minors without means of support, employed the tried-and-true method of controlling the parents by controlling the children. The "former owner" of the minor being apprenticed, it decreed, "shall have the preference." Apprentices were to receive certain protections or privileges, including being taught to read and write, but any runaway was to be remanded "to the service of his or her master or mistress" and subject to "moderate corporal chastisement" (though not "cruel or unusual punishment"). The revised penal code forbade all black persons not in the US military service or possessing the necessary license from owning firearms or deadly weapons, and it prohibited any white person from providing these items, "or any spirituous or intoxicating liquors," to any black person. (Exception was made for white employers to provide black employees with liquor, but insufficient "to produce intoxication.") This law also declared "all the penal and criminal laws" currently governing "crimes and misdemeanors committed by slaves, free negroes, or mulattoes ... to be in full force and effect" (with certain exceptions), and it criminalized a vast array of behaviors by "any freedman, free negro, or mulatto," including involvement in "riots, routs, [and] affrays," "insulting gestures, language, or acts," "exercising the function of a minister of the gospel without a license from some regularly organized church," and "committing any other misdemeanor, the punishment of which is not specifically provided for by law." Any black person convicted under the act and unable or unwilling to pay the resulting costs could be hired out "to any white person" who paid them.

Similarly, the vagrancy act defined "vagrancy" as just about anything a particular situation required. "[A]ll rogues and vagabonds, idle and dissipated persons, beggars, jugglers, or persons practicing unlawful games or plays, runaways, common drunkards, common night-walkers, pilferers, lewd, wanton, or lascivious persons, in speech or behavior, common railers and brawlers" were legally considered to be vagrants, as were "persons who neglect their calling or employment, misspend what they earn, or do not provide for the support of themselves or their families, or dependants, and all other idle and disorderly persons, including all who neglect all lawful business, habitually misspend their time by frequenting houses of ill-fame, gaming-houses, or tippling shops." Lest this definition missed anyone, the act also included a sweeping statement that deemed as vagrants "all freedmen, free negroes and mulattoes" who were "without lawful employment or business" by the start of the new year. For good measure, it imposed an annual poll tax of up to $1 on "every [adult] freedman, free negro, or mulatto" for the support of poor and indigent black people, failure of which to pay would be considered prima facie evidence of vagrancy.

These measures elicited little debate or opposition, but not the civil rights act, which was by far the most contentious measure that made up the code, especially the provisions governing black property rights and black testimony in court. Black property rights spoke to the former slaves' aspirations to escape the plantation system and achieve economic independence. Even Andrew Johnson insisted on this guarantee. Yet to allow black people to acquire real property, land in particular, would potentially deprive planters of the "continuous labor" that was essential to their livelihoods. The act granted all black people – in addition to the right to sue and be sued in court, thereby recognizing their legal existence – the right to own *personal* property "in the same manner and to the same extent that white persons may." However, it conferred no express, corresponding right to *real* property, and it forbade "any freedman, free negro, or mulatto to rent or lease any lands or tenements" outside of cities or towns. This language did not explicitly prohibit black people from owning agricultural homesteads or farms, but many people – for and against, within the state and without – interpreted it as prohibitive. Some legislators insisted that they had voted for this provision of the bill with the understanding that it prevented black landowning, and most of its supporters, especially among the moderates, probably hoped that it would at least inhibit black access to land.[13]

Similarly, the issue of black testimony in court exposed the contradiction between, on the one hand, a foundational legal principle that possessed powerful cultural resonance, and, on the other, a central tenet of southern racial thought that white Southerners were not about to abandon. Predictably, it generated the most controversy. This provision conferred upon black people the right to testify in court, including against white people, but only in cases to which a black person was a party. Advocates argued that the principle was already operative, owing to Governor Sharkey's September proclamation, and that Northerners would insist upon it. They also contended that it was necessary so as to enable black people to defend themselves against white assault on their persons or property. Allowing black people to testify in court, however, would violate the principle that sworn testimony could be relied upon as inviolate truth and was a point of honor. Such a principle could never apply to black people, opponents argued, who had no honor to defend and were inveterate liars. They also warned that accepting black testimony in court would lead to political equality.[14]

The measure generated furious debate in the legislature and in Mississippi society at large. In mid-November, the Mississippi House voted the provision down, resulting in widespread criticism and recrimination. Andrew Johnson telegraphed Provisional Governor Sharkey (directing him to share the

---

[13] Harris, *Presidential Reconstruction in Mississippi*, 130–32. Freedmen's Bureau commissioner O. O. Howard ordered that any attempted prohibition against black landholding not be enforced. *Freedom: L&L-1865*, 730–31.

[14] Jackson (MS) *Daily Clarion*, November 22, 1865. The classic analysis of notions of honor among white Southerners before the Civil War is Wyatt-Brown, *Southern Honor*.

communication with Governor Humphreys) urging the legislature to allow black testimony. Some key opponents, such as Robert S. Hudson, also began to reconsider their position. On November 20, Governor Humphreys intervened, delivering a special message to the legislature. He reminded the lawmakers that the Reconstruction convention, in addition to abolishing slavery, had authorized the enacting of laws to provide for the safety and security of the former slaves in their persons and property. He also pointed out the incongruity of allowing black people to sue and be sued in court without permitting them to testify on their own behalf. "The negro is free – whether we like it or not," Humphreys insisted. While freedom "does not make him a citizen, or entitle him to political or social equality with the white man," he added, "the Constitution and justice do entitle him to protection in his person and property, both real and personal." Black testimony would also protect the white community from "vile and vicious" white men, who, by manipulating the former slaves, would otherwise be able to "plunder our lands with entire security from punishment." The issue "sinks into insignificance," Humphreys continued, compared to the crime, vagrancy, and pauperism that Mississippi faced as a result of abolition. He recommended measures to address these problems, including a militia bill "to protect our people against insurrection or any possible combination of vicious white men and negroes."[15]

The proponents of black testimony forced a reconsideration of the measure, but the opponents seized the opportunity to submit a far more severe substitute for the entire civil rights bill. The substitute bill negated many of the basic rights the former slaves would have gained under the original proposal. It also maintained a key element of slavery by denying freed persons any legal identity. Instead, "agents" would be appointed as the former slaves' representatives to oversee and administer their affairs. Black people could only sue or be sued through their agents, and only white testimony would be allowed in court. The agents would "confirm and ratify all trades and contracts for hire, or the performance of labor made by any freedman," and they – and not the victims – would assume responsibility for reporting assaults against black people and appear in court on their behalf. The agents were also authorized to arrest vagrants and remand laborers who absconded in violation of their contracts. The former slaves would have no legal existence except through their agents. The Senate defeated the substitute, however, and the original bill, with minor revisions, thereupon passed both houses, largely along radical-moderate lines. Humphreys signed the civil rights bill into law.[16]

---

[15] Harris, *Presidential Reconstruction in Mississippi*, 132–34; *PAJ*, 9: 332–34 (Hudson to Johnson), 400–1 (Johnson to Sharkey); Jackson (MS) *Daily Clarion*, November 21, 1865.

[16] The substitute proposal bore certain similarities—mutandis mutatis — to the system of state "warranteeism" that the Mississippi proslavery theorist Henry Hughes, who had died in 1862, had advocated before the war. Ambrose, *Henry Hughes*, esp. chaps. 3–4.

In truth, "civil rights" was a misnomer. The act conferred basic rights on the former slaves, but it also imposed numerous restrictions and obligations. In addition to the aforementioned rights, the act allowed black people to marry on the same basis as white persons, and it legitimized all existing black marriages. It expressly prohibited interracial marriage, however, upon pain of a life sentence – for both parties – in the state penitentiary. The act also enabled any black person, upon affidavit, to charge any white or black person with criminal offense against his or her person or property, and it directed that the state's penal laws, unless otherwise specified, would apply to black people. But the supplementary act provided for penalties against any black person who "falsely and maliciously" caused the arrest and trial of any white person. As far as rights went, that was it. The other provisions of the act required all black people to enter into written labor contracts by the first week of the new year (with greater specificity than the vagrancy act) and provided for their strict enforcement. Both civil officials and private individuals, for instance, were authorized to "arrest and carry back to his or her legal employer" any laborer who quit "without good cause." The act also restricted white behavior by prohibiting the enticement of laborers already under contract. The "civil rights" act was much more about restraining the freed people than empowering them.

"Thrown as we now are upon the wide sea of a new experi[m]ent of what was but yesterday a great domestic institution of the South," opined a moderate Jackson newspaper at the height of debate over the civil rights bill, "[i]t is not unnatural that the wisest and best men of the country, should differ as to the best course of policy to be pursued in regard to the population of which this institution was composed." White Mississippians had indeed vehemently disagreed over "the best course of policy to be pursued" regarding the former slaves. Most of them consequently took satisfaction in having overcome their differences and in surmounting a major obstacle on the road to state restoration. These differences notwithstanding, the Mississippi black code had also emanated from an underlying consensus that viewed slavery as "a great domestic institution of the South." There was no disagreement about that. [17]

As such, it had never dawned on the authors of the black code or their white constituents to ask black Mississippians what they thought. Although excluded from the process of Reconstruction, the latter expressed their disapproval of these laws in a number of local meetings throughout the state. In one such meeting, at Port Gibson in early December, "we the Colorde people" framed a petition to Governor Humphreys that revealed a keen understanding of the code and how it would adversely affect them. The petition also voiced the freed

---

[17] Jackson (MS) *Daily Clarion*, November 23, 1865. On reaction to the Mississippi code and its political repercussions, see Harris, *Presidential Reconstruction in Mississippi*, 140–46.

people's aspirations for freedom while correctly ascertaining the white determination to deny those aspirations.

"[W]e fear from the late acts of the Legeslature that she will not treate us as free," the petition began, observing that the legislation both set black people apart and lumped them all together. "All freedmen Negroes and molattoes is specified in the acts," the petition contended. "[W]hy [not?] colord vagrants that are a n[uisance?] and will not worke for a living be compelde by a law to worke in the fields Set a part for that purpoes[?]" The freed people's detractors were quick to proclaim their faults but never said anything positive about them. "[T]hair is Shureley Some a mong us that is honest, truthful, and industrious." Condemning the contract-enforcement provisions of the code, it noted: "we are to well acquainted with the yelping of bloodhounds and the tareing of our fellow servents To pisces when we were slaves and now we are free we donot want to be hunted by negro-runners and their hounds unless we are guilty of a crimnal crime." The men who had written the code "no meny of us has stood by our owners in thair troubles and thair is some of us who woulde die by them," the petition continued, "but the worde freedom is sweet to us all and greate will be the day when we [are?] assured of our freedom." It likewise acknowledged that some white employers were willing to deal with the freed people fairly, although white public opinion would prevent them from acting on such impulses. Nonetheless, "we are willing to worke for our former masters or eny Stranger that will treate us well and pay us what we earn," the petition asserted, "all we ask is justice and to be treated like humane beings." It beseeched the governor not to ignore their plea. "[W]e think if just men were the majority in the legeslature we woulde get just laws," they speculated. "[W]e hope your honor will not lay us a side but take us in Consideration."

Denying any wish for violence, the petitioners urged the governor not to believe "the falsehood our enimies has got up" that they planned insurrection. "[W]e have [no] [s]uch thought," they avowed. "[N]ow we are free what [would?] we rise for," they asked pointedly. "[W]e owe to much To meny of our white friends that has shown us mercy in bygon dayes To harm their wicked neighbours." They closed by pursuing the theme of Christian forbearance. "Some of us" (though, tellingly, not all) wanted Jefferson Davis to be freed, "for we no worse masters Than he was." Although "he tried hard to keep us all slaves we forgive him," the petitioners concluded. "Some of us know of meny kindenes he shown his slaves on his plantation." The petition ended up in the records of the Freedmen's Bureau, and no evidence indicates that Governor Humphreys ever saw it.[18]

---

[18] *Freedom: L&L-1865*, 856–58. For a similar meeting that took place in Vicksburg in late October, even before the state's black code had been enacted, see *Freedom: L&L-1865*, 816–19.

IV

Even as the Mississippi legislature was hammering out the state's black code, the Federal abolition amendment progressed toward final adoption. The nation also anxiously awaited the convening of the Thirty-Ninth Congress in early December, anticipating in particular how the Republican majority would respond to Johnson's Reconstruction policy. At long last, congressional Republicans would weigh in on the southern state governments – especially those reconstructed by Johnson – and the place of the freed people under them.

As Louisiana's elections – both official and "voluntary" – approached in early November, Freedmen's Bureau Assistant Commissioner Thomas W. Conway became the first casualty in Johnson's war on the bureau. Increasingly under attack from the planters and other conservatives, Conway was removed in October in an action that bureau commissioner General O. O. Howard – who still naïvely believed that he could reconcile Johnson's policy with both the bureau's mission and black aspirations for freedom – did not challenge. While on a tour of the South, not coincidentally, Howard visited New Orleans on the eve of the elections. In an address before an integrated but predominantly black audience, he did not so much as hint at black suffrage. Although moved by Howard's sincerity, the New Orleans *Tribune* expressed black disappointment in his speech – a disenchantment that was destined to grow.[19]

The results of the official election in Louisiana were a foregone conclusion. Wells overwhelmingly won reelection, and conservatives firmly controlled the legislature. In the voluntary election, Henry Clay Warmoth received more than 20,000 votes – nearly as many as Wells, almost all cast by black men – as Louisiana's "territorial" delegate to Congress. Although well organized, the election was limited to the southern part of the state, and – in a preview of things to come – it endured widespread efforts at disruption. At a subsequent mass meeting in New Orleans, meant in part as Warmoth's send-off to Washington, Republican leaders advocated black suffrage and equality before the law. Upon convening later in November, the legislature elected two new US Senators, to replace the current Senators-elect (including Michael Hahn), and commenced work on the state's black code.[20]

By late November, elections had taken place and the legislatures of several southern states had convened or were set to do so. Following South Carolina's qualified ratification of the abolition amendment in mid-November, nullifying

---

[19] McCrary, *Abraham Lincoln and Reconstruction*, 336–38; McFeely, *Yankee Stepfather*, chap. 9.

[20] Taylor, *Louisiana Reconstructed*, 73, 78–81; McCrary, *Abraham Lincoln and Reconstruction*, 338–39. Reports from New Orleans newspapers on the results of Louisiana's voluntary election and its aftermath are reproduced in *Proceedings of the Convention of the Republican Party*, 33–50.

the enforcement clause, Johnson pressured the other states to approve it. Eventually, on December 2, 4, and 6, Alabama, North Carolina, and Georgia, respectively, complied. Georgia's ratification, two days after Congress convened, put the amendment over the top. On December 18, Secretary of State William H. Seward declared the "Thirteenth Amendment" part of the US Constitution. Slavery was no more, including in Kentucky and Delaware, both of which had refused to abolish it. But Mississippi's black code already put the amendment's enforcement clause to the test.[21]

In refusing to ratify the amendment, Mississippi also passed on the opportunity to provide the crucial vote. In truth, the amendment never had a chance in Mississippi. During the state's Reconstruction convention, Provisional Governor Sharkey had doubted that Mississippi would ever accept the enforcement clause. If anything, white opposition had since hardened, despite Johnson's strident urgings to Sharkey that the state ratify the amendment. "The argument is," Johnson wrote, "if the Convention abolished Slavery in good faith, why Should the Legislature hesitate to make it a part of the Constitution of the United States[?]" This was a legitimate question, except that nobody really knew what trouble the second clause might lead to.[22]

What was perhaps most striking about the amendment in Mississippi was the *lack* of commentary – the assumption being that it would not be ratified. Only on November 20 did Governor Humphreys officially notify the legislature of the amendment, recommending approval of the first clause but rejecting the second. (Nothing in the US Constitution has ever provided for a state's qualified, conditional, or partial adoption of an amendment.) To all intents and purposes, the amendment was dead in Mississippi. A legislative joint committee recommended rejection of the entire measure, not just the second clause, and on December 5, the day *before* Georgia provided the decisive vote, the Mississippi House handily defeated the amendment. However inadvertently, Mississippi had declined the distinction of making the Federal abolition amendment operative.[23]

Even as these events were transpiring, scores of congressional members-elect from the seceded states – many having participated in the rebellion but having subsequently been elected under Johnson's Reconstruction policy – were descending upon Washington in anticipation of being seated in the new Congress. This was precisely the situation Maryland Radical Republican Henry Winter Davis had foretold in the spring of 1864. Despite Davis's warning that Congress would be powerless, with no Reconstruction policy in place, to deny

---

[21] Vorenberg, *Final Freedom*, 228–33; Richards, *Who Freed the Slaves?*, 235–40.
[22] *PAJ*, 9: 325.
[23] *PAJ*, 9: 400–1; Harris, *Presidential Reconstruction in Mississippi*, 141–42. Humphreys's message to the legislature was reprinted regularly in Mississippi newspapers during late November and early December.

seats to such claimants, Congress in fact refused to seat them. Instead, it established a Joint Committee on Reconstruction to deal with the matter, making no allowance for the rebellious states that had undergone wartime Reconstruction. Undeterred, Johnson in late December relieved the provisional governors and recognized the elected governors of five southern states, including Mississippi. Meanwhile, within days of the Thirteenth Amendment becoming operative, Louisiana and South Carolina began to enact their black codes, which differed very little from Mississippi's. But this is the beginning of another story.

V

As had their counterparts elsewhere, the freed people and former free people of color of Arkansas were also mobilizing and respectfully demanding racial and civic equality. From November 30 through December 2, even as Congress was preparing to meet, the "Colored Citizens of the State of Arkansas" came together in Little Rock for, according to one participant, "the first Colored Convention ever held in the State of Arkansas." The roughly twenty delegates, mostly hailing from Union-occupied areas during the war, included the black community's religious, professional, and skilled elite. They were meeting for the purpose, as convention president Rev. J. T. White put it, "of conferring with each other, as to our best interest and future prosperity," and "to memorialize the State Legislature and Congress of the United States, to grant us equality before the law and the right of suffrage."[24]

Several members of the state's political and military hierarchy, including Governor Isaac Murphy, attended the convention at various times. William H. Grey delivered the keynote address. Born free in Washington, DC (and likely the son of Virginia congressman and governor Henry A. Wise), Grey had moved his family to St. Louis just prior to the war and relocated to Helena following the 1862 Federal occupation. Although only recently arrived in Arkansas, Grey had already established himself as a leading figure in the state's black community. He would remain deeply involved in public affairs throughout Reconstruction, serving as a delegate at Arkansas's 1868 constitutional convention and later in the legislature. Grey's address sounded the by-now familiar arguments for equal rights. Yet he also consciously centered the events of the previous five years around the black experience even as he articulated the theme – already well-developed in nineteenth-century black thought – of African Americans as a people of destiny. Simply by having survived slavery,

---

[24] Foner and Walker, *Proceedings of the Black National and State Conventions*, 189–94. For a thorough analysis of the Arkansas convention's proceedings and the backgrounds of many delegates, see Rosen, *Terror in the Heart of Freedom*, 98–108. See also Wintory, "African American Legislators," esp. 99–101.

he argued, African Americans were destined for great things. Grey also offered an account of black people's role in the war that Abraham Lincoln himself had recognized but that white Americans would effectually erase in the ensuing decades, only to have it rediscovered a century later.[25]

When the war started, Grey observed, African Americans had "scarcely awakened," mired as they were in what he called the "prison-house of slavery," to the possibility that their condition could ever change. Meanwhile, "the haughty, self-willed" white people of the South had declared, "in the face of an enlightened world, that slavery was divine," and they had made it "the corner-stone of a bastard republic." The slaves were initially thought to have no part in the conflict. Even after "escaping from rebel masters" and serving as Union military laborers, they still faced the hostility of their liberators. Only "after disaster brought the nation to sober reflection," and "in this hour of dire affliction and deep humiliation," did Lincoln and other Unionists realize "the relative strength of the two sections – how the one could be reduced and the other strengthened," Grey contended. "Public sentiment began to change, and from that time the rising star of the Negro has been seen hovering over Washington."

Throughout this ordeal, Grey continued, black people had gained in confidence and self-respect. As slaves, they had shown deference and humility, but their masters "never once dreamed that under this seeming respect there was a human soul, with a will and a purpose of its own." Such subordination was no more. "We have now thrown off the mask, hereafter to do our own talking, and to use all legitimate means to get and to enjoy our political privileges," he declared. "We don't want anybody to swear for us or to vote for us; we want to exercise those privileges for ourselves; and we have met here, under the new order of things, to ask of the people of Arkansas – calmly, dispassionately and respectfully – to give us those rights." Only then would the state enjoy "a Republican form of government."

Black people's contribution to the war – or what Grey called "the last feather that broke the camel's back" – augmented this claim to citizenship. "[I]t was the Negro thrown into the scale on the side of the nation that broke the back of the rebellion and saved the nation." The very government that black people had helped to save, "for the love we bore it," could not now deny them their rights. "The Government of the United States is pledged to secure our rights; we wrote the contract in blood, when her own children were about to destroy her," Grey insisted. "We ask, therefore, that the State do for us what the Government must do eventually." Grey closed by paying homage to his people's past travails and suffering while heralding their destiny. "Our future is sure," he predicted. "[H]ere we have lived, suffered, fought, bled, and many

---

[25] Rosen, *Terror in the Heart of Freedom*, 98–99; Wintory, "African American Legislators," 99–100.

have died. We will not leave the graves of our fathers, but here we will rear our children; here we will educate them to a higher destiny; here, where we have been degraded, will we be exalted – AMERICANS IN AMERICA, ONE AND INDIVISIBLE."

The convention's official *Memorials and Resolutions*, which Grey helped to draft, also linked the demand for legal and political equality to racial uplift. The freed people had endured the "persecutions of two and a half centuries," the document read. Although Arkansas had abolished slavery, "the best means of completing the Emancipation[,] Enfranchisement and elevation of our race" was for the state legislature and Congress "to grant us our oath, before the Civil Courts, and the right of suffrage." Invoking the "fundamental principle" that "taxation and representation are inseparable," the document further insisted that black people, being subject to the law, also deserved its protection. The state and Federal governments must therefore confer upon them equal rights. "We, your humble petitioners, do most earnestly desire and pray that you clothe us with the power of self protection, by giving us our equality before the law and the right of suffrage, so we may become *bona fide* citizens of the State in which we live." Although Arkansas alone among the rebellious states enacted no black code (the legislature merely declared the state's antebellum laws governing free black people to be in effect), the petitioners' request for civic equality would not be granted until congressional Republicans overthrew Johnson's policy and in 1867 implemented Radical Reconstruction.

VI

In mid-December 1865, two weeks after the Little Rock convention, US Army Captain Thomas Kanady was directed by his superiors in New Orleans to proceed to Houma, in Terrebonne Parish. He was to investigate the rumor, "quite current here, that the blacks are going to raise against the whites in that vicinity during the coming holidays." Kanady was also ordered to confer with Robert N. Ogden, the parish district attorney, "and obtain all the facts in the case." Ogden was one of a number of officials, planters, and other prominent individuals from southern Louisiana who had written to state legislators, calling attention to the so-called Christmas Insurrection scare. The freed people, these correspondents alleged, were refusing to sign labor contracts for the coming year, brandishing fire arms and shooting them off during the night, talking openly about the lands they were soon to receive from the government or would take by force if necessary, behaving in a threatening and hostile manner toward the white residents, and causing general mayhem. "There are a great many things said of what has been heard from negroes that if true would indicate a strong probability that they intend to rise before long and put to death the whites and take possession of their lands," wrote Thomas Scott, a judge of East Feliciana Parish.

Such letters to the legislators were among the hundreds, nay thousands, that panicked white Southerners wrote to state and Federal military officials throughout the South during the fall, warning of the calamity that was about to befall them and urging strong measures to prevent it. In turn, twenty Louisiana state legislators warned Governor Wells that "a considerable degree of alarm exists, owing to some movements among the negroes, which, unless properly checked, it is feared, will lead to incalculable mischief." They advised Wells to organize and arm the militia, and that it be authorized "to disarm and disperse all unlawful & insurrectionary assemblages." They beseeched him to "devise some means to avert the impending danger."

The legislators' letter to Wells and the supporting documentation found their way to Federal military authorities, who ordered Kanady to look into the matter. His investigation, completed in late December, revealed the combustible mix of labor, politics, and race in the highly charged atmosphere of Louisiana's November elections – both official and "voluntary" – and the legislative session that would craft the state's black code. Whereas the black mindset oscillated between expectations of land and fears of reenslavement, whites viewed the freed people's determination to resist such reenslavement, by force if necessary, and their efforts at organizing for self-defense as imminent insurrection and slaughter. Kanady betrayed his own condescension in attributing insurrection fever as much to black gullibility in believing grandiose promises as to southern white paranoia and hysteria. But he also offered incontrovertible evidence of the white determination to reduce the former slaves to bondage, and of the continued spirit of resistance to Federal authority.[26]

Finding no basis for the insurrection rumors, Kanady nonetheless discovered that black people in the area – starting before the November elections and continuing since – were holding secret, nightly meetings, from which all white people were excluded except "certain persons" who "had obtained an influence over their minds." As a result of these meetings, the former slaves "had been led to beleive that the Government intended apportioning the confiscated lands among them," Kanady noted, "until every man became impressed with the idea that he was soon to become a landed proprietor." The freed people's refusal to discuss contracts for the new year "arroused the suspicions of the citizens, which soon ripened into a positive beleif, that the object of these meetings and the moroseness of the negroes meant danger to

---

[26] All of the documentation relating to this episode is from *Freedom: L&L-1865*, 873–80. The discussion here combines two separate reports by Kanady, since there is some topic overlap and redundancy between them.

the community." Kanady found "that the fear of an intended rising of the blacks had at one time pervaded the minds of the entire community," leaving "no doubt that the people permitted their fears to magnify the acts of the blacks & upon the evidence of their own fears many of the rumors or reports became current." In other words: a nineteenth-century feedback loop. Yet in conversing with the white residents, Kanady learned "that this fear had given away to one of more security, and that few if any entertained any apprehensions of difficulties with the negroes of a serious nature."

Even as white fears had dissipated, those of the freed people had grown. Their main cause was the reorganization of the militia, under the guise of maintaining law and order, and its use "as an armed and mounted patrol." The former slaves were convinced that "the sole object" of these patrols was "to crush out what freedom they now enjoy and reduce them once more to comparative slavery," once Federal troops had been removed. "They cannot understand why men who but a few months since were in armed rebellion against the government should now have arms put in their hands by that government," Kanady observed. "[T]hey cannot comprehend the fact, how a man can be a rebel today and tomorrow become a loyal citizen, and be appointed to places of trust." While bemoaning what he considered the freed people's naiveté in believing false promises of land, Kanady admitted they had a point. "Knowing so well the character, history and carreer of these men during the late rebellion they have as they think, good cause to distrust their future wellfare, if placed subject to their control." The former slaves would not rise up unprovoked, but "unless the utmost care and prudence be used in the use of this patrol as a local police," Kanady warned, "the most fearful results will ensue, as the blacks unhesitatingly avowed their determination, to me, to resist and if necessary, meet force with force."

As though reviving the patrols were not enough, patrol members were wearing Confederate uniforms and openly displaying Confederate military insignia (violating Federal military orders). The practice – which civil authorities neither countenanced nor discouraged – was clearly having "a bad effect" on the freed people, who, "having been so long kept in bondage, where they knew no law but the will of their masters," Kanady observed, "look with feelings of distrust upon every act that points toward a compulsory system of labor." The "establishing of this militia patrol is viewed with so much distrust and repugnance," he continued, that a mere "slight provocation" would bring the freed people into "armed collision with it, in which event imagination cannot realize the consequences." Indeed, the freed people had "invariably avowed their determination to resist any arrest or interference on the part of the patrol with any of their people," prompting Kanady to caution the white residents "in order that they might be prepared for whatever results might ensue from the acts of their patrol."

Slavery had been abolished throughout the United States, but the old slave patrols had been revived and were being manned by individuals brandishing Confederate paraphernalia. With Louisiana in the process of enacting a black code, moreover, the freed people might have been justified to wonder what had changed with emancipation. Yet one such change was their determination to resist the patrols, with force if necessary – something unthinkable under slavery. In an endorsement of early January 1866, the area's commander, General Thomas W. Sherman, restricted the patrols to routine matters of law and order. They could make no arrests under martial law, which, Sherman noted in a qualifier that spoke volumes, "yet exists in the State to some extent," and any civilian arrests they made must follow due process procedures. "Should the State militia be armed with any further power than this," Sherman warned, "the result may be calamitous."

The donning of Confederate uniforms, in addition to violating Federal military policy, Sherman further observed, was "in bad taste" and "calculated to create effervescence among the loyal people." He advised that the state adopt uniforms and leave no excuse for flaunting Confederate garb. Some months later, civilian uniforms would prevent the police forces of neither Memphis nor New Orleans from stirring up their own form of "effervescence." The consequences, as Sherman had predicted, would be "calamitous."

EPILOGUE

Memphis and New Orleans: May 1–3 and July 30, 1866

The two events, separated in time by nearly three months, are so closely linked as almost to constitute a single episode: the racial violence at Memphis and New Orleans. That the two cities at either end of the lower Mississippi valley would play such a crucial role in the fate of Presidential Reconstruction was only partly coincidental, given everything that had happened during the previous five years. "Race riots" (though "massacres" more accurately conveys what they were) traumatized the black populations of both cities, providing yet further proof that President Andrew Johnson's Reconstruction policy had been a catastrophe. The spirit of rebellion, most Northerners were now convinced, was thriving instead of dissipating in the former seceded states. For the better part of three days in early May in Memphis, and for just under two hours on a sweltering late-July afternoon in New Orleans, white mobs – with the police forces of both cities leading the way – indiscriminately slaughtered scores of black people (and in New Orleans, some of their white allies), who, it was clear, did not enjoy the most elementary protections of life and limb under the law.

It would be an overstatement to say that Memphis and New Orleans, considered together, were the last straw in turning northern opinion against Johnson's Reconstruction policy and in paving the way for "Radical" Reconstruction. The massacres instead must be seen within a complex of events and developments, dating back to the end of the war and continuing forward, that showed Johnson's policy needed either serious modification or complete scrapping. Memphis and New Orleans marked a key turning point in – but did not cause – the northern shift against Johnson. They were the most salient examples of the wave of violence against black people that had swept across the southern landscape since the Confederate surrender. If there were a certain symmetry to the two major cities of the lower Mississippi valley shaping the course of postwar Reconstruction, moreover, the proximate causes – black soldiers in Memphis, black suffrage in New Orleans, black access to public space in both cities – were the most explosive issues that the nation then faced. Nothing enraged white Southerners – even those who accepted the end of slavery – more than the black troops who served in the Union army of occupation, the black men and women who laid equal claim as citizens to public space, and the very idea of black suffrage. These could never be borne.[1]

* * *

By spring 1866, the nation had reached gridlock over the political settlement to the war. Under Johnson's plan of "self-Reconstruction," the former rebellious states had elected new governments and had agreed, however begrudgingly, to end slavery and to meet other minimal conditions. The Thirteenth Amendment had become operative. As far as Johnson was concerned, "Reconstruction" was over and the rebellious states must be admitted. That these governments, under white control, had enacted black codes that left the freed people little removed from slavery was less the problem for Johnson than the solution. Racial violence and the southern state authorities' refusal to grant black people redress bothered Johnson only insofar as they reflected badly on his policy. In response, Republicans and a growing number of Northerners demanded basic guarantees for the former slaves' lives, bodies, and property before readmitting the rebellious states to the Union. These demands included, first, a civil rights bill and, then, an amendment to the Federal Constitution securing, among other things, birthright citizenship and equality before the law. Many Republicans now also advocated black suffrage. Although congressional Republicans overrode Johnson's veto of the Civil Rights bill (and would do the same with a bill to maintain the Freedmen's Bureau), many of them still hoped to reach an accommodation with Johnson, despite his opposition to the amendment.

It was within this context that the three days of violence in Memphis shocked the nation. Even taking historical hindsight into account, the preconditions in the months prior to the episode made some kind of violent confrontation almost inevitable. If the Memphis massacre were indeed, as it has been called, "the first large-scale racial massacre to erupt in the post-Civil War

---

[1] Every general history of Reconstruction or of Presidential Reconstruction places much emphasis on the Memphis and New Orleans massacres. Both events have also received considerable scholarly treatment, although, remarkably, no monograph existed on Memphis until recently. Unless otherwise indicated, the accounts of both episodes presented here are based on the following sources. For Memphis: Ash, *Massacre in Memphis*; Lovett, "Memphis Riots"; Hardwick, "Your Old Father Abe Lincoln Is Dead and Damned"; Rosen, *Terror in the Heart of Freedom*, pt. 1; Bond and O'Donovan, *Remembering the Memphis Massacre*. For New Orleans: Hollandsworth, *Absolute Massacre*; Taylor, *Louisiana Reconstructed*, 103–13; Vandal, *New Orleans Riot of 1866*. Congress conducted thorough investigations of both incidents, producing summary reports and hundreds of pages of eyewitness testimony. For Memphis, see US Congress, House of Representatives, *Memphis Riots and Massacres*. For New Orleans, see US Congress, House of Representatives, *Report of the Select Committee on New Orleans Riots*.

South," it would also prove to be but one of many during Reconstruction. But there is nothing like the shock of the first time.[2]

The population of Memphis had nearly doubled during the war, from about 23,000 to nearly 45,000, with much of that increase made up of the former slaves who had sought refuge in the city. Having increased from about 4,000 in 1860 to 20,000 in 1865, the city's black population by the end of the war nearly equaled the total population at the start. Many of these black residents lived in shanties on the city's outskirts, especially at its southern end, near Fort Pickering, where the Third US Colored Heavy Artillery regiment was stationed. Many of these soldiers' families also squatted in the fort's vicinity. Irish immigrants and their families made up nearly a quarter of the city's 1860 population, largely inhabiting the distinct neighborhood of South Memphis. Overwhelmingly of poor or working-class status, they made up a large majority of the police force and held many patronage jobs with the city government. As was so often the case in the mid-nineteenth-century urban United States, the Irish and black populations vied for the lowest paying jobs, provoking much resentment and animosity between them.

The dramatic increase in the city's black population, along with the visible presence of black soldiers and their deployment in patrolling the city, inflamed relations between the black and Irish populations and with the white population in general. Wartime Tennessee had witnessed considerable conflict between civilian and Federal military authorities, a situation further exacerbated by the presence of the Freedmen's Bureau, which maintained its headquarters toward the southern end of Memphis. Although Federal military authority was being reduced and many city functions were being returned to the civil authorities, a number of near-violent incidents had occurred in the preceding months between black soldiers and city police. Human nature being what it is, off-duty black soldiers occasionally committed petty crimes, especially theft, which the city's white residents, aided by inflammatory newspaper reports, interpreted as an epidemic of criminal mayhem. Neither did the police or white population look kindly on the street parties and other celebrations that black residents held in the public places to which they now claimed equal access. The police frequently mistreated and abused the black soldiers and black residents whom they arrested, often on trumped-up charges, and they were getting pushback from an increasingly frustrated black community.[3]

It was probably an attempt by police to shut down one of these street celebrations that precipitated the massacre. Rumors had circulated throughout

---

[2] "Memories of a Massacre: Memphis in 1866," www.memphis.edu/memphis-massacre/ (accessed August 2019). This website is companion to a symposium, held at the University of Memphis in May 2016 commemorating the sesquicentennial of the massacre, on which Bond and O'Donovan, *Remembering the Memphis Massacre*, is based.

[3] On the black soldiers stationed in Memphis in particular, see Slap, "On Duty in Memphis," 120–31.

the city that something would happen on April 30, the day many soldiers of the Third Colored Heavy Artillery were scheduled to be mustered out of service. Several incidents that day had almost resulted in violence. Although nothing actually developed, false rumors spread through the city. On the afternoon of May 1, several police officers attempted to disperse a street party that included a number of black soldiers. What began as yet another episode of harassment soon escalated into a forceful confrontation before generating an exchange of gunfire that left a police officer dead. From here, the police force mobilized, and groups of armed white men organized to put down the "black insurrection." When city officials requested that the Federal military commander, General George Stoneman, deploy troops to suppress the supposed black rioters, Stoneman, at this critical juncture, acted indecisively. With a force of fewer than 200 men at his disposal, and having listened for months to complaints by officials to be allowed to administer their own city, Stoneman indicated that the civil authorities should handle the situation, even suggesting that they form posses. This was like putting out a fire by throwing gasoline on it.

For the next two terror-filled days, through the afternoon of May 3, when Federal troops finally intervened, white mobs and Memphis policemen and firemen butchered the black population of Memphis, as scores of men, women, and children were attacked, beaten, robbed, and murdered. The marauders raped or sexually assaulted at least five women – and no doubt others – and they burned or destroyed schools, churches, and other institutions, in addition to dozens of residences. They also attacked white teachers and other known white allies of the black community. Most of the violence was indiscriminate, but a number of the perpetrators singled out individual men or women for attack and knew their victims. "The whole evidence discloses the killing of men, women, and children – the innocent, unarmed, and defenceless pleading for their lives and crying for mercy," concluded the congressional investigative report into the affair. The evidence also revealed, the report continued, "the wounding, beating, and maltreatment of a still greater number; burning, pillaging, and robbing; the consuming of dead bodies in the flames, the burning of dwellings, the attempts to burn up whole families in their houses, and the brutal and revolting ravishings of defenceless and terror-stricken women."[4]

By the time order was restored, black Memphis lay in smoldering ruins. The Freedmen's Bureau office in the city conducted an initial investigation, hearing testimony from nearly a hundred witnesses. Even as the bureau was completing its report on May 22, a congressional select committee arrived in Memphis to undertake its own investigation, which it would complete in late July. As would become routine during Reconstruction, the Republican majority and

---

[4] US Congress, House of Representatives, *Memphis Riots and Massacres*, 5.

the Democratic minority reports described diametrically opposed accounts. Yet both reports confirmed that forty-six black persons lost their lives, along with two white men – one policeman and one fireman. Among the black fatalities were fourteen soldiers (nearly one-third of the dead), at least three women, an "Unknown Negro boy," and a "Negro boy." Overall, the identities of sixteen black victims remain unknown. The members of the white mobs wounded another seventy-five persons and "maltreated" ten others; committed 100 "distinct robberies, more or less aggravated," along with the five documented cases of rape, the victims of which testified before the committee; and burned or destroyed four churches, twelve schoolhouses, and ninety-one houses or cabins. "It was called in derision the 'nigger riot,' while, in fact, in the language of General Stoneman, the negroes had nothing to do with it after the first day, except to be killed and abused," noted the majority report, paraphrasing Stoneman's testimony. "They assembled in no bodies," the report continued, now directly quoting Stoneman, "and were engaged in no riotous proceedings."[5]

The Democratic press in Memphis and the nation either shrugged or blamed the victims for the violence. State and local authorities took no action whatsoever, and no grand jury ever convened. No white person so much as faced charges for the death and destruction the perpetrators had wrought. The spasm of violence in Memphis exposed – in contrast to the way the routine reports of murders and assaults in the South since the end of the war had begun to mask – just how badly Reconstruction had gone wrong under Johnson. Yet, however traumatized, the black community of Memphis and the surrounding region would not be cowed. Not two weeks after the massacre, the self-described "Colored Citizens of Helena," just downriver from Memphis, publicly assembled to condemn the violence and express support for the victims.[6]

The nation was still processing the events of early May – and the congressional investigative committee had barely completed its report – when New Orleans conflagrated in late July. Whereas the Memphis massacre involved the presence of black soldiers and the dispute over public space, the one in New Orleans resulted from black suffrage and public space as well. And while the carnage in Memphis unfolded over three interminable days, New Orleans was over in a matter of hours. But the fury and hatred of the white New Orleans mobs were just as intense, and just as deadly.

By mid-1866, the marriage of convenience between Louisiana governor J. Madison Wells and the former Confederates who dominated the state

---

[5] US Congress, House of Representatives, *Memphis Riots and Massacres*, 5 (passage from majority report paraphrasing Stoneman), 35 (list of fatalities), 36 (other assaults, robberies, and destruction of property), 58 (quotation from Stoneman's testimony). Rosen, *Terror in the Heart of Freedom*, offers an important gendered reading of the massacre and of the testimony of the rape victims before the congressional committee.

[6] Rosen, *Terror in the Heart of Freedom*, 82–83 (Helena meeting).

legislature and the New Orleans city government had long since collapsed. Although conservatively inclined and opposed to black suffrage, Wells had vetoed the more draconian provisions of Louisiana's black code, only to be overridden. His vetoes of several other measures had also angered the legislators. The unapologetic former Confederate John F. Monroe, having been elected mayor of New Orleans, purged the city's police force of Unionists from the wartime administration and replaced them with Confederate veterans. Even though Wells headed a government with which Johnson's predecessor had been strongly identified, and Johnson had backed Wells upon first taking office, Johnson now allied with the Democratic legislature and the state's conservatives in opposing black suffrage and the Fourteenth Amendment, both of which Louisiana Republicans advocated.

"It took no political genius," Joe Gray Taylor has written, to recognize that the Louisiana Republican Party's only hope for change was through black suffrage. "When his political survival depended upon it," Taylor further notes, "Wells discovered that black suffrage was not nearly so distasteful as he had once thought." During the September 1865 convention that had brought their party into being, Louisiana Republicans had considered but decided against reconstituting themselves as a constitutional convention. Now, they would try a different tack. They would reconvoke the 1864 constitutional convention, which had adjourned nearly two years earlier. That body had approved a measure allowing the convention president to call the convention back into session. This provision had been intended in the event the voters rejected the constitution, which had not happened, but it included no time limitation. The move was legal, strictly speaking, but it was highly questionable, and the organizers faced any number of logistical complications in reconciling the 1864 situation with the current reality. By modifying the state constitution to allow black suffrage and bar former Confederates from office, the convention clearly intended to precipitate a political revolution in Louisiana. When Wells indicated his support for the proposal, the stage was set for some kind of confrontation.[7]

Planning for the convention, set for July 30, was convoluted. Convention president Judge Edward H. Durrell, who was supposed to have issued the proclamation to meet, declined to participate, anticipating violence and distrusting Wells, so he was replaced by a president pro tem. Several Republican leaders who had had nothing to do with the original convention, including Henry Clay Warmoth and Thomas J. Durant, also avoided involvement (although both men witnessed the bloody *dénouement*). Wells and other convention organizers probably received indications of support from congressional Radicals. Mayor Monroe and other Democrats, including the lieutenant governor, announced that the proposed meeting would be deemed illegal and

---

[7] Taylor, *Louisiana Reconstructed*, 103, 104.

forcibly dispersed. Federal commander General Philip Sheridan was in Texas, and his subordinate, General Absalom Baird, gave mixed signals, ordering that the meeting, even if illegal, should be ignored and not disrupted by the civil authorities. Appeals by both sides to the administration, Democrats to Johnson and Republicans to Secretary of War Edwin M. Stanton, produced no clear instructions. The white population of New Orleans grew restive, especially following congressional approval in June of the Fourteenth Amendment. When state district Judge Edmund Abell, the leader of the conservative Unionists at Louisiana's 1864 constitutional convention, publicly declared participation in the convention a crime, military authorities arrested but soon thereafter released him. It had not gone unnoticed that Memphis authorities, more than two months after the fact, had prosecuted no perpetrators of that city's massacre. Inflammatory speeches by both sides leading up to the meeting did not help matters.

The convention was scheduled to meet at noon on July 30 at the Mechanics' Institute building off Canal Street. For some reason, General Baird thought the meeting time was 6:00 p.m., so no Federal troops were present. The New Orleans police and dozens of white men had undoubtedly organized in advance to interfere with the meeting. The delegates had anticipated being arrested and made the necessary arrangements, but they clearly had no idea what was about to happen. When the delegates first convened, without difficulty, no quorum was present, and so they recessed for an hour. Meanwhile, a group of several dozen black men, many of them Union veterans and armed in self-defense, paraded through the French Quarter toward the Mechanics' Institute in support of the convention, gaining adherents as they marched. By the time they reached their destination, opposing crowds of hundreds of armed white and black men faced off against each other.

The match to this tinderbox was lit when a fracas started at around 1:00 p.m., just as the delegates were reconvening. Before long the police and white mobs set upon the black crowd and the convention itself. A number of black men took shelter in the convention hall and fought back, but the assailants soon overwhelmed them. The delegates Dr. A. P. Dostie, whom conservatives especially detested, and John Henderson were murdered in the hall, as were a number of black men. The situation quickly degenerated into a pogrom against black persons and their white supporters, although former governor Michael Hahn, who was wounded, and several other delegates were arrested and taken into custody for their own protection. Former Confederate general Richard Taylor, who happened to be in the city, and who hardly sympathized with the victims, attested to the savagery of the attacks. For some two hours the slaughter continued until Federal troops finally arrived to restore order. Martial law was declared in New Orleans for the next several days.[8]

---

[8] Taylor, *Destruction and Reconstruction*, 248–50.

Officially, 34 black men and 3 white Republicans were killed, and 17 white and 119 black men wounded, but the true number of casualties was no doubt much higher. Ten policemen were injured, and the assailants evidently killed one of their own men accidentally. When General Philip Sheridan returned to New Orleans and conducted a preliminary investigation, he famously labeled the incident "an absolute massacre," convinced that it was premeditated. The Democratic press in Louisiana and the nation initially downplayed the attack or charged that it had been the result of a Republican conspiracy, but most of the nation echoed Republican outrage. On behalf of the state authorities, Judge Edmund Abell, of all people, impaneled a grand jury in early August to investigate the incident. After hearing testimony from no black witnesses or convention participants, it indicted only the surviving delegates who had been present when the convention met, largely for disturbing the peace. No police official or white citizen faced prosecution. Congress again investigated, taking testimony from scores of witnesses. The Republican majority and Democratic minority reports again told two different stories, but by the time they were finally published, months later, the course of Reconstruction had already been radically altered.

Although the Memphis and New Orleans massacres on their own did not doom Andrew Johnson's Reconstruction policy, they played a critical role in discrediting that policy with the northern public. They further added to the violence that had pervaded the South since the end of war, the black codes, the increasingly open spirit of rebellion, and Johnson's vetoes of the Civil Rights and Freedmen's Bureau bills and his harsh rhetoric in justifying them. Now this. Subsequently, Johnson would take his infamous campaign tour, the "Swing around the Circle," in trying to influence northern voters in the fall 1866 congressional elections. Hecklers called out "Memphis" and "New Orleans" in goading the mercurial Johnson into making intemperate statements, which wasn't difficult. The whole thing was a fiasco.[9]

When the northern voters chose in the congressional elections between Johnson's Reconstruction policy and the Republican program, as embodied in the Fourteenth Amendment, they overwhelmingly chose the latter. The result gave Republicans virtually veto-proof majorities in Congress and solidified the Radicals' position within the party. In early 1867, congressional Republicans would take Reconstruction out of Johnson's hands and pass the Reconstruction Act. Thus, nearly five years after first considering the matter, Congress had finally enacted Reconstruction legislation; and nearly two years after the war ended, a political settlement had been reached. It would require the rebellious states, as conditions for restoration to the Union, to adopt black suffrage and equality before the law and to remove former Confederates from

---

[9] The best account of Johnson's ill-fated campaign tour and its political ramifications remains McKitrick, *Andrew Johnson and Reconstruction*, 428–38.

power. Because Tennessee had approved the Fourteenth Amendment in July 1866, it was the only rebellious state excluded from Radical Reconstruction. Tennessee would also become the only rebellious state to adopt black suffrage voluntarily. The circumstances under which the postwar settlement had been reached did not bode well for its success in the other states, and it unleashed another kind of war.

* * *

If the lower Mississippi valley during the Civil War demonstrated the complexities of emancipation and abolition, it also revealed the inherent difficulty – even impossibility – of ending slavery under the nation's antebellum constitutional system. Owing to the Federal consensus and arduous amending process, along with the white South's determination to preserve slavery, it remains virtually impossible to envision how slavery might have been ended under peacetime conditions. Even allowing that the principle of "property in man" failed to gain constitutional sanction, there was *still* no way to compel the slave states to end slavery against their will. What does it say about the Constitution that that document provided no viable means for putting slavery on a course to "ultimate extinction" short of war, and what does this say about the possibilities for carrying out fundamental change under the Constitution? Is it the case that certain principles and practices are so deeply woven into the fabric of the Constitution that substantive revision on them remains all but impossible, or that certain intractable issues simply defy peaceful resolution? Some abolitionists had predicted that slavery would only end through violence – not by the slaves but rather among white Americans themselves. Many of their critics, both North and South, accused the abolitionists of trying deliberately to foment civil war. Did the American constitutional system lend these predictions and criticisms, whatever the motivations behind them, a certain validity?

The Thirteenth Amendment did not begin as a stand-alone measure to give constitutional sanction to the Emancipation Proclamation. Instead, it must be understood in juxtaposition to the distinct but interrelated problem of *state restoration*, which was the primary goal of Lincoln and most Unionists at the start of the war – even as abolitionists called for a direct assault on slavery. Only after Lincoln issued the proclamation – and largely, though not solely, in response to the contest between free-state and conservative Unionists over state restoration in the lower Mississippi valley – did the challenges of state restoration and the abolition of slavery come to be conjoined. Congressional Republicans and other antislavery advocates subsequently struggled to work this problem out in a manner consistent with the Constitution. The amendment was part of this process. Even those abolitionists who before the war had warned that any attempt by the slave states to secede would result in the freeing of the slaves ultimately came up short, for they had not figured out how to abolish slavery as an institution. It was in the course of confronting the problem of state restoration during the war that antislavery advocates overcame the seemingly insurmountable obstacle that had stymied the abolitionist movement from the founding of the Republic – how, concretely, to abolish slavery.

Antislavery advocates may have finally worked out the difference between military emancipation and abolition, yet not until Lincoln's reelection in November 1864 did contemporaries begin to think seriously of the Federal abolition amendment as a means of ending slavery distinct from that of restoring the seceded states under free-state constitutions. Even though most congressional Republicans, however implicitly, originally envisioned Reconstruction legislation and the abolition amendment as separate elements of a unified strategy, the amendment as of early 1865 was going to the states – including, evidently, the rebellious ones – with no Reconstruction bill having been enacted. The priority was now the amendment, although the consequences of abolition remained entirely unresolved. Ironically, whereas state restoration had been the original Union war goal, and whereas state restoration and abolition gradually converged after January 1863, Federal abolition came to supersede state restoration as a political objective during the final phase of the war.

Yet, even then, the rebellious states would have to undergo some form of political reorganization, else the amendment could never be ratified by the requisite number of states. Paradoxically, the ratifications by Arkansas, Louisiana, and Tennessee (and Virginia) – the states that had undergone wartime Reconstruction – would count toward the amendment (as would those by the states "reconstructed" under Johnson), even though Congress would ultimately refuse to readmit those states under their Unionist governments. No one could have realistically foreseen Lincoln's assassination (although a few of his closest associates did and urged him to take preventative measures). Lincoln, and everyone else, assumed that *he* would be in charge of postwar Reconstruction, and that he and congressional Republicans would eventually overcome their wartime differences and agree on a plan. Nonetheless, the failure to enact Reconstruction legislation – and thus to have a blue-print in place – before the war ended (and before Lincoln's death) gave Lincoln's successor a free hand, with catastrophic consequences for the nation. It may be unfair, even as a matter of historical assessment, to hold Lincoln partly accountable for the failure of Reconstruction. But if war indeed be the continuation of politics by other means, then Lincoln, in making little provision for the postwar order, especially with regard to the consequences of emancipation, perhaps bears some responsibility.

* * *

Having played a central role in transforming the Civil War into a war to end slavery, and in bringing about Radical Reconstruction, the lower Mississippi valley was also destined to play an equally crucial part in the remainder of Reconstruction, and beyond. Lawrence N. Powell has written that a significant part of nineteenth-century (and much of twentieth-century) US history can be told by looking at Louisiana.[10] This observation also holds true for the lower Mississippi valley in general (or what has been called Louisiana "writ large"), especially for the period of Reconstruction and the decades that followed. For instance, in the exercising of political power by African Americans via holding office, which is generally understood to be among the most significant accomplishments of Radical Reconstruction, one-third (502) of the 1,500 black officeholders at all levels of government in the eleven rebellious states hailed from the lower Mississippi valley (Mississippi, 226; Louisiana, 210; Arkansas, 46; Tennessee, 20). The large majority of these officeholders were at the local level, but they also included state and even national office. Eight black delegates from Arkansas, seventeen from Mississippi, and fifty from Louisiana served at the state constitutional conventions mandated by the Reconstruction Act. (Having approved the Fourteenth Amendment, Tennessee was not required to hold a convention.) During Radical Reconstruction, five black state senators and 22 black representatives served in the Arkansas legislature, in addition to 13 senators and 102 representatives in Mississippi (including two Speakers of the House), and 22 senators and 105 representatives in Louisiana. (No black men served in the Tennessee legislature during Reconstruction.)

Likewise, twenty black men (of thirty-two overall in the South) held state-level executive office in the lower Mississippi valley, including State Commissioner, Secretary of State (five from Mississippi and one from Louisiana), Superintendent of Education (only Tennessee did not have a black holder of this office), State Treasurer, and Lieutenant Governor (three from Louisiana and one from Mississippi). In late 1872, P. B. S. Pinchback of Louisiana gained the distinction of becoming (albeit briefly) the first black governor in US history when Henry Clay Warmoth was impeached and thereby suspended from office. At the Federal level, Charles E. Nash of Louisiana served in the US House of Representatives, as did John R. Lynch of Mississippi. Upon his seating in the US Senate in February 1870, the free-born Hiram R. Revels of Mississippi became the first African American to serve in either house of Congress. Several years later, Blanche K. Bruce of Mississippi, who had been born a slave in 1841 in Virginia, became the first African American to serve a full term in the US Senate. A number of black men also held appointive Federal office, especially in the New Orleans Custom House. African Americans never exerted a level of power or influence proportionate to their numbers, or anywhere near to what Reconstruction's

---

[10] Powell, "Why Louisiana Mattered."

detractors would later claim. Still, the ascension of black men to "positions of political authority in the South represented a stunning departure in American government," notes Eric Foner. "The spectacle of former slaves representing the South Carolina rice kingdom and the Mississippi cotton belt in state legislatures, assessing taxes on the property of their former owners, and serving on juries alongside them, epitomized the political revolution wrought by Reconstruction."[11]

Yet events in the lower Mississippi valley also precipitated the undoing of that revolution. In addition to the formation of the Ku Klux Klan in Pulaski, Tennessee, in late 1865, the violence that pervaded the South during Reconstruction would be punctuated by a number of dramatic episodes in the region. These included, in Louisiana, the 1873 Colfax massacre (the bloodiest single episode, in terms of the number of victims killed, during all of Reconstruction), the 1874 Coushatta massacre, and the so-called Battle of Liberty Place in 1874 in New Orleans. It is hardly coincidental that Colfax and Coushatta took place in Louisiana's Red River country, which had remained unvanquished by Federal forces during the war. The success of the 1875 "Mississippi Plan" in overthrowing Republican rule in that state confirmed that the North no longer had the will to counter southern white violence. Although Tennessee and Arkansas were the two southern states that responded most forcefully to the Klan violence of the late 1860s and early 1870s (causing historians of Reconstruction to ponder what-might-have-been had state and Federal authorities elsewhere responded similarly), those states were rife with violence as well.

In addition, the US Supreme Court decision in the 1873 Slaughterhouse Cases, which significantly narrowed the scope of the Fourteenth Amendment, emanated from New Orleans, while the court's 1874 Cruickshank decision, which resulted from the attempt to prosecute the perpetrators of the Colfax massacre, effectively undermined Federal enforcement of black civil rights, even in instances where the state governments were unable or unwilling to protect those rights. The corruption that weakened northern support for Reconstruction was perhaps unmatched in Louisiana. Bitter Republican factionalism in that state – which could be traced to wartime divisions between free-state moderates and radicals, and between the Afro-Creole elite and the rest of the black population – also proved damaging to Reconstruction, as it did in Arkansas, where the debacle of the 1874 Brooks–Baxter War featured armed conflict between rival Republican factions. Although Radical Reconstruction had ended in Tennessee, Arkansas, and Mississippi by the mid-1870s, Louisiana's role in the disputed presidential election of

---

[11] Foner, *Freedom's Lawmakers*, xiv–xvii (quotation, xiv).

1876 and the Compromise of 1877 remains essential to the story of Reconstruction.

Black politics would continue in parts of the lower Mississippi valley, especially in the vicinity of Natchez and in southern Louisiana, after Reconstruction, but by the end of the nineteenth century black voting and officeholding would be shut down. Mississippi was among the first of the southern states, in the early 1890s, to undertake black disfranchisement and to move toward legal segregation. Louisiana would not disfranchise its black voters until the end of the decade, but the state would have the distinction of devising the grandfather clause (which allowed white men to circumvent ostensibly race-neutral literacy or property requirements for voting). And perhaps most notoriously, the 1896 *Plessy v. Ferguson* US Supreme Court decision – which sanctioned legal segregation on the basis of "separate but equal," thereby negating the Fourteenth Amendment's guarantee of the equal protection of the law – would originate in Louisiana. While it is perhaps oddly appropriate that certain elements of Plessy's argument against segregation rested on the privileged position that the free people of color had once enjoyed in Louisiana society, vis-à-vis the enslaved population, the crux of the argument rejected that notion by affirming the equality of *all persons* and the *irrelevance* of race under the law.

The New South plantation regime would also reach its epitome in the lower Mississippi valley. The systems of sharecropping and tenancy that emerged on the cotton plantations of western Mississippi, northeastern Louisiana, and eastern Arkansas would serve as the archetypes for the South as a whole. The Yazoo–Mississippi Delta would be called "the most southern place on Earth," but this statement was equally applicable to the delta regions of Louisiana, Arkansas, and Tennessee. Monthly wage labor and the plantation regimen that took hold in the Louisiana sugar region were exceptional within the postbellum South, but the Thibodaux Massacre of 1887, in which dozens of striking black sugar workers were slain, was one of the most violent instances of labor unrest in the entire nation during the Gilded Age, and it foreshadowed what was to come. By the late nineteenth century, the lower Mississippi valley was virtually synonymous with lynching and other forms of racial violence, systematic political disfranchisement, legal segregation, and repressive labor arrangements. Nowhere did "Jim Crow" become more deeply entrenched than on the cotton and sugar plantations of the lower Mississippi valley, and nowhere would uprooting it prove to be more difficult. That objective has still not been accomplished, and today many communities within the region remain among the poorest and most retrogressive in the nation.

* * *

Chattel slavery violated the nation's founding ideals even as it underpinned much of the nation's development prior to the Civil War. There was little if anything about American antebellum society that slavery did not touch – or corrupt. That conundrum and its legacy have remained central to the American experience right down to the present. A nation that was founded on the principle of universal freedom, that holds that ideal as central to its very identity, and that claims that this ideal distinguishes it from every other nation on earth not only tolerated but also embraced, promoted, and advanced slavery. Many of slavery's defenders did not advocate certain actions or policies for the specific purpose of perpetuating racial slavery, but this objective was usually implied in their avowed, ostensible goal – whether that was removing various American Indian groups from desirable land for (white) settlement, liberating territory from corrupt Mexican rule in the name of Manifest Destiny, spreading the word of God or the benefits of laissez-faire capitalism, or some other purpose. For many others, the extension of slavery was an unfortunate by-product of more pressing aims. Only when a sufficient number of white Americans came to see the perpetuation and expansion of slavery as a potential threat to their own freedom and opportunity did the problem of slavery come to dominate national life. And even then, the large majority of white Americans preferred tolerating slavery to having to deal with the consequences of ending it.

Given what we now know, from the modern disciplines of sociology and psychology, of the overwhelming power of socialization, should it come as any surprise that people who were born and raised in a society that considered slavery to be divinely ordained would have imbibed that belief? Given what we know about how easily the public mind can be inflamed in a mass, democratic society, even without modern technology, should the hysteria that the mere possibility of ending slavery provoked among white Americans startle us? Given what the historical record tells us of the human species' seemingly inexhaustible capacity to inflict pain and suffering on fellow human beings (and on other sentient beings), and to rationalize such behavior on the basis of self-interest or some higher ideal, is it any wonder that the principle of human property was defended for so long and so vigorously by so many? Given the potency of tribalism and the need to belong to something larger than oneself to the human condition, should it shock us that people fought, killed, and died defending a social order and way of life predicated on racial slavery? The large majority of white people who lived under and benefitted from slavery had inherited it from previous generations. They had not consciously chosen to live in a slave society. The point is not to make excuses for persons in the past for actions that later came to be seen as morally wrong, since many people at the time knew better, and since individuals in the past, as today, make moral choices. But neither is the primary purpose of the study of history to pass moral judgment. Given everything we know about the human past, the truly inscrutable problem is not why people owned slaves but rather how humankind ever managed to end the practice.

The abolition of slavery prohibited forever the principle of property in man as a part of national life. But it could not abolish racism and racial hatred, institutionalized racial discrimination, or the white supremacist mindset that has so pervaded the American past and present. These phenomena were essential ancillaries of the slavery regime, but they have also existed independently of it and have outlived it. Racial oppression and subordination were at the heart of the version of slavery that prevailed in the United States and the western hemisphere until it was finally ended near the close of the nineteenth century. Yet just as nonracial forms of slavery have existed throughout history, various modes of racial oppression and subordination have characterized American life since the abolition of slavery, from the quasi-freedom of the Reconstruction era through the rise and fall of Jim Crow to the current era of mass incarceration and Black Lives Matter. Each of these periods had its own historically unique features, circumstances, and conditions, and there was and has been much diversity of experience during each of them, so they cannot all simply be lumped together. But an essential continuity has run through the nation's racial past that predated the end of slavery. White Americans may not have expressly proclaimed the United States "a white man's country" from the very beginning, but many of them began to do so unabashedly in the decades before the Civil War, and many have adhered to this idea, though often employing more muted language, ever since.

If white supremacy has always been at the center of the American project (which is not to say that white supremacy explains *everything* about the American experience, or that the United States was created for the *specific* purpose of oppressing people of color), so too has violence. The geographical outlines of the United States and the other nations of the western hemisphere, as we know them today, were not necessarily inevitable, yet there is no avoiding the fact that they were the product – however historically contingent the process – of imperial conquest. As a settler-state, the United States from its creation was infused with racialized violence. Thomas Jefferson's dream of (white) yeoman farmers moving peaceably across the landscape and making it productive was belied by the violence of systematic land expropriation and the extension of slavery. It was largely through violence that the aboriginal populations were dispossessed of their ancient heritage and that the nation's borders were extended from sea to sea. It was through the violence of the domestic slave trade that more than a million enslaved persons were moved to the old Southwest. And it was through violence that slavery was implanted in the lands beyond the original seaboard states, nurtured, and maintained. It is perhaps oddly appropriate, then, that slavery was destroyed through the most violent conflict that US society has ever directly experienced. Neither is it surprising that many white Americans, once the destruction of slavery had been completed, would resort to violence in trying to salvage what they could of the slave regime. Far from ending racial violence, the abolition of slavery merely transmuted it.

The millions of enslaved persons who endured, in Ira Berlin's words, "generations of captivity" faced the fundamental challenge of finding meaning – and of every day summoning up the will and courage to go on – in an existence of unspeakable oppression and unfathomable suffering. Millions of these persons dreamed of a liberation from bondage that never happened, somehow withstanding unimaginable physical pain, spiritual torment, psychological trauma, and even what historians have called "social death" before a merciful biological death freed them from their earthly sorrows. From the daily material conditions they faced (even weighing these against the conditions of rural peoples throughout the world at the time) to the brutal, even sadistic punishments that their overlords inflicted on them, to the utterly incomprehensible anguish of being separated from loved ones through sale or inheritance, the slaves managed to survive circumstances and conditions that we can barely begin to conceptualize today, and, in doing so, they created a world from which they drew spiritual sustenance and that gave their lives meaning. It detracts not one scintilla from what they accomplished to recognize that the burden of existence allowed them no choice. Despite the contentions of Frederick Douglass, William Lloyd Garrison, Harriet Tubman, Harriet Beecher Stowe, and a God's-Army of other abolitionists that slavery was such an obvious affront to basic human decency, such a gross violation of the spirit of the age, and such a self-evident obstacle to the march of human freedom and progress that its ultimate demise was inevitable, few rational people would have had cause for optimism until slavery's most forceful defenders – blinded by what Elizabeth Fox-Genovese and Eugene D. Genovese called a fatal self-deception – resorted to an undertaking that amounted to self-immolation. But out of the maelstrom of desolation, hopelessness, and despair came deliverance.

BIBLIOGRAPHY

Note: Items published in newspapers and periodicals during the period under study are not listed here; instead, full citations are provided in the footnotes.

Manuscript Collections

Agnew, Samuel A. Diary. Southern Historical Collection, Wilson Special Collections Library. University of North Carolina, Chapel Hill.
Conner, Lemuel P. Family Papers. Louisiana and Lower Mississippi Valley Collections, Hill Memorial Library. Louisiana State University, Baton Rouge.
Ex-Slave Narratives. Louisiana Collection. State Library of Louisiana, Baton Rouge.
Lincoln, Abraham. Papers. Manuscript Division. Library of Congress, Washington, DC.
Louisiana Works Progress Administration. Louisiana Collection. State Library of Louisiana, Baton Rouge.
Louisiana Writers Project. Louisiana Collection. State Library of Louisiana, Baton Rouge.
Minor, William J. Family Papers. Louisiana and Lower Mississippi Valley Collections, Hill Memorial Library. Louisiana State University, Baton Rouge.
Project Files (photostatic copies of documents from the National Archives). Freedmen and Southern Society Project. University of Maryland, College Park.
Steele, Frederick. Papers. Department of Special Collections. Stanford University Libraries, Stanford.

Published Materials: Primary and Secondary

Alexander, Thomas B. *Political Reconstruction in Tennessee.* Nashville: Vanderbilt University Press, 1950; reissue New York: Russell & Russell, 1968.
Ambrose, Douglas. *Henry Hughes and Proslavery Thought in the Old South.* Baton Rouge: Louisiana State University Press, 1996.
Anderson, John Q., ed. *Brokenburn: The Journal of Kate Stone.* Baton Rouge: Louisiana State University Press, 1955.
Aptheker, Herbert. *The Negro in the Civil War.* New York: International Publishers, 1938.

Ash, Stephen V. *A Massacre in Memphis: The Race Riot That Shook the Nation One Year after the Civil War.* New York: Hill and Wang, 2013.

Ash, Stephen V. *Middle Tennessee Society Transformed, 1860–1870: War and Peace in the Upper South.* Baton Rouge: Louisiana State University Press, 1988.

Ash, Stephen V., ed. *Secessionists and Other Scoundrels: Selections from Parson Brownlow's Book.* Baton Rouge: Louisiana State University Press, 1999.

Ash, Stephen V. *A Year in the South: 1865: The True Story of Four Ordinary People Who Lived through the Most Tumultuous Twelve Months in American History.* New York: Palgrave Macmillan, 2002.

Aston, T. H., and C. H. E. Philpin, eds. *The Brenner Debate: Agrarian Class Structure and Economic Development in Pre-Industrial Europe.* Cambridge: Cambridge University Press, 1985.

Atkins, Jonathan M. "The Failure of Restoration: Wartime Reconstruction in Tennessee, 1862–1865." In *Sister States, Enemy States: The Civil War in Kentucky and Tennessee,* edited by Kent T. Dollar, Larry H. Whiteaker, and W. Calvin Dickinson, 299–319. Lexington: University Press of Kentucky, 2009.

Atkins, Jonathan M. *Parties, Politics, and the Sectional Conflict in Tennessee, 1832–1861.* Knoxville: University of Tennessee Press, 1997.

Ayers, Edward L. *In the Presence of Mine Enemies: War in the Heart of America, 1859–1863.* New York: W. W. Norton, 2003.

Ayers, Edward L. *The Thin Light of Freedom: War in the Heart of America, 1859–1863.* New York: W. W. Norton, 2017.

Baker, Jean H. *Affairs of Party: The Political Culture of Northern Democrats in the Mid-Nineteenth Century.* Ithaca: Cornell University Press, 1983.

Ballard, Michael B. *Grant at Vicksburg: The General and the Siege.* Carbondale: Southern Illinois University Press, 2013.

Ballard, Michael B. *Vicksburg: The Campaign That Opened the Mississippi.* Chapel Hill: University of North Carolina Press, 2004.

Banks, Nathaniel Prentiss. *Emancipated Labor in Louisiana.* N.p., [1865?].

Banks, Nathaniel Prentiss. *Letter from Major Gen. N. P. Banks.* N.p., 1864.

Baptist, Edward E. *The Half Has Never Been Told: Slavery and the Making of American Capitalism.* New York: Basic Books, 2014.

Bardaglio, Peter W. *Reconstructing the Household: Families, Sex, and the Law in the Nineteenth-Century South.* Chapel Hill: University of North Carolina Press, 1995.

Barksdale, Kevin T. "Creation of West Virginia." August 8, 2017. Encyclopedia Virginia. www.EncyclopediaVirginia.org/West_Virginia_Creation_of. Accessed September 20, 2019.

Barney, William L. *The Secessionist Impulse: Alabama and Mississippi in 1860.* Princeton: Princeton University Press, 1974.

Basler, Roy P., ed. *The Collected Works of Abraham Lincoln.* 8 vols. New Brunswick: Rutgers University Press, 1953–5.

Bearss, Edwin C. "The Seizure of the Forts and Public Property in Louisiana." *Louisiana History* 2, no. 4 (Autumn 1961): 401–9.

Bearss, Edwin C. "The White River Expedition, June 10–July 15, 1862." *Arkansas Historical Quarterly* 21, no. 4 (Winter 1962): 305–62.

Bearss, Sara. "Constitutional Convention, Virginia (1864)" *Encyclopedia Virginia*. Virginia Humanities, (December 7, 2020). www.EncyclopediaVirginia.org/Virginia_Convention_of_1864. Accessed September 20, 2019.

Beckert, Sven. *Empire of Cotton: A Global History*. New York: Alfred A. Knopf, 2014.

Beckert, Sven, and Seth Rockman, eds. *Slavery's Capitalism: A New History of American Economic Development*. Philadelphia: University of Pennsylvania Press, 2016.

Behrend, Justin. "Rebellious Talk and Conspiratorial Plots: The Making of a Slave Insurrection in Civil War Natchez." *Journal of Southern History* 77, no. 1 (Summer 2011): 17–52.

Behrend, Justin. *Reconstructing Democracy: Grassroots Black Politics in the Deep South after the Civil War*. Athens: University of Georgia Press, 2015.

Bell, Caryn Cossé. *Revolution, Romanticism, and the Afro-Creole Protest Tradition in Louisiana, 1718–1868*. Baton Rouge: Louisiana State University Press, 1997.

Bell, Caryn Cossé. "'Une Chimère': The Freedmen's Bureau in Creole New Orleans." In *The Freedmen's Bureau and Reconstruction: Reconsiderations*, edited by Paul A. Cimbala and Randall M. Miller, 140–60. New York: Fordham University Press, 1999.

Belz, Herman. "The Constitution, the Amendment Process, and the Abolition of Slavery." In *Lincoln and Freedom: Slavery, Emancipation, and the Thirteenth Amendment*, edited by Harold Holzer and Sara Vaughn Gabbard, 160–79. Carbondale: Southern Illinois University Press, 2007.

Belz, Herman. "The Etheridge Conspiracy of 1863: A Projected Conservative Coup." *Journal of Southern History* 36, no. 4 (1970): 549–67.

Belz, Herman. *Reconstructing the Union: Theory and Policy during the Civil War*. Ithaca: Cornell University Press, 1969.

Benedict, Michael Les. *A Compromise of Principle: Congressional Republicans and Reconstruction, 1863–1869*. New York: W. W. Norton, 1974.

Bentley, George R. *A History of the Freedmen's Bureau*. Philadelphia: University of Pennsylvania, 1955.

Bercaw, Nancy. *Gendered Freedoms: Race, Rights, and the Politics of Household in the Delta, 1861–1875*. Gainesville: University Press of Florida, 2003.

Bergeron, Paul H. *Andrew Johnson's Civil War and Reconstruction*. Knoxville: University of Tennessee Press, 2011.

Berlin, Ira. *Generations of Captivity: A History of African-American Slaves*. Cambridge, MA: Harvard University Press, 2003.

Berlin, Ira. *The Long Emancipation: The Demise of Slavery in the United States*. Cambridge, MA: Harvard University Press, 2015.

Berlin, Ira. *The Making of African America: The Four Great Migrations*. New York: Viking, 2010.

Berlin, Ira. *Many Thousands Gone: The First Two Centuries of Slavery in North America*. Cambridge, MA: Harvard University Press, 1998.

Berlin, Ira. *Slaves without Masters: The Free Negro in the Antebellum South.* New York: Pantheon Books, 1974.

Berlin, Ira, Barbara J. Fields, Thavolia Glymph, Joseph P. Reidy, and Leslie S. Rowland, eds. *Freedom: A Documentary History of Emancipation, 1861–1867, Ser. 1. Vol. 1: The Destruction of Slavery.* Cambridge: Cambridge University Press, 1985.

Berlin, Ira, Thavolia Glymph, Steven F. Miller, Joseph P. Reidy, Leslie S. Rowland, and Julie Saville, eds. *Freedom: A Documentary History of Emancipation, 1861–1867, Ser. 1. Vol. 3: The Wartime Genesis of Free Labor: The Lower South.* Cambridge: Cambridge University Press, 1990.

Berlin, Ira, Joseph P. Reidy, and Leslie S. Rowland, eds. *Freedom: A Documentary History of Emancipation, 1861–1867, Ser. 2. The Black Military Experience.* Cambridge: Cambridge University Press, 1982.

Berry, Daina Ramey. *The Price for Their Pound of Flesh: The Value of the Enslaved, from Womb to Grave, in the Building of a Nation.* Boston: Beacon Press, 2017.

Bettersworth, John K. *Confederate Mississippi: The People and Policies of a Cotton State in Wartime.* Baton Rouge: Louisiana State University Press, 1943.

Biographical Directory of the United States Congress, 1774–1989: Bicentennial Edition. Washington, DC: Government Printing Office, 1989.

Blackburn, Robin. *The American Crucible: Slavery, Emancipation, and Human Rights.* London and New York: Verso, 2011.

Blaine, James G. *Twenty Years of Congress from Lincoln to Garfield. With a Review of the Events Which Led to the Political Revolution of 1860.* 2 vols. Norwich, CT: Henry Bill, 1884–86.

[Blair, Montgomery] *Speech of the Hon. Montgomery Blair, (Postmaster General,) on the Revolutionary Schemes of the Ultra Abolitionists, and in Defence of the Policy of the President. Delivered at the Unconditional Union Meeting, Held at Rockville, Montgomery Co., Maryland, on Saturday, October 3, 1863.* New York: D. W. Lee, 1863.

Blair, William A., and James J. Broomall, eds. *Rethinking American Emancipation: Legacies of Slavery and the Quest for Black Freedom.* Cambridge: Cambridge University Press, 2015.

Blair, William A., and Karen Fisher Younger, eds. *Lincoln's Proclamation: Emancipation Reconsidered.* Chapel Hill: University of North Carolina Press, 2009.

Blassingame, John W. *Black New Orleans, 1860–1880.* Chicago: University of Chicago Press, 1973.

Bolton, S. Charles. *Fugitivism: Escaping Slavery in the Lower Mississippi Valley, 1820–1860.* Fayetteville: University of Arkansas Press, 2019.

Bolton, S. Charles. "Slavery and the Defining of Arkansas." *Arkansas Historical Quarterly* 58, no. 1 (Spring 1999): 1–23.

Bond, Beverly Greene, and Susan Eva O'Donovan, eds. *Remembering the Memphis Massacre: An American Story.* Athens: University of Georgia Press, 2020.

Bond, Bradley. *Political Culture in the Nineteenth-Century South: Mississippi, 1830–1899.* Baton Rouge: Louisiana State University Press, 1995.

Botkin, B. A., ed. *Lay My Burden Down: A Folk History of Slavery*. Chicago: University of Chicago Press, 1945.

Boutwell, George S. "The Power of the Government to Suppress the Rebellion [Speech delivered before the National Union League Association, Washington, DC, June 16, 1863]," 216–38, in *Speeches and Papers Relating to The Rebellion and the Overthrow of Slavery*. Boston: Little, Brown, 1867.

Brasher, Glenn David. *The Peninsular Campaign and the Necessity of Emancipation: African Americans and the Fight for Freedom*. Chapel Hill: University of North Carolina Press, 2012.

Brazy, Martha Jane. *An American Planter: Stephen Duncan of Antebellum Natchez and New York*. Baton Rouge: Louisiana State University Press, 2006.

Brooks, Corey M. "Reconsidering Politics in the Study of American Abolitionists." *Journal of the Civil War Era* 8, no. 2 (June 2018): 291–317.

Brown, D. Alexander. *Grierson's Raid: A Cavalry Adventure of the Civil War*. Urbana: University of Illinois Press, 1954.

Brownson, Orestes A. *The Works of Orestes A. Brownson, Collected and Arranged by Henry F. Brownson*. 20 vols. Detroit: Thorndike Nourse, 1882–1907.

Burkhardt, George S. *Confederate Rage, Yankee Wrath: No Quarter in the Civil War*. Carbondale: Southern Illinois Press, 2007.

Burlingame, Michael. *Abraham Lincoln: A Life*. 2 vols. Baltimore: John Hopkins University Press, 2008.

Burlingame, Michael, and John R. Turner Ettlinger, eds. *Inside Lincoln's White House: The Complete Civil War Diary of John Hay*. Carbondale: Southern Illinois University Press, 1997.

Burnham, Walter Dean. *Presidential Ballots, 1836–1892*. Baltimore: Johns Hopkins University Press, 1955.

Butler, Anne M., and Wendy Wolff. *United States Senate Election, Expulsion and Censure Cases 1793-1990*. Washington, DC: Government Printing Office, 1995.

Butler, Benjamin F. *Autobiography and Personal Reminiscences of Major-General Benjamin F. Butler; Butler's Book*. Boston: A. M. Thayer, 1892.

Bynum, Victoria E. *The Free State of Jones: Mississippi's Longest Civil War*. Chapel Hill: University of North Carolina Press, 2001.

Carter, Dan T. "The Anatomy of Fear: The Christmas Insurrection Scare of 1865." *Journal of Southern History* 43, no. 3 (August 1976): 345–64.

Carter, Dan T. *When the War Was Over: The Failure of Self-Reconstruction in the South, 1865–1867*. Baton Rouge: Louisiana State University Press, 1985.

Caskey, Willie Malvin. *Secession and Restoration of Louisiana*. Baton Rouge: Louisiana State University Press, 1938.

Castel, Albert. "The Fort Pillow Massacre: An Examination of the Evidence." In *Black Flag Over Dixie: Racial Atrocities and Reprisals in the Civil War*, edited by Gregory J. W. Urwin, 89–103. Carbondale: Southern Illinois University Press, 2004.

Chenault, William W., and Robert C. Reinders. "The Northern-born Community of New Orleans in the 1850s." *Journal of American History* 51, no. 2 (September 1964): 232–47.

Christ, Mark K. "'They Will Be Armed': Lorenzo Thomas Recruits Black Troops in Helena, April 6, 1863." *Arkansas Historical Quarterly* 72, no. 4 (Winter 2013): 366–83.

Cimbala, Paul A., and Randall M. Miller, eds. *The Freedmen's Bureau and Reconstruction: Reconsiderations*. New York: Fordham University Press, 1998.

Cimprich, John. "Military Governor Johnson and Tennessee Blacks, 1862–65." *Tennessee Historical Quarterly* 39, no. 4 (Winter 1980): 459–70.

Cimprich, John. *Slavery's End in Tennessee, 1861–1865*. Knoxville: University of Tennessee, 1985.

Cleveland, Henry. *Alexander H. Stephens in Public and Private with Letters and Speeches, Before, During, and Since the War*. Philadelphia: National, 1866.

Cobb, James C. *The Most Southern Place on Earth: The Mississippi Delta and the Roots of Regional Identity*. New York: Oxford University Press, 1992.

Coggeshall, William T. *Lincoln Memorial: The Journeys of Abraham Lincoln: From Springfield to Washington, 1861, as President Elect; and from Washington to Springfield, 1865, as President Martyred*. Columbus: Ohio State Journal, 1865.

Cole, Arthur Charles. *The Whig Party in the South*. London: Oxford University Press, 1913.

Congressional Globe, Washington, DC: Government Printing Office, 1863–1865.

Conroy, James. *Our One Common Country: Abraham Lincoln and the Hampton Roads Peace Conference of 1865*. Guilford, CT: Lyons Press, 2014.

Conway, Thomas W. *Annual Report of Thos. W. Conway, Superintendent, Bureau of Free Labor, Department of the Gulf, to Major General Hurlbut, Commanding, for the Year 1864*. N.p.: Times Book and Job Office, n.d.

Conway, Thomas W. *The Freedmen of Louisiana: Final Report of the Bureau of Free Labor, Department of the Gulf, to Major General E. R. S. Canby, Commanding*. New Orleans: Times Book and Job Office, 1865.

Conway, Thomas W. *Report on the Condition of the Freedmen, of the Department of the Gulf, to Major General N. P. Banks, Commanding*. New Orleans: H. P. Lathrop, 1864.

Cooper, William J., Jr. *Jefferson Davis, American*. New York: Alfred A. Knopf, 2000.

Cornish, Dudley Taylor. *The Sable Arm: Negro Troops in the Union Army, 1861–1865*. New York: Longmans, Green, 1956.

Cowen, Ruth Caroline. "Reorganization of Federal Arkansas, 1862–1865." *Arkansas Historical Quarterly* 18, no. 2 (Summer 1959): 32–57.

Cox, LaWanda. *Lincoln and Black Freedom: A Study in Presidential Leadership*. Columbia: University of South Carolina Press, 1981.

Craven, Avery O. *The Coming of the Civil War*. 2nd ed. Chicago: University of Chicago Press, 1957.

Crofts, Daniel W. *Reluctant Confederates: Upper South Unionists in the Secession Crisis*. Chapel Hill: University of North Carolina Press, 1989.

Currie, James T. *Enclave: Vicksburg and Her Plantations, 1863–1870*. Jackson: University Press of Mississippi, 1980.

Dattel, Gene. *Cotton and Race in the Making of America: The Human Costs of Economic Power*. Lanham: Ivan R. Dee, 2009.

Davis, David Brion. *The Problem of Slavery in the Age of Emancipation*. New York: Alfred A. Knopf, 2014.

Davis, Jefferson. *Jefferson Davis, Constitutionalist, His Letters, Papers and Speeches*. Collected and edited by Dunbar Rowland. 10 vols. Jackson: Mississippi Department of Archives and History, 1923.

Davis, Jefferson. *The Rise and Fall of the Confederate Government*. 2 vols. New York: D. Appleton, 1881.

Davis, Ronald L. F. *Good and Faithful Labor: From Slavery to Sharecropping in the Natchez District, 1860–1890*. Westport: Greenwood Press, 1982.

Davis, William C. *"A Government of Our Own": The Making of the Confederacy*. New York: Free Press, 1994.

Dawson, Joseph G. III. *Army Generals and Reconstruction: Louisiana, 1862–1877*. Baton Rouge: Louisiana State University Press, 1982.

Dawson, Joseph G. III, ed. *The Louisiana Governors: From Iberville to Edwards*. Baton Rouge: Louisiana State University Press, 1990.

Debates in the Convention for the Revision and Amendment of the Constitution of the State of Louisiana. New Orleans: W. R. Fish, 1864.

DeBlack, Thomas A. *With Fire and Sword: Arkansas, 1861–1874*. Fayetteville: University of Arkansas Press, 2003.

Degler, Carl N. *The Other South: Southern Dissenters in the Nineteenth Century*. New York: Harper & Row, 1974.

Degler, Carl N. *Place Over Time: The Continuity of Southern Distinctiveness*. Baton Rouge: Louisiana State University Press, 1977.

Dew, Charles B. "The Long-Lost Returns: The Candidates and Their Totals in Louisiana's Secession Election." *Louisiana History* 10, no. 4 (Fall 1969): 353–69.

Dew, Charles. B. "Who Won the Secession Election in Louisiana?" *Journal of Southern History* 36, no. 1 (February 1970): 18–31.

Deyle, Steven. *Carry Me Back: The Domestic Slave Trade in American Life*. New York: Oxford University Press, 2005.

Dimond, E. Grey, and Herman Hattaway, eds. *Letters from Forest Place: A Plantation Family's Correspondence, 1846–1881*. Jackson: University Press of Mississippi, 1993.

Din, Gilbert C. *Spaniards, Planters, and Slaves: The Spanish Regulation of Slavery in Louisiana, 1763–1803*. College Station: Texas A&M University Press, 1999.

Dinges, Bruce J., and Shirley A. Leckie, eds. *A Just and Righteous Cause: Benjamin H. Grierson's Civil War Memoir*. Carbondale: Southern Illinois University Press, 2008.

Dobb, Maurice. *Studies in the Development of Capitalism*. London: George Routledge and Sons, 1946.

Donald, David Herbert. *Lincoln*. New York: Simon and Schuster, 1995.

Donovan, Timothy P., and Willard B. Gatewood, Jr. *The Governors of Arkansas: Essays in Political Biography*. Fayetteville: University of Arkansas Press, 1981.

Dougan, Michael B. *Confederate Arkansas: The Peoples and Policies of a State in Wartime.* Tuscaloosa: University of Alabama Press, 1976.

Downs, Jim. *Sick from Freedom: African-American Illness and Suffering during the Civil War and Reconstruction.* New York: Oxford University Press, 2012.

Drake, Winbourne Magruder. "The Mississippi Reconstruction Convention of 1865." *Journal of Mississippi History* 21, no. 4 (October 1959): 225–56.

Drescher, Seymour. *Abolition: A History of Slavery and Antislavery.* Cambridge: Cambridge University Press, 2009.

Du Bois, W. E. B. *Black Reconstruction: An Essay toward a History of the Part in which Black Folk Played in the Attempt to Reconstruct Democracy in America, 1860–1880.* New York: Harcourt, Brace, 1935.

Dumond, Dwight L. *Southern Editorials on Secession.* New York: Century, 1931.

Dunne, Gerald T. "The Reconstruction Amendments: A Bicentennial Remembrance." In *Our Peculiar Security: The Written Constitution and Limited Government*, edited by Eugene W. Hickok, Jr., Gary L. McDowell, and Philip J. Costopoulos, 179–86. Lanham: Rowman and Littlefield, 1993.

[Durant, Thomas J.] *Letter of Thomas J. Durant to the Hon. Henry Winter Davis.* New Orleans: H. P. Lathrop, 1864.

Eaton, John. *Grant, Lincoln, and the Freedmen: Reminiscences of the Civil War.* New York: Longmans, Green, 1907.

[Eaton, Jr., John] *Report of the General Superintendent of Freedmen, Department of the Tennessee and State of Arkansas for 1864.* Memphis: n.p., 1865.

Edwards, Laura F. *Scarlett Doesn't Live Here Anymore: Southern Women in the Civil War Era.* Urbana: University of Illinois Press, 2000.

Eisenhower, John S. D. *Agent of Destiny: The Life and Times of General Winfield Scott.* New York: Free Press, 1997.

Eiss, Paul K. "A Share in the Land: Freedpeople and the Government of Labour in Southern Louisiana, 1862–65." *Slavery & Abolition* 19, no. 1 (April 1998): 46–89.

Emberton, Carole. "Unwriting the Freedom Narrative: A Review Essay." *Journal of Southern History* 82, no. 2 (May 2016): 377–94.

Engle, Stephen D. *Don Carlos Buell: Most Promising of All.* Chapel Hill: University of North Carolina Press, 1999.

Engs, Robert Francis. *Freedom's First Generation: Black Hampton, Virginia, 1861–1890.* With a new foreword. New York: Fordham University Press, 2004.

Escott, Paul D. *"What Shall We Do with the Negro?": Lincoln, White Racism, and Civil War America.* Charlottesville: University of Virginia Press, 2009.

Eze, Emmanuel Chukwudi, ed. *Race and the Enlightenment: A Reader.* New York: Wiley, 1997.

Faber, Eberhard L. *Building the Land of Dreams: New Orleans and the Transformation of Early America.* Princeton: Princeton University Press, 2016.

Fairclough, Adam. *The Revolution That Failed: Reconstruction in Natchitoches.* Gainesville: University Press of Florida, 2018.

Farmer-Kaiser, Mary J. *Freedwomen and the Freedmen's Bureau: Race, Gender, and Public Policy in the Age of Emancipation*. New York: Fordham University Press, 2010.

Faust, Drew Gilpin. *The Creation of Confederate Nationalism: Ideology and Identity in the Civil War South*. Baton Rouge: Louisiana State University Press, 1988.

Faust, Drew Gilpin. *Mothers of Invention: Women of the Slaveholding South in the American Civil War*. Chapel Hill: University of North Carolina Press, 1996.

Fertig, James Walter. *The Secession and Reconstruction of Tennessee*. Chicago: University of Chicago Press, 1898.

Finkelman, Paul, and Donald R. Kennon, eds. *Lincoln, Congress, and Emancipation*. Athens: Ohio University Press, 2016.

Finley, Randy. *From Slavery to Uncertain Freedom: The Freedman's Bureau in Arkansas 1865–1869*. Fayetteville: University of Arkansas Press, 1996.

Finley, Randy. "The Personnel of the Freedmen's Bureau in Arkansas." In *The Freedmen's Bureau and Reconstruction: Reconsiderations*, edited by Paul A. Cimbala and Randall M. Miller, 93–118. New York: Fordham University Press, 1999.

Finley, Randy. "'This Dreadful Whirlpool' of Civil War: Edward W. Gantt and the Quest for Distinction." In *The Southern Elite and Social Change: Essays in Honor of Willard B. Gatewood, Jr.*, edited by Randy Finley and Thomas A. DeBlack, 53–72. Fayetteville: University of Arkansas Press, 2002.

Fisk, Clinton B. *Plain Counsels for Freedmen: In Sixteen Brief Lectures*. Boston: American Tract Society, 1866.

Fogel, Robert William, and Stanley L. Engerman. *Time on the Cross: The Economics of American Slavery*. New York: Little, Brown, 1974.

Follett, Richard. *The Sugar Masters: Planters and Slaves in Louisiana's Cane World, 1820–1860*. Baton Rouge: Louisiana State University Press, 2005.

Foner, Eric. *Fiery Trial: Abraham Lincoln and American Slavery*. New York: W. W. Norton, 2010.

Foner, Eric. *Freedom's Lawmakers: A Directory of Black Officeholders during Reconstruction*. Revised Edition. Baton Rouge: Louisiana State University Press, 1996.

Foner, Eric, ed. *Our Lincoln: New Perspectives on Lincoln and His World*. New York: W. W. Norton, 2008.

Foner, Eric. *Reconstruction: America's Unfinished Revolution, 1863–1877*. New York: Harper and Row, 1988.

Foner, Eric. *The Second Founding: How the Civil War and Reconstruction Remade the Constitution*. New York: W. W. Norton, 2019.

Foner, Philip S., and George E. Walker, eds. *Proceedings of the Black National and State Conventions, 1865–1900*. Philadelphia: Temple University Press, 1986.

Foner, Philip S., and George E. Walker, eds. *Proceedings of the Black State Conventions, 1840–1865*. 2 vols. Philadelphia: Temple University Press, 1978.

Foreman, Amanda. *A World on Fire: Britain's Crucial Role in the American Civil War*. New York: Random House, 2010.

Fox-Genovese, Elizabeth. *Within the Plantation Household: Black and White Women of the Old South*. Chapel Hill: University of North Carolina Press, 1988.

Fox-Genovese, Elizabeth, and Eugene D. Genovese. *Fruits of Merchant Capital: Slavery and Bourgeois Property in the Rise and Expansion of Capitalism*. New York: Oxford University Press, 1983.

Fox-Genovese, Elizabeth, and Eugene D. Genovese. *The Mind of the Master Class: History and Faith in the Southern Slaveholders' Worldview*. Cambridge: Cambridge University Press, 2005.

Fox-Genovese, Elizabeth, and Eugene D. Genovese. *Slavery in White and Black: Class and Race in the Southern Slaveholders' New World Order*. Cambridge: Cambridge University Press, 2008.

Franklin, John Hope. *The Emancipation Proclamation*. Garden City: Doubleday, 1963.

Frazier, Donald S. *Blood on the Bayou: Vicksburg, Port Hudson, and the Trans-Mississippi*. Buffalo Gap: State House Press, 2015.

Frazier, Donald S. *Fire in the Cane Fields: The Federal Invasion of Louisiana and Texas, January 1861–January 1863*. Buffalo Gap: State House Press, 2009.

Freehling, William W. *The Road to Disunion, Vol. 2: Secessionists Triumphant, 1854–1861*. New York: Oxford University Press, 2007.

Freehling, William W., and Craig M. Simpson, eds. *Showdown in Virginia: The 1861 Convention and the Fate of the Union*. Charlottesville: University of Virginia Press, 2011.

Frisby, Derek W. "The Vortex of Secession: West Tennesseans and the Rush to War." In *Sister States, Enemy States: The Civil War in Kentucky and Tennessee*, edited by Kent T. Dollar, Larry H. Whiteaker, and W. Calvin Dickinson, 46–71. Lexington: University Press of Kentucky, 2009.

Fulkerson, H. S. *A Civilian's Recollections of the War between the States*, ed. Percy Lee Rainwater. Baton Rouge: Otto Claitor, 1939.

Gallagher, Gary W. *The Union War*. Cambridge, MA: Harvard University Press, 2011.

Gantt, Edward W. *Address of Hon. E. W. Gantt to the People of Arkansas*. Little Rock: National Democrat Print, 1863.

Genovese, Eugene D. *A Consuming Fire: The Fall of the Confederacy in the Mind of the White Christian South*. Athens: University of Georgia Press, 1998.

Genovese, Eugene D. *In Red and Black: Marxian Explorations in Southern and Afro-American History*. New York: Pantheon, 1971.

Genovese, Eugene D. *The Political Economy of Slavery: Studies in the Economy and Society of the Slave South*. 2nd ed. Middletown: Wesleyan University Press, 1989.

Genovese, Eugene D. *Roll, Jordan, Roll: The World the Slaves Made*. New York: Pantheon Books, 1974.

Genovese, Eugene D. *The Southern Front: History and Politics in the Cultural War.* Columbia: University of Missouri Press, 1995.

Genovese, Eugene D. *The World the Slaveholders Made: Two Essays in Interpretation.* New York: Random House, 1971.

Genovese, Eugene D., and Elizabeth Fox-Genovese. *Fatal Self-Deception: Slaveholding Paternalism in the Old South.* Cambridge: Cambridge University Press, 2011.

Gerteis, Louis S. *From Contraband to Freedman: Federal Policy toward Southern Blacks, 1861–1865.* Westport: Greenwood Press, 1973.

Gienapp, William E., and Erica L. Gienapp, eds. *The Civil War Diary of Gideon Welles, Lincoln's Secretary of the Navy.* Urbana: University of Illinois Press, 2014.

Glymph, Thavolia. *Out of the House of Bondage: The Transformation of the Plantation Household.* Cambridge: Cambridge University Press, 2008.

Glymph, Thavolia. *The Women's Fight: The Civil War's Battles for Home, Freedom, and Nation.* Chapel Hill: University of North Carolina Press, 2020.

Goleman, Michael J. *Your Heritage Will Still Remain: Racial Identity and Mississippi's Lost Cause.* Jackson: University Press of Mississippi, 2017.

Graf, LeRoy P., Ralph W. Haskins, and Paul H. Bergeron, eds. *The Papers of Andrew Johnson.* 16 vols. Knoxville: University of Tennessee Press, 1967–2000.

Grant, Ulysses S. *Memoirs and Selected Letters: Personal Memoirs of U. S. Grant, Selected Letters 1839–1865.* 2 vols. New York: Library of America, 1990.

Grant, Ulysses S. *Personal Memoirs of U. S. Grant.* 2 vols. New York: Charles L. Webster, 1885–86.

Gudmestad, Robert H. *A Troublesome Commerce: The Transformation of the Interstate Slave Trade.* Baton Rouge: Louisiana State University Press, 2003.

Guelzo, Allen C. *Fateful Lightning: A New History of the Civil War and Reconstruction.* New York: Oxford University Press, 2012.

Guelzo, Allen C. *Lincoln's Emancipation Proclamation: The End of Slavery in America.* New York: Simon and Schuster, 2004.

Guelzo, Allen C. "'Sublime in Its Majesty': Lincoln's Emancipation Proclamation." In *Lincoln and Freedom: Slavery, Emancipation, and the Thirteenth Amendment,* edited by Harold Holzer and Sara Vaughn Gabbard, 60–78. Carbondale: Southern Illinois University Press, 2007.

Guyatt, Nicholas. *Bind Us Apart: How Enlightened Americans Invented Racial Segregation.* New York: Basic Books, 2016.

Hahn, Michael. *Inaugural Address of Michael Hahn, Governor of the State of Louisiana, Delivered at New Orleans, March 4, 1864.* N.p.: n.d.

Hahn, Steven. "Class and State in Postemancipation Societies: Southern Planters in Comparative Perspective." *American Historical Review* 95, no. 1 (February 1990): 75–98.

Hahn, Steven. "'Extravagant Expectations' of Freedom: Rumour, Political Struggle, and the Christmas Insurrection Scare of 1865 in the American South." *Past & Present* 157 (November 1997): 122–58.

Hahn, Steven. *A Nation Under Our Feet: Black Political Struggles in the Rural South from Slavery to the Great Migration.* Cambridge, MA: Belknap Press of Harvard University Press, 2003.

Hahn, Steven. *A Nation Without Borders: The United States and Its World in an Age of Civil Wars, 1830–1910.* New York: Penguin, 2016.

Hahn, Steven. *The Political Worlds of Slavery and Freedom.* Cambridge, MA: Harvard University Press, 2009.

Hahn, Steven, Steven F. Miller, Susan E. O'Donovan, John C. Rodrigue, and Leslie S. Rowland, eds. *Freedom: A Documentary History of Emancipation, 1861–1867.* Ser. 3. Vol. 1, *Land and Labor, 1865.* Chapel Hill: University of North Carolina Press, 2008.

Hall, Gwendolyn Midlo. *Africans in Colonial Louisiana: The Development of Afro-Creole Culture in the Eighteenth Century.* Baton Rouge: Louisiana State University Press, 1992.

Hall, Marshall. "William L. Sharkey and Reconstruction, 1866–1873." *Journal of Mississippi History* 27, no. 1 (February 1965): 1–17.

Hamilton, Daniel W. *The Limits of Sovereignty: Property Confiscation in the Union and the Confederacy during the Civil War.* Chicago: University of Chicago Press, 2007.

Hardwick, Kevin R. "'Your Old Father Abe Lincoln Is Dead and Damned': Black Soldiers and the Memphis Race Riot of 1866." *Journal of Social History* 27, no. 1 (1993): 109–28.

Harris, J. William. *Deep Souths: Delta, Piedmont, and Sea Island Society in the Age of Segregation.* Baltimore: Johns Hopkins University Press, 2001.

Harris, J. William. "Eugene Genovese's Old South: A Review Essay." *Journal of Southern History* 80, no. 2 (May 2014): 327–72.

Harris, William C. *Lincoln and the Border States: Preserving the Union.* Lawrence: University Press of Kansas, 2011.

Harris, William C. *Presidential Reconstruction in Mississippi.* Baton Rouge: Louisiana State University Press, 1967.

Harris, William C. *With Charity for All: Lincoln and the Restoration of the Union.* Lexington: University Press of Kentucky, 1997.

Hearn, Chester G. *The Capture of New Orleans, 1862.* Baton Rouge: Louisiana State University Press, 1995.

Hearn, Chester G. *When the Devil Came Down to Dixie: Ben Butler in New Orleans.* Baton Rouge: Louisiana State University Press, 1997.

Heitmann, John Alfred. *The Modernization of the Louisiana Sugar Industry, 1830–1910.* Baton Rouge: Louisiana State University Press, 1987.

Hepworth, George H. *The Whip, Hoe, and Sword; Or, the Gulf Department in '63.* Boston: Walker, Wise, 1864.

Hermann, Janet Sharp. *The Pursuit of a Dream.* New York: Oxford University Press, 1981.

Hess, Earl J. *The Civil War in the West: Victory and Defeat from the Appalachians to the Mississippi.* Chapel Hill: University of North Carolina Press, 2012.

Hess, Earl J. "Confiscation and the Northern War Effort: The Army of the Southwest at Helena." *Arkansas Historical Quarterly* 44, no. 1 (Spring 1985): 56–75.

Hilton, Rodney, et al. *The Transition from Feudalism to Capitalism*. London: Verso, 1985.

Hollandsworth, James G. *An Absolute Massacre: The New Orleans Race Riot of July 30, 1866*. Baton Rouge: Louisiana State University Press, 2001.

Hollandsworth, James G. *The Louisiana Native Guards: The Black Military Experience During the Civil War*. Baton Rouge: Louisiana State University Press, 1995.

Hollandsworth, James G. *Pretense of Glory: The Life of Nathaniel P. Banks*. Baton Rouge: Louisiana State University Press, 1998.

Holt, Sharon Ann. *Making Freedom Pay: North Carolina Freedpeople Working for Themselves, 1865–1900*. Athens: University of Georgia Press, 2000.

Holzer, Harold. *Lincoln at Cooper Union: The Speech That Made Abraham Lincoln President*. New York: Simon and Schuster, 2004.

Holzer, Harold. *Lincoln President-Elect: Abraham Lincoln and the Great Secession Winter, 1860–1861*. New York: Simon and Schuster, 2008.

Holzer, Harold, and Sara Vaughn Gabbard, eds. *1863: Lincoln's Pivotal Year*. Carbondale: Southern Illinois University Press, 2013.

Holzer, Harold, and Sara Vaughn Gabbard, eds. *Lincoln and Freedom: Slavery, Emancipation, and the Thirteenth Amendment*. Carbondale: Southern Illinois University Press, 2007.

Holzer, Harold, Edna Greene Medford, and Frank J. Williams. *The Emancipation Proclamation: Three Views (Social, Political, Inconographic)*. Baton Rouge: Louisiana State University Press, 2006.

Horn, Huston. *Leonidas Polk: Warrior Bishop of the Confederacy*. Lawrence: University Press of Kansas, 2019.

House Journal of the Extra Session of the Thirty-Third General Assembly of the State of Tennessee which Convened at Nashville, on the First Monday in January, A.D. 1861. Nashville: J. O. Griffith, 1861.

House Journal of the First Session of the General Assembly of the State of Tennessee, 1865, Which Convened at Nashville, Monday, April 3. Nashville: S. C. Mercer, 1865.

House Journal of the Second Extra Session of the Thirty-Third General Assembly of the State of Tennessee, which Convened at Nashville on Thursday, the 25th day of April, A.D. 1861. Nashville: J. O. Griffith, 1861.

Houzeau, Jean-Charles. *My Passage at the New Orleans* Tribune: *A Civil War Memoir*, ed. David C. Rankin. Trans. Gerard F. Denault. Baton Rouge: Louisiana State University Press, 1984.

Howard, Perry H. *Political Tendencies in Louisiana: Revised and Expanded Edition*. Baton Rouge: Louisiana State University Press, 1971.

Hyde, Samuel C., Jr., ed. *A Fierce and Fractious Frontier: The Curious Development of Louisiana's Florida Parishes, 1699–2000*. Baton Rouge: Louisiana State University Press, 2004.

Hyde, Samuel C., Jr. *Pistols and Politics: The Dilemma of Democracy in Louisiana's Florida Parishes, 1810-1899*. Baton Rouge: Louisiana State University Press, 1996.

Hyman, Harold M. *A More Perfect Union: The Impact of the Civil War and Reconstruction on the Constitution*. New York: Alfred A. Knopf, 1973.

Hyman, Harold Melvin. *Era of the Oath: Northern Loyalty Tests during the Civil War and Reconstruction*. Philadelphia: University of Pennsylvania Press, 1954.

Hyman, Harold M., and William M. Wiecek. *Equal Justice under Law: Constitutional Development, 1835-1875*. New York: Harper and Row, 1982.

Ingersoll, Thomas N. *Mammon and Manon in Early New Orleans: The First Slave Society in the Deep South, 1718-1819*. Knoxville: University of Tennessee Press, 1999.

Jacobs, Lawrence, and Desmond King, eds. *The Unsustainable American State*. New York: Oxford University Press, 2009.

James, Dorris Clayton. *Antebellum Natchez*. Baton Rouge: Louisiana State University Press, 1968.

Jeffrey, Katherine B. "The History and Provenance of a (Frequently Misidentified) Baton Rouge Civil War Photograph." *Louisiana History* 57, no. 3 (Summer 2016): 349-58.

Johnson, Ludwell H. *Red River Campaign: Politics and Cotton in the Civil War*. Baltimore: Johns Hopkins University Press, 1958.

Johnson, Michael P. *Toward a Patriarchal Republic: The Secession of Georgia*. Baton Rouge: Louisiana State University Press, 1977.

Johnson, Rashauna. *Slavery's Metropolis: Unfree Labor in New Orleans during the Age of Revolutions*. Cambridge: Cambridge University Press, 2016.

Johnson, Walter. *River of Dark Dreams: Slavery and Empire in the Cotton Kingdom*. Cambridge, MA: Belknap Press of Harvard University Press, 2013.

Johnson, Walter. *Soul by Soul: Life inside the Antebellum Slave Market*. Cambridge, MA: Harvard University Press, 1999.

Joiner, Gary Dillard. *One Damn Blunder from Beginning to End: The Red River Campaign of 1864*. Lanham: Rowman & Littlefield, 2003.

Jones, J. Wayne. "Seeding Chicot: The Isaac H. Hilliard Plantation and the Arkansas Delta." *Arkansas Historical Quarterly* 59, no. 2 (Summer 2000): 147-85.

Jones, Martha S. *Birthright Citizens: A History of Race and Rights in Antebellum America*. Cambridge: Cambridge University Press, 2018.

Jordan, Winthrop D. *Tumult and Silence at Second Creek: An Inquiry into a Civil War Slave Conspiracy*. Rev. ed. Baton Rouge: Louisiana State University Press, 1995.

Journal of Both Sessions of the Convention of the State of Arkansas, which Were Begun and Held in the Capitol, in the City of Little Rock. Little Rock: Johnson and Yerkes, 1861.

Journal of the Convention of Delegates of the People of Arkansas: Assembled at the Capitol, January 4, 1864; Also, Journals of the House of Representatives of the Sessions of 1864, 1864-65, and 1865. Little Rock: Price and Barton, 1870.

Journal of the House of Representatives of the Commonwealth of Kentucky, Begun and Held in the Town of Frankfort, on Monday, the Second Day of September, in the Year of Our Lord 1861, and of the Commonwealth the Seventieth. Frankfort: Yeoman Office, 1861.

Journal of the House of Representatives of the State of Delaware at a Special Session of the General Assembly, Convened and held at Dover, on Monday the 25th Day of November, in the Year of Our Lord, One Thousand Eight Hundred and Sixty-One and of the Independence of the United States, the Eighty-Fifth. N.p., N.d.

Journal of the U.S. House of Representatives, 38th Congress.

Journal of the U.S. Senate, 38th Congress.

Journal of the Proceedings and Debates in the Constitutional Convention of the State of Mississippi, August 1865. Jackson: E. M. Yerger, 1865.

Journal of the Senate of the Commonwealth of Kentucky, Begun and Held in the Town of Frankfort, on Monday, the Second Day of September, in the Year of Our Lord 1861, and of the Commonwealth the Seventieth. Frankfort: Yeoman Office, 1861.

Journal of the Senate of the State of Louisiana. (1865). N.p., N.d.

Journal of the Senate of the State of Mississippi, Called Session, January, 1861. Jackson: E. Barksdale, 1860.

Journal of the State Convention and Ordinances and Resolutions Adopted in January, 1861. Jackson: E. Barksdale, 1861.

Kauffman, Michael W. *American Brutus: John Wilkes Booth and the Lincoln Conspiracies*. New York: Random House, 2004.

Kaye, Anthony E. *Joining Places: Slave Neighborhoods in the Old South*. Chapel Hill: University of North Carolina Press, 2007.

Kennedy, Joseph C. G. *Agriculture of the United States in 1860; Compiled from the Original Returns of the Eighth Census*. Washington, DC: Government Printing Office, 1864.

Kennedy, Joseph C. G. *Population of the United States in 1860; Compiled from the Original Returns of the Eighth Census*. Washington, DC: Government Printing Office, 1864.

Kennington, Kelly M. *In the Shadow of Dred Scott: St. Louis Freedom Suits and the Legal Culture of Slavery in Antebellum America*. Athens: University of Georgia Press, 2017.

Kolchin, Peter. *First Freedom: The Responses of Black to Emancipation and Reconstruction*. Westport: Greenwood Press, 1972.

Kolchin, Peter. "Reexamining Southern Emancipation in Comparative Perspective." *Journal of Southern History* 81, no. 1 (February 2015): 7–40.

Lang, Andrew F. *In the Wake of War: Military Occupation, Emancipation, and Civil War America*. Baton Rouge: Louisiana State University Press, 2021.

LeForge, Judy Bussell. "State Colored Conventions of Tennessee, 1865–1866." *Tennessee Historical Quarterly* 65, no. 3 (Fall 2006): 230–53.

Levine, Bruce. *The Fall of the House of Dixie: The Civil War and the Social Revolution that Transformed the South*. New York: Random House, 2013.

Litwack, Leon F. *Been in the Storm So Long: The Aftermath of Slavery*. New York: Alfred A. Knopf, 1979.

Lovett, Bobby L. "Memphis Riots: White Reaction to Blacks in Memphis, May 1865–July 1866." *Tennessee Historical Quarterly* 38, no. 1 (Spring 1979): 9–33.

Lufkin, Charles L. "Secession and Coercion in Tennessee, the Spring of 1861." *Tennessee Historical Quarterly* 50, no. 2 (Summer 1991): 98–109.

Malone, Ann Patton. *Sweet Chariot: Slave Family and Household Structure in Nineteenth-Century Louisiana*. Chapel Hill: University of North Carolina Press, 1992.

Manning, Chandra. *Troubled Refuge: Struggling for Freedom in the Civil War*. New York: Alfred A. Knopf, 2016.

Marler, Scott P. *The Merchants' Capital: New Orleans and the Political Economy of the Nineteenth-Century South*. Cambridge: Cambridge University Press, 2013.

Marshall, Jessie Ames, ed. *Private and Official Correspondence of Gen. Benjamin F. Butler during the Period of the Civil War*. 5 vols. Norwood, MA: Plimpton Press, 1917.

Marszalek, John F. *Commander of All Lincoln's Armies: A Life of General Henry W. Halleck*. Cambridge, MA: Belknap Press of Harvard University Press, 2004.

Marszalek, John F. *Sherman: A Soldier's Passion for Order*. New York: Free Press, 1993.

Masur, Kate. "'A Rare Phenomenon of Philological Vegetation': The Word 'Contraband' and the Meanings of Emancipation in the United States." *Journal of American History* 93, no. 4 (March 2007): 1050–84.

Masur, Louis P. *Lincoln's Hundred Days: The Emancipation Proclamation and the War for the Union*. Cambridge, MA: Belknap Press of Harvard University Press, 2012.

Masur, Louis P. *Lincoln's Last Speech: Wartime Reconstruction and the Crisis of Reunion*. New York: Oxford University Press, 2015.

Mathisen, Erik. "'It Looks Much Like Abandoned Land': Property and Politics in Reconstruction Mississippi." In *After Slavery: Race, Labor, and Citizenship in the Reconstruction South*, edited by Bruce E. Baker and Brian Kelly, 77–97. Gainesville: University Press of Florida, 2013.

Mathisen, Erik. "The Second Slavery, Capitalism, and Emancipation in Civil War America." *Journal of the Civil War Era* 8, no. 4 (December 2018): 677–99.

McCrary, Peyton. *Abraham Lincoln and Reconstruction: The Louisiana Experiment*. Princeton: Princeton University Press, 1978.

McCurry, Stephanie. *Confederate Reckoning: Power and Politics in the Civil War South*. Cambridge, MA: Harvard University Press, 2010.

McCurry, Stephanie. *Women's War: Fighting and Surviving the American Civil War*. Cambridge, MA: Belknap Press of Harvard University Press, 2019.

McDonald, Roderick A. *The Economy and Material Culture of Slaves: Goods and Chattels on the Sugar Plantations of Jamaica and Louisiana*. Baton Rouge: Louisiana State University Press, 1994.

McFeely, William S. *Yankee Stepfather: General O. O. Howard and the Freedmen*. New Haven: Yale University Press, 1968.

McKaye, James. *The Mastership and Its Fruits: The Emancipated Slave Face to Face with His Old Master. A Supplemental Report to Hon. Edwin M. Stanton, Secretary of War*. New York: William C. Bryant, 1864.

McKitrick, Eric. *Andrew Johnson and Reconstruction*. Chicago: University of Chicago Press, 1960.

McNeilly, Donald P. *The Old South Frontier: Cotton Plantations and the Formation of Arkansas Society, 1819–1861*. Fayetteville: University of Arkansas Press, 2000.

McPherson, Edward. *The Political History of the United States During the Period of Reconstruction (from April 15, 1865 to July 15, 1870)*. Washington, DC: Philip and Solomon, 1871.

McPherson, James M. *Battle Cry of Freedom: The Civil War Era*. New York: Oxford University Press, 1988.

McPherson, James M. *The Negro's Civil War: How American Negroes Felt and Acted During the War for the Union*. New York: Pantheon Books, 1965.

McPherson, James M. *War on the Waters: The Union and Confederate Navies, 1861–1865*. Chapel Hill: University of North Carolina Press, 2012.

Medford, Edna Greene. "The Day of Jubilee." In *1863: Lincoln's Pivotal Year*, edited by Harold Holzer and Sara Vaughn Gabbard, 9–22. Carbondale: Southern Illinois University Press, 2013.

Medford, Edna Greene. *Lincoln and Emancipation*. Carbondale: Southern Illinois University Press, 2015.

Meinig, D. W. *The Shaping of America: A Geographical Perspective on 500 Years of History, Volume 1: Atlantic America, 1492–1800*. New Haven: Yale University Press, 1988.

Memorial of Citizens of Louisiana: Remonstrating Against the Admission of Senators or Representatives from the State of Louisiana into the Congress of the United States, and the Reception of Any Electoral Vote of that State in Counting the Vote for President and Vice-President of the United States, and Praying the Passage of an Act Guaranteeing Republican Government in the Insurrectionary States. [December 7, 1864]. 38th Congress, 2nd Sess. Senate Miscellaneous Documents 2. Serial 1210.

"Memories of a Massacre: Memphis in 1866." University of Memphis. Accessed August 20, 2019. www.memphis.edu/memphis-massacre/.

Messner, William F. *Freedmen and the Ideology of Free Labor: Louisiana, 1862–1865*. Lafayette: Center for Louisiana Studies, University of Southwestern Louisiana, 1978.

Milne, George Edward. *Natchez Country: Indians, Colonists, and the Landscapes of Race in French Louisiana*. Athens: University of Georgia Press, 2015.

Mitchell, Reid. *All on a Mardi Gras Day: Episodes in the History of New Orleans Carnival*. Cambridge, MA: Harvard University Press, 1995.

Moneyhon, Carl H. "From Slave to Free Labor: The Federal Plantation Experiment in Arkansas." *Arkansas Historical Quarterly* 53, no. 2 (Summer 1994): 137–60.

Moneyhon, Carl H. *The Impact of the Civil War and Reconstruction on Arkansas: Persistence in the Midst of Ruin*. Baton Rouge: Louisiana State University Press, 1994.

Moneyhon, Carl H. "The Impact of the Civil War in Arkansas: The Mississippi River Plantation Counties." *Arkansas Historical Quarterly* 51, no. 2 (Summer 1992): 105–18.

Moneyhon, Carl H. "Race and the Struggle for Freedom: African American Arkansans after Emancipation." In *Race and Ethnicity in Arkansas: New Perspectives*, edited by John A. Kirk, 17–30. Fayetteville: University of Arkansas Press, 2014.

Monroe, Haskell M., Jr., James T. McIntosh, and Lynda Lasswell Crist, eds. *The Papers of Jefferson Davis*. 14 vols. Baton Rouge: Louisiana State University Press, 1971–2015.

Moore, Frank, ed. *The Rebellion Record: A Diary of American Events*. 11 vols. and supp. New York: G. P. Putnam, 1861–1864, and D. Van Nostrand, 1864–1868.

Moore, Jessica Parker. "'Keeping All Hands Moving': A Plantation Mistress in Antebellum Arkansas." *Arkansas Historical Quarterly* 74, no. 3 (Autumn 2015): 257–76.

Moore, John Hebron. *The Emergence of the Cotton Kingdom in the Old Southwest: Mississippi, 1770–1860*. Baton Rouge: Louisiana State University Press, 1987.

Narrett, David. *Adventurism and Empire: The Struggle for Mastery in the Louisiana-Florida Borderlands, 1762–1803*. Chapel Hill: University of North Carolina Press, 2017.

Nathans, Sydney. *A Mind to Stay: White Plantation, Black Homeland*. Cambridge, MA: Harvard University Press, 2017.

Neely, Mark E., Jr. *Lincoln and the Democrats: The Politics of Opposition in the Civil War*. Cambridge: Cambridge University Press, 2017.

Neely, Mark E., Jr. *The Union Divided: Party Conflict in the Civil War North*. Cambridge, MA: Harvard University Press, 2002.

Nelson, Bernard H. "Confederate Slave Impressment Legislation, 1861–1865." *Journal of Negro History* 31, no. 4 (October 1946): 392–410.

Nevins, Allan. *Frémont, Pathmaker of the West*. New York: Longmans, Green, 1955.

Nevins, Allan. *The War for the Union*. Vol. 1. *The Improvised War, 1861–1862*. New York: Charles Scribner's Sons, 1959.

Nguyen, Julia Huston. "Preaching Disunion: Clergymen in the Louisiana Secession Crisis." In *The Enigmatic South: Toward Civil War and Its Legacies*, edited by Samuel C. Hyde, Jr., 48–72. Baton Rouge: Louisiana State University Press, 2014.

North, Douglass. *Economic Growth of the United States, 1790–1860*. Englewood Cliffs: Prentice-Hall, 1961.

Northup, Solomon. *Twelve Years a Slave*. 1853. Reprint, ed. Sue Eakin and Joseph Logsdon. Baton Rouge: Louisiana State University Press, 1968.

O'Donovan, Susan Eva. *Becoming Free in the Cotton South*. Cambridge, MA: Harvard University Press, 2007.

Oakes, James. *The Crooked Path to Abolition: Abraham Lincoln and the Antislavery Constitution*. New York, W. W. Norton, 2021.

Oakes, James. *Freedom National: The Destruction of Slavery in the United States, 1861–1865*. New York: W. W. Norton, 2013.

Oakes, James. *The Radical and the Republican: Frederick Douglass, Abraham Lincoln, and the Triumph of Antislavery Politics*. New York: W. W. Norton, 2007.

Oakes, James. "Reluctant to Emancipate?: Another Look at the First Confiscation Act." *Journal of the Civil War Era* 3, no. 4 (December 2013): 458–66.

Oakes, James. *The Ruling Race: A History of American Slaveholders*. New York: Vintage, 1983.

Oakes, James. *The Scorpion's Sting: Antislavery and the Coming of the Civil War*. New York: W. W. Norton, 2014.

Ochs, Stephen J. *A Black Patriot and a White Priest: André Cailloux and Claude Paschal Maistre in Civil War New Orleans*. Baton Rouge: Louisiana State University Press, 2000.

Official Journal of the Proceedings of the Convention for the Revision and Amendment of the Constitution of the State of Louisiana. New Orleans: W. R. Fish, 1864.

Official Journal of the Proceedings of the Convention of the State of Louisiana. New Orleans: J. O. Nixon, 1861.

Official Journal of the Proceedings of the House of Representatives of the State of Louisiana [1864–65]. New Orleans: W. R. Fish, 1864[-65].

Official Journal of the Proceedings of the Senate and House of Representatives of the State of Louisiana and the Legislative Calendar. October 1864–April 1865. [New Orleans: N.p., 1864-65].

Owen, Robert Dale, James McKaye, and Samuel G. Howe. *Final Report of the American Freedmen's Inquiry Commission*. 38th Congress, 1st Sess., 1864. Senate Executive Documents 53. Serial 1176.

Owen, Robert Dale, James McKaye, and Samuel G. Howe. *Preliminary Report of American Freedmen's Inquiry Commission*. 38th Congress, 1st Sess., 1864. Senate Executive Documents 53. Serial 1176.

Painter, Nell Irvin. *Exodusters: Black Migration to Kansas after Reconstruction*. New York: Alfred A. Knopf, 1977.

Palmer, Benjamin M. *Slavery a Divine Trust: The Duty of the South to Preserve and Perpetuate the Institution as It Now Exists*. New York: George F. Nesbitt, 1861.

Palmer, Benjamin M. "A Vindication of Secession and the South." *Southern Presbyterian Review* 14, no. 1 (April 1861): 134–77.

Palmer, Beverly Wilson, ed. *Selected Letters of Charles Sumner*. 2 vols. Boston: Northeastern University Press, 1990.

Paludan, Phillip Shaw. *A People's Contest: The Union and Civil War, 1861–1865*. New York: Harper and Row, 1988.

Paullin, Charles O. *Atlas of the Historical Geography of the United States*, ed. John K. Wright. Washington, DC: Carnegie Institution, 1932. Digital edition ed. Robert K. Nelson et al., 2013. http://dsl.richmond.edu/historicalatlas/.

Paulus, Lawrence. *The Slaveholding Crisis: Fear of Insurrection and the Coming of the Civil War.* Baton Rouge: Louisiana State University Press, 2017.

Penningroth, Dylan C. *The Claims of Kinfolk: African American Property and Community in the Nineteenth-Century South.* Chapel Hill: University of North Carolina Press, 2003.

Perman, Michael. *Reunion without Compromise: The South and Reconstruction, 1865–1868.* Cambridge: Cambridge University Press, 1973.

Petty, A. W. M. *A History of the Third Missouri Cavalry from Its Organization at Palmyra, Missouri, 1861, up to November Sixth, 1864.* Little Rock: J. Wm. Demby, 1865.

Phillips, Christopher. *The Rivers Ran Backward: The Civil War and the Remaking of the American Middle Border.* New York: Oxford University Press, 2016.

Phillips, Christopher. "Southern Cross, North Star: Why the Middle Mattered – and Matters – in Civil War History." *Journal of the Civil War Era* 8, no. 2 (June 2018): 173–86.

Phillips, Paul David. "Education of Blacks in Tennessee, 1865–1870." *Tennessee Historical Quarterly* 46, no. 2 (Summer 1987): 98–109.

Phillips, Ulrich Bonnell. *American Negro Slavery: A Survey of the Supply, Employment and Control of Negro Labor as Determined by the Plantation Régime.* New York: D. Appleton, 1929.

Plater, David D. *The Butlers of Iberville Parish, Louisiana: Dunboyne Plantation in the 1800s.* Baton Rouge: Louisiana State University Press, 2015.

Poe, Ryan M. "The Contours of Emancipation: Freedom Comes to Southwest Arkansas." *Arkansas Historical Quarterly* 70, no. 2 (Summer 2011): 109–30.

Potter, David M. *The Impending Crisis 1848–1861*, completed and ed. Don E. Fehrenbacher. New York: Harper and Row, 1976.

Potter, David M. *Lincoln and His Party in the Secession Crisis.* New Haven: Yale University Press, 1942. Reprinted with a new preface, 1962.

Powell, Lawrence N. *The Accidental City: Improvising New Orleans.* Cambridge, MA: Harvard University Press, 2012.

Powell, Lawrence N. "Why Louisiana Mattered." *Louisiana History* 53, no. 4 (2012): 389–401.

Powell, Lawrence N., and Michael S. Wayne. "Self-Interest and the Decline of Confederate Nationalism." In *The Old South in the Crucible of War*, edited by Harry P. Owens and James J. Cooke, 29–45. Jackson: University Press of Mississippi, 1983.

Proceedings of the Convention of the Republican Party of Louisiana, Held at Economy Hall, New Orleans, September 25, 1865, and of the Central Executive Committee of the Friends of Universal Suffrage of Louisiana. New Orleans: New Orleans Tribune Office, 1865.

Proceedings of the State Convention of Colored Men of the State of Tennessee with the Addresses of the Convention to the Loyal Citizens of Tennessee, and the Colored Citizens of Tennessee Held in Nashville, Tenn., August 7th, 8th, 9th and 10th, 1865. Nashville: Daily Press and Times Job Office, 1865.

Quarles, Benjamin. *The Negro in the Civil War.* Boston: Little Brown, 1969.

Rael, Patrick. *Eighty-Eight Years: The Long Death of Slavery in the United States, 1777–1865.* Athens: University of Georgia Press, 2015.

Rainwater, Percy Lee. *Mississippi: Storm Center of Secession, 1856–1861.* Baton Rouge: Otto Claitor, 1938.

Rankin, David C. "The Origins of Black Leadership in New Orleans during Reconstruction." *Journal of Southern History* 60, no. 3 (August 1974): 417–40.

Ransom, Roger L., and Richard Sutch. *One Kind of Freedom: The Economic Consequences of Emancipation.* 2nd ed. Cambridge: Cambridge University Press, 2001.

Reed, H. Clay. "Lincoln's Compensated Emancipation Plan and Its Relation to Delaware." *Delaware Notes* 7 (1931): 27–78.

Reed, Merl E. *New Orleans and the Railroads: The Struggle for Commercial Empire, 1830–1860.* Baton Rouge: Louisiana State University Press, 1966.

Rehder, John B. *Delta Sugar: Louisiana's Vanishing Plantation Landscape.* Baltimore: Johns Hopkins University Press, 1999.

Reidy, Joseph P. *Illusions of Emancipation: The Pursuit of Freedom and Equality in the Twilight of Slavery.* Chapel Hill: University of North Carolina Press, 2019.

Reinders, Robert C. *End of an Era: New Orleans, 1850–1860.* New Orleans: Pelican, 1964.

Report of the Joint Committee on Reconstruction, at the First Session Thirty-Ninth Congress. Washington, DC: Government Printing Office, 1866.

Richards, Leonard L. *Who Freed the Slaves?: The Fight over the Thirteenth Amendment.* Chicago: University of Chicago Press, 2015.

Richardson, James D. *A Compilation of the Messages and Papers of the Presidents.* 20 vols. New York: Bureau of National Literature, 1897–1916.

Riddle, Charles A. *The Life and Diary of John P. Waddill: The Lawyer who Freed Solomon Northup, 1813–1855.* Lafayette: University of Louisiana at Lafayette Press, 2018.

Ripley, C. Peter. *Slaves and Freedmen in Civil War Louisiana.* Baton Rouge: Louisiana State University Press, 1976.

Roark, James L. *Masters without Slaves: Southern Planters in the Civil War and Reconstruction.* New York: W. W. Norton, 1977.

Robinson, Armstead L. *Bitter Fruits of Bondage: The Demise of Slavery and the Collapse of the Confederacy, 1861–1865.* Charlottesville: University of Virginia Press, 2005.

Robinson, Armstead L. "Day of Jubilo: Civil War and the Demise of Slavery in the Mississippi Valley, 1861–1865." Ph.D. dissertation, University of Rochester, 1977.

Rodrigue, John C. "The Freedmen's Bureau and Wage Labor in the Louisiana Sugar Region." In *The Freedmen's Bureau and Reconstruction: Reconsiderations*, edited by Paul A. Cimbala and Randall M. Miller, 193–218. New York: Fordham University Press, 1999.

Rodrigue, John C. *Lincoln and Reconstruction*. Carbondale: Southern Illinois University Press, 2013.

Rodrigue, John C. *Reconstruction in the Cane Fields: From Slavery to Free Labor in Louisiana's Sugar Parishes, 1862–1880*. Baton Rouge: Louisiana State University Press, 2001.

Roland, Charles P. *Louisiana Sugar Plantations during the American Civil War*. Leiden: E. J. Brill, 1957.

Rose, Willie Lee. *Rehearsal for Reconstruction: The Port Royal Experiment*. Indianapolis: Bobbs-Merrill, 1964.

Rosen, Hannah. *Terror in the Heart of Freedom: Citizenship, Sexual Violence, and the Meaning of Race in the Postemancipation South*. Chapel Hill: University of North Carolina Press, 2009.

Rosenthal, Caitlin. *Accounting for Slavery: Masters and Management*. Cambridge, MA: Harvard University Press, 2018.

Ross, Michael A. *The Great New Orleans Kidnapping Case: Race, Law, and Justice in the Reconstruction Era*. New York: Oxford University Press, 2015.

Ross, Stephen Joseph. "Freed Soil, Freed Labor, Freed Men: John Eaton and the Davis Bend Experiment." *Journal of Southern History* 44, no. 2 (May 1978): 213–32.

Rothman, Adam. *Slave Country: American Expansion and the Origins of the Deep South*. Cambridge, MA: Harvard University Press, 2005.

Rothman, Joshua D. *Flush Times and Fever Dreams: A Story of Capitalism and Slavery in the Age of Jackson*. Athens: University of Georgia Press, 2012.

Rothstein, Morton. "The Antebellum South as a Dual Economy: A Tentative Hypothesis." *Agricultural History* 41, no. 4 (October, 1967): 373–82.

Rugemer, Edward Bartlett. *The Problem of Emancipation: The Caribbean Roots of the American Civil War*. Baton Rouge: Louisiana State University Press, 2008.

Saikku, Mikko. *This Delta, This Land: An Environmental History of the Yazoo-Mississippi Floodplain*. Athens: University of Georgia Press, 2005.

Samito, Christian G. *Lincoln and the Thirteenth Amendment*. Carbondale: Southern Illinois University Press, 2015.

Scarborough, William Kauffman. *Masters of the Big House: Elite Slaveholders of the Mid-Nineteenth-Century South*. Baton Rouge: Louisiana State University Press, 2003.

Schermerhorn, Calvin. *The Business of Slavery and the Rise of American Capitalism, 1815–1860*. New Haven: Yale University Press, 2015.

Schermerhorn, Calvin. *Money over Mastery, Family over Freedom: Slavery in the Antebellum Upper South*. Baltimore: Johns Hopkins University Press, 2011.

Schultz, Robert G. *The March to the River: From the Battle of Pea Ridge to Helena, Spring 1862*. Iowa City: Camp Pope, 2014.

Schurz, Carl. *The Reminiscences of Carl Schurz*. 3 vols. London: John Murray, 1909.

Schurz, Carl. *Report of Carl Schurz on the States of South Carolina, Georgia, Alabama, Mississippi, and Louisiana*. 39th Congress, 1st Sess., 1865. Senate Executive Documents 2. Serial 1237.

Scott, Rebecca J. *Degrees of Freedom: Louisiana and Cuba after Slavery*. Cambridge, MA: Belknap Press of Harvard University Press, 2005.

Scroggs, Jack B. "Arkansas in the Secession Crisis." *Arkansas Historical Quarterly* 12, no. 3 (Autumn 1953): 179–224.

Senate Journal of the Extra Session of the Thirty-Third General Assembly of the State of Tennessee which Convened at Nashville, on the First Monday in January, A.D. 1861. Nashville: J. O. Griffith, 1861.

Senate Journal of the First Session of the General Assembly of the State of Tennessee, 1865, Which Convened at Nashville, Monday, April 3. Nashville: S. C. Mercer, 1865.

Senate Journal of the Second Extra Session of the Thirty-Third General Assembly of the State of Tennessee, which Convened at Nashville on Thursday, the 25th day of April, A.D. 1861. Nashville: J. O. Griffith, 1861.

Sestric, Anthony J. *57 Years: A History of the Freedom Suits in the Missouri Courts*. St. Louis: Reedy Press, 2012.

Sherman, William T. *Memoirs of General William T. Sherman*. 2nd rev and corr. ed. 2 vols. New York: D. A. Appleton, 1886.

Shore, Laurence. *Southern Capitalists: The Ideological Leadership of an Elite, 1832–1885*. Chapel Hill: University of North Carolina Press, 1986.

Shugg, Roger W. *Origins of Class Struggle in Louisiana: A Social History of White Farmers and Laborers during Slavery and after, 1840–1875*. 1939. Reprint. Baton Rouge: Louisiana State University Press, 1968.

Shugg, Roger W. "A Suppressed Co-Operationist Protest against Secession." *Louisiana Historical Quarterly* 19 (January 1936): 199–203.

Siddali, Silvana R. *From Property to Person: Slavery and the Confiscation Acts, 1861–1862*. Baton Rouge: Louisiana State University Press, 2005.

Silber, Nina. *Gender and the Sectional Conflict*. Chapel Hill: University of North Carolina Press, 2008.

Silbey, Joel H. *A Respectable Minority: North Democrats in the Civil War Era, 1860–1868*. New York: W. W. Norton, 1977.

Silkenat, David. *Raising the White Flag: How Surrender Defined the American Civil War*. Chapel Hill: University of North Carolina Press, 2019.

Simon, John Y., and John F. Marszalek, eds. *The Papers of Ulysses S. Grant*. 26 vols. Carbondale: Southern Illinois University Press, 1967–2012.

Simpson, Amos E., and Vaughan Baker. "Michael Hahn: Steady Patriot." *Louisiana History* 13, no. 3 (Summer, 1972): 229–52.

Simpson, Brooks D., Leroy P. Graf, and John Muldowny, eds. *Advice after Appomattox: Letters to Andrew Johnson, 1865–1866*. Special Volume No. 1 of *The Papers of Andrew Johnson*. Knoxville: University of Tennessee Press, 1987.

Sinha, Manisha. *The Slave's Cause: A History of Abolition*. New Haven: Yale University Press, 2016.

Sinisi, Kyle S. *The Last Hurrah: Sterling Price's Missouri Expedition of 1864*. Lanham: Rowan and Littlefield, 2016.

Sitterson, J. Carlyle. *Sugar Country: The Cane Sugar Industry in the South, 1753–1950*. Lexington: University of Kentucky Press, 1953.

Slap, Andrew L. "On Duty in Memphis: Fort Pickering's African American Soldiers." In *Remembering the Memphis Massacre: An American Story*, edited by Beverly Greene Bond and Susan Eva O'Donovan, 120–31. Athens: University of Georgia Press, 2020.

Smith, Adam I. P. *No Party Now: Politics in the Civil War North*. New York: Oxford University Press, 2006.

Smith, Adam I. P. *The Stormy Present: Conservatism and the Problem of Slavery in Northern Politics, 1846–1865*. Chapel Hill: University of North Carolina Press, 2017.

Smith, F. Todd. *Louisiana and the Gulf South Frontier, 1500–1821*. Baton Rouge: Louisiana State University Press, 2014.

Smith, John I. *Courage of a Southern Unionist: A Biography of Isaac Murphy*. Little Rock: Rosa, 1979.

Smith, Timothy B. *Champion Hill: Decisive Battle for Vicksburg*. New York: Savas Beatie, 2004.

Smith, Timothy B. *Grant Invades Tennessee: The 1862 Battles for Forts Henry and Donelson*. Lawrence: University Press of Kansas, 2016.

Smith, Timothy B. *Mississippi in the Civil War: The Home Front*. Jackson: University Press of Mississippi, 2010.

Smith, Timothy B. *The Mississippi Secession Convention: Delegates and Deliberations in Politics and War, 1861–1865*. Jackson: University Press of Mississippi, 2014.

Smith, Timothy B. *Real Horse Soldiers: Benjamin Grierson's Epic 1863 Civil War Raid through Mississippi*. El Dorado Hills: Savas Beatie, 2018.

Smith, Timothy B. "A Victory Could Hardly Have Been More Complete: The Battle of Big Black River Bridge." In *The Vicksburg Campaign: March 29–May 18, 1863*, edited by Steven E. Woodworth and Charles D. Grear, 173–93. Carbondale: Southern Illinois University Press, 2013.

Spurgeon, Ian Michael. *Soldiers in the Army of Freedom: The 1st Kansas Colored, the Civil War's First African American Combat Unit*. Norman: University of Oklahoma Press, 2014.

Stampp, Kenneth M. *And the War Came: The North and the Secession Crisis, 1860–1861*. Baton Rouge: Louisiana State University Press, 1970.

Stanley, Amy Dru. *From Bondage to Contract: Wage Labor, Marriage, and the Market in the Age of Slave Emancipation*. Cambridge: Cambridge University Press, 1998.

Starr, Stephen Z. *Jennison's Jayhawkers: A Civil War Cavalry Regiment and Its Commander*. Baton Rouge: Louisiana State University Press, 1973.

Statutes at Large of the United States of America, 1789–1873. 17 vols. Boston: Little, Brown, 1850–1873.

Sternhell, Yael A. *Routes of War: The World of Movement in the Confederate South.* Cambridge, MA: Harvard University Press, 2012.
Stoker, Donald. *The Grand Design: Strategy and the U.S. Civil War.* New York: Oxford University Press, 2010.
Summers, Mark Wahlgren. *The Ordeal of the Reunion: A New History of Reconstruction.* Chapel Hill: University of North Carolina Press, 2014.
[Sumner, Charles] *No Property in Man. Speech of Hon. Charles Sumner, on the Proposed Amendment of the Constitution Abolishing Slavery through the United States, In the Senate of the United States, April 8th, 1864.* New York: Loyal Publication Society, 1864.
Sumner, Charles. *Slavery and the Rebellion, One and Inseparable: Speech of Hon. Charles Sumner, Before the New York Young Men's Republican Union, Cooper Institute, New York, on the Afternoon of November 5, 1864.* Boston: Wright & Potter, 1864.
Szcodronski, Cheri LaFlamme. "From Contraband to Freedmen: General Grant, Chaplain Eaton, and Grand Junction, Tennessee." *Tennessee Historical Quarterly* 72, no. 2 (Summer 2013): 106–27.
Tadman, Michael. *Speculators and Slaves: Masters, Traders, and Slaves in the Old South.* Madison: University of Wisconsin Press, 1989.
Taliaferro, James G. *A Protest Against the Ordinance of Secession, Passed by the Louisiana Convention, on the 26th January, 1861, Presented to the Convention on that Day, by James G. Taliaferro, the Delegate from the Parish of Catahoula, Who Asked That It Might Be Entered upon the Journal of the Convention, Which Was Refused.* Catahoula: N.p., 1861.
Taylor, Amy Murrell. *Embattled Freedom: Journeys through the Civil War's Slave Refugee Camps.* Chapel Hill: University of North Carolina Press, 2018.
Taylor, Joe Gray. *Louisiana: A History.* New York: W. W. Norton, 1984.
Taylor, Joe Gray. *Louisiana Reconstructed, 1863–1877.* Baton Rouge: Louisiana State University Press, 1974.
Taylor, Richard. *Destruction and Reconstruction: Personal Experiences of the Late War.* New York: D. Appleton, 1879.
Temple, Oliver P. *Notable Men of Tennessee: From 1833 to 1875; Their Times and Their Contemporaries.* New York: Cosmopolitan Press, 1912.
Teters, Kristopher A. *Practical Liberators: Union Officers in the Western Theater during the Civil War.* Chapel Hill: University of North Carolina Press, 2018.
Thomas, Emory M. *The Confederate Nation, 1861–1865.* New York: Harper and Row, 1979.
Thomas, Keith. *In Pursuit of Civility: Manners and Civilization in Early Modern England.* Waltham, MA: Brandeis University Press, 2018.
Tregle, Joseph G., Jr. "Thomas J. Durant, Utopian Socialism, and the Failure of Presidential Reconstruction in Louisiana." *Journal of Southern History* 45, no. 4 (November 1979): 485–512.
Trefousse, Hans L. *Andrew Johnson: A Biography.* New York: W. W. Norton, 1989.

Trefousse, Hans L. *Ben Butler: The South Called Him BEAST!* New York: Twayne, 1957.

Trefousse, Hans L. *The Radical Republicans: Lincoln's Vanguard for Racial Justice.* New York: Alfred A. Knopf, 1969.

Tunnell, Ted. *Crucible of Reconstruction: War Radicalism, and Race in Louisiana, 1862–1877.* Baton Rouge: Louisiana State University Press, 1984.

Tunnell, Ted. *Edge of the Sword: The Ordeal of Carpetbagger Marshall H. Twitchell in the Civil War and Reconstruction.* Baton Rouge: Louisiana State University Press, 2001.

Twitty, Anne. *Before Dred Scott: Slavery and Legal Culture in the American Confluence, 1787–1857.* Cambridge: Cambridge University Press, 2016.

Urwin, Gregory J. W. "'We *Cannot* Treat Negroes . . . as Prisoners of War': Racial Atrocities and Reprisals in Civil War Arkansas." In *Black Flag Over Dixie: Racial Atrocities and Reprisals in the Civil War,* edited by Gregory J. W. Urwin, 132–52. Carbondale: Southern Illinois University Press, 2004.

U.S. Congress, House of Representatives. *Freedmen's Bureau. Message from the President of the United States, Transmitting Report of the Commissioner of the Bureau of Refugees, Freedmen, and Abandoned Lands.* 39th Congress, 1st Session, House Executive Documents 11. Serial 1255.

U.S. Congress. House of Representatives. *Memphis Riots and Massacres.* 39th Congress, 1st Session. House Reports 101. Serial 1274. Washington, DC: U.S. Government Printing Office, 1866.

U.S. Congress. House of Representatives. *Report of the Select Committee on New Orleans Riots.* 39th Congress, 2nd session. House Reports 16. Washington, DC: U.S. Government Printing Office, 1867.

U.S. Congress, Senate. *Letter of the Secretary of War, Communicating, in Compliance with a Resolution of the Senate of December 17, 1866, Reports of the Assistant Commissioners of Freedmen, and a Synopsis of Laws Respecting Persons of Color in the Late Slave States.* 39th Congress, 2nd Session, Senate Executive Documents 6. Serial 1276.

U.S. Congress, Senate. *Report and Testimony of the Select Committee of the United States Senate To Investigate the Causes of the Removal of the Negroes from Southern States to the Northern States. In Three Parts.* 46th Congress, 2nd Session, Senate Reports 693. Washington, DC: Government Printing Office, 1880.

U.S. Department of War. *The War of the Rebellion: A Compilation of the Official Records of the Union and Confederate Armies.* 128 vols. Washington, DC: Government Printing Office, 1880–1901.

Usner, Daniel H. *Indians, Settlers, and Slaves in a Frontier Exchange Economy: The Lower Mississippi Valley Before 1783.* Chapel Hill: University of North Carolina Press, 1992.

Vandal, Gilles. *The New Orleans Riot of 1866: Anatomy of a Tragedy.* Lafayette: Center for Louisiana Studies, University of Southwestern Louisiana, 1983.

Vidal, Cécile, ed. *Louisiana: Crossroads of the Atlantic World.* Philadelphia: University of Pennsylvania Press, 2014.

Volpe, Vernon L. "The Frémonts and Emancipation in Missouri." *Historian* 56, no. 2 (Winter 1994): 339–54.

Vorenberg, Michael. "The Deformed Child: Slavery and the Election of 1864." *Civil War History* 47, no. 3 (September 2001): 240–57.

Vorenberg, Michael. *Final Freedom: The Civil War, the Abolition of Slavery, and the Thirteenth Amendment*. Cambridge: Cambridge University Press, 2001.

Wade, Benjamin F., and Henry Winter Davis. "Protest of Senator Wade and H. Winter Davis, M.C." In *The Radical Republicans and Reconstruction, 1861–1870*, edited by Harold M. Hyman, 137–47. Indianapolis: Bobbs-Merrill, 1967.

Wade, Michael G. "'I Would Rather Be Among the Comanches': The Military Occupation of Southwest Louisiana, 1865." *Louisiana History* 39, no. 1 (Winter 1998): 45–64.

Walker, Clarence E. *Deromanticizing Black History: Critical Essays and Reappraisals*. Knoxville: University of Tennessee Press, 1991.

Walz, Robert B. "Arkansas Slaveholdings and Slaveholders in 1850." *Arkansas Historical Quarterly* 12, no. 1 (Spring 1953): 38–74.

Warmoth, Henry Clay. *War, Politics and Reconstruction: Stormy Days in Louisiana*. New York: MacMillan Company, 1930.

Wayne, Michael. *The Reshaping of Plantation Society: The Natchez District, 1860–1880*. Baton Rouge: Louisiana State University Press, 1983.

Weber, Jennifer L. *Copperheads: The Rise and Fall of Lincoln's Opponents in the North*. New York: Oxford University Press, 2006.

Westwood, Howard C. "Generals David Hunter and Rufus Saxton and Black Soldiers." *South Carolina Historical Magazine* 86, no. 3 (July 1985): 165–81.

Whayne, Jeannie. *Delta Empire: Lee Wilson and the Transformation of Agriculture in the New South*. Baton Rouge: Louisiana State University Press, 2011.

Whayne, Jeannie, and Willard B. Gatewood, eds. *The Arkansas Delta: Land of Paradox*. Fayetteville: University of Arkansas Press, 1993.

Whayne, Jeannie M., ed. *Shadows Over Sunnyside: An Arkansas Plantation in Transition, 1830–1945*. Fayetteville: University of Arkansas Press, 1993.

White, Howard A. *The Freedmen's Bureau in Louisiana*. Baton Rouge: Louisiana State University Press, 1970.

[Whiting, William] *Opinions on "Slavery," and "Reconstruction of the Union," As Expressed by President Lincoln. With Brief Notes by Hon. William Whiting*. New York: John A. Gray & Green, 1864.

Whiting, William. *The Return of the Rebellious States to the Union: A Letter from Hon. Wm. Whiting to the Union League of Philadelphia*. Philadelphia: C. Sherman, 1864.

Wilentz, Sean. *No Property in Man: Slavery and Antislavery at the Nation's Founding*. Cambridge, MA: Harvard University Press, 2018.

Wilkie, Laurie A. *Creating Freedom: Material Culture and African-American Identity at Oakley Plantation, Louisiana, 1840–1950*. Baton Rouge: Louisiana State University Press, 2000.

Williams, Eric. *Capitalism and Slavery*. Chapel Hill: University of North Carolina Press, 1944.
Williams, Frank J. "Under Cover of Liberty." In *Lincoln and Freedom: Slavery, Emancipation, and the Thirteenth Amendment*, edited by Harold Holzer and Sara Vaughn Gabbard, 23–42. Carbondale: Southern Illinois University Press, 2007.
Williams, William H. *Slavery and Freedom in Delaware, 1639–1865*. Wilmington: SR Books, 1996.
Willis, John C. *Forgotten Time: The Yazoo-Mississippi Delta after the Civil War*. Charlottesville: University Press of Virginia, 2000.
Wilson, Henry. *History of the Antislavery Measures of the Thirty-Seventh and Thirty-Eighth United-States Congresses, 1861–64*. Boston: Walker, Wise, 1864.
Winters, John D. *The Civil War in Louisiana*. Baton Rouge: Louisiana State University Press, 1963.
Wintory, Blake. "African American Legislators in the Arkansas General Assembly, 1868–1893: Another Look." In *A Confused and Confusing Affair: Arkansas and Reconstruction*, edited by Mark K. Christ, 87–145. Little Rock: Butler Center Books, 2018.
Wood, Forrest G. *Black Scare: The Racist Response to Emancipation and Reconstruction*. Berkeley: University of California Press, 1968.
Woods, James M. *Rebellion and Realignment: Arkansas's Road to Secession*. Fayetteville: University of Arkansas Press, 1997.
Woods, Thomas H. "A Sketch of the Mississippi Secession Convention of 1861, - Its Membership and Work." *Publications of the Mississippi Historical Society* 6 (1902): 91–104.
Woodworth, Steven E., and Charles D. Grear, eds. *The Vicksburg Assaults, May 19–22, 1863*. Carbondale: Southern Illinois University Press, 2019.
Wooster, Ralph. "The Arkansas Secession Convention." *Arkansas Historical Quarterly* 13, no. 2 (Summer 1954): 172–95.
Wooster, Ralph A. *The Secession Conventions of the South*. Princeton: Princeton University Press, 1962.
Wyatt-Brown, Bertram. *Southern Honor: Ethics and Behavior in the Old South*. New York: Oxford University Press, 1982.
Zietlow, Rebecca E. *The Forgotten Emancipator: James Mitchell Ashley and the Ideological Origins of Reconstruction*. Cambridge: Cambridge University Press, 2017.
Zietlow, Rebecca E. "Ideological Origins of the Thirteenth Amendment." *Houston Law Review* 49, no. 2 (Spring 2012): 393–458.

INDEX

Abell, Edmund, 125, 286–88, 290, 389, 463, 464
abolition (of slavery)
    in Arkansas, 245–46, 250
    in Louisiana, 285–88, 319
    in Mississippi, 426–36
    northern support for, 156–63
    Reconstruction legislation and, 225, 231–34
    Republican support for, 301–6
    in Tennessee, 149–53, 242, 368–72, 378–79
abolitionists, 7–9, 10, 17–21, 61, 162–63, 202, 223, 234, 465
Adams, Henry, 410–13
Adams, Nancy Emily, 410
Alexandria (LA), 283
Allis, Horace B., 293, 325
American Freedmen's Inquiry Commission (AFIC), 176, 271–73, 338
Anaconda Plan, 63
Ashley, James M.
    proposes Federal abolition amendment, 224
    Reconstruction bills, 68, 224–27, 231, 238, 298, 361–63, 372–73, 382
    Reconstruction, views on, 303–5

Baird, Absalom, 463
Baker, Joshua, 191, 197
Banks, Nathaniel P.
    appointed to command, 116
    free-state proposal, endorses, 154
    labor policy of, 166–70, 269–70, 340
    Louisiana Reconstruction, views on, 193, 256, 291, 319, 322, 388

    Port Hudson Campaign, leads, 133
    Reconstruction proposals of, 252–55
    Red River Campaign, leads, 282–85
Barr, Hugh A., 427
Bates, Edward, 108
Baton Rouge, 24, 32, 46, 93, 132, 133, 343
Battle of Liberty Place, 468
Baxter, Elisha, 244, 293, 309–10, 363
Bayou Lafourche, 24, 97, 110, 344
Beaman, Fernando Cortez, 302
Behrend, Justin, 60
Berlin, Ira, 472
Bertonneau, Arnold, 259
Bertrand, Charles P., 148, 244, 326
Bingham, James B., 130, 243
Bisland, Fannie A., 179
Bisland, John, 178
Bisland, William A., 178
black code (Mississippi), 442–48
black soldiers
    atrocities against, 134, 284, 285, 461
    combat experience of, 133–34, 142–43
    Confederate, 57
    endorse black suffrage, 370
    enlistment of, 118
    families of, 347, 459
    guard plantations, 171
    See also Native Guard; U.S. Colored Troops (USCT)
black suffrage
    Arkansas Reconstruction and, 451–53
    Johnson opposes, 394
    Lincoln's support for, 264

black suffrage (cont.)
    Louisiana Reconstruction and, 192, 259, 264, 288, 320, 364–65, 419–20, 438–40, 462
    Reconstruction legislation and, 226, 233, 361–63, 464
    Tennessee Reconstruction and, 370, 422–24
    See also freed people: legal rights of
Blaine, James G., 307
Blair, Frank, 196
Blair, Montgomery, 157
Booth, John Wilkes, 388
Bouligny, John E., 101
Boutwell, George S., 131
Brown, Robert M., 430
Brownlow, William G., 135, 332, 379, 417
    elected governor, 380
    emancipation, views on, 105, 130
    Inaugural Address, 384
    nominated for governor, 369
    secession, opposes, 51
Brownson, Orestes A., 156, 161–62, 201
Bruce, Blanche K., 467
Bullitt, Cuthbert, 389
Bureau of Refugees, Freedmen, and Abandoned Lands. *See* Freedmen's Bureau
Burwell, Armistead, 391
Butler, Benjamin F.
    appointed to command, 63
    contraband policy of, 53
    establishes free labor, 96
    free labor, views on, 98
    fugitive slaves and, 73
    Louisiana Unionists and, 87, 101
    New Orleans, command at, 71–72
    relieved of command, 103

Cailloux, André, 142–43
Camden Expedition, 284–85, 294
Campbell, William B., 69, 105, 130, 149, 151–52, 327, 329, 417
Canby, Edward R. S., 284, 324, 326, 354, 392, 397, 419
Carrods, Frances, 412
Carrods, W. M. C., 411
Carter, Dan T., 443

Chandler, Zachariah, 310
Chase, Salmon P., 87, 128, 157, 183, 274, 276, 311, 338, 386
Chattanooga, 150
Chickamauga (battle), 151
Christmas Insurrection Scare (1865), 443, 453–56
Civil Rights Act (1866), 458
Clark, Charles, 391–92, 416, 425
Colfax Massacre, 468
compensated emancipation, 62, 106–7, 242, 262, 287, 367, 381, 428
Confiscation Acts
    first (1861), 54, 66, 75
    second (1862), 77–80, 91, 169
Congress, US
    fugitive slave policy of, 71
    Reconstruction legislation by, 68, 123, 224–27, 231–34, 298–306, 361–63, 372–73, 381
    seating of claimants, 122, 229–31, 293, 309–10, 363, 373–74, 382, 450
Conner, Elizabeth Frances, 175
Conner, Lemuel P., 46, 58, 175
Conservatives (postwar), 389, 418, 419, 438, 440
contraband camps, 95
conventions
    Arkansas
        black/NERL (1865), 451–53
        constitutional (1864), 186, 245–46
        secession, 49, 50
    Louisiana
        black/NERL (1865), 364–65
        constitutional (1864), 265–67, 285–92, 462
        Republican Party (1865), 438–40
        secession, 46, 138
        Unionist nominating (1864), 258–61
    Mississippi
        constitutional (1865), 391–92, 426–36
        secession, 44
        National Equal Rights League (1864), 321, 332
        Republican-Union (1864), 307
    Tennessee
        black/NERL (1865), 422–24

INDEX 503

constitutional (1865), 368–72
secession (defeated), 51
Unionist (1863), 135–37
Unionist (1864), 241–42, 327
Conway, Thomas W., 339, 342, 366, 398, 408, 420, 449
Cooper, Richard, 429
Cottman, Thomas, 127, 138, 155, 191, 194, 197
Coushatta Massacre, 468
Cox, Samuel S., 196, 300
Cozzens, Samuel W., 179, 180, 270
Crittenden Resolution, 54, 68
Curtis, Samuel R., 67, 76, 85
Cutler, R. King, 319, 363, 366, 382

Dana, Charles A., 150
Dana, Napoleon J. T., 351
Davis Bend (MS), 30–31, 75, 349–52
Davis, Henry Winter, 450
  Federal abolition amendment, views on, 227
  heads select committee, 224
  introduces Reconstruction bill, 231–34
  Reconstruction, views on, 301, 312–15, 376
Davis, Jefferson, 31, 43, 46, 56, 83, 335, 349, 352, 425, 448
Davis, Joseph E., 30–31, 75, 349, 352
Davis, Woodbury, 159
De Soto Parish, 410
Degler, Carl N., 19
Democrats (northern), 68, 234–36, 298–300, 307
Desdunes, Rodolphe Lucien, 128
Donnelly, Ignatius, 303
Dostie, A. P., 128, 463
Downs, Jim, 353, 404
Du Bois, W. E. B., 38
Duncan, Mary, 174
Dunn, Oscar J., 366
Durant, Thomas J., 87, 462
  advocates black suffrage, 192, 439
  free-state radical leader, 128
  Louisiana Reconstruction, views on, 188–89, 263, 322
Durrell, Edward H., 287, 462

East Feliciana Parish, 454
Eaton, John, 170, 175, 182, 275, 338, 351, 401, 408
  appointed General Superintendent of Contrabands, 94–96
  labor views of, 278–80, 345–47
Eggleston, Rev. N. H., 119
elections
  Arkansas
    congressional (1863), 230
    congressional (1865), 440
    general (1864), 246–51
    presidential (1860), 48
    secession, 49
  Louisiana
    congressional (1862), 103
    congressional (1863), 155, 191, 229
    constitutional (1864), 265–67, 283, 319
    general (1864), 319
    presidential (1860), 45
    secession, 45
    state (1864), 253, 261–63
    state (1865), 449
    voluntary (1865), 449
  Mississippi
    constitutional (1865), 425
    general (1865), 441
    presidential (1860), 44
    secession, 44
  presidential (1864), 335–36
  Tennessee
    congressional (1862), 103–5
    constitutional (1865), 369, 378–79
    gubernatorial (1863), 149, 151, 152
    local (1864), 240, 242
    presidential (1860), 50
    presidential (1864), 326–32, 334
    secession, 51
    state (1865), 369, 380
Emancipation Proclamation
  excludes Tennessee, 103–5
  implementation of, 108–11, 375, 390, 404–10, 430–32
  Lincoln presents to Cabinet, 80
  preliminary, 90–93
  See also military emancipation
Etheridge, Emerson, 69, 105, 130, 152, 195–98, 327, 329, 417

Etheridge Plot, 195–98
Ewing, Edwin H., 240

Farragut, David G., 63, 71, 93
Federal abolition amendment
   Andrew Johnson endorses, 241
   defeated in House, 307–8
   House passage of, 374–75
   introduced into Congress, 203, 227–29
   Lincoln endorses, 360–61
   Mississippi rejects, 450
   northern support for, 163
   presidential election and (1864), 335–36
   ratification of, 380, 384, 385, 437, 450
   Senate passage of, 234–36
   See also Thirteenth Amendment
Federal consensus, 7–8, 17–21, 122
Fellows, J. Q. A., 125, 155, 191, 259, 261, 266, 419
Fessenden, William P., 339, 397
Field, A. P., 191, 197, 363, 374
Field, George B., 172
Fishback, William M., 49, 244, 249, 363, 364
   denied Senate seat, 309–10
   elected to Senate, 293
Fisher, Ephraim S., 441
Fisk, Clinton B., 408, 422
Flanagin, Harris, 418
Flanders, Benjamin F., 87, 127, 189, 229, 262, 265, 366
   elected to Congress, 102
   gubernatorial nomination of, 259
   Louisiana Reconstruction, views on, 254
   supervises plantation labor, 339–44
Follett, Richard, 273
Foner, Eric, 468
Forrest, Nathan Bedford, 285, 296
Fort Pillow Massacre, 285
Fourteenth Amendment, 462, 465
Fox-Genovese, Elizabeth, 406, 472
Franklin (battle), 368
free people of color
   advocate black suffrage, 192, 259, 289, 320, 364–65
   divisions among, 128, 364–66
   freed people and, 321, 364–66
   labor views of, 343
   military experience of, 142–43
   See also freed people; slaves
freed people
   attacks against, 406–7, 410–13, 457–65
   free people of color and, 321, 364–66
   freedom, notions of, 167, 170, 175, 178–80, 279–80, 344, 347–52, 370, 402, 404–13, 420–24, 438–40, 447–48, 451–56
   geographic mobility of, 346–47, 420
   land, desire for, 344, 347–52, 365
   legal rights of, 231–34, 289–90, 292–93, 320, 361–63, 382, 385–88, 392–95, 434, 439, 441–48, 451–53
   officeholding by, 467–68
   political mobilization of, 332, 421
   reenslavement of, 93, 173, 275, 285, 345, 354–55
   See also free people of color; slaves
Freedmen and Southern Society Project (FSSP), 14, 404, 406, 421
Freedmen's Aid Association, 366
Freedmen's Bureau, 338, 383, 408–9, 420, 426, 434, 449, 459, 460
Frémont, John C., 55
Friends of Universal Suffrage, 419–20, 438–40
Fugitive Slave Act, 71

Gallagher, Gary W., 6
Gantt, Edward W., 146, 186, 244, 247, 418
   advocates abolition, 148
   Arkansas Reconstruction, views on, 310
Genovese, Eugene D., 291, 406, 472
Gillem, Alvan C., 240
Goode, Edmund J., 430
Goodrich's Landing (LA), 173
Grant, Ulysses S., 56, 64, 83, 94, 172, 174, 187, 349
   black soldiers, views on, 134
   captures Forts Henry and Donelson, 65
   fugitive slaves, policy on, 67
   Vicksburg Campaign, leads, 93, 116, 132

INDEX

Grey, William H., 451–53
Grierson's Raid, 132

Hahn, Michael, 87, 127, 189, 252, 264, 319, 321, 366, 380, 419, 463
   elected governor, 263
   elected to Congress, 102, 110, 121, 229
   elected to Senate, 366
   gubernatorial candidacy of, 255–56, 261–62
   Inaugural Address, 263–64
   Louisiana constitutional convention and, 288–91
   Louisiana Reconstruction, views on, 139, 320
   resigns as governor, 380
Hahn, Steven, 352
Halleck, Henry W., 66
Hampton Roads, 381
Hanks, George H., 271
Harris, Ira, 123
Harris, Isham G., 50–52
Harris, Ransom, 332
Harris, William C., 443
Harrison, James T., 433
Hawkins, John P., 183
Hay, John, 197, 310, 361
Helena, 32, 76, 84, 105, 172, 278, 345, 348, 451, 461
Henderson, John, 463
Hood, John Bell, 367
Houzeau, Jean-Charles, 128, 192, 320, 398
Howard, O. O., 408, 449
Hudson, Robert S., 428, 430, 433, 446
Humphreys, Benjamin G., 441–42
Hurlbut, Stephen A., 147, 151, 323, 339, 397–98, 399

Ingraham, James H., 364, 398

Jacks, Thomas M., 245, 246, 250
Johnson, Andrew
   abolition, support for, 149–51, 187, 242, 295, 327, 332–34, 368, 371, 379
   appointed military governor, 69–71
   conservative Unionists, challenged by, 135–37, 296, 327
   Crittenden Resolution, cosponsors, 54
   elected vice president, 334
   emancipation, views on, 130
   endorses Federal abolition amendment, 241
   "Moses" speech, 332–34
   nominated vice president, 295–96, 307
   opposes black suffrage, 394
   Reconstruction policy of, 392–95, 415, 425–26, 438, 457–58, 464–65
   Reconstruction proposal of, 237–41, 328–29
   resigns as military governor, 379
   Tennessee elections, authorizes, 104
Johnson, Bradish, 138
Johnson, James M., 50, 186, 230, 244, 246, 293
Johnson, Reverdy, 88
Johnson, Walter, 22, 39
Johnston, Amos R., 429
Johnston, Joseph E., 367
Jones, Henry, 178

Kanady, Thomas, 453–56
Kelley, William D., 374
Kennedy, Hugh, 101, 125, 191, 388, 419
Kentucky, 16, 55, 61, 66, 93, 118, 201, 302, 360, 390, 431, 450
Kimball, Nathan, 247
Knoxville, 150
Kolchin, Peter L., 12
Ku Klux Klan, 468

L'Union, 128, 192, 320
Lafourche Parish, 344
land, 183, 184, 273, 274, 404
   freed people's desire for, 344, 347–52, 365, 421, 423, 445
Lellyett, John, 136, 329
Life on the Mississippi (Twain), 25
Lincoln, Abraham
   Annual Messages, 106–7, 199–203, 360–61

506 INDEX

Lincoln, Abraham (cont.)
  appoints Andrew Johnson military governor, 69–71
  April 15 proclamation, 48
  Arkansas Reconstruction, views on, 147–48, 247–48, 309
  Arkansas Unionists, meets with, 247
  black military enlistment, support for, 117
  black suffrage, support for, 264, 385–88
  cease-and-desist proclamation (1862), 80
  colonization, support for, 62
  compensated emancipation, proposals for, 62, 106–7, 381
  congressional elections (1862), support for, 101–2, 103–5
  Emancipation Proclamation, issues, 108–11
  Emancipation Proclamation, presents draft to Cabinet, 80
  Federal abolition amendment, endorses, 360–61, 375
  free black delegation, meets with, 264
  Frémont emancipation order, countermands, 55–56
  Inaugural Addresses, 47, 383
  "last address," 385–88, 440
  Louisiana conservative Unionists, meets with, 138, 194
  Louisiana Reconstruction, views on, 129, 140–41, 153–54, 189–90, 193–94, 257–58, 291, 323–24, 385–88
  New Orleans, approves expedition against, 63
  preliminary Emancipation Proclamation, 90–93
  Proclamation of Amnesty and Reconstruction (ten-percent plan), 199–203
  Reconstruction, views on, 48, 61, 360–63, 383, 385–88, 394–95
  reelected president, 336
  southern Unionists, views on, 86–90
  Tennessee Reconstruction, views on, 150, 240, 330
  Tennessee, excludes from Emancipation Proclamation, 105
  vetoes Wade–Davis bill, 310–12
Little Rock, 24, 32, 76, 145, 148, 186, 230, 244, 251, 284, 292, 325, 418, 421
Locket, Herry, 178
Longyear, John W., 303
Lookout Mountain (battle), 187
Lynch, James (Rev.), 422
Lynch, John R., 467

Maistre, Claude Paschal, 142
Malhiot, E. E., 127, 138, 155
Manning, Chandra, 95, 316
Mansfield (battle), 283
Marks' Mill, 284
Marler, Scott P., 32, 72
Marshall, Thomas A., 430
Martin, William T., 430
Masur, Louis, 311
Maxwell, H. J., 422
Maynard, Horace, 69, 104, 105, 130, 135, 238, 307
McCollam, Andrew, 155, 341
McCrary, Peyton, 267, 286, 382
McCurry, Stephanie, 168
McKaye, James, 271–73
Meador, Cincinnatus Vann, 244
Meinig, D. W., 2
Mellen, William P., 183, 274–76, 338, 397
Memphis, 32, 51, 70, 74, 83, 130, 147, 165, 173, 238, 240, 274, 296, 334, 349, 378, 403, 456
  violence at, 457–61, 464–65
Mendiverri, Antonio, 290
Mercer, Samuel C., 130
military emancipation, 62, 67, 71, 127, 135, 226
  implementation of, 72–76, 90, 94–98, 109
  origins of, 53–55
  versus constitutional abolition, 3–13, 80, 106–7, 118–21, 141, 148, 156–63, 202, 302, 372, 375, 430–32, 466
  See also Emancipation Proclamation
military laborers, 53, 56, 72, 82–84, 85, 94, 97, 146, 167, 171, 404, 452
Militia Act (1862), 79

INDEX 507

Milligan, Samuel, 368
Milliken's Bend (battle), 134
Minor, William J., 59, 176, 400–1
Missionary Ridge (battle), 187
Missouri, 16
Monroe, John F., 462
Montgomery, Benjamin, 352
Montgomery, Isaiah, 352
Montgomery, Thornton, 352
Moore, Thomas O., 45, 46
Mound Bayou (MS), 352
Murphy, Isaac, 440, 451
   elected governor, 250
   free-state leader, 244
   gubernatorial administration of, 324–26, 385, 418–19
   inauguration of, 292–93
   nominated for governor, 186
   provisional governor, 246
   secession, opposes, 49–50

Nash, Charles E., 467
Nashville, 9, 26, 32, 65, 94, 135, 238, 240, 295, 327, 330, 332, 334, 359, 367, 368, 384, 422
Nashville (battle), 368
Natchez, 24, 32, 45, 57, 146, 170, 174, 181, 345, 347, 402, 416, 469
Natchez District, 24, 27, 30, 31, 37, 53, 175, 280, 400
National Equal Rights League (NERL), 321, 332, 364–65, 370, 399, 421
Native Guard, 57, 117, 133, 142–43, 364, *see also* black soldiers; U.S. Colored Troops (USCT)
Nelson, Thomas A. R., 130, 241, 329
New Orleans, 28, 29, 32, 45, 52, 63, 71, 87, 101, 108, 125, 127, 137, 138, 143, 155, 191, 192, 262, 285, 343, 364, 389, 419, 438, 449
   violence at, 461–65
Nicolay, John G., 197
Northup, Solomon, 39
Norton, Jesse O., 303

Oakes, James, 6, 18–20, 80, 235
Odin, Jean-Marie, 143
Ogden, Robert N., 453

Palmer, Benjamin M., 45
paternalism
   decline of, 169, 174, 176, 271–73
   defined, 33
Pea Ridge (battle), 67
Pendleton, George H., 300
Perryville (battle), 93
Pettus, John J., 44
Phelps, John S. (Arkansas military governor), 84, 105, 243
Phelps, John W. (Union general), 74
Phillips, U. B., 39
Pierce, S. E., 178
Pinchback, P. B. S., 192, 467
plantation labor
   conflict over, 178–80, 270, 271–73, 275, 277–78, 339–41, 344–45, 401–4
   military policy on, 94–98, 166–68, 177, 269–70, 339, 397–98
   Treasury Department policy on, 397
plantations
   antebellum development of, 29–32
   attacks against, 172, 181, 275, 345
   leasing of, 169, 170–74, 178–83, 270, 274–79
   military policy on, 170–74, 349–52
   regional distribution of, 23–25
   Treasury Department policy on, 182, 270, 274–76, 338
planters
   economic dominance of, 37
   emancipation, responses to, 75–76, 83, 85–86, 98, 111, 127, 174, 181, 186, 404–13
   fugitive slaves, responses to, 66–67
   ideology of, 32–37, 169, 176–77, 182, 354–55, 410, 435
   labor views of, 167–69, 175, 178–80, 271, 279–80, 339, 341–42, 400–1, 402
   northern, 169, 173
   slave insurrection scare, response to, 57–60
Pleasant Hill (battle), 283
Plessy v. Ferguson, 469
Poison Spring, 284
Polk, Leondis, 56

Port Hudson, 116, 117, 133–34, 141, 168
Porter, David, 132, 174, 181
Potter, George L., 427–28, 430–32, 433
Powell, Lawrence N., 467
Proclamation of Amnesty and Reconstruction, 149, 199–203, *see also* ten-percent plan
Pugh, Alexander Franklin, 344

Radical Reconstruction, 258, 273, 411, 421, 453
Reconstruction
  abolition and, 156–63
  congressional legislation on, 69, 224–27, 361–63, 372–73, 381
  Johnson's policy on, 392–95
  Lincoln's views on, 61, 383
  Republicans' views on, 61–62, 68–69, 118–23, 156–58, 376
Rector, Henry, 48, 49
Red River Campaign, 282–85, 350
Republicans
  Federal abolition amendment, views on, 227–29, 234–36
  Reconstruction, views on, 61–62, 68–69, 118–23, 156–58, 224, 301–6, 372–73, 376
Revels, Hiram R., 467
Reynolds, Joseph, 325, 363
Richards, Leonard L., 5
Riddell, James L., 191, 194
Rogers, Anthony A. C., 244, 250, 294, 309
Roselius, Christian, 124, 256, 257, 260, 266, 286
Roudanez, Jean Baptiste, 259, 366
Roudanez, Louis Charles, 128, 320
Rozier, Joseph A., 125, 256, 259, 260

Schurz, Carl, 394–95, 435
Scott, Thomas, 454
Sebastian, William K., 147–48
secession
  in Arkansas, 48–50
  in Louisiana, 45–46
  in Mississippi, 44–45
  in Tennessee, 50–52
Second Creek (MS), 57–60

Seward, William H., 140, 157, 374, 381, 450
Sharkey, William L., 432, 434, 441, 445
  appointed provisional governor, 393, 416–17
  gubernatorial administration of, 424–26
Shepley, George F., 87, 101–2, 129, 137, 153, 154, 187, 189–94, 229, 252, 265
Sheridan, Philip, 463, 464
Sherman, Thomas W., 456
Sherman, William T., 83, 93, 187, 284, 350, 367
Shiloh (battle), 67
Shreveport, 133, 283, 390, 410–13
Sickles, Daniel L., 249
slave insurrection scare, 57–60
slaveholders. *See* planters
slaves
  Confederate impressment of, 56, 76
  cultural life of, 38
  geographical distribution of, 25–28
  seek freedom, 53–54, 66–67, 72–76, 82–86, 94–98, 146, 283, 352–53, 404–13
  See also free people of color; freed people
Smith, Charles, 319, 363, 366, 382
Smith, Edmund Kirby, 283, 390
Snow, William D., 364
Sprague, John W., 408
St. James Parish, 168
Stanton, Edwin M., 154, 157, 224, 463
Steele, Frederick
  appointed to command, 85
  Arkansas Reconstruction, oversees, 243, 246–51, 294–95
  Arkansas Reconstruction, views on, 326
  Camden Expedition, leads, 284
  relieved of command, 325
  Union capture of Little Rock and, 148
Stephens, Alexander H., 43, 374, 381
Stone, Kate, 57, 75, 170, 174
Stoneman, George, 460, 461
Stones River (or Murfreesboro, battle), 94

INDEX

Sumner, Charles, 158, 224, 297, 310
  defeats Louisiana claimants, 382
  Federal abolition amendment, views on, 227
  Reconstruction, views on, 159–60

Taylor, Amy Murrell, 171
Taylor, Joe Gray, 125, 462
Taylor, Richard, 283, 463
ten-percent plan
  announced, 199–203
  conservative opposition to, 241
  Johnson's policy and, 394–95
  Reconstruction legislation and, 226
  Republican criticism of, 301–6, 312–15
  See also Proclamation of Amnesty and Reconstruction
Terrebonne Parish, 178, 344, 453
Thibodaux Massacre, 469
Thirteenth Amendment, 118, 450, 458, 465, 466, *see also* Federal abolition amendment
Thomas, George H., 368
Thomas, Lorenzo, 117, 146, 170–74, 180–83, 277–79
Thomas, Samuel, 280, 350, 408
Trévigne, Paul, 128, 320
Trumbull, Lyman, 228, 309, 373
Twain, Mark, 25

U.S. Colored Troops (USCT), 117, *see also* black soldiers; Native Guard
Unionists, conservative
  Arkansas
    oppose abolition, 245–46
    organize in, 244
  Louisiana
    election plan of, 155
    meet with Lincoln, 138, 194
    oppose abolition, 286–88, 290–91
    organize in, 127
    Reconstruction proposals of, 138–41, 191, 259–61
  Tennessee
    election plan of, 149, 151–52, 327, 329–31
    oppose abolition, 378–79
  organize in, 130
  Reconstruction proposals of, 135–37, 296
Unionists, free-state
  Arkansas
    attacks against, 294–95
    difficulties of, 324–26, 363
    organize in, 186, 244
  Louisiana
    black suffrage and, 192–93
    divisions among, 192–93, 252–55, 259, 286, 321–23, 389, 419–20, 438–40
    organize in, 127–28
    organize Republican Party in, 419–20, 438–40
    Reconstruction proposals of, 129, 137–38, 153–55, 187–90
  Tennessee
    abolish slavery in, 368–72
    organize in, 130
    Reconstruction proposals of, 151
Unionists, southern
  emancipation, views on, 123–24, 129–31
  Lincoln's views on, 86–90
  Louisiana, organize in, 87, 101
  Tennessee, hold convention in (1863), 135–37

Van Bergen, John P., 178
Vicksburg, 24, 30, 32, 75, 146, 180, 345, 346, 348, 351, 390, 416
Vicksburg Campaign, 93, 116, 132, 134, 141, 165, 168, 170, 172, 274, 349
Vorenberg, Michael, 5, 8, 12, 118, 157, 162, 163, 224, 228, 235, 307, 308, 335

Wade–Davis bill, 362
  amendments to, 306
  Democratic criticism of, 298–300
  introduced, 231–34
  Lincoln vetoes, 310–12
  Louisiana Reconstruction and, 322
  Republican commentary on, 301–6
Wade–Davis Manifesto, 312–15, 322
Wadsworth, James S., 176, 182

wages
  conflict over, 178–80, 278
  rates, 97, 167, 171, 269, 274, 277, 338, 398
Warmoth, Henry Clay, 420, 438–40, 449, 462, 467
Weitzel, Godfrey, 97
Welles, Gideon, 174
Wells, J. Madison, 258, 438, 454, 461
  becomes governor, 366, 381
  elected lieutenant governor, 262
  gubernatorial administration of, 388–90, 419
Western Sanitary Commission, 182

White, J. T. (Rev.), 451
White, Robert J. T., 325
Whiting, William, 158–59, 224
Wilentz, Sean, 18
Williams, Thomas, 303
Wise, Henry A., 451
woodyards, 346

Yeatman, James E., 182
Yerger, J. Shall, 425
Yerger, William, 416, 425, 427, 432, 435

Zietlow, Rebecca E., 5, 225

CPSIA information can be obtained
at www.ICGtesting.com
Printed in the USA
LVHW050345210123
737604LV00001B/21